THIRD EDITION

MicroSim™ PSpice®
and Circuit Analysis

JOHN KEOWN
Southern Polytechnic State University

Prentice Hall
Upper Saddle River, New Jersey   **Columbus, Ohio**

Library of Congress Cataloging-in-Publication Data

Keown, John.
    MicroSim PSpice and circuit analysis / John Keown. — 3rd ed.
        p.   cm. —
    Includes index.
    ISBN 0-13-235458-6 (alk. paper)
    1. Electric circuit analysis—Data processing.   2. PSpice.
I. Title. II. Series.
TK454.K46 1998
621.3815′0285′5369—dc21   97-6639
                                                 CIP

Editor: Linda Ludewig
Production Editor: Mary M. Irvin
Design Coordinator: Julia Zonneveld Van Hook
Cover Designer: Brian Deep
Production Manager: Pamela D. Bennett
Marketing Manager: Debbie Yarnell
Production Coordination: Spectrum Publisher Services

This book was set in Times Roman by TCSystems and was printed and bound by R. R. Donnelley & Sons. The cover was printed by Phoenix Color Corp.

 © 1998 by Prentice-Hall, Inc.
Simon & Schuster/A Viacom Company
Upper Saddle River, New Jersey 07458

Earlier editions entitled *PSpice and Circuit Analysis,* © 1993 and 1991, by Macmillan Publishing Company.

Printed in the United States of America

10 9 8 7 6 5 4 3 2 1

ISBN: 0-13-235458-6

Prentice-Hall International (UK) Limited, *London*
Prentice-Hall of Australia Pty. Limited, *Sydney*
Prentice-Hall of Canada, Inc., *Toronto*
Prentice-Hall Hispanoamericana, S. A., *Mexico*
Prentice-Hall of India Private Limited, *New Delhi*
Prentice-Hall of Japan, Inc., *Tokyo*
Simon & Schuster Asia Pte. Ltd., *Singapore*
Editora Prentice-Hall do Brasil, Ltda., *Rio de Janeiro*

Preface

Methods of circuit analysis vary widely, depending on the complexity of the problem. Whereas some circuits require nothing more complicated than the writing of a single equation for their solution, others require that several equations be solved simultaneously. When the response of a circuit is to be performed over a wide range of frequencies, the work is often both tedious and time consuming. Various tools ranging from trig tables and slide rules to calculators and computers have been used by those anxious to ease the burden of lengthy computations.

In many cases the problem to be solved requires that the student have an understanding of which basic laws and principles are involved in the solution. In some cases, if the topology of a network is known, along with complete descriptions of the elements that are connected among the various nodes, computer programs can be used to perform the analyses.

Such programs have been under development for several decades. If you have access to a computer language such as BASIC, Pascal, or FORTRAN, you can devise your own programs to readily solve certain types of problems. More powerful programs, capable of solving many types of electrical networks under a variety of conditions, require years to develop and update.

What is SPICE?

Such a program is SPICE, which stands for *Simulation Program with Integrated Circuit Emphasis.* The version of SPICE used in this book is PSpice, a commercial product developed by the MicroSim Corporation. The evaluation version of the program, which is available at no cost, is sufficient to perform all the exercises and programs in this book.

The SPICE program is both powerful and flexible. At the same time, it can be intimidating and bewildering to the beginner, who might well ask, How do I use this mighty tool in the most elementary way?

Although it might appear foolish to use a powerful hammer to drive a tack, if novices can solve problems with SPICE *for which they already know the answers,* they will gain confidence to move ahead. Thus this text begins with dc circuit analysis, proceeds with ac circuit analysis, then goes into the various topics involving semiconductors.

PSpice is a development of the MicroSim Corporation. It is widely used in industry for the main purpose of allowing the designer to investigate the behavior of a circuit without having to actually breadboard the circuit in the laboratory. This allows for a considerable savings in materials and labor. If the design needs to be modified or tweaked, changes can easily be submitted to the computer for another look at the results. The designer is familiar with the components that will eventually be used in the actual circuit. He or she understands their electrical properties and behavior. How large numbers of these components will interact, however, is sometimes difficult to predict. This is where the computer program takes over, going through the tedious solutions much more quickly and with far less chance for mistakes than the human approach.

Should every electrical student, practitioner, and designer learn SPICE and use it? I believe the answer is an unqualified yes. It has become a standard in both the academic and professional worlds. Your education will not be complete without an exposure to this valuable tool.

Will SPICE teach you what you need to know to perform both circuit analysis and design? I believe the answer is an unqualified no. A study of the basic laws that govern circuit behavior is just as important today as it ever was. SPICE and other computer aids of the same nature will merely free you of the drudgery of lengthy and repetitive computations. You will surely gain some additional knowledge in the process, which you might otherwise overlook. You will also enjoy using Probe, a feature of PSpice that allows you to plot circuit response involving functions of frequency and time, among other things.

The motivation for this book comes from a desire to present a simple, easy-to-follow guide to PSpice to all those who want to learn more about computer aids to circuit analysis. The material is presented in such a way that anyone who is studying or has studied the various electrical topics will be able immediately to put PSpice to practical use.

An important feature of the book is the development of models for such devices as the bipolar junction transistor, the field-effect transistor, and the operational amplifier. The models need be no more complicated than necessary for the problem at hand. For example, if you are interested in bias voltages and currents for the BJT, there is no need for a model of the transistor that takes ac quantities into account. It is hoped that the readers will be able to develop their own models for other devices, especially those where linear approximations are all that is needed.

When reading this book be aware that you will learn much more by going through each example on the computer. It is important that you produce the required input (circuit) files, submit them to the PSpice program, then look at the output files and/or Probe to see the results. Only by actual experience with the computer will you begin to appreciate the power at your disposal and the satisfaction that comes from seeing the solutions appear on your monitor and printer.

Schematics

Schematics is a MicroSim product that allows the circuit designer to place the various components of a circuit on a drawing board prior to carrying out the analysis in PSpice. The components, or parts, use standard symbols. These parts are available in several libraries, or categories. For example, there is a library of sources; dc and ac voltages and currents and dependent sources are available.We will not be using Schematics in the early chapters, because PSpice will be more easily understood if the study begins with what was available in SPICE in its infancy. From a hand-drawn sketch of an electrical or electronic circuit, we begin by assigning nodes in the circuit using a simple numbering sequence. The ground point is zero node, and we must label all other nodes. Then we identify the elements of the circuit one by one on a single line of a file that we call a circuit (or input) file. When the entire circuit has been characterized, the analysis (or simulation) takes place. The results will tell us a great deal (sometimes more, sometimes less) about the behavior of the circuit under a variety of conditions.

If we choose to use Schematics, the entire electrical or electronic circuit is placed on a drawing board (on the screen) and we choose from among the available options the kind of analysis we would like to perform. The end result is the same as we would get if we went directly to the PSpice program. Whether to use PSpice directly or to let Schematics create the circuit file, the choice is ours to make.

WHAT'S NEW IN THE THIRD EDITION

There have been numerous improvements and changes in the capabilities of PSpice since the material for the first and second editions was developed. The MicroSim Corporation issues two releases of their products each year. The material for this edition is based on the evaluation software, version 6.3, revision 2. This software (or a later version if available) is included with this text in the form of a CD-ROM. It was copyrighted in 1996 by MicroSim Corporation.

One of the main features of the newest software is that all the programs and on-line documentation are Windows-based. Whether you are using Windows 3.1x or Windows 95 will make little difference. If you are moving from one version of Windows to another, the programs should behave in the same fashion.

Chapters 1–13 cover most of the topics that are included in dc and ac circuit analysis, semiconductor devices and circuits, operational amplifiers, two-port networks, and filters.

Chapters 14–17 are devoted to the same topics using the tools available in Schematics.

Appendix C on the installation of the MicroSim software is all new, dealing with Windows and the CD-ROM installation.

Appendix E has been expanded to reflect the wider availability of digital parts in the device library.

All the example problems have been reworked using the Windows version of PSpice, and all the Probe traces have been revised to show the new look of Probe output. In some cases, the results are not quite the same as those obtained using an earlier version of the software.

IMPORTANT NOTICE

After the printer had finalized the third edition, MicroSim made available a later evaluation version of the software. This version of the DesignLab Evaluation Software, v. 7.1, is included in the back of the book.

The reader should be aware of several changes that affect the material presented in the book.

1. The new version of the software is designed for Windows 95 and Windows NT. Since it uses 32-bit file handling exclusively, it will not run on Windows 3.1 or Windows for Workgroups, which have 16-bit operating systems.

2. After the evaluation software has been installed, you will see no reference to a PSpice icon in the MicroSim Eval 7.1 program group. Since one of the main features of the early chapters of this book is to be able to use PSpice without going through Schematics, the user should make a few changes on the desktop.

3. Select Start, Programs, and run the Windows Explorer. Select the *msimev71* file folder in the left column; then size the Explorer window to allow a portion of the desktop to be seen in the background. Find the Pspice icon in the right column. Using the mouse, drag this icon to the desktop, where a shortcut will be created. This will allow easy access to PSpice.

4. You may also want to create a shortcut to the Notepad on the desktop and/or create a shortcut to the MicroSim Text Editor in the same manner as described in item 3. The Text Editor then becomes the preferred tool for creating circuit files. When you save a file in the Text Editor, the extension *.cir* is assumed.

ACKNOWLEDGMENTS

My sincere thanks to the reviewers of the third edition for their comments and insights: Seyed Akhavi, Jefferson Technical College; T. E. Brewer, Georgia Institute of Technology; Dr. Victor Gerez; John D. Polus, Purdue University; Russell E. Puckett, Texas A&M; and Stephen Titcomb, University of Vermont.

Contents

1

DC Circuit Analysis   25

2

AC Circuit Analysis (for Sinusoidal Steady-State Conditions)   71

3

Transistor Circuits   115

4

Multistage Amplifiers, Frequency Response, and Feedback   157

5

The Operational Amplifier   189

6

Transients and the Time Domain   223

7

Fourier Series and Harmonic Components   249

8

Stability and Oscillators   267

9
An Introduction to PSpice Devices   285

10
The BJT and Its Model   315

11

The Field-Effect Transistor

347

12

Two-Port Networks and Passive Filters

367

13
Nonlinear Devices   401

14
Schematics   415

15

Transistor Circuits in Schematics   451

16

Operational Amplifiers in Schematics   479

17

Other Topics in Schematics   497

Appendix A   541

Brief Summary of PSpice Statements

Introduction

PSpice and Circuit Analysis, 3d edition, will reinforce basic circuit analysis principles using the version of SPICE called PSpice. It is not a complete text on circuit analysis; it is intended to serve as a supplement or reference to a more detailed, conventional textbook. Here the reader can take an active part in learning new ideas through the use of PSpice on the IBM PC (or the various other brands of personal computers) using Windows 3.1x or Windows 95.

The examples shown in this book were run using the MicroSim Evaluation Software, Version 6.3, Revision 2. The MicroSim company has made a practice of giving their evaluation software to faculty members of electrical departments in technical institutes, colleges, and universities free of charge. They have graciously permitted this CD-ROM to be included in its entirety with this book.

At the same time, users should be aware that the full-fledged version of the MicroSim products are available directly from the company. Paying customers are entitled to such services as free technical support, annual maintenance of the programs, a trade-up policy, and a generous educational discount.

For further information write

MicroSim Corporation
20 Fairbanks
Irvine, CA 92718 USA
General Offices: 714 770-3022
Sales: 800 245-3022
E-mail: sales@microsim.com
WWW: http://www.microsim.com

The material in this book may be used in a variety of settings, beginning with elementary dc circuit analysis; progressing through ac analysis including polyphase circuits, electronic devices and circuits; as well as more advanced topics such as operational amplifiers, frequency response, transients, Fourier analysis, nonlinear devices, and active filters. As you move through the material, it is important that you actually work the exercises and problems on the computer. This gives you an immediate feel for the ease or difficulty of a particular problem. It also allows you to build the confidence that is needed to move ahead with a thorough understanding of basic principles and concepts.

Whether your main interest is in dc/ac circuits or electronics, we advise you to start at the beginning. The mechanics of using the computer as a learning device are best applied to simple models in the first examples. As you become more familiar with the mechanics you will find that the more difficult concepts require only a little more effort.

As you move to more advanced topics, you should feel more comfortable jumping about from chapter to chapter as your interests and studies dictate. The sequence of topics is not critical beyond the introductory chapters dealing with circuit analysis.

The examples in this text were first run on a Zeos 486 DX-2 (Intel processor) computer using Windows for Workgroups (v. 3.11), then on an IBM Pantera using Windows 95. The numerical results that you obtain when running the example programs may agree exactly with those shown in the text. If they do not, differences in equipment or software may be responsible. In all cases the differences should be insignificant.

A BIT OF BACKGROUND

SPICE is widely used in the academic and industrial worlds to simulate the operation of various electric circuits and devices. It was developed at the University of California and used initially on mainframe computers. The successor to the original, SPICE2, is more powerful. Later versions, such as PSpice by the MicroSim Corporation, are designed to operate on PCs, Macintoshes, and minicomputers.

The material in this book is designed to be used with PCs under Windows. Earlier versions of PSpice may be run under DOS.

In order to perform a SPICE analysis of a circuit an input file, or circuit file, must be produced. This can be done using any suitable text editor; in Windows it is easily done through the Windows Notepad. To allow for compatibility between various versions of Windows, the standard 8.3 file format is recommended. A file name might be *firstone.cir* for example.

It is the author's belief that the use of MicroSim Schematics, which allows a circuit to be drawn from its various components, should be postponed until a fundamental knowledge of PSpice is developed. For this reason, Schematics is developed beginning with Chapter 10.

GETTING STARTED

The educational (evaluation) version of the MicroSim software on CD-ROM is included with this book.

If you are using Windows 3.1x, install the software by the usual method of selecting File, Run from the Program Manager. On the Command Line, type

d:\setup.exe

assuming that *d* is the designation for the CD-ROM drive. The setup program will then guide you through the installation process. You may have to install the Win32 applications software in order to use the MicroSim text editor. Do this by executing the program *d:\ole32s\130\disk1\setup.exe* on the installation disk.

If you are using Windows 95, install the software from the Windows Explorer. Right-click on the CD-ROM icon, then select Autoplay.

After the software has been installed, the MicroSim Eval 6.3 software workgroup will appear as shown in Fig. I.1. Note that the Windows Notepad has been placed in the workgroup for convenience.

Before you begin working with PSpice, it is recommended that you do the following: In File Manager, create a new directory by going to the root directory and selecting File, Create Directory. Name the new directory *p*. Go to the MicroSim Workgroup and select the PSpice icon (click only once), then in Program Manager select Properties. In the Program Item Properties change the working directory to *c:\p*. Repeat this process for all the icons within the MicroSim workgroup.

Our plan will include creating input files for PSpice analysis using Notepad. This is the reason for putting a copy of the Notepad icon in the MicroSim Workgroup. The input files will have descriptive names and the extension *cir*. For more details and illustrations on loading the MicroSim software into your computer, refer to Appendix C.

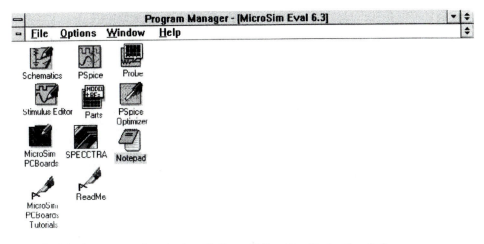

Fig. I.1 Display screen after the installation of MicroSim Evaluation Software.

A FEW HELPFUL POINTS

When you create an input file for the circuit under investigation, always begin with a complete sketch of the circuit. Label the nodes using a distinct marking, such as red or blue ink. There must always be a zero (0) node, which will be the *reference* node. The other nodes can have either numerical or alphabetical designations (numbers are usually easier to use). Decide on a name for the input file, for example, *dctwo.cir*. The extension *cir* designates a circuit (or input) file.

Include a statement in your input file for every element in the circuit. The order of the statements for the elements is of little consequence; however, the first statement in your input file must be a title or description. If it describes an element, it will be ignored. The last statement must be the .END (upper- or lowercase) statement.

In general, upper- and lowercase alphabetic characters may be used interchangeably; use whichever is more suitable for the particular circuit. Some prefer uppercase for dc circuits and lowercase for ac circuits.

When dealing with either large or small values, observe the following SPICE conventions:

Value	Symbolic Form	Exponential Form
10^{-15}	F	1E-15
10^{-12}	P	1E-12
10^{-9}	N	1E-9
10^{-6}	U	1E-6
10^{-3}	M	1E-3
25.4×10^{-6}	MIL	25.4E-6
10^{3}	K	1E3
10^{6}	MEG	1E6
10^{9}	G	1E9
10^{12}	T	1E12

Remember that the symbolic form may be shown as either upper- or lowercase letters. For example, M or m will be correct for the prefix milli.

In describing a capacitor, a statement such as this might be used:

```
C 4 5 25NF
```

This means that a capacitor is connected between nodes *4* and *5*. The value of the capacitor is 25 nanofarads. The statement could have been given simply as

```
C 4 5 25n
```

Thus the unit symbol is optional.

Pay particular attention to the fact that the symbolic form for the prefix is immediately adjacent to the numeric value. Do not put a space between the number and the prefix. This also should be done when using the exponential form of the prefix, as in

```
C 4 5 25E-9
```

As another example,

```
R3 2 3 33kilohms
```

obviously describes a 33-kΩ resistor connected between nodes *2* and *3*. It would also be correct to use

```
R3 2 3 33k
```

An independent-voltage source is shown, for example, as

```
V 1 0 DC 40V
```

The DC designation is optional, as is the final V (after the 40). Thus an alternative form for this statement might be

```
V 1 0 40
```

Some readers of the earlier editions have asked for a more detailed introduction to the mechanics of creating an input (circuit) file for PSpice on the PC. Before you begin working on the material of Chapter 1, you may want to look at this complete example as well as the material in the following PSpice Overview.

HERE'S HOW IT'S DONE

A dc circuit with a voltage source and four resistors is shown in Fig. I.2. The nodes have been given numbers ranging from 0 to 3. A SPICE analysis requires that all nodes be numbered (or given alphabetic designation). There must also be a reference node, which is called node zero.

Creating the Input File

Thus we might create an input file called *ex1.cir* to be analyzed by the PSpice processor. Double-click (dbl-clk) on the Notepad icon and begin typing at the blinking icon:

```
First Circuit for PSpice
VS 1 0 24V
R1 1 2 10
R2 2 0 1k
R3 2 3 300
```

Fig. I.2   First circuit for PSpice.

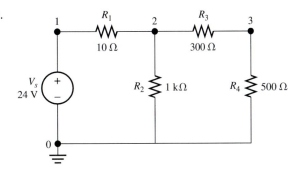

```
R4 3 0 500
.OPT nopage
.OP
.END
```

Use the File Save command and name the file *ex1.cir*.

Running the PSpice Analysis

When you are satisfied that the file is correct and complete, Exit and dbl-clk on the PSpice icon. In PSpice, select File, Open. Either type *ex1* or select *ex1.cir* from the list of files. When OK is chosen, the simulation will take place, and the message "Simulation completed successfully" should appear. Select OK.

Examining the Output File

Now you have a choice in examining the output. You may select File, Examine Output in PSpice (which invokes the MicroSim text Editor) or you may use Notepad to open the file *ex1.out*. The results of the simulation are shown in Fig. I.3, using the MicroSim Text Editor. In order to show the important elements of the output file, several blank lines have been removed.

Conventional circuit analysis will confirm that $V_{20} = 23.472$ V and $V_{30} = 14.67$ V. The current I is the (negative of the) current shown in the output file as the

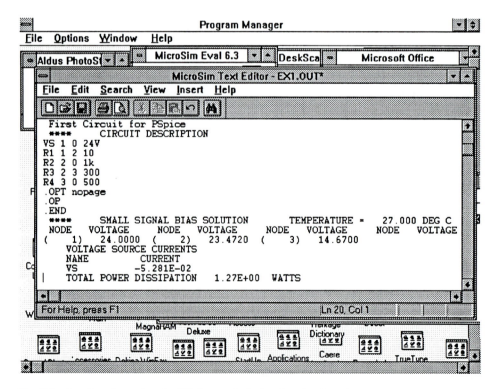

Fig. I.3 Results of running the PSpice analysis for the circuit *ex1.cir*.

voltage-source current of 52.81 mA. The total power dissipated, which is the product of V_S and I, is 1.27 W.

Turning our attention to the input file, notice that this file contains an entry for every element in the circuit. Each element is shown on a separate line with enough information for PSpice to determine what the element is, which pair of nodes the element is placed between, and the size (value) of the element. The *.OPT* (short for .OPTIONS) *no page* entry prevents unnecessary page breaks in the output file. The *.OP* entry is generally used to supply bias-point information in transistor-circuit analysis. For the dc circuit it may be omitted. The *.END* entry is required for every input file.

Changing the Input File

In order to get more information from the PSpice analysis, revise the input file (with the .cir extension) to include two additional lines, as follows:

```
.DC VS 24V 24V 24V
.PRINT DC I(R1) I(R2) I(R3)
```

```
    **** 08/02/96 13:50:55 ******* Win32s Evaluation PSpice (April 1996) *********

     First Circuit for PSpice

     ****        CIRCUIT DESCRIPTION

    VS 1 0 24V
    R1 1 2 10
    R2 2 0 1k
    R3 2 3 300
    R4 3 0 500
    .DC VS 24V 24V 24V
    .PRINT DC I(R1) I(R2) I(R3)
    .OPT nopage
    .OP
    .END

     ****        DC TRANSFER CURVES              TEMPERATURE =   27.000 DEG C

       VS          I(R1)         I(R2)        I(R3)
        2.400E+01    5.281E-02    2.347E-02    2.934E-02

     ****        SMALL SIGNAL BIAS SOLUTION      TEMPERATURE =   27.000 DEG C

     NODE   VOLTAGE      NODE   VOLTAGE      NODE   VOLTAGE      NODE   VOLTAGE
     (   1)   24.0000  (    2)   23.4720  (    3)   14.6700

        VOLTAGE SOURCE CURRENTS
        NAME          CURRENT
        VS            -5.281E-02

        TOTAL POWER DISSIPATION   1.27E+00  WATTS

     ****        OPERATING POINT INFORMATION     TEMPERATURE =   27.000 DEG C

        JOB CONCLUDED

        TOTAL JOB TIME            1.21
```

Fig. I.4

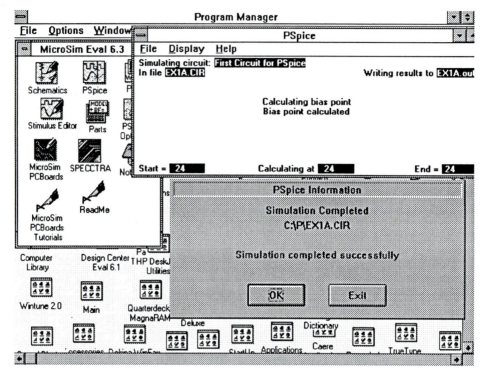

Fig. I.5 A PSpice simulation is successfully completed.

The placement of these lines is not critical, but you may refer to Fig. I.4 (which also shows a listing of the results) for their suggested location in the file. Save the new version of the input file as *ex1a.cir;* then run the PSpice analysis, following the same procedure as before. At the conclusion of the job, the screen should contain the information shown in Fig. I.5. Next, consider the new output file shown in Fig. I.4.

The output file contains some new information. It shows the currents that were called for in the *.PRINT* statement. Verify by conventional circuit analysis that the branch currents are $I_{R1} = 52.81$ mA, $I_{R2} = 23.47$ mA, $I_{R3} = 29.34$ mA. The explanation of the two new lines in the input file will be found in Chapter 1.

The Current Directions

Note that resistor R_1 is described by

```
R1  1  2  10
```

The resistor is connected between nodes *1* and *2;* the *1, 2* order means that the current is referenced from node *1* toward node *2.* If the current through R_1 is in that direction, it will be given as a positive value by PSpice. Note that this is in agreement with the results shown in the output file. If the resistor had been described by the input line

```
R1  2  1  10
```

the results would show that the current I(R1) is a negative number. The same reasoning applies for the other resistors in the circuit.

The treatment of the voltage source V_S is different, however. It is described by

```
VS 1 0 24V
```

When sources are involved, the *1, 0 order* means that the current inside the source is references from node *1* toward node *0*. Since the current is actually out of node *1*, it is given as *–5.281E-02* (amperes).

FURTHER READING

Many of the example problems in this text are references to similar examples that have been worked by conventional means in other texts. The following texts will serve as resource material for further study and explanation of the topics briefly covered in this book:

Circuit Analysis
Irving L. Kosow, Wiley, 1988

Electronic Devices and Circuits, 2d ed.
Theodore F. Bogart, Jr., Merrill/Macmillan, 1990

Electronic Devices
William D. Stanley, Prentice-Hall, 1989

Integrated Electronics
Millman and Halkais, McGraw-Hill, 1972

PSpice Overview

This section gives an overview of some of the things that can be done using PSpice. Explanations will be given in detail in later chapters of the book. After you see a feature that is of special interest, you may want to move ahead to the chapter that covers the topic in more detail.

DC CIRCUIT ANALYSIS

Figure P.1 represents a dc circuit with a voltage source and three resistors. The Spice solution for the various currents and voltages in the circuit can easily be found. If you have read the "Getting Started" section of the introduction, you will be ready to construct an input file using Notepad. For the first analysis, it should look like this:

```
Resistive Circuit with Voltage Source
Vs 1 0 dc 12V
R1 1 2 50ohms
R2 2 0 100ohms
R3 2 0 200ohms
.END
```

Follow the exact format shown above; for example, do not put a space between the "12" and the "V", do not put a space between the "50" and the "ohms", and so forth. Now save the file, using the name *preview.cir,* exit Notepad, and choose the PSpice icon (dbl-click). Choose File, Open and select the file *preview.cir.*

The analysis produces what is called the *small-signal bias solution.* You can view the results by using Notepad and opening the file *preview.out* or by simply selecting File, Examine Output while still in the PSpice program. The complete out-

Fig. P.1   A dc circuit for SPICE analysis.

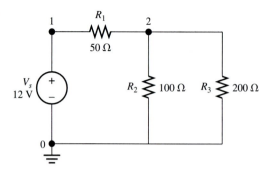

put file is shown in Fig. P.2. If you are interested in producing a printed copy of this output file, it is desirable to use a word-processing program (MS Word) and select the *Courier New* font. This will assure that horizontal spacing is properly maintained (it is lost in Times New Roman). You will want to reset for smaller left and right margins so that the long lines will not wrap-around to the next line. Also edit out the unnecessary blank lines and the page-feed characters; otherwise, the output will waste paper and be more difficult to follow.

The output file gives three items of interest: (1) the voltage at node *2,* (2) the current furnished by the voltage source, and (3) the total power dissipation. Identify each of these and verify the values from your pencil-and-paper solution.

It would be helpful to obtain more information about the circuit. The various currents can be shown if the input file contains two additional lines: a dc voltage statement and a PRINT dc statement. The extra page feeds are easily eliminated by including an option (.OPT) statement. The new input file is

```
Resistive circuit with voltage Source
Vs 1 0 12V
R1 1 2 50
R2 2 0 100
R3 2 0 200
.OPT nopage
.dc Vs 12V 12V 12V
.PRINT dc I(R1) I(R2) I(R3)
.END
```

The first four lines of the file have been modified slightly. The dc description of V_S is not required. The ohms designation for each resistor is not required; in fact, it makes the value more difficult to read. The PRINT statement will not produce the desired results unless a dc sweep statement is included. The sweep begins at 12 V, ends at 12 V, and uses a 12-V step. This means that there is no actual sweep of voltages, involving several different voltage values.

Run the PSpice analysis and examine the output file. There is a section called DC TRANSFER CURVES, which shows the current through each resistor. Note, however, that the node voltages are missing. They can be restored to the output by the use of the OP statement. This gives the operating-point information of node voltages and source currents.

```
**** 08/02/96 14:42:13 ****** Win32s Evaluation PSpice (April 1996) *********

Resistive Circuit with Voltage Source

****      CIRCUIT DESCRIPTION

********************************************************************************

Vs 1 0 dc 12V
R1 1 2 50ohms
R2 2 0 100ohms
R3 2 0 200ohms
.END

**** 08/02/96 14:42:13 ****** Win32s Evaluation PSpice (April 1996) *********

Resistive Circuit with Voltage Source

****      SMALL SIGNAL BIAS SOLUTION      TEMPERATURE =   27.000 DEG C

********************************************************************************

 NODE   VOLTAGE     NODE   VOLTAGE     NODE   VOLTAGE     NODE   VOLTAGE

(   1)   12.0000  (   2)    6.8571

     VOLTAGE SOURCE CURRENTS
     NAME            CURRENT

     Vs             -1.029E-01

     TOTAL POWER DISSIPATION   1.23E+00   WATTS

        JOB CONCLUDED

        TOTAL JOB TIME              .93
```

Fig. P.2

In order to obtain still more information from the analysis, a transfer function
statement is included in the input file. The final version of this file is

```
Resistive circuit with Voltage Source
Vs 1 0 12V
R1 1 2 50
R2 2 0 100
R3 2 0 200
.OPT nopage
.OP.
PRINT dc I(R1) I(R2) I(R3)
.dc Vs 12V 12V 12V
.TF V(2) Vs
.END
```

The output file is shown in Fig. P.3. The small-signal bias solution has been restored
with the OP statement. The TF statement gives the ratio V(2)/Vs along with the
input resistance at Vs and the output resistance at V(2). Check the results against
your own solution. What should be the value of the input resistance? Note that the
output resistance is found with V_S shorted, placing the three resistors in parallel.

```
**** 08/02/96 15:29:38 ******* Win32s Evaluation PSpice (April 1996) *********

 Resistive Circuit with Voltage Source

 ****     CIRCUIT DESCRIPTION

 *******************************************************************************

Vs 1 0 dc 12V
R1 1 2 50
R2 2 0 100
R3 2 0 200
.OPT nopage
.dc Vs 12V 12V 12V
.PRINT dc I(R1) I(R2) I(R3)
.TF V(2) Vs
.END

 ****     DC TRANSFER CURVES                  TEMPERATURE =    27.000 DEG C

   Vs           I(R1)         I(R2)         I(R3)

    1.200E+01    1.029E-01    6.857E-02    3.429E-02

 ****     SMALL SIGNAL BIAS SOLUTION          TEMPERATURE =    27.000 DEG C

 NODE    VOLTAGE     NODE   VOLTAGE     NODE   VOLTAGE     NODE    VOLTAGE

 (   1)  12.0000  (    2)    6.8571

     VOLTAGE SOURCE CURRENTS
     NAME            CURRENT

     Vs            -1.029E-01

    TOTAL POWER DISSIPATION   1.23E+00  WATTS

 ****     SMALL-SIGNAL CHARACTERISTICS

     V(2)/Vs =  5.714E-01

     INPUT RESISTANCE AT Vs =  1.167E+02

     OUTPUT RESISTANCE AT V(2) =  2.857E+01

        JOB CONCLUDED

        TOTAL JOB TIME            .33
```

Fig. P.3

AC CIRCUIT ANALYSIS

An ac circuit example will show some of the features available for steady-state sinusoidal circuits.

Figure P.4 shows a circuit with a source voltage of 100 V at a frequency of 100 Hz. This could be the effective (rms) value or the peak value; all other voltages and currents will be shown accordingly. The circuit has resistance, capacitance, and inductance. The input file is named *acpre.cir* and contains the following:

```
Series-Parallel ac Circuit
Vs I 0 ac 100V
R1 1 2 10
R2 2 3 10
L 3 0 100mH
C 2 0 10uF
.ac LIN 1 100Hz 100Hz
.PRINT ac I(R1) IP(R1) V(2) VP(2)
.PRINT ac I(C) IP(C) I(R2) IP(R2)
.OPT nopage
.END
```

Since the source voltage is ac rather than dc, it must be shown as such. The inductance is 100 mH; the H is optional but is used for appearance sake. The ac statement provides an ac sweep. It is a linear sweep (LIN), although either an octave or a decade sweep could be chosen. The sweep involves only a single value of frequency, but without it the desired results could not be printed. The *OPT* statement prevents unnecessary title banners and page feeds. In most of the examples in the rest of the book, this statement will not be used; it can always be included if desired.

The results of the PSpice analysis are shown in Fig. P.5. The small-signal bias solution is of no interest. It would apply only if there were dc sources involved. This portion of the output file is often edited out before the results are printed. The current I(C) is the magnitude of the current in the C branch; IP(C) is the phase angle in degrees of this current. The current I(R2) is the magnitude of the current in the branch with R2 *and* L; IP(R2) is the phase angle of this current.

Using a calculator, verify that the sum of these currents is the same as the current shown through RI. In rectangular form these are

$$I_C + I_{R2} = (0.0548, 0.60823) + (0.32, -0.873)$$
$$= 0.9298/\underline{-69.87°}$$

Note that the statement for RI is given as

```
R1 1 2 10
```

The nodes are given in the order *1, 2*. This will reference the current in the direction away from the source. When an attempt is made to add currents, the reference directions should be carefully noted and placed on the circuit diagram.

Fig. P.4 An ac circuit for SPICE analysis.

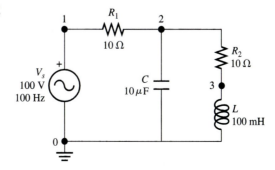

```
Series-Parallel ac Circuit

 ****      CIRCUIT DESCRIPTION

 ****************************************************************************

Vs 1 0 ac 100V
R1 1 2 10
R2 2 3 10
L 3 0 100mH
C 2 0 10uF
.ac LIN 1 100Hz 100Hz
.PRINT ac I(R1) IP(R1) V(2) VP(2)
.PRINT ac I(C) IP(C) I(R2) IP(R2)
.OPT nopage
.END

 ****      SMALL SIGNAL BIAS SOLUTION       TEMPERATURE =   27.000 DEG C

 NODE   VOLTAGE      NODE   VOLTAGE      NODE   VOLTAGE      NODE   VOLTAGE

 (   1)    0.0000  (   2)    0.0000  (   3)    0.0000

     VOLTAGE SOURCE CURRENTS
     NAME          CURRENT

     Vs           0.000E+00

     TOTAL POWER DISSIPATION   0.00E+00  WATTS

 ****      AC ANALYSIS                      TEMPERATURE =   27.000 DEG C

   FREQ        I(R1)        IP(R1)       V(2)         VP(2)

   1.000E+02   9.295E-01   -6.988E+01   9.719E+01   5.152E+00

 ****      AC ANALYSIS                      TEMPERATURE =   27.000 DEG C

   FREQ        I(C)         IP(C)        I(R2)        IP(R2)

   1.000E+02   6.107E-01    9.515E+01   1.528E+00   -7.580E+01

             JOB CONCLUDED

             TOTAL JOB TIME            1.15
```

Fig. P.5

A more interesting ac analysis can be obtained when the frequency is swept between two chosen limits. In our example, a rough approximation of the resonant frequency shows it to be near $f_o = 160$ Hz. The input file is changed as follows:

```
Series-Parallel ac Circuit
Vs 1 0 ac 100V
R1 1 2 10
R2 2 3 10
L 3 0 100mH
C 2 0 10uF
.ac LIN 151 50Hz 200Hz
.probe
.end
```

The *.ac* statement will give a linear sweep of *151* values of frequency in the range from 50 Hz to 200 Hz. This means that calculations will be performed for each integer frequency in the chosen range. The *.probe* statement will place the results in a probe data file, which in this case is called *acpre.dat*.

Probe

When the PSpice analysis is run, the results will automatically be available to you in the Probe program. In PSpice select <u>F</u>ile, <u>R</u>un Probe. The screen will show the axes for a graph with frequency along the horizontal axis. Now select <u>T</u>race, <u>A</u>dd, and type for the <u>T</u>race Command.

```
IP(R1)
```

This produces a plot, called a trace, of the phase of the current through R1, which is the total circuit current from the source. The plot may now be changed as follows: Select <u>P</u>lot, <u>X</u> Axis Settings . . . Then select the <u>U</u>ser Defined and enter the values "50Hz" to "200 Hz" Finally, select the Li<u>n</u>ear button and click OK.

Next, for a title, choose T<u>o</u>ols, <u>L</u>abel, <u>T</u>ext . . . and type

```
Phase angle of circuit current
```

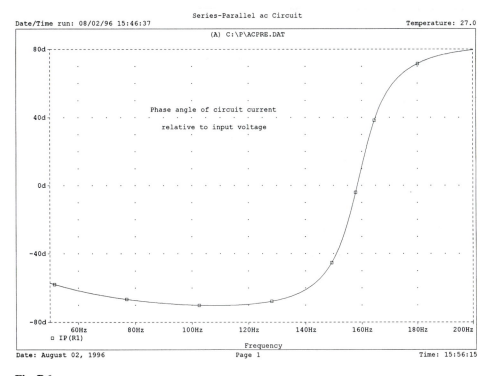

Fig. P.6

Repeat the process for the second line, which is

`relative to input voltage`

Use the mouse to move the text to a convenient location on the graph. Now you are ready to obtain a printed copy of the plot. This is done by selecting File, Print, OK. The plot should be like the one shown in Fig. P.6.

While still in Probe, choose the cursor mode by using the "Toggle Display of cursor" icon near the top right of the screen. (As you move among the icons, their descriptions are shown on the bottom left. See Fig. P.7 and note that the desired icon shows crosshairs and a check mark.)

The Probe Cursor display near the bottom of the screen shows the following:

```
A1 =      50.000,    -57.073
A2 =      50.000,    -57.073
dif =      0.000,      0.000
```

The *A1* values are for the beginning frequency (*X*-axis) and phase-shift angle (the IP plot). Since the cursor has not been moved, the A2 values are a repeat of the *A1* values. Use the mouse to select the point on the curve where the phase shift is near zero. Then use the left and right arrows to move to the exact desired spot. The cursor display should now be

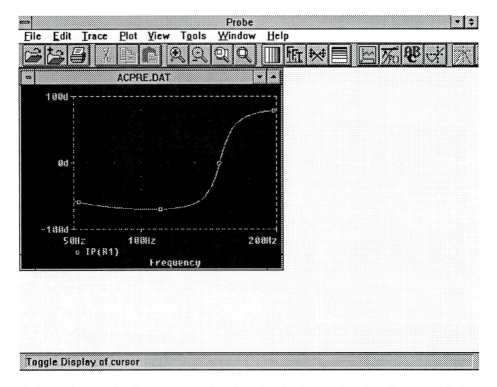

Fig. P.7   Phase angle of current in Probe. Note that the "Toggle Display of cursor" is being selected.

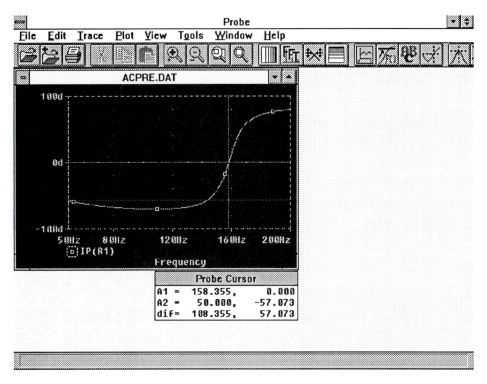

Fig. P.8 The cursor is being used to find the location of the resonant frequency.

```
A1 =      158.355      0.000
A2 =       50.000    -57.073
dif =     108.355     57.073
```

The A1 values show the new frequency of *158.355* Hz and the phase shift of *0°*. The *A2* values are retained as they were initially. The dif (difference) values are self-explanatory. Note that the *0.000* values for phase shift may not be exactly obtained. A very small value may instead appear. If you run the simulation again, the results may differ slightly in Probe. See Fig. P.8 for this display.

Remove the cursor display (the icon toggles) and select Plot, Add Plot. A new plot area now appears above the original plot. See if you can add plots of the currents through *R1, C,* and *L,* respectively. Then label the plots as shown in Fig. P.9 and obtain a printed copy. Note that the magnitude of the total current is less than the magnitude of the inductive-branch current. It is also sometimes less than the magnitude of the capacitive-branch current.

TRANSISTOR CIRCUIT ANALYSIS

The next preview circuit is for a bipolar-junction (BJT) with a typical biasing set of resistors. This circuit is shown in Fig. P.10. PSpice allows the use of *built-in* models

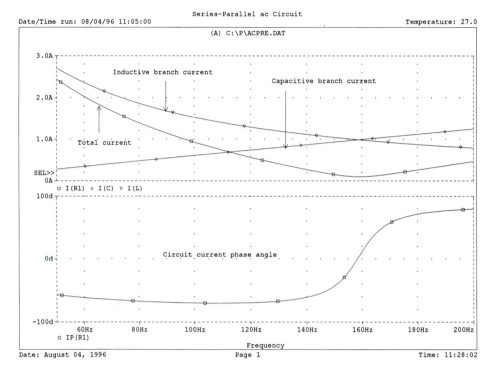

Fig. P.9

for BJTs and other devices. Assume that the transistor has a large-signal current gain, $h_{FE} = 80$, and that under typical forward-bias conditions $V_{BE} = 0.8$ V.

Before going to the PSpice solution, we will consider the usual method for finding bias currents and voltages. It is assumed that from your studies you are familiar with these methods, and this will serve as a brief review. When the circuit is opened at the base, the Thevenin voltage is found using voltage division:

$$V_{Th} = \frac{V_{CC}R_2}{R_1 + R_2} = \frac{(12)(5)}{45} = 1.333 \text{ V}$$

To find the Thevenin resistance, V_{CC} is shorted, placing R_1 and R_2 in parallel. The Thevenin resistance is

$$R_{Th} = R_1 \parallel R_2 = 40 \text{ k}\Omega \parallel 5 \text{ k}\Omega = 4.444 \text{ k}\Omega$$

Applying KVL to the loop containing R_{Th} and R_E, we have

$$V_{Th} = R_{Th}I_B + V_{BE} + R_E(h_{FE} + 1)$$
$$1.333 \text{ V} = (4.444 \text{ k}\Omega)I_B + 0.8 \text{ V} + (100 \text{ }\Omega)(80 + 1)$$

Fig. P.10 A BJT biasing circuit.

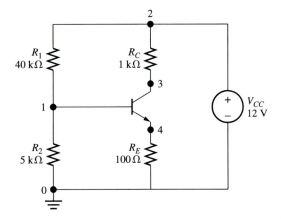

Solving for I_B yields

$$I_B = 42.5 \ \mu\text{A}$$

Since $I_C = h_{FE}I_B$, this gives a collector current of *3.4* mA. The emitter current is the sum of the collector and base currents and is *3.44* mA. The voltages at nodes *3, 4*, and finally node *1* are now found using the known currents.

The voltage at the collector is

$$V_3 = V_{CC} - R_C I_C = 12 - (1 \ \text{k}\Omega)(3.4 \ \text{mA}) = 8.6 \ \text{V}$$

The voltage at the emitter is

$$V_4 = R_E I_E = (100 \ \Omega)(3.44 \ \text{mA}) = 0.344 \ \text{V}$$

The voltage at the base is

$$V_1 = V_{BE} + V_4 = 0.8 + 0.344 = 1.144 \ \text{V}$$

Although the solution has not been difficult, it is certainly time consuming. If some of the parameters of the circuit change, the solution must again be found. PSpice will allow these repetitive solutions to be found more easily. The input file is

```
BJT Biasing Circuit
VCC 2 0 12V
R1 2 1 40k
R2 1 0 5k
RC 2 3 1k
RE 4 0 100
Q1 3 1 4 QN
.MODEL QN NPN(BF=80)
.dc VCC 12V 12V 22V
.OP
.OPT nopage
.PRINT dc I(R1) I(R2) I(RC) I(RE)
.END
```

```
**** 05/19/96 20:35:32 ******* Win32s Evaluation PSpice (April 1995) *********
 BJT Biasing Circuit
*****      CIRCUIT DESCRIPTION
VCC 2 0 12V
R1 2 1 40k
R2 1 0 5k
RC 2 3 1k
RE 4 0 100
Q1 3 1 4 QN
.MODEL QN NPN(BF=80)
.dc VCC 12V 12V 12V
.OP
.OPT nopage
.PRINT dc I(R1) I(R2) I(RC) I(RE)
.END


    ****      BJT MODEL PARAMETERS
               QN
               NPN
          IS  100.000000E-18
          BF   80
          NF    1
          BR    1
          NR    1


    ****      DC TRANSFER CURVES              TEMPERATURE =   27.000 DEG C
     VCC          I(R1)        I(R2)       I(RC)       I(RE)

    1.200E+01    2.713E-04    2.293E-04    3.366E-03    3.408E-03

    ****      SMALL SIGNAL BIAS SOLUTION        TEMPERATURE =   27.000 DEG C

  NODE    VOLTAGE      NODE    VOLTAGE      NODE    VOLTAGE      NODE    VOLTAGE

 (   1)    1.1464  (    2)   12.0000  (    3)    8.6345  (    4)     .3408


     VOLTAGE SOURCE CURRENTS
     NAME           CURRENT

     VCC          -3.637E-03


     TOTAL POWER DISSIPATION    4.36E-02   WATTS

   ****      OPERATING POINT INFORMATION        TEMPERATURE =   27.000 DEG C

**** BIPOLAR JUNCTION TRANSISTORS
NAME          Q1
MODEL         QN
IB            4.21E-05
IC            3.37E-03
VBE           8.06E-01
VBC          -7.49E+00
VCE           8.29E+00
BETADC        8.00E+01
GM            1.30E-01
RPI           6.15E+02
RX            0.00E+00
RO            1.00E+12
CBE           0.00E+00
CBC           0.00E+00
CBX           0.00E+00
CJS           0.00E+00
BETAAC        8.00E+01
FT            2.07E+18
```

Fig. P.11

The chosen name for the BJT must begin with *Q*. The numbers *3, 1,* and *4* are the nodes of the *collector, base,* and *emitter,* respectively. *QN* is our chosen model name for an *npn* transistor. The .MODEL statement contains our chosen model name and the required NPN designation for the *built-in* model of an *npn* BJT. The *BF=80* gives a dc beta of *80.* The results of the PSpice analysis are shown in Fig. P.11. The values given for the currents and voltages are close to those predicted.

In the chapter on bipolar-junction transistors (Chapter 3), this circuit will be the foundation for a case study that will involve using the BJT as a common-emitter amplifier. Among other things, the voltage gain, current gain, input resistance, and output resistance will be found.

1

DC Circuit Analysis

Direct-current circuits are important not only in themselves, but also because many of the techniques used in dc analysis will carry over into ac circuit analysis. In fact, many of the electronic devices and circuits can be analyzed using these same methods.

AN INTRODUCTORY EXAMPLE

Figure 1.1 shows a series circuit with a dc voltage source and three resistors connected in series. The most important feature of this circuit is that all elements carry the same current. If the current through any element is known, the current through all other elements will of necessity be the same. Another important feature of this circuit is that the applied voltage (in this case 50 V) will divide among the resistors in direct proportion to their respective resistances. For example, the voltage drop across the 150-Ω resistor will be three times as great as the voltage drop across the 50-Ω resistor. Using the concept of voltage division, it is easy to find the voltage drops without knowing the circuit current. Thus the voltage drop across R_3 is

$$V_{R3} = V\left(\frac{R_3}{R_1 + R_2 + R_3}\right) = 50 \cdot \frac{150}{100 + 50 + 150} = 25 \text{ V}$$

Likewise, the voltage drop across R_2 is

$$V_{R2} = V\left(\frac{R_2}{R_1 + R_2 + R_3}\right) = 50 \cdot \frac{50}{100 + 50 + 150} = 8.333 \text{ V}$$

Fig. 1.1 Series circuit with three resistors.

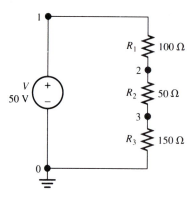

The current is easily found from either of these voltages:

$$I = \frac{V_{R3}}{R_3} = \frac{25}{150} = 0.1667 \ A$$

or

$$I = \frac{V_{R2}}{R_2} = \frac{8.333}{50} = 0.1667 \ A$$

USING SPICE TO INVESTIGATE THE CIRCUIT

Use the Notepad to enter the statements for the PSpice analysis. After entering the lines of the file, give it a name, such as *prob1.cir*. Be sure that each line is entered exactly as shown:

```
Spice Analysis of a Series Circuit
V 1 0 50V
R1 1 2 100
R2 2 3 50
R3 3 0 150
.OP
.END
```

There is a statement for each element of the circuit. Each line of the input file is a statement. If you have a very long statement, begin the second line with a plus (+) sign. The statements include the voltage source and the three resistors. The beginning statement is necessary for PSpice and serves to identify the circuit. The *V* statement is for the independent voltage. Nodes *1* and *0* are the plus and minus nodes, respectively; *50V* is for the value 50 volts. Note that there is no space between *50* and *V*. The *V* may be omitted if desired. Each *R* statement identifies a particular resistor and its associated nodes along with the resistance in ohms. The *.OP* statement is a control statement that will give the maximum amount of information, and the *.END* statement is needed as a signal that there are no more statements.

After you have completed entering the file, saved it, and exited from the Notepad, select the PSpice icon in the MicroSim workgroup, then File, Open . . . .

(In Program Manager, using File, Properties, the Working Directory for all the icons should have already been set to *c:\p*. If this has not been done, do so at this time.)

The Simulation of the Circuit

When the file *prob1.cir* is selected, the simulation of the circuit will proceed. In a moment the screen should show

```
Reading and checking errors
Bias point calculated
No errors
```

after which a window appears with the message

```
Simulation completed successfully
```

Choose OK to remain in the PSpice program. Now, (1) choose File, Examine Output to invoke the MicroSim text editor, or (2) examine the output outside the PSpice program by using the Notepad and opening the file *c:.\p\prob1.out*, or (3) examine the output in a word processor such as Microsoft Word, Word Pro, or WordPerfect. The last choice gives you more flexibility in formatting the output text using the Courier New TrueType font, eliminating unnecessary blank lines, repetitive lines, and page-feed characters.

Examining the Output File

You may want to eliminate lines containing merely asterisks and the line that pertains to temperature. Now, print the file using the File, Print command in whatever editor you are using. The most important part of the output file contains information about the various node voltages. You should see the following:

```
Node Voltage  Node Voltage   Node Voltage
( 1) 50.0000  ( 2) 33.3330   ( 3) 25.0000
```

Node voltage *1* is the voltage V_{10}, the source voltage. Node voltage *2* is the voltage V_{20}, the voltage drop across both R_2 and R_3. Node voltage *3* is the voltage V_{30}, the voltage drop across R_3.

We predicted that V_{R3} (which is V_{30}) would be 25 V, so the PSpice analysis seems correct. How can you check for V_{R2}? This will be $V_2 - V_3$, which is actually $V_{20} - V_{30}$.

$$V_2 - V_3 = 33.333 - 25.000 = 8.333 \text{ V}$$

The PSpice analysis also gives the voltage-source current; the voltage source is called *V*, and the current is given as $-1.667E-01$. The current has the correct numerical value, but what is the reason for the minus sign? SPICE shows source currents from plus to minus inside the source. Since the current is actually from minus to plus inside the source, it is given as a negative value. Or simply stated, when a source current is negative, it is from the positive terminal to the external circuit.

Note that the statement describing the voltage source was correctly given as

```
V 1 0 50V
```

As previously stated, this means that the positive terminal is at node *1*, the negative terminal is at node *0*, and the value of the voltage is 50 V (dc implied). Incidentally, independent voltages must begin with the letter *V* and are typically written as *V1*, *V2*, *VIN*, and so forth.

Notice that the total power dissipation is also given in the SPICE analysis as 8.33 watts. This is simply the product of *V* and *I*, $50 \cdot 0.1667 = 8.33$ W.

How much more information can you obtain for the circuit in Fig. 1.1? After you have thought of other things that might be found, look at another simple, common circuit.

Another Simple Circuit for Analysis

Consider the circuit in Fig. 1.2. This is a tee (*T*) circuit with a 50-V source and a load resistance $R_4 = 150 \ \Omega$. This resistor is the load attached to the *T* portion of the circuit and might be changed to other values as needed. The load resistor is sometimes thought of as the output resistor.

Can you find the voltage across the load resistor and the current through it? To be specific, find V_3 and *I* (the current in the direction from node *3* to *0*).

The input resistance R_{in} is found by adding R_2 and R_4 (sum of 200 Ω), putting this in parallel with R_3(200 ∥ 200 = 100 Ω), and adding R_1(sum of 200 Ω). Thus $R_{in} = 200 \ \Omega$.

The source (input) current is $V/R_{in} = 50/200 = 0.25$ A (out of the plus side of *V*).

The voltage drop across R_1 is $IR_1 = 0.25 \cdot 100 = 25$ V. The voltage drop across R_3 is $V - V_{R1} = 50 - 25 = 25$ V.

The voltage drop across R_4 is found by voltage division as

$$V_{R4} = \frac{V_{R3}R_4}{R_2 + R_4} = 25 \cdot \frac{150}{50 + 150} = 18.75 \text{ V}$$

The current *I* is found as $V_{R4}/R_4 = 18.75/150 = 0.125$ A.

In Fig. 1.2, the voltage across R_4 is called V_3, meaning precisely V_{30}. You may analyze this circuit by other methods, and you are encouraged to do so.

Fig. 1.2 Tee (*T*) circuit.

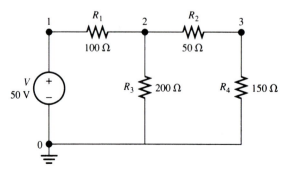

After you have obtained your pencil-and-paper results, it is time to look at what can be done with PSpice. Create a file called *prob2.cir* containing the following statements:

```
Spice Analysis of a Tee Circuit
V 1 0 50V
R1 1 2 100
R2 2 3 50
R3 2 0 200
R4 3 0 150
.OP
.OPTIONS NOPAGE
.TF V (3) V
.END
```

As usual, the file contains a title statement and is completed with the .END statement. Another statement that requires consideration is the .TF statement. This is a transfer function; it contains an output and input reference, respectively. The output is V(3), representing the voltage across R_4, and the input is V, which is the source voltage. It is your choice as to what you will call the output variable; it might be the voltage across another resistor, for example. Simply stated, the transfer function will give the ratio V(3) /V. In this example it will be 18.75/50 = 0.375.

The .OPTIONS statement with the option *NOPAGE* prevents unnecessary banners and page headings. You may want to include such a statement in all your input files. It is preferable to edit out all unnecessary lines from the output file. In this case, it makes little difference whether the NOPAGE option is used or not. For this reason this statement will not be found in the ensuing examples.

Run the PSpice analysis and look at the file PROB2.OUT. Remember to strip the file of unwanted lines and form feeds; then obtain a printed copy for further study. Verify the voltage drop across R_3. This is V(2) in the PSpice output. Also verify the voltage drop across R_4. This is V(3) as shown in Fig. 1.2. The voltage-source current is given as $-2.5E-1$, for -0.25 A. Is this the expected value?

Now look for the bonus information obtained by using the .TF statement. The ratio V(3)/V is given as 0.375. Is this correct?

Also, we now have values shown for both input and output resistances. What is meant by each of these? The input resistance is the resistance as seen by the source V, which is referred to as the second parameter in the .TF statement. This parameter is always an input source name. Recall our calculation of R_{in} = 200 Ω. Your PSpice value should confirm this.

What is meant by output resistance? The output variable was specified in the .TF statement as V(3). We must look back into the circuit between nodes *3* and *0* with the source voltage V deactivated (shorted, not simply removed). Thus R_1 and R_3 are in parallel, and this combination is in series with R_2, with that combination in parallel with R_4. Verify that this will yield R_{out} = 65.63 Ω.

In many circuits, it is desirable to compare an output variable with an input source. Sometimes this is referred to as a *gain*. If both of these values are voltages, the result is called a *voltage gain*. In circuits containing only passive devices such as the resistors of Fig. 1.2, along with the independent source, this gain will be less than 1. The value of the voltage gain is 0.375.

In summary, we have looked at simple resistive circuits for the purpose of seeing how they are analyzed by pencil-and-paper methods and how the results are verified using PSpice. Keep in mind that you will not want to use the PSpice tool as a substitute for understanding basic theory. If you do not understand how resistors in series and parallel may be combined to find equivalent resistances, do not assume that a computer analysis will take you through. Actually, you will find that in order to get the most out of a tool such as SPICE, you must know a great deal about circuit analysis.

At this point, you might ask why bother with SPICE? There are two reasons. After you apply SPICE to simple circuits and thoroughly understand what you are doing, you can use the same tools on circuits that are far more complicated than you care to solve by other methods. In addition, SPICE is so widely used that it is considered by many to be a necessary tool of the trade.

Remember, independent-voltage statements begin with V and resistance statements begin with R. Use labels for voltage and resistance that will be easy to recognize in the circuit you are modeling. VS or VIN might be chosen for source voltages, and RS could represent the internal resistance of the source.

Next, we will look at some important circuit-analysis techniques and how SPICE can be used to verify important theorems.

BASIC CIRCUIT LAWS

In the study of electric circuits, it is well known that the algebraic sum of the voltages around a closed path is equal to zero. This is Kirchoff's voltage law. Kirchoff's current law is that the algebraic sum of the currents entering a junction is equal to zero. Figure 1.3 demonstrates the correctness of these two laws. Since the circuit contains three meshes and four nodes (in addition to the reference node), do not

Fig. 1.3   Circuit with three meshes.

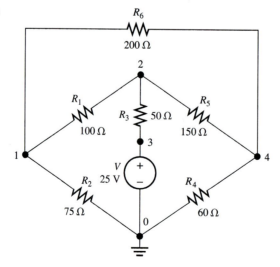

attempt to solve it by pencil-and-paper methods at this time, but set up the SPICE file instead. Do this yourself; then compare your results with the file given here.

```
Bridge Circuit for Use with Basic Circuit Laws
V  3  0  25V
R1  1  2  100
R2  1  0  75
R3  2  3  50
R4  4  0  60
R5  2  4  150
R6  1  4  200
.OP
.END
```

Run the PSpice analysis and obtain a printed copy for further study and work. We recommend that you leave room on your PSpice printed copy to show a sketch of the circuit, with all known values indicated. Show the location of the various nodes that go with the statements. It is easy to see the node labels if they are shown in a different color.

Find the sum of the voltages around the loop at the left, namely,

$$V_{12} + V_{23} + V_{30} + V_{01}$$

Remember that V_{12} is actually $V_1 - V_2$, and so forth. Check your values against these respective numbers:

$$-9.7039 - 8.632 + 25.000 - 6.6641 = 0$$

The zero sum is a verification of Kirchoff's voltage law. Now write the symbolic equation for the loop on the right and check to see that the sum is zero. After you have done this, consider the following loop voltages:

$$V_{13} + V_{34} + V_{41} = 0$$

In the figure, note that V_{13} can be found as $V_1 - V_3$; you do not have to follow a wired path, going from node *1* to node *2* and then from node *2* to node *3*. In the laboratory, if you measured the voltage V_{13}, you would place the red lead at node *1* and black lead at node *3*. The voltmeter should read -18.34 V. Check your calculations for the sum of the voltages, which should be

$$-18.3359 + 19.9727 - 1.6368 = 0$$

Remember that the order of the subscripts determines whether a voltage will be given as a positive or negative value. That is, if V_{12} is positive (say, 6.5 V), then V_{21} is negative (-6.5 V). The importance of giving the proper sign to a voltage cannot be overstated.

Find the sum of the currents entering node *1*. Call these I_{21}, I_{01}, and I_{41}. Show these in symbolic form, then substitute the values. Thus

$$I_{21} = \frac{V_2 - V_1}{R_1} = 97.039 \text{ mA}$$

$$I_{01} = \frac{-V_1}{R_2} = -88.855 \text{ mA}$$

$$I_{41} = \frac{V_4 - V_1}{R_6} = -8.184 \text{ mA}$$

The sum of the currents equals zero, verifying Kirchoff's current law. Incidentally, the value for I_{01} is rounded to five significant digits. Otherwise, the sum will be slightly different.

Currents are often shown with a single subscript rather than a double subscript. If a single subscript is to be used, you should show the direction of the currents in the diagram; otherwise, the solution is ambiguous! This is just as important as giving the proper sign to a voltage.

Getting More from the Output File

Can we obtain more information from the simulation, especially more about the branch currents? Revise the input file to include the statements

```
.PRINT DC I(R1) I(R2) I(R3)
.PRINT DC I(R4) I(R5) I(R6)
.DC V 25V 25V 25V
.OPT nopage
```

The *.OPT nopage* statement is an abbreviated version of *.OPTIONS NOPAGE*. Now, save the new version of the circuit file and run the simulation again. The results are shown in Fig. 1.4. The *.PRINT* statements were used, along with the *.DC* statement, to produce the desired listing of currents through the various resistors.

Current Directions

Some currents are given as positive and some as negative. For example the current I(R1) $= -9.704E-02$ means that $I_{R1} = -97.04$ mA. The line in the input file describing R_1 contains

```
R1 1 2 100
```

Now, since PSpice gives the current I(R1) as a negative value, it means that the positive direction of current is actually from node *2* toward node *1*.

To check the current law again, find the sum of the currents at node *2*. Set up the symbolic form of the equations, then substitute the values.

CIRCUIT WITH TWO VOLTAGE SOURCES

Figure 1.5 shows a circuit with two voltage sources. Although it is not an involved circuit, finding the various currents and voltages will require significant effort. We assume that you will not attempt mesh or nodal analysis at this time. (More on these methods will follow). Another technique, almost intuitive, is to consider the effects of each source taken one at a time. That is, consider the circuit *a* with source V_1 in place and source V_2 inactive (replaced by a short circuit); then consider the circuit *b* with source V_2 in place and source V_1 inactive.

Draw the original circuit; then draw the circuit *a* and also the circuit *b*. Find the voltage at node *2* for each of the circuits. After you have done this, compare your values with these values: $V_2(a) = 6.75$ V, $V_2(b) = 5.06$ V. By using the con-

```
Bridge Circuit for Use with Basic Circuit Laws

 ****        CIRCUIT DESCRIPTION

V 3 0 25V
R1 1 2 100
R2 1 0 75
R3 2 3 50
R4 4 0 60
R5 2 4 150
R6 1 4 200
.PRINT DC I(R1) I(R2) I(R3)
.PRINT DC I(R4) I(R5) I(R6)
.DC V 25V 25V 25V
.OP
.OPT nopage
.END

   V            I(R1)       I(R2)       I(R3)
    2.500E+01  -9.704E-02   8.885E-02  -1.726E-01

   V            I(R4)       I(R5)       I(R6)
    2.500E+01   8.379E-02   7.560E-02   8.184E-03

  NODE    VOLTAGE     NODE    VOLTAGE     NODE    VOLTAGE     NODE    VOLTAGE
 (    1)   6.6641  (    2)   16.3680  (    3)   25.0000  (    4)    5.0273

      VOLTAGE SOURCE CURRENTS
      NAME          CURRENT
      V            -1.726E-01

    TOTAL POWER DISSIPATION   4.32E+00  WATTS
```

Fig. 1.4

cept of *superposition*, the actual voltage at node *2* will be the sum of these two values; thus, $V_2 = 11.81$ V.

You can find the source current from V_1. In symbols,

$$I_{12} = \frac{V_1 - V_2}{R_1}$$

$$I_{12} = \frac{20 - 11.81}{100} = 81.9 \text{ mA}$$

Superposition is useful in circuits containing resistors and more than one source; however, three or more sources might make the calculations very tedious.

Now use SPICE to verify your work. Your file should look something like this:

```
Circuit with Two Voltage Sources
V1 1 0 20V
V2 3 0 12V
R1 1 2 100
R2 2 3 80
R3 2 0 140
.OP
.TF V(2) V1
.END
```

Fig. 1.5 Circuit with two voltage sources.

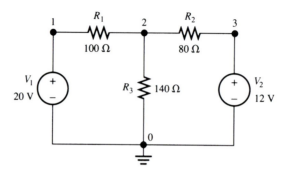

The PSpice results will show V(2) = 11.807 V, in close agreement with the calculations using superposition. The voltage-source current for V_1 is given by PSpice as $-8.193\text{E}-2$. Recall that this means that the current will be from the positive node of the source V_1.

What does the PSpice value for the input resistance mean? The resistance is referred to source V_1. It is the resistance seen by this source when the other source V_2 is inactive. This places the 80-Ω resistor and the 140-Ω resistor in parallel and adds the 100-Ω resistor to that combination, giving R_{in} = 150.9 Ω.

Can you explain the output resistance? Recall that the .TF statement listed V(2) as the output variable. Visualize the output resistance as being seen between nodes 2 and 0 with all voltage sources inactive (shorted out). This gives R_1, R_2, and R_3 all in parallel. It is easily verified that the equivalent resistance of this combination is 33.7 Ω.

THEVENIN'S THEOREM AND APPLICATIONS

What is Thevenin's theorem, and why is it so important and useful? If you consider a nontrivial circuit and would like to work with a variety of load resistances for the circuit, Thevenin's theorem provides the ideal method.

Refer to Fig. 1.6(a), which contains a voltage source and several resistors, including a load resistor, R_L. Find the voltage across R_L and the current through it. If you find the equivalent resistance of the circuit, then the source current, and next the voltage drop across R_1, and so forth, you will eventually be able to find the voltage drop across R_L. However, if R_L changes in value, the entire solution must be reworked. The Thevenin theorem will help solve this problem.

Begin by removing the load resistance. Your method is to be independent of R_L, and this is important. Now, find the voltage V_{30}. Simply stated, this is the voltage across the load terminals with the load resistance removed. This may be called V_{Th}.

Next, find the resistance as seen at the load terminals. This might be called R_{Th}.

Now, replace the circuit with a practical voltage source consisting of V_{Th} in series with R_{Th}. Then the load resistance R_L may be put back in the circuit. As far as this resistance is concerned, the voltage drop across it, the current through it, and the power consumed by it will be the same as in the original circuit.

For Fig. 1.6, find V_{Th} and R_{Th}. Remove R_L; then use the voltage division to find V_{20} = 50 V. To find R_{Th}, make V inactive by replacing it with a short circuit. Now

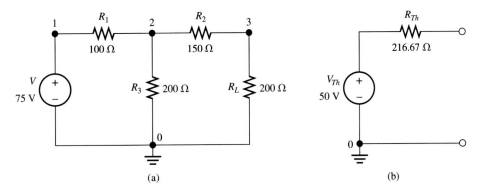

(a)

(b)

Fig. 1.6 (a) Circuit to illustrate Thevenin's theorem. (b) Thevenin voltage and series resistance.

looking at the network from terminals *3* and *0*, you calculate the resistance is R_{Th} = 216.67 Ω. The practical voltage source consists of V_{Th} in series with R_{Th}. Thus in Fig. 1.6(b) you have the new circuit. It can now be easily solved with any value of R_L in place. For example, when R_L = 200 Ω, use voltage division to find V_{30} = 24 V. On the other hand, when R_L = 300 Ω, V_{30} = 29 V.

SPICE and Thevenin's Theorem

Continuing with the circuit of Fig. 1.6, now use PSpice to verify your solution. Instead of simply removing R_L, replace the actual R_L with a very large load resistance, say, R_L = 1 teraohm (1E12). The circuit file will be

```
Thevenin Circuit for Spice
V 1 0 75V
R1 1 2 100
R2 2 3 150
R3 2 0 200
RL 3 0 1E12
.OP
.TF V(3) V
.END
```

After running the PSpice analysis, note that V(2) = 50.0000 V and V(3)= 50.0000 V. Be sure that you can explain these results before going on. What is the value of V_{Th}?

The .TF statement gave the output resistance at V(3) as 216.7 Ω. This is the R_{Th}. Note that R_4 was many orders of magnitude larger than any of the other resistors in the circuit. Thus R_4 has a negligible loading effect on the circuit. You may want to use a smaller value for this resistance and compare the results.

Practical Application of Thevenin's Theorem

The previous example was easy enough to solve without calling on PSpice. If the problem gets more involved, like Fig. 1.7, PSpice can save a great deal of time. Set up the file for solving this problem, then check your results against those given here.

Fig. 1.7 Bridge-tee circuit and Thevenin equivalent.

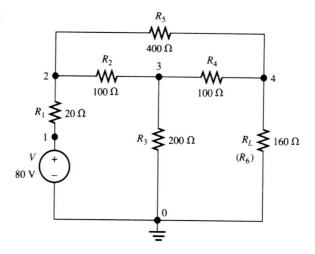

```
Thevenin Analysis of Bridged-Tee Circuit
V  1  0  80V
R1 2  1  20
R2 2  3  100
R3 3  0  200
R4 3  4  100
R5 2  4  400
R6 4  0  1E8
.OP
.TF V(4) V
.END
```

The output file is shown in Fig. 1.8. The voltage V(4) = 57.143 V is V_{Th}. The output resistance at V(4) = 128.6 Ω is R_{Th}. Note that both the open-circuit voltage and the resistance looking into the circuit at the load terminals with the load resistance removed are found by the simple technique of replacing the actual load resistance with a very large resistance value.

From the results of the analysis, draw the Thevenin practical voltage source, containing V_{Th} and R_{Th} in series. The original diagram showed a value R_L = 160 Ω. You have not needed this value until this point in the solution. Now, with R_L in place, you may find the values of load voltage and load current.

Was it worth the effort of using PSpice to find the Thevenin values for this problem? Try to find V_{Th} and R_{Th} by pencil-and-paper methods, and you will agree it was.

What do you think would happen if you omitted R_6 in the circuit file for the problem you just finished? You should try this, verifying that the results are the same. The reason that R_6 can be omitted is that node *4* will not be left hanging without a return path to ground.

Circuit for Thevenin Replacement

The circuit of Fig. 1.9 offers another opportunity to use Thevenin's theorem. In this circuit, several different values of R_L are to be used, and you desire to find the volt-

```
    **** 05/20/96 11:33:25 ******* Win32s Evaluation PSpice (April 1995) *********

    Thevenin Analysis of Bridged-Tee Circuit

    ****       CIRCUIT DESCRIPTION

    ***********************************************************************************
    V 1 0 80V
    R1 2 1 20
    R2 2 3 100
    R3 3 0 200
    R4 3 4 100
    R5 2 4 400
    R6 4 0 1E8
    .OP
    .OPT nopage
    .TF V(4) V
    .End

    ****       SMALL SIGNAL BIAS SOLUTION        TEMPERATURE =   27.000 DEG C

    NODE    VOLTAGE        NODE    VOLTAGE        NODE    VOLTAGE        NODE    VOLTAGE

    (   1)    80.0000  (    2)    74.7250  (    3)    52.7470  (    4)    57.1430

        VOLTAGE SOURCE CURRENTS
        NAME            CURRENT

        V               -2.637E-01

        TOTAL POWER DISSIPATION   2.11E+01   WATTS

    ****       OPERATING POINT INFORMATION       TEMPERATURE =   27.000 DEG C

    ****       SMALL-SIGNAL CHARACTERISTICS

        V(4)/V =  7.143E-01

        INPUT RESISTANCE AT V =  3.033E+02

        OUTPUT RESISTANCE AT V(4) =  1.286E+02

            JOB CONCLUDED

            TOTAL JOB TIME              .66
```

Fig. 1.8

age and current associated with each one. Create your PSpice file for the circuit. You will see that R_L can be omitted without using a very large resistance in its place. Check your file against the one shown here.

```
Bridge Circuit for Thevenin
V 4 3 40V
R1 1 2 100
R2 2 0 150
R3 1 4 200
R4 4 0 200
R5 2 3 50
.OP
.TF V(1) V
.END
```

Fig. 1.9 Circuit for Thevenin replacement.

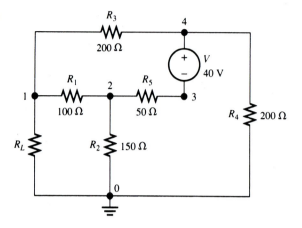

Run the analysis and then draw the Thevenin practical voltage source. Be sure to include the labels for the nodes involved. The results should agree with Fig. 1.10. The nodes are labeled *1* and *0*. Note that the open-circuit voltage at node *1* is negative with respect to node *0*. The PSpice results show $V(1) = -2.9091$ V. The .TF statement gave the output resistance at $V(1)$ as 152.7 Ω. This is R_{Th}. Now you may choose a wide range of values for R_L and complete the circuit analysis.

Using Thevenin's theorem allows you to replace a complicated network with a practical voltage source. Recall that as far as R_L is concerned, it does not matter whether it is being supplied from the original circuit or from the Thevenin practical voltage source. The two circuits are not equivalent, however.

Return to the example of Fig. 1.6, our first Thevenin example. With the load removed, $V_{Th} = 50$ V and $R_{Th} = 216.7$ Ω. With $R_L = 200$ Ω, the current is 0.12 A. Because this is the current throughout the series circuit, the power furnished by the source voltage V_{Th} is 6 W. Since the load power is 2.88 W, the remaining 3.12 W is used by R_{Th}. But in the original circuit, the source voltage is 75 V and the source current will be 0.33 A. This requires a source power of 24.8 W. Since the 200-Ω load requires only 2.88 W, the rest of the power goes to the three resistors in the tee.

The point of this example is simply that the Thevenin practical voltage source is not equivalent to the original circuit. But the statement is still valid that as far as R_L is concerned the results are the same.

Fig. 1.10 Thevenin values for Fig. 1.9.

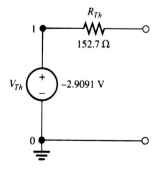

Fig. 1.11 Practical voltage
source with load.

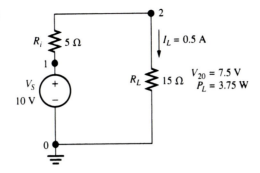

PRACTICAL CURRENT SOURCE VS. PRACTICAL VOLTAGE SOURCE

So far, you have worked with only a single type of source of electrical energy, the
voltage source. In many situations, circuits behave as though they were supplied
from a practical current source instead. Figure 1.11 shows a practical voltage source.
It has an open-circuit voltage of 10 V. This is also called its ideal-voltage source value. To make it a practical voltage source, it must contain an internal resistance in
series with it. This is given as $R_i = 5\ \Omega$. The circuit is completed with the addition
of $R_L = 15\ \Omega$.

Solving for $V_{20} = 7.5$ V and $I_L = 0.5$ A, now attempt to find a practical current source that will take the place of the practical voltage source. This means
that the load resistance should not know the difference as far as its voltage and
current (and power) are concerned. It is easily verified that the ideal current source
of 2 A in parallel with $R_i = 5\ \Omega$ will do the job. To find I_S, simply find the ratio
V_S/R_i.

Figure 1.12 shows the practical current source. In each case the voltage across
the load resistance and the current through this resistance are the same, with $V_{20} =$
7.5 V and $I_L = 0.5$ A. The power to the load resistance is $V_{20}I_L = 3.75$ W. Are the
practical voltage source of Fig. 1.11 and the practical current source of Fig. 1.12
equivalent? To answer that, find the power furnished by each source. Verify that in
the former case the power is 5 W, while in the latter case the power is 15 W. To
explain the difference, compare the power in R_i in each case.

Fig. 1.12 Practical current
source with same load as Fig. 1.11.

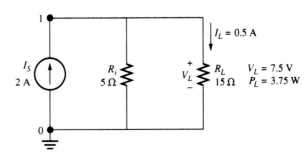

SPICE ANALYSIS OF CIRCUIT WITH CURRENT SOURCE

The solutions for circuits with current sources are more readily done with nodal analysis rather than loop analysis. The SPICE solutions are based on nodal analysis. Recall that each node in a circuit must be identified and that all circuit elements must be accounted for in terms of their respective nodes. With a voltage source, the first node listed in the SPICE statement is the positive node. With a current source, the first node listed is the one at the tail of the current arrow. A simple example is given in Fig. 1.13. Solve the circuit for currents and voltages.

Since the two resistive branches contain 200 Ω each, the 500-mA source current divides equally, giving $I_1 = I_2 = 250$ mA. Find $V_{10} = R_iI_1 = 200 \cdot 0.250 = 50$ V. Then find $V_{20} = R_LI_2 = 100 \cdot 0.250 = 25$ V.

Now, we will look at the PSpice file that gives the circuit solution.

```
Simple Circuit with Current Source
I 0 1 500mA
RT 1 0 200
R1 1 2 100
RL 2 0 100
.OP
.TF V(2) I
.END
```

Note the use of *mA* as the symbol for *milliamperes*. Sometimes this is given instead of *M* or *MA*. Be careful! The symbol for *mega-* is *MEG*. The current source is shown with the nodes *0* and *1*, respectively, for tail to tip. The transfer function shows V(2) as the output variable and *I* as the input source. A statement such as this gives the transfer function as well as the input and output resistances.

Run the analysis and note these results: V(1) = 50 V, V(2) = 25 V. Then note that V(2)/I = 50. This transfer function is the ratio of output voltage to input current (ohms). It may not be of interest in this analysis. The input resistance is 100 Ω, as is easily verified. The output resistance is 75 Ω. This is the resistance as seen from nodes *2* and *0* with the current source inactive. This means that the current source is opened (or removed from the circuit). Verify that the value of the output resistance is 75 Ω. See Fig. 1.14 for the output file.

Your output will show a heading for voltage-source currents, but none is named because there are no voltage sources. Next is a line that gives the total

Fig. 1.13 Simple circuit with current source.

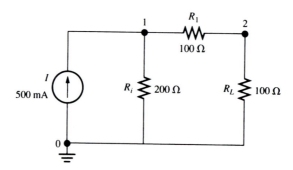

```
Simple Circuit with Current Source

I 0 1 500mA
RI 1 0 200
R1 1 2 100
RL 2 0 100
.OP
.TF V(2) I
.END

****        SMALL SIGNAL BIAS SOLUTION        TEMPERATURE =   27.000 DEG C

NODE    VOLTAGE      NODE    VOLTAGE      NODE   VOLTAGE       NODE    VOLTAGE

(    1)   50.0000  (    2)    25.0000

      VOLTAGE SOURCE CURRENTS
      NAME           CURRENT

      TOTAL POWER DISSIPATION    0.00E+00  WATTS

****        OPERATING POINT INFORMATION       TEMPERATURE =   27.000 DEG C

****        SMALL-SIGNAL CHARACTERISTICS

      V(2)/I =  5.000E+01

      INPUT RESISTANCE AT I =  1.000E+02

      OUTPUT RESISTANCE AT V(2)  =  7.500E+01
```

Fig. 1.14

power dissipation as zero. This is easily misunderstood. It means that the product of source voltages and their respective currents is zero. The .OP statement gives powers for voltage sources only. Can you determine the total power dissipation? Use the sum of the I^2R values for the three resistors and verify that 25 W is the total power. A simpler method of finding the total power is to use the product of I, the source current, and V(1), the voltage across the source. Verify that this gives the same result of 25 W.

NORTON'S THEOREM

Norton's theorem is used to produce a practical current source with its accompanying shunt resistance as an alternative to the Thevenin practical voltage source with its series resistance. The relationship between the sources is

$$I_N = \frac{V_{Th}}{R_{Th}}$$

and the resistance value for both sources is the same. The technique for finding I_N is to replace the load resistance with a short circuit and find the current through this short-circuited branch. This current is I_N. In some circuits it is more convenient to find I_N, while in others it is more convenient to find V_{Th}. After one or the other is found, the conversion between the two is made by applying the equation given previously.

Using Norton's Theorem

The circuit of Fig. 1.15, with the load resistor R_4 removed, is to be replaced by the Norton equivalent. In order to find the short-circuit current, a short is placed across node *3*, thereby eliminating this node. The input file becomes

```
Norton's Theorem; Find Isc
V  1  0  48V
R1  1  2  20k
R2  2  0  20k
R3  2  0  5k
.DC V 48V 48V 48V
.OP
.OPT nopage
.PRINT DC I (R3) V(1,2)
.END
```

Run the analysis and verify that the short-circuit current is the current through R_3 and that it is I(R3) = 1.6 mA.

Short-Circuit Current in Missing Element

Refer to the circuit in Fig. 1.7, where the load resistor R_L must be shorted in order to find the short-circuit current. The obvious problem is that there is no remaining element that will carry this current. In situations like this, R_L may be replaced by a very small resistor. The input file will be

```
Norton's Theorem with RL Replaced by Small R
V  1  0  80V
R1  2  1  20
R2  2  3  100
R3  3  0  200
R4  3  4  100
R5  2  4  400
RL  4  0  0.001
.DC V 80V 80V 80V
.OP
.PRINT DC I(RL)
.END
```

Fig. 1.15 Tee circuit for Norton analysis.

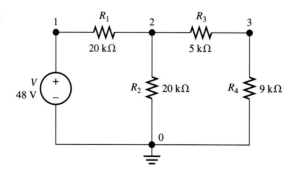

The PSpice analysis gives I(RL) = 0.444 A, which is the desired short-circuit current, I_N. In the preceding input file, it would not be helpful to include a .TF statement in an attempt to find the output resistance at V(4). The reason is that the output resistance includes the R_L value of 0.001 Ω that was used to find the short-circuit current.

We conclude that finding V_{Th} and R_{Th} using PSpice is easier, since one input file provides both values.

CIRCUIT WITH CURRENT AND VOLTAGE SOURCES

Circuits with both current and voltage sources can be solved by superposition. If the circuits are not complicated, this provides a simple and convenient method of solution. Figure 1.16 shows a circuit with a current source I and a voltage source V. Use superposition to find the voltage V_{10}. Check your results against this solution. With I active and V replaced with a short circuit, $V_{10}(a) = 5$ V; with V active and I replaced with an open circuit, $V_{10}(b) = 10$ V. Add these two values to obtain the actual voltage, $V_{10} = 15$ V.

Turn to PSpice for an analysis of the circuit. Your input file should look like this:

```
Simple Current and Voltage Sources
I 0 1 1A
V 2 0 20
R1 1 0 10
R2 1 2 10
.OP
.TF V(1) V
.END
```

The output file shows V(1) = 15 V, in agreement with the superposition results. The .OP statement allowed you to find the voltage-source current of 0.5 A. Verify that this is the correct value. Remember that the *total power dissipation* given by PSpice is for the voltage source only; it is simply the product of V and the source current, which is 10 W. Use I^2R for each resistor and verify that $P_1 = 22.5$ W, $P_2 = 2.5$ W, giving $P_t = 25$ W. The .TF statement allows you to find input and output resistances. Check these values, remembering that the current source is replaced by an open circuit to find R_{in} and R_{out}.

In summary, when current sources are present, beware of how you use the total power dissipation. It represents only the power associated with the voltage

Fig. 1.16 Simple current and voltage sources.

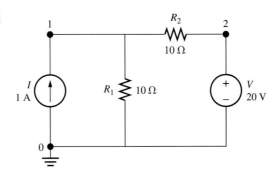

sources. If there are two or more voltage sources, the power shown in PSpice is for *all* voltage sources.

MAXIMUM POWER TRANSFER

In a circuit where a load resistance can be made to vary or be selected to fill a particular need, the question is sometimes asked, What value of R_L will allow maximum power to be developed in the load resistor? Figure 1.17 shows R_L as such a resistor. When the value of R_L is chosen to be equal to the resistance looking back into the network from the load terminals (nodes *3* and *0*), then the power to R_L will be the maximum.

 The resistance of the network as seen at the load terminals with the load removed is simply the Thevenin resistance. For this circuit it is 30 Ω. Thus when $R_L = 30 \ \Omega$, it will dissipate the maximum power. This means that with all other values in the circuit fixed, either a smaller or larger value of R_L will take less power. We will demonstrate this with a SPICE analysis. The input file is

```
Maximum Power Transfer to R Load
V  1  0  12V
R1  1  2  20
R2  2  0  20
R3  2  3  30
RL  3  0  30
.OP
.END
```

 The results show $V(3) = 3$ V, from which $P_L = V(3)^2/R_L = 0.3$ W. Now you see the real advantage of using SPICE when R_L is made either smaller or larger. Go back to the input file and replace only the value of 30 Ω and quickly see the new results.

 For example, with $R_L = 29 \ \Omega$, $V(3) = 2.9492$ V, and $P_L = 0.2999$ W; on the other hand, with $R_L = 31 \ \Omega$, $V(3) = 3.0492$ V, and again $P_L = 0.2999$ W. Try several other values for R_L and notice that the power to the load resistor will invariably be less than 0.3 W. Remember that the maximum power to R_L occurred when R_L was matched to the resistance seen looking back into the circuit with R_L removed. This is easily found for more complicated circuits by using the Thevenin technique.

Fig. 1.17   Maximum power transfer to R load.

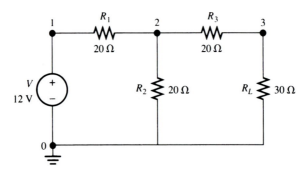

The computer analysis allows more time for us to concentrate on understanding the principles that govern circuit behavior, and spend less time on the mundane, repetitive calculations.

DEPENDENT SOURCES IN ELECTRIC CIRCUITS

A dependent (controlled) source might represent either a voltage source or a current source that is dependent on another voltage or current somewhere else in the circuit.

Voltage-Dependent Voltage Source

An example, Fig. 1.18 shows a circuit with a source voltage V, an independent source, along with another source voltage E, which is a dependent (or controlled) source. It is also labeled $2V_a$. In what way is E dependent? It is a function of the voltage drop across resistor R_1, which is shown as V_a. The factor 2 means that the voltage E will be twice the voltage drop V_a. The factor 2 is also called k.

The circuit voltages and currents may be found by conventional analysis. In the loop on the left,

$$V = R_1I_{12} + E = R_1I_{12} + 2V_a$$

where I_{12} is the current through R_1. Since $V_a = R_1I_{12}$, the expression becomes

$$V = R_1I_{12} + 2R_1I_{12} = 3R_1I_{12}$$
$$10 \text{ V} = (3) (250 \text{ }\Omega)I_{12}$$
$$I_{12} = 13.33 \text{ mA}$$
$$V_{12} = V_a = R_1I_{12} = (250 \text{ }\Omega)(13.33 \text{ mA}) = 3.333 \text{ V}$$
$$E = 2V_a = 6.667 \text{ V}$$

Since this is the voltage applied across R_2, the current through R_2 and the current through R_3 and R_L branch are readily found:

$$I_{R2} = \frac{6.667 \text{ V}}{100 \text{ k}\Omega} = 66.67 \text{ }\mu\text{A}$$

Fig. 1.18 Voltage-controlled voltage source.

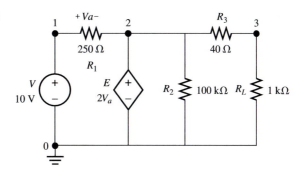

$$I_{R3} = \frac{6.667 \text{ V}}{1.04 \text{ k}\Omega} = 4.41 \text{ mA}$$

The current through source E is directed downward and is

$$I_E = 13.33 \text{ mA} - 66.67 \text{ }\mu\text{A} - 6.41 \text{ mA} = 6.85 \text{ mA}$$

How is a problem of this kind solved using PSpice? The input file for Fig. 1.18 is

```
Voltage-Controlled Voltage Source
V 1 0 10V
E 2 0 1 2 2
R1 1 2 250
R2 2 0 100k
R3 2 3 40
RL 3 0 1k
.OP
.TF V(3) V
.END
```

```
Voltage-Controlled Voltage Source

   ****        CIRCUIT DESCRIPTION

   V 1 0 10V
   E 2 0 1 2 2
   R1 1 2 250
   R2 2 0 100k
   R3 2 3 40
   RL 3 0 1k
   .OP
   .OPT nopage
   .TF V(3) V
   .END


   NODE   VOLTAGE      NODE   VOLTAGE      NODE   VOLTAGE      NODE   VOLTAGE

   (   1)   10.0000  (   2)    6.6667  (   3)    6.4103


      VOLTAGE SOURCE CURRENTS
      NAME            CURRENT

      V            -1.333E-02

      TOTAL POWER DISSIPATION   1.33E-01   WATTS

   **** VOLTAGE-CONTROLLED VOLTAGE SOURCES

   NAME          E
   V-SOURCE      6.667E+00
   I-SOURCE      6.856E-03

    ****        SMALL-SIGNAL CHARACTERISTICS

        V(3)/V =  6.410E-01

        INPUT RESISTANCE AT V =   7.500E+02

        OUTPUT RESISTANCE AT V(3) =  3.846E+01
```

Fig. 1.19

The new statement in this input file is a description of the dependent source E. Nodes 2 and 0 are its *plus* and *minus* nodes, respectively. Nodes 1 and 2 are the *plus* and *minus* nodes of the voltage upon which E is dependent. The final 2 is the factor k. The output file, Fig. 1.19, shows $V(2) = 6.6667$ V and $V(3) = 6.4103$ V, as predicted. The voltage-source current for source V is given as 13.33 mA, also as predicted. Note that the source current for E is given as 6.856 mA. It is shown as positive, which means from plus to minus inside E.

The PSpice analysis shows the input resistance is 750 Ω. This is simply the ratio of V to I_{12}. In finding the output resistance, each voltage source is considered as a short. This puts a short between nodes 2 and 0, giving $R_3 \parallel R_L$ for a resistance of 38.46 Ω.

Figure 1.20 shows a modification of the circuit. The input file for this circuit is

```
Another Voltage-Controlled Voltage Source
V 1 0 10V
E 3 0 2 0 2
R1 1 2 250
R2 2 0 100k
R3 3 4 40
RL 4 0 1k
.OP
.TF V(4) V
.END
```

In this simplified model for a voltage amplifier, the results are easily predicted by circuit analysis. The current in the loop on the left is

$$I_{12} = \frac{V}{R_1 + R_2} = \frac{10 \text{ V}}{250 \text{ } \Omega + 100 \text{ k}\Omega} = 99.75 \text{ } \mu\text{A}$$

The voltage drop across R_2 is

$$V_2 = V_a = I_{12}R_2 = (99.75 \text{ } \mu\text{A})(100 \text{ k}\Omega) = 9.975 \text{ V}$$

and

$$E = 2V_a = (2)(9.975 \text{ V}) = 19.95 \text{ V}$$

From the PSpice analysis, we find $V(2) = 9.9751$ V, $V(3) = 19.95$ V, and $V(4) = 19.183$ V. The source current through V is 99.75 μA, and the source current through

Fig. 1.20 Revised circuit with voltage-controlled voltage source.

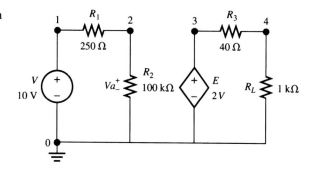

E is -19.18 mA. The negative sign indicates that the current from plus to minus inside E is negative, or alternatively, that the positive current is upward through E.

Current-Dependent Voltage Source

Sometimes a dependent (controlled) voltage source is dependent on a *current* somewhere else in the circuit, as shown in Fig. 1.21. The dependent source is shown to have a value $0.5I$, where I is the current through resistor R_1. The current is in the direction from node *1* toward node *2*. The dependent voltage source has its positive terminal at node *3*, which means that it tends to furnish current clockwise in the loop on the right. It is important to note these features, since they play a role in assigning polarities and directions in the solution.

The circuit is easily analyzed. In the loop on the left, the 15-V source will give a current $I = V/(R_1 + R_2) = 15/(10 + 5) = 1$ A. The dependent voltage source is labeled $0.5I$. This will be equal to $0.5 \cdot 1 = 0.5$ V. Thus $V_{30} = 0.5$ V. How is this dimensionally a voltage? The value $k = 0.5$ is not dimensionless; it is in ohms. In general, the notation kI will be used for this CDVS (current-dependent voltage source). The k factor must be in ohms for the product of k and I to give volts.

The current in the loop on the right is found to be $I_L = 0.5/(25 + 25) = 10$ mA. The voltage $V_{40} = R_L I_L = 0.25$ V.

Using PSpice, solve the problem as an introduction to other, more elaborate circuits. The input file will contain a statement for the current-dependent voltage source. Here is what the file should look like:

```
Circuit with Current-Dependent Voltage Source
V 1 0 15V
H 3 0 V -0.5
R1 1 2 10
R2 2 0 5
R3 3 4 25
R4 4 0 25
.OP
.TF V(4) V
.END
```

Look carefully at the entry for the CDVS shown on the line beginning with the symbol H. On the same line the *3* and *0* represent the plus and minus terminals of

Fig. 1.21 Circuit with current-dependent voltage source.

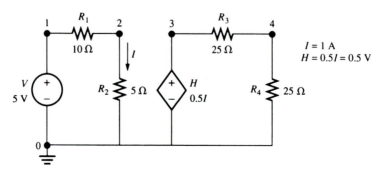

the dependent voltage source. This is followed by the symbol V, which represents the independent voltage through which the controlling current I is carried. The last entry on this line is -0.5. The 0.5 is the factor k, but the minus sign requires explanation. In SPICE, a voltage-source current such as the current through V would be positive if it were directed from plus to minus through V. Since the reference current I is oppositely directed, the H statement requires the minus sign for the factor k. Study this feature, as it can easily be confusing. Had the minus sign been omitted, voltages V(3) and V(4) would have had the wrong sign in your PSpice results.

When you are sure you are ready to continue, run the analysis and look at the results in the output file. Note that V(3) = 0.5 V and V(4) = 0.25 V. The voltage-source current of V is -1.0 A. Recall that this means that the current is actually out of the plus side of V, and that I in Fig. 1.21 is a positive value. Thus V(3) is positive.

At the expense of being repetitive, also recall that the value shown in the output file for total power is simply VI and is not really total power. Under the section in the output file called *Current-Controlled Voltage Sources*, there are two lines of entries. The first gives a V-source entry of 0.5 V. This is the voltage value of the dependent-source voltage. More puzzling is the next entry, which gives an I-source value of -10 mA. Can you figure out what this means? It means that the current through the CDVS is 10 mA from the minus to the plus terminal inside the source. This is in agreement with what we already know about how SPICE shows source currents.

Current-Dependent Current Source

Another type of dependent source, one that is frequently encountered in electronics, is the current-dependent current (CDCS) source. Figure 1.22 shows the basic circuit. The dependent source has a value of $3I$, where I is the current through the resistor R_1. As in the previous example, the current is in the direction from node *1* toward node *2*, clockwise in the loop on the left. The factor $3I$ is generally given as kI, where k is the multiplier for the referenced current that appears somewhere else in the circuit. Simply stated, if $I = 2$ A in the loop on the left, then the current through F will be $(3)(2) = 6$ A in the direction of the arrow shown in F. In this example, we can easily solve for $I = 20/(1500 + 2500) = 5$ mA, as the current in the loop on the left. The current in F is thus $(5 \text{ mA})(3) = 15$ mA (downward). This current

Fig. 1.22 Current-controlled current source.

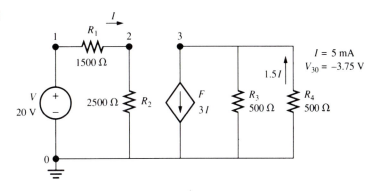

will divide evenly between R_3 and R_4, giving 7.5 mA through each resistor. The currents go from node *0* toward node *3*, putting node *3* at a negative potential. The voltage V(3) = (− 500)(7.5 mA) = − 3.75 V.

As a prelude to more elaborate circuits with dependent sources, how will Fig. 1.22 look in a PSpice file? Here it is:

```
Current-Controlled Current Source
V  1  0  20V
F  3  0  V  -3
R1  1  2  1500
R2  2  0  2500
R3  3  0  500
R4  3  0  500
.OP
.TF  V  (3)  V
.END
```

Your output should show V(2) = 12.5 V and V(3) = −3.75 V. Under the heading *Current-Controlled Current Sources*, the *I*-source called *F* has a value of 15 mA. Since this is three times the current in the loop on the left, it is correct. The positive value means that the current is in the direction from node *3* toward node *0* inside *F*. It is necessary to show the proper values in the input-file statement for *F*. On the line describing *F*, the first two values are for the tail and tip nodes of *F*. The next value, *V*, refers to the voltage source that carries the current *I*. This current *I* is related to the dependent-source current by the relationship *kI*. The factor *k* is a multiplier for *I*; it is dimensionless. The *k* in this example has a value of −3 because of how the voltage *V* relates to the current *I* as explained in several previous examples. Study this example carefully, as it is where mistakes are often made. If you fully understand the simpler examples, you will be able to handle the more involved ones with confidence.

In the output file the value given for R_{in} is 4 kΩ, which is obviously correct. Also of interest is the value for R_{out} = 250 F. In the portion of the circuit in Fig. 1.22 on the far right, we see R_3 and R_4 in parallel. The current source is made inactive by opening it (or removing it).

Another Current-Dependent Current Source

A slightly different situation involving the CDCS, which often appears in electric circuit analysis, is one in which the controlling current is in a branch containing no independent voltage source, that is, no *V*-type element. Figure 1.23(a) shows a typical example. Note that *I* is the current through R_3. It is this current that appears with its multiplier *k* through the current-dependent current source *F*. Recall that the line in the input file that describes *F* must show a *V-type* value. How do you handle this? Simply insert a zero-valued voltage source in the branch where *I* appears, as shown in the detail of Fig. 1.23(b). Call this source *V0* to remind you that it is a zero-valued source. Look at the PSpice input file for this circuit:

```
Another CDCS Example
V  1  0  35V
V0  2A  2  0V
F  3  0  V0  -3
```

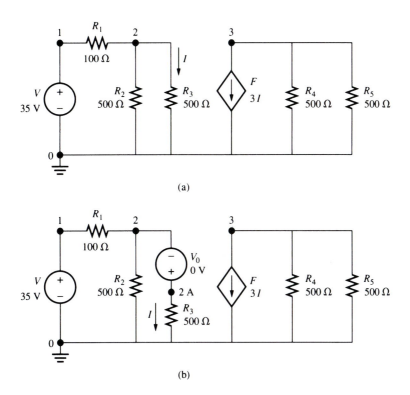

Fig. 1.23 (a) Another CDCS example. (b) The circuit modified to include zero-volt source.

```
R1  1  2  100
R2  2  0  500
R3  2A 0  500
R4  3  0  500
R5  3  0  500
.OP
.TF V (3) V
.END
```

Notice the line describing F. It refers to the independent voltage $V0$ because this branch of the circuit contains the current I, the controlling current. Compare this statement with the F statement of the previous example to see the difference. Also note the addition of a line describing $V0$. The two nodes are $2A$ and 2. Note carefully that the plus node (always the first node) tends to furnish current in the direction shown for I in the figure. This follows the same convention used in the previous example, where I was also shown out of the plus source node.

We have not previously used an alphabetic character to designate a node, but this is all right. In fact, combinations of letters and numbers may be used. Thus nodes might be called $a1, b12, 1c$, and so forth. Also, the fact that this is a zero-valued source means that its presence does not alter the behavior of the circuit. The line describing $R3$ has been changed to show the presence of the new node $2A$.

Run the simulation and look at the results. The values are V(2) = 25 V, V(3) = −37.5 V, and as expected V(2A) = 25 V also. You should be able to easily verify that

I = 50 mA, giving 3I = 150 mA as shown in the output file; this is the current in F. This current splits equally between R_4 and R_5, giving a current of 37.5 mA upward (node 0 toward node 3) in each. Thus V(3) = $-$37.5 V

As an additional exercise, see what happens when two lines of the input file are changed as follows:

```
VO 2 2A OV
F  3 0 VO 3
```

This is simply an alternative way of describing the relationship between the CDCS and its controlling current. Try to visualize that they are equally valid, and use whichever one you feel more comfortable using.

Voltage-Dependent Current Source

A dependent current source that is a function of a voltage somewhere else in the circuit is described by a G entry for SPICE. Figure 1.24 shows an example. This circuit is easily analyzed by pencil-and-paper methods. Voltage v_2 is found by voltage division to be 9 V. The current through the dependent source is thus (0.02)(9) = 180 mA. The k value of 0.02 is dimensionally conductance or ohms^{-1}. This current divides equally between R_3 and R_4, giving 90 mA through each resistor. This produces V_{30} = ($-$0.09)(200) = $-$18 V. The PSpice input file is

```
Voltage-Controlled Current Source
V 1 0 12V
G 3 0 2 0 0.02
R1 1 2 300
R2 2 0 900
R3 3 0 200
R4 3 0 200
.OP
.TF V (3) V
.END
```

The line showing G gives the first two nodes as 3 and 0. These are for the tail and tip, respectively, of the dependent-current arrow. The next two nodes are 2 and 0, for the plus and minus nodes of the controlling voltage, v_2. Run the PSpice analysis and verify that V(2) = 9 V, V(3) = $-$18 V, R_{in} = 1200 Ω, and R_{out} = 100 Ω.

The ratio V(3)/V = $-$1.5 is the gain. Later you will see how this type of analysis can be used for active circuits containing transistors and various integrated circuits.

Fig. 1.24 Voltage-controlled current source.

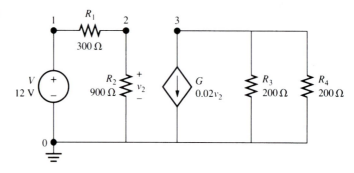

Another Current-Dependent Voltage Source

Recall that a voltage source that is controlled by a current elsewhere in the circuit is called a current-controlled, or current-dependent, voltage source. Figure 1.25 gives a type of example different from the one previously considered. The controlling current in this example is i_2, the current down through R_3 (toward node 0). The CCVS is marked H. The value of k is 400. Solving for the source current from V, you get $I_s = 15/(50 + 250) = 50$ mA. This current divides equally between R_2 and R_3, giving $i_2 = 25$ mA as the controlling current. The value of H is then $(400) \cdot (25$ mA$) = 10$ V. The current in the loop at the right of the diagram is $10/(200) = 50$ mA. The PSpice input file is

```
Current-Controlled Voltage Source
V  1  0  15V
VO 2A 2  0V
H  3  0  VO -400
R1 1  2  50
R2 2  0  500
R3 2A 0  500
R4 3  4  50
R5 4  0  150
.OP
.TF V(4) V
.END
```

Run the analysis and confirm that V(2) = 12.5 V, V(3) = 10 V, and V(4) = 7.5 V. The PSpice statement for H gives 3 and 0 as the plus and minus nodes of the controlled voltage. It also shows $V0$ as a named voltage source in the path of the controlling current i_2. The polarity of $V0$ is correct to give i_2 as a positive value in the direction shown in Fig. 1.25. The last value in the H statement is -400, representing k. The minus sign is required, as in earlier examples, in keeping with how SPICE treats currents through voltage sources.

Note that the output file gives the current through V as -50 mA, which means 50 mA out of the positive terminal of V, and the current through $V0$ as -25 mA, which means 25 mA out of the positive terminal of $V0$. Under the heading *Current-Controlled Voltage Sources* you find a voltage value of 10 V; this is shown as *V-source*. The value of -50 mA, which is shown as *I-source*, is the current through H. Once again, the minus sign means that the direction of positive current through H is from the minus to the plus terminal.

Fig. 1.25 Current-controlled voltage source.

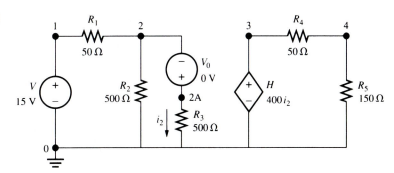

In summary, we have looked at each of the four types of controlled sources, E (for VCVS), F (for CCCS), G (for VCCS), and H (for CCVS). Controlled sources play an important part in the analysis of most circuits with active devices such as transistors. It is important to be able to analyze simple circuits with such devices, thus paving the way for an understanding of more elaborate circuits. The basic ideas are best treated in the dc circuits with which we are dealing in this chapter.

POLYNOMIAL DEPENDENT SOURCES

This topic is usually not included in an introductory course. If you are not interested in polynomial sources at this time, skip over this material, moving ahead to the section on mesh analysis.

The possibility of using a nonlinear dependent source might sometimes arise, so let us see what this means and how it may be applied to an actual example. Figure 1.26 shows a voltage source V supplying two equal resistors $R_1 = R_2 = 1$ kΩ. The VCVS is E, and in this case there is no simple k factor relating E to another voltage in the circuit. Suppose that E is to be based on V_{20} in a nonlinear fashion, given by the polynomial

$$f(x) = 3 + 2x + x^2$$

Let E be related to V_{20} by the polynomial expression. This would mean, for example, that if $V_{20} = -1$ V, $E = 2$ V, or if $V_{20} = 2$ V, $E = 11$ V. Verify this in the equation before going on. Now consider the input file:

```
Circuit with Controlled Source
V 1 0 1V
E 3 0 POLY(1) 2, 0 3 2 1
R1 1 2 1k
R2 2 0 1k
R3 3 4 2k
R4 4 0 2k
.DC V −4 4 1 : this is a dc "sweep" of the source voltage V
.PRINT DC V(2) V(3) V(4)
.END
```

Before running this analysis, look carefully at the statement describing E. The nodes 3 and 0 are the plus and minus nodes of E, as we would expect. The *POLY(1)* means that we will use a polynomial to describe the functional relationship between E and some other voltage. The *(1)* means that only one pair of nodes is referenced as a controlling voltage. The *2,0* identifies the controlling *plus* and *minus* nodes for voltage v_1.

Now for the polynomial itself, the *3 2 1* values represent the a, b, and c values of the general case

$$f(x) = a + bx + cx^2$$

giving us the desired polynomial shown above the input file. Note that if either value a or b is zero, a zero must be shown. Otherwise the statement would not completely describe the degree of the polynomial. This means that a third-degree polynomial would require 4 values (for a, b, c, and d).

Since the SPICE manuals are not very clear on this subject, you may want to spend some extra time looking over this example. Remember this when the need for the nonlinear source arises.

The .DC statement gives a range of voltages for V from -4 V to 4 V. This is called a *sweep* of voltage, and this statement will override the V statement that shows $V = 1$ V. The last value in the .DC statement shows the increment of V, which in the example is 1 V. Other uses of the .DC statement in this chapter will provide further clarification.

Run the analysis and verify our predictions for the relationship between V(3), which is E, and V(2).

Dependent Source as a Function of Two Other Voltages

Letting a dependent source depend on more than one other source can be done using a POLY form in the dependent statement. For example, in Fig. 1.26 make E a function of both v_1 and v_2. This requires part of the statement to be POLY(2) 2,0 4,0. The commas are optional and are added for clarity. The rest of the statement must contain coefficients. Determining what these coefficients represent will require some thought and planning. When two controlling voltages are involved, the terms represent $k_0, k_1v_1, k_2v_2, k_3v_1{}^2, k_4v_1v_2$, and $k_5v_2{}^2$. The pattern may look complicated, but with a little study it becomes clear. The k factors are multipliers for each possible voltage or combination of voltages. The voltages are listed in order of degree beginning with the first voltage, called v_1. In our example, v_1 represents V_{20}, and v_2 represents V_{40}.

Now, consider the entire statement involving the two controlling voltages:

```
E 3 0 POLY(2) 2,0 4,0 0 2 3
```

The last three values, *0 2 3*, represent k_0, k_1, and k_2. This stands for $0k_0 + 2v_1 + 3v_2$. Thus the dependent voltage E will be the sum of twice the voltage drop across R_2 and three times the voltage drop across R_4. Note again that the commas are optional. They are often added for clarity.

The input file is

```
Polynomial Form for Two Inputs
V 1 0 1V
E 3 0 POLY(2) 2,0 4,0 0 2 3
```

Fig. 1.26 Circuit with polynomial-controlled source.

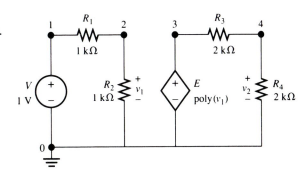

```
R1 1 2 1k
R2 2 0 1k
R3 3 4 2k
R4 4 0 2k
.DC V -4 4 1
.PRINT DC V(2) V(3) V(4)
.END
```

Run the analysis and verify that E is given by the expression $2V_{20} + 3V_{40}$.

You might need to use this multidependent tool when there are circuits where the addition, subtraction, or multiplication of several voltages or currents is to take place. Using the proper choice of E, F, G, and H for the dependent source along with the POLY feature will allow the circuit to be simulated.

MESH ANALYSIS AND PSPICE

Introductory circuits courses contain a treatment of how to write loop and mesh equations to solve for currents in circuits. The standard form to solve for three mesh currents is

$$R_{11}I_1 + R_{12}I_2 + R_{13}I_3 = V_1$$
$$R_{21}I_1 + R_{22}I_2 + R_{23}I_3 = V_2$$
$$R_{31}I_1 + R_{32}I_2 + R_{33}I_3 = V_3$$

where R_{11} is the self-resistance of mesh 1, R_{12} is the mutual resistance between meshes 1 and 2, R_{13} is the mutual resistance between meshes 1 and 3, and V_1 is the net source voltage tending to furnish the current in the direction of I_1. Similar statements can be made about the other equations, where R_{22} and R_{33} represent self-resistances and all other R terms represent mutual resistances. A pencil-and-paper solution for three simultaneous equations is tedious and error prone. When there are more than three equations, the job becomes a much more difficult chore. Numerous versions of computer programs are available for solving these equations.

As an exercise, you may wish to write the mesh equations for Fig. 1.27 and solve for I_1, I_2, and I_3, using a computer program or a calculator designed for this purpose.

Can you solve such equations using SPICE? In a word, no. However, you can use a few tricks to get the job done, as the next example will show. Figure 1.27 shows

Fig. 1.27 Mesh analysis with PSpice.

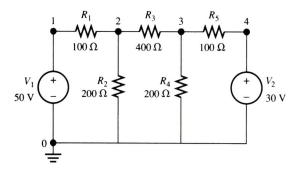

the circuit with its three meshes. If you set up three equations following the standard format, you can solve for $I_1, I_2,$ and I_3. You may wish to do this as an exercise before looking at the input file for PSpice, which is given here.

```
Mesh Analysis with PSpice
V1 1 0 50V
V2 4 0 30V
R1 1 2 100
R2 2 0 200
R3 2 3 400
R4 3 0 200
R5 3 4 100
.OP
.DC V1 50 50 10
.PRINT DC I(R1) I (R3) I(R5)
.END
```

Two interesting statements are shown in the input file. The first is the .DC statement. This is a dc-sweep statement, which was introduced in the Norton's theorem example. It allows you to sweep through a set of source voltages V_1. The next two values, *50* and *50*, are for the start and stop voltage values of the sweep, and the last value, *10*, is an increment. If you had wanted to sweep V_1 in 10-V increments, beginning at zero, the statement would have been

```
.DC V1 0 50 10
```

Since you are not actually interested in a sweep, you force a sweep of a single voltage. The concept of the sweep is needed for the next statement. The .PRINT statement includes the term DC, which is the sweep parameter previously chosen. In this type of .PRINT statement, you can obtain such things as currents I(R1) and voltages V(2,3) as needed. If you omit the .DC sweep, the print statement of this form will be invalid.

Run the PSpice analysis and look at the results. Values obtained include I(R1) = 0.1833 A, I(R3) = 25 mA, and I(R5) = −83.33 mA. These are the mesh currents that would be obtained from the standard mesh analysis if you solved three simultaneous equations. The PSpice solution is actually more like a nodal analysis, but you have forced more calculations to be made, giving the desired mesh currents (actually, branch currents also).

DC SWEEP

Since the mesh problem introduced the concept of a dc sweep, let us look at an example where the sweep is used in the normal fashion, with a range of input voltages. The familiar tee circuit of Fig. 1.28 will be used. You do not need a preliminary analysis, so look at the input file for the PSpice analysis.

```
Spice Sweep Analysis of Tee Circuit
V 1 0 50V
R1 1 2 100
R2 2 3 50
R3 2 0 200
R4 3 0 150
```

Fig. 1.28   Tee circuit and a
voltage sweep.

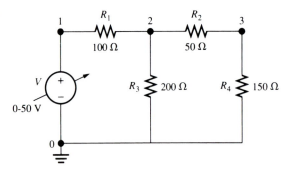

```
.OP
.TF V(3) V
.DC V 0 50 10
.PRINT DC V(2,3) I(R3)
.END
```

The dc sweep will begin with $V = 0$ and continue through $V = 50$ in 10-V
increments. Two output tables will be produced, the first showing the relation
between V and V(2,3) and the second showing the relation between V and I(R3) as
directed by the print statement. Run the PSpice analysis and look at the results.
Notice how the tables are shown. How might the tables be used? If you are looking
for the V required to give a current I(R3) of 50 mA, the table shows that $V = 20$ V
is required. You could easily ratio this result yourself, but if there are many *ifs* to
look at, PSpice can do the work for you.

USING THE .PROBE STATEMENT

The MicroSim software includes the Probe program, which has been used in the
introductory chapter. The program may be run by selecting the Probe icon in the
MicroSim workgroup but is usually invoked by simply including a .PROBE statement in the circuit file you wish to simulate.

To illustrate how this statement is put to good use, the tee circuit will be reex-
amined. The circuit file is named *satc.cir* (Sweep Analysis Tee Circuit) and is a slight
modification of the one previously given.

```
Sweep Analysis of Tee Circuit
V 1 0 50V
R1 1 2 100
R2 2 3 50
R3 2 0 200
R4 3 0 150
.OP
.TF V(3) V
.DC V 0 50 10
.PROBE
.END
```

Now, perform the PSpice analysis and see what happens. At the conclusion of the
simulation, you may look at the output file or you may choose to produce various

graphs. In PSpice select File, Run Probe, the select Trace, Add and see that the Add Traces window contains suggestions of trace quantities such as V, V(1), V(2), and V(3) along with the currents I(R1), I(R2), and so forth. Select I(R3), then repeat the process to select I(R1). This produces a second trace on the same graph (or plot); on the screen they are shown in different colors for easy distinction. If you wish to obtain a printed copy of the traces, you can easily label each trace by using the Tools, Label, Text command. Refer to Fig. 1.29 for this plot.

As a matter of added interest, select the cursor icon (showing cross hairs and a check mark) to obtain a cross-hair display on the screen. Use the mouse and the left and right arrows if necessary to verify that when $V = 15.0$ V, I(R3) $= 37.5$ mA. Then press Ctrl-right arrow (to select the other trace) and verify that when $V = 15.0$ V, I(R1) $= 75.0$ mA. Recall that the simulation called for a source-voltage sweep for $V = 0, 10, 20, 30\ 40$, and 50 V. The Probe processor produced a curve-fit analysis so that intermediate values of voltage and current could be investigated.

For another interesting example of using Probe, go back to Fig. 1.26 and the example where we introduced the dependent polynomial voltage source (Circuit with Controlled Source). Add a .PROBE statement to the circuit file and run the simulation again. Now, instead of looking at the tabulated results in the output file, use Probe to plot the relationships among voltages V(2), V(3), and V(4). Work with the traces until you feel comfortable using Probe. Use the cursor to verify the numerical results compared with using the .PRINT statement.

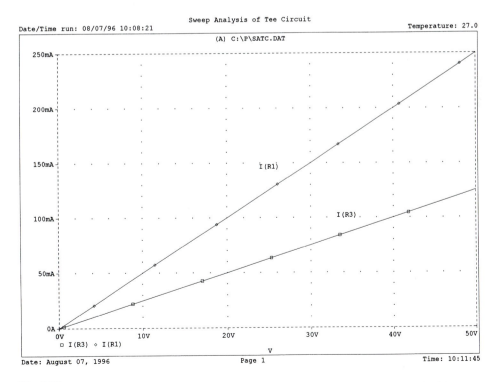

Fig. 1.29

Many more features are available in Probe. These features will be explored in examples throughout the text.

NODAL ANALYSIS AND PSPICE

Introductory circuits courses cover the topic of nodal analysis using standard equations. These equations are more easily written if all practical voltage sources are replaced by practical current sources. This has the disadvantage of physically changing the circuit, but the advantage is that fewer nodes appear and this allows for fewer equations. After you find the node voltages, if necessary you can convert the sources back to their original forms. The standard form for node voltages looks like this:

$$G_{11}V_1 + G_{12}V_2 + G_{13}V_3 = I_1$$
$$G_{21}V_1 + G_{22}V_2 + G_{23}V_3 = I_2$$
$$G_{31}V_1 + G_{32}V_2 + G_{33}V_3 = I_3$$

where G_{11} is the self-conductance at node I, G_{12} is mutual conductance between nodes 1 and 2, G_{13} is mutual conductance between nodes 1 and 3, and the term I_1 is the net source current directed toward node 1. In nodal analysis, all self-conductances are positive, and all mutual conductances are negative.

The circuit in Fig. 1.30 will be used for the nodal example. As an exercise, see if you can write the nodal equations and solve them with either a computer program or a calculator designed for the solution of simultaneous equations. Writing the standard equations and understanding them is important, but solving such equations over and over is not fun.

The PSpice solution for the circuit in Fig. 1.30 is simple, involving nothing that is new at this point. The input file should look something like this:

```
Nodal Analysis of Circuit with Several Current Sources
I1 0 1 20mA
I2 0 2 10mA
I3 0 3 15mA
R1 1 0 500
R2 1 2 500
```

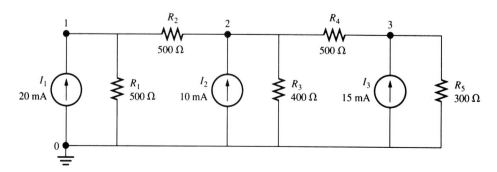

Fig. 1.30   Nodal analysis with several current sources.

```
R3  2  0  400
R4  2  3  500
R5  3  0  300
.OP
.END
```

The input file contains enough information to allow for all the node voltages to be found. Run the analysis and verify the voltages: V(1) = 7.694 V, V(2) = 5.3947 V, V(3) = 4.8355 V. The total power dissipation is shown as zero, an obviously incorrect value. Remember that this is because there are no independent voltage sources.

It is instructive to convert the current sources to voltage sources in Fig. 1.30 and create an input file for this resulting circuit. Figure 1.31 shows the revised circuit. You will notice that nodes *1, 2,* and *3* have been preserved for easy reference. There are three additional nodes, and your input file must be modified accordingly.

```
Nodal Analysis with Current Sources Converted to Voltage Sources
V1  1A  0  10V
V2  2A  0  4V
V3  3A  0  4.5V
R1  1A  1  500
R2  1  2  500
R3  2  2A  400
R4  2  3  500
R5  3  3A  300
.OP
.END
```

When you run this analysis, verify that V(1) = 7.6974 V, V(2) = 5.3947 V, and V(3) = 4.8355 V, as before. Three additional node voltages are given as V(1A) = 10 V, V(2A) = 4V, and V(3A) = 4.5 V as given in the input file for the source voltages. As a bonus, you obtain the three source currents. For example, the current in V_1 is given as −4.605 mA. This means that positive current in the amount of 4.605 mA is out of the plus side of V_1. Verify that the other source currents are correct, and state their true directions as positive numbers. Since all sources were voltage sources instead of current sources, the total power is correctly given as 27.1 mW.

A NONPLANAR CIRCUIT

When a circuit is nonplanar, it cannot be drawn in two dimensions without a crossing of the lines connecting the nodes. Such a circuit is shown in Fig. 1.32, which con-

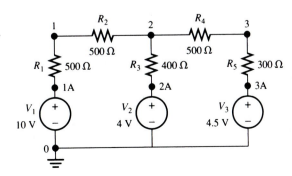

Fig. 1.31 Current sources converted to voltage sources.

Fig. 1.32   A nonplanar circuit.

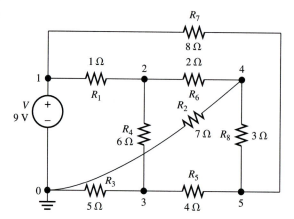

tains a voltage source and eight resistors for a total of nine elements. Using circuit-analysis techniques, mesh analysis may be applied to planar circuits, but nodal or loop analysis must be used on nonplanar ones. PSpice is a more convenient tool for handling circuits with large numbers of elements. For the circuit illustrated, the input file is

```
Nonplanar Circuit Containing Nine Elements
V 1 0 9V
R1 1 2 1
R2 4 0 7
R3 3 0 5
R4 2 3 6
R5 5 3 4
R6 2 4 2
R7 1 5 8
R8 4 5 3
.DC V 9V 9V 9V
.PRINT DC V(1,2) V(2,3) V(2,4)
.PRINT DC V(4,5) V(5,3) V(1,5)
.OP
.OPT nopage
.END
```

This input file produces the voltage drops across the individual elements, which is desirable if branch currents are needed. Alternatively, the print statements could call for the currents through the resistors, such as I(R1). Note that without the .OP entry, the node voltages would not be obtained.

Verify that $V(1,2) = 1.367$ V, $V(2,4) = 1.685$ V, and $V(1,5) = 3.031$ V. Also verify numerically that $V(1) = V(1,2) + V(2,3) + V(3)$.

SUMMARY OF PSPICE STATEMENTS USED IN THIS CHAPTER

The designation [...] means an optional item; <...> is a required item.

E[*name*] <+*node*> <−*node*> <[+*controlling node*> <−*controlling node*]>
<*gain*>

For example,

```
E 2 3 1 0 5
```

means a voltage-controlled voltage source between nodes *2* and *3*, dependent on the voltage between nodes *1* and *0*. Voltage *E* will be five times voltage V_{10}.

F[*name*] *<+node> <−node> <controlling V device name> <gain>*

For example,

```
F 4 2 VA 50
```

means a current-controlled current source between terminals *4* and *2* with the current through the source from node *4* to node *2*. The current is dependent on the current through source V A, having a gain factor of 50. If necessary, V A may be set at zero volts.

G[*name*] *<+node> <−node> <+controlling node> <−controlling node> <transconductance>*

For example,

```
G 5 1 2 0 0.05
```

means a voltage-controlled current source between nodes *5* and *1* that is dependent on the voltage between nodes *2* and *0*. The g_m value is 50 mS.

H[*name*] *<+node> <−node> <controlling V device name> <transresistance>*

For example,

```
H 6 4 VB 20
```

means a current-controlled voltage source between nodes *6* and *4* that is dependent on the current through the voltage source VB. If necessary, VB may be set at zero volts. The transfer-resistance value is 20.

I[*name*] *<+node> <−node>* **[DC]** *<value>*

For example,

```
I 0 1 DC 2A
```

means a direct current from an ideal current source directed from node *0* to node *1* internally. The value of the current is 2 A.

R[*name*] *<+node> <−node> <value>*

For example,

```
R1 1 2 100
```

means a resistor between nodes *1* and *2* with a value of 100Ω. Since a resistor is bilateral, either node may be called the +node (or the −node). If it is desired to find the current through the resistor, the node designation is significant. In this example if the current is called I(R1) and it is actually moving from node *1* to node *2*, it will be shown as a positive number in PSpice.

V[*name*] <+*node*> <−*node*> [DC] <*value*>

For example,

```
V 1 0 DC 50V
```

means a source voltage with the positive terminal at node *1* and the negative terminal at node *0*. It is an ideal dc voltage source of 50 V. [DC] appears in brackets, meaning that this portion of the statement is optional. The V following the 50 is also optional but should be included for clarity. Other forms of the *V* statement are found in later chapters. Some involve ac voltages, and some include a transient specification.

DOT COMMANDS USED IN THIS CHAPTER

.DC[LIN] [OCT] [DEC] <*sweep variable*> <start> <end> <increment>

For example,

```
.DC LIN VS 0V 10V 0.1V
```

means that the source voltage VS will assume values from 0 V to 10 V, in 0.1-V increments. The sweep in voltages is linear.

.END

This statement must come at the end of the input file. It tells PSpice that there are no more statements in the file.

.OP

This statement is used to produce detailed bias-point information.

.OPTIONS

For example,

```
.OPTIONS NOPAGE
```

means the option has been selected that will suppress paging and printing of a banner for each major section of output. Other options are

ACCT to produce accounting information

LIST giving a summary of circuit devices

NODE producing a node table

NOECHO to suppress listing of the input file

NOMOD suppressing listing of model parameters

OPTS to show which options are chosen

WIDTH to set the number of columns for output

.PRINT DC < *output variable* >

For example,

```
.PRINT DC V(5) I(RL)
```

means that the output file will contain a listing that includes V(5), the voltage at node *5*, and I(RL), the current through resistor RL.

.PROBE

means that the waveform analyzer Probe is to be used in the analysis. All voltages and currents are available for use in Probe. It is up to you to select which item to plot, assuming that a range of values has been included in the analysis. The range could be one of input voltages or, in the case of ac, a frequency range.

In Probe, arithmetic expressions of output variables may be used. The simple +, −, /, * (add, subtract, divide, and multiply) operators are frequently used. Available functions include ABS(x), SGN(x), DB(x), EXP(x), LOG(x), LOG10(x), PWR(x,y), SQRT(x), SIN(x), COS(x), TAN(x), ARCTAN(x), d(x), s(x), AVG(x), and RMS(x).

.TF< *output variable* > < *input source* >

For example,

```
.TF V(5) VS
```

means that the transfer function V(5)/VS is produced. This is described as a small-signal transfer function. It also produces the input and output resistances.

The **POLY** form of source

For example,

```
E1 5 2 POLY(1) 3 1 1 2 3
```

means that the VCVS E1 is dependent on the voltage between nodes *3* and *1* in a nonlinear form as described by a polynomial. The (1) means that there is a single controlling voltage V_{31}. The next three terms are for k_0, k_1, and k_2 in the formula

$$k_0 + k_1 v_1 + k_2 v_1^2$$

If there are more k values, it means that the polynomial is of higher degree.

When a line in an input file begins with an asterisk (*), it is a comment line rather than a statement to be processed. A comment may also be placed at the end of a statement if the comment is preceded by a semicolon (;).

In describing PSpice statements, the notation [...] means an optional item; the notation <...> means a required item. When an asterisk is placed at the end of a PSpice statement, it means that the item may be repeated.

PROBLEMS

1.1 For the circuit in Fig. 1.33, find the current I. Your PSpice input file should include a method for finding the current directly. Verify the results by finding the current as V_{12}/R_1 and V_{23}/r_2.

Fig. 1.33

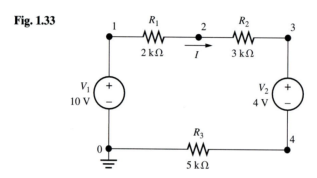

1.2 For the circuit in Fig. 1.34, find the power furnished by each of the voltage sources V_1 and V_2. Your input file should provide for finding the current through each voltage source. Verify the results by finding the power absorbed by all the resistors. Find each resistor power by using either I^2R or V^2/R.

Fig. 1.34

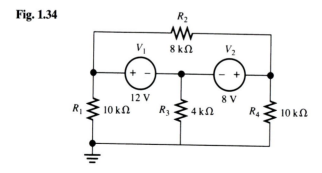

1.3 Find V_{ab} (the Thevenin voltage) and R_{ab} (the Thevenin resistance) for the circuit of Fig. 1.35. Your input file should follow the method suggested in the text for finding these values.

Fig. 1.35

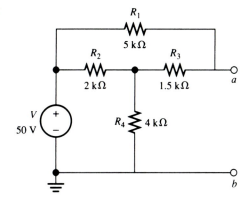

1.4 For the ladder network shown in Fig. 1.36, find R_{in}, the resistance seen by the source. Include the necessary statements in your PSpice input file to find the input resistance directly.

Fig. 1.36

$R = 1.5 \, k\Omega$

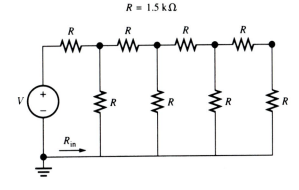

1.5 For the circuit in Fig. 1.37, find voltage V_{12}. This may be found simply from $V(1) - V(2)$. Verify the results by including provisions in your input file to find the current through R_2 directly.

Fig. 1.37

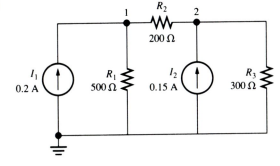

1.6 For the circuit in Fig. 1.38, find the current through the 6-Ω resistor and the voltage v.

Fig. 1.38

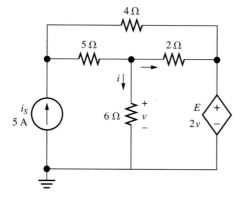

1.7 For the circuit in Fig. 1.39, find the voltage v_{23} and the current i.

Fig. 1.39

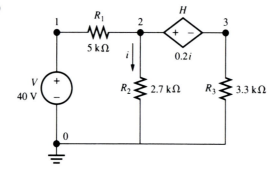

1.8 For the circuit in Fig. 1.40, find the voltage across resistor R_4.

Fig. 1.40

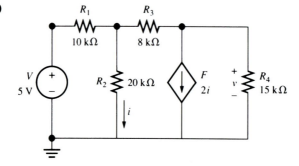

1.9 For the circuit in Fig. 1.41, find the voltage v_{ab}.

Fig. 1.41

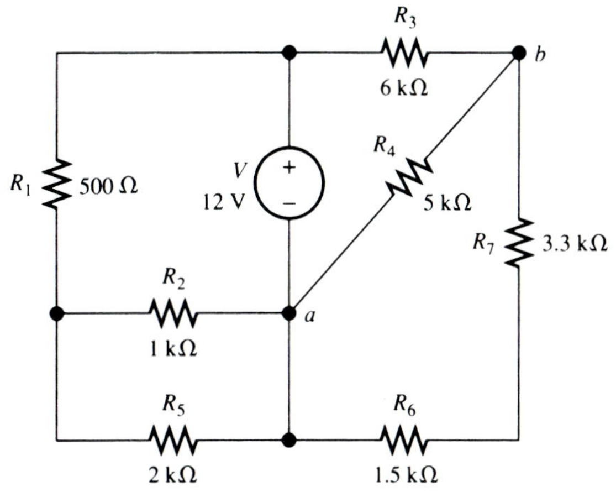

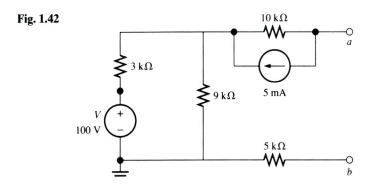

1.10 For the circuit in Fig. 1.42, find V_{ab} and R_{ab}, the Thevenin equivalents.

Fig. 1.42

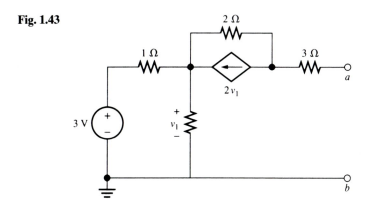

1.11 For the circuit in Fig. 1.43, find the Thevenin equivalent circuit at terminals *ab*.

Fig. 1.43

AC Circuit Analysis (for Sinusoidal Steady-State Conditions)

SPICE gives dc node voltages without any special requirements, since the dc voltages are part of the normal calculations for operating points that are necessary for transistor biasing and the like. If you want an ac analysis, you must specifically ask for it. An introductory example will show how this is done.

SERIES AC CIRCUIT WITH *R* AND *L*

The series circuit of Fig. 2.1 shows an ac source voltage of 1 V in series with a resistance and an inductance. The *R* and *L* combination might be a coil, for example. Values are $R = 1.5 \, \Omega$, $L = 5.3$ mH, and $f = 60$ Hz. Find the current in the circuit and the impedance of the coil. The input file might be

```
AC Circuit with R and L in Series (Coil)
V 1 0 AC 1V
R 1 2 1.5
L 2 0 5.3mH
.AC LIN 1 60Hz 60Hz
.PRINT AC I(R) IR(R) II(R) IP(R)
.END
```

The .AC statement gives a LIN (linear) sweep for one frequency only, with beginning and ending frequencies of 60 Hz. The .PRINT statement with the sweep parameter AC is required to print the variables chosen, which are:

I(R) is the magnitude of the current through *R*.

IM(R) is (also) the magnitude of the current through *R*.

Fig. 2.1   Series R and L.

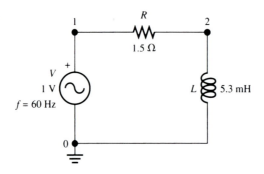

IR(R) is the real component of the current through R.

II(R) is the imaginary component of the current through R.

IP(R) is the phase angle in degrees of the current through R.

If we wanted to express the voltage drop V_2 across the inductor in like manner we might use:

V(2) is the magnitude of the voltage (between nodes *2* and *0* respectively).

VM(2) is (also) the magnitude of the voltage.

VR(2) is the real component of the voltage.

VI(2) is the imaginary component of the voltage.

VP(2) is the phase angle in degrees of the voltage.

Run the PSpice analysis. The node voltages are shown as zero. This means that there are no biasing, dc values. Voltage-source currents and power dissipation also refer to biasing. These values are also zero. The interesting part of the result shows FREQ = 60 Hz, I(R) = 0.4002 A for the magnitude of the ac current. IR(R) = 0.2403 A for the real part of this current, II(R) = −0.3201 A as the imaginary part of the current, and IP(R) = −53.1° as the angle of the current.

In ac problems of this type, it is helpful to draw phasor diagrams. Figure 2.2 shows such a diagram. The voltage is taken as the reference at zero degrees. The current is shown at its angle of −53.1°. You may find the impedance of the coil as

$$Z = \frac{V}{I} = \frac{1\underline{/0^\circ}}{0.4\,\underline{/-53.1^\circ}} = 2.5\underline{/53.1^\circ}\ \Omega$$

Since the voltage was given as a unit value, this is the same as the reciprocal of the I phasor.

Fig. 2.2   Phasor diagram for series R and L.

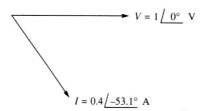

Fig. 2.3 Series R and C.

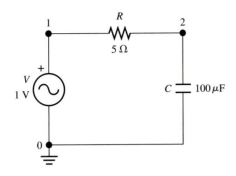

SERIES AC CIRCUIT WITH *R* AND *C*

If a capacitor is used in place of an inductor, the circuit is as shown in Fig. 2.3. The values are $R = 5\ \Omega$, $C = 100\ \mu\text{F}$, and $f = 318$ Hz. The input file then might become

```
AC Circuit with Resistance and Capacitance in Series
V 1 0 AC 1V
R 1 2 5
C 2 0 100uF
.AC LIN 1 318Hz 318Hz
.PRINT AC I(R) IP(R) V(2) VP(2)
.END
```

In the .PRINT statement, V(2) and VP(2) are for the magnitude and phase of the capacitor voltage. Run the PSpice analysis; then plot the phasor diagram of current and voltages. Your results should agree with Fig. 2.4.

PARALLEL BRANCHES IN AC CIRCUIT

The next example, shown in Fig. 2.5, is for R and L in parallel, using a current source. Values chosen are $I = 100\ \underline{/0°}$ mA, $R = 8\frac{1}{3}\ \Omega$, and $L = 6.36$ mH. For this circuit, find the voltage across the parallel branches, the currents through each branch, and the admittance of the RL combination. The input file should look like this:

```
AC Circuit with Parallel Branches R and L
I 0 1 AC 100mA
R 1 0 8.33333
```

Fig. 2.4 Phasor diagram for series R and C.

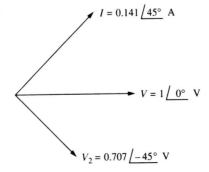

Fig. 2.5   Parallel R and L.

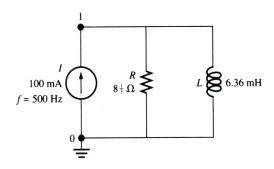

```
L 1 0 6.36mH
.AC LIN 1 500Hz 500Hz
.PRINT AC V(1) VP(1) I(R) IP(R) I(L) IP(L)
.END
```

The voltage is found as V(1) and VP(1) for the magnitude and phase angle, and the current through each branch is found in the usual way. Run the analysis, verifying that V(1) = 0.7691 and VP(1) = 22.64°. The admittance of the RL combination is $Y = I/V(1) = (0.100 \ /0°)/(0.7691 \ /22.6°) = (0.13 \ /-22.6°)$ S.

Construct the phasor diagram for this circuit, showing all currents and voltage V_1. Check your results against those shown in Fig. 2.6.

As an exercise in circuit analysis, convert the branch currents from polar to rectangular form, then add them and compare the value with the source current.

PARALLEL BRANCHES WITH CAPACITIVE BRANCH

Figure 2.7 shows another parallel circuit. Values are $I = 100 \ /0°$ mA, $R = 8\frac{1}{3}$ Ω, $C = 14.14$ μF, and $f = 500$ Hz.

Before running the PSpice analysis, calculate the admittance of the RC combination. This is given as $Y = G + jB$, where $G = 1/R$ and $B = 2\pi fC$. The input file is

```
AC Circuit with Parallel R and C
I 0 1 AC 100mA
R 1 0 8.333333
C 1 0 14.14uF
.AC LIN 1 500Hz 500Hz
.PRINT AC V(1) VP(1) I(R) IP(R) I(C) IP(C)
.END
```

Run the analysis; then construct a complete phasor diagram for the circuit. Compare your results with Fig. 2.8. The results show $V = 0.7815 \ /-20.3°$ V. Verify your predicted value of Y. Use the formula $Y = I/V$.

Fig. 2.6   Phasor diagram for parallel R and L.

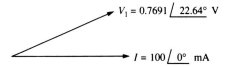

Fig. 2.7 Parallel R and C.

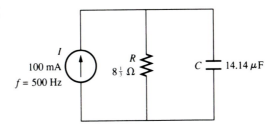

MAXIMUM POWER TRANSFER IN AC CIRCUIT

Recall that in a dc circuit, maximum power is delivered to a load resistance when $R_L = R_s$. In an ac circuit, the source impedance is often complex, or the Thevenin equivalent of everything excluding the load is most likely complex, containing resistance and reactance. The maximum power theorem tells you that for maximum power to be delivered in the case of a source impedance that contains resistive and reactive components, the load should be its conjugate. For example, if $Z_s = (600 + j150)$ Ω, for maximum power to be delivered to the load, it should be adjusted to $Z_L = (600 - j150)$ Ω. For this circuit, refer to Fig. 2.9. Of course, the X values must be converted to inductance and capacitance values. If we choose $f = 1$ kHz, then $L = 23.873$ mH, and $C = 1.061$ μF. The input file is

```
Maximum Power Transfer in AC Circuits
V 1 0 AC 12V
RS 1 2 600
L 2 3 23. 873mH
RL 3 4 600
C 4 0 1. 06uF
.AC LIN 1 1000Hz 1000Hz
.PRINT AC I(RL) V(3) VP(3)
.END
```

Run the analysis and verify that the current in the circuit is 10 mA at an angle of (almost) zero degrees. Also, observe that V(3) = 6.18 V at an angle of −14°. The power delivered to the load is easily found as $P = |I|^2 R = 60$ mW. This series circuit is resonant at the frequency of 1 kHz.

Note that using the calculated values of L and C as fixed (or given) and changing the frequency to some other value, the X values would change and the current would change to a smaller value.

RESONANCE IN SERIES *RLC* CIRCUIT

Series resonance occurs in a circuit with R, L, and C when the input impedance is purely resistive. Thus the inductive reactance and the capacitive reactance cancel, and the current is a maximum. As a result, the phase angle of the circuit is zero. That

Fig. 2.8 Phasor diagram for parallel R and C.

$I = 100 \underline{/\ 0°}$ mA

$V = 0.7815 \underline{/\ {-20.3°}}$ V

Fig. 2.9 Maximum power to load impedance.

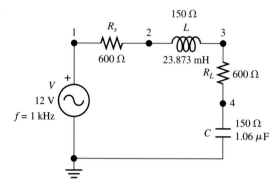

is, the current and the applied voltage are in phase.
The resonant frequency is easily founded from

$$f_o = \frac{1}{2\pi\sqrt{LC}}$$

Figure 2.10 shows such a circuit. The values are $R = 50\ \Omega$, $L = 20$ mH, and $C = 150$ nF. For this example, this gives $f_o = 2905.8$ Hz. The applied voltage is chosen to be $1\ \underline{/0°}$ V. Work with the following input file:

```
Series Resonance with RLC
V  1  0  AC  1V
R  1  2  50
L  2  3  20mH
C  3  0  150nF
.AC LIN 99 100Hz 5000Hz
.PROBE
.END
```

The .AC statement calls for a linear sweep beginning at 100 Hz and ending at 5000 Hz in 99 steps, giving 50-Hz increments.

Run the PSpice analysis, and when it is done, select File, Run Probe. When the dark screen appears with the range of frequencies displayed along the X-axis you may produce a graph of any of several variables. Do the following:

1. Plot IP(R) over a linear frequency range extending from 2 kHz to 4 kHz. Do this by typing in the desired variable, *IP(R)*, in the Trace Command field and choos-

Fig. 2.10 Series resonance with *RLC*.

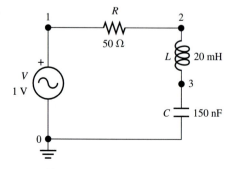

ing OK. In order to obtain the desired *X*-axis range, choose Plot, X-axis Settings ... Data Range, User Defined. Next type in *2kHz* (no space) to *4kHz*, then select Scale Linear, OK. If you should produce an incorrect graph, select Trace, Delete All, then repeat the process to get the desired trace. Your graph should pass through zero degrees at a frequency near 2.9 kHz. Verify this by selecting the cursor mode icon (it has cross hairs and a *check* symbol), then using the mouse or the right (and left) arrow to find the zero-phase-shift location, which should be at *f* = 2.9059 kHz. See Fig. 2.11.

2. Plot V(1)/I(R) over the same frequency range (2 kHz to 4 kHz). Force the *Y*-axis values to the range of 0 to 300. The plot will represent the magnitude of *Z*. Use the cursor to find the following values: at 2 kHz, *Z* = 284 Ω; at 2.9 kHz, *Z* = 50 Ω; and at 4 kHz, *Z* = 243 Ω.

3. Plot two graphs on the screen together, one giving V(3) and the other giving I(R). Use Plot, Add Plot to obtain the second graph. Let the frequency range extend from 0 to 5 kHz, linear. Your results should show a maximum for V(3) of about 7.3 V and maximum for I(R) of 20 mA. Check these values for accuracy using pencil-and-paper methods. See Fig. 2.12 for comparison.

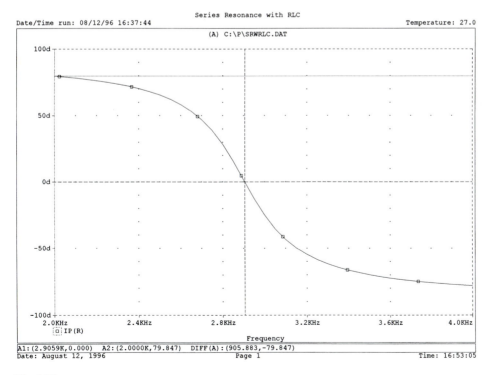

Fig. 2.11

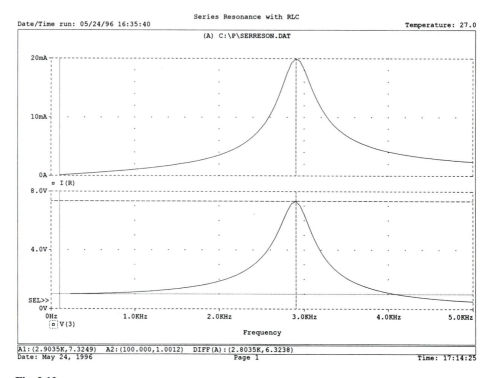

Fig. 2.12

FREQUENCY SWEEP FOR SERIES-PARALLEL AC CIRCUIT

Figure 2.13 shows another ac network. Values are $V = 100 \underline{/0°}$ V, $R_1 = 10$ Ω , $R_2 = 10 \,\Omega$, $L = 100$ mH, and $C = 10$ μF. Assume that the resonant frequency is unknown and that a preliminary investigation is required. The input file might be

```
Series-Parallel AC Circuit
V 1 0 AC 100V
R1 1 2 10
R2 2 3 10
L 3 0 100mH
```

Fig. 2.13 Series-parallel ac circuit.

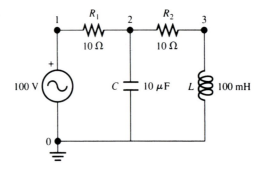

```
C 2 0 10uF
.AC LIN 100 50Hz 1000Hz
.PRINT AC I(R1) IP(R1)
.END
```

The .AC statement is a guess for the resonant frequency somewhere in the range 50 Hz to 1000 Hz. If this is not close to the actual range, you can choose a new set of values. The .PRINT statement calls for the circuit current magnitude and phase. This will allow you to look for unity power factor, because when this condition occurs, the angle on the current will be zero.

Run the analysis and look at the output file. Do not bother to print the file, since you will want to change the range of frequencies before you are through. You should confirm that between $f = 155$ Hz and $f = 165$ Hz, resonance occurs. Now revise the input file by modifying the ac sweep statement to become

```
.AC LIN 101 100 200
```

Now look at all the whole-number frequencies between 100 Hz and 200 Hz. Run the analysis and see that resonance comes between $f = 158$ Hz and $f = 159$ Hz. Also the current close to resonance is approximately 98 mA.

Now you are in a position to look at a powerful feature of the PSpice analysis. Does resonance occur at the series-resonance-formula predicted value of $1/(2\pi \sqrt{LC}\,)$? Use your calculator to compute this formula value. It should be $f = 159.155$ Hz. This does not quite agree with our prediction that f_o lies between 158 Hz and $f = 159$ Hz. Is the difference merely round-off error?

Revise the input file to give the ac sweep as

```
.AC LIN 51 155Hz 160Hz
```

This will give a frequency increment of 0.1 Hz in the analysis. Run the study again and find where the sign of the current angle IP(R1) changes. The results should show that this is between a frequency of 158.3 Hz and 158.4 Hz. From your study of resonance, you should confirm that the series-resonance formula is incorrect for this series-parallel circuit. Note that the minimum current comes not at the resonant frequency but at $f = 159.2$ Hz, where the phase angle of the current is about 5.97°.

For an interesting exercise, replace the .PRINT statement with a .PROBE statement in this analysis. You will be able to show in graphical form what you have seen with the numerical results. The graphs have the advantage of allowing you to look at many variables without having to revise the input file.

EFFECT OF CHANGES IN COIL RESISTANCE

In Fig. 2.13, one of the parallel branches contains $R = 10\ \Omega$ and $L = 100$ mH. This might be a coil with a small resistance. The question might be asked, What effect does the resistance of the coil have on the behavior of the circuit? Modify the input file by making $R_2 = 50\ \Omega$ and confirm that $f_o = 138$ Hz. Then make $R_2 = 80\ \Omega$ and see that $f_o = 95$ Hz. Would you have guessed that the change in resonant frequency would have been that great?

Note how easily PSpice lets you vary the circuit parameters and carry out a new set of calculations. If you want numerical accuracy, the .PRINT statement provides it, and if you want to see the actual plot of variables, the .PROBE statement is invaluable.

A PARALLEL-RESONANT CIRCUIT

The equations for analyzing a parallel resonant circuit are considerably more tedious than those for the series-resonant circuit. You may refer to an introductory text for a full treatment of these equations. However, the analysis using PSpice will allow you to find the resonant frequency and the input impedance at resonance (or near resonance) with ease. In this example you will also again look at the cursor available in Probe.

The circuit shown in Fig. 2.14 contains one branch with a coil and another branch with a capacitor. Values are $R_L = 10\ \Omega$, $L = 2.04$ mH, $R_C = 5\ \Omega$, and $C = 0.65\ \mu$F. Note that a small sampling resistor $R = 1\ \Omega$ has been added in series with the voltage source, making V a 1-V practical source. A preliminary estimate indicates that the resonant frequency is between 4 kHz and 5 kHz. Consider the input file as shown here.

```
Parallel Resonant Circuit
V 1 0 AC 1V
RL 1A 2 10
RC 1A 3 5
R 1 1A 1
L 2 0 2.04mH
C 3 0 0.65uF
.AC LIN 1001 4000Hz 5000Hz
.PROBE
.END
```

The input file shows a frequency sweep extending from 4 kHz to 5 kHz in 1-Hz increments. Run the analysis, then using Probe, plot IP(R). The X-axis shows a range extending from 1 kHz to 10 kHz, anticipating a logarithmic plot. This will mean that a selected trace will appear over a small portion of the graph. Change the X-axis range so that it extends from 4 kHz to 5 kHz on a linear scale. By inspection, f_o is near 4.3 kHz. Refer to Fig. 2.15 for this trace.

Fig. 2.14 Parallel resonant circuit.

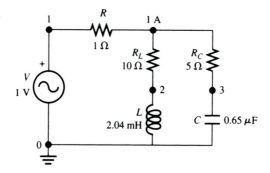

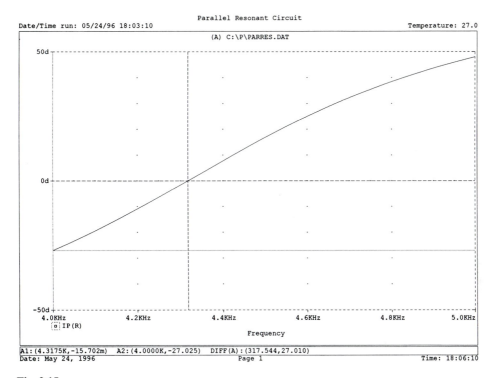

Fig. 2.15

Using the Probe Cursor

From the menu line choose T<u>o</u>ols, <u>C</u>ursor, <u>D</u>isplay and see that a Probe Cursor box appears on the screen. It will appear at the bottom right, but it may be moved to other locations if desired. The box contains the following:

```
A1 =  4.0000K,  -27.025
A2 =  4.0000K,  -27.025
dif = 0.000,      0.000
```

The *A1* line represents the *X* and *Y* values of frequency and IP(R) at the left end of the plot. These are $f = 4$ kHz and phase angle $-27.025°$. This is, at $f = 4$ kHz, the current is at $-27.025°$ relative to the input voltage with an implied angle of zero.

With the right-arrow key, move the hairline until you find the point where the phase shift is zero (or almost zero). When we ran this analysis, the probe cursor values were

```
A1 =  4.3175K,  -15.702m
A2 =  4.0000K,  -27.025
dif = 317.544,   27.010
```

Your values may differ slightly. In fact, if you remove the trace and add it back, the values may change slightly, since a curve-fit routine is used to achieve the plot. The *A1* line tells you that when $f = 4.3175$ kHz, the phase angle of the current is near zero. Thus the resonant frequency $f_o = 4.3175$ kHz, since the input current is in phase with the applied voltage at this frequency. Incidentally, the resistance R in the circuit is necessary to make the input voltage a *practical* voltage source.

It is also of interest to find the input impedance (or admittance) of the circuit at resonance. Recall that the value should be purely resistive (or conductive) at resonance. With this in mind, plot I(R). Since $V = 1$ V, the circuit current can also be thought of as representing the input admittance. Explain why. From this plot again use the cursor mode. Move the hairline until you find the predicted $f_o = 4.3175$ kHz. What is the value of I at this frequency? Confirm that $I = 4.683$ mA at the resonant frequency. Also confirm that $Z_o = R_o = 213.5 \ \Omega$. Note that this is not the minimum current.

FINDING THE INPUT IMPEDANCE OF AN AC CIRCUIT

Consider a box containing an unknown impedance network, such as the one shown in Fig. 2.16. In a PSpice analysis you can call for both V(1) and I(R) in a print statement. However, the statement cannot call for V(1)/I(R). The various mathematical operators are not allowed. If you use Probe to obtain a trace of a desired variable, you may use the following operators:

$$+ \quad - \quad * \quad / \quad \text{and parentheses.}$$

In addition a variety of functions may be employed, including the following:

abs(x)	$\|x\|$
sgn(x)	$+1$ (if $x>0$), 0 (if $x = 0$), -1 (if $x<0$)
sqrt(x)	$\sqrt{x}$
exp(x)	e^x
log(x)	$\ln(\|x\|)$
log10(x)	$\log(\|x\|)$
m(x)	magnitude of x
p(x)	phase of x
r(x)	real part of x
img(x)	imaginary part of x
g(x)	group delay of x
pwr(x,y)	$\|x\|^y$
sin(x)	sin(x)

Fig. 2.16 Box containing unknown impedance network.

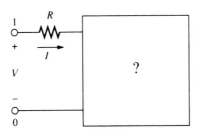

Fig. 2.17 Circuit with current-sensing resistor.

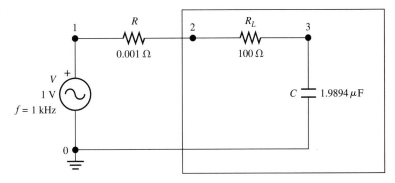

cos(x)	cos(x)
tan(x)	tan(x)
atan(x)	$\tan^{-1}(x)$
arctan(x)	$\tan^{-1}(x)$
d(x)	derivative of x
s(x)	integral of x
avg(x)	running average of x
rms(x)	running RMS average of x
min(x)	minimum of the real part of x
max(x)	maximum of the real part of x

Thus in order to find the input impedance of the circuit in Fig. 2.16, let R be a very small resistor (used to sense the current), and the input impedance V(1)/I(R) you can find in Probe by using r(V(1)/I(R)) for the real part of Z and img(V(1)/I(R)) for the imaginary part of Z. This gives the same result as using r(VM(1)/IM(R)) and img(VM(1)/IM(R)). To obtain the phase angle of Z, p(V(1)/I(R)) may be used. An example will clarify the technique.

Figure 2.17 shows a circuit with a current-sensing resistor and an "unknown" impedance in the box. In order to find the impedance, you need a simulation that will involve Probe. An ac sweep is included in the circuit file:

```
Input Impedance Using a Small Current-Sensing Resistor
V 1 0 AC 1V
R 1 2 0.001; this is the current-sensing resistor
RL 2 3 100
C 3 0 1.9894uF
.AC LIN 501 500Hz 1500Hz
.PROBE
.END
```

Run the analysis and in Probe plot the real and imaginary components of Z_{in}. The results are shown in Fig. 2.18. Use the cursor mode and verify that when $f = 1$ kHz, $R_{in} = 100\,\Omega$ (the real part of Z_{in}) and $X_{in} = -80\,\Omega$ (the imaginary part of Z_{in}).

Input Impedance of a Two-Branch Network

In the previous circuit the results were easy enough to find without using Probe. In a more complex circuit, such as that in Fig. 2.19, the input impedance is not found

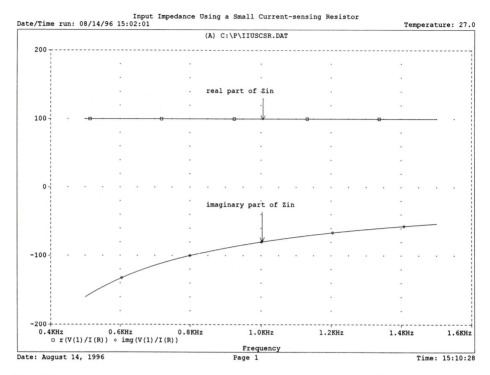

Fig. 2.18

by pencil-and-paper methods without considerable effort. Using Probe, the results are easily obtained. The input file is

```
Input Impedance of Two-Branch Network
V 1 0 AC 12V
Rs 1 2 50
R1 2 3 100
R2 3 5 80
R3 3 4 75
R4 5 6 60
```

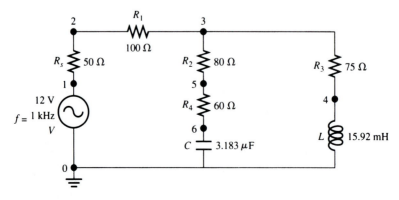

Fig. 2.19   Input impedance of two-branch network.

```
L 4 0 15.92mH
C 6 0 3.183uF
.AC LIN 501 500Hz 1500Hz
.PROBE
.END
```

In Probe, find the input impedance (at node *2* looking to the right) at $f =$ 1 kHz. You should verify that $Z_{in} = (178.9 + j29.33)$ Ω. You may prefer to show complex values simply as an ordered pair; in this case $Z_{in} = (178.9, 29.33)$ Ω. Compare your traces with Fig. 2.20.

A PHASE-SHIFT NETWORK

A simple phase-shifting circuit using only capacitors and resistors is shown in Fig. 2.21. This bridged-*T* circuit uses the following values: $C_1 = C_2 = 10$ nF, $R_1 = 200$ Ω, $R_2 = 250$ Ω, $R_L = 100$ Ω, and $R = 1$ Ω (sampling resistor). The PSpice analysis is to investigate the phase-shifting property of this network. Determine at what frequency the network will produce the maximum phase shift of current relative to input voltage and what the phase shift will be. Trial-and-error may be used to find the proper range of frequencies for this analysis. This is the input file:

```
Phase-Shift Network
V 1 0 AC 1V
R 1 1A 1
R1 1A 3 200
R2 2 0 250
```

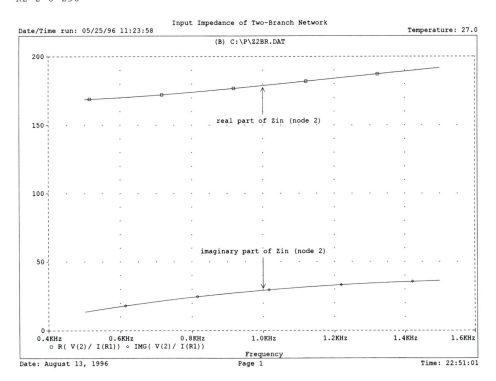

Fig. 2.20

Fig. 2.21   Phase-shift network.

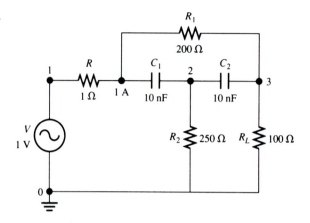

```
RL 3 0 100
C1 1A 2 10nF
C2 2 3 10nF
.AC LIN 501 5kHz 500kHz
.PROBE
.END
```

Run the Pspice analysis, then plot IP(R) using a linear frequency range of 5 kHz to 500 kHz. You can readily see that the maximum phase shift is slightly less than 30° and that this occurs at a frequency near 300 kHz. For a more accurate answer, use the cursor mode and verify that the maximum phase shift is 29.67° at $f = 281.4$ kHz.

While still in Probe, obtain a trace of IP(RL). This will indicate the phase shift of the bridged-T network itself. Find the frequency at which the network produces zero phase shift. Notice that this occurs at a frequency of less than 50 kHz.

Revise the input file to allow for an ac sweep beginning at 5 kHz and ending at 50 kHz. Now run the analysis and determine the frequency for zero phase shift, with a plot of IP(RL). Using the cursor, verify that $f = 29.32$ kHz. Your plot should look like Fig. 2.22.

LOCUS OF ADMITTANCES

A graphical technique that is often used in ac circuit analysis is based on finding the locus of impedances or admittances. If elements are in series, impedances are used, and the total effect is found by adding the various loci. If elements are in parallel, admittances are used, since the total effect is again found by adding the admittances of the various branches.

The circuit of Fig. 2.23 contains two parallel branches with values $C = 0.318$ μF, $R_L = 50$ Ω, and $L = 3.18$ mH. The input file is created using an ac sweep from 5 Hz to 10 kHz and is

```
Locus of Admittances
V 1A 0 AC 1V
R 1A 1 1
RL 1 2 50
L 2 0 3.18mH
```

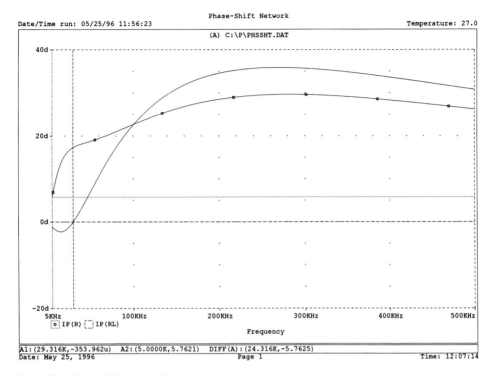

Date/Time run: 05/25/96 11:56:23   Temperature: 27.0

Fig. 2.22   Phase-shift network.

```
C 1 0 0. 318uF
.AC LIN 201 5Hz 10kHz
.PROBE
.END
```

Run the analysis and plot IP(R) to find the resonant frequency. Using the cursor, verify that $f_o = 4.336$ kHz.

Now change the X-axis, letting it represent the real component of admittance. Since $V = 1$ V, $Y = I/V = I/1$. Thus Y is numerically the same as the current, and you can plot I and Y interchangeably. In the Y-plane, G is shown on the horizontal axis and B on the vertical axis.

Fig. 2.23   Circuit for locus of admittances.

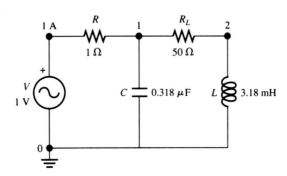

Before you attempt to change the X-axis, delete the trace that is currently on the screen and select Plot, X-axis settings ..., specify Auto Range, Linear, then Axis Variable; type in IR(R) for the X-axis Variable, followed by OK (twice). Now obtain a trace of II(R). Because I and Y are numerically the same, the axes can be thought of as the Y-plane values for G (X-axis) and B(Y-axis). This graph contains important information that is not readily seen. The point at the top left is for $f = 10$ kHz. Moving down the graph takes you to lower frequencies, where the values of B and G may be obtained. Move the cursor to the point where $B = $ (nearly) 0 and confirm that $G = 5$ mS. This indicates that the impedance of the network is 200 Ω at the resonant frequency of 4.336 kHz.

Obtain a printed copy of the Y-plane graph. Mark the X-axis G (in mS) and the Y-axis B (in mS) for further study. Your graph should look like Fig. 2.24. You know where two frequencies are located on this graph, but how can you identify others? A simple method involves going back to the circuit file and changing the top frequency in the ac sweep statement. For starters, let the top frequency be 6 kHz and run the simulation again. When you see the Y-plane values, carefully note where the graph begins (6 kHz), and transfer this to your previous graph using B and G values. Try this for several other top frequencies, marking each new top value of f on the original graph.

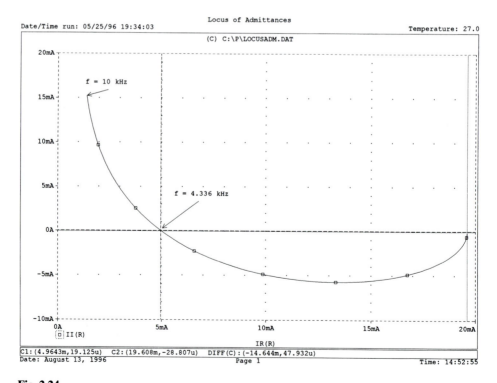

Fig. 2.24

Fig. 2.25 Series circuit for admittance locus.

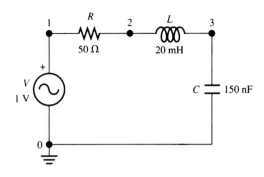

Admittance Locus for Series *RLC*

The admittance locus for a series *RLC* circuit takes an interesting shape. Can you predict what it will look like for a sweep of frequencies? It will be a circle (if *B* and *G* are shown to the same scale). The circuit shown in Fig. 2.25 uses the values *R* = 50 Ω, *L* = 20 mH, and *C* = 150 nF. The input file is

```
Admittance Locus for Series RLC Circuit
V 1 0 AC 1V
R 1 2 50
L 2 3 20mH
```

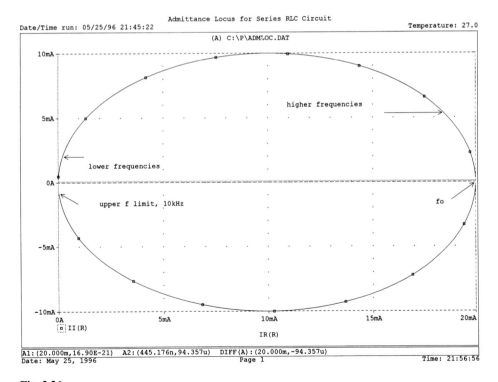

Fig. 2.26

```
C 3 0 150nF
.AC LIN 5001 100Hz 10kHz
.PROBE
.END
```

The sweep of frequencies takes you well beyond the resonant frequency of 2906 Hz. Run the analysis and plot IR(R) on the *X*-axis vs. II(R) on the *Y*-axis. Watch carefully as the curve is drawn on the screen. This will occur too quickly to see unless many points are used in the sweep statement (.AC). Note that the curve begins on the left of the screen and moves in a clockwise direction. The first portion of the curve is drawn quickly, but the last part, completing the circle, appears to be drawn slowly. This is due to the relative locations of low and high frequencies on the graph. From the 9 o'clock position moving clockwise to the 3 o'clock position, there is a range of frequencies from 0 Hz to the resonant frequency of 2906 Hz. The entire lower half of the circle extends from the resonant frequency to the upper frequency limit.

Obtain a printed copy of the trace for further study. Note that you can make the graph look more like a true circle by careful selection of the *X*- and *Y*-ranges, although this may mean losing some portion of the circle. Figure 2.26 shows this graph.

Now remove the trace and select frequency as the *X*-axis variable. Plot I(R) as a function of frequency and in the cursor mode use the "Position cursor at next peak value" icon (on the far right) to verify f_o.

MULTIPLE SOURCES IN AC NETWORKS

When there is more than a single source in an ac network, you must specify the relative phase angles of the sources. In each statement describing a voltage source in the example of Fig. 2.27, note that the value of the voltage is shown with a magnitude followed by an angle. Thus V_2, which is 10 V at an angle of $-90°$, is shown as 10V -90. For this example, your assignment is to find the current through each of the elements *C, L,* and *R* and to find voltage V(2). The input file is

```
AC Network with More Than One Source
V1 1 0 ac 20V 0
V2 0 4 ac 10V -90
```

Fig. 2.27   An ac network with more than one source.

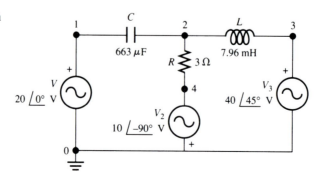

```
V3 3 0 ac 40V 45
R 2 4 3
L 2 3 7.96mH
C 1 2 663uF
.ac LIN 1 60Hz 60Hz
.print ac i(C) ir(c) ii(C) ip(C)
.print ac i(L) ir(L) ii(L) ip(L)
.print ac i(R) ir(R) ii(R) ip(R)
.print ac v(2) vr(2) vi(2) vp(2)
.opt nopage
.end
```

Run the simulation in PSpice and look at the results in the output file. What are the directions of the currents that have been found? You must look at the element statements to be sure of this. For example, the statement describing the capacitor shows the nodes as *1* and *2,* respectively. This means that on the circuit diagram you should show the current in the direction from node *1* toward node *2.* Failure to do this would leave you with an incomplete (or ambiguous) solution. Looking at the statements for *R* and *L,* assign current-direction arrows to these elements to complete the solution. Refer to Fig. 2.28 for the output file. Note that irrelevant lines have been edited out. It is a good practice to do this when you print such a file.

Three-phase networks will be considered in a later section. The source voltages will be specified in much the same way as in the present example.

```
AC Network with More Than One Source

****      CIRCUIT DESCRIPTION

V1 1 0 ac 20V 0
V2 0 4 ac 10V -90
V3 3 0 ac 40V 45
R 2 4 3
L 2 3 7.96mH
C 1 2 663uF
.ac LIN 1 60Hz 60Hz
.print ac i(C) ir(C) ii(C) ip(C)
.print ac i(L) ir(L) ii(L) ip(L)
.print ac i(R) ir(R) ii(R) ip(R)
.print ac v(2) vr(2) vi(2) vp(2)
.opt nopage
.end

****      AC ANALYSIS                    TEMPERATURE =    27.000 DEG C

   FREQ          I(C)          IR(C)        II(C)         IP(C)
   6.000E+01     2.050E+00     8.907E-01    -1.846E+00    -6.424E+01

   FREQ          I(L)          IR(L)        II(L)         IP(L)
   6.000E+01     8.243E+00     -8.238E+00   2.994E-01     1.779E+02

   FREQ          I(R)          IR(R)        II(R)         IP(R)
   6.000E+01     9.377E+00     9.129E+00    -2.145E+00    -1.323E+01

   FREQ          V(2)          VR(2)        VI(2)         VP(2)
   6.000E+01     2.762E+01     2.739E+01    3.564E+00     7.414E+00
```

Fig. 2.28

TRANSFORMERS

When using transformers in SPICE, you need a descriptive entry to show the self-inductance of each of the two windings, primary and secondary, and the coefficient of coupling k. Figure 2.29 is an example showing a voltage source of 20 V at a frequency of 1 kHz. Values for the transformer are known to be $R_1 = 20\ \Omega$, $L_1 = 25$ mH, $R_2 = 20\ \Omega$, $L_2 = 25$ mH, and $M = 20$ mH (mutual inductance). Find current in the primary, current in the secondary, power to the secondary, and power to the load impedance.

The coefficient of coupling may be found from

$$k = \frac{M}{\sqrt{L_1 L_2}}$$

For the example, this value will be 20/25 = 0.8. With this, you are ready to create the input file.

```
Circuit with Mutual Inductance
V 1 0 AC 20V
R1 1 2 20
R2 3 4 20
L1 2 0 25mH
L2 3 0 25mH
RL 4 5 40
CL 5 0 5.3uF
K L1 L2 0.8
.AC LIN 1 1kHz 1kHz
.PRINT AC I(R1) IR(R1) II(R1)
.PRINT AC I(R2) IR(R2) II(R2)
.END
```

Run the analysis and obtain a printed copy of the output file. Verify that the primary current is (0.1767, −0.1441) A and that the secondary current is (0.1979, −0.04904) A. Note that these answers are simply given as ordered pairs for the real and imaginary components. The results do not give the desired powers directly, since the .PRINT statements cannot contain expressions such as $I*I*R$. Use the calculator to verify that the power to the secondary is 2.49 W and that the power to the load impedance is 1.66 W.

Fig. 2.29 Circuit with mutual inductance.

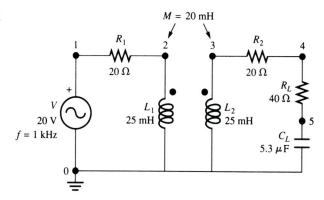

The dot convention is important in some transformer situations. In this example the dots are assumed to be at node *2* for L_1 and node *3* for L_2. The dots are thus assumed to be at the first-named node for each *L*.

FREQUENCY RESPONSE OF TUNED CIRCUIT

Tuned circuits are used in various electronic circuits such as those found in radio and television sets. Capacitors are placed in shunt with the transformer windings to create resonant conditions. At and near the resonant frequency, the power delivered to the secondary is large, but away from the resonant frequency, little power is delivered. Figure 2.30 shows a typical circuit fed from an ac current source: $I = 19.6$ mA, $R_1 = R_2 = 1\ \Omega$, $L_1 = L_2 = 25$ mH, $C_1 = C_2 = 1.013\ \mu$F, $R_L = 5$ kΩ, and $k = 0.05$. The *LC* combination produces a resonant frequency $f_o = 1$ kHz.

You are interested in investigating the behavior of the circuit at a range of frequencies near the resonant frequency. This is done by using the input file shown here.

```
Frequency Response of Tuned Circuit with Mutual Impedance
I 0 1 AC 19.6mA
C1 1 0 1.013uF
C2 3 0 1.013uF
R1 1 2 1
R2 3 4 1
L1 2 0 25mH
L2 4 0 25mH
K L1 L2 0.05
RL 3 0 5k
.AC LIN 401 800Hz 1200Hz
.PROBE
.END
```

The frequency sweep will extend from 800 Hz to 1200 Hz. Run the analysis and plot V(3) over the desired range of frequencies. Use a linear *X*-axis. Examine the shape of the voltage across the load. Notice that it rises on either side of the resonant frequency, dipping at f_o. Obtain a printed copy of this graph for further study. Figure 2.31 shows the graph.

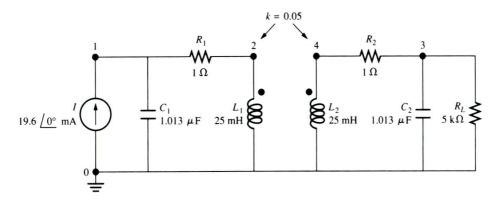

Fig. 2.30 Tuned circuit with mutual inductance.

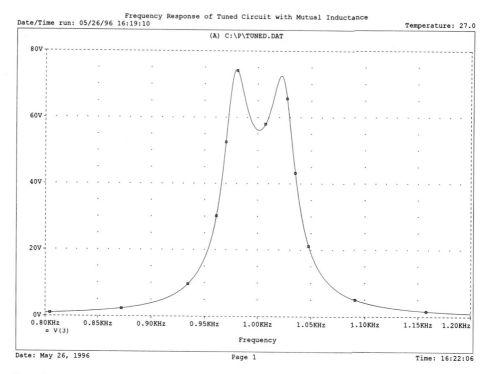

Frequency Response of Tuned Circuit with Mutual Inductance

Date/Time run: 05/26/96 16:19:10 — Temperature: 27.0

(A) C:\P\TUNED.DAT

Date: May 26, 1996   Page 1   Time: 16:22:06

Fig. 2.31

The value of $k = 0.05$, which was specified for this example, produced over-coupling. This gives a usable band of frequencies that are passed with little attenuation. For frequencies where the voltage level falls below 0.7 of its peak value, we have moved outside the usable bandwidth. Can you determine the bandwidth for this tuned circuit? Use the cursor and verify that at the peak $V(3) = 74.321$ V and $f = 980$ Hz. Seven-tenths of this value is 52 V; this level occurs when $f_1 = 970$ Hz and $f_2 = 1032$ Hz, giving a $BW = 62$ Hz.

In the circuit file, change the value of k to 0.03. Run the simulation again and note that the peak is higher and the bandwidth is smaller. In this case the peak is $V(3) = 82.156$ V. The largest peak voltage to the load will be achieved at a value of k giving critical coupling. For this circuit this peak voltage occurs with $k = 0.0155$. Run the simulation once more using this value of k. Verify that $V(3) = 99.238$ V at the peak.

THREE-PHASE AC CIRCUITS

Three-phase ac circuits may be treated as though they were single-phase circuits if the load is equally balanced among the phases. When the load is unbalanced, the solution becomes more tedious. This example will show the method of solution for the unbalanced case.

Fig. 2.32 Unbalanced three-phase load.

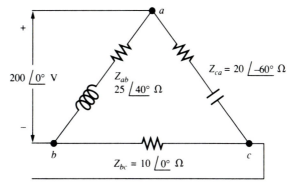

Figure 2.32 shows an unbalanced three-phase load. In the statement of the problem the delta-connected impedances are given as $Z_{ab} = 25 \angle 40° \, \Omega$, $Z_{bc} = 10 \angle 0° \, \Omega$, and $Z_{ca} = 20 \angle -60° \, \Omega$. The line voltages are balanced, 200 V, 60 Hz, with V_{ab} at 0°, using positive phase sequence. This means that $V_{ab} = 200 \angle 0° \, V$, $V_{bc} = 200 \angle -120° \, V$, and $V_{ca} = 200 \angle 120° \, V$.

Begin the solution by solving for the values of L and C. These are readily found by pencil-and-paper methods using known impedances and the frequency. In the circuit diagram, include small source resistances although none was stated in the problem. If these are omitted, PSpice will give an error message indicating a voltage loop. The line resistances are added to allow you to find the line currents. Figure 2.33 shows the revised diagram. The input file then becomes

```
Three-Phase Unbalanced Load
VAB 12 2 AC 200V 0
VBC 20 0 AC 200V -120
VCA 10 1 AC 200V 120
RS1 12 1 0.01
RS2 20 2 0.01
```

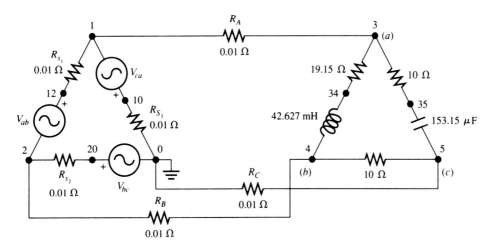

Fig. 2.33 Unbalanced three-phase load revised.

```
RS3 10 0 0.01
RA 1 3 0.01
RB 2 4 0.01
RC 0 5 0.01
RAB 3 34 19.15
LAB 34 4 42.627mH
RBC 4 5 10
RCA 3 35 10
CCA 35 5 153.15uF
.AC LIN 1 60Hz 60Hz
.PRINT AC I(RA) IP(RA) IR(RA) II(RA)
.PRINT AC I(RB) IP(RB) IR(RB) II(RB)
.PRINT AC I(RC) IP(RC) IR(RC) II(RC)
.OPT nopage
.END
```

Run the PSpice analysis and verify the currents shown in the output of Fig. 2.34. For example $I(RA) = (16.09, -5.136)$ A $= 16.89 \underline{/-17.7°}$ A. Note that the value listed as $I(RA)$ in the output file is the magnitude of the current; it could also have been specified as $IM(RA)$. Show the reference directions for each of the currents on your circuit diagram, for the solution is incomplete without these. As a check, add the line currents to see that they total zero. Expect slight round-off errors in the results.

```
Three-Phase Unbalanced Load

  ****        CIRCUIT DESCRIPTION

VAB 12 2 AC 200V 0
VBC 20 0 AC 200V -120
VCA 10 1 AC 200V 120
RS1 12 1 0.01
RS2 20 2 0.01
RS3 10 0 0.01
RA 1 3 0.01
RB 2 4 0.01
RC 0 5 0.01
RAB 3 34 19.15
LAB 34 4 42.627mH
RBC 4 5 10
RCA 3 35 10
CCA 35 5 153.15uF
.AC LIN 1 60Hz 60Hz
.OPT nopage
.PRINT AC I(RA) IP(RA) IR(RA) II(RA)
.PRINT AC I(RB) IP(RB) IR(RB) II(RB)
.PRINT AC I(RC) IP(RC) IR(RC) II(RC)
.END

  ****      AC ANALYSIS                        TEMPERATURE =   27.000 DEG C

    FREQ         I(RA)         IP(RA)        IR(RA)        II(RA)
    6.000E+01    1.689E+01    -1.770E+01    1.609E+01    -5.136E+00
    FREQ         I(RB)         IP(RB)        IR(RB)        II(RB)
    6.000E+01    2.016E+01    -1.430E+02    -1.609E+01   -1.215E+01
    FREQ         I(RC)         IP(RC)        IR(RC)        II(RC)
    6.000E+01    1.728E+01    9.001E+01     -3.292E-03   1.728E+01
```

Fig. 2.34

POWER-FACTOR IMPROVEMENT

An induction motor requires a larger-than-necessary current when used without a capacitor. For example, if a 5-hp induction motor takes 53 A at 117 V, operating single phase with an efficiency of 78.5%, let us do some preliminary calculations in preparation for an analysis. The power input to the motor is

$$P_{in} = \eta/P_{out} = \frac{(5)(746)}{0.785} = 4.75 \text{ kW}$$

The volt-ampere product will be

$$S = VI = (117)(53) = 6.2 \text{ kVA}$$

With P and S known, Q is found as the missing side of the volt-ampere triangle:

$$S = P + jQ$$

giving

$$Q = 3.985 \text{ kVA}$$

The resistance of the motor is

$$R = \frac{V^2}{P} = \frac{(117)^2}{4750} = 2.88 \text{ }\Omega$$

and the reactance of the motor is

$$X = \frac{V^2}{Q} = \frac{(117)^2}{3985} = 3.44 \text{ }\Omega$$

At a frequency $f = 60$ Hz, this represents an inductance of

$$L = \frac{X}{\omega} = 9.12 \text{ mH}$$

Having analyzed the problem with pencil-and-paper techniques, it might appear that we have little left to do with PSpice. However, in order to see the effects of placing various capacitors across the line, the computer analysis will be helpful. Refer to Fig. 2.35, which shows the resistance R and the inductance L of the motor, along with a pair of sensing resistors, R_A and R_B. Their roles will become apparent when a capacitor is added.

An input file is needed that will show the total current and the branch currents in relation to the applied voltage. This file is

```
Single-Phase Motor, 5 hp
V 1 0 ac 117V
RA 1 2 0.001
RB 2 3 0.001
R 3 0 2.88
L 3 0 9.12 mH
.ac LIN 1 60Hz 60Hz
.PRINT ac i(RA) ip(RA) i(RB) ip(RB)
.PRINT ac i(R)  ip(R)
.PRINT ac I(L) ip(L)
.END
```

Fig. 2.35 Circuit for power-factor improvement.

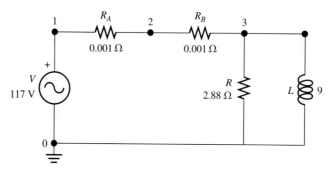

The PSpice output file will show the following currents:

```
I(RA) =  5.296E+01,  IP(RA) = -3.992E+01
I(RB) =  5.296E+01,  IP(RB) = -3.992E+01
 I(R) =  4.060E+01,   IP(R) =  3.331E-02
 I(L) =  3.401E+01,   IP(L) = -8.997E+01
```

The current I(RA) is the line current, in close agreement with the stated current of 53 A, at an angle near $-40°$. The power factor *(pf)* is found as the cosine of the angle of line current with respect to line voltage, so

$$pf = \cos(-40°) = 0.76$$

The two branch currents, through the motor resistance and inductance, have a phasor sum equal to the line current. It is now easy to show the effect of placing a capacitor across the line, which will be from node *2* to node *0*. Add the following statement to the input file

```
C 2 0 380uF
```

and modify one of the print statements to include the current through the capacitor. Now run the analysis again. The output file will show the following:

```
I(RA) = 4.411E+01,   IP(RA) = -2.299E+01
I(RB) = 5.296E+01,   IP(RB) = -3.993E+01
 I(C) = 1.676E+01,    IP(C) =  9.001E+01
 I(R) = 4.060E+01,    IP(R) =  2.510E-02
 I(L) = 3.401E+01,    IP(L) = -8.997E+01
```

Observe that the line current I(RA) has been reduced to 44.11 A at a lagging angle near 23°, clearly showing the effects of power-factor improvement. The power factor is now

$$pf = \cos(-23°) = 0.92$$

The capacitor draws a current of 16.76 A at an angle of 90°, bringing about the change in line current. Note that the current through the sensing resistor R_B is the same as the line current before the capacitor was added, as you would expect.

THREE-PHASE POWER-FACTOR IMPROVEMENT

A three-phase motor is represented by the components shown on the right side of Fig. 2.36, with a delta connection assumed. R_1 and L_1 are the per-phase resistance and inductance, respectively, of the motor. The other phases have the same values of

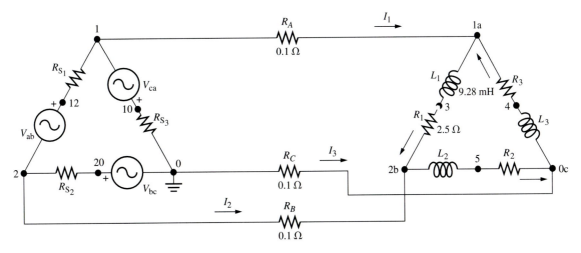

Fig. 2.36 A delta-connected, three-phase motor.

components. Line-voltage dropping resistors are included in each of the three-phase lines. An input file is prepared that will show the various voltages and currents. It is shown along with the output in Fig. 2.37.

The order of the subscripts in each statement must be given careful attention. For each passive element the subscripts are in keeping with the current directions shown in Fig. 2.36. A phasor diagram of currents and voltages is shown in Fig. 2.38. The angle between the phase voltage V(1a, 2b) and the phase current I(R1) is 3.22 + 51.23 = 54.45°. The current lags the voltage by 54.45°. The cosine of this angle is the power factor

$$pf = \cos(-54.45°) = 0.581$$

It is our desire to improve the power factor by adding a bank of capacitors as shown in Fig. 2.39. The input file is modified to show the presence of the capacitors. When the PSpice analysis is run, the results will be as shown in Fig. 2.40.

Observe that each of the line currents is 75.51 A compared with 92.64 A before the addition of the capacitor bank. The reduction in current is accompanied by an improvement in the power factor. The power-factor angle will be found as the angle between phase voltage and phase current, as was the case before the addition of the capacitors. The phase voltage will be taken as $V(1a, 2b) = 230 \underline{/2.26°}$ V. The phase current is found (indirectly) from the current $I(RA) = 75.52 \underline{/-72.2°}$ A. Since this is a line current, the corresponding phase current has a magnitude

$$I_f = \frac{75.52}{\sqrt{3}} = 43.6 \text{ A}$$

at an angle of −42.2°. This angle is obtained by adding 30° to the angle on the line current. Both the magnitude and the angle values are based on the presence of a balanced load. The power factor angle is 2.26° + 42.2° = 44.46°, and the power factor is

$$pf = \cos(-44.46°) = 0.71$$

Fig. 2.37

```
Circuit for Power-Factor Correction

VAB 12 2 AC 240V 0
VBC 20 0 AC 240V -120
VCA 10 1 AC 240V 120
RS1 12 1 0.01
RS2 20 2 0.01
RS3 10 0 0.01
RA 1 1a 0.1
RB 2 2b 0.1
RC 0 0c 0.1
R1 3 2b 2.5
R2 5 0c 2.5
R3 4 1a 2.5
L1 1a 3 9.28mH
L2 2b 5 9.28mH
L3 0c 4 9.28mH
.AC LIN 1 60Hz 60Hz
.PRINT AC I(RA) IP(RA)
.PRINT AC I(RB) IP(RB)
.PRINT AC I(RC) IP(RC)
.PRINT AC V(1a,2b) VP(1a,2b)
.PRINT AC V(2b,0c) VP(2b,0c)
.PRINT AC V(0c,1a) VP(0c,1a)
.PRINT AC I(R1) IP(R1)
.PRINT AC I(R2) IP(R2)
.PRINT AC I(R3) IP(R3)
.OPT nopage
.END

    FREQ          I(RA)        IP(RA)
    6.000E+01     9.264E+01    -8.123E+01

    FREQ          I(RB)        IP(RB)
    6.000E+01     9.264E+01    1.588E+02

    FREQ          I(RC)        IP(RC)
    6.000E+01     9.264E+01    3.877E+01

    FREQ          V(1a,2b)     VP(1a,2b)
    6.000E+01     2.300E+02    3.222E+00

    FREQ          V(2b,0c)     VP(2b,0c)
    6.000E+01     2.300E+02    -1.168E+02

    FREQ          V(0c,1a)     VP(0c,1a)
    6.000E+01     2.300E+02    1.232E+02

    FREQ          I(R1)        IP(R1)
    6.000E+01     5.348E+01    -5.123E+01

    FREQ          I(R2)        IP(R2)
    6.000E+01     5.348E+01    -1.712E+02

    FREQ          I(R3)        IP(R3)
    6.000E+01     5.348E+01    6.877E+01
```

An alternative approach to finding the phase current, which applies to unbalanced loads as well, is to add the current in one phase of the load to the corresponding current in a capacitor. Thus by adding I(R1) and I(C1), we obtain

$$I(R1) + I(C1) = 53.53 \,\underline{/-52.19°}\ \text{A} + 13.02 \,\underline{/92.226°}\ \text{A} = 43.6 \,\underline{/-42.18°}\ \text{A}$$

in agreement with the previous calculation. Before the capacitors were added, the power factor was 0.58.

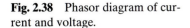

Fig. 2.38 Phasor diagram of current and voltage.

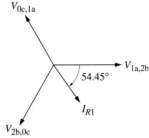

If necessary, the PSpice analysis can readily be performed with other values of capacitance for comparison.

A THREE-PHASE RECTIFIER

A three-phase Y-connected rectifier is shown in Fig. 2.41. Each phase voltage has a peak value of 10 V at 60 Hz. The diodes allow current to reach the load without falling to a zero value at any time. The input file is

```
Three-Phase Rectifier
v1 1 0   sin(0 10V 60Hz 0 0 0)
v2 2 0   sin(0 10V 60Hz 0 0 -120)
v3 3 0   sin(0 10V 60Hz 0 0 120)
DA 1 4 D1
DB 2 4 D1
DC 3 4 D1
RL 4 0 100
.MODEL D1 D
.TRAN 0.1ms 33.33ms
.PROBE
.END
```

Run the analysis and using Probe verify the result shown in Fig. 2.42. Then remove the traces of voltage and obtain a trace of the load current I(RL). Verify that it varies between a minimum value of 43.4 mA and a maximum value of 91.67 mA.

Fig. 2.39 Motor circuit with capacitor bank added.

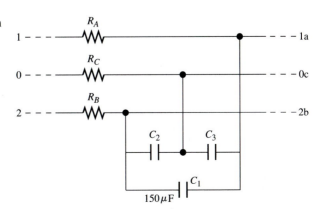

```
Circuit for Power-Factor Correction with Capacitor Bank Added
VAB 12 2 AC 240V 0
VBC 20 0 AC 240V -120
VCA 10 1 AC 240V 120
RS1 12 1 0.01
RS2 20 2 0.01
RS3 10 0 0.01
RA 1 1a 0.1
RB 2 2b 0.1
RC 0 0c 0.1
R1 3 2b 2.5
R2 5 0c 2.5
R3 4 1a 2.5
L1 1a 3 9.28mH
L2 2b 5 9.28mH
L3 0c 4 9.28mH
C1 1a 2b 150uF
C2 2b 0c 150uF
C3 0c 1a 150uF
.AC LIN 1 60Hz 60Hz
.PRINT AC I(RA) IP(RA) I(C1) IP(C1)
.PRINT AC I(RB) IP(RB) I(C2) IP(C2)
.PRINT AC I(RC) IP(RC) I(C3) IP(C3)
.PRINT AC V(1a,2b) VP(1a,2b)
.PRINT AC V(2b,0c) VP(2b,0c)
.PRINT AC V(0c,1a) VP(0c,1a)
.PRINT AC I(R1) IP(R1)
.PRINT AC I(R2) IP(R2)
.PRINT AC I(R3) IP(R3)
.OPT nopage
.END

    FREQ         I(RA)        IP(RA)       I(C1)       IP(C1)
    6.000E+01    7.552E+01    -7.220E+01   1.302E+01   9.226E+01

    FREQ         I(RB)        IP(RB)       I(C2)       IP(C2)
    6.000E+01    7.552E+01    1.678E+02    1.302E+01   -2.774E+01

    FREQ         I(RC)        IP(RC)       I(C3)       IP(C3)
    6.000E+01    7.552E+01    4.780E+01    1.302E+01   -1.477E+02

    FREQ         V(1a,2b)     VP(1a,2b)
    6.000E+01    2.302E+02    2.260E+00

    FREQ         V(2b,0c)     VP(2b,0c)
    6.000E+01    2.302E+02    -1.177E+02

    FREQ         V(0c,1a)     VP(0c,1a)
    6.000E+01    2.302E+02    1.223E+02

    FREQ         I(R1)        IP(R1)
    6.000E+01    5.353E+01    -5.219E+01

    FREQ         I(R2)        IP(R2)
    6.000E+01    5.353E+01    -1.722E+02

    FREQ         I(R3)        IP(R3)
    6.000E+01    5.353E+01    6.781E+01
```

Fig. 2.40

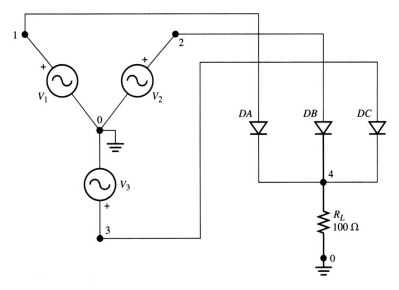

Fig. 2.41 Three-phase rectifier.

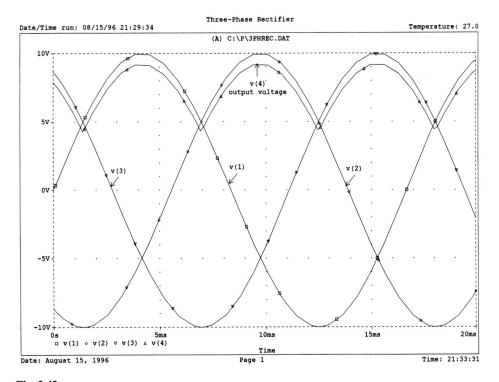

Fig. 2.42

The *.MODEL* statement is used to describe a diode. The diode is one of many devices supported by PSpice. The description *D1* is our choice, but the *D* is required and may not be changed. The statements calling for three diodes (all alike) state that *DA, DB,* and *DC* are based on the same type diode, which we have named *D1.* For other examples, refer to Appendix B.

VOLTAGE REGULATION IN A THREE-PHASE SYSTEM

A power feeder line must be designed to allow for no greater voltage drop between the source and load than an allowed amount. Often the allowed amount must provide a voltage regulation of 5% or less. The circuit in Fig. 2.43 will be used to illustrate voltage-regulation requirements. Observe that each line contains both resistance and inductance. With $R = 0.077\ \Omega$ and $L = 0.244$ mH in the feeder line, will the desired voltage regulation be achieved? A PSpice simulation will be used to find the load voltage.

The Y-connected load represents a 440-V, three-phase, 60-Hz motor. The source voltage is given as 460 V, from which the phase voltage is obtained:

$$V_A = \frac{460}{\sqrt{3}} = 265.58\ \text{V}$$

The input file should require no further explanation. It is shown in Fig. 2.44 with the results of the analysis. The voltage regulation is

$$\text{Voltage regulation} = \frac{V_{NL} - V_{FL}}{V_{FL}} = \frac{265.58 - 257}{257} = 3.34\%$$

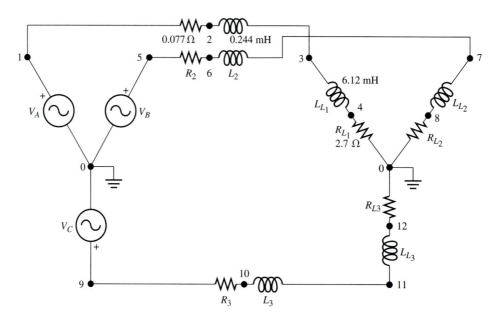

Fig. 2.43   Circuit for voltage regulation.

Fig. 2.44

```
Voltage Regulation for Three-Phase Load

VA 1 0 AC 265.58V 0
VB 5 0 AC 265.58V -120
VC 9 0 AC 265.58V 120
R1 1 2 0.077
R2 5 6 0.077
R3 9 10 0.077
L1 2 3 0.244mH
L2 6 7 0.244mH
L3 10 11 0.244mH
RL1 4 0 2.7
RL2 8 0 2.7
RL3 12 0 2.7
LL1 3 4 6.12mH
LL2 7 8 6.12mH
LL3 11 12 6.12mH
.AC LIN 1 60Hz 60Hz
.PRINT AC I(R1) IP(R1) I(R2) IP(R2)
.PRINT AC I(R3) IP(R3)
.PRINT AC V(3) VP(3) V(7) VP(7)
.PRINT AC V(11) VP(11)
.OPT nopage
.END

  FREQ        I(R1)       IP(R1)       I(R2)       IP(R2)
   6.000E+01   7.237E+01   -4.083E+01   7.237E+01   -1.608E+02

  FREQ        I(R3)       IP(R3)
   6.000E+01   7.237E+01   7.917E+01

  FREQ        V(3)        VP(3)        V(7)        VP(7)
   6.000E+01   2.570E+02   -3.108E-01   2.570E+02   -1.203E+02

  FREQ        V(11)       VP(11)
   6.000E+01   2.570E+02   1.197E+02
```

A TWO-PHASE SYSTEM

A two-phase electrical system is little more than a curiosity, but its analysis can be readily undertaken using PSpice. The diagram in Fig. 2.45 shows such a system, where the load is shown in terms of equal impedances of $Z = (25 + j50)$ Ω for each phase. At a frequency of 60 Hz, the reactance of 50 Ω becomes an inductance $L = 0.133$ H. The preparation of the input file is similar to that of other examples previ-

Fig. 2.45　A two-phase circuit.

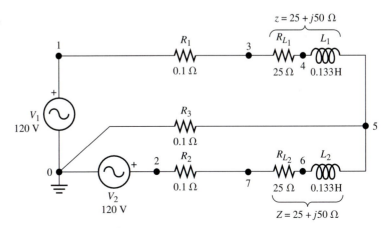

ously shown. It is included in Fig. 2.46, which shows the output voltages and currents. The phase voltages at the load are almost the same value (120 V) and are about 90° apart. The line currents I(RL1) and I(RL2) are almost the same value (2.15 A) and are also about 90° apart. Note that I(RL1) is at an angle of −63.27°, which is the same as the angle on the impedance of the load. The neutral current I(R3) is greater than the two line currents.

$$Z = R + jX_L = 25 + j50 = 55.9 \text{ } \underline{/63.4°} \text{ } \Omega$$

Draw a phasor diagram showing the phase voltages at the load and each of the three line currents.

It is interesting to see what happens when the resistance of each line increases. Let us use 10-Ω values for R1, R2, and R3 and run the simulation again. The new output file is shown in Fig. 2.47. Note that V(3,5) = 111 $\underline{/19.3°}$ and V(7,5) = 89.1 $\underline{/-82.2°}$. The voltages are now unbalanced and are 105.5° apart. The line currents are also unbalanced, and again the current in the neutral (ground) is larger than either of the other two currents.

```
Two-phase system

V1 1 0 AC 120 0
V2 2 0 AC 120 -90
R1 1 3 0.10
R2 2 7 0.10
R3 0 5 0.10
RL1 3 4 25
RL2 7 6 25
L1 4 5 0.133H
L2 6 5 0.133H
.AC LIN 1 60Hz 60Hz
.OPT nopage
.PRINT AC V(3,5) VP(3,5)
.PRINT AC V(7,5) VP(7,5)
.PRINT AC I(RL1) IP(RL1)
.PRINT AC I(RL2) IP(RL2)
.PRINT AC I(R3) IP(R3)
.END

****     AC ANALYSIS                    TEMPERATURE =    27.000 DEG C

    FREQ         V(3,5)        VP(3,5)
    6.000E+01    1.200E+02     2.284E-01

    FREQ         V(7,5)        VP(7,5)
    6.000E+01    1.196E+02     -8.986E+01

    FREQ         I(RL1)        IP(RL1)
    6.000E+01    2.142E+00     -6.327E+01

    FREQ         I(RL2)        IP(RL2)
    6.000E+01    2.135E+00     -1.534E+02

    FREQ         I(R3)         IP(R3)
    6.000E+01    3.022E+00     7.178E+01
```

Fig. 2.46

```
Two-phase system with large values of line resistance

V1 1 0 AC 120 0
V2 2 0 AC 120 -90
R1 1 3 10
R2 2 7 10
R3 0 5 10
RL1 3 4 25
RL2 7 6 25
L1 4 5 0.133H
L2 6 5 0.133H
.AC LIN 1 60Hz 60Hz
.OPT nopage
.PRINT AC V(3,5) VP(3,5)
.PRINT AC V(7,5) VP(7,5)
.PRINT AC I(RL1) IP(RL1)
.PRINT AC I(RL2) IP(RL2)
.PRINT AC I(R3) IP(R3)
.END

  ****      AC ANALYSIS                  TEMPERATURE =   27.000 DEG C

    FREQ        V(3,5)      VP(3,5)
    6.000E+01   1.110E+02   1.926E+01

    FREQ        V(7,5)      VP(7,5)
    6.000E+01   8.909E+01   -8.220E+01

    FREQ        I(RL1)      IP(RL1)
    6.000E+01   1.981E+00   -4.424E+01

    FREQ        I(RL2)      IP(RL2)
    6.000E+01   1.590E+00   -1.457E+02

    FREQ        I(R3)       IP(R3)
    6.000E+01   2.280E+00   9.265E+01
```

Fig. 2.47

SUMMARY OF NEW PSPICE STATEMENTS USED IN THIS CHAPTER

C[*name*] <+*node*> <−*node*> <*value*>

For example,

```
C 4 5 0.5uF
```

means that a capacitor of value 0.5 μF is located between nodes *4* and *5*. Another form of the C statement adds *IC = value* at the end of the line for an initial voltage value. For example,

```
C 4 5 0 0.5uF IC = 3V
```

means that the capacitor has an initial voltage of 3 V, with node *4* positive.

I[*name*] <+*node*> <−*node*> AC <*mag*> [<*phase*>]

For example,

```
IS 1 2 AC 0.35 45
```

means an ac source of 350 mA between nodes *1* and *2* at a phase angle of 45°. Remember that currents and voltages default to dc unless otherwise shown.

K[*name*] L[*name*] L[*name*] <*coupling value*>

For example,

```
K L1 L2 0.1
```

means a coupled circuit, perhaps a transformer, with two coupled inductors L1 and L2. The coefficient of coupling is $k = 0.1$. Another form of this statement that relates to a coupled circuit with an iron core will be introduced later.

L[*name*] <+*node*> <−*node*> <*value*>

For example,

```
L1  3  0  25mH
```

means an inductor of 25 mH between nodes *3* and *0*. To show an initial current, use *IC* = *value* at the end of the line.

V[*name*] <+*node*> <−*node*> AC <*mag*> [*phase*]

For example,

```
V2  4  1  AC  110  120
```

means an ac source of 110 V between nodes *4* and *1* at a phase angle of 120°.

DOT COMMANDS USED IN THIS CHAPTER

.AC [LIN] [OCT] [DEC] <*points*> <*f start*> <*f end*>

For example,

```
.AC DEC 20 1kHz 1MEG
```

means that PSpice will run a simulation with frequency as a variable. The frequency range is from 1 kHz to 1 Mhz using 20 points per decade. If LIN is chosen (instead of DEC), the *points* value represents the total number of points in the frequency range.

.MODEL <name> <type>[<param>=<value>[<tol>]]

This statement may be used with any of the models available in PSpice. These include resistors, inductors, capacitors, diodes, transistors (bipolar and JFET) and other devices. The device *name* for a diode must begin with a D, and could be D1, D2, DA, etc. The device *type* must be the same as that given under .MODEL in Appendix B. Examples are RES for resistor, IND for inductor, D for diode.

.PRINT <[DC] [AC] [NOISE] [TRAN]> <*output variable list*>

For example,

```
.PRINT AC V(2) V(5,4) VP(5,4) I(R1) IP(R1)
```

means to print to the output file the ac values shown. V(2) will give the magnitude of V_2; V(5,4) will give the magnitude of V_{54}; I(R1) will give the magnitude of the current through resistor R_1; and IP (R1) will give the phase angle of the current through R_1.

Note that one (and only one) of the items in the list DC, AC, NOISE, and TRAN must be chosen.

.PROBE

This statement was introduced in Chapter 1 but is being repeated here in more detail. When you include a Probe statement in an input (circuit) file and run the PSpice simulation, the output file will be created along with a data file. The output file has the extension *.out,* and the data file has the extension *.dat.*

To run the Probe program, click on its icon in the MicroSim workgroup. This brings up a screen with the Probe heading followed by a menu line displaying

File Edit Trace Plot View Tools Window Help

Another row contains symbolic icons. The symbols are described in the bottom line of the screen display. Use the mouse to point to a symbol and learn what it does. For example, the first icon in the fourth group elicits the explanation

Toggle X axis type between Log and Linear

The first thing to do in Probe is to select File, Open . . . , then specify the data file of interest. Next, select Trace, Add. In the Add Traces box a list of suggested variables is shown. Selecting one places it on the Trace Command line. As explained earlier in this chapter, various mathematical operators may be used along with a set of functions.

When you have produced a plot worth keeping, choose File, Print to obtain a printed version of what you see on the screen. Many of the plots shown in this book have been obtained in this manner. A laser printer (HP LaserJet) produces a fine plot; we have used a color printer (HP DeskJet 855C) with less than satisfactory results, since the plot lines are too thin.

PROBLEMS

2.1 Find the equivalent impedance of the circuit shown in Fig. 2.48 as seen by the source. Since the inductive and capacitive values are given in ohms, use the fre-

Fig. 2.48

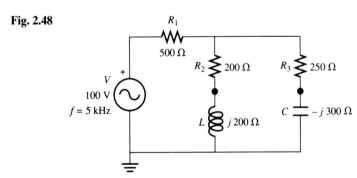

quency $f = 5$ kHz to solve for L and C values needed in the input file. Check your results using conventional circuit-solving methods.

2.2 The circuit shown in Fig. 2.49 has a low Q. Find the resonant frequency by using a sweep of frequencies in the range 3 kHz to 6 kHz. Verify that $f_o = 3.56$ kHz. Find the current at resonance and the minimum current. At what frequency does minimum current occur?

Fig. 2.49

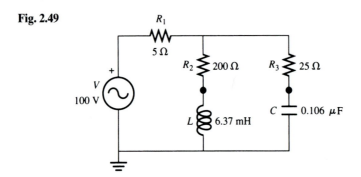

2.3 Rework Problem 2.2 with $R_2 = 20 \, \Omega$.

2.4 This problem investigates the voltage variations across R, L, and C in the vicinity of resonance. With the elements shown in Fig. 2.50, $f_o = 159.15$ Hz. Prepare an input file to obtain plots of V_R, V_L, and V_C for the frequency range 10 Hz to 300 Hz. Demonstrate that V_R maximum is at f_o, while V_{Lmax} is below f_o, and V_{Cmax} is above f_o.

Fig. 2.50

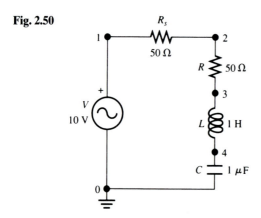

2.5 For the circuit shown in Fig. 2.51 find the impedance as seen by the source at $f = 1$ kHz.

Fig. 2.51

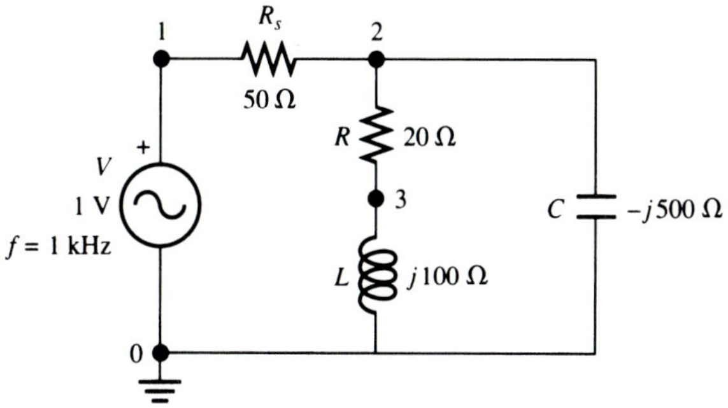

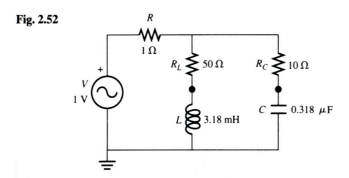

2.6 The circuit in Fig. 2.52 is to be used to obtain a plot of locus of admittances for a typical two-parallel-branch circuit. It is similar to one used in an example in this chapter. Run a Probe analysis and plot IP(R) to determine the resonant frequency. Then produce an admittance plot and find the values of G and B at resonance.

Fig. 2.52

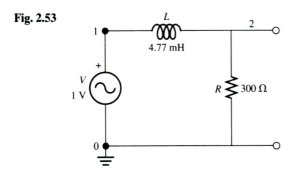

2.7 Find the frequency at which $V_2 = 0.707$ V by obtaining a Bode plot of V_2/V_1 for the circuit shown in Fig. 2.53. Show what the phase shift is at this frequency.

Fig. 2.53

2.8 Find the frequency at which the output voltage is minimum, and find the value of the output voltage at this frequency (magnitude and phase). Find the stop band of frequencies, representing the frequency range where the output is down by 3 dB or more. Refer to Fig. 2.54.

Fig. 2.54

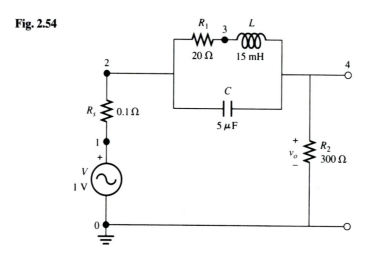

2.9 Figure 2.55 is an example of a double-resonant factor. It has a pass-band frequency at 150 kHz. Obtain plots for the circuit that show the details of the output voltage magnitude and phase in the region of interest.

Fig. 2.55

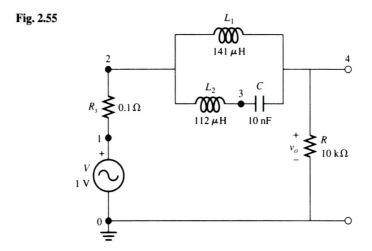

2.10 For the circuit in Fig. 2.56 find i_1 and i_2. Also find V_{40}. *Hint:* Since reactance values cannot be used directly in SPICE, assume that $\omega = 1000$ rad/s and solve for L and C.

Fig. 2.56

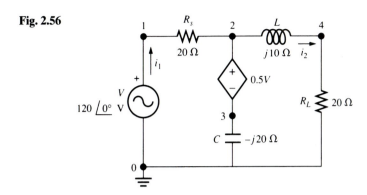

2.11 To check the answers found in Problem 2.10, find V_{20}; then use the voltage across L to find current i_2. Compare these values with the results previously obtained.

2.12 For the circuit shown in Fig. 2.57 find i and V_2. Convert the current sources to voltage sources, and use conventional pencil-and-paper methods to verify your results.

Fig. 2.57

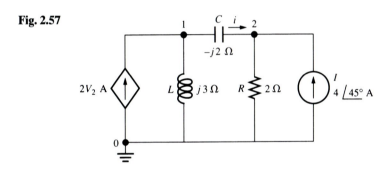

2.13 A phase-sequence indicator is shown in Fig. 2.58. It is assumed that $f = 60$ Hz and that R_1 and R_2 are identical lamps. Given $V_{12} = 100\ \underline{/0°}$ V and $V_{23} = 100\ \underline{/-120°}$ V, verify that the phase sequence (which obviously is ABC) may be

Fig. 2.58

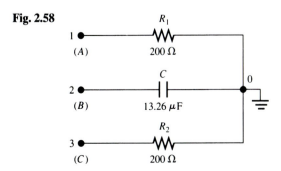

determined by the relative brightness of lamps R_1 and R_2. Use a PSpice analysis to verify that.

2.14 A three-phase, 60-Hz, unbalanced load is Y-connected and is fed from balanced supply voltages $V_{ab} = 208 \underline{/0°}$ V, $V_{bc} = 208 \underline{/-120°}$ V, and $V_{ca} = 208 \underline{/120°}$ V. The phase impedances are $Z_{a0} = 8 \underline{/30°}$ Ω, $Z_{b0} = 4 \underline{/-50°}$ Ω, and $Z_{c0} = 6 \underline{/20°}$ Ω. Find the three line currents and the neutral current. *Hint:* Convert the impedances to R and X values; then convert each X to either L or C depending on the sign of the reactance. Verify that phase a has $R = 6.928$ Ω and $L = 10.61$ mH, phase b has $R = 2.571$ Ω and $C = 865.7$ μF, and phase c has $R = 5.638$ Ω and $L = 5.433$ mH.

3

Transistor Circuits

SPICE has built-in models for bipolar-junction transistors and field-effect transistors. These models are more complicated than the models used in introductory electronics courses. It is customary to study biasing circuits and amplifier circuits separately. This is done in order to give the student a more complete understanding of the dc and ac analysis of BJTs and FETs.

The analysis of transistor circuits will be more meaningful if the built-in models are not used in the beginning. Therefore a simplified model for the dc forward-biased transistor will be used when it is appropriate.

THE BIPOLAR-JUNCTION TRANSISTOR (BJT)

Bipolar-junction transistors are the first topic of study in this chapter. As an example, Fig. 3.1 shows a typical transistor biasing circuit. The transistor is type *npn* silicon, with $h_{FE} = 80$ and $V_{BE} = 0.7$ V (assumed for the active region). No other information is known about the transistor. Circuit values are $R_1 = 40$ kΩ:, $R_2 = 5$ kΩ, $R_C = 1$ kΩ, $R_E = 100$ Ω, and $V_{CC} = 12$ V.

A Model Suitable for Bias Calculations

In order to use a SPICE analysis, we propose that you devise a suitable model for the bipolar-junction transistor. This model will allow you to find the quiescent values of voltages and currents in the bias circuit. Figure 3.2 shows the model along with the other components that you will need for the analysis. The transistor contains a current-dependent current source F to handle h_{FE} and an independent voltage source VA to represent the active-region voltage V_{BE}.

Fig. 3.1 Typical transistor biasing circuit.

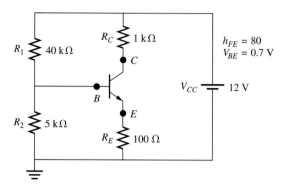

The input file is

```
Transistor Bias Circuit
VCC 4 0 12V
VA 1 2 0.7V
F 3 2 VA 80
R1 4 1 40k
R2 1 0 5k
RC 4 3 1k
RE 2 0 100
.OP
.OPT nopage
.END
```

    Perform the analysis in PSpice; then verify that V(3) = 7.961 V and V(2) = 0.4089 V, giving $V_{CE} = V_3 - V_2 = 7.552$ V. Draw current-direction arrows on the circuit diagram, then compute the collector current

$$I_C = \frac{V_4 - V_3}{R_C}$$

Fig. 3.2 Bias model for bipolar *npn* transistor.

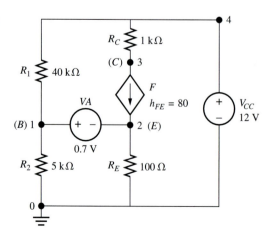

It should be 4.039 mA. What is the base current? Verify from the voltage-source currents that $I_B = 50.49$ μA. Compute I_B from the value of h_{FE} and compare it with this answer. Compute the emitter current $I_E = V_2/R_E$. It should be 4.089 mA. Verify that $I_E = I_B + I_C$.

If you are interested in getting the currents directly from the PSpice analysis, you can use the dc sweep method as shown in this modified input file:

```
Transistor Bias Circuit with Currents Shown in Output File
VCC 4 0 12V
VA 1 2 0.7V
F  3 2 VA 80
R1 4 1 40k
R2 1 0 5k
RC 4 3 1k
RE 2 0 100
.DC VCC 12V 12V 12V
.OP
.OPT nopage
.PRINT DC I(RC) I(RE) V(3,2)
.END
```

Verify that this gives I(RC) = 4.039 mA, I(RE) = 4.089 mA, and V(3,2) = 7.552 V as previously calculated. Note that in the first analysis you were able easily to calculate the currents. It may not be worth the extra effort to use the dc sweep technique; however, the choice is available.

Saturation Considerations

A precautionary note is needed for the situation involving biasing conditions that produce saturation. From your study of transistors you will recall that the value of h_{FE} in the active region of operation is not the same as h_{FE} in saturation. This means that if saturation occurs, the predicted value for I_C using the active region h_{FE} will be too large. You should suspect that this condition exists when the calculated V_{CE} drops below a few tenths of a volt. Several problems at the end of the chapter deal with the question of active-region vs. saturation biasing.

In summary, we have introduced the bias model for the *npn* Si transistor. This model can be used with various bias configurations and multistage amplifiers. Can you modify the model for (a) *pnp* Si transistors and (b) *pnp* Ge transistors?

Biasing Example for a Germanium Transistor

For another example of transistor biasing, see Fig. 3.3, which shows a *pnp* germanium transistor, with $h_{FE} = 60$ and $V_{BE} = -0.2$ V. Component values are $R_F = 50$ kΩ, $R_E = 50$ Ω, $R_C = 1$ kΩ, and $V_{CC} = -12$ V. Draw the SPICE model for the transistor and include the resistor values to complete the circuit. Figure 3.4 shows the results. Compare the treatment of the current-dependent current source shown here with the one of the previous example. Since this is a *pnp* transistor, the current arrow is away from the internal junction. Now decide how much information you would like to obtain from the PSpice analysis. Your input file might be

Fig. 3.3 Bias circuit using *pnp* germanium transistor.

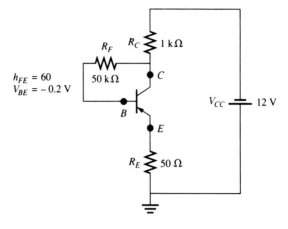

```
Transistor Bias Circuit for PNP Ge
VCC 0 4 12
VA 1 2 0.2
F 1 3 VA 60
RF 2 3 50k
RE 1 0 50
RC 3 4 1k
.DC VCC 12 12 12
.PRINT DC I(RC) I(RE) I(RF)
.OP
.END
```

     Run the analysis; then draw current-direction arrows in their proper directions for the *pnp* transistor. Verify that $I_E = 6.311$ mA and $I_B = 103.5$ μA. Why are some of the resistor currents shown positive while others are shown negative? This has to do with the order of the subscripts in the R statements. For example, the statement

```
RE 1 0 50
```

Fig. 3.4 Bias model for germanium *pnp* transistor.

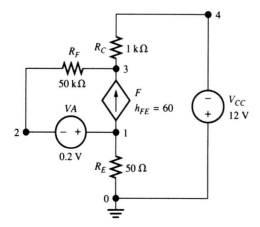

produced a negative current I(RE). This is because the current is actually from node *0* toward node *1* in R_E. A careful comparison of the current-reference directions shown in the diagram should be made with those implied in the SPICE statements. Note that the current in R_C is actually the emitter current, rather than the collector current. Do you understand why? The collector current is shown in the PSpice output under *current-controlled current sources* as 6.208 mA. Add the base and collector currents, and compare the sum with the emitter current.

SMALL-SIGNAL *h*-PARAMETER MODEL OF THE BIPOLAR TRANSISTOR

An accurate model for the bipolar transistor, widely used in small-signal analysis, is the *h*-parameter model, shown in Fig. 3.5. This model, with appropriate values, is used for common-emitter, common-base, or common-collector configurations. Our task is to produce a version of this model for use with SPICE. The model will contain a current-dependent current source for use with h_f and a voltage-dependent voltage source for use with h_r. Figure 3.6 shows the model with *RI* for h_i, *E* to specify h_r, *RO* as $1/h_o$, and *F* to specify h_f.

Common-Emitter Transistor Analysis Using *h*-Parameter Model

Figure 3.7 shows a typical circuit for analysis. Even if the circuit is more complicated than this figure, you can often reduce it to this form by using various theorems and reduction techniques. Values given are $V_s = 1$ mV, $R_s = 1$ kΩ, $R_i = 1.1$ kΩ (h_{ie}), $h_r = 2.5 \times 10^{-4}$ (to be used with *E*), $h_f = 50$ (to be used with *F*), $R_o = 40$ kΩ = $1/h_o$, and $R_L = 10$ kΩ. $V0 = 0$ V is needed to give an independent source for the *F* statement.

Although we are interested in small-signal response, we will not use an ac analysis. The reason is simple and should be completely understood at this time. As long as you are dealing with small signals (ac steady state) and there are no reactive elements in the circuit, you can get more information from the PSpice analysis by letting the dc analysis represent either ac effective or peak values. The PSpice program cannot tell the difference! Be sure that you understand that the results will be small-signal results and have nothing to do with the dc biasing. Of course, we assume that the Q point has been established properly for active-region operation. Here is the input file:

Fig. 3.5   The *h*-parameter model for the transistor.

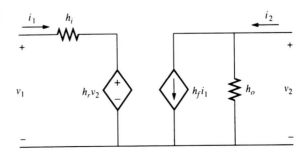

Fig. 3.6 The PSpice version of the *h*-parameter mode.

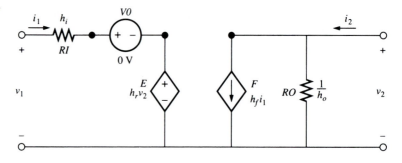

```
Small-Signal Analysis of Transistor Circuit Using h Parameters
VS  1  0  1mV
VO  3  3A  0
E  3A  0  4  0  2.5E-4
F  4  0  VO  50
RS  1  2  1k
RI  2  3  1.1k
RO  4  0  40k
RL  4  0  10k
.OP
.TF  V(4)  VS
.END
```

Run the analysis and get a printed copy of the results for further study. Verify that $I_b = 0.5$ μA, $I_c = 20$ μA (from V(4)/R_L), the overall voltage gain is -200 (V(4)/VS), $R_i = 2$ kΩ, and $R_o = 8.4$ kΩ.

Since R_i includes R_s, what is the input resistance looking into the base of the transistor? It is $R_i - R_s = 1$ kΩ. Also, since R_o includes R_L, what is the output resistance looking into the collector (not including R_L)? Find this by using conductances.

CE connection, typical *h* parameters

$h_{ie} = 1.1$ kΩ $h_{fe} = 50$
$h_{re} = 2.5 \times 10^{-4}$ $\dfrac{1}{h_{oe}} = 40$ kΩ

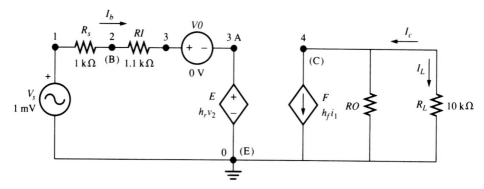

Fig. 3.7 *CE h*-parameter model with source and load.

$1/R_o = 1.1905 \times 10^{-4}$; subtract $1/R_L = 1 \times 10^{-4}$ from this, giving $1/R_o' = 0.1905 \times 10^{-4}$. Thus $R_o' = 52.5$ kΩ.

The voltage gain from base to collector is $V(4)/V(2) = -400$. The current gain is $A_I = I_L/I_b = -20 \ \mu\text{A}/0.5 \ \mu\text{A} = -40$. Refer to Fig. 3.8 for the output file.

In summary, the PSpice analysis has saved you some calculations; but without an understanding of the current-reference directions and voltage polarities, your solution will be incomplete. You should have an understanding of h-parameter theory to go along with the PSpice model, which we have developed. Remember, the choice of h-parameter values depends on the configuration.

Some authors use models other than those based on the h parameters. These other models are often simpler and less accurate. However, you should have little trouble taking the other models through the analyses for comparison with the re-

```
Small-Signal Analysis of Transistor Circuit Using h Parameters

VS 1 0 1mV
VO 3 3A 0
E 3A 0 4 0 2.5E-4
F 4 0 VO 50
RS 1 2 1k
RI 2 3 1.1k
RO 4 0 40k
RL 4 0 10k
.OP
.TF V(4) VS
.OPT nopage
.END

****      SMALL SIGNAL BIAS SOLUTION          TEMPERATURE =    27.000 DEG C

NODE   VOLTAGE      NODE   VOLTAGE      NODE   VOLTAGE      NODE    VOLTAGE
(    1)     .0010   (    2) 500.0E-06   (    3)-50.00E-06   (    4)     -.2000
(   3A)-50.00E-06

    VOLTAGE SOURCE CURRENTS
    NAME            CURRENT
    VS            -5.000E-07
    VO             5.000E-07

    TOTAL POWER DISSIPATION     5.00E-10  WATTS

****      OPERATING POINT INFORMATION        TEMPERATURE =    27.000 DEG C

**** VOLTAGE-CONTROLLED VOLTAGE SOURCES
NAME          E
V-SOURCE   -5.000E-05
I-SOURCE    5.000E-07

**** CURRENT-CONTROLLED CURRENT SOURCES
NAME          F
I-SOURCE    2.500E-05

****       SMALL-SIGNAL CHARACTERISTICS
     V(4)/VS = -2.000E+02

    INPUT RESISTANCE AT VS =  2.000E+03

    OUTPUT RESISTANCE AT V(4) =  8.400E+03
```

Fig. 3.8

sults given in this and other examples to follow. Problem 3.14 deals with an alternative simplified model and will serve as an introduction to this topic.

It is relatively easy to develop the models for the common-base and common-collector configurations.

Common-Collector Transistor Analysis Using *h*-Parameter Model

Another widely used circuit is the common-collector configuration, shown in Fig. 3.9. Again, the circuit may be more elaborate than this, but it can often be reduced to this by use of Thevenin's theorem and other circuit simplification techniques. The input signal is fed through R_s to the base of the transistor, and the output is taken at the emitter. Figure 3.10 shows the circuit with the *h*-parameter model for the transistor. The circuit is almost identical with that of Fig. 3.7, but the *h* parameters for the *CC* connection must be used. This gives the following input file:

```
Common-Collector Circuit Analysis with h Parameters
VS 1 0 1mV
VO 3 3A 0
E 3A 0 4 0 1
F 4 0 VO -51
RS 1 2 1k
RI 2 3 1.1k
RO 4 0 40k
RL 4 0 10k
.OP
.TF V(4) VS
.END
```

Run the PSpice analysis, and verify that V(4)/VS = 0.9949, I_L = 0.949E−8, I_b = 2.438E−9, $A_I = I_L/I_b$ = 40.8, R_o' = 40.97 Ω (including R_L), and R_i' = 410 kΩ (including R_s). Determine the input resistance at the base and the output resistance excluding R_L. These should be R_i = 409.1 kΩ and R_o = 41.14 Ω. Show the currents in the circuit diagram, and label the locations of the various input and output impedances. Note that the voltage gain is almost 1 with no phase reversal. The current gain also shows no phase reversal.

Fig. 3.9 *CC* transistor amplifier.

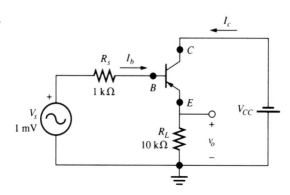

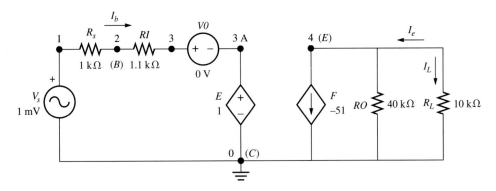

Fig. 3.10 *CC h*-parameter model with source and load.

Common-Base Transistor Analysis Using *h*-Parameter Model

The common-base circuit shown in Fig. 3.11 uses the same values for external components as in the previous examples. Figure 3.12 shows the circuit with the *h* parameters added. Using typical *h* parameters for the *CB* configuration, the input file becomes

```
Common-Base Circuit Analysis with h Parameters
VS 1 0 1mV
VO 3 3A 0
E 3A 0 4 0 2.9E-4
F 4 0 VO -0.98
RS 1 2 1k
RI 2 3 21.6
RO 4 0 2.04MEG
RL 4 0 10k
.OP
.TF V(4) VS
.END
```

Run the analysis and verify that $A_V = 9.52$, $I_L = 0.95$ μA, $I_e = 0.976$ μA, $R_i' = 1024$ Ω, $R_o' = 9.924$ kΩ. Solve for R_i at the emitter and R_o without including R_L. These should be $R_i = 24$ Ω and $R_o = 1.3$ MΩ. Show that the voltage gain from emitter to collector is $A_V = 406$.

Fig. 3.11 *CB* transistor amplifier.

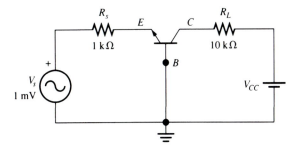

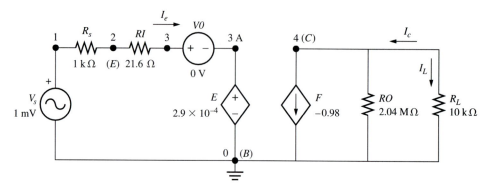

Fig. 3.12   *CB h*-parameter model with source and load.

Figure 3.13 shows the output from PSpice for this example. Unnecessary information was deleted from the file before it was printed.

In summary, we have presented the three basic transistor configurations, *CE*, *CC*, and *CB*. The *h*-parameter model for each is used in the PSpice solution. We have used typical *h* parameters for each configuration; sometimes these must be estimated, but data sheets should be used as available.

Other Configurations

When the transistor circuits do not simplify to the basic models of Figs. 3.7, 3.10, and 3.12, you must take care to maintain the positioning of the elements among the nodes. For example, in Fig. 3.14, a resistor is connected between the collector and the base in a *CE* circuit.

USING A CIRCUIT INVOLVING MILLER'S THEOREM

In your study of electronic circuits, you should learn that the bridging resistor R_1 interferes with an easy application of the gain equations. The resistor is often replaced with two other resistors using Miller's theorem. If you are familiar with Miller's theorem, use it to solve this problem with pencil-and-paper technique to see what is involved before continuing. Using SPICE, it is unnecessary to apply Miller's theorem. Keeping the bridging resistor in the circuit, the *h*-parameter model is shown in Fig. 3.15. The SPICE treatment is almost identical with the standard *CE* analysis. The input file becomes

```
Common-Emitter Circuit with Bridging Resistor
VS 1 0 1mV
VO 3 3A 0
E 3A 0 4 0 2.5E-4
F 4 0 VO 50
RS 1 2 10k
RI 2 3 1.1k
RO 4 0 40k
RL 4 0 10k
```

```
**** 05/27/96 20:15:40 ******* Win32s Evaluation PSpice (April 1995) *********

 common-Base Circuit Analysis with h Parameters

 ****        CIRCUIT DESCRIPTION

VS 1 0 1mV
V0 3 3A 0
E 3A 0 4 0 2.9E-4
F 4 0 V0 -0.98
RS 1 2 1k
RI 2 3 21.6
RO 4 0 2.04MEG
RL 4 0 10k
.OP
.OPT nopage
.TF V(4) VS

 NODE   VOLTAGE      NODE   VOLTAGE      NODE   VOLTAGE      NODE    VOLTAGE

 (    1)    .0010  (    2) 23.85E-06  (    3) 2.761E-06  (    4)     .0095
 (   3A) 2.761E-06

     VOLTAGE SOURCE CURRENTS
     NAME            CURRENT

     VS          -9.762E-07
     V0           9.762E-07

     TOTAL POWER DISSIPATION   9.76E-10  WATTS

 **** VOLTAGE-CONTROLLED VOLTAGE SOURCES

 NAME          E
 V-SOURCE      2.761E-06
 I-SOURCE      9.762E-07

 **** CURRENT-CONTROLLED CURRENT SOURCES

 NAME          F
 I-SOURCE     -9.566E-07

   ****       SMALL-SIGNAL CHARACTERISTICS

       V(4)/VS =  9.520E+00

     INPUT RESISTANCE AT VS =  1.024E+03

     OUTPUT RESISTANCE AT V(4) =  9.924E+03
```

Fig. 3.13

```
R1 2 4 200k
.OP
.TF V(4) VS
.END
```

Run the analysis and obtain the output file for comparison with the previous *CE* results. Verify that $A_V = V(4)/VS = -12.7$ (voltage gain from source to load), $I_L = -1.27$ μA, and $I_b = 33.02$ nA, giving a current gain $A_I = I_L/I_b = -38.46$. From the overall input resistance $R_i' = 10.34$ kΩ, calculate the input resistance at the base, and from the overall output resistance $R_o' = 2.834$ kΩ, calculate the output resistance with R_L removed. These should be $R_i = 340$ Ω and $R_o = 3.95$ kΩ. If you

Fig. 3.14 *CE* amplifier with bridging resistor.

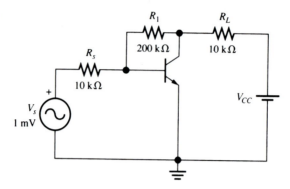

worked this problem using Miller's theorem, you can appreciate how much work was saved using PSpice to obtain the results. It is difficult to go through the Miller method without making mistakes.

Compare the results of this analysis with those of the basic common-emitter amplifier (without the bridging resistor). Notice the effect of the bridging resistor on the gains and the input and output resistances. Figure 3.16 shows the output file.

The Dual of Miller's Theorem

Another circuit configuration is often analyzed using the dual of Miller's theorem. In Fig. 3.17, the emitter resistor R_e is replaced with two other resistors (one in series with the base, the other in series with the collector). If you are familiar with this technique, use it to solve for the gains in this example. Then compare the results with those obtained here using PSpice.

You will not need to replace R_e in the PSpice analysis. The circuit, using the *h*-parameter model, is shown in Fig. 3.18. The input file is as follows:

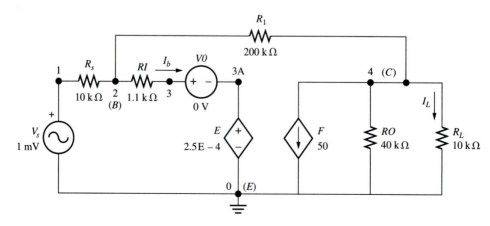

Fig. 3.15 *CE h*-parameter model with bridging resistor.

```
Common-Emitter Circuit with Bridging Resistor

VS 1 0 1mV
V0 3 3A 0
E 3A 0 4 0 2.5E-4
F 4 0 V0 50
RS 1 2 10k
RI 2 3 1.1k
RO 4 0 40k
RL 4 0 10k
R1 2 4 200k
.OP
.OPT nopage
.TF V(4) VS

   NODE   VOLTAGE    NODE   VOLTAGE    NODE   VOLTAGE    NODE   VOLTAGE
 (   1)     .0010  (    2) 33.15E-06  (    3)-3.175E-06  (    4)     -
.0127
(   3A)-3.175E-06

     VOLTAGE SOURCE CURRENTS
     NAME           CURRENT

     VS          -9.669E-08
     V0           3.302E-08


     TOTAL POWER DISSIPATION   9.67E-11  WATTS

  ****      OPERATING POINT INFORMATION      TEMPERATURE =   27.000 DEG C

  **** VOLTAGE-CONTROLLED VOLTAGE SOURCES

  NAME           E
  V-SOURCE    -3.175E-06
  I-SOURCE     3.302E-08

  **** CURRENT-CONTROLLED CURRENT SOURCES

  NAME           F
  I-SOURCE     1.651E-06

   ****       SMALL-SIGNAL CHARACTERISTICS

       V(4)/VS = -1.270E+01

     INPUT RESISTANCE AT VS =  1.034E+04

     OUTPUT RESISTANCE AT V(4) =  2.834E+03
```

Fig. 3.16

```
Common-Emitter Amplifier with Emitter Resistor
VS 1 0 1mV
V0 3 3A 0
E 3A 4 5 4 2.5E-4
F 5 4 V0 50
RS 1 2 1k
RI 2 3 1.1k
RO 5 4 40k
RL 5 0 10k
RE 4 0 330
.OP
.TF V(5) VS
.END
```

Fig. 3.17 *CE* amplifier with emitter resistor.

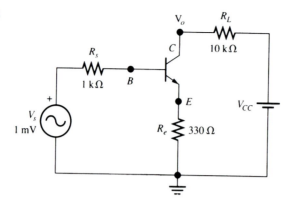

Run the analysis, obtain a printed copy, and verify that the overall voltage gain $A_V = V(5)/VS = -25.74$, $R'_i = 15.44$ kΩ, and $R'_o = 9.752$ kΩ. Calculate and verify that A_V (at the base) $= -27.5$, $A_I = I_L/I_b = -39.7$, $R_i = 14.44$ kΩ (at the base), and $R_o = 393$ kΩ (without R_L).

The effect of the emitter resistor on the input and output resistances is of particular interest in this analysis. The input resistance increases by the factor $(1 + h_{fe})R_e$. The voltage gain is usually approximated by the expression $-R_L/R_e$. Check to see how accurate this is in the example. Figure 3.19 shows the output file.

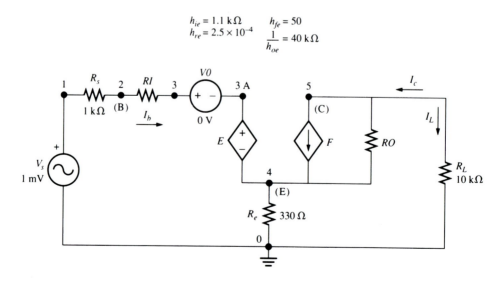

Fig. 3.18 PSpice *CE* amplifier with emitter resistor.

```
Common-Emitter Amplifier with Emitter Resistor

 ****        CIRCUIT DESCRIPTION

VS 1 0 1mV
VO 3 3A 0
E 3A 4 5 4 2.5E-4
F 5 4 VO 50
RS 1 2 1k
RI 2 3 1.1k
RO 5 4 40k
RL 5 0 10k
RE 4 0 330
.OP
.OPT nopage
.TF V(5) VS
.END

 NODE   VOLTAGE      NODE   VOLTAGE      NODE   VOLTAGE      NODE   VOLTAGE

(    1)     .0010  (    2) 935.2E-06  (    3) 864.0E-06  (    4) 870.6E-06
(    5)    -.0257  (   3A) 864.0E-06

     VOLTAGE SOURCE CURRENTS
     NAME          CURRENT

     VS           -6.477E-08
     VO            6.477E-08

     TOTAL POWER DISSIPATION   6.48E-11  WATTS

**** VOLTAGE-CONTROLLED VOLTAGE SOURCES

NAME        E
V-SOURCE   -6.651E-06
I-SOURCE    6.477E-08

**** CURRENT-CONTROLLED CURRENT SOURCES

NAME        F
I-SOURCE    3.239E-06

 ****      SMALL-SIGNAL CHARACTERISTICS

     V(5)/VS = -2.574E+01

     INPUT RESISTANCE AT VS =  1.544E+04

     OUTPUT RESISTANCE AT V(5) =  9.752E+03
```

Fig. 3.19

COMMON-COLLECTOR CIRCUIT WITH COLLECTOR RESISTOR

Another circuit of interest is a slight variation of the usual common-collector circuit. It contains an external collector resistor, added to protect the transistor from a short circuit across the emitter resistor. This modified circuit is shown in Fig. 3.20, and the PSpice model is shown in Fig. 3.21. If you want to analyze this by conventional pencil-and-paper techniques, the presence of R_c presents a problem that might call for the application of the dual of Miller's theorem. The derivation of formulas is tedious and adds little insight to the operation of the circuit. Look at the input file; then compare the results with those of the amplifier without R_c.

Fig. 3.20 *CC* circuit with collector resistor.

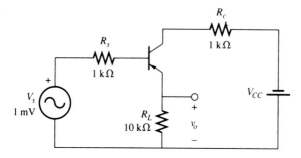

```
Common-Collector Circuit with Collector Resistor
VS 1 0 1mV
VO 3 3A 0
E 3A 4 5 4 1
F 5 4 VO -51
RS 1 2 1k
RI 2 3 1.1k
RC 4 0 1k
RO 5 4 40k
RL 5 0 10k
.OP
.TF V(5) VS
.END
```

Run the analysis and compare the results with those obtained for the simple *CC* amplifier. You will see that the voltage gain is almost identical in both cases and that the input and output resistances changed very little. We conclude that the addition of R_c to the basic circuit has minimal effect on the operation of the circuit.

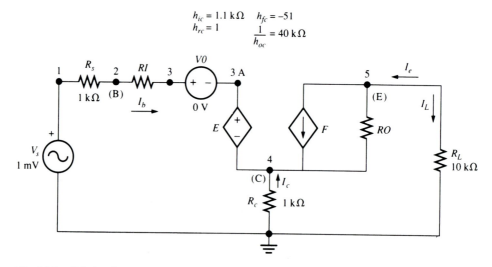

Fig. 3.21 *CC* circuit model with collector resistor.

HIGH-INPUT-RESISTANCE AMPLIFIER

When you need an amplifier with high input resistance, you might choose the Darlington circuit of Fig. 3.22. The circuit consists of a pair of common-collector transistors, often produced in a single package. Note that the first stage can be thought of as having an infinite external emitter resistor $R_{e1} = \infty$. Using the h-parameter model for the cascaded CC stages results in Fig. 3.23, from which the following input file is created:

```
Darlington-Pair (High-Input-Resistance) Amplifier
VS 1 0 1mV
VO1 3 3A 0
VO2 5 5A 0
E1 3A 0 4 0 1
E2 5A 0 6 0 1
F1 4 0 VO1 -51
F2 6 0 VO2 -51
RS 1 2 1k
RI1 2 3 1.1k
RO1 4 0 40k
RI2 4 5 1.1k
RO2 6 0 40k
RL 6 0 4k
.OP
.TF V(6) VS
.END
```

Run the analysis and verify that the voltage gain $V(6)/VS = 0.9929$, $R'_i = 1.682$ MΩ, and $R'_o = 22.24\ \Omega$. From your calculations show that $R_i = 1.681$ MΩ at the base of the first transistor $Q1$ and that $R_o = 22.36\ \Omega$ with R_L removed. Also find $A_I = I_L/I_b = 417.5$, which is much higher than for the single-stage CC amplifier. This analysis has assumed that the h parameters for both stages are the same. In reality, the quiescent currents of the first stage are less than those of the second stage. Figure 3.24 shows the output file.

Fig. 3.22 Darlington circuit for high input resistance.

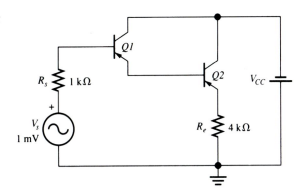

$$h_{ic} = 1.1 \text{ k}\Omega \qquad h_{fc} = -51$$
$$h_{rc} = 1 \qquad \frac{1}{h_{oc}} = 40 \text{ k}\Omega$$

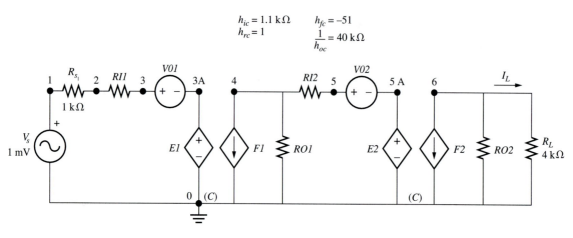

Fig. 3.23 Darlington *CC h*-parameter circuit model.

TWO-STAGE AMPLIFIERS

The treatment of two-stage amplifiers is much simplified using SPICE rather than wading through the usual formula calculations, which are tedious and error prone. If you understand the basic principles of amplifier analysis, you should not hesitate to use PSpice for multistage analysis. As an illustration, consider the *CE-CC* amplifier in Fig. 3.25. The input is to the base of the first transistor. The output from its collector goes directly to the base of the second transistor, with the output taken on the emitter at R_{e2}. The *h* parameters are shown in Fig. 3.26, differing slightly from those of previous examples. The input file is

```
Two-Stage Amplifier; CE and CC Stages
VS 1 0 1mV
VO1 3 3A 0
VO2 5 5A 0
E1 3A 0 4 0 6E-4
F1 4 0 VO1 50
E2 5A 0 6 0 1
F2 6 0 VO2 -51
RS 1 2 1k
RI1 2 3 2k
RO1 4 0 40k
RC1 4 0 5k
RI2 4 5 2k
RO2 6 0 40k
RE2 6 0 5k
.OP
.TF V(6) VS
.END
```

After running the analysis, you should verify that V(6)/VS = −75.31 is the overall voltage gain. From your calculations, show that $A_I = I_L/I_{b1} = -43.2$, $R_i = 1.869 \text{ k}\Omega$ (at the base of *Q1*), and $R_o = 130 \ \Omega$. Figure 3.27 shows the output file.

```
Darlington-Pair (High-Input-Resistance) Amplifier

  ****        CIRCUIT DESCRIPTION

VS 1 0 1mV
V01 3 3A 0
V02 5 5A 0
E1 3A 0 4 0 1
E2 5A 0 6 0 1
F1 4 0 V01 -51
F2 6 0 V02 -51
RS 1 2 1k
RI1 2 3 1.1k
RO1 4 0 40k
RI2 4 5 1.1k
RO2 6 0 40k
RL 6 0 4k
.OP
.OPT nopage
.TF V(6) VS
.END

  ****        SMALL SIGNAL BIAS SOLUTION       TEMPERATURE =    27.000 DEG C

NODE    VOLTAGE     NODE    VOLTAGE     NODE    VOLTAGE     NODE    VOLTAGE
(    1)     .0010  (    2) 999.4E-06  (    3) 998.8E-06  (    4) 998.8E-06
(    5) 992.9E-06  (    6) 992.9E-06  (   3A) 998.8E-06  (   5A) 992.9E-06

    VOLTAGE SOURCE CURRENTS
    NAME        CURRENT
    VS          -5.946E-10
    V01          5.946E-10
    V02          5.354E-09

    TOTAL POWER DISSIPATION    5.95E-13  WATTS

  **** VOLTAGE-CONTROLLED VOLTAGE SOURCES
NAME         E1          E2
V-SOURCE     9.988E-04   9.929E-04
I-SOURCE     5.946E-10   5.354E-09

  **** CURRENT-CONTROLLED CURRENT SOURCES

NAME         F1          F2
I-SOURCE    -3.032E-08  -2.730E-07

  ****        SMALL-SIGNAL CHARACTERISTICS
      V(6)/VS =  9.929E-01

    INPUT RESISTANCE AT VS =  1.682E+06

    OUTPUT RESISTANCE AT V(6) =  2.224E+01
```

Fig. 3.24

SIMPLIFIED *h*-PARAMETER MODEL

The examples thus far have been based on the full h-parameter model for the transistor that is normally used for small-signal, low-frequency analysis. Another model that is often used for certain BJT circuits is the simplified h-parameter model. In this model h_{fe} and h_{ie} are used, and the other h parameters are omitted. There is little justification for using the simplified model with SPICE. It is often in error by 10%

Fig. 3.25 Two-stage amplifier;
CE and *CC* stages.

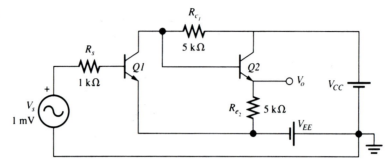

or more. It is given here for reference, along with another look at the common-emitter amplifier. Remember that the values for h_{ie} and h_{fe} are used for all three configurations, *CE*, *CB*, and *CC*.

The *CE* Amplifier Using the Simplified *h*-Parameter Model

Figure 3.28 shows the simplified model, using PSpice notation, and Fig. 3.29 shows the common-emitter circuit using the model. The input file for the analysis is given here:

```
Simplified h-Parameter Analysis
VS 1 0 1mV
VO 3 0 0V
F 4 0 VO 50
RS 1 2 1k
RI 2 3 1.1k
RL 4 0 10k
.OP
.TF V(4) VS
.END
```

You can easily predict the results of this analysis using pencil-and-paper methods. Compare your predictions with the PSpice answers.

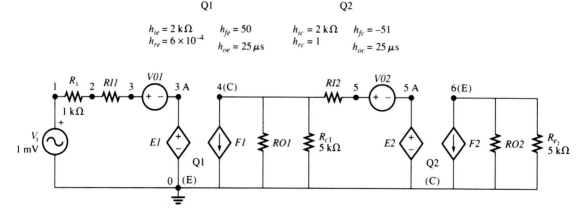

Fig. 3.26 Two-stage amplifier; *CE* and *CC* stages.

```
Two-Stage Amplifier; CE and CC Stages

  ****        CIRCUIT DESCRIPTION

VS 1 0 1mV
VO1 3 3A 0
VO2 5 5A 0
E1 3A 0 4 0 6E-4
F1 4 0 VO1 50
E2 5A 0 6 0 1
F2 6 0 VO2 -51
RS 1 2 1k
RI1 2 3 2k
RO1 4 0 40k
RC1 4 0 5k
RI2 4 5 2k
RO2 6 0 40k
RE2 6 0 5k
.OP
.OPT nopage
.TF V(6) VS
.END

  ****      SMALL SIGNAL BIAS SOLUTION        TEMPERATURE =   27.000 DEG C

  NODE   VOLTAGE     NODE    VOLTAGE     NODE    VOLTAGE     NODE    VOLTAGE
 (   1)    .0010   (    2) 651.5E-06   (    3)-45.58E-06   (    4)    -.0760
 (   5)   -.0753   (    6)    -.0753   (   3A)-45.58E-06   (   5A)    -.0753

     VOLTAGE SOURCE CURRENTS
     NAME          CURRENT
     VS           -3.485E-07
     VO1           3.485E-07
     VO2          -3.322E-07

     TOTAL POWER DISSIPATION    3.49E-10   WATTS

 **** VOLTAGE-CONTROLLED VOLTAGE SOURCES
 NAME        E1            E2
 V-SOURCE   -4.558E-05  -7.531E-02
 I-SOURCE    3.485E-07  -3.322E-07

 **** CURRENT-CONTROLLED CURRENT SOURCES
 NAME        F1            F2
 I-SOURCE   1.743E-05   1.694E-05

  ****      SMALL-SIGNAL CHARACTERISTICS
      V(6)/VS = -7.531E+01

     INPUT RESISTANCE AT VS =   2.869E+03

     OUTPUT RESISTANCE AT V(6) =  1.267E+02
```

Fig. 3.27

FIELD-EFFECT TRANSISTOR (FET) AMPLIFIERS

The FET amplifier is often simple enough not to require computer analysis. In the cases where an extra resistance is present (either R_d or R_s), the situation is more interesting. Our first example involves a common-source FET with the output taken across R_d at the drain. The extra resistance is R_s. Figure 3.30 shows the amplifier, and Fig. 3.31 gives the model. From your study of FETs, predict what the voltage gain and the load current will be.

Fig. 3.28 Simplified *h*-parameter model.

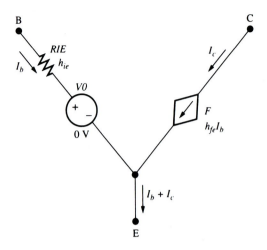

We often show the input floating in the model (the gate is not connected), but this will not work in a SPICE analysis. The solution is to place a large resistor from gate to drain. In our example, $R_{GD} = 10$ MΩ, $g_m = 2$ mS, $r_d = 40$ kΩ, $R_L = 2$ kΩ, $R_s = 500$ Ω, and the input voltage is 1 mV. The input file becomes

```
Common-Source FET with RS
VI 1 0 1mV
G 2 3 1 3 2mS
RD 2 3 40k
RL 2 0 2k
RS 3 0 500
RG 1 2 10MEG
.OP
.TF V(2) VI
.END
```

After running the analysis, verify that V(2)/VI = -1.939 and $R'_o = 1.95$ kΩ. From your calculations, show that $R_o = 79.6$ kΩ and $I_L = -950$ nA.

Fig. 3.29 *CE* amplifier using simplified *h*-parameter model.

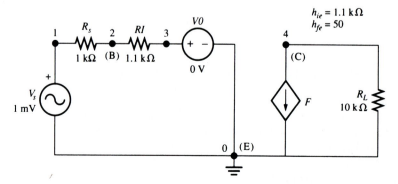

Fig. 3.30 Common-source FET with R_s.

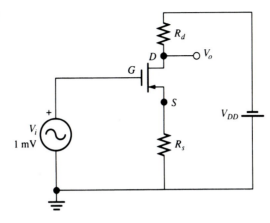

Common-Drain FET with External Drain Resistor

In Fig. 3.30 if the output is taken across R_s, this is a common-drain amplifier. Assuming that R_d is still in place, you are interested in the analysis. The SPICE model shown in Fig. 3.32 produces this input file:

```
Common-Drain FET with Drain Resistor
VI 1 0 1mV
G 3 2 1 2 2mS
RD 2 3 40k
RD1 3 0 1k
RS 2 0 2k
RG 1 3 10MEG
.OP
.TF V(2) VI
.END
```

From your study of FETs, predict what the voltage gain for this source-follower circuit should be; then run the PSpice analysis and verify that V(2)/VI = 0.7882 and $R'_o = 403.9\ \Omega$. Calculate $R_o = 506\ \Omega$ and $I_L = 394$ nA.

Fig. 3.31 FET model and common-source amplifier.

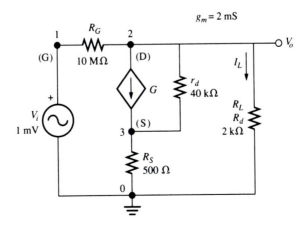

Fig. 3.32 Common-drain FET with drain resistor.

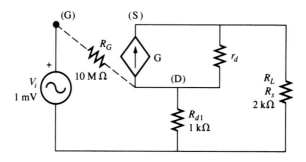

Frequency Response of FET Amplifiers

When you use the FET amplifier over a wide range of frequencies, you need to account for the internal node capacitances. Figure 3.33 shows a common-source amplifier model including C_{gd}, C_{gs}, and C_{ds}. Usually these internal capacitances are small. In our example, we choose $C_{gs} = 3$ pF, $C_{ds} = 1$ pF, and $C_{gd} = 2.8$ pF. Other values include $g_m = 1.6$ mS, $r_d = 44$ kΩ, along with $R_s = 1$ kΩ and $R_L = 100$ kΩ. For the SPICE analysis, we will choose a frequency range of 100 Hz to 100 kHz. The capacitances will be of interest only at high frequencies. The input file is as follows:

```
Common-Source Amplifier; High-Frequency Model
VI 1 0 AC 1mV
G 3 0 2 0 1.6mS
RD 3 0 44k
RL 3 0 100k
RS 1 2 1k
CGS 2 0 3pF
CGD 2 3 2.8pF
CDS 3 0 1pF
.AC DEC 20 100 10MEG
.PROBE
.END
```

Run the analysis and obtain a printed output of the Probe results using a log-frequency X-axis, with V(3) on the Y-axis. Can you identify at what frequency the

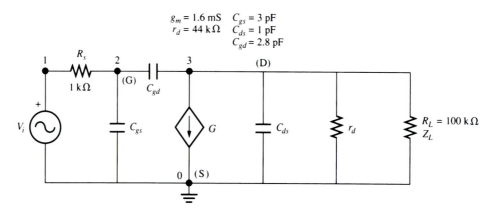

Fig. 3.33 Common-source amplifier; high-frequency model.

output becomes seriously attenuated? Because this is not quite a Bode plot, it is difficult to be specific. Remove this trace and add a new logarithmic trace. The trace that you call for should be

$$20*\log10(V(3)/49mV)$$

The plot is now in standard Bode form. In the expression, 49 mV represents the midfrequency gain as shown on the first plot. We used this value to normalize the plot. The vertical axis now shows 0 at the top followed by −5, −10, and so forth. Adjust the X-axis to show the frequency range 100 Hz to 5 MHz. Use the cursor to verify that the −3 dB point is at $f = 619$ kHz. Obtain a printed copy of this, and draw lines tangent to both linear portions of the curve. The point where these lines intersect indicates where the frequency response is down 3 dB. Figure 3.34 shows the plot.

HIGH-FREQUENCY MODEL OF THE BIPOLAR-JUNCTION TRANSISTOR

For the *CE* circuit, we often use the hybrid-π model. Figure 3.35 shows this model along with V_s, R_s, and R_L, the external components. In this model an extra node B' is required to account for the behavior at high frequencies. Parameters used in this model are resistors $r_{ce}, r_{bb'}, r_{b'e}, r_{b'c}$ and capacitors C_c and C_e. The gain is represented by a voltage-dependent current source $g_m V_{b'e}$. Figure 3.35 shows the values used in this example. These lead to the following input file:

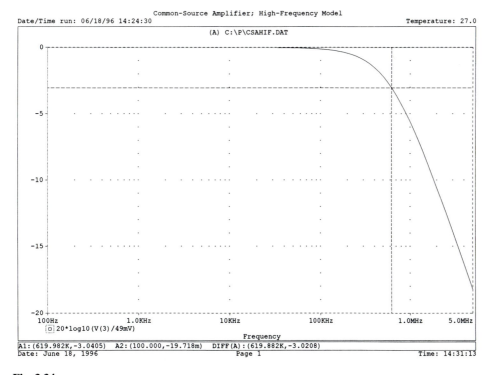

Date/Time run: 06/18/96 14:24:30

Common-Source Amplifier; High-Frequency Model

Temperature: 27.0

(A) C:\P\CSAHIF.DAT

A1: (619.982K,-3.0405)   A2: (100.000,-19.718m)   DIFF(A): (619.882K,-3.0208)
Date: June 18, 1996   Page 1   Time: 14:31:13

Fig. 3.34

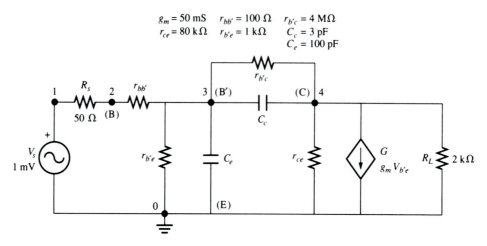

Fig. 3.35   Hybrid-π model for BJT, common-emitter circuit.

```
High-Frequency Model of Bipolar-Junction Transistor
VS 1 0 AC 1mV
G 4 0 3 0 50mS
RS 1 2 50
RBB 2 3 100
RBE 3 0 1k
RBC 3 4 4MEG
RCE 4 0 80k
RL 4 0 2k
CE 3 0 100pF
CC 3 4 3pF
.AC DEC 50 100k 10MEG
.PROBE
.END
```

Run the analysis and determine the midfrequency voltage output at V(4). Verify that it is approximately 85 mV. Then obtain a plot of

$$20*\log10(V(4)/85mV)$$

This will allow you to find the 3 dB point. Verify that it is at $f = 2.8$ MHz. Figure 3.36 shows the plot.

Without the aid of a powerful tool such as PSpice, the equations needed to correctly solve problems such as this become very difficult to drive and employ. The circuit has four independent nodes, and the elements are complex. For the mathematical treatment simpler models often are used instead.

EMITTER FOLLOWER AT HIGH FREQUENCIES

We now present a variation of the high-frequency analysis. This circuit includes a load impedance Z_L, consisting of R_L and C_L. The amplifier has low output resistance and is used as a driver for a capacitive load. Figure 3.37 shows the circuit with the hybrid-π model. Note that the current arrow on G still points toward the emitter node. The input file is

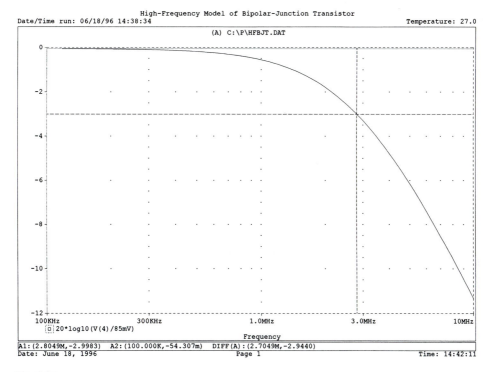

Fig. 3.36

```
Emitter Follower High-Frequency Model
VS 1 0 AC 1mV
G 0 4 3 4 50mS
RS 1 2 50
RBB 2 3 100
```

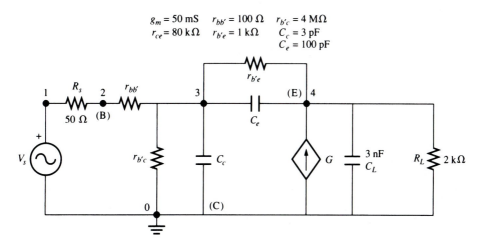

Fig. 3.37   Hybrid-π model, emitter follower with capacitive load.

```
RBE 3 4 1k
RBC 3 0 4MEG
RL 4 0 2k
CL 4 0 3nF
CC 3 0 3pF
CE 3 4 100pF
.AC DEC 50 100k 1OMEG
.PROBE
.END
```

Run the analysis, then plot V(4). Note that the gain is slightly less than unity, as expected for the emitter follower. To obtain the Bode plot, use the trace for

$$20*\log10(V(4)/0.99\text{mV})$$

Then using the cursor mode, verify that the 3 dB point is at $f = 2.7$ MHz. Add a second graph that is a plot of the phase shift of V(4). To do this simply plot VP(4). See that the phase shift at the -3 dB frequency is about $-57°$. Note that at the lowest frequency of the plot, 100 kHz, there is already a phase shift of a few degrees due to the capacitive nature of the load. Figure 3.38 shows the phase-shift and magnitude plots for this circuit.

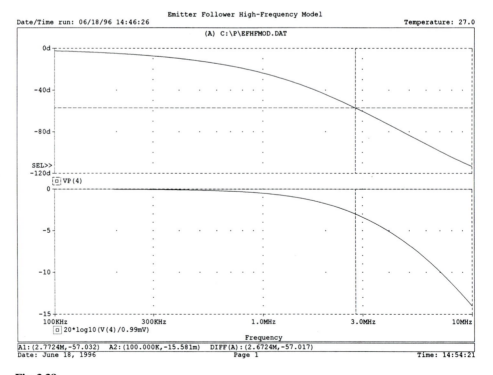

Fig. 3.38

DC SENSITIVITY

Variations in component values can cause circuits to operate improperly. In some cases, expected voltages and currents fall outside acceptable values. In other cases, an improper biasing condition might lead to distortion problems, and so forth. Using PSpice, the sensitivity of an output variable may be determined by including the .SENS statement.

For example, in a series circuit as shown in Fig. 3.39, the resistor R_2 represents the load resistance. The voltage across this resistor is 1.25 V. The input file will contain a statement to determine the sensitivity of this voltage with respect to the other elements in the circuit. The file is

```
Sensitivity of Load Voltage in Series Circuit
Vs 1 0 5V
R1 1 2 300
R2 2 0 100
.sens V(2)
.end
```

The output from this analysis is shown in Fig. 3.40. The dc sensitivities of the output voltage V_2 are shown in relation to the various elements in the circuit. The first element listed is R_1, with its value of 300 Ω. Its sensitivity is given as $-3.125E-03$ volts per unit. Since R_1 is a resistor, the *unit* is the ohm. The sensitivity is then $-3.125E-03$ V/Ω. The sensitivity of V_2 to changes in the R_2 value of 9 Ω is $9.375E-03$ V/Ω. Finally, the sensitivity of V_2 to changes in V_s is 0.25 V/V. We would like to discover how these values are found and what they mean.

The concept of sensitivity was introduced by Bode in *Network Analysis and Feedback Amplifier Design*. He was interested in how a transfer function T would change when there were changes in one element in the system. The symbol S was introduced, with superscript and subscript, to represent sensitivity. The superscript is the output parameter, and the subscript is the element in question. In our series circuit, using voltage division,

$$V_2 = V_s \frac{R_2}{R_1 + R_2}$$

First consider that R_1 becomes the variable while the other elements are held constant. R_1 might increase by a small amount. ΔR_1, bringing about a small change

Fig. 3.39 Circuit to illustrate sensitivity.

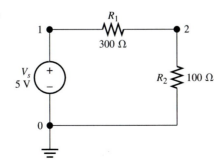

```
Sensitivity of Load Voltage in Series Circuit

 ****        CIRCUIT DESCRIPTION
Vs 1 0 5V
R1 1 2 300
R2 2 0 100
.sens V(2)
.opt nopage
.end

 ****        SMALL SIGNAL BIAS SOLUTION         TEMPERATURE =   27.000 DEG C

 NODE    VOLTAGE        NODE    VOLTAGE     NODE    VOLTAGE     NODE    VOLTAGE
 (   1)    5.0000  (     2)    1.2500

      VOLTAGE SOURCE CURRENTS
      NAME            CURRENT
      Vs            -1.250E-02

      TOTAL POWER DISSIPATION    6.25E-02   WATTS

 ****        DC SENSITIVITY ANALYSIS                TEMPERATURE =   27.000 DEG C

 DC SENSITIVITIES OF OUTPUT V(2)
               ELEMENT          ELEMENT          ELEMENT          NORMALIZED
               NAME             VALUE            SENSITIVITY      SENSITIVITY
                                                 (VOLTS/UNIT)  (VOLTS/PERCENT)
               R1            3.000E+02          -3.125E-03        -9.375E-03
               R2            1.000E+02           9.375E-03         9.375E-03
               Vs            5.000E+00           2.500E-01         1.250E-02
```

Fig. 3.40

in V_2, which will be ΔV_2. In the limit, $\Delta R_1 \rightarrow \partial R_1$ and $\Delta V_2 \rightarrow \partial V_2$. The element sensitivity for element R_1 is defined as

$$\frac{V_2}{R_1} S_{R_1}^{V_2} = \frac{V_2 \, \partial \ln V_2}{R_1 \, \partial \ln R_1} = \frac{\partial V_2}{\partial V_1}$$

$$\frac{\partial V_2}{\partial R_1} = \frac{\partial V_s}{\partial R_1} \frac{R_2}{R_1 + R_2} = \frac{V_s(-R_2)}{(R_1 + R_2)^2}$$

In our example

$$\frac{\partial V_2}{\partial R_1} = \frac{-5(100)}{(400)^2} = -0.003125$$

which is in agreement with the element sensitivity shown in the output file.

The sensitivity of V_2 with respect to R_1 is defined as

$$\frac{V_2}{R_2} S_{R_2}^{V_2} = \frac{V_2 \, \partial \ln V_2}{R_2 \, \partial \ln R_2} = \frac{\partial V_2}{\partial R_2}$$

$$\frac{\partial V_2}{\partial R_2} = \frac{\partial V_s}{\partial R_2} \frac{-R_2}{R_1 + R_2} = \frac{V_s R_1}{(R_1 + R_2)^2}$$

In our example

$$\frac{\partial V_2}{\partial R_2} = \frac{5(300)}{(400)^2} = 0.009375$$

which is also in agreement with the element sensitivity shown in the output file.

Normalized values are shown in the last column of the PSpice analysis of Fig. 3.40. These are found as the product of element value and element sensitivity.

Now that we have seen how the sensitivity values are found, our next step is to determine what they mean. Suppose that there is an incremental change in the value of R_1. For example, let R_1 increase by 1%. This gives $R_1 = 303 \ \Omega$ and $\Delta R_1 = 3 \ \Omega$. Based on the value $\partial V_2/\partial R_1 = -0003125$, $\Delta V_2 = 3(-0.003125) = -0.009375$, and the new value of $V_2 = 1.240625$ V.

In like manner, suppose that there is an increase in the value of R_2 by 1%. This gives $R_2 = 101 \ \Omega$ and $\Delta R_2 = 1 \ \Omega$. Based on the value of $\partial V_2/\partial R_2 = 0.009375$, $\Delta V_2 = 0.009375$ V, and the new value of $V_2 = 1.259375$ V.

But wait—could we not find the new value of V_2 in each case by the voltage-division formula? Thus when $R_1 = 303 \ \Omega$.

$$V_2 = V_s \frac{R_2}{R_1 + R_2} = 5\frac{100}{403} = 1.240695 \text{ V}$$

On the other hand, when $R_2 = 101 \ \Omega$,

$$V_2 = V_s \frac{R_2}{R_1 + R_2} = 5\frac{101}{401} = 1.25935 \text{ V}$$

Careful comparison of the two methods for predicting the new value of V_2 shows that they are not in exact agreement. In fact, had we used changes greater than 1%, the disagreement would have been greater. It now becomes obvious that sensitivity values are not to be used for predicting actual values of the output voltage. Instead, they are to be used in determining which elements are more critical in maintaining a stable circuit.

When the normalized sensitivities for our circuit are compared, we look at the larger values and conclude that these are the more critical. For example, the largest value shown in the last column of Fig. 3.40 is the value for V_s, which is 0.0125. Thus V_s becomes the most critical element. The normalized sensitivities for R_1 and R_2 are the same in magnitude. Thus they are equally sensitive elements.

DC SENSITIVITY OF BIAS CIRCUIT

The circuit in Fig. 3.41 is our model for a BJT bias circuit. In this example the transistor has $V_{BE} = 0.7$ V and $h_{FE} = 80$. The output voltage is taken as the collector-to-emitter voltage V(3,2). This voltage will be the subject of the sensitivity analysis. Here is the input file:

Fig. 3.41 Simple BJT model for sensitivity

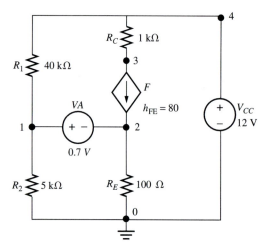

```
Sensitivity of Model Transistor Bias Circuit
VCC 4 0 12V
VA 1 2 0.7V
F 3 2 VA 80
R1 4 1 40k
R2 1 0 5k
RC 4 3 1k
RE 2 0 100
.SENS V(3,2)
.END
```

Run the analysis and study the listings for element sensitivity. This output is shown in Fig. 3.42. Verify that for a 0.12-V increase in V_{CC}, V(3,2) will increase by 0.02636 V. Also verify that of the various resistors in the circuit, R_1 is the most sensitive in determining V(3,2). As an exercise, use the element sensitivity values to approximate V(3,2) when first R_1 increases by 1% and then when R_2 increases by 1%. Remember that the results obtained by this method will be approximate and will apply only to incremental changes in the element values.

SENSITIVITY OF LIBRARY BJT CIRCUIT

When the PSpice model of a BJT is used in a sensitivity analysis, sensitivity of the output variable to changes in transistor parameter values are obtained, as well as the information previously given. For example, the circuit shown in Fig. 3.43 uses one of the BJTs in the evaluation library, the *Q2N2222*. It is our desire to obtain the sensitivity of V(3,4), the collector-to-emitter voltage. The input file is

```
Sensitivity of BJT Biasing Circuit
VCC 2 0 12V
R1 2 1 40k
R2 1 0 3.3k
RC 2 3 7.7k
RE 4 0 220
```

```
Sensitivity of Model Transistor Bias Circuit

   ****       CIRCUIT DESCRIPTION

VCC 4 0 12V
VA 1 2 0.7V
F 3 2 VA 80
R1 4 1 40k
R2 1 0 5k
RC 4 3 1k
RE 2 0 100
.SENS V(3,2)
.OPT nopage
.END


   ****       SMALL SIGNAL BIAS SOLUTION        TEMPERATURE =    27.000 DEG C

   NODE    VOLTAGE      NODE    VOLTAGE      NODE    VOLTAGE      NODE    VOLTAGE
   (    1)    1.1089  (    2)     .4089  (    3)    7.9610  (    4)   12.0000

       VOLTAGE SOURCE CURRENTS
       NAME          CURRENT
       VCC          -4.311E-03
       VA            5.049E-05

       TOTAL POWER DISSIPATION   5.17E-02  WATTS

   ****       DC SENSITIVITY ANALYSIS              TEMPERATURE =    27.000 DEG C

DC SENSITIVITIES OF OUTPUT V(3,2)
           ELEMENT          ELEMENT          ELEMENT          NORMALIZED
           NAME             VALUE            SENSITIVITY      SENSITIVITY
                                             (VOLTS/UNIT)  (VOLTS/PERCENT)
           R1             4.000E+04          2.125E-04         8.499E-02
           R2             5.000E+03         -1.385E-03        -6.923E-02
           RC             1.000E+03         -4.039E-03        -4.039E-02
           RE             1.000E+02          2.463E-02         2.463E-02
           VCC            1.200E+01          2.197E-01         2.636E-02
           VA             7.000E-01          7.023E+00         4.916E-02
```

Fig. 3.42

Fig. 3.43 Built-in model for
sensitivity.

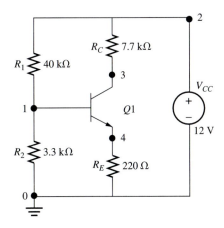

```
Q1 3 1 4 Q2N2222
.SENS V(3,4)
.LIB EVAL.LIB
.END
```

The output file, shown in Fig. 3.44, gives dc sensitivities of V(3,4) not only to the external components but also to the transistor parameters as well. In the

```
Sensitivity of BJT Biasing Circuit
VCC 2 0 12V
R1 2 1 40k
R2 1 0 3.3k
RC 2 3 7.7k
RE 4 0 220
Q1 3 1 4 Q2N2222
.SENS V(3,4)
.LIB EVAL.LIB
.OPT nopage
.END

    ****      BJT MODEL PARAMETERS
                  Q2N2222
                  NPN
            IS   14.340000E-15
            BF   255.9

    ****      SMALL SIGNAL BIAS SOLUTION      TEMPERATURE =   27.000 DEG C

  NODE    VOLTAGE      NODE    VOLTAGE      NODE    VOLTAGE      NODE    VOLTAGE
  (   1)    .8926   (    2)   12.0000   (    3)    3.4815   (    4)    .2450

      VOLTAGE SOURCE CURRENTS
      NAME            CURRENT
      VCC           -1.384E-03

      TOTAL POWER DISSIPATION   1.66E-02  WATTS

    ****      DC SENSITIVITY ANALYSIS        TEMPERATURE =   27.000 DEG C

DC SENSITIVITIES OF OUTPUT V(3,4)
            ELEMENT          ELEMENT          ELEMENT         NORMALIZED
            NAME             VALUE          SENSITIVITY       SENSITIVITY
                                            (VOLTS/UNIT)    (VOLTS/PERCENT)
            R1              4.000E+04         6.263E-04         2.505E-01
            R2              3.300E+03        -7.395E-03        -2.440E-01
            RC              7.700E+03        -1.086E-03        -8.363E-02
            RE              2.200E+02         3.186E-02         7.009E-02
            VCC             1.200E+01        -1.274E+00        -1.529E-01
Q1
            RB              1.000E+01         2.127E-04         2.127E-05
            RC              1.000E+00         2.020E-05         2.020E-07
            RE              0.000E+00         0.000E+00         0.000E+00
            BF              2.559E+02        -1.586E-03        -4.059E-03
            ISE             1.434E-14         2.022E+13         2.899E-03
            BR              6.092E+00         3.790E-11         2.309E-12
            ISC             0.000E+00         0.000E+00         0.000E+00
            IS              1.434E-14        -6.888E+13        -9.878E-03
            NE              1.307E+00        -4.250E+00        -5.555E-02
            NC              2.000E+00         0.000E+00         0.000E+00
            IKF             2.847E-01        -1.831E-02        -5.213E-05
            IKR             0.000E+00         0.000E+00         0.000E+00
            VAF             7.403E+01         6.382E-04         4.725E-04
            VAR             0.000E+00         0.000E+00         0.000E+00
```

Fig. 3.44

latter category, note that under *Q1* in the sensitivity analysis, *RB* is the (internal) base resistance, *RC* is the collector ohmic resistance, *RE* is the emitter ohmic resistance, and so forth. Of particular interest is the sensitivity with respect to the dc beta, *BF*.

SUMMARY OF NEW PSPICE STATEMENTS USED IN THIS CHAPTER

E[name]<+node><−node><+controlling node><−controlling node><gain>

For example,

```
E 6 5 2 1 18
```

means that a voltage-controlled voltage source is connected between nodes *6* and *5*. It is dependent on the voltage between nodes *2* and *1*, and it has a voltage gain of 18. This statement (along with the *F* and *G* statements) was given in Chapter 1; it is repeated here since it is a fundamental amplifier equation. Some of the examples and problems in this chapter require its use. Like other dependent sources, its form could also involve a POLY expression. Note that the gain is a dimensionless voltage ratio.

F[name]<+node><−node><+controlling V device name><gain>

For example,

```
F 4 3 VA 80
```

means that a current-controlled current source is connected between nodes *4* and *3*. The current arrowhead is at node *3*. The current through the dependent source is greater than the current through VA by a factor of 80. The voltage source *VA* may be an actual source or a dummy source of zero volts. The dummy source is often needed to specify the path for the controlling current.

The *h*-parameter model of the transistor requires the use of the *F* statement. The gain is h_{fe} and is dimensionless. Other transistor models involving beta also require the *F* statement.

G[name]<+node><−node><+controlling node><−controlling node> <transconductance>

For example,

```
G 8 7 5 3 20mS
```

means that a voltage-controlled current source is connected between nodes *8* and *7*. The current arrowhead is at node *7*. The current through the dependent source is a function of the voltage between nodes *5* and *3* as specified by the transconductance of 20 mS. This means, for example, that if $v_{53} = 10$ mV, then $i_{87} = (10$ mV) $\cdot$ (20 mS) = 200 μA.

DOT COMMANDS USED IN THIS CHAPTER

.TF <output variable><input source>

For example,

```
.TF V(4) VS
```

When used with the *h*-parameter model as introduced in this chapter, this statement will give the small-signal gain V_4/V_S. This is possible when we are using ac voltages in circuits where the passive components are purely resistive. As far as PSpice is concerned, the analysis could be ac or dc.

.LIB<file name>

For example,

```
.LIB EVAL.LIB
```

means that the library *EVAL.LIB* will be searched for the models used in the input file. In the example based on the BJT biasing circuit, the transistor Q_1 was used. This is based on the model for the *Q2N2222*. This model is found in the library *EVAL.LIB* that comes with the evaluation version of PSpice.

.SENS<output variable>

For example,

```
.SENS V(2)
```

means that the dc sensitivities of the output voltage V(2) will be computed in relation to the various elements in the circuit.

PROBLEMS

3.1 A biasing circuit for a silicon transistor with $h_{FE} = 100$ is shown in Fig. 3.45. Assume that $V_{BE} = 0.7$ V in your PSpice model. Find currents I_B and I_C. Find the bias voltage V_{CE}. Your results should show $I_B = 21.5$ µA, $I_C = 2.15$ mA, and $V_{CE} = 3.55$ V. Is the transistor operating in the active region?

Fig. 3.45

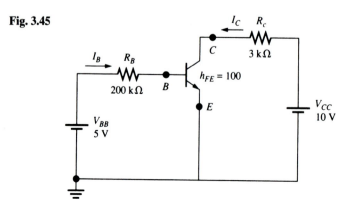

3.2 Change the value of R_B in Problem 3.1 to 50 kΩ. Assume that all other values remain the same, and use PSpice to find I_B, I_C, and V_{CE}. Study your results carefully, and explain why the values are incorrect. *Hint:* Recall that relatively large values of base current may put the transistor into saturation.

3.3 Using the PSpice bias model with $V_{BE} = 0.7$ V, solve for I_B, I_C, and V_{CE} in Fig. 3.46. Is the transistor operating in the active region?

Fig. 3.46

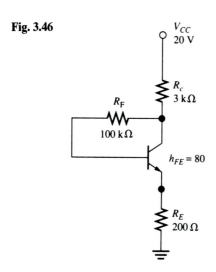

3.4 From the PSpice bias model with $V_{BE} = 0.7$ V, determine I_B, I_C, and V_{CE} in Fig. 3.47. *Note:* Use the h parameters given in Fig. 3.7 for each of the following problems where h-parameter analysis is required.

Fig. 3.47

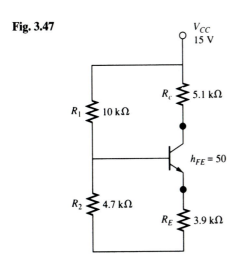

3.5 Use the PSpice model based on the full set of h parameters to solve this problem. In Fig. 3.48 find $A_I = I_o/I_i$, $A_v = V_c/V_b$, and $A_{V_s} = V_c/V_s$. *Hint:* For small-
signal, low-frequency analysis, the capacitor can be replaced by a short circuit.

Fig. 3.48

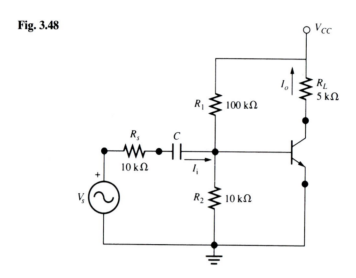

3.6 Use the same PSpice model as in Problem 3.5. For the circuit shown in Fig. 3.49
with R_E added to the circuit, solve for A_I, A_V, and A_{V_s}.

Fig. 3.49

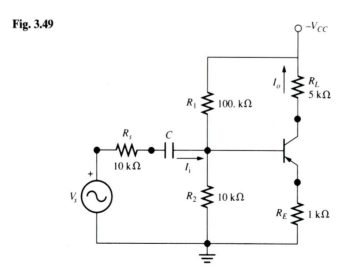

3.7 For each of the amplifiers of Problems 3.5 and 3.6, find the input resistance as
seen by the source using PSpice.

3.8 Using the full h-parameter model, find A_I, A_V, and R_i for the circuit of Fig. 3.50.

Fig. 3.50

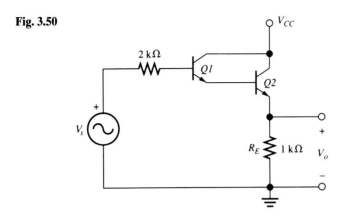

3.9 A *CS* FET amplifier is shown in Fig. 3.51. When the input voltage $V_i = 4$ mV, what will be the output voltage from drain to ground? What is the voltage gain of the amplifier? Is the gain positive or negative? What does this mean?

Fig. 3.51

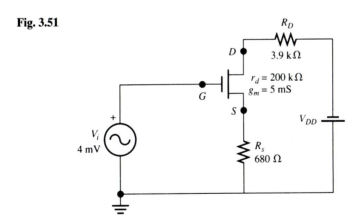

3.10 When the output voltage of the amplifier in Problem 3.9 is taken from the source terminal, it becomes a *CD* amplifier. Using the same values as previously given, what will be the output voltage from source to ground? What is the voltage gain of the amplifier? Is the gain positive or negative?

3.11 A *CS* FET amplifier is to be used over a wide range of frequencies. Given: $R_s = 1$ kΩ, $C_{gs} = 2$ pF, $C_{gd} = 3$ pF, $C_{ds} = 1.5$ pF, $R_L = 48$ kΩ, $g_m = 3$ mS, and $r_d = 100$ kΩ, run a PSpice analysis and obtain a plot of frequency response for the amplifier. Find the upper 3 dB frequency. What is the midfrequency gain of the amplifier?

3.12 A common-emitter amplifier is shown in Fig. 3.52. It has the following parameters: $g_m = 70$ mS, $R_{ce} = 100$ kΩ, $r_{bb'} = 120$ Ω, $r_{b'e} = 1100$ Ω, $r_{b'c} = 2$ MΩ,
$C_c = 2.5$ pF, and $C_e = 80$ pF. In the external circuit $R_s = 1050$ Ω, $R_L = 2.4$ kΩ,
and $V_s = 5$ mV. Run a PSpice analysis to determine the frequency response.
Determine the midfrequency output voltage and the voltage gain. Find the upper 3 dB frequency.

Fig. 3.52

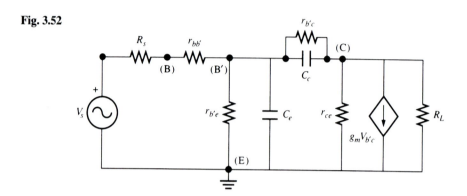

3.13 Run a Probe analysis for the amplifier of Problem 3.12 to determine the input
impedance at $f = 50$ kHz.

3.14 Instead of using the simplified h-parameter model for the BJT, and equivalent
model is shown in Fig. 3.53. Clearly, $r_{bb'} + r_{b'e} = h_{ie}$ and $g_m v_{b'e} = h_{fe} i_b$. Given
$h_{fe} = 100$, $h_{ie} = 1200$ Ω, and $r_{bb'} = 100$ Ω, and using the model shown, find the
midfrequency gain (from source to collector) of the amplifier shown in Figure
3.54). In the figure $R_1 = 20$ kΩ, $R_2 = 10$ kΩ, $R_c = 4.8$ kΩ, and $R_e = 800$ Ω. Treat
C_1 and C_2 as short circuits.

Fig. 3.53

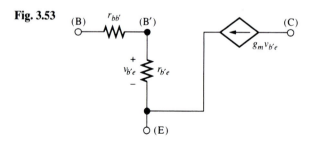

Fig. 3.54

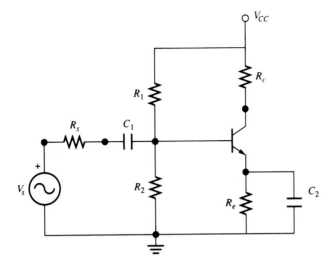

Multistage Amplifiers, Frequency Response, and Feedback

This chapter covers a variety of topics based on frequency response. We will look at how frequency affects Bode plots, decibel notation, and high-frequency models for the BJT and FET. We will also present the effects of feedback on single-stage and multistage amplifiers.

LOW-PASS FILTER

For an introduction and a bit of a review, consider the low-pass RC circuit shown in Fig. 4.1(a). Values are $R = 100$ kΩ, $C = 1$ nF, and $V = 1\underline{/0°}$ V. The output is across the capacitor at V(2). The input file for this circuit will allow for a Probe investigation extending from 1 Hz to 1 MHz.

```
High-Frequency Response of Simple Filter
V 1 0 AC 1V
R 1 2 100k
C 2 0 1nF
.AC DEC 20 1HZ 1MEG
.PROBE
.END
```

Run the analysis; then spend some time looking at various aspects of the response. First plot V(2) and look at the shape of the curve. The output level varies from 1 V at $f = 1$ Hz to almost 0 V at $f = 1$ MHz. When the frequency is low, the value of X is large, allowing most of the source voltage of 1 V to appear across node 2. As the frequency increases, X becomes smaller and V(2) diminishes. When $|V_R| = |V_C|$, what will be the value of each voltage? Remember that you are dealing with phasors and that these two voltages are always 90° apart as shown in Fig. 4.1(b). When the two voltages are equal in magnitude, $v_C = 0.707 \underline{/-45°}$ V.

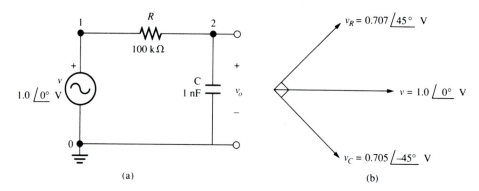

(a)   (b)

Fig. 4.1   (a) Low-pass filter. (b) Phasor diagram for low-pass filter.

On the Probe screen, use the cursor to find the frequency that gives $V(2) =$ 0.707 V. Verify that this is at $f = 1.591$ kHz. In ac analysis, the formula is easily shown to be $f_H = 1/(2\pi RC)$, agreeing with your results.

Add a plot of VP(2) and verify that when $f = 1.591$ kHz, $\theta \approx -45°$. This would be exactly $\theta = 45°$ if more points were used in the plot. Change the Y-axis to go from $-90°$ to $0°$, and look for the midway point $(-45°)$ on the Y-axis. Note that again $f = 1.591$ kHz and that this is the point of inflection on the phase-angle plot. Figure 4.2 shows the Bode phase plot.

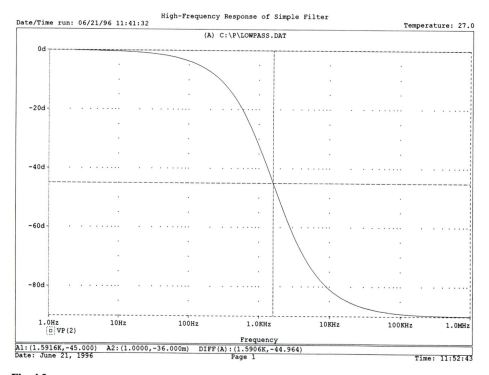

Fig. 4.2

Fig. 4.3 High-pass filter.

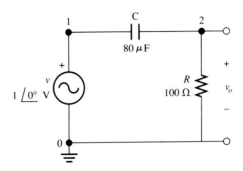

LOW-FREQUENCY RESPONSE OF HIGH-PASS *RC* NETWORK

The counterpart of the low-pass filter of the previous example is the high-pass network shown in Fig. 4.3. The circuit is again an *RC* combination, but here the output is taken across *R*. Values are $R = 100\ \Omega$, $C = 80\ \mu F$, and $V = 1.0\ \underline{/0°}$. The input file is

```
Low-Frequency Response of Simple Filter
V 1 0 AC 1V
R 2 0 100
C 1 2 80uF
.AC DEC 20 0.01Hz 10kHz
.PROBE
.END
```

Run the analysis; then plot V(2). Using the cursor mode, find the frequency at which the output is down 3 dB. Verify that when V(2) = 0.707 V, f = 19.89 Hz. Figure 4.4 shows this response curve. Note that it is not a Bode plot, since the *Y*-axis is not logarithmic.

Remove the trace of V(2) and plot VP(2). Using a phase range from 0° to 90°, find the 45° point. You should see that at $\theta = 45.0°$, f = 19.89 Hz. Remove the trace of VP(2) and plot I(R). Verify that when f = 19.89 Hz, $I = 7.07\underline{/45°}$ mA. These values are easily checked with ac circuit theory, and you are encouraged to do so.

COMMON-EMITTER AMPLIFIER WITH BYPASS CAPACITOR

It is customary to use a bypass capacitor such as C_e in Fig. 4.5 across R_e in the common-emitter amplifier. This allows for a larger voltage gain than if C_e was omitted. The problem is to choose a large enough value for C_e so that at the lowest usable frequency the gain will not be down below 3 dB (and consequently the phase shift will not be greater than 45° due to the Z_e value). The ac analysis will be based on the model shown in Fig. 4.6 The *h*-parameter values used here are the same as those used in the previous *CE* transistor examples of Chapter 3. Additional values are $R_s = 50\ \Omega$, $R_1 = 50\ k\Omega$, $R_2 = 8\ k\Omega$, $R_e = 1\ k\Omega$, $R_c = 2\ k\Omega$, $C_b = 50\ \mu F$, $C_e = 100\ \mu F$, and $V = 1$ mV. The analysis extends from 0.01 Hz to 10 kHz, requiring this input file:

```
Common-Emitter Amplifier with Emitter-Bypass Capacitor
V 1 0 AC 1mV
VO 4 4A 0
E 4A 5 6 5 2.5E-4
```

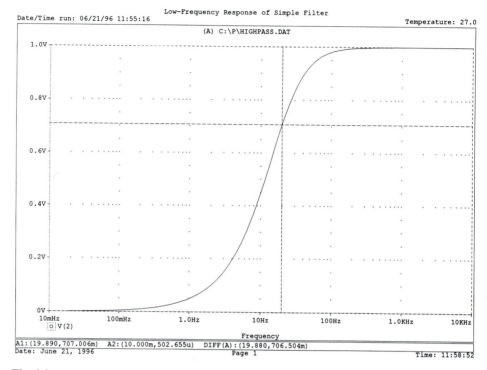

Fig. 4.4

```
F  6 5 VO 50
RS 1 2 50
R1 3 0 50k
R2 3 0 8k
RI 3 4 1.1k
RE 5 0 1k
RO 6 5 40k
```

Fig. 4.5   *CE* amplifier with
bypass capacitor.

$$h_{fe} = 50 \qquad h_{re} = 2.5E - 4$$
$$h_{ie} = 1.1 \text{ k}\Omega \qquad \frac{1}{h_{oe}} = 40 \text{ k}\Omega$$

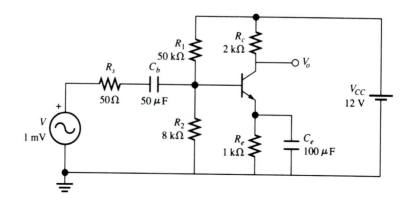

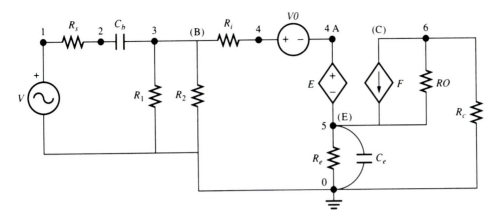

Fig. 4.6 Circuit model for *CE* amplifier with C_e and C_b.

```
RC 6 0 2k
CB 2 3 50uF
CE 5 0 100uF
.AC DEC 20 0.01Hz 10kHz
.PROBE
.END
```

Run the analysis and in Probe plot V(6), the output voltage. The curve should look like that obtained from the example of the *RC* high-pass filter. Use the cursor mode to determine the midfrequency output voltage. Verify that at 5 kHz the output voltage V(6) = 83.99 mV.

Now, look at the *Y*-axis in terms of decibels. Remove this trace and replace it with

$$20*\log10(V(6)/84mV)$$

Suddenly, the plot takes on a strange appearance. The information that was essentially hidden in the linear plot now adds more detail to the dB plot. Refer to Fig. 4.7 for this plot. Where are the two curved portions located, and what causes them? The answers will require further investigation.

Set the *Y*-axis for −20 to 0 range, and the *X*-axis for 1 Hz to 10 kHz. Use the cursor to locate the −3 dB point. Verify that this is at about *f* = 74 Hz. This frequency is called a *pole frequency*, but because the circuit also has another capacitor C_b, it will produce a secondary pole at a lower frequency.

In order to concentrate on the effects of C_e alone, modify your input file to eliminate C_b. This is easily done by changing the *CB* statement to become

```
RB 2 3 0.001
```

Make this change and run the analysis again. In Probe, plot

$$20*\log10(V(6)/84mV)$$

as before. Verify that close to the −3 dB point, *f* = 69.8 Hz. Thus the presence of C_b does not greatly change the location of the first pole. There is also a zero in this circuit, indicated by the frequency at which the response is up by 3 dB from its lowest

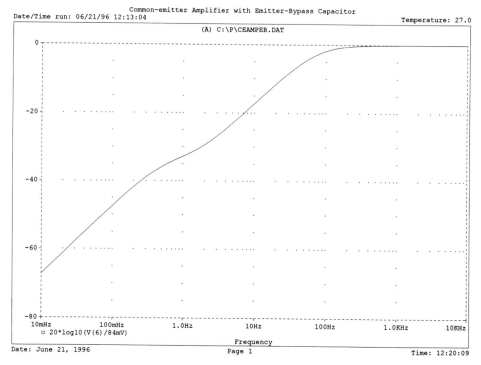

Fig. 4.7

level. Using the cursor mode, see that on the far left on the plot, the response is −32.91 dB. Verify that when 3 dB is added to this (giving −29.91 dB), the frequency $f = 1.577$ Hz. Thus the zero is located at a frequency of about 1.6 Hz.

If you have interest in seeing what happens when C_e is not responsible for the first pole, simply change the value of R_e to 0.001 Ω and rerun the analysis with C_b restored. This gives a single pole at 3.26 Hz.

TWO-STAGE AMPLIFIER AT HIGH FREQUENCIES

A two-stage CE amplifier based on a simplified hybrid-π model is shown in Fig. 4.8. The values are $V = 1$ mV, $R_s = 50$ Ω, $R_{L1} = R_{L2} = 2$ kΩ, $r_{bb'} = 100$ Ω, $r_{b'e} = 1$ kΩ, $g_m = 50$ mS, $C_e = 100$ pF, and $C_c = 3$ pF. The input file becomes

```
Two-Stage CE Amplifier at High Frequencies
V  1  0  AC  1mV
G1  4  0  3  0  50mS
G2  6  0  5  0  50mS
RS  1  2  50
RBB1  2  3  100
RBE1  3  0  1k
RL1  4  0  2k
RBB2  4  5  100
RBE2  5  0  1k
RL2  6  0  2k
```

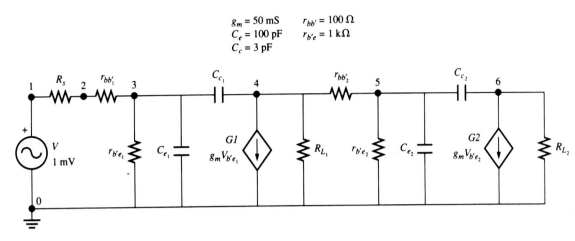

$$g_m = 50 \text{ mS} \quad r_{bb'} = 100 \ \Omega$$
$$C_e = 100 \text{ pF} \quad r_{b'e} = 1 \text{ k}\Omega$$
$$C_c = 3 \text{ pF}$$

Fig. 4.8 Two-stage *CE* amplifier at high frequencies.

```
CE1  3  0  100pF
CC1  3  4  3pF
CE2  5  0  100pF
CC2  5  6  3pF
.AC DEC 20 100Hz 1MEG
.PROBE
.END
```

Run the analysis and in Probe plot V(6). Using the cursor, verify that at mid-frequencies, V(6) = 2.805 V. Remove this trace; then plot

$$20*\log10(V(6)/2.806V)$$

Use the cursor mode to show that the $-$ 3 dB point is at $f = 541.2$ kHz. You will notice that the plot does not show an exact straight-line region needed to find the -3 dB point by the Bode technique. This is because the amplifier has more than one pole frequency. There is a pole frequency for each capacitor, hence a total of 4 poles. The poles are usually not close together in networks of this type. When one pole is dominant, it will be close to the -3 dB point. From a practical standpoint, finding the -3 dB frequency is more important than locating the frequencies of all the poles. Refer to Fig. 4.9 for this Bode plot.

Next look at VP(6) and show that at $f = 541.3$ kHz, $\theta = -48°$, completing the analysis.

TWO-STAGE *CE* AMPLIFIER WITH VOLTAGE-SERIES FEEDBACK

Using conventional feedback development, the circuit shown in Fig. 4.10 is analyzed only with a degree of difficulty. Keeping the full set of *h* parameters in the analysis leads to a complicated set of formulas. On the other hand, with the help of SPICE, the nodal analysis is greatly simplified. In the small-signal study of the circuit, assume that all capacitors have been selected to represent short circuits for the chosen range of frequencies. This gives the circuit model shown in Fig. 4.11. Find the

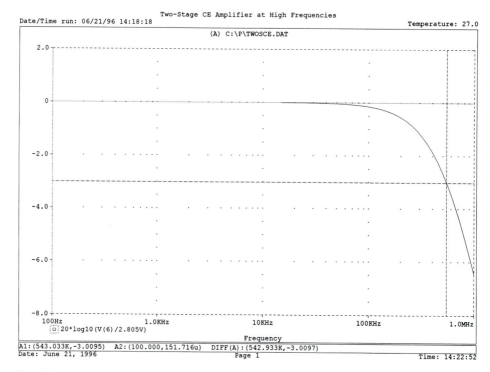

Fig. 4.9

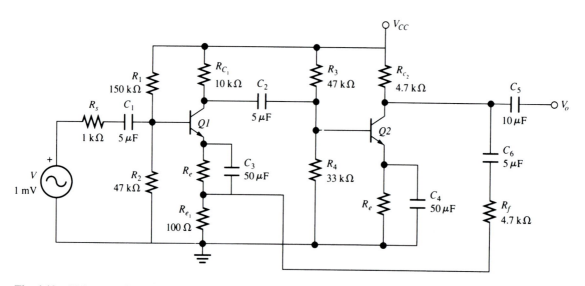

Fig. 4.10   Voltage-series feedback with two *CE* stages.

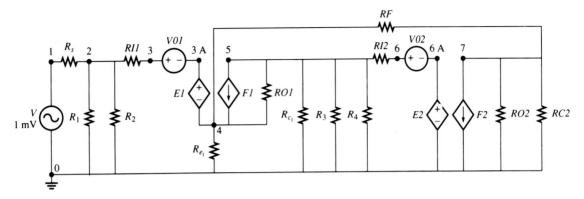

Fig. 4.11 Small-signal, low-frequency model voltage-series feedback, *CE*.

voltage gain, R_i and R_o. Carefully label each node; then create the input file. Compare your file with the one given here:

```
Small-signal Model Voltage-series Feedback, CE Pair
V  1  0  1mV
VO1  3  3A  0
VO2  6  6A  0
E1  3A  4  5  4  2.5E-4
E2  6A  0  7  0  2.5E-4
F1  5  4  VO1  50
F2  7  0  VO2  50
RS  1  2  1k
R1  2  0  150k
R2  2  0  47k
RI1  2  3  1.1k
RE1  4  0  100
RO1  5  4  40k
RC1  5  0  10k
R3  5  0  47k
R4  5  0  33k
RI2  5  6  1.1k
RO2  7  0  40k
RC2  7  0  4.7k
RF  7  4  4.7k
.TF  V(7)  V
.OP
.END
```

Run the analysis and produce a printed copy of the output file. With careful editing of unnecessary lines, you should be able to print the results on a single page. Refer to Fig. 4.12 for comparison with your results. The analysis shows that V(7)/ V = 43.58. This is the overall voltage gain. From the result $R'_o = 148.6\ \Omega$, verify that $R_o = 153.5\ \Omega$ with the load removed. From the result $R'_i = 27.29\ k\Omega$, verify that $R_i = 99.01\ k\Omega$ at the base of the first transistor.

How do the results of the analysis using feedback compare with those obtained when R_f is removed? Simply run the analysis again with the *RF* statement omitted. The results show V(7)/V = 1223, $R_o = 42.9\ k\Omega$, and $R_i = 6.06\ k\Omega$. See Fig. 4.13.

```
Small-signal Model Voltage-series Feedback, CE Pair

V 1 0 1mV
V01 3 3A 0
V02 6 6A 0
E1 3A 4 5 4 2.5E-4
E2 6A 0 7 0 2.5E-4
F1 5 4 V01 50
F2 7 0 V02 50
RS 1 2 1k
R1 2 0 150k
R2 2 0 47k
RI1 2 3 1.1k
RE1 4 0 100
RO1 5 4 40k
RC1 5 0 10k
R3 5 0 47k
R4 5 0 33k
RI2 5 6 1.1k
RO2 7 0 40k
RC2 7 0 4.7k
RF 7 4 4.7k
.TF V(7) V
.OP
.OPT nopage
.END

     NODE    VOLTAGE     NODE    VOLTAGE     NODE    VOLTAGE     NODE    VOLTAGE
    (   1)    .0010    (   2) 963.4E-06   (   3) 952.7E-06   (   4) 953.0E-06
    (   5)-416.6E-06   (   6) 10.89E-06   (   7)    .0436    (  3A) 952.7E-06
    (  6A) 10.89E-06

       VOLTAGE SOURCE CURRENTS
       NAME         CURRENT
       V           -3.664E-08
       V01          9.719E-09
       V02         -3.886E-07

       TOTAL POWER DISSIPATION   3.66E-11  WATTS

     ****       OPERATING POINT INFORMATION     TEMPERATURE =    27.000 DEG C

    **** VOLTAGE-CONTROLLED VOLTAGE SOURCES
    NAME         E1          E2
    V-SOURCE   -3.424E-07   1.089E-05
    I-SOURCE    9.719E-09  -3.886E-07

    **** CURRENT-CONTROLLED CURRENT SOURCES
    NAME         F1          F2
    I-SOURCE    4.860E-07  -1.943E-05

     ****       SMALL-SIGNAL CHARACTERISTICS

         V(7)/V =  4.358E+01

         INPUT RESISTANCE AT V =  2.729E+04

         OUTPUT RESISTANCE AT V(7) =  1.486E+02
```

Fig. 4.12

```
Small-signal Model Voltage-series Feedback, CE Pair (with RF removed)

V 1 0 1mV
V01 3 3A 0
V02 6 6A 0
E1 3A 4 5 4 2.5E-4
E2 6A 0 7 0 2.5E-4
F1 5 4 V01 50
F2 7 0 V02 50
RS 1 2 1k
R1 2 0 150k
R2 2 0 47k
RI1 2 3 1.1k
RE1 4 0 100
R01 5 4 40k
RC1 5 0 10k
R3 5 0 47k
R4 5 0 33k
RI2 5 6 1.1k
RO2 7 0 40k
RC2 7 0 4.7k
.TF V(7) V
.OP
.OPT nopage
.END

NODE    VOLTAGE      NODE    VOLTAGE      NODE    VOLTAGE      NODE    VOLTAGE
(    1)     .0010   (    2) 838.3E-06  (    3) 686.3E-06  (    4) 688.0E-06
(    5)    -.0061   (    6) 305.9E-06  (    7)   1.2235   (   3A) 686.3E-06
(   6A) 305.9E-06

      VOLTAGE SOURCE CURRENTS
      NAME          CURRENT
      V             -1.617E-07
      V01            1.382E-07
      V02           -5.818E-06

      TOTAL POWER DISSIPATION   1.62E-10  WATTS

**** VOLTAGE-CONTROLLED VOLTAGE SOURCES
NAME          E1            E2
V-SOURCE     -1.695E-06    3.059E-04
I-SOURCE      1.382E-07   -5.818E-06

**** CURRENT-CONTROLLED CURRENT SOURCES
NAME          F1            F2
I-SOURCE      6.911E-06   -2.909E-04

  ****     SMALL-SIGNAL CHARACTERISTICS

      V(7)/V =  1.223E+03

      INPUT RESISTANCE AT V =  6.186E+03

      OUTPUT RESISTANCE AT V(7) =  4.236E+03
```

Fig. 4.13

TWO-POLE AMPLIFIER MODEL WITH FEEDBACK

As a continuation of the PSpice analysis of frequency response and related topics, consider the circuit of Fig. 4.14. The circuit consists of the resistance, inductance, and capacitance such that it may be used to illustrate important properties of a two-pole

Fig. 4.14   Two-pole circuit
model, amplifier with feedback.

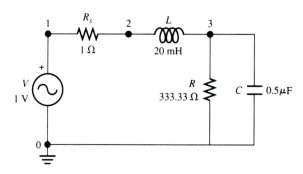

feedback amplifier. Although the circuit does not physically contain the active
devices associated with amplifiers, it nevertheless has the same frequency, phase, and
transient response as an amplifier. Look closely at this circuit, because many of the
terms associated with frequency response and transient response may be better
understood from a simple circuit such as this.

We will begin our analysis by using the following elements: $V = 1$ V, $R_s = 1\ \Omega$,
$L = 20$ mH, $R = 333.33\ \Omega$, and $C = 0.5\ \mu$F. The undamped resonant frequency of
this circuit is given by

$$f_o = \frac{1}{2\pi \sqrt{LC}} = 1.59\ \text{kHz}$$

The angular frequency is

$$\omega_o = 2\pi f_o = 10\ \text{krad/s}$$

Other quantities of interest are $Q = R/(\omega_o L)$ and $k = 1/2Q$ (the damping factor). Later, you will see the effects of changing k by changing R; however, in the
beginning analysis use $R = 333.33\ \Omega$ and $k = 0.3$. It is interesting to look at the frequency response of this two-pole circuit, keeping in mind that it behaves like an
amplifier with feedback. The input file is

```
Two-Pole Circuit Model for Amplifier with Feedback
V 1 0 AC 1
RS 1 2 1
L 2 3 20mH
R 3 0 333.33 Ω
C 3 0 0.5uF
.AC DEC 50 100 10kHz
.PROBE
.END
```

Run the analysis and plot V(3) over the range 100 Hz to 5 kHz. The vertical
axis shows that over a certain range of frequencies, the output voltage V(3) exceeds
the input voltage of 1 V. From the transfer function you find that the peak occurs at
$\omega = \omega_o \sqrt{1 - 2k^2}$. Also the peak value is

$$V_p = \frac{1}{2k \sqrt{1 - k^2}}$$

Calculate what these values should be for this example; then use the cursor mode in Probe to verify these values. The results should indicate a peak at $f = 1.445$ kHz, with $V_p = 1.73$ V. Refer to Fig. 4.15 for this plot.

The next portion of the analysis involves using a step function for the input voltage to see the degree of ringing, or overshoot, associated with this value of k. For this step input voltage, the V statement is changed to include a pulse, *PWL*. The values in parentheses are ordered pairs for time and voltage. Thus at the beginning $(0, 0)$ means that at zero time, the voltage is zero. Then $(0.01\text{ms}, 1)$ means that at 0.01 ms, the voltage is 1 V. The rise is taken to be linear in the time interval. The voltage remains at 1 V until $t = 2$ ms. The *.TRAN* statement uses two values, the first of which deals with the print interval (for printing and plotting) and can be ignored for the Probe analysis. The second value represents the final time, 1 ms. Thus the input file is

```
Transient Response of Two-Pole Circuit Model for Amplifier with Feedback
V 1 0 PWL (0,0 0.01ms,1 2ms,1)
RS 1 2 1
R 3 0 333.33
L 2 3 20mH
C 3 0 0.5uF
.TRAN 0.05ms 1.5ms
.PROBE
.END
```

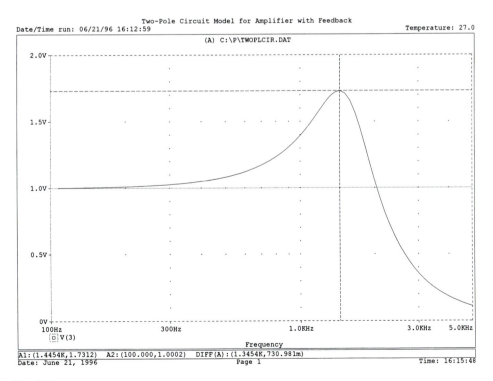

Fig. 4.15

Fig. 4.16 Step response of a two-pole network.

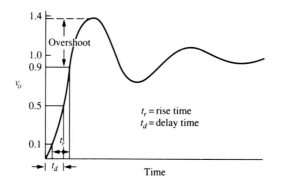

Run the analysis and in Probe plot V(3). Note that the *X*-axis represents time, because you called for a transient analysis. It extends to 1.5 ms. The *Y*-axis shows the overshoot of the circuit with its damped oscillatory response. There are several important times that you will find by using the cursor mode. Refer to Fig. 4.16 for the designation of these times. The time $t_{0.1}$ is the time when the response reaches 0.1 of its final value. The time $t_{0.5}$ is the time when the response reaches 0.5 of its final value (the delay time), and so forth. Using the cursor, verify that $t_{0.1} = 52$ μs, $t_{0.5} = 124$ μs, and $t_{0.9} = 186$ μs. This gives a rise time of $(t_{0.9} - t_{0.1}) = 134$ μs. Also verify that the voltage reaches a peak value of 1.368 V at $t = 326$ μs. Figure 4.17 shows the transient response.

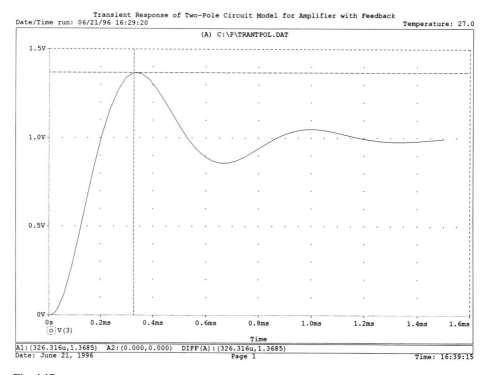

Fig. 4.17

Thus PSpice and Probe have given you information that would be very time consuming to obtain from pencil-and-paper methods. Using such methods, you could hope to find only a few critical points of the plots without enormous effort.

Of equal importance, you can now change the value of k and quickly run another analysis. Return to the input file for frequency response, and change the value of resistance to $R = 141.41\ \Omega$. This is in keeping with the fact that when $2k^2 > 1$, there will be no peak in the frequency response. When $R = 141.41\ \Omega$, $k = 0.707$. Run the frequency analysis with this value of R, and confirm that the response does not peak but begins to drop at a lower frequency. Use other values of k if you would like to continue this analysis. Remember that larger values of R (smaller values of k) will give peaks in the response. Suggested values are $k = 0.4$ and $k = 0.6$.

The transient analysis for each value of k should also be investigated. We have used $k = 0.3$ in the transient analysis. When $k = 0.707$, although there is no peaking in the frequency plot, demonstrate that there is still some overshoot and consequent ringing in the transient response to the step input voltage. According to theory, when $k = 1$, critical damping will be reached and overshoot will be eliminated. This will also mean that the frequency response will show more attenuation for lower frequencies. Run the analysis with $k = 1$, and verify that $t_{0.1} = 59\ \mu s$, $t_{0.5} = 173\ \mu s$, and $t_{0.9} = 403\ \mu s$. Also show that the response is down 3 dB (to 0.707 V) at $f = 1.016$ kHz.

In summary, we have looked at the frequency and transient responses of a two-pole circuit that has the characteristics of a feedback amplifier. Study the results until you have a clear picture of the roles played by Q, k, R, L, and C in the circuit.

CE AMPLIFIER WITH VOLTAGE-SHUNT FEEDBACK

For an actual amplifier example, Fig. 4.18 shows the simplified hybrid-π model for a *CE* amplifier with voltage-shunt feedback. Since we are interested in the high-frequency response, we will use an ac analysis and a frequency range extending from 1 kHz to 10 MHz. The input file is

Fig. 4.18 *CE* amplifier with voltage-shunt feedback.

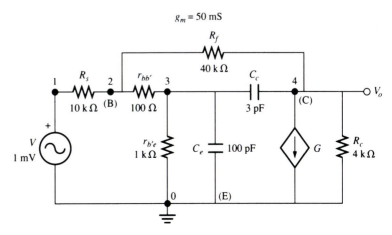

```
CE Amplifier with Voltage-Shunt Feedback
V 1 0 AC 1mV
G 4 0 3 0 50mS
RS 1 2 10k
RBB 2 3 100
RBE 3 0 1k
RF 2 4 40k
RC 4 0 4k
CE 3 0 100pF
CC 3 4 3pF
.AC DEC 40 1kHz 10MEGHz
.PROBE
.END
```

Run the analysis; then verify using the cursor mode that V(4) = 3.199 mV in the midfrequency range. With that knowledge, remove the trace and plot

$$20*\log10(V(4)/3.2mV)$$

Use the cursor to find the 3 dB point at $f = 1.37$ MHz.

To demonstrate the effect of R_f on the circuit, remove the input-file statement for RF and run the analysis again. Verify that with R_f removed, V(4) = 18.02 mV at midfrequencies and that the 3 dB point is at $f = 246$ kHz. As you expect from your study of feedback, R_f stabilizes the circuit, producing a lower voltage gain and a larger bandwidth.

CURRENT-SHUNT FEEDBACK TWO-STAGE *CE* AMPLIFIER

To further illustrate the effects of feedback over a range of frequencies, Fig. 4.19 shows a current-shunt feedback pair of *CE* stages. The hybrid-π simplified model is again chosen, and $R_f = 1.2$ kΩ is used between the emitter of Q_2 and the base of Q_1. Use this input file to run the analysis:

```
Current-Shunt Feedback Pair
I 0 1 AC 1mA
G1 3 0 2 0 50mS
```

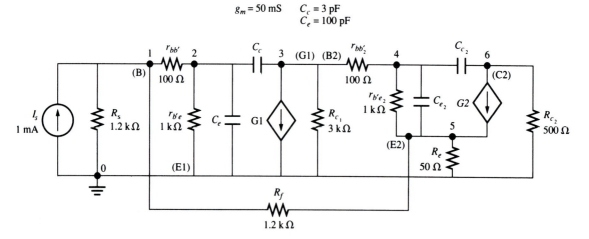

Fig. 4.19   Current-shunt feedback pair, *CE* amplifier.

```
G2  6  5  4  5  40mS
RS  1  0  1.2k
RBB  1  2  100
RBE  2  0  1k
RC1  3  0  3k
RBB2  3  4  100
RBE2  4  5  1k
RE  5  0  50
RC2  6  0  500
RF  5  1  1.2k
CE  2  0  100pF
CC  2  3  3pF
CE2  4  5  100pF
CC2  4  6  3pF
.AC DEC 40 10kHz 100MEGHz
.PROBE
.END
```

Verify in Probe that I(RC2) = 22.82 mA (which is 27.16 dB above I_s) at mid-frequencies with a current peak of 26.35 mA at f = 6.68 MHz. Then use

$$20*\log10(I(RC2)/22.82mA)$$

to obtain the dB plot of the output current. In order to see the peak more clearly, let the X-axis extend from 10 kHz to 20 MHz, and let the Y-axis go from −5 to 5. Use the cursor to verify that the −3 dB point is at f = 11.73 MHz. The plot should look like Fig. 4.20.

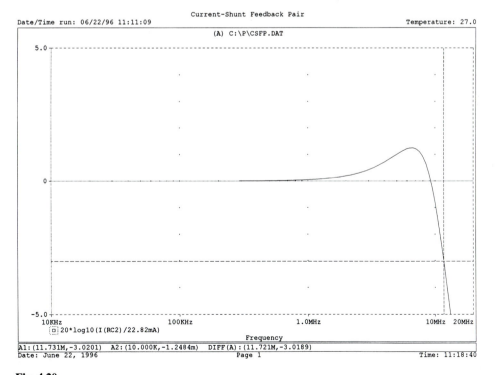

Fig. 4.20

Run the analysis with R_f removed from the circuit to show that I(RC2) = 508.9 mA at midfrequencies without the feedback path.

THREE-STAGE *CE* AMPLIFIER FREQUENCY RESPONSE

We will now look at a case study of a three-stage *CE* amplifier. The circuit is too difficult to analyze without the help of a computer. We will find that SPICE comes to our aid, allowing for an in-depth analysis of the circuit with various parameters. First, we will look at the frequency response of the amplifier without feedback. After that we will introduce a feedback resistor, connected between the collector of the last stage and the base of the first stage. Finally, we will see what needs to be done to correct a problem with severe peaking of the feedback amplifier.

The circuit is shown in Fig. 4.21. Again the simplified hybrid-π model is used for each transistor. For simplicity, the load resistor of each stage is chosen as 2 kΩ. Actually, the load resistor of each of the first two stages represents the parallel combination of biasing and collector resistors. The source is $V = 0.1$ mV, with $R_s = 50 \ \Omega$. The input file is

```
Three-Stage CE Amplifier Frequency Response
V 1 0 AC 0.1mV
G1 4 0 3 0 50mS
G2 6 0 5 0 50mS
G3 8 0 7 0 50mS
RS 1 2 50
RBB1 2 3 100
RBE1 3 0 1k
RL1 4 0 2k
RBB2 4 5 100
RBE2 5 0 1k
RL2 6 0 2k
RBB3 6 7 100
RE3 7 0 1k
RL3 8 0 2k
CE1 3 0 100pF
CC1 3 4 3pF
```

$$g_m = 50 \text{ mS} \quad C_c = 3 \text{ pF} \quad R_s = 50 \ \Omega$$
$$r_{b'e} = 1 \text{ k}\Omega \quad C_e = 100 \text{ pF} \quad R_{L_1} = 2 \text{ k}\Omega$$
$$r_{b'b} = 100 \ \Omega \quad R_{L_2} = 2 \text{ k}\Omega$$
$$R_{L_3} = 2 \text{ k}\Omega$$

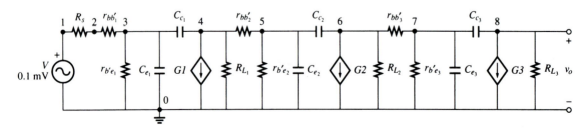

Fig. 4.21   Three-stage *CE* amplifier frequency response.

```
CE2 5 0 100pF
CC2 5 6 3pF
CE3 7 0 100pF
CC3 7 8 3pF
.AC DEC 20 10kHz 1MEGHz
.PROBE
.END
```

Run the analysis, showing that V(8) = 9.046 V at midfrequencies. Then plot

$$20*log10(V(8)/9.05V)$$

and check to see that the −3 dB point is located at f = 419 kHz. The gain is probably considerably greater than needed, and the frequency response is somewhat limited compared to what it might be with feedback. Refer to Fig. 4.22 for comparison with your results.

Effects of Circuit Modifications

The second portion of the analysis will be performed with a slightly modified circuit. Change the voltage source to a current source, based on the Norton equivalent, and change the load resistor to let R_{L3} = 50 Ω. The modifications give

```
I 2 0 AC 2uA
RS 2 0 50
RL3 8 0 50
.AC DEC 20 10kHz 10MEGHz
```

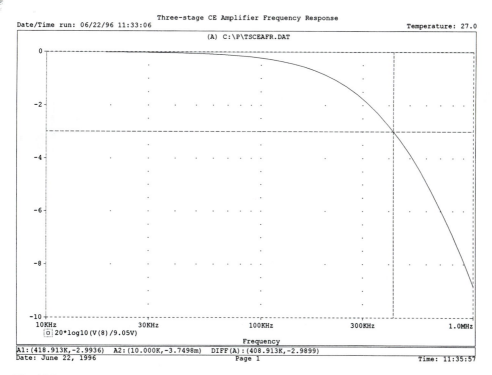

Fig. 4.22

Note that the *RS* statement was changed because node *1* has been eliminated. Refer to Fig. 4.23 for this detail. Run the analysis and verify that I(RL3) = 4.52 mA at midfrequencies. Then using

$$20*log10(I(RL3)/4.53mA)$$

to obtain the dB plot, verify that the response is down 3 dB at $f = 777$ kHz. This simply demonstrates that the smaller value of *RL* extends the bandwidth.

Three-Stage Amplifier with Voltage-Shunt Feedback

Next, consider a more significant change. Insert a feedback resistor, $R_f = 5$ kΩ, between nodes *8* and *2*, that is, from the collector of stage *3* back to the base of stage *1*. This produces voltage-shunt feedback, which you have seen in previous examples. Modify the input file by adding the statement for R_f:

```
RF 8 2 5k
```

Then run the analysis to $f = 20$ MHz, verifying that I(RL3) = 191 μA at midfrequencies. This leads to the desired trace, which is

$$20*log10(IRL3)/191\mu A)$$

Adjust the *Y*-axis range to run from -20 to 20 dB. Verify that the current peak is 17.89 dB at $f_p = 7.94$ MHz. Also show that the -3 dB point is at $f = 11.16$ MHz. Fig. 4.24 shows this trace.

The sudden, steep rise in the output response is, of course, undesirable. Consider eliminating this feature by placing a suitable capacitor across the feedback resistor, R_f. The capacitor will introduce another zero into the gain expression. The obvious choice for the location of this zero is at f_p. This is accomplished using $C_f = 1/2\pi R_f f_p$. Using $f_p = 8$ MHz gives $C_f = 4$ pF. Insert the statement

```
CF 8 2 4pF
```

in the input file and run the analysis again. Your Probe results should show a gain response that is almost flat well beyond the former peak location, with a peak of 0.652 dB at $f = 7.9$ MHz and the -3 dB point at $f = 11.62$ MHz. Refer to Fig. 4.25 for this frequency plot.

Fig. 4.23 Modified three-stage *CE* amplifier.

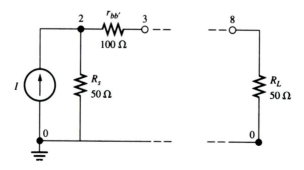

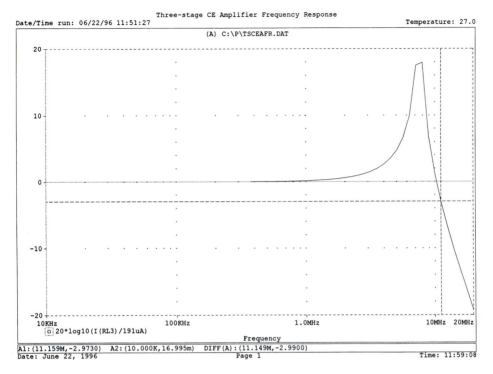

Fig. 4.24

Spend some time looking over the results of these studies. It is important to realize that without the computer as a tool, the analyses would have been far too difficult to attempt.

SUMMARY OF NEW PSPICE TREATMENT USED IN THIS CHAPTER

V[*name*] <+*node*> <−*node*> [*transient specification*]

For example,

```
V 1 0 PWL (0us 0V 1us 1V 1s 1V)
```

means that the voltage source connected between nodes *1* and *0* is a waveform described as *PWL* (piecewise linear). At time = 0, the voltage is zero; then at $t = 1$ μs, $V = 1$ V, and at $t = 1$ s, $V = 1$ V. The progression from one voltage to the next is linear.

Various Forms of Transient Specification

Several forms of transient specifications are available in PSpice for describing independent voltage or current sources. These are useful when the source is not simply dc or ac and you want to run a transient analysis. We will now describe these sources in detail, including simple examples of each.

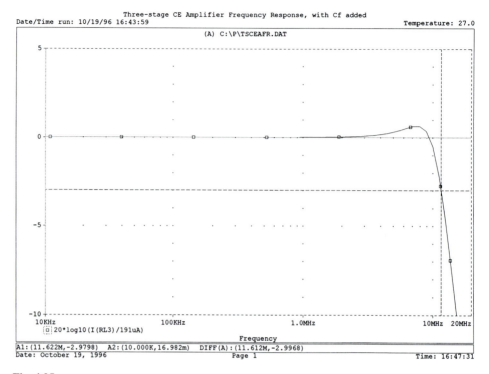

Fig. 4.25

The Exponential Source

This transient specification has the form

exp(<*v1*> <*v2*> <*td1*> <*t1*> <*td2*> <*t2*>)

where

$v1$ = initial voltage

$v2$ = peak voltage

$td1$ = rise delay time

$\tau1$ = rise time constant

$td2$ = fall delay time

$\tau2$ = fall time constant

As an example, consider the following input file:

```
The Exponential Source
V 1 0 exp(2V 12V 2s 1s 7s 1s)
R 1 0 1
.tran 0.1s 12s
.probe
.end
```

Figure 4.26 shows the Probe output of v(1). The trace shows $V = 2$ V as the initial value; then at $t = 2$ s the voltage begins an exponential rise toward 12 V with a rise time constant of $\tau 1 = 1$ s. At $t = 7$ s, the voltage begins to fall exponentially toward its initial voltage with a fall time constant of $\tau 2 = 1$ s. Note that $td1$ and $td2$ are specified with respect to $t = 0$.

The Pulse Source

This transient specification has the form

pulse(<*v1*> <*v2*> <*td*> <*tr*> <*tf*> <*pw*> <*per*>)

where

$v1$	=	initial voltage
$v2$	=	pulsed voltage
td	=	delay time
tr	=	rise time
tf	=	fall time
pw	=	pulse width
per	=	the period if the wave recurs

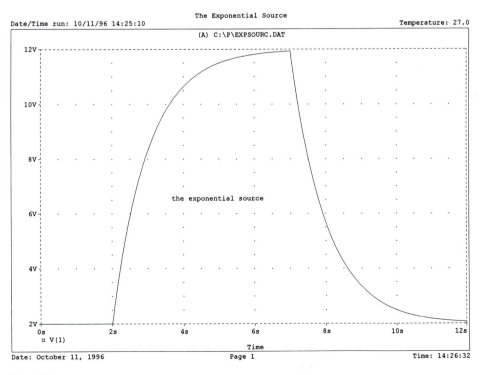

Date/Time run: 10/11/96 14:25:10   The Exponential Source   Temperature: 27.0

(A) C:\P\EXPSOURC.DAT

the exponential source

□ V(1)

Time

Date: October 11, 1996   Page 1   Time: 14:26:32

Fig. 4.26

For example, look at this input file:

```
The Pulse Source
V 1 0 pulse (0 5V 0.5ms 0.1ms 0.1ms 0.8ms 2ms)
R 1 0 1
.tran 0.02ms 4ms
.probe
.end
```

Figure 4.27 shows the Probe output of v(1). The trace shows $V = 0$ V until 0.5 ms (the delay time); then the voltage rises toward 5 V with a rise time of 0.1 ms. The pulse width is 0.8 ms, followed by a fall time of 0.1 ms. The period is 2 ms, after which the pulse repeats. Note the slope on both the leading and the trailing edges of the pulse; this is due to the rise and fall times of 0.1 ms.

The Piecewise-Linear Source

This transient specification has the form

PWL(<*t1*> <*v1*> <*t2*> <*v2*> · · · <*tn*> <*vn*>)

where *tl* = time associated with voltage *vl*, *t2* = time associated with voltage *v2*, and

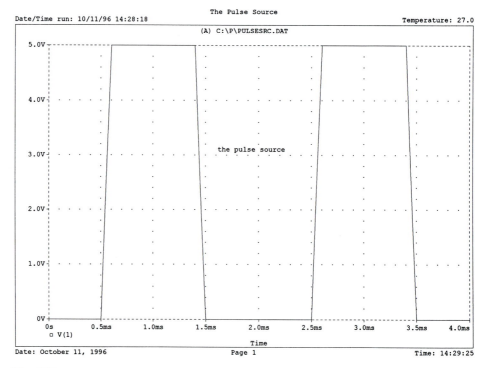

Fig. 4.27

so forth. The progression from one voltage level to another is linear, as you would get by "connecting the dots." As an example, consider this input file:

```
The Piecewise-Linear Source
V 1 0 PWL(0s 0V 0.2s 3V 0.4s 5V 0.6s −5V 0.8s −3V 1s 0V)
R 1 0 1
.tran 0.01s 1s
.probe
.end
```

Figure 4.28 shows the Probe output of v(1). Note that in the *PWL* statement, times are given first, followed by the corresponding voltages. Successive times must be given; the voltages can be either positive or negative values.

The Frequency-Modulated Source

This transient specification has the form

SFFM(*<vo> <va> <fc> <m> <fs>*)

where

vo = offset voltage

va = amplitude of voltage

fc = carrier frequency

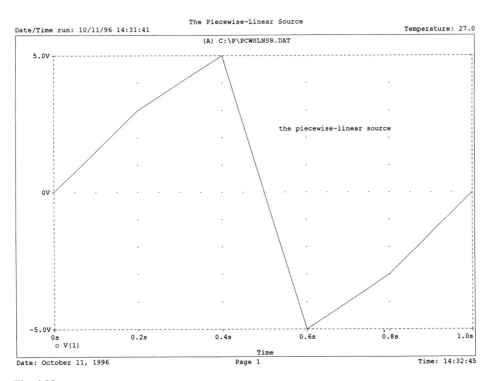

Fig. 4.28

m = index of modulation

fs = signal frequency

For example, look at this input file:

```
Single-Frequency FM Source
V 1 0 sffm(0V 5V 10kHz 3 1kHz)
R 1 0 1
.tran 0.005ms 1ms
.probe
.end
```

Figure 4.29 shows the Probe output of v(1). Since the carrier frequency f_c = 10 kHz, the time display on the X-axis shows 10 cycles of the carrier in the time of 1 ms. The carrier is modulated at the rate determined by the signal frequency and the index of modulation. Note the larger spacing of the waves toward the center of the trace. When a small value of m is used, the shifting of the carrier is less noticeable. When a larger value of m is used, the shifting is more pronounced.

As an exercise, run the SFFM analysis using $m = 6$, and compare the results with those shown here.

The Sine-Wave Source

This transient specification has the form

sin(<vo> <va> <f> <td> <df> <phase>)

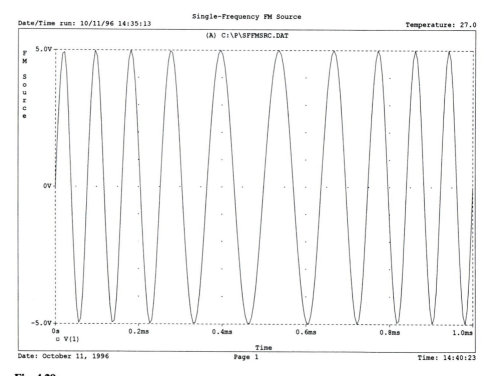

Fig. 4.29

where

vo = offset voltage

va = voltage amplitude

f = frequency

td = time delay

df = damping factor

phase = the phase of the sine wave

An example will clarify the use of this transient specification.

```
The Sine-Wave Source
V 1 0 sin(0.3V 1V 500Hz 0 500 0)
R 1 0 1
.tran 0.06ms 6ms
.probe
.end
```

Figure 4.30 shows the results. The Probe output of v(1) is for 6 ms, representing 3 cycles of the damped sine wave. The damping is of the form

$$e^{-at}$$

where *a* is the damping factor, which in our example is 500. Note that when $t = 2$ ms, this represents

$$e^{-1}$$

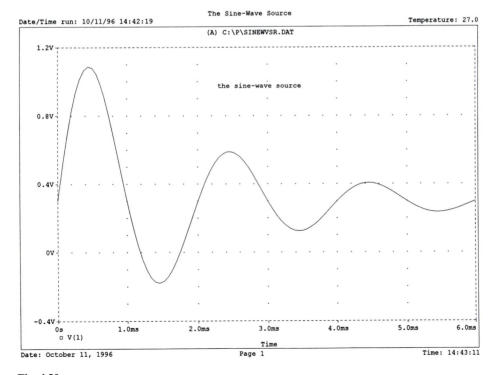

Fig. 4.30

It is obvious that smaller values of a will produce less damping and that when $a = 0$, the wave is undamped.

In summary, the transient specifications for independent sources (voltages or currents) may be shown in a variety of ways. These specifications are designed to be used with transient analyses, requiring the use of the .tran statement in the input file.

PROBLEMS

4.1 As an extension of the low-pass filter shown in Fig. 4.1, Fig. 4.31 shows a circuit with two resistors and two capacitors. Using a PSpice analysis, produce a graph showing magnitude and phase of the output voltage. Identify the 3 dB frequency.

Fig. 4.31

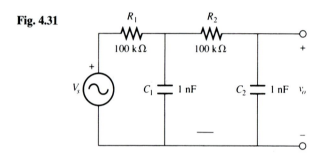

4.2 Analyze the CE amplifier of Fig. 4.5 using the simplified h-parameter model. Compare the results with those obtained using the full h-parameter model.

4.3 Use the simplified h-parameter model with $h_{ie} = 1.1$ kΩ and $h_{fe} = 80$ for each of the two stages of the amplifier shown in Fig. 4.32. Note that the first stage is CE and the second stage is CC. Given $R_s = 100$ Ω, $R_c = 4$ Ω, and $R_e = 2$ kΩ, and with $V_s = 2$ mV, find the output voltage at midfrequencies.

Fig. 4.32

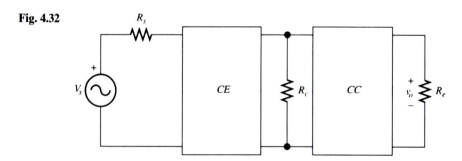

4.4 A cascode amplifier is often used for high-frequency applications. Assume in Fig. 4.33 that both FETs have $g_m = 5$ mS, $r_d = 50$ kΩ, $C_{gs} = 5$ pF, $C_{gd} = 4$ pF, $C_{ds} = 0.5$ pF, $C_1 = C_2 = C_3 = C_4 = 50$ μF, $R_1 = 470$ kΩ, $R_2 = 100$ kΩ, $R_3 = 180$ kΩ, $R_s = 800$ Ω, and $R_d = 4$ kΩ. Find the midfrequency gain of the amplifier and the upper 3 dB frequency based on a PSpice analysis.

Fig. 4.33

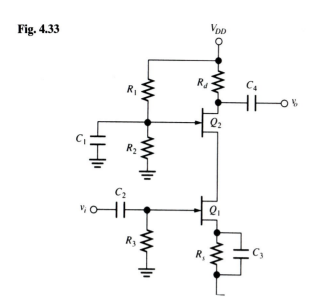

4.5 Use the high-frequency model of the FET with $C_{gs} = 5$ pF, $C_{gd} = 3$ pF, $C_{ds} = 0.4$ pF, $g_m = 6$ mS, and $r_d = 500$ kΩ. A source follower is shown in Fig. 4.34. Using $V_s = 1$ mV, obtain a plot of frequency showing the upper 3 dB point when (a) $R_s = 2$ kΩ and (b) $R_s = 10$ kΩ.

Fig. 4.34

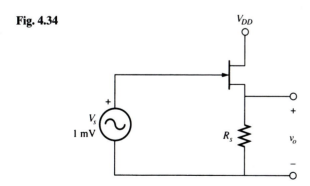

4.6 Use the hybrid-π model for the current-series feedback amplifier shown in Fig. 4.35. Given: $g_m = 50$ mS, $r_{bb'} = 100$ Ω, $r_{b'e} = 1$ kΩ, $C_c = 4$ pF, $C_e = 80$ pF, $r_{ce} = 80$ kΩ. With $R_s = 500$ Ω, $V_s = 1$ mV, and $R_L = 4$ kΩ, plot the frequency response when (a) $R_e = 300$ Ω and (b) $R_e = 500$ Ω.

Fig. 4.35

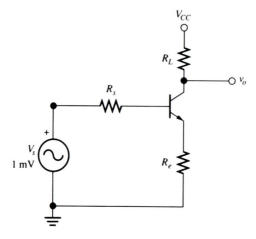

4.7 Figure 4.36 shows an example of voltage-shunt feedback. Use the simplified h-parameter model with $h_{fe} = 100$ and $h_{ie} = 1.1$ kΩ. Given: $R_s = 500$ Ω and $R_e = 4$ kΩ. Find the midfrequency voltage gain and the input and output resistances with $V_s = 1$ mV when (a) $R_f = 27$ kΩ and (b) $R_f = 40$ kΩ.

Fig. 4.36

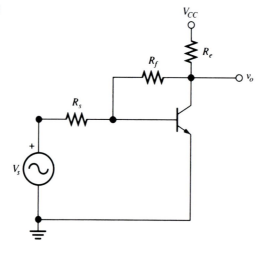

4.8 A CE amplifier uses a shunt-peaking coil as shown in Fig. 4.37(a) to enhance its high-frequency response. The Miller-approximation model of the circuit is shown in Fig. 4.37(b). Given: $R_L = 500$ Ω, $R_1 = 100$ Ω, $R_i = 1.1$ kΩ, $L = 5$ μH, $g_m = 0.2$ mS, and $r_b = 100$ Ω. Using $C_c = 5$ pF and $C_e = 100$ pF, verify that $C_i = 605$ pF. Create a PSpice input file to determine the frequency response of the circuit. Find the midfrequency gain of the amplifier. Compare the upper 3 dB frequencies with and without the peaking coil in the circuit.

Fig. 4.37

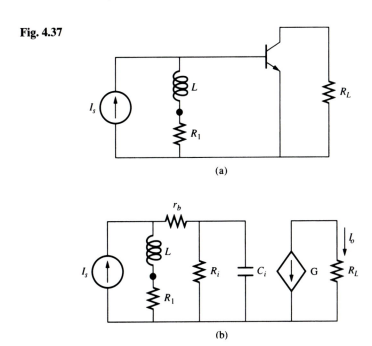

(a)

(b)

4.9 Wiring often introduces series inductance that has an effect on frequency response in an amplifier. In Fig. 4.38 a simplified amplifier model is shown that includes series inductance $L = 0.5$ mH. Run a PSpice analysis to determine the frequency response of the circuit. Given $v = 1$ mV, find v_o over the frequency range from 100 Hz to 10 MHz. For comparison, assume that L is neglected, and run the analysis again.

Fig. 4.38

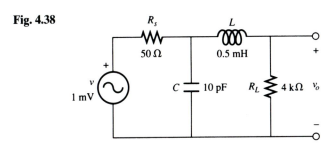

The Operational Amplifier

The operational amplifier (op amp) is an integrated-circuit device widely used in electronics. The actual circuitry is complex and has many features that may or may not be needed in our model. Therefore we will begin with only the essential components and refer to this model as the ideal op amp.

THE IDEAL OPERATIONAL AMPLIFIER

The ideal operational amplifier will be modeled for SPICE as an amplifier with high input resistance, zero output resistance, and high voltage gain. Typical values of these parameters are shown in Fig. 5.1, where $R_i = 1$ GΩ, $A = 200,000$, and $v_o = A(v_2 - v_1)$. Note that v_1 is an inverting input and v_2 is a noninverting input. This model will serve for dc and low-frequency analysis. We will add other features to the model as needed.

Although you do not need SPICE in the analysis of simple op amp circuits, it is desirable to see what information you can obtain even in these situations. There are also some limitations that deserve your attention.

The circuit of Fig. 5.2(a) shows the op amp being used in a negative feedback connection. The feedback resistor, R_2, is connected from the output to v_1, the inverting *minus* input terminal. The noninverting input is grounded. Figure 5.2(b) shows the PSpice version of the circuit. The input file is

```
Ideal Operational Amplifier
VS 1 0 1V
E 3 0 0 2 200E3
RI 2 0 1G
```

Fig. 5.1 The ideal operational amplifier.

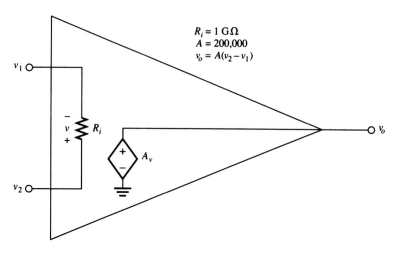

$$R_i = 1 \text{ G}\Omega$$
$$A = 200,000$$
$$v_o = A(v_2 - v_1)$$

Fig. 5.2 The ideal inverting op amp.

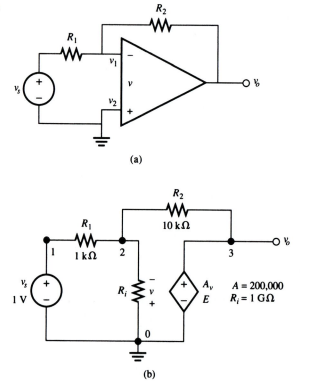

(a)

$$R_2$$
$$10 \text{ k}\Omega$$

$$R_1$$
$$1 \text{ k}\Omega$$

$$v_s$$
$$1 \text{ V}$$

$$A_v$$
$$A = 200,000$$
$$R_i = 1 \text{ G}\Omega$$

(b)

Fig. 5.3 Noninverting ideal op amp.

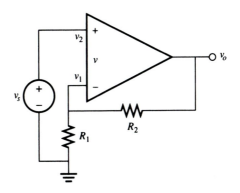

```
R1 1 2 1k
R2 3 2 10k
.OP
.TF V(3) VS
.END
```

Run the analysis and look at the results in the output file. Verify that $V(3)/VS = -9.999$. The gain is very close to -10 and is sometimes approximated as $v_o/v_s = -R_2/R_1$. Using nodal analysis, write the equations required to solve for the ratio v_o/v_s. Demonstrate that the results depend on the value of A and that only when A becomes infinite is the approximation equation correct.

Your analysis should show $R_{in} = 1$ kΩ. Can you explain this? Remember that the inputs to the operational amplifier can be thought of as a virtual ground. This means that the input resistance is seen as R_1.

NONINVERTING IDEAL OPERATIONAL AMPLIFIER

Figure 5.3 shows another simple circuit for the op amp. This circuit has v_s connected to the noninverting (+) input. Figure 5.4 shows the model along with the components. The input file is

Fig. 5.4 Noninverting ideal op amp model.

$A = 200,000$
$R_1 = 1$ kΩ
$R_2 = 9$ kΩ

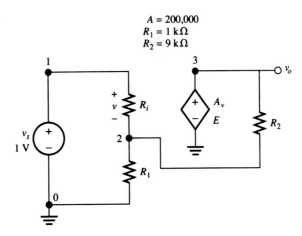

```
Ideal Operational Amplifier, Noninverting
VS 1 0 1V
E 3 0 1 2 200E3
RI 1 2 1G
R1 2 0 1k
R2 3 2 9k
.OP
.TF V(3) VS
.END
```

Verify that V(3)/VS = 10, in keeping with the formula $v_o/v_s = 1 + R_2/R_1$. Also verify that $R_{in} = 2.0E13$. Why is the input resistance so large a value? Since the ideal draws virtually no current, the source v_s sees what appears to be almost an open circuit in this case.

OP AMP GIVING VOLTAGE DIFFERENCE OUTPUT

If the op amp has inputs to both its plus and minus terminals, it may be used to find the difference of these two voltages, with appropriate amplification. To keep the analysis simple, assume that $R_1 = R_3 = 5$ kΩ and $R_2 = R_4 = 10$ kΩ in Fig. 5.5. The SPICE model for the ideal op amp and its external components is shown in Fig. 5.6. The input file is

```
Op Amp Giving Voltage Difference Output
VA 1 0 3V
VB 4 0 10V
E 5 0 3 2 200E3
RI 2 3 1G
R1 1 2 5k
R2 5 2 10k
R3 4 3 5k
R4 3 0 10k
.OP
.TF V(5) VB
.END
```

The analysis will show that V(5) = 14 V. Using nodal analysis on the ideal op amp, you should verify that

$$v_a = \frac{R_2(v_b - v_a)}{R_1}$$

Fig. 5.5   Op amp giving voltage difference output.

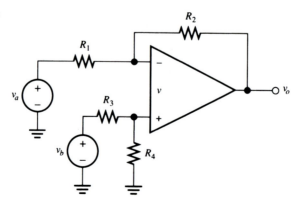

Fig. 5.6 Op amp model for voltage difference.

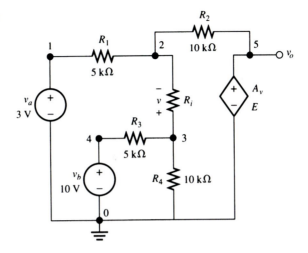

which agrees with our results. A few more pencil-and-paper calculations will give insight. Begin by finding the voltage at the plus input of the op amp. This is easily done when you recall that ideally the op amp inputs draw no current. The voltage v_b divides (using voltage division) to give $v+ = 6.667$ V. This means that $v-$ is also 6.667 V (actually PSpice gives this as 6.666 V). Using this voltage, you can easily find the current through R_1 and R_2. The output file is shown in Fig. 5.7.

Remember that SPICE should not be used simply as a way to get numerical results in problems such as this. It is hoped that you will ask yourself some questions about the results, which will help you learn more about circuit analysis and the devices being investigated.

FREQUENCY RESPONSE OF THE OPERATIONAL AMPLIFIER

When you consider the frequency response of an op amp, you must use a model that accounts for the rolling off that will occur as the frequency increases. Using typical op amp characteristics, we propose the model of Fig. 5.8. Study the model, which includes $R_{in} = 1$ MΩ, $R_o = 50$ Ω, $R_{i1} = 1$ kΩ, $C = 15.92$ μF, and EG with a voltage gain of 100,000. The latter is referred to as A_o, the low-frequency or dc open-loop gain. Using these values, we desire to produce $f_c = 10$ Hz, where f_c represents the frequency at which the open-loop response is down by 3 dB.

In order to verify the design, we will use the circuit of Fig. 5.9, but *without the feedback resistor R_2*. The input file for the test becomes

```
Op Amp Model with 3 dB Frequency at 10 Hz for Open-Loop Gain
VS 2 0 AC 1mV
EG 3 0 2 1 1E5
E 6 0 4 0 1
RI1 3 4 1k
RO 6 5 50
R1 0 1 10k
RL 5 0 22k
RIN 1 2 1MEG
```

```
Op Amp Giving Voltage Difference Output

   ****       CIRCUIT DESCRIPTION

VA 1 0 3V
VB 4 0 10V
E 5 0 3 2 200E3
RI 2 3 1G
R1 1 2 5k
R2 5 2 10k
R3 4 3 5k
R4 3 0 10k
.OP
.OPT nopage
.TF V(5) VB
.END

 NODE    VOLTAGE      NODE   VOLTAGE      NODE   VOLTAGE      NODE   VOLTAGE

 (   1)    3.0000  (    2)    6.6666  (    3)    6.6667  (    4)   10.0000
 (   5)   14.0000

    VOLTAGE SOURCE CURRENTS
    NAME           CURRENT

    VA          7.333E-04
    VB         -6.667E-04

    TOTAL POWER DISSIPATION   4.47E-03   WATTS

 **** VOLTAGE-CONTROLLED VOLTAGE SOURCES

NAME          E
V-SOURCE    1.400E+01
I-SOURCE   -7.333E-04

   ****       SMALL-SIGNAL CHARACTERISTICS

      V(5)/VB =   2.000E+00

      INPUT RESISTANCE AT VB =   1.500E+04

      OUTPUT RESISTANCE AT V(5) =   0.000E+00
```

Fig. 5.7

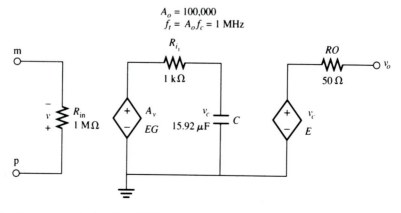

$A_o = 100{,}000$
$f_t = A_o f_c = 1\text{ MHz}$

Fig. 5.8   Op amp mode for $f_c = 10$ Hz.

Fig. 5.9 Frequency response of
op amp model.

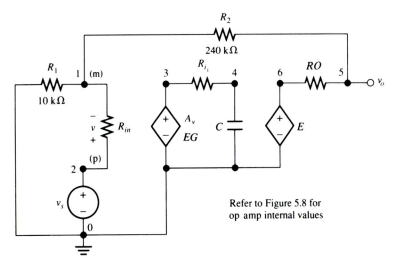

```
C 4 0 15.92uF
.AC DEC 40 1 1MEG
.PROBE
.END
```

Run the simulation and in Probe trace V(5), the output voltage, as shown in Fig.
5.10. As predicted, the output voltage falls from $v_o \approx 100$ V at $f = 1$ Hz to $v_o \approx 70$ V

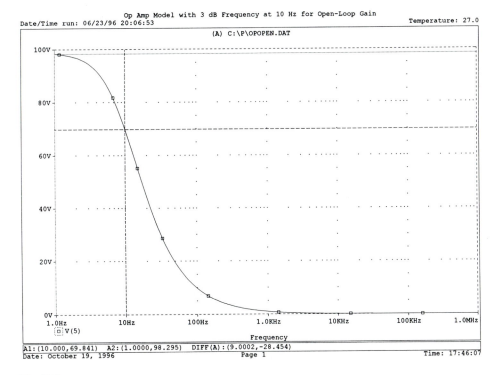

Fig. 5.10

at $f = 10$ Hz. This is the frequency at which the gain is down by 3 dB, as predicted. It is represented by the symbol f_c. The output voltage of almost 100 V corresponds to the open-loop gain $A_o = 100,000$.

To view another aspect of the model op amp circuit, remove the trace of V(5) and trace

$$20*\log10(V(5)/V(2))$$

This decibel plot clearly indicates an attenuation of 20 dB/decade, as shown in Fig. 5.11. Return to the input file and add a line for the resistor R_2, as follows:

```
R2 5 1 240k
```

This becomes a practical circuit with an output voltage limited to a reasonable value. In Probe obtain a trace of v_o, which will now be near 25 mV at midfrequency. Obtain a log trace, or Bode plot, of the output voltage relative to the input voltage as you did previously. The results are shown in Fig. 5.12.

Verify that at midfrequencies the gain $A_{mid} = 27.96$ dB and that the frequency where the gain is down by 3 dB is $f = 39.2$ kHz. In order to check the accuracy of these values, recall that $f_t = A_o f_c$, representing the unity-gain frequency. The model assumes that $f_t = 1$ MHz, which is a typical value for the unity-gain frequency. It also assumes that $f_c = 10$ Hz, giving $A_o = 1E5$. The value of f_c is set by $R_{i1} = 1$ kΩ and $C = 15.92$ μF.

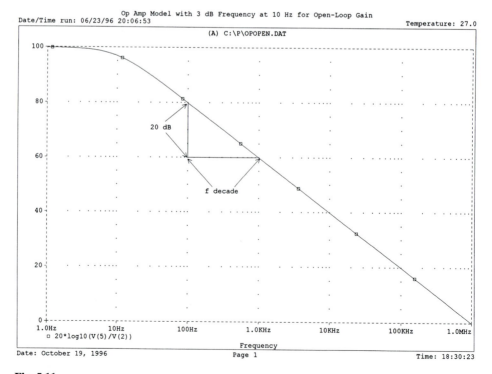

Fig. 5.11

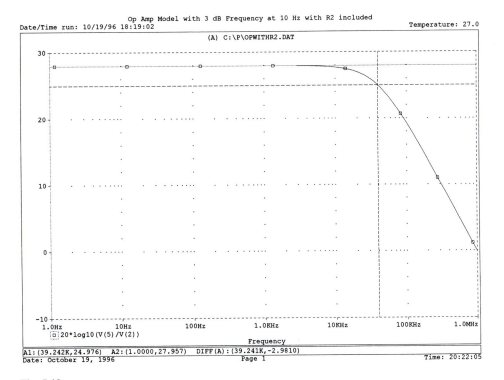

Fig. 5.12

Note that the closed-loop bandwidth is given approximately by $CLBW = f_t\beta$ and

$$\beta = \frac{R_1}{R_1 + R_2}$$

In our example, $\beta = 10/250 = 0.04$, and $f_t\beta = 40$ kHz. This is an approximation and is in close agreement with our model that gave $f = 39.55$ kHz as the 3 dB frequency.

As a further investigation of the model, change the value of the feedback resistor, using $R_2 = 15$ kΩ, and run the analysis again. Verify that $A_{\mathrm{mid}} = 7.959$ dB and $f_{3\mathrm{dB}} = 393.6$ kHz. Using the approximate formula and the new β, what is the predicted value of $f_{3\mathrm{dB}}$?

USING A SUBCIRCUIT FOR THE OPERATIONAL AMPLIFIER

The model we used for the op amp in the previous example contains enough elements to make it a good candidate for use in a subcircuit. This will also serve as an introduction to the concept of subcircuits. The model is shown in Fig. 5.13. Observe that the nodes and the elements are shown using lowercase letters. This is not necessary, since PSpice is not case-sensitive. That is, upper- and lowercase can be used interchangeably. However, to make the subcircuit and its elements easier to identify, we chose lowercase node labels. We chose letters rather than numbers so that

Fig. 5.13 Subcircuit for op amp with nodes designated.

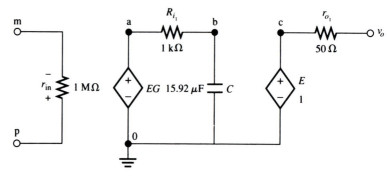

the nodes will not be confused with elements external to the subcircuit. The subcircuit will be given as an independent portion of an input file, but it is not a complete input file in itself. The statements in the subcircuit will be

```
.subckt opamp m p vo
 eg a 0 p m 1e5
 e c 0 b 0 1
 rin m p 1meg
 ril a b 1k
 c b 0 15.92uf
 rol c vo 50
.ends
```

Each subcircuit begins with a *.subckt* statement. The first item in its list is the subcircuit name, which is *opamp* in this example. This is followed by a set of nodes, which link the subcircuit to the rest of the input file. You can think of these as externally available nodes. In this example they are *m, p,* and *v_o.* The reference node is always given as node *0,* and this need not be included in the node list.

Identify the elements in the subcircuit in the usual manner. Since this is a subcircuit and not a complete input file, it does not matter that some of the nodes appear to be floating. The element statements are indented to make them easy to identify, but this is not a requirement. Finally, the statement *.ends* marks the end of the subcircuit.

Now you are ready to look at a new version of the analysis of the op amp using the subcircuit. The complete circuit is shown in Fig. 5.9 and is repeated as Fig. 5.14. After you have more experience, you may want to represent the subcircuit simply by using a box or a triangle. In the figure you will see that the nodes *m, p,* and *v_o* have new designations. These are called nodes *1, 2,* and *3,* respectively. In order to use the subcircuit, the main circuit file must contain a statement such as this:

```
X 1 2 3 opamp
```

The *X* designates a subcircuit call. Nodes *1, 2,* and *3* are in the proper order to conform to nodes *m, p,* and *v_o* in the subcircuit. This allows the subcircuit to receive the node designation being passed from the main circuit file. The statement also contains the subcircuit name, *opamp.* Now look at the entire input file:

```
Op Amp Analysis Using Subcircuit
VS 2 0 AC 1mV
R1 1 0 10k
```

Fig. 5.14 Model showing subcircuit to be called by main circuit.

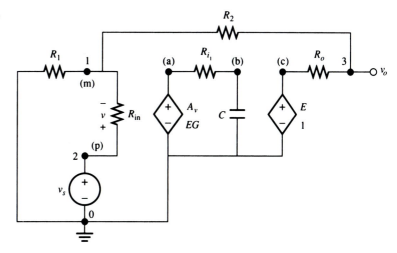

```
R2  3  1  240k
X  1  2  3  opamp
.AC DEC 40 100 1MEG
.PROBE

.subckt opamp m p vo
 eg a 0 p m 1e5
 e c 0 b 0 1
 rin m p 1meg
 ril a b 1k
 c b 0 15.92uf
 rol c vo 50
.ends
.END
```

Run the analysis and verify that it gives the same result as the previous analysis in which the subcircuit was not used.

OP AMP DIFFERENTIATOR CIRCUIT

A differentiator circuit based on an ideal op amp is shown in Fig. 5.15. With the inverting input at a potential of zero volts, $v_c = v$. It is easily shown that with $R = 0.5\,\Omega$,

$$v_o = \frac{-dv}{dt}$$

Thus when the input voltage is a triangle as shown in Fig. 5.15(b), the output should be a square wave. Use this input file to test the conclusion:

```
Differentiator Circuit
v 1 0 PWL (0, 0 1s, 1V 2s, 0)
C 1 2 2
R 2 3 0.5
X 2 0 3 iop
.subckt iop m p vo
 ri m p 1meg
```

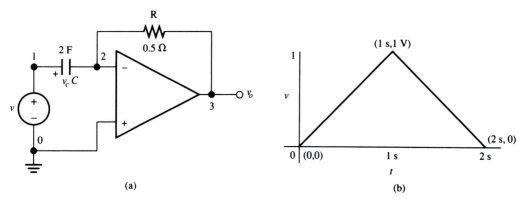

Fig. 5.15   Differentiator using ideal op amp.

```
 e vo 0 p m 2e5
.ends
.TRAN 0.05s 2s
.PROBE
.END
```

Run the analysis and verify that the output is a square wave alternating from −1.0 V to 1 V. The polarity of the output voltage indicates the inversion that takes place in the op amp also. Plot v(3) along with v(1). Refer to Fig. 5.16 for the results.

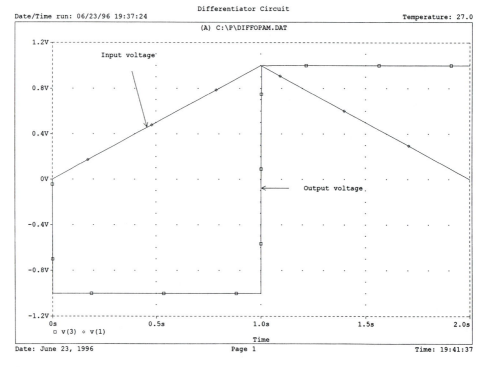

Fig. 5.16

Note that the input-file statement for *C* should *not* be given as

```
C 1 2 2F
```

where the *F* is intended to represent farads. The *F* will be taken as a prefix, giving the value of 2 fF (femtofarads). If you like to use unit symbols whenever possible, you might use this alternative form:

```
C 1 2 2E6UF
```

OP AMP INTEGRATOR CIRCUIT

The counterpart of the differentiator is the integrator. In the circuit of Fig. 5.17(a) the positions of *R* and *C* are interchanged when compared with Fig. 5.15. The new circuit is an (inverting) integrator. In order to test its properties, use the waveshape shown in Fig. 5.17(b) and this input file:

```
Integrator Circuit
v 1 0 PWL (0 0 0.01ms, −1V 1s, −1V 1000.01ms, 0V 2s, 0V 2000.01ms, 1V
+ 3s, 1V)
R 1 2 0.5
C 2 3 2
X 2 0 3 iop
.subckt iop m p vo
 ri m p 1meg
 e vo 0 p m 2e5
.ends
```

Fig. 5.17 Integrator using ideal op amp.

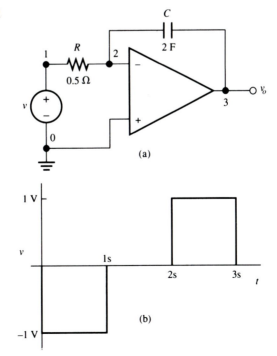

(a)

(b)

```
.tran 0.05s 3s
.probe
.end
```

Run the analysis and plot v(1) along with v(3). Verify that the output starts out as a ramp, reaching a peak value of 1 V, then begins to fall back to zero between 2 s and 3 s. Refer to Fig. 5.18 for the results.

As an additional exercise, use the input waveform from the differentiator example and see what output voltage you obtain. Verify its parabolic shape with a final value of −1 V. Figure 5.19 shows this plot.

RESPONSE TO UNIT STEP FUNCTION

A unit step function is shown in Fig. 5.20(b). By definition, it remains at zero volts until $t = 0$, and from that time forward it is 1 V. The circuit shown in Fig. 5.20(a) has for its external components $R = 2\ \Omega$, $R_1 = 1\ \Omega$, and $C = 0.125$ F. An analysis of the circuit shows that

$$v_o(t) = (3 - 2e^{-4t})u(t)$$

You may want to sketch this response before beginning the PSpice analysis, in order to know what you will be looking for. The input file is

```
Response to Unit Step Function
vs 1 0 PWL (0, 0 1us, 1V 5s, 1V)
```

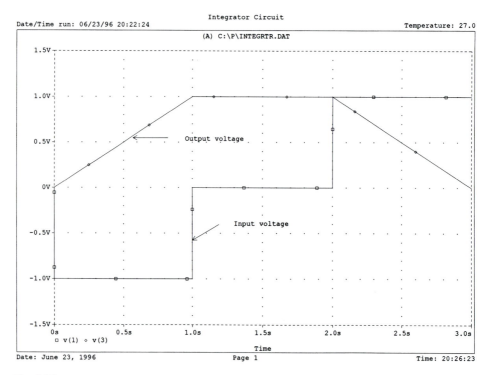

Fig. 5.18

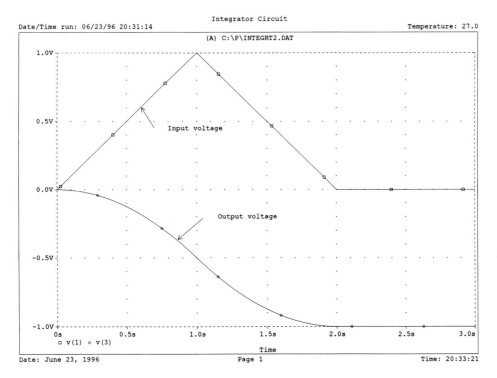

Fig. 5.19

```
C  2  3  0.125
R  2  3  2
R1 2  0  1
X  2  1  3  iop
.subckt iop m p vo
  ri  m  p  1meg
  e  vo  0  p  m  2e5
.ends
.TRAN 0.05s 3s
.PROBE
.END
```

When you run the Probe analysis verify, using the cursor, that at $t = 0.5$ s, $v_o = 2.73$ V. This is in agreement with the equation given for this circuit. The results are shown in Fig. 5.21.

DOUBLE OP AMP CIRCUIT

Unless there is a need to use a device such as the op amp more than once in an input file, there is little to gain by setting up the subcircuit. But in some situations, there may be several of the same devices. In these cases, it is much easier to work with the subcircuit. Suppose that you would like to compare the frequency responses of the two op amp circuits we looked at previously (in the section "Frequency Response

Fig. 5.20 Response of first-order circuit to unit step function.

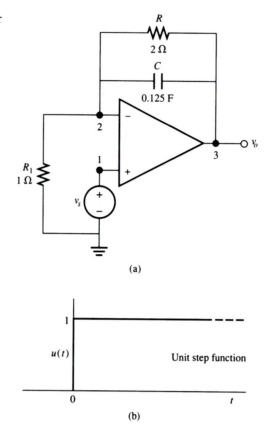

(a)

(b)

of the Operational Amplifier"). Recall that the circuits were alike except that in the first case R_2 was 240 kΩ, while in the second case R_2 was 15 kΩ. By looking at their frequency characteristics on the same graph, you can get a better comparison.

In order to do this, simply extend the circuit so that both cases are covered at the same time. We will define the op amp in the subcircuit and use Fig. 5.22 to provide for easy identification of the nodes. Note that the *Op1* and *Op2* are shown merely as triangles, but because you are already familiar with their model, there is no need to repeat the internal details. Now your input file is easily obtained:

```
Double Op Amp Circuit for Gain-Bandwidth Analysis
VS1 2 0 AC 1mV
R1 1 0 10k
R2 3 1 240k
X1 1 2 3 opamp
VS2 5 0 AC 1mV
R3 4 0 10k
R4 6 4 15k
X2 4 5 6 OPAMP
.AC DEC 40 100 10MEG
.PROBE
.subckt opamp m p vo
   eg a 0 p m 1e5
```

Fig. 5.21

```
e  c  0  b  0  1
rin  m  p  1meg
ril  a  b  1k
c  b  0  15.92uf
rol  c  vo  50
.ends
.END
```

The subcircuit is described as before. Once you develop the subcircuit, you can merely copy it into any input file where it is needed. It is called twice, first by the *X1* statement, then next by the *X2* statement. The list of nodes used in each case is in keeping with Fig. 5.22.

Run the analysis; then plot

$$20*\log 10(V(3)/V(2))$$

and

$$20*\log 10(V(6)/V(5))$$

Use the cursor mode to find the 3 dB point of the first trace. Note that the first trace is automatically selected when you use the cursor mode. Verify that $A_{mid} = 27.96$ dB and $f_{3dB} = 39.8$ kHz.

Now follow the second trace with the cursor. Press [*Ctrl*] [*Rt arrow*] to activate the cursor for the second trace. Then move along the second trace until you find the

Fig. 5.22 Double op amp circuit.

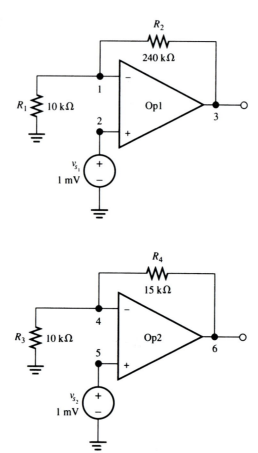

desired information. Note that the second trace shows A_{mid} = 7.96 dB, which is down 20 dB from the first trace. The frequency to look for will correspond to a gain of 4.96 dB (7.96 − 3.00). Verify that this gives f_{3dB} = 398 kHz. These results are in agreement with the previous examples. Refer to Fig. 5.23 for this double plot.

ACTIVE FILTERS

Active filters can be used to provide low-pass, high-pass, and band-pass filters with improved cutoff properties when compared with simple single-pole filters, which contain only a single capacitor, for example. The Butterworth filter serves as a classic example of an active filter.

  We often use the operational amplifier in the construction of active filters because it is available with high gain–bandwidth products. We will not attempt to include the theory of filters in this discussion. If you are studying active filters for the first time, refer to a good reference to understand better the elegance and simplicity of these circuits.

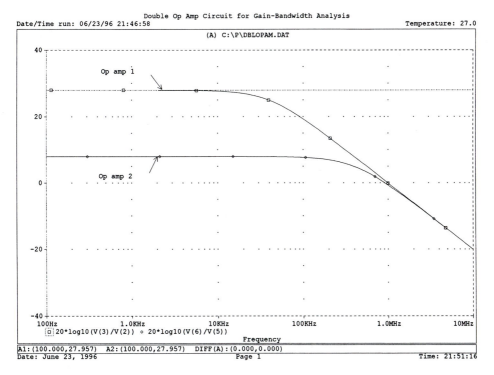

Fig. 5.23

Second-Order Butterworth Low-Pass Filter

Using a table of normalized Butterworth polynomials, we find these factors for the second-order filter:

$$s^2 + 1.414s + 1$$

The second-order filter is shown in Fig. 5.24. For an introductory example, we would like to find the elements R_1, R_2, R, and C for a Butterworth filter with a cutoff frequency at $f_c = 5$ kHz. As usual, the cutoff frequency is taken as the frequency at which the response is down by 3 dB. According to theory, the low-frequency gain is given by

$$A_{vo} = 3 - 2k$$

where k represents the damping factor, defined as half the coefficient of s in the quadratic given from the Butterworth polynomial table.* For this example, $k = 0.707$ and

$$A_{vo} = 3 - 1.414 = 1.586$$

---

*See Hillburn and Johnson. *Manual of Active Filter Designs*, McGraw-Hill, 1973.

Fig. 5.24 Second-order Butterworth filter, low pass.

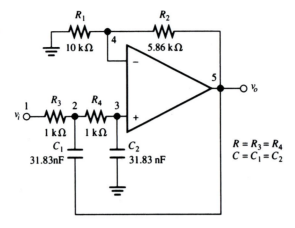

Let $R_1 = 10 \text{ k}\Omega$. Since

$$A_{vo} = \frac{R_1 + R_2}{R_1}$$

then $R_2 = 5.86 \text{ k}\Omega$. If we let $R = 1 \text{ k}\Omega$, then since $f_c = 1/(2\pi RC)$, we find $C = 31.83 \text{ nF}$. To test the Butterworth theory, use the ideal model of the op amp as a subcircuit, as shown in Fig. 5.25. Now construct the input file as follows:

```
Second-Order Butterworth Filter
VI 1 0 AC 1mV
R3 1 2 1k
R4 2 3 1k
R1 4 0 10k
R2 5 4 5.86k
C1 2 5 31.83nF
C2 3 0 31.83nF
X 4 3 5 iop
.AC DEC 40 1 100kHz
.PROBE
.subckt iop m p vo
  e vo 0 p m 2e5
```

Fig. 5.25 Ideal op amp subcircuit.

```
.subckt iop m p vo
  e vo 0 p m 2e5
  rin m p 1meg
.ends
```

$v_o = A(v_p - v_m)$

$A = 200,000$

```
rin m p 1meg
.ends
.END
```

Run the analysis and plot $V(5)/V(1)$. Check to see that $A_{vo} = 1.586$, in agreement with our prediction. Then remove the trace and plot

$$20*\log 10(V(5)/(V(1)*1.587V))$$

to confirm that $f_c = 5$ kHz. This second-order filter should have about twice the attenuation rate of a first-order filter. Recall that a first-order filter has an attenuation rate of 20 dB/decade. Verify that at $f = 10$ kHz, A_v is down 12.31 dB, and at $f = 100$ kHz, A_v is down by 52.05 dB. This is approximately 40 dB/decade. This plot is shown in Fig. 5.26.

Fourth-Order Butterworth Low-Pass Filter

For another example, consider a fourth-order Butterworth filter designed to give $f_c = 1$ kHz. From the polynomial table, we find these factors:

$$(s^2 + 0.765s + 1)\ (s^2 + 1.848s + 1)$$

The damping factor k is half the coefficient of s in each quadratic factor, giving $k_1 = 0.383$ and $k_2 = 0.924$.

$$A_{v1} = 3 - 2k_1 = 3 - 0.765 = 2.235 \text{ and } A_{v2} = 3 - 2k_2 = 1.152$$

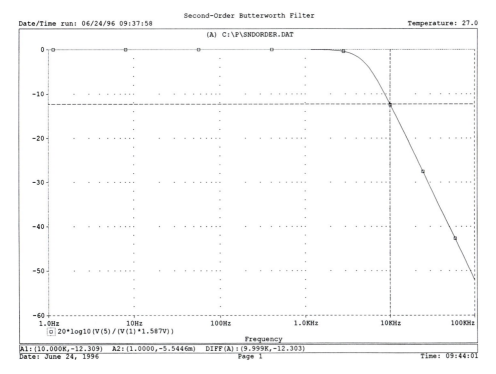

Fig. 5.26

For the first stage, let $R_1 = 10$ kΩ, and using

$$A_{v1} = \frac{R_1 + R_2}{R_1}$$

we find that $R_2 = 12.35$ kΩ. For the second stage, let $R_1 = 10$ kΩ, giving $R_2 = 1.52$ kΩ. For $f_c = 1$ kHz, if we let $R = 1$ kΩ, then $C = 0.16$ μF. The circuit is shown in Fig. 5.27. Note that since each element must have a unique designation, the R and C values shown are expanded from those given here. The input file becomes

```
Fourth-Order Butterworth Filter
VI 1 0 AC 1mV
R3 1 2 1k
R4 2 3 1k
R1 4 0 10k
R2 5 4 12.35k
R7 5 6 1k
R8 6 7 1k
R5 8 0 10k
R6 9 8 1.52k
C1 2 5 0.16uF
C2 3 0 0.16uF
C3 6 9 0.16uF
C4 7 0 0.16uF
.AC DEC 40 1 10kHz
.PROBE
.subckt iop m p vo
 e vo 0 p m 2e5
 rin m p 1meg
.ends
X1 4 3 5 iop
X2 8 7 9 iop
.END
```

Run the analysis; then make traces together for V(5)/V(1), V(9)/V(5), and V(9)/V(1). These represent the gain of the first stage, the gain of the second stage, and the overall gain, respectively. Since these are not decibel plots, you should be

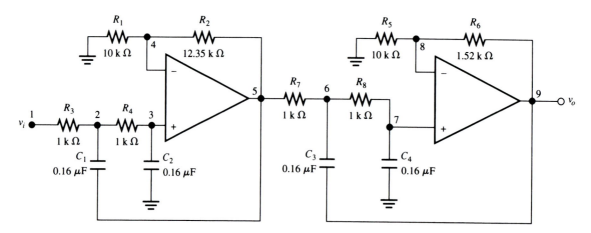

Fig. 5.27 Fourth-order Butterworth filter, low pass.

able to easily verify that $A_{v1} = 2.235$, $A_{v2} = 1.152$, and A_v (overall) $= A_{v1}A_{v2} = 2.575$. You can find these values by using the cursor mode at low frequencies. Press [*Ctrl*] [*Rt arrow*] to select among the traces. Refer to Fig. 5.28 for these plots.

Obtain a printed copy of this graph including all three traces for further study. Note the interesting peak in the A_{v1} graph. This is compensated for in the graph of A_{v2} so that the trace of overall gain is flat over almost all of its pass band of frequencies; then it drops off steeply near the frequency 1 kHz.

The rate of attenuation can be determined more easily from the decibel plot. Use the method involving 20*log10(V(9)/V(1)), and so forth, to replace the three traces with logarithmic traces. Verify that for the overall circuit, $f_c = 1$ kHz. Also observe the rate of attenuation for each of the three traces. You should be able to show that for each of the two stages, the rate of attenuation is about 10 dB/decade compared with about 20 dB/decade for the combined stages. Looking at the results of this example, you will feel some of the delight that comes from seeing the main ideas conveyed in such a graphical manner. You should also appreciate how much time and effort are spared by using such a powerful computational tool as PSpice. Refer to Fig. 5.29 for these plots.

We can show one additional feature of the Butterworth filter by using a slight modification of the previous input file. Compare the two-stage filter with the four-stage filter. A few calculations will be necessary because you do not have data for a two-stage filter with $f_c = 1$ kHz.

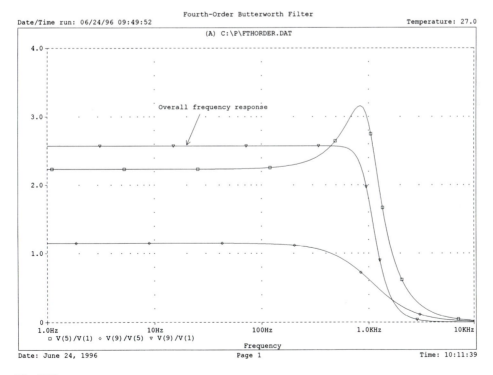

Fig. 5.28

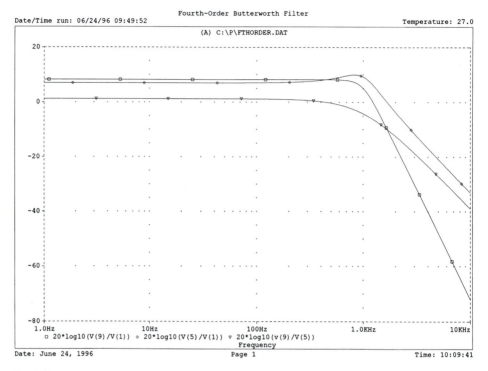

Fourth-Order Butterworth Filter

(A) C:\P\FTHORDER.DAT

□ 20*log10(V(9)/V(1))   ◇ 20*log10(V(5)/V(1))   ▽ 20*log10(v(9)/V(5))
Frequency

Date: June 24, 1996   Page 1   Time: 10:09:41

Fig. 5.29

The low-frequency gain will be the same as before for the two-stage filter, namely, $A_v = 1.586$. Let $R_1 = 10$ kΩ, giving $R_2 = 5.86$ kΩ. Using $R = 1$ kΩ, find that $C = 0.159$ μF. The circuit extension for this filter is shown in Fig. 5.30. Note that the extension involves an extension of node numbering more than anything else; this filter has its own input and is not physically linked with the four-stage filter. When this information is added to the original input file, it becomes

Fig. 5.30   Circuit extension to include second-order filter.

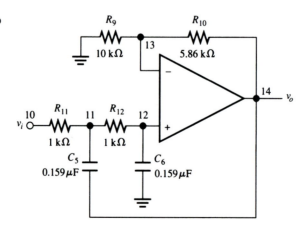

```
Fourth-Order Butterworth Filter Compared with Second-Order
VI  1 0 AC 1mV
R3  1 2 1k
R4  2 3 1k
R1  4 0 10k
R2  5 4 12.35k
R7  5 6 1k
R8  6 7 1k
R5  8 0 10k
R6  9 8 1.52k
C1  2 5 0.16uF
C2  3 0 0.16uF
C3  6 9 0.16uF
C4  7 0 0.16uF
VI1 10 1 AC 1mV
R9  13 0 10k
R10 14 13 5.86k

R11 10 11 1k
R12 11 12 1k
C5  11 14 0.159uF
C6  12 0 0.159uF
X1  4 3 5 iop
X2  8 7 9 iop
X3  13 12 14 iop
.AC DEC 40 1 10kHz
.PROBE
.subckt iop m p vo
  e vo 0 p m 2e5
  rin m p 1meg
.ends
.END
```

Run the analysis and plot decibel traces of V(9)/V(1) for the fourth-order filter and V(14)/V(10) for the second-order filter. You should find that $A_v = 4.006$ dB (second order) and $A_v = 8.214$ dB (fourth order). We want to show these on a comparable basis, so plot

$$20*\log10(V(14)/V(10))$$

and

$$20*\log10(V(9)/V(1)) - 4.208$$

The value of 4.208 represents the offset of the second trace from the first, normalizing the second trace with respect to the first. This graph with its two overlapping traces in the low-frequency range clearly shows that both Butterworth filters have the same f_c at 1 kHz. This will apply to Butterworth filters of all orders. See Fig. 5.31 for these traces.

ACTIVE RESONANT BAND-PASS FILTER

A simple resonant circuit can give steep cutoff characteristics by making use of the resonant properties of a *RLC* combination. Figure 5.32 shows an input loop containing V_s, R, L, and C. We will choose the component values to provide a particular bandwidth B and quality factor Q as outlined here.

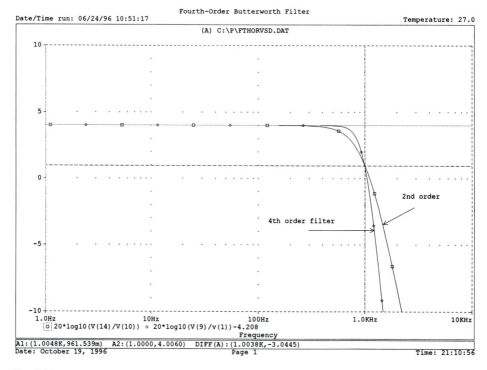

Fig. 5.31

The center frequency is taken as the frequency at which L and C resonate, which is given by

$$f = \frac{1}{2\pi \sqrt{LC}}$$

Fig. 5.32   Active resonant band-pass filter With $Q = Z$.

for $Q = 2$ $L = 0.289$ H
       $R = 10$ kΩ $C = 0.724$ nF

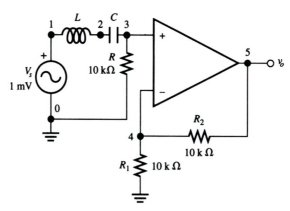

The quality factor Q is defined as $Q = \omega_o L/R$. In this type of filter circuit, $B = f_o/Q = R/(2\pi L)$. For example, we will chose $Q = 2$, $f_o = 11$ kHz, and $R = 10$ kΩ. This leads to $L = 0.289$ H, and $C = 0.724$ nF. To complete the circuit, we chose $R_1 = 10$ kΩ and $R_2 = 10$ kΩ for feedback and to produce a suitable A_v for this non-inverting amplifier. The input file is

```
Active Resonant Band-Pass Filter
VS 1 0 AC 1mV
R 3 0 10k
R1 4 0 10k
R2 5 4 10k
L 1 2 0.289H
C 2 3 0.724nF
X 4 3 5 iop
.AC DEC 40 1kHz 100kHz
.PROBE

.subckt iop m p vo
  e vo 0 p m 2e5
  rin m p 1meg
.ends
.END
```

Run the analysis and look at the ratio of output to source voltage (V(5)/V(1)) on a logarithmic scale. Verify the predicted center frequency and the bandwidth. Values to look for at the 3 dB points are about $f_1 = 8.6$ kHz and $f_2 = 14.1$ kHz, giving $B = 5.5$ kHz. You will see that the center frequency turns out to be at about 11.2 kHz.

Also obtain a trace of VP(5) to observe the phase shift changes near the resonant frequency.

It is interesting to compare two circuits of this type that have different values of Q, the quality factor. We have seen the results when $Q = 2$, and now we will add another circuit with $Q = 5$. Refer to Fig. 5.33, which shows the added circuit. The bandwidth $B = 2.2$ kHz, and retaining $R = 10$ kΩ gives $L = 0.723$ H, and $C = 0.289$ nF. The nodes are numbered in such a way that the original input file can be

Fig. 5.33 Circuit extension for band-pass filter with $Q = 5$.

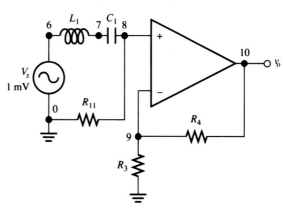

appended. This will allow us to look at the response of both circuits at the same time in Probe.

Add the following statements to the input file shown previously.

```
VS1  6  0  AC  1mV
R11  8  0  10k
R3   9  0  10k
R4   10 9  10k
L1   6  7  0.723H
C1   7  8  0.289nF
X1   9  8  10  iop
```

Run the analysis and plot together

$$20*\log10(V(5)/V(1))$$

and

$$20*\log10(V(10)/V(6))$$

to see the effects of $Q = 5$ along with $Q = 2$. Verify the bandwidth of the $Q = 5$ case using the cursor mode. This should be almost exactly $B = 2.2$ kHz. Figure 5.34 shows these curves.

Obtain another plot, using VP(5) for one trace and VP(10) for the other. This will show the comparison of phase shifts for the two cases. Refer to Fig. 5.35 for the results.

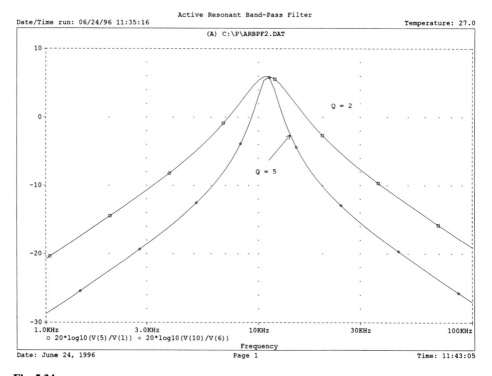

Fig. 5.34

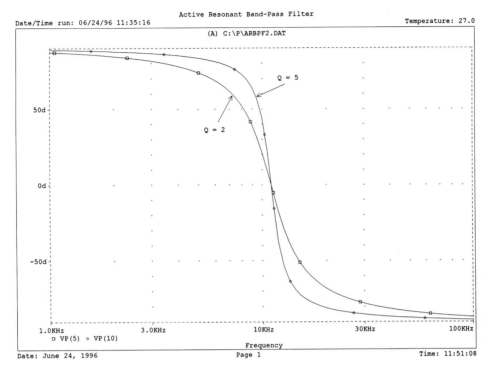

Fig. 5.35

ACTIVE *RC* BAND-PASS FILTER

The use of an inductor in the band-pass filter is not always desirable, especially since in some cases the inductance value is large. The circuit shown in Fig. 5.36 provides an alternative. Here any capacitors and resistors are used to obtain the band pass. Formulas are

$$R_1 = \frac{Q}{A_o \omega_o C_1}$$

$$R_3 = \frac{Q}{\dfrac{\omega_o C_1 C_2}{C_1 + C_2}}$$

$$R_p = R_1 \| R_2 = \frac{1}{\omega_o^2 R_3 C_1 C_2}$$

For an example, we will choose $A_o = 50$, $f_o = 160$ Hz, and $B = 16$ Hz. For convenience we will let $C_1 = C_2 = 0.1$ μF. Solve for $Q = f_o/B$. Also find R_1, R_2, and R_3. Check your answers with those shown on page 218. Note that the resistance values have been slightly rounded. The input file is

Fig. 5.36 Active *RC* band-pass filter.

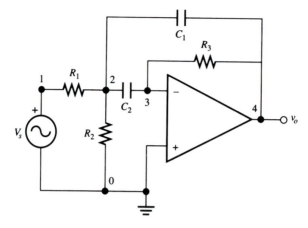

```
Active RC Band-Pass Filter
VS 1 0 AC 1mV
R1 1 2 2k
R2 2 0 667
R3 4 3 200k
C1 2 4 0.1uF
C2 2 3 0.1uF
X 3 0 4 iop
.AC DEC 100 1 1kHz
.PROBE
.subckt iop m p vo
 e vo 0 p m 2e5
 rin m p 1meg
.ends
.END
```

Run the analysis and plot V(4)/V(1) to show that $A_o = 50$ at $f_o = 158$ Hz; then remove this trace and plot the same voltage ratio on a logarithmic scale to find the bandwidth. You should verify that $f_1 = 151$ Hz and $f_2 = 167$ Hz, giving $B = 16$ Hz. Figure 5.37 shows the results, with the cursor at one of the 3 dB points.

NEW PSPICE STATEMENT USED IN THIS CHAPTER

X[*name*] [*<node>*]* *<sname>*

For example

```
X1 9 8 10 iop
```

means that a subcircuit is connected at nodes *9, 8,* and *10* in the (main) circuit. The name of the subcircuit is *iop.* The input file contains a description of the subcircuit. It might look like this, for example:

```
.subckt iop 1 2 3
. . .

. . .
.ends
```

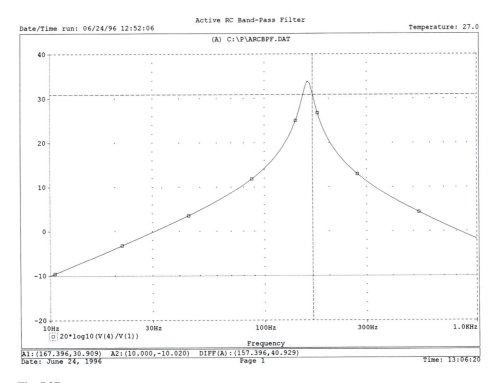

Active RC Band-Pass Filter

Date/Time run: 06/24/96 12:52:06   Temperature: 27.0

(A) C:\P\ARCBPF.DAT

A1:(167.396,30.909)   A2:(10.000,-10.020)   DIFF(A):(157.396,40.929)
Date: June 24, 1996   Page 1   Time: 13:06:20

Fig. 5.37

where the name *iop* identifies the subcircuit, and the nodes *1, 2,* and *3* refer to nodes *8, 9,* and *10,* respectively, of the *X* statement. The line with *.ends* shows the end of the subcircuit description.

The use of subcircuits is most convenient when it is necessary to use a device, model, or group of elements more than once in an input file. For example, *X1, X2,* and *X3* could all refer to the same device *iop*.

PROBLEMS

5.1 An ideal inverting op amp as shown in Fig. 5.2 has $R_1 = 2$ kΩ, $R_2 = 15$ kΩ, $A = 100,000$ and $R_i = 1$ MΩ. Run a PSpice analysis to determine the voltage gain, the input resistance, and the output resistance. A value of 1 MΩ for R_i is a practical value. When $R_i = 1$ GΩ is used in the PSpice analysis, what differences are obtained in the results?

5.2 Design an ideal noninverting op amp as shown in Fig. 5.3 to have a voltage gain of 20. Select values for R_1 and R_2, and run a PSpice analysis to verify your design.

5.3 An ideal op amp as shown in Fig. 5.5 is to be used with inputs $v_a = 3$ V and $v_b = 10$ V. When $R_1 = 5$ kΩ, $R_2 = 10$ kΩ, $R_3 = 10$ kΩ, and $R_4 = 5$ kΩ, find the output voltage using PSpice. Compare the results with those obtained in the text example where $R_1 = R_3$ and $R_2 = R_4$. Define the role of R_3 and R_4 in determining the voltage gain.

5.4 The op amp model in Fig. 5.8 assumes that $f_t = 1$ MHz and $f_c = 10$ Hz. Revise the model to allow for $f_t = 2$ MHz and $f_c = 10$ Hz. Use $R_1 = 10$ kΩ, and $R_2 = 240$ kΩ. Find the midfrequency gain and the upper 3-dB frequency. Compare your results with those given in the text example.

5.5 In Fig. 5.15 the product of R and C equals 1 (second). Using the more practical values $C = 50$ μF and $R = 20$ kΩ with the same input should produce the same results as those given in the text example. Demonstrate that this is the case. Then using $C = 50$ μF and $R = 10$ kΩ, run the analysis again. Explain the difference between these and the previous results.

5.6 Using the circuit of Fig. 5.17 with $C = 50$ μF and $R = 20$ kΩ, run the PSpice analysis with the same input as shown in the figure. Compare your results with Fig. 5.18. Then using $C = 50$ μF and $R = 10$ kΩ, run the analysis again. Explain the difference between these and the previous results.

5.7 Figure 5.38 shows a first-order op amp circuit, which has

$$v_s = 4 - 4u(t) \text{ V}$$

where $u(t)$ represents a unit step function. Analysis shows that

$$v_c(t) = 10e^{-4t} \text{ V}$$

and

$$v_o(t) = -v_c(t) \text{ V}$$

for $t \geq 0$. Run the PSpice analysis to verify the predicted results.

Fig. 5.38

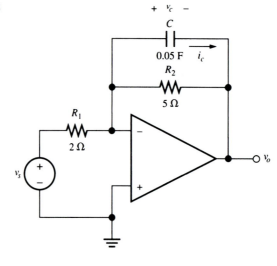

5.8 Figure 5.39 shows an op amp circuit where

$$v_s(t) = 3 - 3u(t) \text{ V}$$

find (a)$v_o(0)$, (b) $i_c(0)$, (c)$i_o(0)$, and (d) the plot of $v_o(t)$ using PSpice analysis.

Fig. 5.39

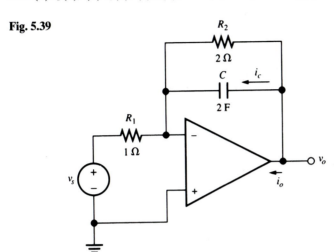

5.9 Design a first-order, low-pass filter such as that shown in Fig. 5.40 with a cutoff frequency of $f_o = 5$ kHz. Use $R = R_1 = 1$ kΩ and solve for C. Find the midfrequency gain; then use Probe to verify your design.

Fig. 5.40

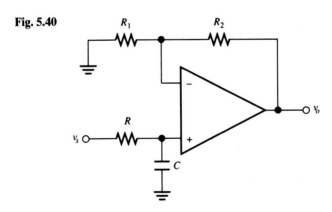

Transients and the Time Domain

One of the important features of PSpice is its transient analysis capability. Transients can be tedious from the mathematical point of view. Lengthy derivations often involve differential equations with specified boundary conditions and assumptions for the solutions. PSpice allows you to gain additional insight, especially when you need plots of voltages and currents as a function of time.

SWITCH CLOSING IN AN *RL* CIRCUIT

Every circuit, when first energized, experiences at least a brief period of transient conditions. As an example, Fig. 6.1 shows a circuit with a 1-V source (a battery), a switch (to be closed at the beginning of the time measurements), a resistor R, and an inductor L. See what happens immediately after the switch closes. From your study of circuit analysis, you know that the current will not immediately reach its final value V/R, but that it will rise exponentially. The time constant $\tau = L/R$ represents the time required for the current to reach 63.2% of its final value. After about 5τ, the current will have reached its final value within less than 1%.

In PSpice, we will investigate this response using the PWL (piecewise linear) function. It will be used in the statement describing the applied voltage, as follows:

```
V 1 0 PWL(0,0 10us, 1V 10ms, 1V)
```

The statement shows that the voltage is between nodes *1* and *0* and that its form is given as piecewise linear. The arguments in parentheses represent time, voltage pairs. In this example at $t = 0$, $V = 0$; then at $t = 10$ μs, $V = 1$ V; then at $t = 10$ ms, $V = 1$ V. If you move from point to point between successive pairs with a

Fig. 6.1   Switch closing in an
RL circuit.

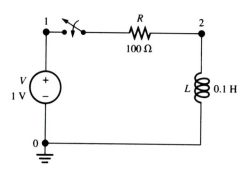

straight line between, you will see how the voltage looks as a function of time. Now you are ready to look at the complete input file:

```
Switch Closing in RL Circuit
V 1 0 PWL(0,0 1us, 1V 10ms, 1V)
R 1 2 100
L 2 0 0.1H
.TRAN 1ms 10ms
.PROBE
.END
```

Incidentally, the first *time* shown in the .TRAN statement is a print-step value (make it about one-tenth of the second value), and the second value indicates the length of the time for the analysis.

Run the analysis and plot I(R). Note that the current begins to build exponentially as expected, reaching a final value of 10 mA. Use the cursor mode to determine the initial rate of change of current $\Delta i/\Delta t$. You might choose to do this for a time interval of about 50 μs. Verify that this initial $\Delta i/\Delta t = 10$ A/s. If the current continued to increase at this linear rate, when would it reach its final value of 10 mA?

As you know, after one time constant the current should reach 0.632 of its final value. Verify on the graph that this value, 6.32 mA, is reached at $t = 1$ ms. Refer to Fig. 6.2 for this graph.

If you are just learning about time constants, make another graph to help you with this concept. Remove the current trace and plot three curves V(1), V(2), and V(1,2). The voltage V(1,2) is the same as V(1) − V(2). If you change the time scale to run from −1 ms to 10 ms, you can see the initial switch closing more readily. What do the curves represent? V(1) is the applied voltage, which rises suddenly from zero to 1 V; V(2) is the inductor voltage, which begins at 1 V when $t = 0$. Can you apply Kirchhoff's voltage law to explain why? V(1,2) is the voltage drop across the resistor. This plots in the same fashion as the current, obviously, since $v_R = Ri$. Since $v_R + v_L$ must equal V (the applied voltage) at all times, v_R and v_L appear to be mirror images. Figure 6.3 shows these relationships.

NONZERO INITIAL CURRENT IN THE TRANSIENT ANALYSIS

The circuit of Fig. 6.4 contains an open switch before $t = 0$. After that, the switch is closed, creating a transient condition. You can use PSpice to allow for the initial cur-

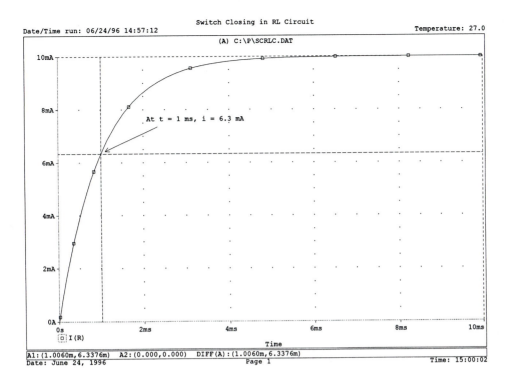

Fig. 6.2

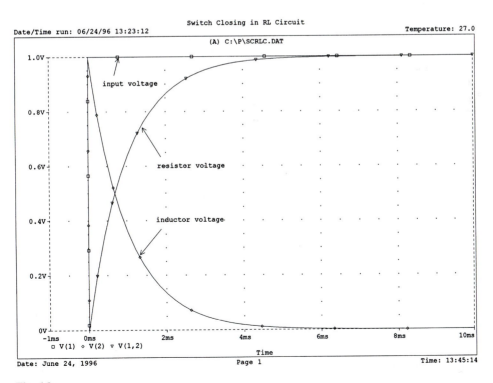

Fig. 6.3

Fig. 6.4 Circuit with nonzero initial current.

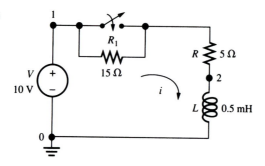

rent in the circuit if you do some preliminary work. As an example, let $R_1 = 15 \, \Omega$, $R = 5 \, \Omega$, $L = 0.5$ mH, and $V = 10$ V. Before the switch is closed, the current is

$$i(0) = \frac{V}{R_1 + R} = 0.5 \text{ A}$$

After the switch is closed, the current will rise exponentially as in the previous example. Use the initial current of 0.5 A in the input file, which looks like this:

```
Transient with Nonzero Initial Current
V 1 0 PWL(0, 2.5V 1us, 10V 1ms, 10V)
R 1 2 5
L 2 0 0.5mH IC=0.5A
.TRAN 10us 1ms
.PROBE
.END
```

Note that the L statement contains $IC = 0.5$ A. This is a *guess* for the initial current. In reality it is more than a guess, but it is called that in SPICE. This alone will not make the analysis run correctly, however. Notice that our *PWL* contains 0, 2.5 V. Where did that come from? Before the switch is closed, with $i = 0.5$ A, the voltage drop across R is given by $v_R = Ri = 0.5 \cdot 5 = 2.5$ V. You must help the analysis along by using this as the initial voltage. Recall that R_1 drops out of the picture during the PSpice analysis, and there is no node for R_1. With only R and L in the loop along with V, initially all of V appears across R.

Now you are ready to run the analysis and look at the current. Plot I(R) and verify that the initial current is 0.5 A and that the final current is 2 A. After one time constant, the current should reach what value? The total change is 1.5 A; in one time constant the current should reach $0.632 \cdot 1.5 = 0.948$ of that change. Add this to 0.5 A, giving the current $i = 1.448$ A. Verify this on the plot, using the cursor mode. Refer to Fig. 6.5 for this plot.

RESISTOR AND CAPACITOR IN THE TRANSIENT ANALYSIS

If a capacitor is used in series with a resistor, as shown in Fig. 6.6, there will be an initial inrush of current when the switch is closed. Our analysis is based on $\tau = 1$ ms and $C = 0.1 \, \mu$F, giving $R = \tau/C = 10 \, \text{k}\Omega$. The input file is simply

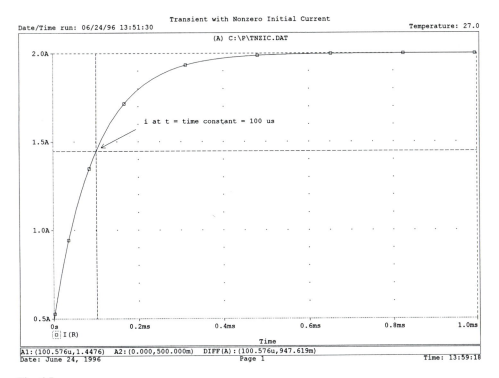

Fig. 6.5

```
Switch Closing in RC Circuit
V 1 0 PWL(0,0 1us, 1V 10ms, 1V)
R 1 2 10k
C 2 0 0.1uF
.TRAN 1ms 10ms
.PROBE
.END
```

Run the analysis and plot I(R). What is the value of current at the instant the switch is closed? What will be the value of current when $t = \tau$? If the current continues to drop at its initial rate, when will it become zero? Refer to Fig. 6.7 for this trace.

Fig. 6.6 Switch closing in *RC* circuit.

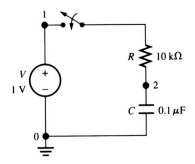

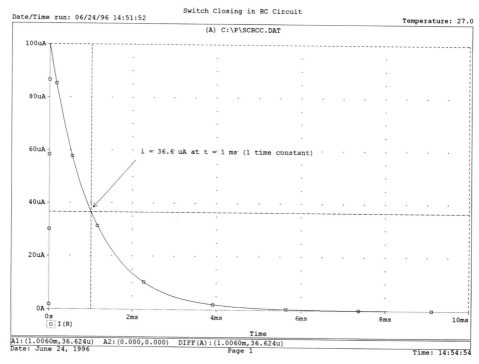

Fig. 6.7

Remove the current trace and plot V(1), V(2), and V(1,2)—the applied voltage, the capacitor voltage, and the resistor voltage, respectively. Note the exponential rise in capacitor voltage as the resistor voltage decreases exponentially. Figure 6.8 shows these features.

A DOUBLE-ENERGY CIRCUIT

A double-energy circuit is one that contains an inductor and a capacitor in addition to one or more resistors.

When a circuit contains R, L, and C in series, the transient response is classically divided into three categories. The first is for overdamping, the second for critical damping, and the third for underdamping or oscillatory conditions. We will begin with the overdamped case.

Overdamped *RLC* Series Circuit

Figure 6.9 shows the circuit with a 12-V source. The switch is to be closed just after $t = 0$, causing the transient conditions to begin. Values are $C = 1.56$ μF, $L = 10$ mH, and $R = 200$ Ω. The value of R will be adjusted later to allow for the other conditions. With $R = 200$ Ω, the circuit is overdamped. A time of 1 ms will be sufficient to allow the current to rise to a peak value and then exponentially decay. A mathe-

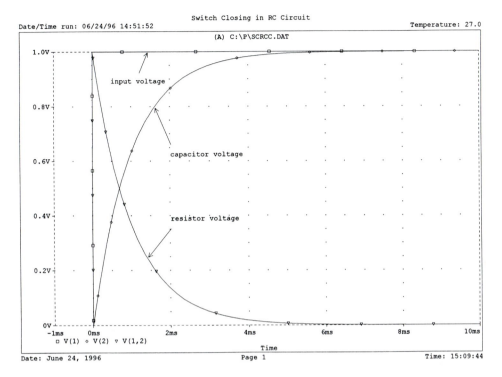

Fig. 6.8

matical analysis of this circuit shows that there are two exponential components of current, which combine to give the actual current that you will see on the graph. The input file is

```
Double-Energy Circuit, Overdamped
V 1 0 PWL(0,0 1us,12V 10ms,12V)
R 1 2 200
L 2 3 10mH
C 3 0 1.56uF
.TRAN 10us 1ms
.PROBE
.END
```

Fig. 6.9   A double-energy circuit, overdamped.

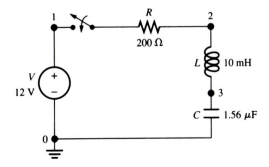

Run the analysis; then plot I(R). Verify that the current peaks at $i = 47.4$ mA when $t = 125$ μs. Figure 6.10 shows the overdamped response.

Now you can make an interesting discovery relating to the voltage components in the circuit. Remove the current trace and plot V(1), V(3), V(2,3), and V(1,2). These nodes are readily identified in the circuit diagram, Fig. 6.9. Observe that the resistor voltage reaches a peak of $v_R = 9.46$ V at $t = 125$ μs. Also observe that the inductor voltage appears to suddenly rise to nearly $v_L = 11.8$ V and then passes through zero to a negative peak of $v_L = -1.201$ V at $t = 226$ μs. Fig. 6.11 shows these traces.

The Critically Damped *RLC* Circuit

Use the same circuit as in Fig. 6.9. Analysis shows that for critical damping.

$$R^2 = \frac{4L}{C}$$

Keep the former values of L and C. When $R = 160$ Ω, the critical condition exists. To see the results, simply change the value of R in the input file to the required value and run the analysis again.

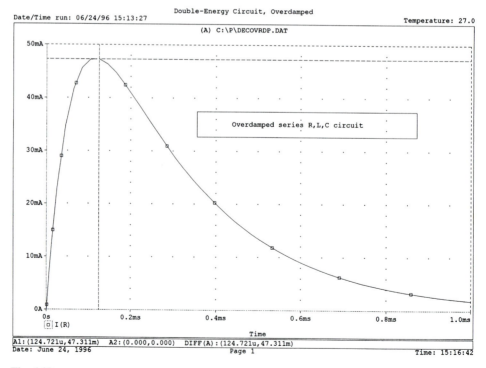

Fig. 6.10

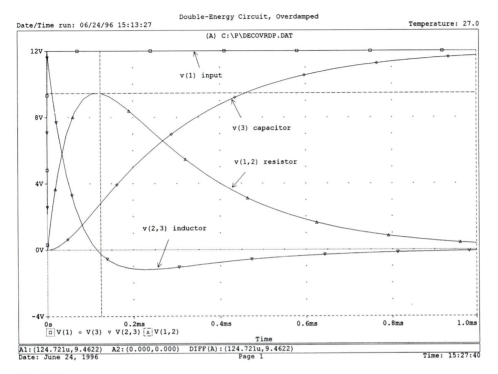

Fig. 6.11

After running the analysis, verify that the current reaches a peak value of $i =$ 55.36 mA at $t = 125$ μs. Remove the current trace and plot the various voltages as in the previous analysis. These curves will have the same appearance as those of the former case involving overdamping. Refer to Fig. 6.12 for these plots.

The Underdamped *RLC* Circuit

To show the effects of underdamping, you need to reduce the resistance to less than the critical value of 160 Ω. Run the analysis using $R = 60$ Ω. Change this value in the input file and look at the plot of current using I(R). Verify that the current peaks at $i = 92.7$ mA when $t = 171$ μs. Also observe that the current goes negative, then positive once again. This oscillatory pattern is typical for the underdamped case. Of course, smaller values of R produce a more extended period of oscillation. Refer to Fig. 6.13 for the oscillatory current trace. You may want to try several other smaller values of resistance and observe the effect on the transient response.

After looking at the current plot, remove the trace and plot V(1), V(3), V(2,3), and V(1,2). It is interesting to see that the capacitor voltage rises above the applied voltage of 12 V, reaching its peak as the inductor voltage is rising from its negative peak. If you try other values of R, you will see a variation of the ways in which the component voltages interact, always in keeping with Kirchhoff's voltage law, of course. Figure 6.14 shows these plots.

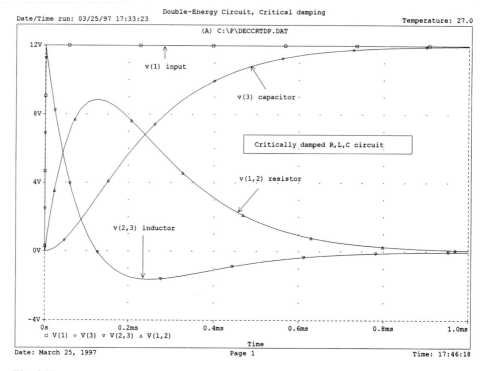

Fig. 6.12

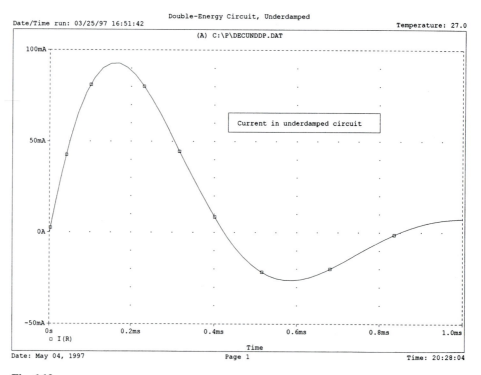

Fig. 6.13

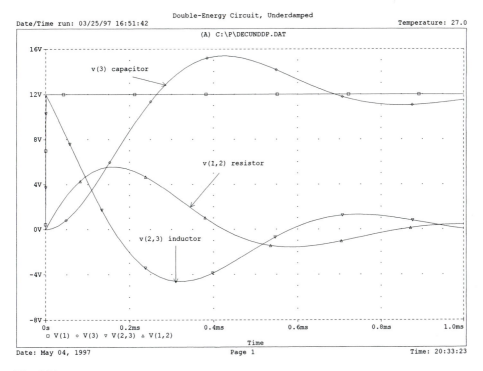

Double-Energy Circuit, Underdamped
Date/Time run: 03/25/97 16:51:42   Temperature: 27.0
(A) C:\P\DECUNDDP.DAT

Date: May 04, 1997   Page 1   Time: 20:33:23

Fig. 6.14

STEP RESPONSE OF AN AMPLIFIER

When a step of voltage is applied to an amplifier, the high-frequency response will determine whether or not the output wave closely resembles the input wave. Consider the amplifier as a low-pass circuit as shown in Fig. 6.15. The output voltage will show exponential rise and fall. Specifically, during the rise the output is given by

$$v_o = V(1 - e^{-t/RC})$$

The rise time t_r is a measure of how fast the amplitude of the output can respond to the step of input voltage. Since

$$f_H = \frac{1}{2\pi RC}$$

the rise time is

$$t_r = 2.2RC = \frac{0.35}{f_H}$$

We suggest that to avoid excessive distortion you let $f_H = 1/t_p$, where t_p is the pulse width. This means that $t_r = 0.35t_p$.

To illustrate these features, choose a low-pass circuit model with $R = 10$ kΩ and $C = 796$ pF, giving $f_H = 20$ kHz. From the equations, $t_p = 50$ μs and $t_r = 17.5$ μs. See how closely these values are matched in the PSpice analysis. The input file is

Fig. 6.15 Step response of an amplifier.

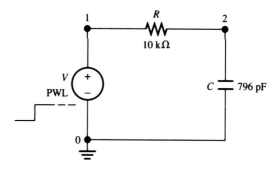

```
Pulse Response When fH=1/tp
V 1 0 PWL(0,0 0.5us, 1V 50us, 1V 50.5us, 0)
R 1 2 10k
C 2 0 796pF
.TRAN 0.5us 100us
.PROBE
.END
```

Run the analysis, and in Probe plot v(1) and v(2), the input and output voltages. Verify on the output wave that $t_{0.1} = 1.1$ μs and $t_{0.9} = 18.6$ μs. These represent the times when the output voltage is at one-tenth and at nine-tenths of its peak value. The difference in the two times is the rise time. This gives $t_r = 17.5$ μs, in close agreement with our prediction. Refer to Fig. 6.16 for this plot.

What would be the result of using a value of capacitance that is twice as large as the recommended maximum value? Simply run the analysis with the new value, $C = 1.592$ nF. Observe that the output wave does not reach the desired value of 1 V and is generally more distorted.

It is also instructive to see the results when the capacitance is smaller than the maximum recommended value. Run the analysis with $C = 398$ pF. You will see that the square wave is much more faithfully reproduced in the output wave.

LOW-FREQUENCY RESPONSE OF AN AMPLIFIER

When a high-pass circuit such as shown in Fig. 6.17 is used to simulate the low-frequency response of an amplifier, the output is given by

$$v_o - Ve^{-t/RC}$$

When the time constant $\tau = RC$ is too small, the output wave will display an undesirable tilt. Since R is probably fixed as the input resistance to an amplifier stage, the value of C must be made large enough to avoid excessive tilt. For an example, choose $R = 1.59$ kΩ and $C = 10$ μF, and use a 50-Hz square wave for testing. The input file is

```
Tilt of Square Wave for Low-Frequency Response
V 1 0 PWL(0,0 1us, 1V 10ms, 1V 10.001ms, −1V 20ms, −1V 20.001ms, 1V 30ms, 1V)
C 1 2 10uF
R 2 0 1.59k
```

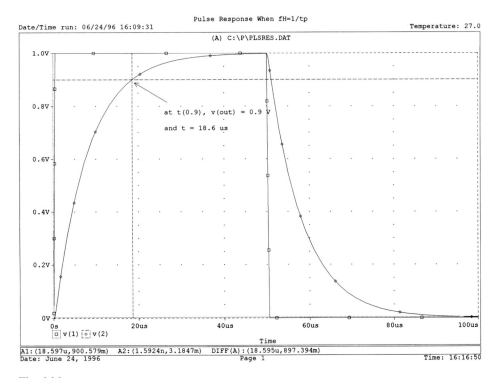

Pulse Response When fH=1/tp

Date/Time run: 06/24/96 16:09:31   Temperature: 27.0

(A) C:\P\PLSRES.DAT

at t(0.9), v(out) = 0.9 V

and t = 18.6 us

A1: (18.597u,900.579m)   A2: (1.5924n,3.1847m)   DIFF(A): (18.595u,897.394m)
Date: June 24, 1996   Page 1   Time: 16:16:50

Fig. 6.16

```
.TRAN 0.15ms 30ms
.PROBE
.END
```

Run the analysis; then plot v(1) and v(2). Find the tilt of the output by comparing the peak on the leading and trailing edges. Verify that these values are 1 V and 0.533 V, giving a tilt of 46.7%. Often a tilt of no more than about 10% is considered desirable. Obviously, a larger value of capacitance is needed. Let $C = 50 \ \mu F$ and run the analysis again. Verify that the tilt is no less than 12%. Figure 6.18 shows this plot.

Fig. 6.17 Low-frequency response of an amplifier.

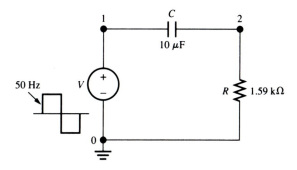

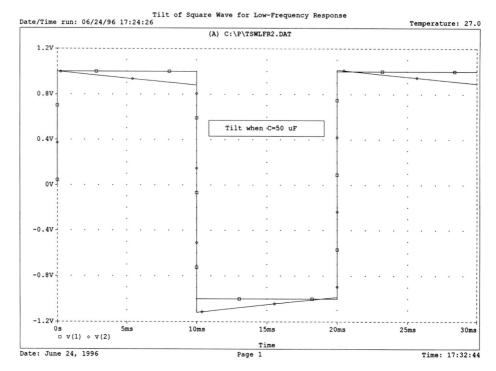

Fig. 6.18

In the laboratory, the response would be observed with an oscilloscope connected to the amplifier output when the input is a square wave of the proper frequency.

CIRCUIT WITH CHARGED CAPACITOR

The circuit in Fig. 6.19 contains capacitance in one branch and inductance in another branch.* A voltage source is present to charge the capacitor; then the voltage source is effectively shorted.

Before a PSpice analysis can be performed, the initial voltages and currents that affect the analysis must be determined. In the description for v_s, it is seen that the applied voltage is constant at 6 V for $t < 0$. In this dc circuit the capacitor is an open circuit, and the inductor is a short circuit. The current from the 6-V source becomes $6 \text{ V}/3 \ \Omega = 2 \text{ A}$, and the voltage at node 1 is 4 V. This is the voltage that appears across the capacitor at $t = 0$. The current of 2 A passes through R_1, R_2, and L.

At $t = 0$, the applied voltage $v_s = 0$ V, and the circuit becomes Fig. 6.20. This circuit is the subject of the PSpice analysis. The input file becomes

---

*This example is from Bobrow (see "Further Reading," p.5)

Fig. 6.19 Circuit with capacitive branch and inductive branch.

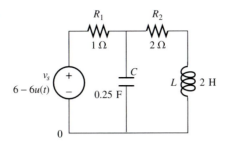

```
Initial Conditions Example
R1 0 1 1
R2 1 2 2
C 1 0 250mF IC=4V
L 2 0 2H IC=2A
.TRAN 0.01ms 4s UIC
.PROBE
.END
```

The input file contains in the C statement an IC value of 4 V, which is the initial capacitor voltage; in the L statement there is an IC of 2 A, which is the initial current through L. Note that an initial condition for a capacitor is limited to a voltage value and that an initial condition for an inductor can be only a current. It is also necessary to append to the .*TRAN* statement the term *UIC*, which means that the transient analysis is to begin with the specified initial values.

Run the analysis and plot both the capacitor voltage and the inductor voltage. Verify that at $t = 0.5$ s, $v_C(0.5$ s$) = -0.860$ V and $v_L(0.5$ s$) = -3.49$ V. The plot is shown in Fig. 6.21.

As an additional exercise, plot both the capacitor current and the inductor current. Observe that $i_C(0) = -6$ A. Since $R_1 = 1$ Ω and $R_2 = 2$ Ω, we expect twice the initial current through R_1 as the current through R_2. This gives 4 A through R_1 and 2 A through R_2. Sketch the circuit and correctly show the directions of the various branch currents. While you are observing the current traces, verify that at $t = 0.5$ s, $i_C(0.5$ s$) = -0.457$ A and $i_L(0.5$ s$) = 1.316$ A. Note that if you have two traces on the same plot, you may choose which one to follow with the cursor by choosing *Cursor;* then with the mouse click on the selected trace marker. For example, click on the small diamond to select the second trace.

Fig. 6.20 Circuit at $t = 0$.

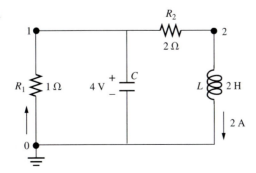

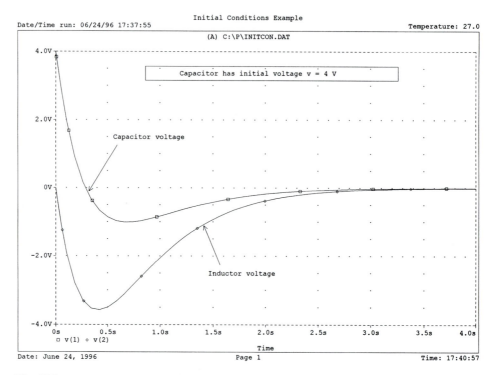

Date/Time run: 06/24/96 17:37:55

Initial Conditions Example

Temperature: 27.0

(A) C:\P\INITCON.DAT

Capacitor has initial voltage v = 4 V

Capacitor voltage

Inductor voltage

□ v(1) ◇ v(2)

Time

Date: June 24, 1996   Page 1   Time: 17:40:57

Fig. 6.21

Before leaving Probe, plot the currents through both resistors. Verify that at $t = 0$, $i_{R1}(0) = -4$ A and $i_{R2}(0) = 2$ A. Observe the directions of the current arrows in Fig. 6.20 in order to understand the current signs (positive and negative).

SWITCH-OPENING CIRCUIT WITH *L* AND *C*

Another circuit in which the source voltage is removed at $t = 0$ is shown in Fig. 6.22. We will find the initial conditions before attempting the PSpice analysis. There is a dc voltage $V_s = 6$ V applied at $t < 0$. Under this condition, the circuit appears as R_1 and R_2 in parallel. By current division, current $I_{R1} = 3$ A and current $I_{R2} = 2$ A. This current also passes through the indicator L. The current through R_2 produces a voltage.

$$V(1,2) = R_2 I_{R2} = (3)(2) = 6 \text{ V}$$

This is the initial capacitor voltage.

At $t = 0$, the switch is opened, and the circuit for PSpice is as shown in Fig. 6.23. The initial values are shown in the figure. Note the polarity of the initial capacitor voltage and the direction of the initial inductor current. The input file thus becomes

Fig. 6.22 Circuit with switch opening at $t = 0$.

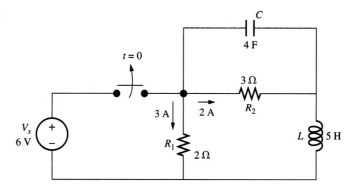

```
Switch-Opening Circuit with L, C
R1  1  0  2
R2  1  2  3
C  1  2  4000mF  IC=6V
L  2  0  5H  IC=2A
.TRAN 0.01ms 16s UIC
.PROBE
.END
```

Run the analysis and verify that when the switch is opened at $t = 0$, $v_C(0) = 6$ V and $i_L(0) = 2$ A, in keeping with our initial-condition statements. Also verify that $v_L(0) = -10$ V by plotting $v(2)$, and verify that $i_C(0) = 0$.

How can $v_L(0)$ be predicted using simple circuit analysis just after the switch is opened? Since the current through the inductor cannot change instantaneously, the current in R_1 suddenly becomes 2 A (upward) rather than its former value of 3 A (downward). This current of 2 A produces a voltage drop of 4 V with the polarity shown in Fig. 6.23. Applying KVL to the loop containing R_1, C, and L gives $v_L(0) = -10$ V, confirming the PSpice results. Figure 6.24 shows $v(1,2)$ which is v_C.

While you are still in the Probe analysis, verify currents and voltages at $t = 2$ s, as follows:

Fig. 6.23 Conditions when switch is opened.

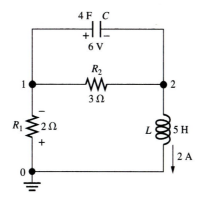

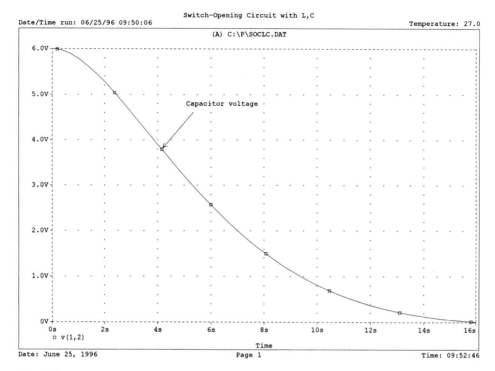

Fig. 6.24

$$v_C(2 \text{ s}) = 5.2778 \text{ V}$$

$$v_L(2 \text{ s}) = -3.94 \text{ V}$$

$$i_C(2 \text{ s}) = -2.428 \text{ A}$$

$$i_L(2 \text{ s}) = -0.675 \text{ A}$$

The currents are shown in Fig. 6.25.

CIRCUIT WITH CURRENT SOURCE

The circuit shown in Fig. 6.26 shows a source producing a steady current of 3 A for $t < 0$. Then at $t = 0$, the current becomes 0. Initial conditions for L and C must be determined before the PSpice analysis is undertaken. Prior to $t = 0$, the current through R is 3 A, while the current through the other branch is zero, since C appears open for dc conditions. Thus $i_L(0) = 0$. The voltage drop across R is $(2 \ \Omega)(3 \text{ A}) = 6$ V, with the polarity as shown in Fig. 6.27. Since, under dc conditions, there can be no voltage across L, the voltage $v_C(0) = 6$ V. This is enough information to perform the PSpice analysis. The input file is

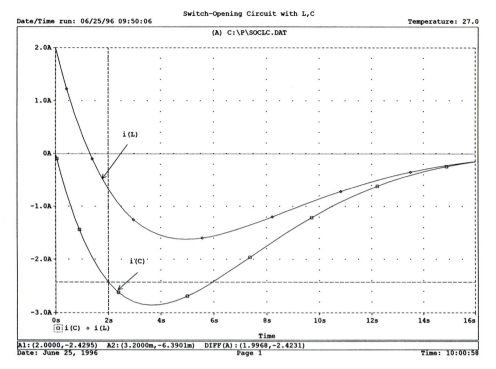

Switch-Opening Circuit with L,C

Date/Time run: 06/25/96 09:50:06   Temperature: 27.0

(A) C:\P\SOCLC.DAT

A1:(2.0000,-2.4295)   A2:(3.2000m,-6.3901m)   DIFF(A):(1.9968,-2.4231)
Date: June 25, 1996   Page 1   Time: 10:00:58

Fig. 6.25

```
Initial Conditions from Current Source
R 1 0 2
L 1 2 3H
C 2 0 4000mF IC=6V
.TRAN 0.001ms 24s UIC
.PROBE
.END
```

Run the analysis and plot the resistor voltage and the capacitor voltage. Verify the initial conditions for both these voltages. As an exercise, verify that $v_C(4 \text{ s}) = 4.2095 \text{ V}$ and $v_R(4 \text{ s}) = 4.5476 \text{ V}$. Without obtaining a trace of v_L, what should be its

Fig. 6.26 Circuit with current source.

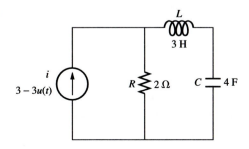

Fig. 6.27   Circuit at $t = 0$.

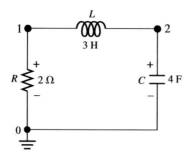

value at $t = 4$ s? Use KVL to find this value. Resistor and capacitor voltages are shown in Fig. 6.28.

Now plot current i_C. Note that it has an initial value of zero, since it must have the same current as the inductor. Verify that $i(4$ s$) = -2.2738$ A. This is the current

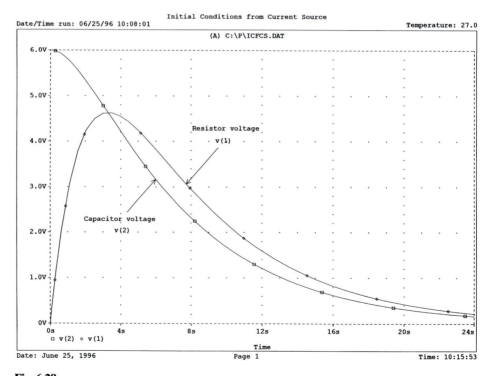

Fig. 6.28

Fig. 6.29 Circuit with switch opening at $t = 0$.

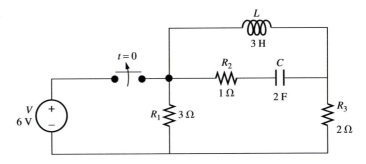

through each element in the CCW direction. Also verify that the maximum current is $i_{max} = -2.313$ A at $t = 3.48$ s.

BRIDGE CIRCUIT WITH INITIAL CURRENT

The circuit of Fig. 6.29 has a switch that opens at $t = 0$. Before the switch is opened, the circuit appears as in Fig. 6.30. The inductance has been replaced by a short circuit, indicating that 6 V appears across both R_1 and R_3. This voltage produces a current of 2 A in R_1 and a current of 3 A in R_2 as shown. Because there is no current through the capacitor branch, the current of 3 A must also appear in the inductor. Since the voltage V(1,3) is zero, $v_C = 0$. This information allows us to set the PSpice initial conditions, producing the following input file:

```
Switch Opening in Bridge Circuit
R1 0 1 3
R2 1 2 1
R3 3 0 2
L 1 3 3H IC=3A
C 2 3 2000mF
.TRAN 0.001ms 16s UIC
.PROBE
.END
```

Fig. 6.30 Circuit conditions before switch is opened.

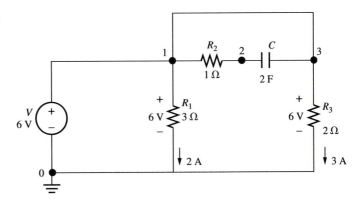

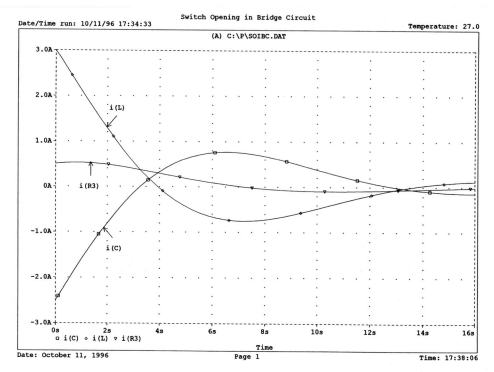

Fig. 6.31

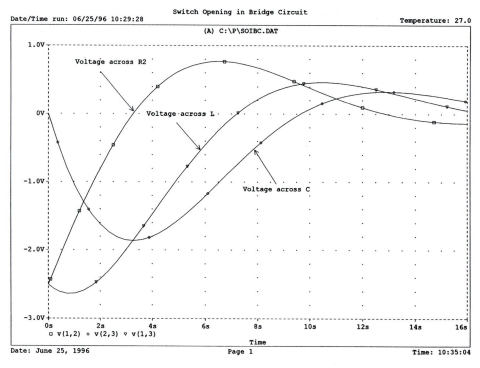

Fig. 6.32

Fig. 6.33 A ringing circuit.

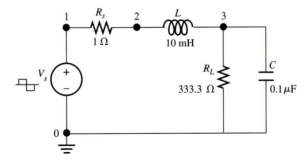

Run the analysis and verify the following: $i_C(0) = -2.5$ A, $i_L(0) = 3$ A, $i_{R3}(0) = 0.5$ A, $v_{12}(0) = -2.5$ V, $v_{23}(0) = 0$, and $v_{13}(0) = -2.5$ V. (*Note:* $v_{12}(0)$ means $v(1,2)$ at $t = 0$.) The current traces are shown in Fig. 6.31, and the voltage traces are shown in Fig. 6.32.

As an exercise, apply KVL to the loop containing R_1, R_2, C, and R_3 to predict i_C at $t = 0$.

A RINGING CIRCUIT

The circuit of Fig. 6.33 might represent a network to be tested with a square-wave input. The input voltage is given as a 1-V source that abruptly changes from 0 to 1 V; then at 2 ms there is a 2-V change to -1 V; then at 4 ms there is another abrupt change to 1 V. The problem is to determine how accurately the square wave is reproduced as a voltage across R_L. The input file is

```
Ringing Circuit
Vs 1 0 PWL(0s, 0V 0.01ms, 1V 2ms, 1V 2.01ms, -1V 4ms, -1V 4.01ms, 1V)
Rs 1 2 1
L 2 3 10mH
RL 3 0 333.3
C 3 0 0.1uF
.TRAN 0.05ms 6ms
.PROBE
.END
```

The Probe results of plotting V(3) are shown in Fig. 6.34. In probe you may also want to display V_s in order to see the deviation in the two traces. Before leaving Probe, remove the voltage traces and plot each of the currents. Of particular interest is current I(C). The current traces should give you a better understanding of this type of circuit.

Run the analysis again with C decreased by an order of magnitude, and compare the results.

PROBLEMS

6.1 Given the circuit shown in Fig. 6.35, with $V = 10$ V, $R_1 = R = 1$ kΩ, and $C = 200$ μF, obtain a plot of $v_C(t)$ for a time range extending from before the switch is

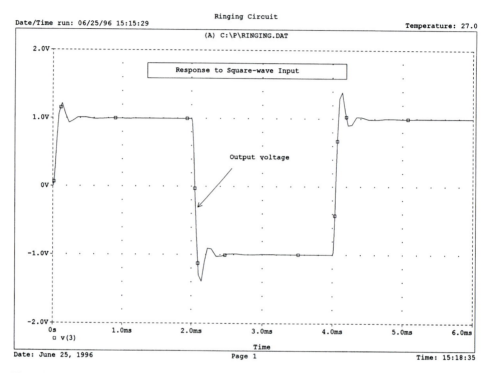

Fig. 6.34

opened to when the capacitor voltage approaches zero. Perform the required PSpice analysis and obtain the Probe graph of v_C.

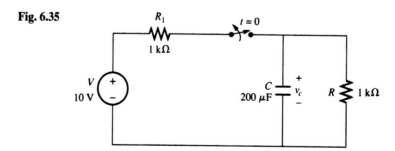

Fig. 6.35

6.2 For the circuit in Fig. 6.36, $V = 10$ V, $R_1 = R = 100$ Ω, and $L = 2$ H. Obtain a plot of $v_L(t)$ for a time range extending from before the switch is opened to when the inductor voltage approaches zero. Perform the required PSpice analysis and obtain the Probe graph of v_L.

Fig. 6.36

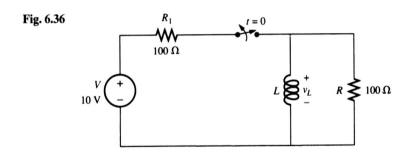

6.3 A double-energy circuit, which is shown in Fig. 6.37, has $V = 20$ V, $R = 100$ Ω, $L = 20$ mH, and $C = 2$ μF. Obtain a plot that shows the current as a function of time, beginning when the switch is closed. Because this circuit has an R value that gives underdamping, plot at least a full cycle of the oscillatory current.

Fig. 6.37

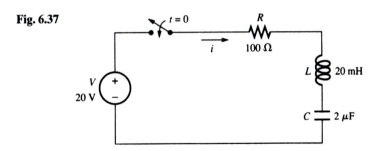

6.4 (a) Increase the value of R in Problem 6.3 to give critical damping, and obtain plots of current and component voltages. Find the maximum positive and negative current values.

(b) Using $R = 250$ Ω, repeat part a. Find the maximum positive and negative values of all component voltages.

6.5 At high frequencies the output capacitance of a voltage amplifier must be taken into account. In Fig. 6.38, $R = 10$ kΩ and $C = 1$ nF in order to model the output. With a pulse input voltage of 1 V applied for $t_p = 100$ μs, the output voltage should be a reasonable replica of the input pulse.

(a) Use the method described in the section "Step Response of an Amplifier" to determine the nature of the output voltage. Using Probe, see if the output voltage across C is a reasonable replica of the input pulse.

(b) If you desire a more exact replica of the input voltage, select a new value for t_p and run the analysis again. What are the f_H value for parts a and b?

Fig. 6.38

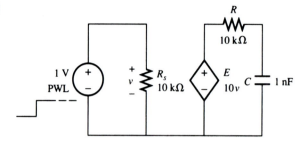

6.6 The discussion on low-frequency response of an amplifier in this chapter stated that often a tilt of no more than 10% is desirable. An approximate formula for tilt is

$$\text{tilt} = \frac{\pi f_L}{f}$$

where $f_L = 1/(2\pi RC)$ and f is the frequency of the square wave. Use an analysis based on the method shown in the example where the test is to be based on a 60-Hz square wave.

(a) Using $R = 1.59\ \text{k}\Omega$ and $C = 10\ \mu\text{F}$, find the tilt on the output by comparing the peak on the leading and trailing edges.

(b) What value of C is required to give a tilt of approximately 10%? Verify your choice with a Probe plot.

7

Fourier Series and Harmonic Components

One of the powerful features of PSpice is its ability to analyze systems with nonlinear response. For example, a power amplifier that is subjected to large input-signal swings will begin to operate over the nonlinear portion of its characteristics. This will introduce distortion in the output waveshape. In this chapter you will find out how much distortion is present, and you will analyze the harmonic content of the amplifier output.

FUNDAMENTAL AND SECOND-HARMONIC FREQUENCY

We will begin with a simple circuit that will introduce the concepts that are needed for more elaborate circuits. Figure 7.1 shows an input voltage $V_{in,p} = 1$ V. This is a sine wave with $f = 1$ kHz and a peak value of 1 V. ($V_{in} = 1/\sqrt{2}$ rms.) The voltage-dependent voltage source E is used to give an output that is a nonlinear function of the input. In this example, let

$$f(x) = 1 + x + x^2$$

This functional relationship is shown in the E statement in terms of the polynomial coefficients. Recall the polynomial form,

$$f(x) = k_0 + k_1 x + k_2 x^2$$

In our example this means that each of the last three numbers in the E statement will be *one*. We want to perform a Fourier analysis to see which harmonics are present in the output, but first we need to know more about what to expect.

A transient analysis must be performed in order to allow for the Fourier

Fig. 7.1 Output voltage is a nonlinear function of input.

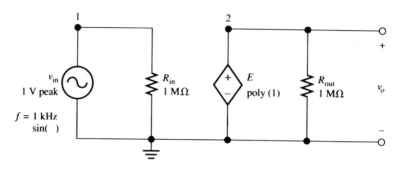

analysis to take place. We will need both a .TRAN and a .FOUR statement. It is customary to run the transient analysis for a full period of the fundamental frequency. In this example, $f = 1$ kHz; therefore $T = 1/f = 1$ ms. The Fourier analysis will produce frequency components through the ninth harmonic. This should be more than adequate for most purposes. If higher harmonics were shown, they would have little meaning due to the accumulation of round-off error in the results.

In order to give a more complete description of the input voltage V_{in}, use the *sin* form for the source. The arguments of $\sin(a, b, c, \ldots)$ are a = offset voltage, b = peak value, c = frequency, d = delay, e = damping factor, and f = phase.

The .FOUR statement produces the Fourier analysis, giving the Fourier components of the results of the transient analysis. Arguments for this statement include the frequency and the variables with which you are working. In this example, you will look at V(1) and V(2), which represent the input and output voltage waveforms. The input file is

```
Fourier Analysis; Decomposition of Polynomial
Vin 1 0 sin(0 1 1000); arguments are offset, peak, and frequency
Rin 1 0 1MEG
E 2 0 poly(1) 1,0 1 1 1; last 3 1s are for k0, k1, k2
Rout 2 0 1MEG
.TRAN 1us 1ms
.FOUR 1000 V(1) V(2)
.PROBE
.END
```

Run the analysis; then plot V(1) and V(2). Verify that V(1) is a replica of the input voltage V_{in}. The output voltage should show a dc component and a composite wave peaking at 3 V. From your study of Fourier series, you may observe that this looks like a wave consisting of a fundamental and second harmonic. You may want a printed copy of this graph for future study. Figure 7.2 shows these plots.

We are not through with this analysis. Look at the output file for this circuit, shown in Fig. 7.3, and note the following features. The node voltages show V(1) = 0 V and V(2) = 1 V. This means that the input wave has no offset, but the output has a 1-V offset, since $k_0 = 1$.

Figure 7.3 includes a table of Fourier components of V(1), but only a few of the values have real significance. The dc component of *3.5E − 10* is close to zero. It is not quite zero due to accumulation of round-off error. Harmonic no. 1 represents

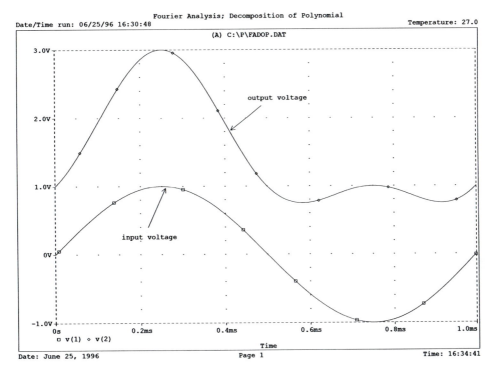

Fig. 7.2

the fundamental at $f = 1$ kHz. It shows a Fourier component of 1 and a phase of $2.4E - 7$ (almost zero). If you think of the components as

$$b_n \sin(nx)$$

then this corresponds to $b_1 = 1$, $n = 1$, where x is the fundamental frequency. The other harmonics can be ignored, since their values are many orders of magnitude smaller than the fundamental. It is from these components that we obtained the Probe trace of V(1). Refer to Fig. 7.3 for these data.

There is another table of Fourier components in Fig. 7.3; these are for V(2). Before looking at the various harmonics, note that there is a dc component in the composite wave of 1.5 V. Why 1.5 V? The value $k_0 = 1$ V is part of it, but the other 0.5 V is associated with b_2. Theory shows that in second-harmonic distortion, $b_0 = b_2$, where b_0 is a dc component introduced into the output. The fundamental frequency is present with $b_1 = 1$ V, and the second harmonic shows $b_2 = 0.5$ V at $-90°$. The higher harmonics are much smaller in magnitude, and they may be ignored.

As an exercise in wave synthesis, you may want to sketch the individual waves to see how you might predict the Probe result that you obtained as V(2). Remember to include proper amplitudes and phases for the fundamental and second harmonic as well as the total dc component.

After you have attempted to sketch the composite wave, you will be glad to know that PSpice can do this for you.

```
Fourier Analysis; Decomposition of Polynomial
Vin 1 0 sin(0 1 1000); arguments are offset, peak, and frequency
Rin 1 0 1MEG
E 2 0 poly(1) 1,0 1 1 1; last 3 1s are for k0, k1, k2
Rout 2 0 1MEG
.TRAN 1us 1ms
.FOUR 1000 V(1) V(2)
.PROBE
.END
```

NODE	VOLTAGE	NODE	VOLTAGE	NODE	VOLTAGE	NODE	VOLTAGE
(1)	0.0000	(2)	1.0000				

FOURIER COMPONENTS OF TRANSIENT RESPONSE V(1)

DC COMPONENT =   2.936647E-08

HARMONIC NO	FREQUENCY (HZ)	FOURIER COMPONENT	NORMALIZED COMPONENT	PHASE (DEG)	NORMALIZED PHASE (DEG)
1	1.000E+03	1.000E+00	1.000E+00	1.115E-06	0.000E+00
2	2.000E+03	1.994E-08	1.994E-08	-9.308E+01	-9.308E+01
3	3.000E+03	7.381E-09	7.381E-09	-9.083E+01	-9.083E+01
4	4.000E+03	4.388E-09	4.388E-09	-8.993E+01	-8.993E+01
5	5.000E+03	3.134E-09	3.134E-09	-9.107E+01	-9.107E+01
6	6.000E+03	1.525E-09	1.525E-09	-6.706E+01	-6.706E+01
7	7.000E+03	1.511E-09	1.511E-09	-1.392E+02	-1.392E+02
8	8.000E+03	1.237E-09	1.237E-09	-3.990E+01	-3.990E+01
9	9.000E+03	7.642E-10	7.642E-10	3.320E+01	3.320E+01

TOTAL HARMONIC DISTORTION =   2.208405E-06 PERCENT

FOURIER COMPONENTS OF TRANSIENT RESPONSE V(2)

DC COMPONENT =   1.500000E+00

HARMONIC NO	FREQUENCY (HZ)	FOURIER COMPONENT	NORMALIZED COMPONENT	PHASE (DEG)	NORMALIZED PHASE (DEG)
1	1.000E+03	1.000E+00	1.000E+00	-2.888E-07	0.000E+00
2	2.000E+03	5.000E-01	5.000E-01	-9.000E+01	-9.000E+01
3	3.000E+03	7.971E-08	7.971E-08	-1.546E+02	-1.546E+02
4	4.000E+03	5.126E-08	5.126E-08	-1.439E+02	-1.439E+02
5	5.000E+03	3.918E-08	3.918E-08	-1.420E+02	-1.420E+02
6	6.000E+03	3.327E-08	3.327E-08	-1.299E+02	-1.299E+02
7	7.000E+03	3.606E-08	3.606E-08	-1.268E+02	-1.268E+02
8	8.000E+03	2.859E-08	2.859E-08	-1.316E+02	-1.316E+02
9	9.000E+03	2.584E-08	2.584E-08	-1.189E+02	-1.189E+02

TOTAL HARMONIC DISTORTION =   4.999939E+01 PERCENT

Fig. 7.3

DECOMPOSITION AND RECONSTRUCTION OF WAVE

We will create a new input file based on Fig. 7.4, where we introduce two independent current sources. These are added to aid our analysis. They are not intended to modify or interfere with the original circuit in any way.

We used the two current sources so that you can look at the fundamental and second-harmonic frequencies. They supply a 1-Ω resistor in the parallel connection. The new input file is an extension of the previous file and looks like this:

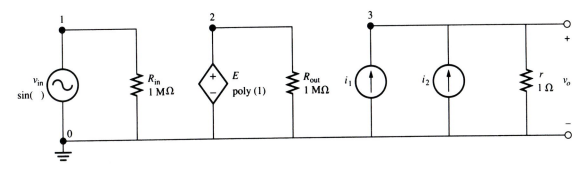

Fig. 7.4 Decomposition and reconstruction of waves.

```
Fourier Analysis; Decomposition of Polynomial
Vin 1 0 sin(0 1 1000); arguments are offset, peak, and frequency
Rin 1 0 1MEG
E 2 0 poly(1) 1,0 1 1 1; last 3 1s are for k0, k1, k2
Rout 2 0 1MEG
il 0 3 sin(1 1 1000)
i2 0 3 sin(0.5 0.5 2000 0 0 −90); offset, peak, freq., time delay, damping, phase
r 3 0 1
.TRAN 1us 1ms
.FOUR 1000 V(1) V(2) V(3)
.PROBE
.END
```

Before running the analysis, look carefully at the descriptions for il and i2. The information used for the reconstruction of the waves comes from your Fourier results of the previous study. Be sure that you understand the various arguments; then run the analysis. In Probe, plot $I(i1)$, $I(i2)$, and $I(r)$. Although these are currents, they may be thought of as numerically equal to voltages, since they are in parallel with $r = 1\ \Omega$. Figure 7.5 shows the results. Now you can see that the first trace represents the fundamental, the second represents the second harmonic, and the third represents the addition of these in the resistor r. Of course, if you prefer, you may plot $V(3)$ instead of $I(r)$. This may be more attractive since the Y-axis will no longer be marked in amperes. Verify that the first two waves add together to give the third wave at various times. In order to show a more compact plot, we used a 1-V offset for the fundamental and a 0.5-V offset for the second harmonic. Actually, the fundamental has a zero offset.

SECOND-HARMONIC DISTORTION IN A POWER AMPLIFIER

When an amplifier is driven so that it no longer follows the linear portion of its characteristic curve, it will introduce some distortion. A first approximation to this distortion is often made by including the second harmonic, indicating that the transfer function relating i_c to i_b (the collector current and base current) is somewhat parabolic. Usually, the distortion is much less than that indicated by our first, introductory example, which was shown in Fig. 7.1. The polynomial might be more like

$$f(x) = 0.1 + x + 0.2x^2$$

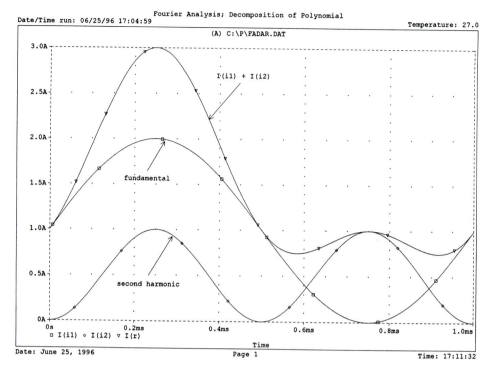

Fig. 7.5

It is a simple matter to convert the original input file to handle this situation. The *E* statement becomes

```
E 2 0 poly(1) 1.0 0.1 1 0.2; last 3 terms are for k0, k1, k2
```

The entire input file is

```
Fourier Analysis; Second-Harmonic Distortion, Power Amplifier
Vin 1 0 sin(0 1 1000)
Rin 1 0 1MEG
E 2 0 poly(1) 1.0 0.1 1 0.2
Rout 2 0 1MEG
.TRAN 1us 1ms
.FOUR 1000 V(1) V(2)
.PROBE
.END
```

Run the analysis and in Probe plot V(1) and V(2). You will see that both waves look very much like true sine waves. For a more accurate comparison, remove the V(2) trace and plot V(2) − 0.1 instead. This allows both waves to align more closely. When comparing the waves, remember that V(1) is the true sine wave and V(2) is the combination of the fundamental and the second harmonic. In this example, the second-harmonic content is considerably smaller in amplitude than in the previous example. You may want a printed copy of these waves for further study. Figure 7.6 shows the results.

After leaving Probe, look at the output file for this case. The input voltage V(1) is exactly the same as in the previous example, but V(2) is, of course, different. Note that the overall dc component of the output voltage is *0.2* V, and the second harmonic at $f = 2$ kHz has an amplitude of *0.1* V and an angle of $-90°$. The other frequency components are much smaller and can be ignored. Finally, look at the total harmonic distortion, which is very close to 10%, as expected. The second harmonic distortion is defined as b_2/b_1, where the b values are the coefficients of the second harmonic and the fundamental, respectively. Refer to Fig. 7.7 for these data.

INTERMODULATION DISTORTION

We will use the simple circuit shown in Fig. 7.8 to show how two sine waves combine in a nonlinear device using frequencies that are fairly close together, namely, $f_1 = 1$ kHz and $f_2 = 1.5$ kHz. The nonlinear mixing occurs in the voltage-dependent voltage source e. The polynomial describing the relationship is an extension of that used in the previous example and is

$$f(x) = 1 + x + x^2 + x^3$$

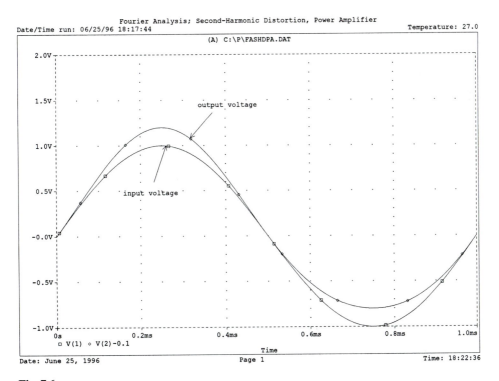

Fourier Analysis; Second-Harmonic Distortion, Power Amplifier

Date/Time run: 06/25/96 18:17:44   Temperature: 27.0

(A) C:\P\FASHDPA.DAT

□ V(1) ◇ V(2)-0.1

Date: June 25, 1996   Page 1   Time: 18:22:36

Fig. 7.6

```
Fourier Analysis; Second-Harmonic Distortion, Power Amplifier

****      CIRCUIT DESCRIPTION

Vin 1 0 sin(0 1 1000)
Rin 1 0 1MEG
E 2 0 poly(1) 1,0 0.1 1 0.2
Rout 2 0 1MEG
.TRAN 1us 1ms
.FOUR 1000 V(1) V(2)
.PROBE


NODE    VOLTAGE     NODE    VOLTAGE     NODE    VOLTAGE     NODE    VOLTAGE

(   1)   0.0000   (   2)     .1000

FOURIER COMPONENTS OF TRANSIENT RESPONSE V(1)

DC COMPONENT =   2.936647E-08

HARMONIC    FREQUENCY    FOURIER      NORMALIZED     PHASE        NORMALIZED
  NO          (HZ)       COMPONENT    COMPONENT      (DEG)        PHASE (DEG)

   1       1.000E+03    1.000E+00    1.000E+00    1.115E-06     0.000E+00
   2       2.000E+03    1.994E-08    1.994E-08   -9.308E+01    -9.308E+01
   3       3.000E+03    7.381E-09    7.381E-09   -9.083E+01    -9.083E+01
   4       4.000E+03    4.388E-09    4.388E-09   -8.993E+01    -8.993E+01
   5       5.000E+03    3.134E-09    3.134E-09   -9.107E+01    -9.107E+01
   6       6.000E+03    1.525E-09    1.525E-09   -6.706E+01    -6.706E+01
   7       7.000E+03    1.511E-09    1.511E-09   -1.392E+02    -1.392E+02
   8       8.000E+03    1.237E-09    1.237E-09   -3.990E+01    -3.990E+01
   9       9.000E+03    7.642E-10    7.642E-10    3.320E+01     3.320E+01

    TOTAL HARMONIC DISTORTION =   2.208405E-06 PERCENT

FOURIER COMPONENTS OF TRANSIENT RESPONSE V(2)

DC COMPONENT =   2.000000E-01

HARMONIC    FREQUENCY    FOURIER      NORMALIZED     PHASE        NORMALIZED
  NO          (HZ)       COMPONENT    COMPONENT      (DEG)        PHASE (DEG)

   1       1.000E+03    1.000E+00    1.000E+00    7.683E-07     0.000E+00
   2       2.000E+03    1.000E-01    1.000E-01   -9.000E+01    -9.000E+01
   3       3.000E+03    1.756E-08    1.756E-08   -1.336E+02    -1.336E+02
   4       4.000E+03    1.430E-08    1.430E-08   -1.348E+02    -1.348E+02
   5       5.000E+03    9.547E-09    9.547E-09   -1.365E+02    -1.365E+02
   6       6.000E+03    8.100E-09    8.100E-09   -1.232E+02    -1.232E+02
   7       7.000E+03    6.463E-09    6.463E-09   -1.342E+02    -1.342E+02
   8       8.000E+03    5.743E-09    5.743E-09   -9.544E+01    -9.544E+01
   9       9.000E+03    6.931E-09    6.931E-09   -1.092E+02    -1.092E+02

    TOTAL HARMONIC DISTORTION =   9.999880E+00 PERCENT
```

Fig. 7.7

The currents add in $R = 1 \ \Omega$, making V(1) numerically equal to the current in R. Thus the input voltage is V(1), which might be thought of as the voltage into a non-linear mixer. Because the sine waves are of different frequencies, their sum appears as a complex waveform. The input file is

```
Intermodulation Distortion
i1 0 1 sin(0 1 1000)
i2 0 1 sin(0 1 1500)
```

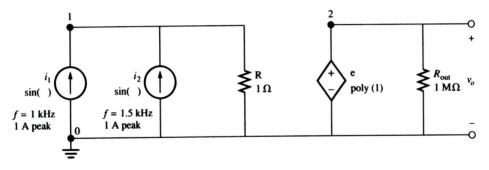

Fig. 7.8 Illustrating intermodulation distortion.

```
r 1 0 1
e 2 0 poly(1) 1,0 1 1 1 1
rout 2 0 1MEG
.tran 50us 50ms 50us
.probe
.end
```

Run the simulation and in Probe trace V(1). Select Plot, X-Axis Settings . . . , User Defined, and set the range from *0* to *10* ms to give a clearer view of the trace. The display shows five cycles of the composite input voltage. Figure 7.9 shows this graph.

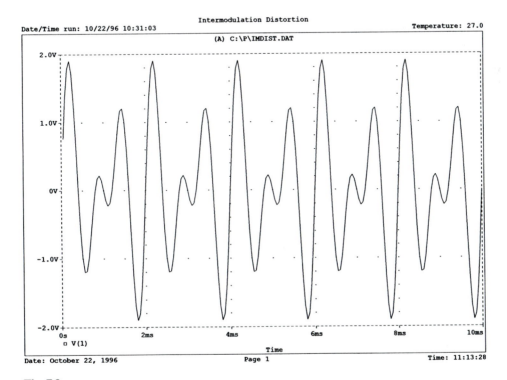

Fig. 7.9

To confirm that this is actually the addition of the *1*-kHz and *1.5*-kHz waves, select Trace, Fourier, converting from the time domain to the frequency domain. The display now extends to a frequency $f = 10$ kHz. Change the range to extend only to *4* kHz. Verify that the components are at the proper frequency with the expected amplitudes. Actually at $f = 1$ kHz, the voltage is *0.991* V, and at $f = 1.5$ kHz, the voltage is *0.979* V. Remember that in this synthesis, some accumulated error is present. Refer to Fig. 7.10 for the frequency display.

Next, select Trace, End Fourier to return to the time domain, delete the trace of V(1), and plot V(2). This represents the output of the mixer, which has been operated on by the polynomial relationship given by $f(x)$. The time domain plot looks a bit like what you saw at the input V(1), but closer observation will tell you that the two waves differ considerably. There is little hint of the frequency components making up this complex wave, so you will need to select the Fourier display for this wave; then expand the display of frequency components by letting the *X*-range extend from *0* to *5* kHz. Obtain a printed copy of this frequency spectrum for further study. From your studies of modulation-frequency components, you can predict and verify the results. Note that there is a dc component of *2* V along with significant components at *0.5*-kHz spacing in the range from *0.5* kHz to *4.5* kHz. See Fig. 7.11 for the frequency spectrum.

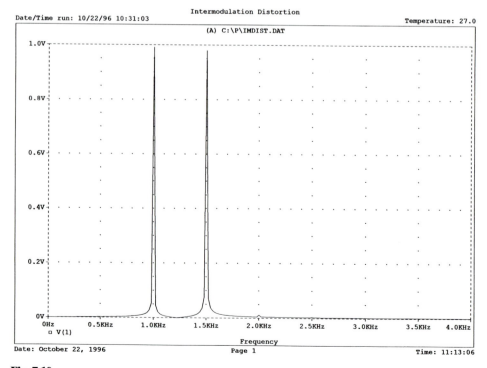

Fig. 7.10

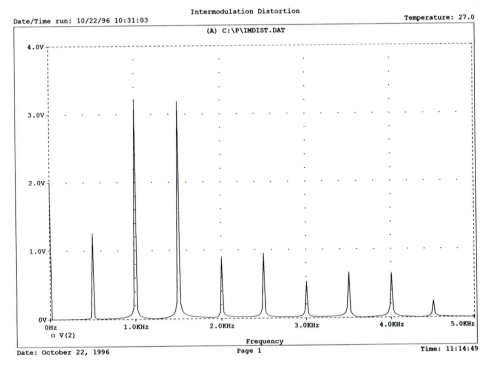

Fig. 7.11

ADDING SINE WAVES

One of the first things you learn in ac steady-state circuit analysis is that when a sine-wave voltage is used in a circuit containing linear elements such as resistors, inductors, and capacitors, the resulting current is also a sine wave of the same frequency. The various voltage drops in the circuit are all sine waves as well, obviously at the same frequency and differing only in amplitude and phase. We will use a simple circuit model to illustrate some of these features. Figure 7.12 shows three voltage sources feeding a circuit containing $R = 1\ \Omega$ along with $R_1 = R_2 = 0.001\ \Omega$. The latter two resistors are required to make the voltage sources practical. With this circuit we can show the addition of sine waves in Probe. The input file is

```
Addition of Sine Waves of the Same Frequency
v1 1 0 sin(0 1 1kHz)
*In the complete expression for sin the terms are
*offset, peak, frequency, delay, damping factor, and phase
v2 2 0 sin(0 1 1kHz 0 0 45); phase=45 degrees
v3 3 0 sin(0 1 1kHz 0 0 90); phase=90 degrees
r1 1 2 0.001
r2 2 3 0.001
R 3 0 1
.tran 0.1ms 2ms
.probe
.end
```

Fig. 7.12 Adding sine waves of the same frequency.

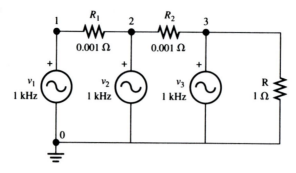

Run the simulation, and in Probe trace v(1), v(2), and v(1) + v(2). The resulting traces show v_2 peaking about 45° ahead of v_1, and the sum of v_1 and v_2 peaking at a point in between. Verify that the peak of v_1 is *1* V a *251* μs (90°), the peak of v_2 is *1* V at *131* μs (47.16°), and the peak of $v_1 + v_2$ is *1.8381* V at *171* μs (61.56°). Remove these traces and try other combinations, such as v(1), v(3), and v(1) + v(3). Try to predict what the peak value of the resultant will be, based on your study of the addition of sinusoids, before you look at the graph, which is shown in Fig. 7.13.

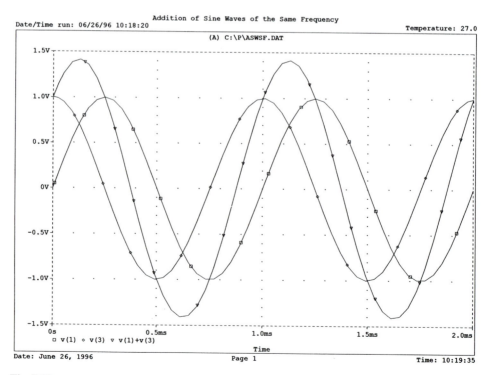

Fig. 7.13

ADDING FUNDAMENTAL AND SECOND HARMONIC

The input file based on Fig. 7.12 can easily be modified for a variety of source combinations. Remove v_3 and let v_2 be the second harmonic of v_1. Of course, the resulting wave will have a shape that is no longer a sine wave. In fact, its form will depend on the relative phasing of v_1 and v_2. For our example, we will let the two waves reach their positive peaks together. The input file is

```
Adding Sine Waves; Fundamental and 2nd Harmonic Peaking Together
v1 1 0 sin(0 1 1kHz)
v2 2 0 sin(0 1 2kHz 0 0 −90)
R1 1 2 0.001
R 2 0 1
.tran 0.1ms 1ms
.probe
.end
```

Run the analysis and in Probe plot v(1), v(2), and v(1) + v(2). Since v_1 and v_2 reach their positive peaks together, the resultant wave peaks at 2 V, but when the fundamental reaches its negative peak, the second harmonic has returned to its positive peak, giving a result of zero. The wave of $v_1 + v_2$ is clearly not a sine wave. See Fig. 7.14 for these plots.

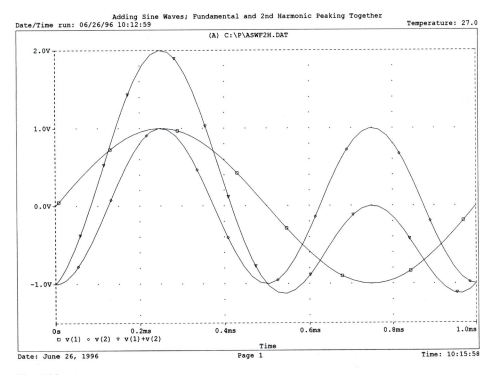

Fig. 7.14

AMPLITUDE MODULATION

An interesting plot of an amplitude-modulated wave may be obtained in PSpice by using a multiplier function on sine waves of widely differing frequency. Figure 7.15 shows the simulator circuit model. The first sinusoidal source is v_1 with a frequency of 1 kHz. The second source is v_2 with a frequency of 20 kHz. The multiplication takes place in the dependent voltage source e. The resistors are required to avoid floating sources. The input file is

```
Multiplier for Modulated Wave
v1 1 0 sin(0 1 1000)
R1 1 0 10k
v2 2 0 sin(0 1 20000)
R2 2 0 10k
e 3 0 poly(2) 1,0 2,0 0 0 0 0 1
R3 2 0 10k
.tran lus 1ms
.four 1000 v(1) v(2) v(3)
.probe
.end
```

The polynomial statement has for its last five terms $0\ 0\ 0\ 0\ 1$. Recall that these are coefficient values for k_0, $k_1 v_1$, $k_2 v_2$, $k_3 v_1{}^2$, $k_4 v_1 v_2$. All k values are zero except for the last, with $k_4 = 1$. Run the analysis; then in Probe plot v(1) and v(3). This plot deliberately omits the 20-kHz wave, making the results easier to interpret. The composite wave v(3) clearly shows the classical appearance of an amplitude-modulated wave. In this example, both of the input waves v_1 and v_2 have 1-V amplitudes. See these traces in Fig. 7.16.

Before leaving Probe, add the plot of the other input voltage v(2), so that you are now displaying v(1), v(2), and v(3). This trace now shows the carrier along with the other two waves, giving the complete picture. Print this if you would like a copy of it; then remove the v(2) trace and choose Trace, Fourier. Let the X-axis range extend from 0 to 30 kHz. The frequency domain now shows the 1-kHz, 19-kHz, and 21-kHz components. The latter components are the upper- and lower-sideband frequencies produced by this modulation. Observe the amplitude of each wave. Recall the trigonometric identity

Fig. 7.15 Multiplier for modulated wave.

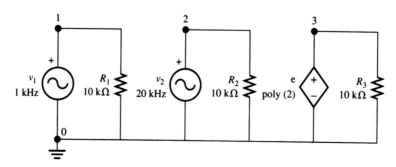

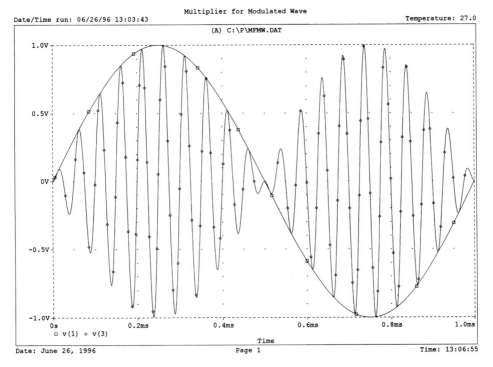

Date/Time run: 06/26/96 13:03:43 — Multiplier for Modulated Wave — Temperature: 27.0

(A) C:\P\MFMW.DAT

Fig. 7.16

$$(\sin \alpha)(\sin \beta) = \tfrac{1}{2}[\cos(\alpha - \beta) - \cos(\alpha + \beta)]$$

which accounts for the amplitudes of 0.5 V for the sideband frequencies. Refer to Fig. 7.17 for the frequency spectrum. (The markers were removed to avoid clutter.)

Run the analysis with various relative amplitudes for the modulating voltage v_1 to see what effect this has on the modulation factor m. For example, when v_1 has an amplitude of 0.8, what is the modulation factor, and what does the composite wave look like?

NEW DOT COMMAND USED IN THIS CHAPTER

.FOUR*<frequency>***<output variable>*

For example,

```
.FOUR 1kHz V(1) V(2)
```

means perform a decomposition into Fourier components. The decomposition will be done only if a transient analysis has been specified in the input file by using

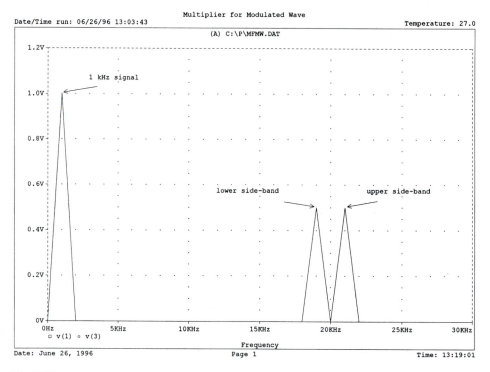

Fig. 7.17

.TRAN <step value><final time>

The Fourier analysis gives the dc component, the fundamental, and all harmonics through the ninth. They are shown in magnitude and phase with actual and normalized values. In the preceding example, both V(1) and V(2) will be analyzed into their components.

It is customary to use the *.PROBE* statement in connection with the Fourier analysis; however, *.PRINT* or *.PLOT* may be used as well.

PROBLEMS

7.1   In Fig. 7.18, the polynomial for *E* is of the form

$$f(x) = x + x^2$$

Using $v_{i\text{peak}} = 1$ V, $f = 1$ kHz, and $V = 1$ V, we wish to compare v_o with v_i. Predict what the approximate harmonic content in the output will be; then run a PSpice analysis, which will show the harmonic content of both the input and output voltages. In the .FOUR statement use voltages V(2,1) and V(3). Look at the output file and determine the harmonic content in V(3).

Fig. 7.18

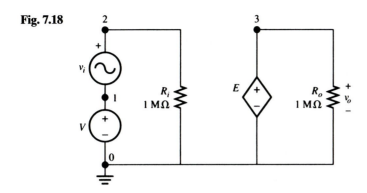

7.2 In Problem 7.1, use Trace, Fourier to observe the harmonic content in V(3). Let the X-axis run from 0 to 5 kHz displaying V(2,1) and V(3).

7.3 Run the analysis for Problem 7.1 with

$$f(x) = 2 + 0.1x^2$$

Predict the approximate harmonic content in the output; then plot V(2,1) and V(3) to verify the accuracy of your predictions.

7.4 Figure 7.4 shows a polynomial source. The source E was given as

$$f(x) = 1 + x + x^2$$

Change the source to

$$f(x) = x + x^2$$

and perform the decomposition and reconstruction analysis, modifying i_1 and i_2 as required so that I(r) will be the same shape as V(2).

7.5 In the section "Second-Harmonic Distortion in a Power Amplifier," change the polynomial to

$$f(x) = 0.05 + x + 0.1x^2$$

and run a PSpice analysis as suggested in the text. Plot V(1) and V(2) − 0.05 to compare the ac components of input and output voltage. Predict the dc component of the output voltage, the amplitude and phase of the second harmonic, and the total harmonic distortion. Verify your predictions using Probe and your output file.

7.6 In the section "Intermodulation Distortion," we combined two sine waves of different frequencies. Perform an analysis using $f_1 = 2$ kHz and $f_2 = 2.5$ kHz with the $f(x)$ expression remaining the same. Modify the .TRAN statement as necessary. Follow the steps as given in the text example in order to verify your predictions of frequency components in the output.

7.7 In the section "Adding Sine Waves," Fig. 7.12 showed parallel branches with three voltage sources. The adding of waves was mathematical rather than physical. Modify the circuit so that the voltage sources are all in series; then perform the analysis again. Are the results the same?

7.8   Perform an analysis to add sine waves of the same frequency $f = 1$ kHz, given

$$v_1 = 0.5\underline{/0°} \text{ V} \quad v_2 = 1\underline{/45°} \text{ V} \quad v_3 = 1.5\underline{/90°} \text{ V}$$

(a) Find the peak value of $v_1 + v_2$ and the time and phase angle at which the peak occurs.
(b) Repeat part *a* for $v_1 + v_3$.
When using the cursor mode, and several traces are shown on the same plot, use the [*Ctrl*] key to select among the traces.

7.9   To illustrate the effect of adding sine waves of slightly different frequencies rather than adding harmonics, perform an analysis as in Problem 7.8 using $v_1 = 1$ V, 1 kHz, 0° ; $v_2 = 1$ V, 1.2 kHz, 0° ; and $v_3 = 1$ V, 1.4 kHz, 0° .
(a) Plot v_1, v_2, and $v_1 + v_2$. Find the peak value of $v_1 + v_2$.
(b) Plot v_1, v_3, and $v_1 + v_3$. Find the peak value of $v_1 + v_3$.

7.10 Based on the section dealing with amplitude modulation, let $v_1 = 1$ V, 1 kHz and modify v_2 so that the index of modulation will be 0.5. Run the PSpice analysis to illustrate the desired results.

8

Stability and Oscillators

Amplifiers, especially those involving several stages, may be stable or may go into oscillation. When oscillations occur, they are prone to settle at a certain frequency, depending on the combination of components used, including any stray inductance and capacitance. When a portion of the output signal is fed back to the input, there is the possibility that oscillations will be produced.

THE FEEDBACK LOOP

Figure 8.1 shows a block diagram of the basic feedback loop. It includes a mixing junction where the input signal v_i and the feedback signal v_f combine. Actually, the mixing junction gives a phase inversion to the feedback signal as shown by the minus sign in the figure, so that this component appears as a negative input. The difference voltage is

$$v_d = v_i - v_f$$

This voltage is fed into the amplifier, which has a voltage gain A. This creates the output voltage

$$v_o = Av_d = A(v_i - v_f)$$

The output is returned to the summing junction after passing through a feedback network labeled β. The ratio v_f/v_o defines β as the portion of the output voltage that is fed back or returned to the summing junction.

It is assumed that you will study this topic more thoroughly in another text-

Fig. 8.1   The basic feedback loop.

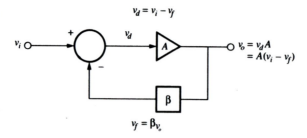

$$v_d = v_i - v_f$$

$$v_o = v_d A$$
$$= A(v_i - v_f)$$

$$v_f = \beta v_o$$

book. However, some authors use different symbols for the various quantities shown here. In this text the loop gain or transmission gain is given by $A\beta$, the product of the gain of the amplifier and the feedback factor. If the effect of the phase inversion is taken into account, the loop gain is $-A\beta$. It is not difficult to show that

$$A_f = \frac{A}{1 + A\beta}$$

This represents the closed-loop gain, which is the gain of the circuit with the feedback network in place.

   If the signal fed back, including its inversion, is identical to the input signal, the external input may be removed, and the amplifier will continue to produce the same output as before. This is expressed by stating that

$$-A\beta = 1$$

is the condition required for oscillation, which is called the *Barkhausen criterion*. From a practical standpoint, $|A\beta|$ should be slightly greater than unity. Nonlinearity in the circuit components allows the oscillations to continue without building up to larger and larger amplitudes.

   In Fig. 8.1, all voltages may be replaced by currents, producing the dual of the previous situation. This means that the input is i_i, the difference is i_d, the output is $i_o = i_d A$, and the feedback signal becomes $i_f = \beta i_o$, making

$$i_d = i_i - i_f$$

The loop gain is still $A\beta$, which becomes $-A\beta$ taking the phase inversion into account. The closed-loop gain is still

$$A_f = \frac{A}{1 + A\beta}$$

THE WIEN-BRIDGE OSCILLATOR WITH INITIAL HELP

As an introduction to the study of oscillators, consider the Wien-bridge circuit of Fig. 8.2. The circuit components have been chosen to give $f_o = 25$ kHz with

Fig. 8.2   Wien-bridge oscillator.

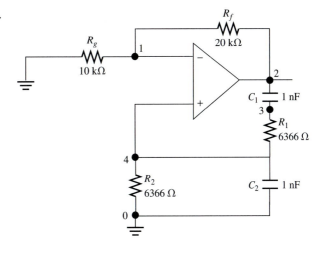

$$f_o = \frac{1}{2\pi RC}$$

where $R = R_1 = R_2$, and $C = C_1 = C_2$. If C is chosen as 1 nF, then $R = 6366\ \Omega$. For oscillations to be sustained, R_f/R_g must be 2. If R_f is chosen as 20 kΩ, then $R_g = 10$ kΩ. Our problem is to use PSpice to show that oscillations will occur at the desired frequency. This input file is proposed:

```
Wien-Bridge Oscillator
E 2 0 4 1 2E5
Ri 4 1 1E6
Rg 1 0 10k
R1 3 4 6366
R2 4 0 6366
Rf 2 1 20k
C1 2 3 1nF IC=2V; initial charge to begin oscillations
C2 4 0 1nF
.PROBE
.TRAN 0.05us 50us UIC
.END
```

The capacitor C_1 is given an initial charge (with specified voltage) in order to create the priming condition required to begin the oscillations. Without this, the PSpice analysis will show that the output voltage is a steady zero value.

The results obtained in Probe are shown in Fig. 8.3. The trace shows the output voltage v(2). Note that the output is a sine wave with a frequency $f = 25$ kHz and an amplitude of 6 V.

Can the actual oscillator be expected to produce a peak output voltage of 6 V? In an attempt to answer this question, run the analysis again, but change the capacitor voltage using IC = 1 V. We will also look at the oscillator from the standpoint of loop gain and phase shift later in this chapter.

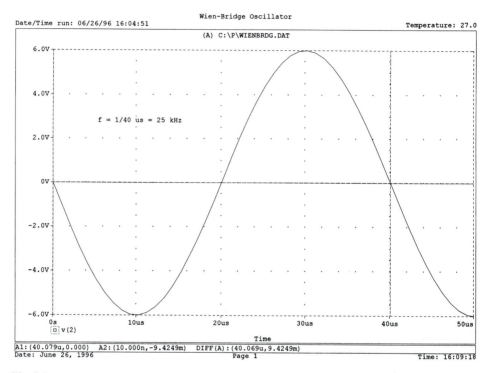

Fig. 8.3

THE *LC* OSCILLATOR WITH INITIAL HELP

A tuned-circuit oscillator using two capacitors and one inductor in the feedback loop is called a *Colpitts oscillator*. The Hartley oscillator is similar, but it uses two inductors and one capacitor. The Colpitts circuit and its components are shown in Fig. 8.4. The input file is

```
Colpitts Oscillator
E 3 0 0 2 2E5
Ri 0 2 1E6
R1 2 1 10k
R2 2 3 20k
R 3 4 1k
C1 1 0 0.005uF
C2 4 0 0.05uF IC=2V
L 1 4 5mH
.PROBE
.TRAN 0.3us 60us UIC
.END
```

In Probe, when the output voltage V(3) is plotted, the results are as shown in Fig. 8.5. Observe that the oscillations appear to be increasing in amplitude. Since we are using an ideal op amp in the circuit, the onset of nonlinearity does not appear. In the practical circuit the sine wave would begin to show some distortion as well as

Fig. 8.4 Colpitts oscillator.

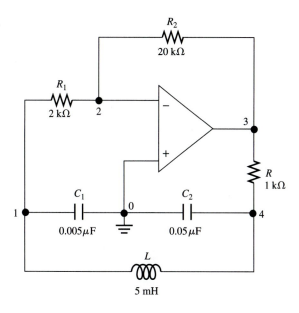

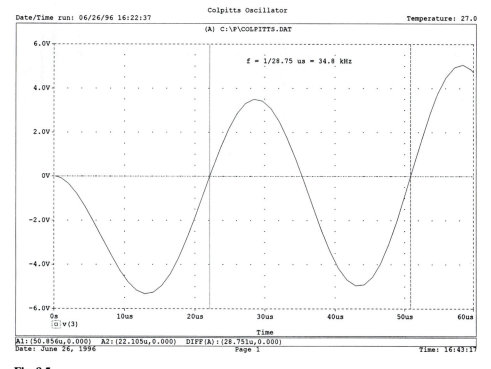

Fig. 8.5

leveling off. The amplitude of the sine wave would be determined largely by the biasing voltage present in the op amp circuit. Note that the frequency is found by using the (reciprocal of the) time between two axis crossings.

MEASUREMENTS WITH A TEST CIRCUIT

In order to take measurements of the loop gain and phase shift of the feedback loop, we will introduce a test circuit as shown in Fig. 8.6. The circuit consists of an independent ac voltage $V = 1$ V at nodes TV_o and TV_i (o for *out* and i for *in*). There are also two voltage-dependent voltage sources. EV_i and EV_o. The independent voltage source is inserted at a convenient break point in the feedback path of an oscillator. Each dependent voltage has its accompanying internal resistance so that nodes V_i and V_o will not appear to be floating. The measuring technique will be illustrated in the following examples.

THE PHASE-SHIFT OSCILLATOR

The classic RC phase-shift oscillator is shown in Fig. 8.7. The output of the op amp is connected to three RC phase-shifting networks. Each network will produce a certain phase shift, and if the total phase shift produced in the three networks is 180°, oscillations may occur. It is further required that $|A\beta| = 1$. An analysis of the circuit shows the frequency of oscillation is

$$f_o = \frac{1}{2\pi RC\sqrt{6}}$$

For example, let the desired frequency of oscillation be $f_o = 100$ Hz, and let $C = 0.5\ \mu$F. Then R becomes 1.3 kΩ. The analysis of this circuit also shows that at f_o, $\beta = 1/29$; therefore $|A|$ should equal 29 if oscillations are to be sustained. In practice, $|A|$ is made slightly greater than 29 to account for slight variations in components and operating conditions.
    This circuit is an inverting op amp where

$$A = \frac{-R_f}{R_1}$$

Fig. 8.6   Test circuit for voltage measurement.

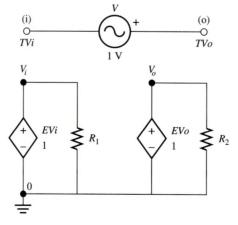

Fig. 8.7 Phase-shift oscillator.

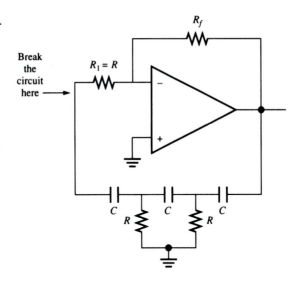

Since $R_1 = R$, this relation yields

$$A = -29 = \frac{-R_f}{1.3 \text{ k}\Omega}$$

and solving for R_f, we find that $R_f = 37.7$ kΩ. If this value is increased by 5% to allow for the variations previously mentioned, the value of R_f becomes 39.58 kΩ.

In order to look at the loop gain, we will break the feedback loop to allow for measurements with our test circuit. The break will take place at the point marked in Fig. 8.7. The node at this point will thus become two nodes. These two nodes will appear to be floating unless they are shown in a subcircuit. For this reason, the oscillator is redrawn in Fig. 8.8, where the break involves the two nodes i (for *in*) and o (for *out*). The figure includes labeling of the other nodes in preparation for PSpice input file. It is convenient to put the op amp in a subcircuit as we have done in other examples. The simplified op amp model will have this subcircuit:

```
.subckt iop m p vo; m is inverting, p is noninverting
 rin m p 1E6
 e vo 0 p m 2E5
.ends
```

The next portion of the input file involves the circuit shown in Fig. 8.8, showing the break point that will allow for the loop-gain analysis. The op amp is called from its subcircuit with the X statement. This portion of the input file is

```
.subckt rc i o; i and o are in and out labels for break point
 x 2 1 3 iop; this calls the opamp circuit
 vi 1 0 1V
 rf 3 2 39.58k
 rl o 2 1.3k
 r2 5 0 1.3k
 r3 4 0 1.3k
```

Fig. 8.8 Phase-shift oscillator
with feedback loop broken.

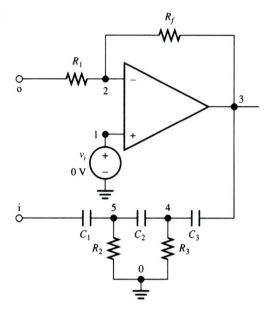

```
cl i 5 0.5uF
c2 5 4 0.5uF
c3 4 3 0.5uF
.ends
```

The last portion of the input file shows the reference to the oscillator subcircuit *rc*;
it also contains the statements required to perform the test of the feedback loop.
The input statements are

```
* loop-gain test statements
X TVi TVo rc
V TVo TVi AC 1
EVi Vi 0 0 TVi 1
R1 Vi 0 1E6
EVo Vo 0 TVo 0 1
R2 Vo 0 1E6
.AC DEC 20 1Hz 10kHz
.PROBE
.END
```

Create an input file by combining all three of the preceding segments and run
the analysis. Then plot

$$20*\log 10(V(Vi)/V(Vo))$$

The plot indicates the open-loop gain of the feedback network. Remember that if
oscillations are to be sustained, $|A\beta|$ must equal 1. On the logarithmic plot, the value
corresponds to zero rather than one. Verify that at $f = 100$ Hz, the plot gives a near-
zero response. See Fig. 8.9 for this plot.

Now plot the phase shift with

$$VP(Vi) - VP(Vo)$$

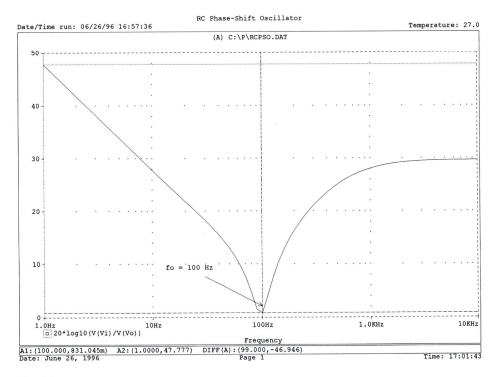

Fig. 8.9

which will compare the phases of the fed-back signal and the output signal. Confirm that at $f = 100$ Hz, the angle of the trace is $-187°$. Since the open-loop analysis does not include the phase inversion at the input, the total phase shift under closed-loop conditions is actually 367°. This is close to the desired 360°, which would mean that the amplifier cannot distinguish between an input signal and a feedback signal, thereby sustaining oscillations. Figure 8.10 shows the phase-shift plot.

THE WIEN-BRIDGE OSCILLATOR

For another oscillator example, consider Fig. 8.11, which shows the Wien-bridge oscillator. The bridge involves series elements R_1, C_1, and parallel elements R_2, C_2. An analysis of this circuit shows that

$$f_o = \frac{1}{2\pi RC}$$

We will choose $f_o = 25$ kHz, $C_1 = C_2 = 1$ nF, and $R_g = 10$ kΩ. This leads to $R = R_1 = R_2 = 6366\ \Omega$. In this circuit, $|A\beta| = 1$ is required for oscillations to be sustained. The analysis also shows that at resonance, $\beta = \frac{1}{3}$, calling for an amplifier gain of $A = 3$. Since the gain of the noninverting op amp is

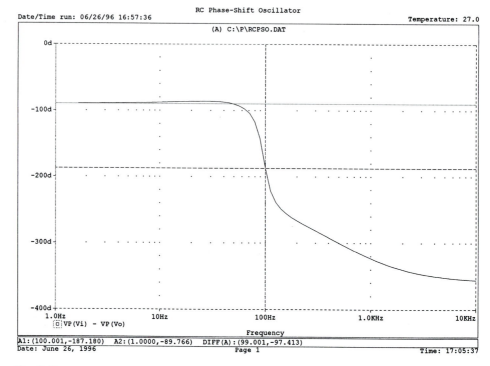

Fig. 8.10

$$A = \frac{R_g + R_f}{R_g}$$

this gives $R_f = 20$ kΩ.

We redraw the circuit in Fig. 8.12 to show the break for the test measurements and the labeling of the nodes. The subcircuit for the oscillator thus becomes a portion of the input file. The entire input file is

```
Wien-Bridge Oscillator with Test Circuit
.subckt wien i o
 x 2 4 i iop
 vi 1 0 0V
 rg 1 2 10k
 rf 2 i 20k
 r1 3 4 6366
 r2 4 0 6366
 c1 o 3 1nF
 c2 4 0 1nF
.ends
.subckt iop m p vo
 rin m p 1E6
 e vo 0 p m 2E5
.ends
X TVi TVo wien
V TVo TVi AC 1
```

Fig. 8.11 Wien-bridge oscillator.

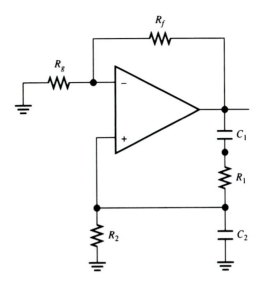

```
EVi Vi 0 0 TVi 1
R1 Vi 0 1E6
EVo Vo 0 TVo 0 1
R2 Vo 0 1E6
.AC DEC 40 1kHz 1 MegHz
.PROBE
.END
```

Run the analysis and plot

$$20*log10(V(Vi)/V(Vo))$$

Fig. 8.12 Wien-bridge oscillator
with feedback loop open.

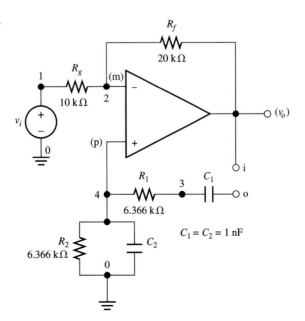

Verify that at $f = 25.12$ kHz, the gain is at its maximum. This corresponds to a unity gain since this is a dB plot.

Now select <u>P</u>lot and add another plot that will show the phase shift of the feedback loop. The desired trace is

$$VP(Vi) - VP(Vo)$$

which will tell you whether or not the phase-shift circuit produces the desired phase shift required to sustain oscillations. Verify that the phase-shift plot shows that at $f = 25.3$ kHz, the phase shift is $-180°$. Refer to Fig. 8.13 for these plots.

Another Wien-Bridge Example

For another example, suppose that we are given the component values for the bridge portion of a Wien-bridge oscillator, but we have not solved for the frequency of oscillation. We wish to see whether or not oscillations will be sustained and if so at what frequency. The circuit diagram is essentially the same as in the previous example, and Fig. 8.14 shows the component values. The input file is

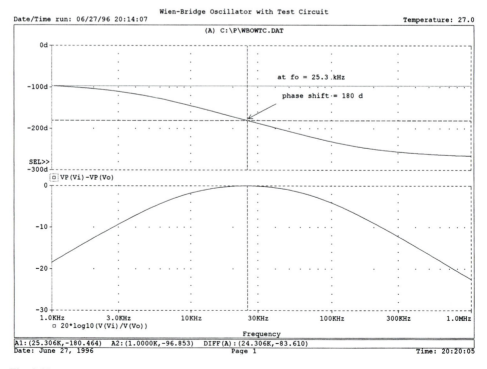

Fig. 8.13

Fig. 8.14 Another Wien-bridge oscillator with feedback loop broken.

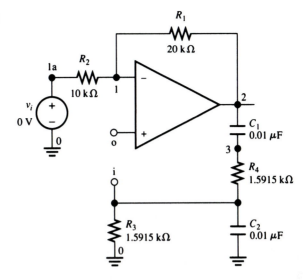

```
Another Wien-Bridge Example
.subckt wien i o
 vi 1a 0 0V
 x 1 o 2 iop
 r1 1 2 20k
 r2 1 1a 20k
 r3 i 0 1.5915k
 r4 3 i 1.5915k
 c1 2 3 0.01uF
 c2 i 0 0.01uF
.ends
.subckt iop m p vo
 rin m p 1E6
 e vo 0 p m 2E5
.ends
X TVi TVo wien
V TVo TVi AC 1
EVi Vi 0 0 TVi 1
R1 Vi 0 1E6
EVo Vo 0 TVo 0 1
R2 Vo 0 1E6
.AC DEC 20 100Hz 0.1MegHz
.PROBE
.END
```

Run the analysis, and as in the previous example, plot

$$20*log10(V(Vi)/V(Vo))$$

Use the cursor mode to show that the peak of this plot is at $f = 10$ kHz. In order to verify that this is the frequency at which oscillations will be sustained, plot

$$VP(Vi) - VP(Vo)$$

and show that the phase shift is $-180°$ at a frequency of 10 kHz. Figure 8.15 shows these plots.

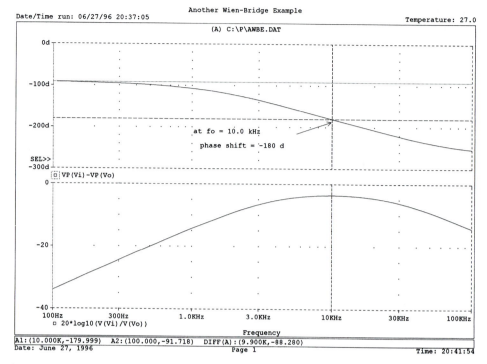

Fig. 8.15

THE COLPITTS OSCILLATOR

We often use a general type of oscillator circuit to describe either the Colpitts or the Hartley oscillator. Figure 8.16 shows the general circuit. The impedances are Z_1, Z_2, and Z_3. For oscillations to be produced, it is found that

$$Z_1 + Z_2 + Z_3 = 0$$

The impedances are usually assumed to be pure reactances, with X_1 and X_2 the same type and X_3 the opposite type. In the Colpitts, X_1 and X_2 are capacitive while X_3 is inductive. Let us choose $C_1 = 0.005\ \mu F$ and $C_2 = 0.05\ \mu F$, which gives $L = 5$ mH.

The frequency of oscillation is found to be

$$f_o = \frac{1}{2\pi} \frac{C_1 + C_2}{LC_1 C_2}$$

which gives $f_o = 33.38$ kHz. This is the circuit previously shown in Fig. 8.4. The other components are $R = 1\ k\Omega$, $R_1 = 10\ k\Omega$, and $R_2 = 20\ k\Omega$.

The circuit is broken for test purposes, giving Fig. 8.17. The input file then becomes

```
Colpitts Oscillator
.subckt colpitts i o
  x 2 1a 3 iop
```

Fig. 8.16 Basic circuit for resonant-type oscillator.

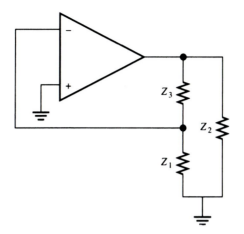

```
vi 1a 0 0V
r1 o 2 10k
r2 2 3 20k
r 3 4 1k
c1 i 0 0.005uF
c2 4 0 0.05uF
L i 4 5mH
.ends
.subckt iop m p vo
 rin m p 1E6
 e vo 0 p m 2E5
.ends
X TVi TVo colpitts
V TVo TVi ac 1
EVi Vi 0 0 TVi 1
```

Fig. 8.17 Colpitts oscillator test circuit.

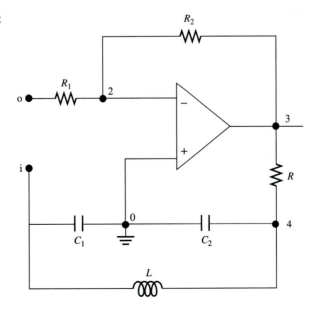

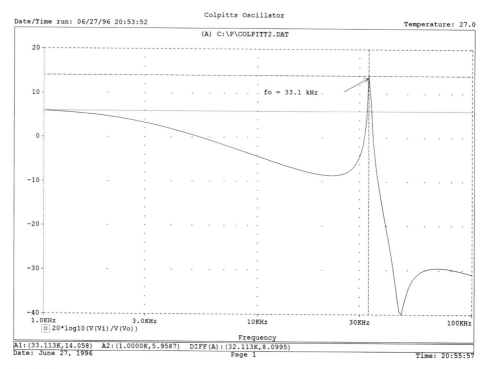

Fig. 8.18

```
R1 Vi 0 1E6
EVo Vo 0 TVo 0 1
R2 Vo 0 1E6
.ac DEC 100 1kHz 100kHz
.PROBE
.END
```

Run the analysis and obtain a plot like the one shown in Fig. 8.18. Note that there is a resonant point at $f = 33.1$ kHz, which is close to the predicted frequency of oscillation. Plot the difference in phase between the input and output voltages, and verify that at $f = 33.5$ kHz, the phase shift is $-180°$.

PROBLEMS

8.1 A phase-shift oscillator as shown in Fig. 8.7 is to oscillate at $f_o = 1$ kHz. Using $C = 1 \, \mu\text{F}$, select the required components and run an analysis by one of the methods suggested in the text. Using Probe, verify that the circuit performs as expected. Document your results with a Probe plot.

8.2 Using the Wien-bridge oscillator as shown in Fig. 8.11, it is desired to have $f_o = 10$ kHz. Make the required changes in the input file given in the text, and run a PSpice analysis that includes an initial charge of C_1. Using Probe, verify that the circuit is capable of sustaining oscillations at the desired frequency.

8.3 Design a Colpitts oscillator to operate at $f_o = 100$ kHz. The circuit shown in Fig. 8.4 may be used as a model. Use the technique of opening the feedback loop to show that oscillations will be sustained at the desired frequency and to demonstrate the phase shift at this frequency.

8.4 For the Colpitts oscillator of Problem 8.3, close the feedback loop and use the stimulus method to show that oscillations occur at $f_o = 100$ kHz. Verify sinusoidal oscillations using Probe.

8.5 Refer to Fig. 8.16 for the general LC oscillator configuration. Design a Hartley oscillator where X_1 and X_2 are inductors and X_3 is a capacitor, such that $f_o = 50$ kHz. Let $L_1 = L_2 = 20$ mH. Assume that there is no mutual coupling between the inductors. Use PSpice/Probe to verify the design.

8.6 An FET phase-shift oscillator equivalent circuit is shown in Fig. 8.19. For oscillations to occur, $|A|$ must be at least 29, requiring an FET with $\mu \geq 29$. Given: $g_m = 5$ mS, $r_d = 500$ kΩ, $C = 0.5$ μF, $R = 1.3$ kΩ, and $R_d = 10$ kΩ, use the method of opening the feedback loop to determine if oscillations will occur and if so at what frequency.

Fig. 8.19

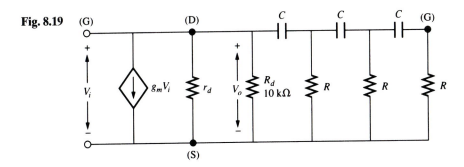

9

An Introduction to PSpice Devices

In the previous chapters, we have emphasized creating our own models. The models have been those that are customarily used in circuit analysis. These models have been linear and bilateral. Such models should be used whenever possible in order to keep the analysis clear and simple.

Often there is a need for a more complicated model, perhaps one that will require the use of equations that will convey the characteristics of the device. One of the strengths of PSpice is that several such models are available for your use. These models contain features that are usually associated with actual components.

A HALF-WAVE RECTIFIER

To introduce you to the concept of device models, consider the circuit shown in Fig. 9.1. This is the basic circuit for a half-wave rectifier, consisting of an ac-voltage source, a diode, and a resistor. The use of the diode presents a problem. You might model the diode as a closed switch for the positive half cycles of the input voltage and as an open switch for the negative half cycles. If you did this, you would then break the problems into two parts because your models would call for two different representations.

There is no need to do this, however, because PSpice has a built-in model for the diode. In order for you to use this built-in model, you must include a .MODEL statement in your input file. It has the following form:

.MODEL <*model name*> <*model type*>

Fig. 9.1   Half-wave rectifier
using diode model.

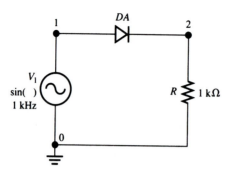

For this example, we will choose *D1* as the model name, and we must use *D* as the
model type. This is required if PSpice is to recognize the device as a diode of the
built-in model type. In order to see the circuit in action, use this input file:

```
Half-Wave Rectifier Using Built-in Model
v1 1 0 sin (0 12V 1000Hz)
DA 1 2 D1
R 2 0 1k
.MODEL D1 D
.TRAN 0.1ms 1ms
.PROBE
.END
```

The transient analysis will allow you to look at a full cycle of both the input
sine wave at f = 1 kHz and the output voltage across the resistor as a function of
time. Note the form of the diode statement:

```
DA 1 2 D1
```

The designation *DA* is our choice for this diode name. The name must begin
with *D*. It is located between nodes *1* (p) and *2* (n). The last item on the list is *D1*.
This must agree with the diode *model name.*
Run the analysis and in Probe plot v(1) and v(2) for a full cycle. This will be for
t = 1 ms. Observe that the input is a sine wave and that the output has been rectified
such that the negative half cycle is missing. The output voltage differs from the input
voltage during the positive half cycle by the voltage drop across the diode. Use the
cursor mode to determine the diode drop when the input voltage is at its peak. Verify
that this voltage drop is 0.72 V. Figure 9.2 shows the input and output waves.
The listing of the model type in the .MODEL statement could be extended to
include other parameters. For example, silicon diodes and germanium diodes have
different cut-in voltages and different saturation currents. You can specify up to 14
parameters in order to customize a diode. A complete list of these parameters is
given in Appendix D under "*D* Diode."

THE BUILT-IN MODEL FOR A DIODE

If you would like to see the characteristic curve for the built-in model of a diode in
PSpice, you might consider using the dc sweep. The circuit is shown in Fig. 9.3. This
will enable you to look at the point-by-point response, obtaining a characteristic

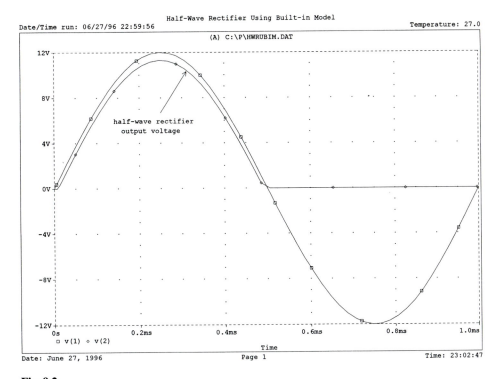

Fig. 9.2

curve in much the same manner as you would in the laboratory. The input file will look like this:

```
Built-in Diode Model for PSpice
V 1 0 10V
R 1 2 100
D1 2 0 DMOD
.DC V   −0.5V 10V 0.02V
.MODEL DMOD D
.PROBE
.END
```

Fig. 9.3 Circuit for diode characteristic curve.

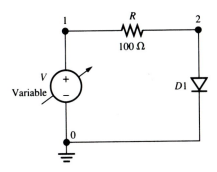

For this example, we called the diode *D1*, and it is located between nodes *2* and *0*. We chose the model name *DMOD*. The name is specified in the .MODEL statement as the first argument.

In Probe, change the *X*-axis to represent V(2) in the range up to 0.8 V, and plot I(D1) in the range up to 50 mA. This produces a characteristic curve for the built-in diode with no changes in the predefined parameters. See Fig. 9.4 for the diode characteristic curve. You may want to modify the diode model to fit a particular need. For example, the parameter *EG* represents the barrier height. Normally this is 1.1 eV. Changing this to 0.72 eV would be in keeping with a Ge diode. If you change any parameter, you may want to look at the resulting characteristics before proceeding with an analysis of an elaborate circuit using your revised model.

THE FILTERED HALF-WAVE RECTIFIER

In order to smooth the output voltage, place a capacitor across the load resistance, as shown in Fig. 9.5. The capacitor must be large enough to keep the output voltage from dropping significantly during the time when the diode is not conducting.

For this classic problem, choose $R = 1 \text{ k}\Omega$, $C = 25 \text{ }\mu\text{F}$, and $f = 60$ Hz. The frequency is chosen to represent an ordinary voltage supply such as you would expect to find in home or commercial situations. The input file is

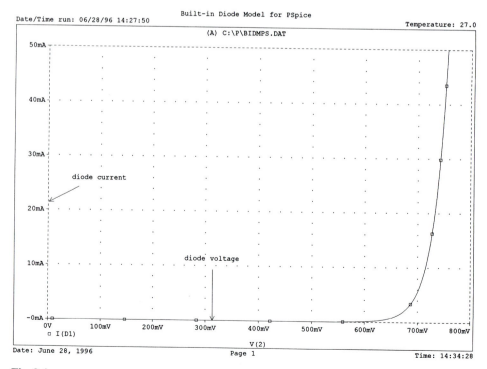

Fig. 9.4

Fig. 9.5 Half-wave rectifier with capacitor filter.

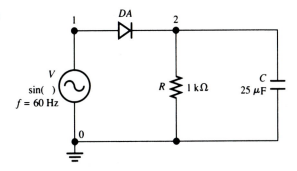

```
Half-Wave Rectifier with Capacitor Filter
V 1 0 sin (0 12 60)
DA 1 2 D1
R 2 0 1k
C 2 0 25uF
.MODEL D1 D
.TRAN 0.1ms 33.33ms
.PROBE
.END
```

Run the analysis, and choose a time range from zero to 25 ms. Plot v(1) and v(2). Note that the output voltage follows a pattern like that of the first example until a time just past when the voltages reach their peaks. Then, because the capacitor was charged to the peak voltage, the diode stops conducting. This allows the capacitor to discharge exponentially until the time when the input voltage is large enough to allow conduction to begin again. Refer to Fig. 9.6 for the details of this wave-shape.

The mathematical treatment of this circuit usually neglects the diode drop. The equation for peak diode current is then

$$I_m = V_m \sqrt{\frac{1}{R_L^2} + \omega^2 C^2}$$

Verify that, using the given values, this gives $I_m = 113.7$ mA.

Remove the traces of voltage and plot I(DA), the diode current. Using the cursor mode, check the on-screen current maximum against the calculated value. There should be close agreement.

Fig. 9.6 Ideal diode in half-wave, capacitor-filtered circuit.

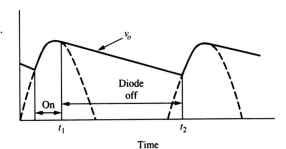

The equations for determining the cutout angle are

$$\theta = \arctan \omega C R_L$$

and

$$\omega t_1 = \pi - \theta = 180° - \theta$$

Using these values leads to $\theta = 83.94°$ and $\omega t_1 = 96.06°$. Verify that cut-in occurs at 18.26 ms, which corresponds to 34.4°.

Remove the trace of diode current and plot v(2) again. Verify that the cutout occurs at the predicted location. At $t = 4.55$ ms the current drops to the microamp region. Assuming this to be cutoff gives a cutoff angle of 98°.

The maximum value of output voltage is simply the maximum value of the input voltage minus the diode drop. This is found to be $v(2)_{max} = 11.23$ V. The ripple voltage is $V_r = 11.3 - 6.49 = 4.81$ V. See Fig. 9.7 for the traces of v(1) and v(2).

Now it is possible to observe the effects of changing the value of C in order to lessen the ripple voltage. Change the value of capacitance to $C = 50$ μF and run the analysis again. Plot v(1) and v(2). Verify that the ripple is reduced to $V_r = 2.802$ V.

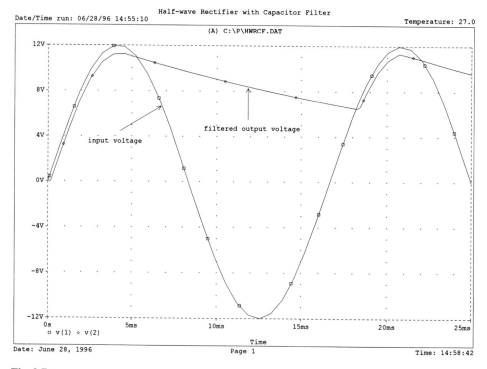

Fig. 9.7

THE FULL-WAVE RECTIFIER

In order to better utilize the input voltage, use a full-wave rectifier, such as that shown in Fig. 9.8. The voltages v_1 and v_2 are taken from a center-tapped transformer with the ground connection at the center tap. The output voltage is v_o across R. For this connection, the input file becomes

```
Full-Wave Rectifier
v1 1 0 sin (0 12 60Hz)
v2 0 3 sin (0 12 60Hz)
R 2 0 1k
D1 1 2 DA
D2 3 2 DA
.MODEL DA D
.TRAN 0.1ms 25ms
.PROBE
.END
```

Run the analysis and in Probe plot v(1), v(3), the two input voltages, and v(2), the output voltage. Here you see full-wave rectification with conduction over the entire cycle. These traces are shown in Fig. 9.9. Remove the voltage traces; then plot i(R), the output current. Verify that the current reaches a peak $i(R)_{max} = 11.27$ mA each half cycle. Does this agree with your calculated value? See Fig. 9.10 for the load-current plot.

FULL-WAVE RECTIFIER WITH FILTER

Place a 25-µF capacitor across R and add the statement

```
C 2 0 25uF
```

to the input file of the example used in the previous section.

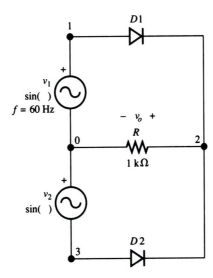

Fig. 9.8 Full-wave rectifier, PSpice-model circuit.

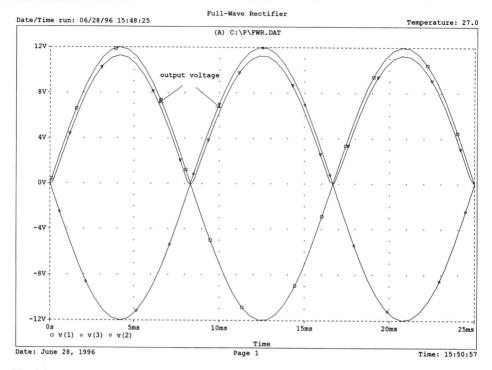

Fig. 9.9

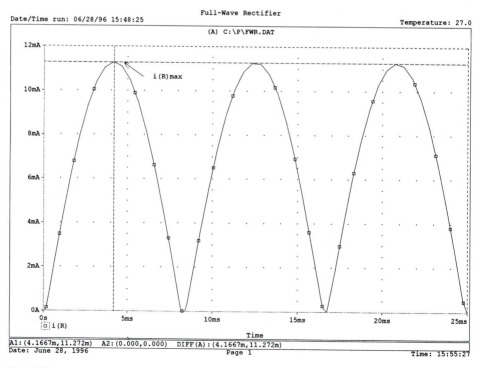

Fig. 9.10

After you run the analysis, plot the output voltage v(2) along with the input voltages v(1) and v(3). Observe the effects of the capacitor on the ripple voltage. Using the cursor mode, verify that $v(2)_{max} = 11.28$ V and $v(2)_{min} = 8.76$ V, giving $V_r = 2.52$ V. These traces are shown in Fig. 9.11.

SIMPLE DIODE CLIPPER

A clipper is used to transmit part of an input voltage of an arbitrary waveform to its output terminals. When a diode is biased by placing it in series with a dc voltage, the clipping action takes place. Figure 9.12 shows one such circuit. The input file is

```
Diode Clipping Circuit
vi 1 0 sin(0 12V 60Hz)
DA 2 3 D1
R 1 2 1k
VR 3 0 8V
.MODEL D1 D
.TRAN 0.1ms 25ms
.PROBE
.END
```

Run the analysis and plot the input voltage v(1) and the output voltage v(2). Can you predict what will be the clipping level? Why is it not at 8 V? These traces are shown in Fig. 9.13.

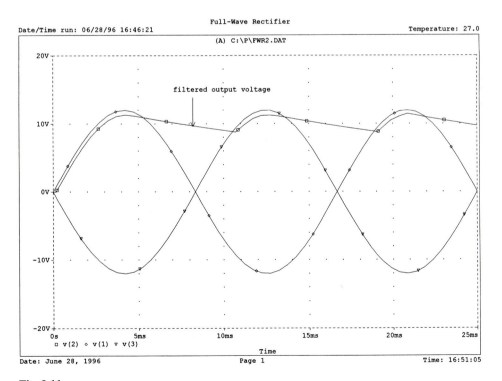

Date/Time run: 06/28/96 16:46:21   Full-Wave Rectifier   Temperature: 27.0

(A) C:\P\FWR2.DAT

filtered output voltage

□ v(2) ◇ v(1) ▽ v(3)

Time

Date: June 28, 1996   Page 1   Time: 16:51:05

Fig. 9.11

Fig. 9.12 A simple diode clipper.

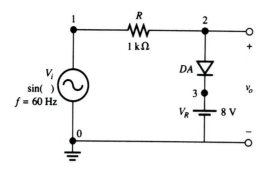

A DOUBLE-ENDED CLIPPER

Double-ended clipping is used to convert a sine wave into a square wave. A simple back-to-back connection of two avalanche diodes is shown in Fig. 9.14. The avalanche diodes are selected to have a Zener (breakdown) voltage of 2.4 V. The built-in diode model can easily be converted to an avalanche diode through the use of the parameter *BV* for breakdown voltage. This is shown in the input file:

```
Double-Ended Clipper Using Avalanche Diodes
vi 1 0 sin(0 24V 60Hz)
DA 3 2 D1
DB 3 0 D1
R 1 2 1k
```

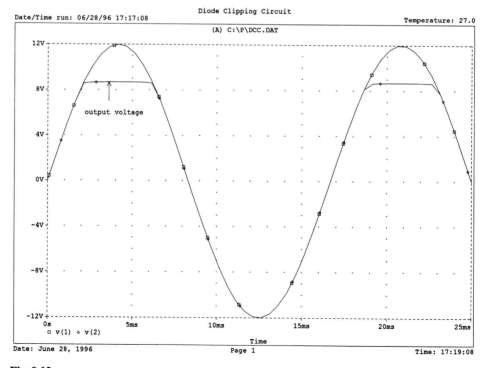

Fig. 9.13

Fig. 9.14 Double-ended clipper using avalanche diodes.

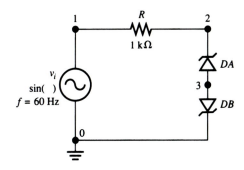

```
.MODEL D1 D(BV=2.4V)
.TRAN 0.1ms 25ms
.PROBE
.END
```

Run the analysis; then plot the input voltage v(1) and the output voltage v(2). Note that the output is clipped on both ends due to the action of the back-to-back diodes. Does the clipping occur such that the output voltage swings between ±2.4 V? Verify that the output voltage peaks at 3.628 V. You should also look at v(2) alone, where the squared output is more evident. Refer to Fig. 9.15 for these traces.

The transfer characteristic is often shown for this circuit. You can look at this curve by changing the X-axis to represent v(1), then plotting v(2). This plot shows the output voltage over the complete range of input-voltage swings. Note that this plot shows some overtracing. This is because the transient analysis is based on the sine-wave input. You can avoid this problem by using a dc sweep. Revise the input file as follows:

```
Double-Ended Clipper Using Avalanche Diodes
VI 1 0   24V
DA 3 2 D1
DB 3 0 D1
R 1 2 1k
.MODEL D1 D(BV=2.4V)
.DC VI   -24 24 0.1
.PROBE
.END
```

Run the analysis and obtain the improved transfer characteristic. The input voltage *VI* is shown on the X-axis. Plot V(2) on the Y-axis. Refer to Fig. 9.16 for this trace.

VARIABLE LOAD RESISTOR FOR MAXIMUM POWER

We have considered the maximum power theorem for both dc and ac circuits. In both cases the load was set and the analysis made. If we desired to change the load, we made the change in the input file and ran the analysis again. There is a way, however, to let the load resistance change without running another analysis. We will outline this method next.

The circuit of Fig. 9.17 shows a 12-V dc source with $R_i = 5\Omega$ connected to a variable R_L. In order to produce the variable R_L, it is necessary to use a .MODEL statement for the resistor. It looks like this:

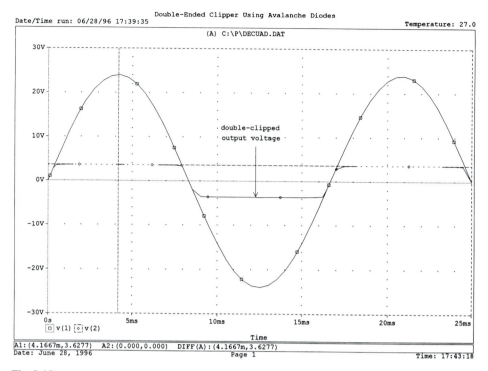

Fig. 9.15

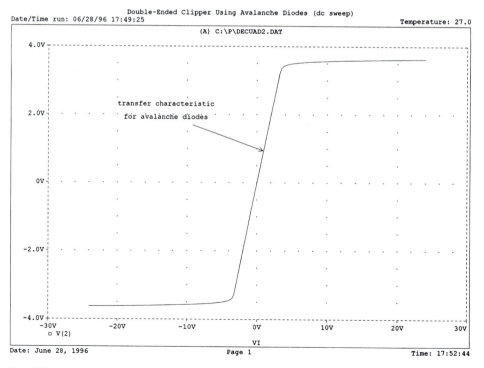

Fig. 9.16

```
.MODEL RL RES
```

where *RL* is the chosen model name and *RES* is the required model type. By using the model, you will be able to include a .DC sweep statement showing a range of values for *RL*. This statement is

```
.DC RES RL(R) 0.1 10 0.1
```

where *RES* is the required sweep-variable name and RL(R) uses our choice for the model name; the (R) is the required resistor-device name. The entire input file is

```
Maximum Power with Variable Load Resistor
V 1 0 12V
RI 1 2 5
RLOAD 2 0 RL 1
.MODEL RL RES
.DC RES RL(R) 0.1 10 0.1
.PROBE
.END
```

Note the statement for *RLOAD*. The last parameter given is a scale factor of 1. This is a required value, and the analysis will not run without it. Its purpose is to allow for various scale factors (multipliers) if required. This might be useful if there are several resistors, each based on the same model.

Run the analysis and plot

$$I(RI)*V(2)$$

giving the power delivered to the load resistor. Verify that the peak occurs when $R = 5\Omega$, representing $RLOAD = 5\Omega$. Use the cursor to show that $P_{max} = 7.2$ W. Figure 9.18 shows this plot.

BUILT-IN MODEL FOR THE BIPOLAR-JUNCTION TRANSISTOR

We have waited a long time to introduce the built-in model for the BJT. Although one of the main strengths of PSpice lies in the wide range and versatility of its built-in models, at the same time these complex models can strike fear into the heart of the beginner. For example, the BJT device Q has 40 parameters that the user may specify. If you take a look under "Q Bipolar Transistor" in Appendix D, you will see

Fig. 9.17 Maximum power with variable load resistor.

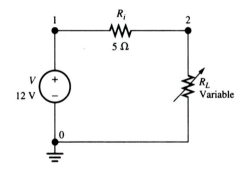

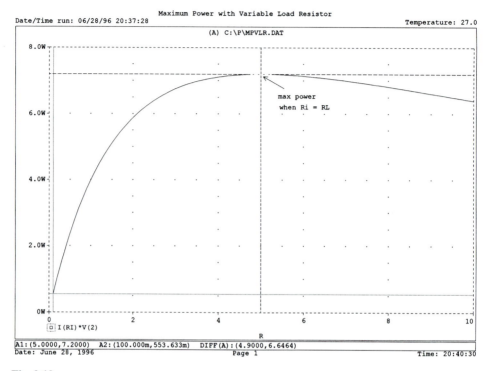

Maximum Power with Variable Load Resistor

(A) C:\P\MPVLR.DAT

max power
when Ri = RL

A1:(5.0000,7.2000)   A2:(100.000m,553.633m)   DIFF(A):(4.9000,6.6464)

Fig. 9.18

just how comprehensive these parameters are. Many of them will probably be unfamiliar to you, and they are beyond the scope of our discussion.

OUTPUT CHARACTERISTICS OF THE COMMON-EMITTER TRANSISTOR

To introduce the BJT model, we will use the common-emitter biasing circuit of Fig. 9.19. If you were to do a laboratory investigation of the output characteristics of a BJT, you might use this circuit. You would obtain one characteristic curve by keep-

Fig. 9.19   BJT in *CE* connection to show output characteristics.

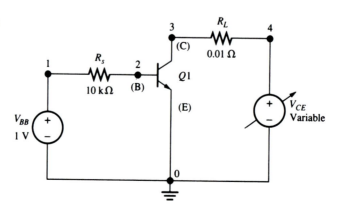

ing the input current I_B constant while varying the voltage V_{CE}. Most students are familiar with this exercise. We will look at this from the SPICE point of view.

We call the transistor $Q1$ and use model name BJT. We choose both of these, and the required statement becomes

```
Q1 3 2 0 BJT
```

The nodes are in the order *collector*, *base*, and *emitter*, respectively. The model statement is

```
.MODEL BJT NPN
```

where BJT is chosen to agree with our $Q1$ designation and NPN is the required model type for an *npn* transistor. The entire input file is

```
BJT PSpice Model Characteristics
VBB 1 0 1V
RS 1 2 10k
RL 3 4 0.01
Q1 3 2 0 BJT; 3=collector, 2=base, 1=emitter
VCE 4 0 5V
.MODEL BJT NPN
.DC VCE 0 15V 0.1V
.PROBE
.END
```

Run the analysis and plot $-I(RL)$. The minus sign is correct with respect to the R_L statement shown in the file. Use the cursor mode to find I_{Cmax}. This should be $I_{Cmax} = 2.07$ mA. This characteristic curve is shown in Fig. 9.20. Remove this trace and plot I(RS) to obtain the input current I_B. Verify that this has a maximum value of $I_B = 20.7$ μA. It is obvious from these two values that $h_{FE} = 100$, in agreement with the model parameter BF. You may specify other values for BF as necessary for a particular transistor model. See Appendix D under "Q Bipolar Transistor" for a list of all the transistor parameters.

INPUT CHARACTERISTICS OF THE COMMON-EMITTER TRANSISTOR

The input characteristics may be obtained from an input file that contains reference to the built-in model as follows:

```
BJT Input Characteristics
IBB 0 1 100uA
Rs 1 0 1000k
RL 2 3 1k
Q1 2 1 0 BJT
VCC 3 0 12V
.MODEL BJT NPN
.DC IBB 0 100uA 1uA
.PROBE
.END
```

Reference to Fig. 9.21 shows that this *npn*-transistor model has a value for V_{BE} in the active region of about 0.8 V. Since this is about 0.1 V too high for a BJT, the standard model will produce results that differ from those obtained when you created your own model for bias analysis.

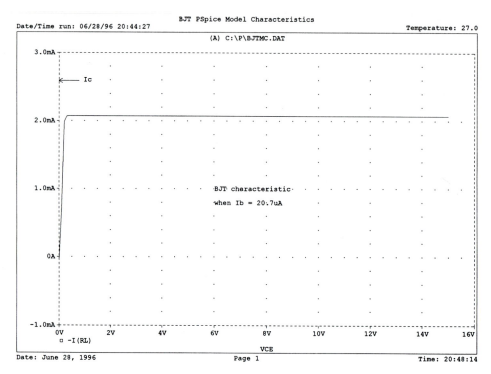

Fig. 9.20

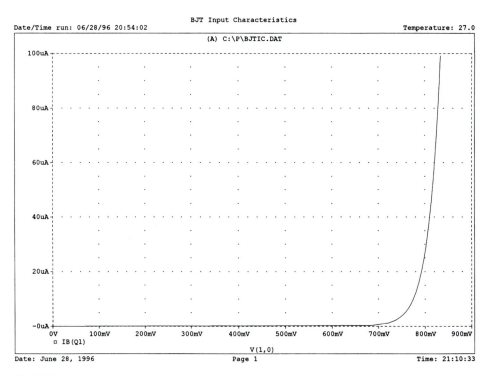

Fig. 9.21

OUTPUT CHARACTERISTICS OF THE JFET

A family of curves representing the output characteristics of the JFET are of value in determining the drain current saturation value, the pinch-off voltage, and so forth. The construction of these curves is left as an exercise for you and is the subject of Problem 9.8.

OTHER ACTIVE SEMICONDUCTOR DEVICES

Appendices A, B, and D contain listings of other active devices including "*B* GaAsFET" and "*M* MOSFET." From an academic point of view you are encouraged to use your own models for transistors and other devices. This will allow you to decide which model is most appropriate for which situation. In more advanced applications, the built-in models will allow you to set parameters that could not otherwise be taken into account.

THE DIFFERENTIAL AMPLIFIER

The differential amplifier is used as the first stage of the operational amplifier. In its elementary form it looks like Fig. 9.22. For an analysis we will use the built-in model for the *npn* transistor, giving a matched pair for *Q1* and *Q2*. Also, we will choose $R_{s1} = R_{s2} = 1$ kΩ and $R_{c1} = R_{c2} = 2$ kΩ.

Difference-Mode Gain

The difference-mode gain of the differential amplifier is found by setting $V_{s1} = -V_{s2} = V_s/2$. The gain is approximated as

Fig. 9.22 The difference amplifier (difference mode).

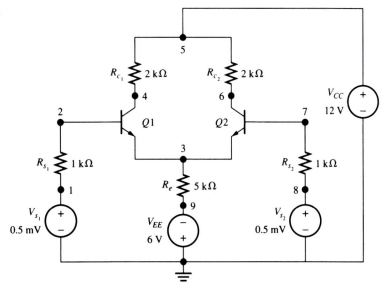

$$A_d = \frac{v_o}{v_s} = \frac{h_{fe}R_c}{2(R_s + h_{ie})}$$

For our analysis, choose $V_s = 1$ mV, giving $V_{s1} = 0.5$ mV and $f = 1$ kHz. Based on the built-in model, calculate the expected value for A_d. The input file will look at bias voltages and ac operation. In order to obtain the ac voltages in the output file, use the .PRINT statement. This leads to the following input file:

```
Model for Differential Amplifier
VS1 1 0 AC 0.5mV ; Vs1 = -Vs2 = Vs/2
VS2 0 8 AC 0.5mV ; This gives difference-mode operation
RS1 2 1 1k
RS2 7 8 1k
RE 3 9 5k
RC1 4 5 2k
RC2 5 6 2k
VCC 5 0 12V
VEE 0 9 6V
Q1 4 2 3 BJT
Q2 6 7 3 BJT
.AC LIN 1 1000Hz 1000Hz
.MODEL BJT NPN
.PRINT AC V(1) V(2) V(3) V(4) V(5) V(6) V(7) V(8)
.TF V(4) VS1
.END
```

Run the analysis and obtain a printed copy of the output file. If you remove the unnecessary information, you should be able to reduce this file to a single page of less than 60 lines. Verify that $A_d = V_o/V_{s1} = V(4)/V(1) = 33.4$. Note how the input voltages V_{s1} and V_{s2} are referenced in the input file with respect to their nodes. Figure 9.23 shows this output file.

Common-Mode Gain

For common-mode operation it is necessary to set $V_{s1} = V_{s2} = V_s$. The common-mode gain may be approximated by

$$A_c = \frac{-h_{fe}R_c}{R_s + h_{ie} + (1 + h_{fe})2R_e}$$

Using the known values for the transistor, predict what this gain will be. Modify the input file so that the input voltages are shown as

```
VS1 1 0 AC 1mV; Vs1 = Vs2
VS2 8 0 AC 1mV; This gives common-mode operation
```

After making these changes, run the analysis and obtain a printed copy of the output file as before. Verify that $A_c = V(4)/V(1) = 0.197$. This output file is shown in Fig. 9.24.

```
Model for Differential Amplifier

   ****        CIRCUIT DESCRIPTION

VS1 1 0 AC 0.5mV ; Vs1 = -Vs2 = Vs/2
VS2 0 8 AC 0.5mV ; This gives difference-mode operation
RS1 2 1 1k
RS2 7 8 1k
RE 3 9 5k
RC1 4 5 2k
RC2 5 6 2k
VCC 5 0 12V
VEE 0 9 6V
Q1 4 2 3 BJT
Q2 6 7 3 BJT
.AC LIN 1 1000Hz 1000Hz
.MODEL BJT NPN
.PRINT AC V(1) V(2) V(3) V(4) V(5) V(6) V(7) V(8)
.TF V(4) VS1
.END

   ****        BJT MODEL PARAMETERS

BJT
                NPN
          IS   100.000000E-18
          BF   100
          NF   1
          BR   1
          NR   1

 NODE    VOLTAGE      NODE    VOLTAGE      NODE    VOLTAGE      NODE    VOLTAGE

 (     1)   0.0000  (     2)   -.0052  (     3)   -.7624  (     4)   10.9630
 (     5)   12.0000 (     6)   10.9630 (     7)   -.0052  (     8)   0.0000
 (     9)   -6.0000

     VOLTAGE SOURCE CURRENTS
     NAME        CURRENT
     VS1        -5.186E-06
     VS2         5.186E-06
     VCC        -1.037E-03
     VEE        -1.048E-03

     TOTAL POWER DISSIPATION   1.87E-02  WATTS

   ****        SMALL-SIGNAL CHARACTERISTICS
        V(4)/VS1 = -1.680E+01

        INPUT RESISTANCE AT VS1 =  1.191E+04
        OUTPUT RESISTANCE AT V(4) =  2.000E+03

 FREQ        V(1)        V(2)        V(3)        V(4)        V(5)
    1.000E+03   5.000E-04   4.165E-04   1.389E-17   1.670E-02   1.000E-30
 FREQ        V(6)        V(7)        V(8)
    1.000E+03   1.670E-02   4.165E-04   5.000E-04
```

Fig. 9.23

Transfer Characteristics of the Differential Amplifier

An important aspect of differential-amplifier operation is found by investigating its transfer-characteristic curve. The use of the built-in model for the transistor will make this task easy. Since we are interested in small values of differential input volt-

```
Model for Differential Amplifier--Common Mode

 ****      CIRCUIT DESCRIPTION

VS1 1 0 AC 1mV ; Vs1 = Vs2
VS2 8 0 AC 1mV ; This gives common-mode operation
RS1 2 1 1k
RS2 7 8 1k
RE 3 9 5k
RC1 4 5 2k
RC2 5 6 2k
VCC 5 0 12V
VEE 0 9 6V
Q1 4 2 3 BJT
Q2 6 7 3 BJT
.AC LIN 1 1000Hz 1000Hz
.MODEL BJT NPN
.PRINT AC V(1) V(2) V(3) V(4) V(5) V(6) V(7) V(8)
.TF V(4) VS1
.END

 ****      BJT MODEL PARAMETERS

BJT
             NPN
          IS  100.000000E-18
          BF  100
          NF  1
          BR  1
          NR  1
```

NODE	VOLTAGE	NODE	VOLTAGE	NODE	VOLTAGE	NODE	VOLTAGE
(1)	0.0000	(2)	-.0052	(3)	-.7624	(4)	10.9630
(5)	12.0000	(6)	10.9630	(7)	-.0052	(8)	0.0000
(9)	-6.0000						

```
   VOLTAGE SOURCE CURRENTS
   NAME           CURRENT
   VS1           -5.186E-06
   VS2           -5.186E-06
   VCC           -1.037E-03
   VEE           -1.048E-03

   TOTAL POWER DISSIPATION   1.87E-02  WATTS

 ****      SMALL-SIGNAL CHARACTERISTICS
      V(4)/VS1 = -1.680E+01

      INPUT RESISTANCE AT VS1 =  1.191E+04
      OUTPUT RESISTANCE AT V(4) =  2.000E+03
```

FREQ	V(1)	V(2)	V(3)	V(4)	V(5)
1.000E+03	1.000E-03	9.990E-04	9.941E-04	1.969E-04	1.000E-30

FREQ	V(6)	V(7)	V(8)
1.000E+03	1.969E-04	9.990E-04	1.000E-03

Fig. 9.24

age, we will use a dc sweep for the input voltage range of -0.5 V to 0.5 V. For this analysis, V_{s2} will be given a fixed value of 1 mV; the sweep will apply to V_{s1}. Thus the input file becomes

```
Transfer Characteristics of Differential Amplifier
VS1 1 0 1mV ; this input will vary from  -0.5 V to 0.5 V
```

```
VS2 8 0 1mV ; this input will remain fixed
RS1 2 1 1k
RS2 7 8 1k
RE  3 9 5k
RC1 4 5 2k
RC2 5 6 2k
VCC 5 0 12V
VEE 0 9 6V
Q1 4 2 3 BJT
Q2 6 7 3 BJT
.MODEL BJT NPN
.OP
.DC VS1    -0.5 0.5 0.01
.PROBE
.END
```

Run the analysis and in Probe plot $-I(RC1)$. Compare the results with the transfer characteristics given in a text dealing with this subject. Note that the linear portion of this transfer curve is somewhat limited. Can you approximate the linear range for V_{s1} and I_{RC1}? The X-axis is usually normalized to the volt-equivalent of temperature and is given as

$$\frac{V_{B1} - V_{B2}}{V_T}$$

Recall that $V_T = 26$ mV at room temperature and the linear portion of the curve is limited to about ± 26 mV. Refer to Fig. 9.25 for the transfer-characteristic curve.

The differential amplifier is a good limiter, and if the input voltage exceeds ± 100 mV at room temperature, the output becomes saturated. Verify these statements from your printed copy of the transfer curve. Can you produce the mirror image of this transfer curve? This can be obtained by keeping V_{s1} fixed while varying V_{s2}.

LOGIC GATES

The evaluation version of PSpice contains well over 100 of the logic devices that are available in the production version of the software. Most of the *7400*-series gates, flip-flops, counters, and so forth are available. A complete listing of the logic devices in the evaluation version of PSpice can be found in Appendix E.

THE 7402 NOR GATE

A circuit involving a single NOR gate is shown in Fig. 9.26. The two inputs, *A* and *B*, are shown as pulse trains of various widths and amplitudes of 1 V. The NOR gate is referenced with a subroutine call (in the *X* statement), where nodes *1, 2,* and *3* refers to inputs *A* and *B* and output *Y*, respectively. The subroutine call lists the device as *7402*. The complete input file is

```
Digital Circuit Using NOR gate
VCC 4 0 5V
X 1 2 3 7402
V1 1 0 PWL(0s 0V 0.1ms 1V 1s 1V 1.0001s 0V
+2s 0V 2.0001s 1V 3s 1V 3.0001s 0V 4s 0V 4.0001s 1V 5s 1V)
```

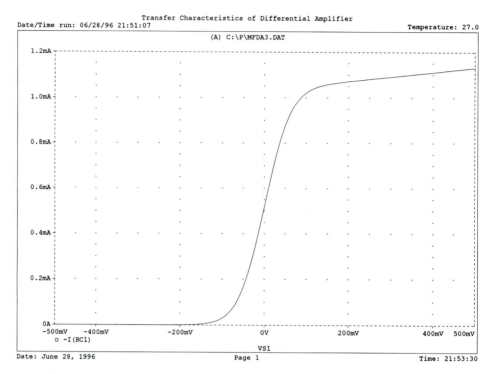

Fig. 9.25

```
V2 2 0 PWL (0s 0V 1.5s 0V 1.50001s 1V 2.5s 1V 2.50001s 0V
+3.5s 0V 3.50001s 1V 3.7s 1V 3.70001s 0V 5s 0V)
R 4 3 100k
.lib eval.lib
.tran 0.01ms 5s
.probe
.end
```

Fig. 9.26 NOR gate with two inputs.

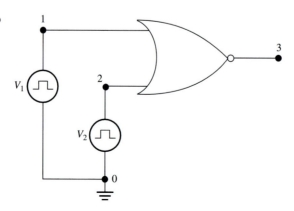

Refer to Appendix E, where you will find the entry

```
.subckt 7402 A B Y . . .
```

which shows the entire subroutine. The subroutine does not need to be included in the input file, since there is a reference to the library *EVAL.LIB,* which contains the necessary information. In Probe trace v(1) and v(2) and the input waves *A* and *B,* along with v(3), the output wave *Y.* Your results should agree with Fig. 9.27, which shows the waves as three separate plots. This is a simple timing diagram for our gate circuit.

In the output listing of Fig. 9.28 only a portion of the total file is shown. The listing of the model parameters has been omitted to save space. Note that analog-to-digital interface statements in the form of subroutine calls are automatically generated from the 7402 subroutine. These are for each of the three nodes of the NOR gate. Statements for the digital power supply are also automatically produced. Note the listing of $G\_DPWR = 5$ V along with the other node voltages.

As an exercise, change the timing patterns for the two inputs so that their region of coincidence will be different from that previously used and run the simulation again. From your knowledge of the operation of the NOR gate, it is easy to verify the results.

Finally, replace the 7402 NOR gate with a 7408 AND gate and perform a similar analysis.

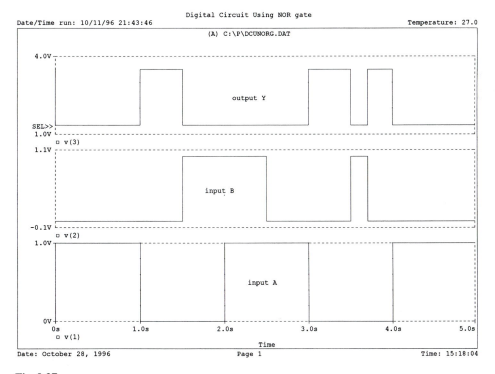

Fig. 9.27

```
Digital Circuit Using NOR gate
VCC 4 0 5V
X 1 2 3 7402
V1 1 0 PWL(0s 0V 0.1ms 1V 1s 1V 1.0001s 0V
+2s 0V 2.0001s 1V 3s 1V 3.0001s 0V 4s 0V 4.0001s 1V 5s 1V)
V2 2 0 PWL(0s 0V 1.5s 0V 1.50001s 1V 2.5s 1V 2.50001s 0V 3.5s 0V 3.50001s 1V
+3.7s 1V 3.70001s 0V 5s 0V)
R 4 3 100k
.lib eval.lib
.tran 0.01ms 5s
.probe
.end

**** Generated AtoD and DtoA Interfaces ****
* Analog/Digital interface for node 3
* Moving X.U1:OUT1 from analog node 3 to new digital node 3$DtoA
X$3_DtoA1
+ 3$DtoA
+ 3
+ $G_DPWR
+ $G_DGND
+ DtoA_STD
+       PARAMS: DRVH=  96.4    DRVL= 104    CAPACITANCE=    0
*
* Analog/Digital interface for node 1
* Moving X.U1:IN1 from analog node 1 to new digital node 1$AtoD
X$1_AtoD1
+ 1
+ 1$AtoD
+ $G_DPWR
+ $G_DGND
+ AtoD_STD
+       PARAMS: CAPACITANCE=    0
* Analog/Digital interface for node 2
* Moving X.U1:IN2 from analog node 2 to new digital node 2$AtoD
X$2_AtoD1
+ 2
+ 2$AtoD
+ $G_DPWR
+ $G_DGND
+ AtoD_STD
+       PARAMS: CAPACITANCE=    0
* Analog/Digital interface power supply subcircuits
X$DIGIFPWR 0 DIGIFPWR
  ****       Diode MODEL PARAMETERS
  ****       BJT MODEL PARAMETERS
  ****       Digital Input MODEL PARAMETERS
  ****       Digital Output MODEL PARAMETERS
  ****       Digital Gate MODEL PARAMETERS
  ****       Digital IO  MODEL PARAMETERS

  ****       INITIAL TRANSIENT SOLUTION        TEMPERATURE =   27.000 DEG C
  NODE   VOLTAGE     NODE   VOLTAGE     NODE   VOLTAGE     NODE   VOLTAGE
(    1)   0.0000  (    2)    0.0000  (    3)   3.5028  (    4)    5.0000
($G_DGND)    0.0000                  ($G_DPWR)    5.0000
(X$1_AtoD1.1)      .0915             (X$1_AtoD1.2)      .0457
(X$1_AtoD1.3)      .8277             (X$2_AtoD1.1)      .0915
(X$2_AtoD1.2)      .0457             (X$2_AtoD1.3)      .8277
 DGTL NODE : STATE  DGTL NODE : STATE  DGTL NODE : STATE  DGTL NODE : STATE
(  2$AtoD) : 0     (  3$DtoA) : 1     (  1$AtoD) : 0
```

Fig. 9.28

NEW PSPICE STATEMENTS USED IN THIS CHAPTER

D[*name*] <+*node* > <−*node* > < *model name* > [*area*]

For example,

```
D1 1 2 D1
```

means that a certain diode *DA* is used in the circuit between nodes *1* (p) and *2* (n). The model for the diode is to be described in a .MODEL statement that bears the model name *D1*. There might be several diodes, *DA, DB,* and *DC,* for example, based on the same model.

J[*name*] <*drain node* > < *gate node* > < *source node* > < *model name* > [*area*]

For example,

```
J 5 4 2 JFET
```

means that a certain junction FET is used in the circuit connected among nodes *5* (drain), *4* (gate), and *2* (source). The model for the FET is to be described in a .MODEL statement that has the model name *JFET.* The circuit may contain several FETs, *J, J1,* and *J2,* for example, based on the same model.

Q[*name*] <*collector node* > < *base node* > < *emitter node* > [*substrate node*] <*model name* > [*area*]

For example,

```
Q1 3 2 0 BJT
```

means that a certain bipolar transistor *Q1* is connected among nodes *3* (collector), *2* (base), and *0* (emitter). The model for the bipolar transistor is to be described in a .MODEL statement that bears the model name *BJT.* There might be several transistors, *Q1, Q2,* and *Q3,* for example, that are based on the same model.

R[*name*] <+*node* > < −*node* > [*model name*] <*value* >

For example,

```
RLOAD 2 0 RL 1
```

means that a resistor *RLOAD* is connected between nodes *2* and *0.* Also, this resistor is modeled as *RL* in a .MODEL statement. The last value (shown after *RL* as *1*) represents a scale factor of unity. It or some other scale factor must be included. A scale factor of 2 would indicate a doubling of the value described in the model.

One of the reasons for using a resistor based on a model is to allow for a .DC statement where *RES* is chosen as the sweep variable. Refer to the dot statements for more information.

NEW DOT COMMANDS

.MODEL *<model name> <type>*

For example,

```
.MODEL D1 D
```

is used to define a diode model. The *D* is used to show that the model is in the PSpice library of devices. The list of library models includes the following:

>   CAP (capacitor)
>   IND (inductor)
>   RES (resistor)
>   D (diode)
>   NPN (*npn*-type BJT)
>   PNP (*pnp*-type BJT)
>   NFJ (*n*-channel JFET)
>   PFJ (*p*-channel JFET)
>   NMOS (*n*-channel MOSFET)
>   PMOS (*p*-channel MOSFET)
>   GASFET (*n*-channel GaAs MOSFET)
>   ISWITCH (current-controlled switch)
>   VSWITCH (voltage-controlled switch)
>   CORE (nonlinear, magnetic-core transformer)

A more complete form of the model statement is

.MODEL *<model name> <type>* [(*<parameter name>* = *<value>*)]*

For example,

```
.MODEL D1 D(IS=1E-12 N=1.2 VJ=0.9 BV=10)
```

means that some of the 14 possible diode parameters have been selected to have values other than their default ones. The asterisk positioned after the brackets means that the enclosed item may be repeated. Appendix D contains a list of each library device with its various model parameters and their default values.

PROBLEMS

9.1 A half-wave rectifier as shown in Fig. 9.1 is to have the following parameters: $IS = 1E - 9$ A, $VJ = 0.8$ V, $IBV = 1E - 6A$, $EG = 0.72$ eV. Run an analysis like the one described in the text, and compare the results with those previously obtained. What differences are observed?

9.2 A diode circuit containing a biasing voltage in series with an ac source is shown in Fig. 9.29. Use the built-in diode model in your analysis. Given: $V = 0.8$ V and $R = 1$ kΩ. Describe the ac voltage as a sin( ) function with a 0.2-V peak at $f = 1$ kHz.

(a) Perform an analysis to plot voltages v(2,1) and v(3) in Probe. Does the diode conduct for a full cycle? Verify and explain the results.

(b) Run the analysis again with $V = 0.6$ V. Explain the results.

(c) Run the analysis again with $V = 0.4$ V. Explain the results.

Fig. 9.29

9.3 The diode characteristic curve shown in Fig. 9.4 is for the built-in diode model. Produce a diode characteristic for the diode of Problem 9.1 Describe any differences in the two curves.

9.4 A full-wave rectifier with a capacitor filter using $C = 25$ μF is discussed in the text. Use an analysis like the one suggested to determine the ripple and the average value of output voltage when $C = 10$ μF.

9.5 The circuit shown in Fig. 9.30 is similar to Fig. 9.12 except that the diode is reversed. When $v_i = 12$ V peak, $f = 60$ Hz, and $V_R = 8$ V, run an analysis to show the input and output voltages. Predict the output voltage waveshape and compare with the Probe results.

Fig. 9.30

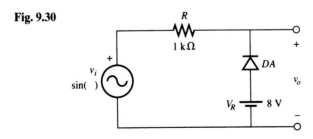

9.6 The circuit shown in Fig. 9.31 uses the same values as those of Problem 9.5. The output is taken across R and V_R in series. Predict the output voltage waveshape; then run the PSpice analysis for comparison.

Fig. 9.31

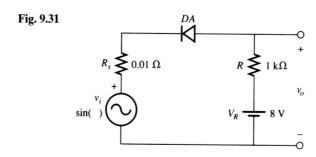

9.7 Using the circuit shown in Fig. 9.32 with the built-in model for the .BJT, find the Q-point voltages and currents. Let $h_{FE} = 80$ (BF = 80 in the .MODEL statement). Note that the circuit is the same as Fig. 3.1. Compare the results obtained here with those given in Chapter 3. Note that there are noticeable differences in the two sets of values. In Fig. 3.2, VA was chosen as 0.7 V, representing a realistic value for V_{BE} in the active region. Using the built-in model, your output file should show $V_{BE} = 0.806$ V. This difference is responsible for the change in base current and so forth between the two sets of answers. This problem points out one of the reasons why your own models (such as those developed in Chapter 3) are often preferred over the built-in models.

Fig. 9.32

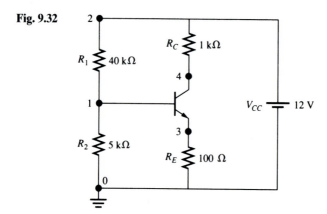

9.8 The circuit shown in Fig. 9.33 is to be used to obtain the drain characteristics of the FET. Let V_{DS} vary from 0 to 18 V in 0.2-V increments. Use the built-in model for the JFET, with the designation *NJF* (for the *n*-channel junction FET).

(a) On the first analysis, use $V_{GS} = 0$ V. Find the maximum drain current and the pinch-off voltage.

(b) Change the value of V_{GS} to -1 V and rerun the analysis.

Fig. 9.33

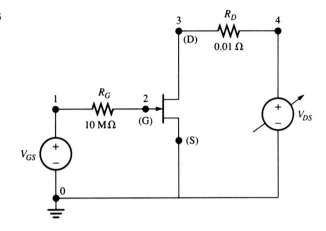

9.9 Figure 3.7 shows a *CE h*-parameter model for a BJT. If the *h* parameters are not used and the built-in model is chosen, the circuit must be modified to show V_{CC} and a dc biasing voltage for the base. Typically, the full circuit might look like Fig. 9.34. Use the built-in model for the BJT with $h_{FE} = 50$ (BF = 50), and create an input file that will find the low-frequency voltage gain. Use $f = 5$ kHz for a single-frequency analysis. Compare the results with those obtained using the *h*-parameter model. Which method is preferred for this type of problem? Why?

Fig. 9.34

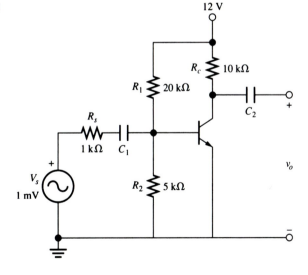

10

The BJT and Its Model

THE BIPOLAR-JUNCTION TRANSISTOR (BJT)

This chapter emphasizes the use of the library model of the BJT as compared with the *h*-parameter model or other simplified models. PSpice has a generic, built-in model for the BJT that uses the parameters shown in Appendix D under the topic "*Q* Bipolar Transistor." It will prove helpful to look at both the input and the output characteristics of this model. This will provide an introduction to the use of such models, which will be desirable if we are to use the models in various circuits.

Output Characteristics

A test circuit is shown in Fig. 10.1. The circuit shows a variable voltage supply V_{CC} and a variable current supply I_B. The transistor is called Q_1. When the built-in model for a BJT is used, the designation for the device must begin with Q. The input file becomes

```
BJT Output Characteristics
VCC 4 0 10V
IB 0 1 25uA
RB 1 2 0.01
RC 4 3 0.01
Q1 3 2 0 BJT; the designation BJT is our choice
.MODEL BJT NPN (BF=80)
.dc VCC 0 10V 0.05V IB 5uA 25uA 5uA
.PROBE
.END
```

The .MODEL statement shows our choice *BJT* for the model name and *NPN* (required) for the model type. The default value for *BF*, which represents the for-

Fig. 10.1 Test circuit for BJT characteristics.

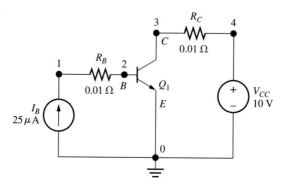

ward beta (h_{FE}), is *100;* it has been changed to *80* as an item of choice. Other parameters may be changed as desired; otherwise, default values will be used.

The *.dc* statement contains an outer loop to sweep V_{CC} and an inner loop to sweep I_B. *Caution:* If you attempt to let the value of I_B begin at 0 μA, the dc sweep will not run successfully.

Run the analysis and in Probe plot I(RC). This graph is shown in Fig. 10.2. It is helpful to label the various traces with their input current values. The *Y*-axis range was changed to read 0 2.1 mA.

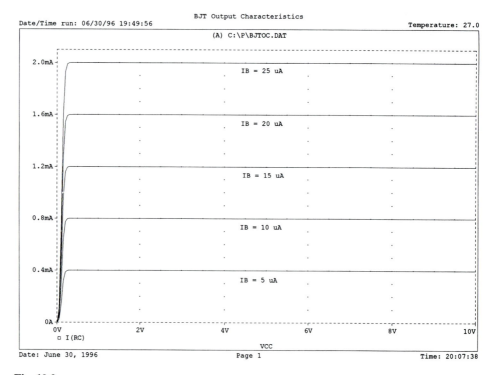

Fig. 10.2

Note that when $I_B = 25$ μA and V_{CC} (actually V_{CE}) is above a fraction of a volt, the collector current I_C, shown on the graph as I(RC), is 2.0 mA. This is in keeping with the value $h_{FE} = 80$.

Input Characteristics

To obtain the input characteristics, an alternative circuit, shown in Fig. 10.3, may be used. The current source I_{BB} is made practical by being placed in parallel with the resistor R_s. The input file is

```
BJT Input Characteristics
IBB 0 1 100uA
Rs 1 0 1000k
RL 2 3 0.01
Q1 2 1 0 BJT
VCC 3 0 10V
.MODEL BJT NPN(BF=80)
.dc IBB 0 100uA 1uA VCC 0V 10V 2V
.PROBE
.END
```

When the analysis is completed, change the X-axis to show V(1), and plot I(IBB). You will obtain a plot that shows only two distinct traces. The first, nearest the origin, is for $V_{CE} = 0$ V. The other is for all other values of V_{CE}. These are shown in Fig. 10.4. You may wish to run the analysis with the zero value for V_{CC} omitted. The results will confirm that the first trace is no longer shown. Note that when the built-in model for Q is used, V_{BE} will be approximately 0.8 V for typical values of base current.

A COMMON-EMITTER BJT AMPLIFIER

A simple common-emitter circuit is shown in Fig. 10.5. The input loop might be the result of applying Thevenin's theorem to a more complicated network. There is no coupling capacitor. We will assume that our analysis is for a frequency of 5 kHz, where the capacitor might be considered as a short circuit. The given value of h_{FE} is 50. The input file is

Fig. 10.3 Test circuit for BJT input characteristics.

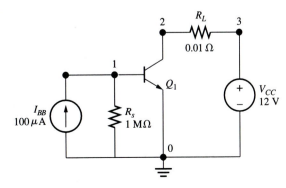

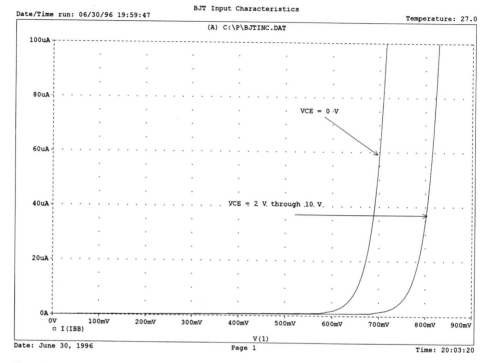

Fig. 10.4

```
CE Amplifier, BJT Model
VCC 5 0 18V
VBB 3 2 0.8V
RS 1 2 1k
RL 4 5 10k
Q1 4 3 0 BJT
MODEL BJT NPN(BF=50)
.TF V(4) VS
.OP
vs 1 0 ac 1mV
.AC lin 1 5kHz 5kHz
.PRINT ac I(RS) I(RL) V(3) V(4)
.END
```

Fig. 10.5 Common-emitter BJT amplifier.

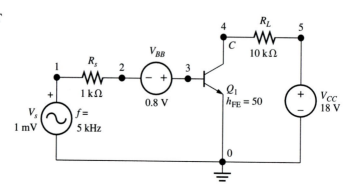

```
CE Amplifier, BJT Model
VCC 5 0 18V
VBB 3 2 0.8V
RS 1 2 1k
RL 4 5 10k
Q1 4 3 0 BJT
.MODEL BJT NPN(BF=50)
.TF V(4) VS
.OP
.OPT nopage
vs 1 0 ac 1mV
.AC lin 1 5kHz 5kHz
.PRINT ac I(RS) I(RL) V(3) V(4)
.END

   ****      BJT MODEL PARAMETERS
             BJT
             NPN
         IS  100.000000E-18
         BF  50
         NF  1
         BR  1
         NR  1

   NODE   VOLTAGE    NODE   VOLTAGE    NODE   VOLTAGE    NODE   VOLTAGE
   (   1)   0.0000  (   2)    -.0226  (   3)    .7774  (   4)   6.6929
   (   5)  18.0000

      VOLTAGE SOURCE CURRENTS
      NAME          CURRENT
      VCC          -1.131E-03
      VBB          -2.261E-05
      VS           -2.261E-05

      TOTAL POWER DISSIPATION   2.04E-02  WATTS

   **** BIPOLAR JUNCTION TRANSISTORS
   NAME          Q1
   MODEL         BJT
   IB            2.26E-05
   IC            1.13E-03
   VBE           7.77E-01
   VBC          -5.92E+00
   VCE           6.69E+00
   BETADC        5.00E+01
   BETAAC        5.00E+01

   ****      SMALL-SIGNAL CHARACTERISTICS
         V(4)/VS = -2.332E+02

         INPUT RESISTANCE AT VS =  2.144E+03

         OUTPUT RESISTANCE AT V(4) = 1.000E+04

   ****      AC ANALYSIS                    TEMPERATURE =   27.000 DEG C
    FREQ        I(RS)      I(RL)      V(3)       V(4)
   5.000E+03   4.665E-07  2.332E-05  5.335E-04  2.332E-01
```

Fig. 10.6

A frequency of 5 kHz is shown in the .AC statement. The .*PRINT ac* statement will allow us to find the specified currents and voltages. The output file from the PSpice analysis is shown in Fig. 10.6. Various formulas might be used to predict the voltage gain V(4)/V(3); for example,

$$A_V = -h_{fe}\frac{R_L}{h_{ie}} = \frac{-50(10 \text{ k}\Omega)}{1.1 \text{ k}\Omega} = -455$$

using an assumed value $h_{ie} = 1.1$ kΩ. Then using voltage division between R_s and h_{ie}, the voltage gain from the source V(4)/VS is found to be -238. From the PSpice output file under small-signal characteristics V(4)/VS is given as -233. The results are in close agreement.

The input resistance at VS given by PSpice is 2.144 kΩ. Subtracting R_s (1 kΩ) from this gives $h_{ie} = 1.144$ kΩ, which is close to the assumed value. The output resistance is given as 10 kΩ. In the actual case, this would be the parallel equivalent of R_L and h_{oe}. But if we assume that $h_{oe} \ge R_L$, then the value is approximately R_L. Note that if a capacitor had been included in the input loop, this method of finding the small-signal characteristics would not have given useful results.

The last lines of output contain the ac analysis. The frequency is 5 kHz, the base current is 0.46665 μA, and the collector current is 23.32 μA. In order to check these values by conventional circuit analysis, we must find the ac base current. This is

$$I_b = \frac{V_s}{R_s + h_{ie}} = \frac{1 \text{ mV}}{1 \text{ k}\Omega + 1.14 \text{ k}\Omega} = 0.476 \text{ }\mu\text{A}$$

The ac collector current is

$$I_c = h_{fe}I_b = 50(0.476 \text{ }\mu\text{A}) = 23.37 \text{ }\mu\text{A}$$

These values are in close agreement with the PSpice results.

Returning to the dc analysis, it is our desire to calculate the dc base current, given by

$$I_B = \frac{V_{BB} - V_{BE}}{R_s} = \frac{0.8 \text{ V} - 0.7774 \text{ V}}{1 \text{ k}\Omega} = 22.6 \text{ }\mu\text{A}$$

This is a presumptuous calculation, since V_{BE} has been taken from the PSpice results. Now it becomes obvious that this circuit is more useful for illustration than for practical purposes, since slight changes in V_{BB} or V_{BE} will cause large changes in I_B. Next, the dc collector current is found as $h_{FE}I_B$, giving a value of 1.13 mA, and the collector voltage is

$$V_C = V_{CC} - R_LI_C = 18 \text{ V} - (10 \text{ k}\Omega)(1.13 \text{ mA}) = 6.7 \text{ V}$$

The total power dissipation shown by PSpice is the product of the magnitudes of the dc source voltages and currents. Verify that this is 20.4 mW.

A final item of interest in Fig. 10.6 is the listing called BIPOLAR-JUNCTION TRANSISTORS. Our selected name *Q1*, along with the selected model name *BJT*, is shown, followed by a list of 16 quiscent-point values (not all are shown in Fig. 10.6). These values apply to the actual bias conditions of the circuit. They will change when the *Q*-point currents and voltages change. For example, if the transistor should go into saturation, the *BETADC* value would be much lower. After you have studied the results, move to a more practical circuit and do a more comprehensive analysis.

BIASING CASE STUDY

A circuit with a more stable operating point than the previous one is shown in Fig. 10.7. This is called a self-bias or emitter-bias circuit. The input file is

```
Biasing Case Study
VCC 2 0 12V
R1 2 1 40k
R2 1 0 3.3k
RC 2 3 4.7k
RE 4 0 220
Q1 3 1 4 Q2N2222
.LIB EVAL.LIB ; this calls in the library file EVAL.LIB
.DC VCC 12V 12V 12V
.PRINT DC I(RC) I(R1) I(R2) I(RE)
.OP
.OPT nopage
.END
```

There is no *.MODEL* statement in this input file. Instead, the transistor is identified as *Q2N2222 (npn)*. This is the designation for one of the transistors that is modeled in the evaluation version of PSpice. Other BJTs in the library are shown in Appendix E and include the *Q2N2907A (pnp)*, the *Q2N3904 (npn)*, and the *Q2N3906 (pnp)*. The line beginning with *.LIB* is required to make use of the resources in the library. The production version of PSpice contains many more transistors than those listed here. The library is in a file called *eval.lib*. Find the *.model Q2N2222* listing in Appendix E, which begins with

Fig. 10.7 Self-bias circuit.

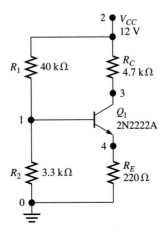

```
.model Q2N2222 NPN (Is=14.34f Xti=3 Eg=1.11 Vaf = 74.03
Bf=255.9 . . .
```

The various model parameters are assigned values in this statement. Thus the value of *Is* represents the *pn* saturation current, and so forth. A complete listing of the bipolar transistor parameters is given in Appendix D (look under "*Q* Bipolar Transistor").

Run the simulation and check the operating-point voltages and currents. Verify that $V_{CE} = 6.5185$ V and that the collector current $I_C = 1.114$ mA. Note that although *Q1* has a maximum forward beta h_{FE} of 255.9, under the operating-point information *BETADC* is given as *160*, in keeping with a base current IB = 6.96 mA. The output file is shown in Fig. 10.8. (Not all the model parameters are shown.)

The AC Analysis

In order to illustrate how this circuit behaves as a common-emitter amplifier we will add several components. Refer to Fig. 10.9 for the new circuit. An ac source voltage of 10 mV (peak value), a source resistance R_s of 50 Ω, and capacitors C_b and C_e have been added. The input file becomes

```
Biasing Case Study Extended
VCC 2 0 12V
Vs 1a 0 ac 10mV
Rs 1a 1b 50
Cb 1b 1 15uF
Ce 4 0 15uF
R1 2 1 40k
R2 1 0 3.3k
RC 2 3 4.7k
RE 4 0 220
Q1 3 1 4 Q2N2222
.DC VCC 12V 12V 12V
.PRINT DC I(RC) I(R1) I(R2) I(RE)
.OP
.opt nopage nomod ; suppress banner and model parameters
.ac LIN 1 5kHz 5kHz ; a sweep is necessary for ac analysis
.PRINT ac i(RC) i(RE) i(RS)
.PRINT ac v(1) v(1b) v(3) v(4)
.LIB EVAL.LIB
.END
```

In this input file, V_s is identified as an ac voltage, and an ac sweep is called for. Without the *.ac LIN* statement there will be no ac analysis information in the output file.

Run the analysis and verify that the bias voltage and current values have not changed from what they were in the previous output file. In fact, all the operating-point information is the same as before. Refer to Fig. 10.10 for the output file.

In addition to the previous results, we have asked for several ac currents and voltages. Verify that v(3)/v(1) = 188 and v(3)/vs = 182.7. The ac output current is

```
Biasing Case Study
VCC 2 0 12V
R1 2 1 40k
R2 1 0 3.3k
RC 2 3 4.7k
RE 4 0 220
Q1 3 1 4 Q2N2222
.LIB EVAL.LIB
.DC VCC 12V 12V 12V
.PRINT DC I(RC) I(R1) I(R2) I(RE)
.OP
.OPT nopage
.END


****        BJT MODEL PARAMETERS
                Q2N2222
                  NPN
            IS   14.340000E-15
            BF   255.9
            NF   1
            VAF  74.03


****      DC TRANSFER CURVES              TEMPERATURE =   27.000 DEG C
   VCC          I(RC)        I(R1)        I(R2)        I(RE)
  1.200E+01   1.114E-03   2.777E-04   2.707E-04   1.121E-03

   ****      SMALL SIGNAL BIAS SOLUTION      TEMPERATURE =   27.000 DEG C


 NODE    VOLTAGE      NODE    VOLTAGE      NODE    VOLTAGE      NODE    VOLTAGE
(   1)    .8933    (    2)   12.0000    (    3)    6.7651    (    4)     .2466


      VOLTAGE SOURCE CURRENTS
      NAME            CURRENT
      VCC           -1.391E-03


      TOTAL POWER DISSIPATION   1.67E-02   WATTS


   ****      OPERATING POINT INFORMATION     TEMPERATURE =   27.000 DEG C

**** BIPOLAR JUNCTION TRANSISTORS
NAME         Q1
MODEL        Q2N2222
IB           6.96E-06
IC           1.11E-03
VBE          6.47E-01
VBC         -5.87E+00
VCE          6.52E+00
BETADC       1.60E+02
GM           4.29E-02
RPI          4.12E+03
RX           1.00E+01
RO           7.17E+04
CBE          5.40E-11
CBC          3.47E-12
CBX          0.00E+00
CJS          0.00E+00
BETAAC       1.77E+02
FT           1.19E+08
```

Fig. 10.8

Fig. 10.9 Common-emitter
amplifier.

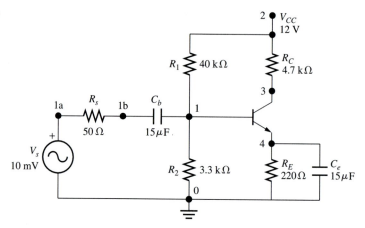

0.3888 mA, and the ac input current is 5.523 μA, giving a current gain of 70.4 from the source.

As an exercise, place a small resistor $R_B = 0.01\ \Omega$ in series with the base of the transistor. Call for the current through R_B in the .*PRINT ac* statement; then run the analysis and find the current gain from base to collector. It will not be the same as the current found as I_c/h_{fe}, where h_{fe} is *BETAAC*. Can you give an explanation for this?

It is instructive to use Probe to look at the ac voltages at various points in the circuit. Change the input file to contain the following:

```
Biasing Case Study Extended for Probe
VCC 2 0 12V
Vs 1a 0 sin (0 10mV 5kHz) ; arguments are offset, peak, and frequency
Rs 1a 1b 50
Cb 1b 1 15uF
Ce 4 0 15uF
R1 2 1 40k
R2 1 0 3.3k
RC 2 3 4.7k
RE 4 0 220
Q1 3 1 4 Q2N2222
.opt nopage nomod
.TRAN 0.02ms 0.6ms
.PROBE
.FOUR 5kHz V(3)
.LIB EVAL.LIB
.END
```

The voltage source is now shown not simply as an *ac* source but rather as a *sin ( )* source. The arguments are *offset, amplitude,* and *frequency.* The waveshapes may be displayed by including the .*PROBE* statement. Run the analysis; then plot v(3) and v(1) as shown in Fig. 10.11. In this figure, the cursor has been used to find the maximum value of collector voltage. Note that the collector voltage is 180° out of phase with the base voltage. Use the cursor to find the maximum and minimum

```
Biasing Case Study Extended

VCC 2 0 12V
Vs 1a 0 ac 10mV
Rs 1a 1b 50
Cb 1b 1 15uF
Ce 4 0 15uF
R1 2 1 40k
R2 1 0 3.3k
RC 2 3 4.7k
RE 4 0 220
Q1 3 1 4 Q2N2222
.DC VCC 12V 12V 12V
.PRINT DC I(RC) I(R1) I(R2) I(RE)
.OP
.opt nopage nomod ; suppress banner and model parameters
.ac LIN 1 5kHz 5kHz ; a sweep is necessary for ac analysis
.PRINT ac i(RC) i(RE) i(RS)
.PRINT ac v(1) v(1b) v(3) v(4)
.LIB EVAL.LIB
.END

  ****      DC TRANSFER CURVES             TEMPERATURE =   27.000 DEG C
   VCC         I(RC)        I(R1)       I(R2)      I(RE)
   1.200E+01   1.114E-03   2.777E-04   2.707E-04   1.121E-03


  ****      SMALL SIGNAL BIAS SOLUTION     TEMPERATURE =   27.000 DEG C
 NODE   VOLTAGE      NODE   VOLTAGE     NODE   VOLTAGE      NODE   VOLTAGE
(   1)    .8933  (    2)  12.0000  (    3)   6.7651  (    4)     .2466
(  1a)   0.0000  (   1b)   0.0000


    VOLTAGE SOURCE CURRENTS
    NAME          CURRENT
    VCC          -1.391E-03
    Vs            0.000E+00

    TOTAL POWER DISSIPATION   1.67E-02   WATTS


  ****      OPERATING POINT INFORMATION    TEMPERATURE =   27.000 DEG C

**** BIPOLAR JUNCTION TRANSISTORS
NAME          Q1
MODEL         Q2N2222
IB            6.96E-06
IC            1.11E-03
VBE           6.47E-01
VBC          -5.87E+00
VCE           6.52E+00
BETADC        1.60E+02
BETAAC        1.77E+02


  ****      AC ANALYSIS                    TEMPERATURE =   27.000 DEG C

   FREQ        I(RC)       I(RE)        I(RS)
   5.000E+03   3.888E-04   3.772E-06   5.523E-06
   FREQ        V(1)        V(1b)        V(3)         V(4)
   5.000E+03   9.724E-03   9.725E-03   1.827E+00   8.299E-04
```

Fig. 10.10

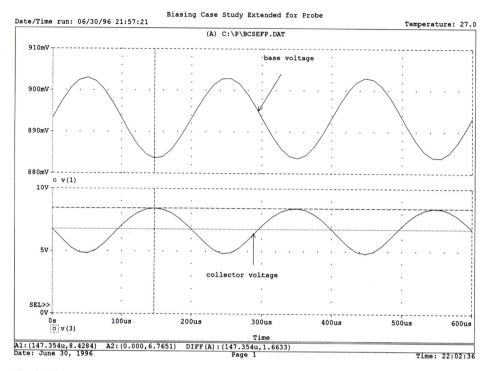

Fig. 10.11

values. Verify that the base voltage has a peak-to-peak value of 19.4 mV, while the collector has a corresponding value of 3.62 V. This gives a voltage gain $A_V = 187$, in agreement with the previous ac analysis.

Finally, the output file shown in Fig. 10.12 contains the results of the Fourier analysis of the output voltage V(3). The dc component is 6.75 V, which is not quite the same as the bias voltage at the collector due to the harmonic content of the output voltage. The fundamental frequency (5 kHz) shows a value of 1.781 V. This is the peak value, with the peak-to-peak value being 3.562 V. The plot of collector voltage shows a peak-to-peak value of 3.634 V. The two are not expected to be the same, again due to harmonic content. The second harmonic of the output voltage is 0.1342 V, which is an order of magnitude less than the fundamental. Higher harmonics are almost negligible, giving a total harmonic distortion of about 7.5%.

CE AMPLIFIER WITH UNBYPASSED EMITTER RESISTOR

When a common-emitter amplifier uses an unbypassed emitter resistor, the voltage gain of the circuit is reduced, but the frequency response is improved. The circuit, with its current-series feedback, is shown in Fig. 10.13. In this analysis, the built-in model for the BJT will be used, and the value of h_{FE} will be *80*. This is the input file:

```
Biasing Case Study Extended for Probe

VCC 2 0 12V
Vs 1a 0 sin(0 10mV 5kHz) ; arguments are offset, peak, and frequency
Rs 1a 1b 50
Cb 1b 1 15uF
Ce 4 0 15uF
R1 2 1 40k
R2 1 0 3.3k
RC 2 3 4.7k
RE 4 0 220
Q1 3 1 4 Q2N2222
.opt nopage nomod
.TRAN 0.02ms 0.6ms
.PROBE
.FOUR 5kHz V(3)
.LIB EVAL.LIB
.END

    ****     INITIAL TRANSIENT SOLUTION      TEMPERATURE =   27.000 DEG C
   NODE    VOLTAGE      NODE   VOLTAGE      NODE    VOLTAGE      NODE   VOLTAGE
   (   1)    .8933   (    2)  12.0000   (    3)   6.7651   (    4)     .246
   (  1a)   0.0000   (   1b)   0.0000

       VOLTAGE SOURCE CURRENTS
       NAME          CURRENT

       VCC          -1.391E-03
       Vs            0.000E+00

       TOTAL POWER DISSIPATION   1.67E-02  WATTS

    ****     FOURIER ANALYSIS               TEMPERATURE =   27.000 DEG C

   FOURIER COMPONENTS OF TRANSIENT RESPONSE V(3)

   DC COMPONENT =   6.757350E+00

   HARMONIC   FREQUENCY     FOURIER     NORMALIZED      PHASE        NORMALIZED
      NO        (HZ)       COMPONENT    COMPONENT       (DEG)       PHASE (DEG)

       1       5.000E+03   1.780E+00    1.000E+00     -1.752E+02     0.000E+00
       2       1.000E+04   1.343E-01    7.541E-02      1.019E+02     2.771E+02
       3       1.500E+04   4.445E-03    2.496E-03     -1.089E+01     1.643E+02
       4       2.000E+04   2.902E-03    1.630E-03     -1.114E+02     6.384E+01
       5       2.500E+04   2.710E-03    1.522E-03     -1.204E+02     5.485E+01
       6       3.000E+04   2.695E-03    1.514E-03     -1.277E+02     4.750E+01
       7       3.500E+04   2.638E-03    1.482E-03     -1.337E+02     4.154E+01
       8       4.000E+04   2.563E-03    1.440E-03     -1.402E+02     3.502E+01
       9       4.500E+04   2.430E-03    1.365E-03     -1.442E+02     3.100E+01

       TOTAL HARMONIC DISTORTION =     7.553840E+00 PERCENT
```

Fig. 10.12

```
Analysis of CE Amplifier with Unbypassed RE
VCC 4 0 12V
R1 4 1 40k
R2 1 0 5k
RC 4 2 1k
RE 3 0 100
```

Fig. 10.13 *CE amplifier with unbypassed emitter resistor.*

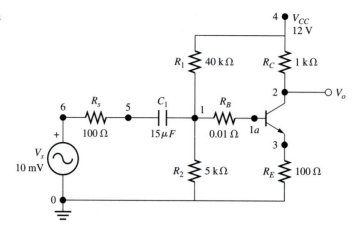

```
Rs 6 5 100
Rb 1 1a 0.01
C1 5 1 15uF
Q1 2 1a 3 BJT
.MODEL BJT NPN (BF=80)
.OP
vs 6 0 ac 10mV
.ac LIN 1 5kHz 5kHz
.PRINT ac i(RB) i(RC) i(RS) v(1) v(2) v(3)
.END
```

The dc analysis of this circuit was given in the "PSpice Overview" chapter at the beginning of the book and will not be repeated here.

Turning our attention to the ac analysis, using conventional circuit analysis, the voltage gain (from base to collector) is approximated as

$$A_V = \frac{-R_C}{R_E} = \frac{-1000\ \Omega}{100\ \Omega} = -10$$

But for small values of R_C, this could introduce up to about a 10% error (on the high side). A more accurate equation is

$$A_V = \frac{-R_C}{R_i} = \frac{-R_C}{h_{ie} + (1 + h_{fe})R_E} = \frac{-1000\ \Omega}{1100\ \Omega + (1 + 80)100\ \Omega} = -8.7$$

Since this is the voltage gain from base to collector, voltage division is used to find the voltage gain from the source to the collector:

$$A_{Vs} = \frac{A_V R_p}{R_p + R_s} = \frac{-8.7(3000\ \Omega)}{3000\ \Omega + 100\ \Omega} = -8.4$$

where R_p is the parallel combination of R_1, R_2, and R_i.

Now examine the output file, Fig. 10.14, to see how the PSpice analysis compares with the conventional results. PSpice shows an overall voltage gain V(2)/vs = −8.878. The two values differ by a little more than 5%.

```
Analysis of CE Amplifier with Unbypassed RE

VCC 4 0 12V
R1 4 1 40k
R2 1 0 5k
RC 4 2 1k
RE 3 0 100
Rs 6 5 100
Rb 1 1a 0.01
C1 5 1 15uF
Q1 2 1A 3 BJT
.MODEL BJT NPN(BF=80)
.OP
.OPT nopage nomod
vs 6 0 ac 10mV
.ac LIN 1 5kHz 5kHz
.PRINT ac i(RB) i(RC) i(RS) v(1) v(2) v(3)
.END


   NODE   VOLTAGE     NODE   VOLTAGE     NODE   VOLTAGE     NODE   VOLTAGE
 (   1)    1.1464   (   2)    8.6345   (   3)    .3408   (   4)   12.0000

 (   5)    0.0000   (   6)    0.0000   (  1a)    1.1464


     VOLTAGE SOURCE CURRENTS
     NAME          CURRENT
     VCC         -3.637E-03
     vs           0.000E+00


     TOTAL POWER DISSIPATION   4.36E-02  WATTS

**** BIPOLAR JUNCTION TRANSISTORS

NAME          Q1
MODEL         BJT
IB            4.21E-05
IC            3.37E-03
VBE           8.06E-01
VBC          -7.49E+00
VCE           8.29E+00
BETADC        8.00E+01
GM            1.30E-01
RPI           6.15E+02
RX            0.00E+00
RO            1.00E+12
CBE           0.00E+00
CBC           0.00E+00
CBX           0.00E+00
CJS           0.00E+00
BETAAC        8.00E+01
FT            2.07E+18


  ****      AC ANALYSIS                  TEMPERATURE =   27.000 DEG C

   FREQ        I(RB)       I(RC)       I(RS)        V(1)        V(2)
   5.000E+03   1.110E-06   8.878E-05   3.286E-06   9.671E-03   8.878E-02
 FREQ        V(3)
   5.000E+03   8.989E-03
```

Fig. 10.14

Fig. 10.15 Finding the input
resistance.

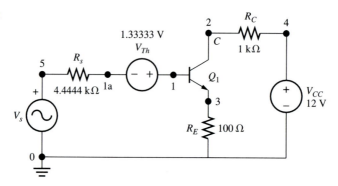

Finding the Input Resistance

It is desirable to find the input resistance as seen by the ac source. If we simply use
a statement such as

```
.TF v(4) vs
```

the results will be disappointing. You might try this and see what happens.
Removing the capacitor C_1 from the circuit will not work either, since this will upset
the bias conditions.

Another approach is shown in Fig. 10.15, where the Thevenin voltage and
Thevenin resistance are shown in the input loop along with V_s. This maintains the
proper bias voltages and currents and will allow for the transfer function to be used.

Study the output file of Fig. 10.16 (which also contains the input listing) to see
that the bias voltages have not changed. This listing shows the input resistance as
13.16 kΩ. At the base of the transistor, R_i = 13.16 kΩ − 4.444 kΩ = 8.7 kΩ. The calculated value of 9.2 kΩ differs from this by slightly more than 5%. We conclude that
the methods are in adequate agreement.

USING OUR OWN MODEL WITH THE *h* PARAMETERS

We will now compare finding voltage gains, current gains, and input resistance using
the PSpice model with the use of our own model for the *CE* amplifier based on the
h parameters. The method was introduced in Chapter 3, "Transistor Circuits."

The *h*-Parameter Analysis

The circuit of Fig. 10.13 is considered from the ac point of view. The supply V_{CC}
becomes a ground, C_1 is assumed to be a short circuit, and R_1 is in parallel with R_2.
The circuit for analysis becomes Fig. 10.17, and using the *h* parameters this becomes
Fig. 10.18.

Recall that the maximum amount of information can be obtained by pretend-
ing that we are doing a dc analysis rather than an ac analysis. This allows us to find

```
Find Input Resistance

VCC 4 0 12V
VTh 1 1a 1.33333V
RC 4 2 1k
RE 3 0 100
Rs 5 1a 4.4444k
Q1 2 1 3 BJT
.MODEL BJT NPN(BF=80)
.TF v(2) vs
.OP
vs 5 0 ac 10mV
.ac LIN 1 5kHz 5kHz
.PRINT ac i(Rs) i(RC) v(1) v(2) v(3)
.END

  NODE    VOLTAGE      NODE    VOLTAGE      NODE    VOLTAGE      NODE    VOLTAGE

(    1)    1.1464  (    2)    8.6345  (    3)    .3408  (    4)   12.0000
(    5)    0.0000  (   1a)   -.1870

     VOLTAGE SOURCE CURRENTS
     NAME              CURRENT

     VCC             -3.366E-03
     VTh             -4.207E-05
     vs              -4.207E-05

     TOTAL POWER DISSIPATION    4.04E-02   WATTS

****      SMALL-SIGNAL CHARACTERISTICS

        V(2)/vs = -6.079E+00

     INPUT RESISTANCE AT vs =   1.316E+04

     OUTPUT RESISTANCE AT V(2)  =   1.000E+03

   FREQ        I(Rs)        I(RC)        V(1)        V(2)        V(3)

   5.000E+03   7.599E-07   6.079E-05   6.623E-03   6.079E-02   6.155E-03
```

Fig. 10.16

the desired small-signal characteristics, including voltage gain and input resistance. The input file will not be repeated here, but it is shown in the output listing of Fig. 10.19. The results compare favorably with those obtained by using the built-in model for the BJT.

PHASE RELATIONS IN THE *CE* AMPLIFIER

When a *CE* amplifier uses an emitter resistor R_E for bias stability, it is bypassed with a capacitor C_E so that the input signal will see the emitter as a ground point in the circuit. If we look at the ac waveshapes at the collector and the emitter, it is of inter-

Fig. 10.17 *CE* amplifier for ac
analysis.

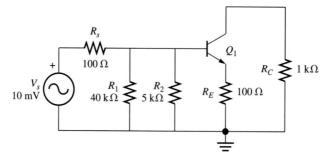

est to compare what the gain will be with and without C_E. This will also allow us to examine a potential problem when we use the *.TRAN* statement to look at ac steady-state values.

The Amplifier without the Emitter Capacitor

Refer to Fig. 10.13 for the circuit that is shown without C_E. The input file for the analysis is

```
Phase Relations in CE Amplifier
VCC 4 0 12V
R1 4 1 40k
R2 1 0 5k
RC 4 2 1k
RE 3 0 100
Rs 6 5 100
RB 1 1A 0.01
C1 5 1 15uF
Q1 2 1A 3 BJT
.MODEL BJT NPN (BF=80)
vs 6 0 sin (0 10mV 5kHz)
.TRAN 0.02ms 0.2ms
.PROBE
.END
```

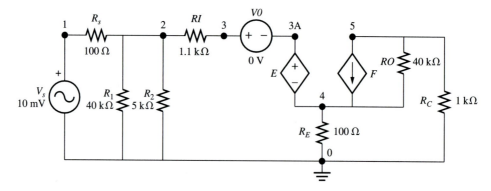

Fig. 10.18 *CE* amplifier using *h*-parameter model.

```
CE Amplifier with Re

vs 1 0 10mV
VO 3 3A 0
E 3A 4 5 4 2.5E-4
F 5 4 VO 80
Rs 1 2 100
R1 2 0 40k
R2 2 0 5k
RI 2 3 1.1k
RO 5 4 40k
RC 0 5 1k
RE 4 0 100
.TF V(5) Vs
.OP
.dc vs 10mV 10mV 10mV
.PRINT dc i(RC) i(Rs) i(RI) i(RE)
.END

   vs           I(RC)         I(Rs)         I(RI)         I(RE)

   1.000E-02   8.402E-05   3.256E-06   1.079E-06   8.510E-05
NODE   VOLTAGE      NODE   VOLTAGE      NODE   VOLTAGE      NODE   VOLTAGE

(   1)     .0100  (   2)     .0097  (   3)     .0085  (   4)     .0085
(   5)    -.0840  (  3A)     .0085


     VOLTAGE SOURCE CURRENTS
     NAME           CURRENT

     vs           -3.256E-06
     VO            1.079E-06


     TOTAL POWER DISSIPATION   3.26E-08  WATTS

**** VOLTAGE-CONTROLLED VOLTAGE SOURCES

NAME         E
V-SOURCE    -2.313E-05
I-SOURCE     1.079E-06

**** CURRENT-CONTROLLED CURRENT SOURCES

NAME         F
I-SOURCE     8.634E-05

  ****      SMALL-SIGNAL CHARACTERISTICS

       V(5)/vs = -8.402E+00

       INPUT RESISTANCE AT vs =  3.071E+03

       OUTPUT RESISTANCE AT V(5) =  9.987E+02
```

Fig. 10.19

Run the analysis and in Probe plot the collector voltage $v(2)$, the source voltage $v(6)$, and the emitter voltage $v(3)$. Note that the source voltage and the emitter voltage are in phase, while the collector voltage is 180° out of phase. Verify that the ac peak value of $v(2)$ is 88.75 mV and the ac peak value of $v(3)$ is 9 mV, compared with the ac peak value of $v(6)$, which is 10 mV. The transient analysis has successfully been used to allow us to look at steady-state values, and the results have been what

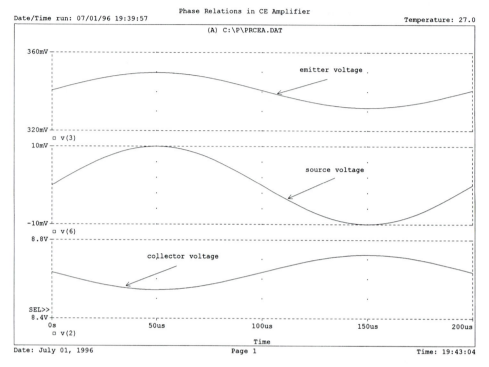

Fig. 10.20

we would expect when compared with those obtained by conventional analysis methods. Compare your plots with those shown in Fig. 10.20.

The Amplifier with the Emitter Capacitor

The amplifier is designed, however, to use a capacitor C_E across R_E. Let us insert the required line in the input file:

```
CE  3  0  10uF
```

and run the analysis again. In Probe plot the emitter voltage alone (to fill the entire screen), and notice that the wave appears distorted. If we plot several cycles of this voltage, we will see that the wave appears to be going through a transient phase before it begins to settle down to what we would have expected to see in the beginning. In the laboratory, the oscilloscope would show the wave correctly, so why does Probe show it differently? It is because we are using a transient analysis in a circuit with reactive elements. Therefore, we must be careful and look for potential problems such as this.

Plot v(2) and verify that v(2) = 0.929 V ac peak and that v(3) max = 3.5 mV ac peak. Note that the collector voltage also appears slightly distorted, with an axis-crossing value of 8.6345 V as shown in Fig. 10.21, a peak = 9.614 V, and a valley = 7.756 V.

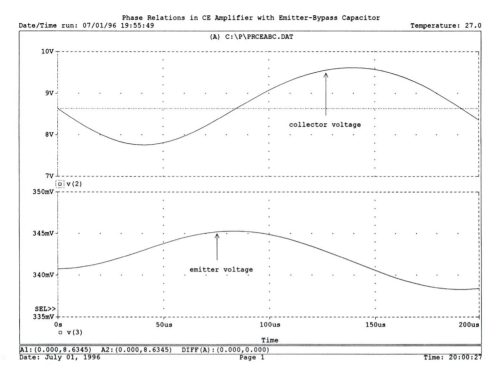

Fig. 10.21

Verify that at $f = 5$ kHz, the capacitor is not an ideal short circuit. Compute the impedance of the parallel combination of R_E and C_E. It is $Z = 3.18\ \underline{/-88°}\ \Omega$.

As an exercise, plot the current through C_E and the current through R_E. The emitter current can be plotted as $-\text{IE}(Q1)$ for comparison. Note the phase relations among the various currents and between the emitter voltage and the source voltage.

THE BJT FLIP-FLOP

A BJT flip-flop using *npn* transistors is shown in Fig. 10.22. For proper operation, this bistable multivibrator (or binary) should allow one transistor to operate well below cutoff while the other transistor is in saturation. Let us assume in the beginning that Q_1 is off and Q_2 is on. Using conventional analysis techniques.

$$V_1 = \frac{V_{BB}R_2}{R_2 + R_3} = -1.57\ \text{V}$$

This is sufficient back bias to cut off Q_1. To determine the collector current for the other transistor, I_{RC2} and I_{R2} will be found:

$$I_{RC2} = \frac{V_{CC}}{R_{C2}} = 5.45\ \text{mA}$$

Fig. 10.22 A BJT flip-flop.

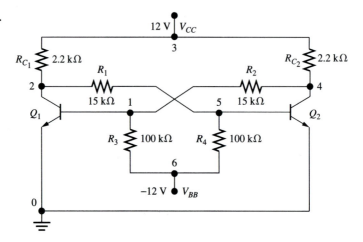

$$I_{R2} = \frac{V_{CC}}{R_2 + R_3} = 0.104 \text{ mA}$$

assuming that $V_4 = 0$.

The collector current in Q_2, which will be called I_{C2}, is the difference of these:

$$I_{C2} = I_{RC2} - I_{R2} = 5.35 \text{ mA}$$

It should be noted that the minimum base current I_{B2} required to saturate Q_2 is

$$I_{B2\text{min}} = \frac{I_{C2}}{h_{FE}} = \frac{5.35 \text{ mA}}{30} = 0.18 \text{ mA}$$

The base current is found by calculating its two components:

$$I_{R1} = \frac{V_{CC}}{R_{C1} + R_1} = 0.70 \text{ mA}$$

$$I_{R4} = \frac{0 - V_{BB}}{R_4} = 0.12 \text{ mA}$$

assuming that $V_5 = 0$.

The base current in Q_2, which is called I_{B2}, is the difference of these:

$$I_{B2} = I_{R1} - I_{R4} = 0.58 \text{ mA}.$$

a value well above the minimum required for saturation.

Since the circuit is symmetrical, had we assumed that Q_1 was on and Q_2 was off, the analysis would have produced similar results with the roles of the transistors swapped.

The PSpice Analysis

In order to run a PSpice analysis, we will assume that Q_1 is off, as we did in the conventional analysis. To allow for this in the input file, a *.NODESET* statement is required. The input file then becomes

```
BJT Flip-flop (Q1 off)

VCC 3 0 12V
VBB 6 0 -12V
RC1 3 2 2.2k
RC2 3 4 2.2k
R1 2 5 15k
R2 4 1 15k
R3 1 6 100k
R4 5 6 100k
Q1 2 1 0 QN
Q2 4 5 0 QN
.MODEL QN NPN(IS=1E-9 BF=30 BR=1 TF=0.2ns TR=5ns
.NODESET V(4)=0.15V
.OP
.DC VCC 12V 12V 12V
.PRINT DC I(RC1) I(RC2) I(R1) I(R2)
.END


    ****      BJT MODEL PARAMETERS
                 QN
                 NPN
              IS    1.000000E-09
              BF    30
              NF    1
              BR    1
              NR    1
              TF  200.000000E-12
              TR    5.000000E-09


   VCC         I(RC1)       I(RC2)       I(R1)       I(R2)
    1.200E+01   6.742E-04    5.421E-03    6.742E-04   1.050E-04

   NODE   VOLTAGE     NODE    VOLTAGE     NODE   VOLTAGE     NODE   VOLTAGE
  (   1)   -1.5012   (   2)   10.5170   (   3)   12.0000   (   4)     .0736
  (   5)     .4037   (   6)  -12.0000

     VOLTAGE SOURCE CURRENTS
     NAME          CURRENT
     VCC          -6.095E-03
     VBB           2.290E-04

     TOTAL POWER DISSIPATION    7.59E-02   WATTS

**** BIPOLAR JUNCTION TRANSISTORS
NAME        Q1          Q2
MODEL       QN          QN
IB         -1.05E-09    5.50E-04
IC          1.02E-09    5.32E-03
VBE        -1.50E+00    4.04E-01
VBC        -1.20E+01    3.30E-01
VCE         1.05E+01    7.36E-02
BETADC     -9.78E-01    9.66E+00
GM          0.00E+00    2.19E-01
RPI         3.00E+13    1.29E+02
RX          0.00E+00    0.00E+00
RO          1.00E+12    7.40E+01
CBE         2.00E-22    4.65E-11
CBC         5.00E-21    6.76E-11
CBX         0.00E+00    0.00E+00
CJS         0.00E+00    0.00E+00
BETAAC      0.00E+00    2.83E+01
FT          0.00E+00    3.06E+08
```

Fig. 10.23

```
BJT Flip-flop (Q1 on)

VCC 3 0 12V
VBB 6 0 -12V
RC1 3 2 2.2k
RC2 3 4 2.2k
R1 2 5 15k
R2 4 1 15k
R3 1 6 100k
R4 5 6 100k
Q1 2 1 0 QN
Q2 4 5 0 QN
.MODEL QN NPN(IS=1E-9 BF=30 BR=1 TF=0.2ns TR=5ns
.NODESET V(2)=0.15V
.OP
.DC VCC 12V 12V 12V
.PRINT DC I(RC1) I(RC2) I(R1) I(R2)
.END


****      BJT MODEL PARAMETERS
              QN
              NPN
          IS    1.000000E-09
          BF    30
          NF    1
          BR    1
          NR    1
          TF  200.000000E-12
          TR    5.000000E-09


 VCC           I(RC1)      I(RC2)      I(R1)       I(R2)
  1.200E+01    5.421E-03   6.742E-04   1.050E-04   6.742E-04


  NODE   VOLTAGE     NODE   VOLTAGE     NODE   VOLTAGE     NODE   VOLTAGE
(    1)    .4037  (    2)    .0736  (    3)  12.0000  (    4)  10.5170
(    5)  -1.5012  (    6) -12.0000


    VOLTAGE SOURCE CURRENTS
    NAME          CURRENT
    VCC          -6.095E-03
    VBB           2.290E-04

    TOTAL POWER DISSIPATION   7.59E-02  WATTS


**** BIPOLAR JUNCTION TRANSISTORS
NAME          Q1           Q2
MODEL         QN           QN
IB            5.50E-04    -1.05E-09
IC            5.32E-03     1.02E-09
VBE           4.04E-01    -1.50E+00
VBC           3.30E-01    -1.20E+01
VCE           7.36E-02     1.05E+01
BETADC        9.66E+00    -9.78E-01
GM            2.19E-01     0.00E+00
RPI           1.29E+02     3.00E+13
RX            0.00E+00     0.00E+00
RO            7.40E+01     1.00E+12
CBE           4.65E-11     2.00E-22
CBC           6.76E-11     5.00E-21
CBX           0.00E+00     0.00E+00
CJS           0.00E+00     0.00E+00
BETAAC        2.83E+01     0.00E+00
FT            3.06E+08     0.00E+00
```

Fig. 10.24

```
BJT Flip-flop
VCC 3 0 12V
VBB 6 0 -12V
RC1 3 2 2.2k
RC2 3 4 2.2k
R1 2 5 15k
R2 4 1 15k
R3 1 6 100k
R4 5 6 100k
Q1 2 1 0 QN
Q2 4 5 0 QN
.MODEL QN NPN (IS=1E-9 BF=30 BR=1 TF=0.2ns TR=5ns)
.NODESET V(4)=0.15V; guess for Q2 on (in saturation)
.OP
.DC VCC 12V 12V 12V
.PRINT DC I(RC1) I(RC2) I(R1) I(R2)
.END
```

The .NODESET value for V(4) = 0.15 V is a preliminary guess that is used in the beginning of the PSpice solution. When the iteration process of the solution is completed, this value is likely to change.

Run the PSpice analysis and observe that the node voltages and quiescent currents are in close agreement with those obtained by conventional circuit analysis. Also note that under the heading BIPOLAR-JUNCTION TRANSISTORS the operating-condition values of voltages, currents, and betas are close to those that were expected. The results are shown in Fig. 10.23.

It is interesting to run the analysis with the opposite initial conditions, setting Q_1 on and Q_2 off. This is brought about by using an initial guess for V(2) = 0.15 V instead of setting V(4) at that value. The results show that the roles of the two BJTs have reversed, and the various voltages and currents assume their counterpart values. Refer to Fig. 10.24 for the output file.

THE ASTABLE MULTIVIBRATOR

The collector-coupled astable multivibrator is a free-running circuit (astable means "not stable"). This circuit can be difficult to handle using PSpice, and unless some trial-and-error is used, the iteration process may fail to converge. The circuit of Fig. 10.25 shows two BJTs in a symmetrical configuration. A transistor is chosen with $h_{FE} = 80$. We may predict the period of oscillation as

$$T = 0.693 (R_1C_1 + R_2C_2) = 1.386RC$$

assuming that $R_1 = R_2 = R$ and $C_1 = C_2 = C$. Using off-the-shelf component values for the resistor and capacitor values, let $R = 56 \text{ k}\Omega$ and $C = 100 \text{ pF}$. In our example, this gives a period $T = 7.762 \text{ μs}$ and a frequency $f = 128.8 \text{ kHz}$. The input file is

```
Astable Multivibrator
VCC 5 0 5V
RC1 5 1 1k
RC2 5 2 1k
R1 5 3 56k
R2 5 4 56k
```

Fig. 10.25   Collector-coupled
astable multivibrator.

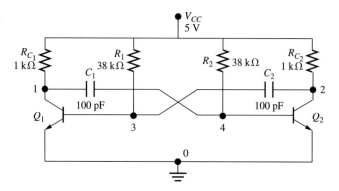

```
C1 1 4 100pF
C2 2 3 100pF
Q1 1 3 0 QN
Q2 2 4 0 QN
.MODEL QN NPN (IS=1E-12 BF=80 BR=1 TF=0.2ns TR=5ns)
.NODESET V(1)=0 V(3)=0
.OP
.PRINT DC I(RC1) I(RC2) I(R1) I(R2)
.TRAN 0.18us 18us
.PROBE
.END
```

The *.TRAN* statement deserves discussion. Since the period is known to be slightly over 7 μs, the analysis should run for perhaps 15 μs to 20 μs, in order to give the waveshapes enough time to settle to their expected forms. When a time of 20 μs was used, the iterations did not converge, and the plots were incorrect. Attempts to use other step times were also unsuccessful, although some combinations might be found that will produce proper results. The interval of 18 μs and the step of 0.18 μs did produce good results, however. Collector-voltage waveshapes are shown in Fig. 10.26, and base-voltage waveshapes are shown in Fig. 10.27. Using the cursor, you should verify that $T = 7.865$ μs, giving $f = 127$ kHz. These values are in close agreement with our predictions. Small-signal bias voltages and the initial transient voltages are shown in the output file of Fig. 10.28.

AN EMITTER-COUPLED BJT MULTIVIBRATOR

Another multivibrator is shown in Fig. 10.29. This is an emitter-coupled multivibrator, using off-the-shelf components. The details of the analysis are found in Millman and Taub, *Pulse, Digital, and Switching Waveforms*. For their analysis, it is assumed that Q_1 saturates and Q_2 does not. We set the initial voltage at the collector of Q_1 to a value of 25 V. You may want to try several different values of nodeset voltage and compare the results. The Millman and Taub analysis estimates the period of oscillation to be $T = 145.6$ μs.

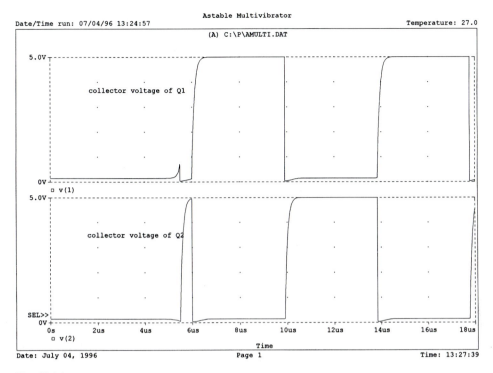

Fig. 10.26

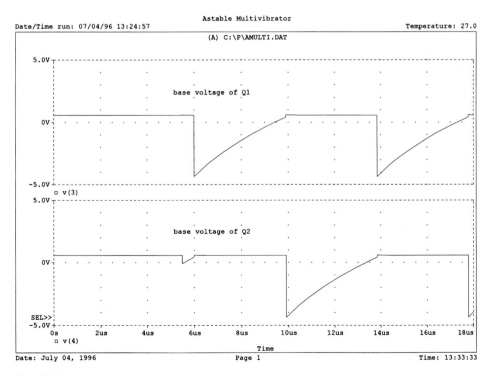

Fig. 10.27

```
Astable Multivibrator
VCC 5 0 5V
RC1 5 1 1k
RC2 5 2 1k
R1 5 3 56k
R2 5 4 56k
C1 1 4 100pF
C2 2 3 100pF
Q1 1 3 0 QN
Q2 2 4 0 QN
.MODEL QN NPN (IS=1E-12 BF=80 BR=1 TF=0.2ns TR=5ns)
.NODESET V(1)=0 V(3)=0
.OP
.PRINT DC I(RC1) I(RC2) I(R1) I(R2)
.TRAN 0.18us 18us
.PROBE
.END


   ****      BJT MODEL PARAMETERS
QN

              NPN
         IS   1.000000E-12
         BF   80
         NF   1
         BR   1
         NR   1
         TF   200.000000E-12
         TR   5.000000E-09


  ****       SMALL SIGNAL BIAS SOLUTION        TEMPERATURE =   27.000 DEG C
NODE    VOLTAGE      NODE   VOLTAGE      NODE    VOLTAGE      NODE    VOLTAGE
(    1)    .1452  (    2)      .1452  (    3)      .5770  (    4)      .5770
(    5)   5.0000


    VOLTAGE SOURCE CURRENTS
    NAME          CURRENT
    VCC           -9.868E-03


    TOTAL POWER DISSIPATION   4.93E-02  WATTS

  ****       OPERATING POINT INFORMATION      TEMPERATURE =   27.000 DEG C
  **** BIPOLAR JUNCTION TRANSISTORS
NAME           Q1           Q2
MODEL          QN           QN
IB             7.90E-05     7.90E-05
IC             4.85E-03     4.85E-03
VBE            5.77E-01     5.77E-01
VBC            4.32E-01     4.32E-01
VCE            1.45E-01     1.45E-01
BETADC         6.15E+01     6.15E+01
BETAAC         7.97E+01     7.97E+01


  ****       INITIAL TRANSIENT SOLUTION        TEMPERATURE =   27.000 DEG C
NODE    VOLTAGE      NODE   VOLTAGE      NODE    VOLTAGE      NODE    VOLTAGE
(    1)    .1452  (    2)      .1452  (    3)      .5770  (    4)      .5770
(    5)   5.0000


    VOLTAGE SOURCE CURRENTS
    NAME          CURRENT
    VCC           -9.868E-03


    TOTAL POWER DISSIPATION   4.93E-02  WATTS
```

Fig. 10.28

Fig. 10.29 Emitter-coupled multivibrator.

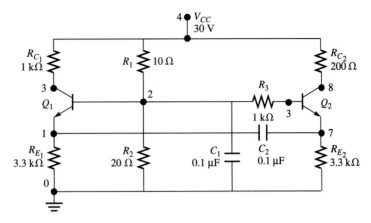

As an exercise, create your own input file for this circuit. Verify that the Probe results show $T = 151.4$ μs. The traces of collector voltages are shown in Fig. 10.30. Note that the X-axis has been plotted for the time interval 0.6 ms to 1.0 ms. This was done by changing the X-axis range to 0.6m 1.0m. The output file is shown in Fig. 10.31.

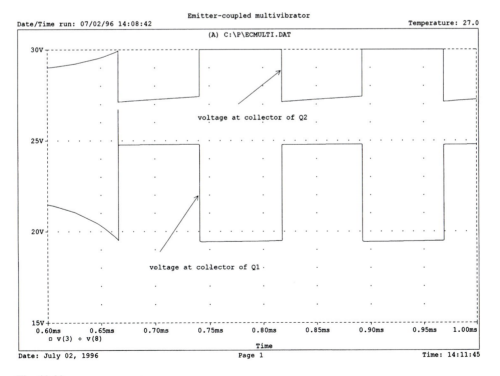

Fig. 10.30

```
Emitter-coupled multivibrator
VCC 4 0 30V
R1 4 2 10
R2 2 0 20
R3 2 3 1k
RC1 4 3 1k
RC2 4 8 200
RE1 1 0 3.3k
RE2 7 0 3.3k
C1 2 0 0.1uF
C2 1 7 0.1uF
Q1 3 2 1 QN
Q2 8 3 7 QN
.MODEL QN NPN(IS=1E-12 BF=30 BR=1 TF=0.2ns TR=5ns)
.NODESET V(3)=25V
.OP
.PRINT DC I(RC1) I(RC2) I(RE1) I(RE2)
.TRAN 0.5us 1ms
.PROBE
.END

    ****      BJT MODEL PARAMETERS

QN

            NPN
        IS    1.000000E-12
        BF    30

    ****       SMALL SIGNAL BIAS SOLUTION        TEMPERATURE =   27.000 DEG C
NODE    VOLTAGE      NODE    VOLTAGE    NODE    VOLTAGE    NODE    VOLTAGE
(    1)  19.4310  (    2)   20.0120  (    3)   22.0520  (    4)    30.0000
(    7)  21.4680  (    8)   28.7410

    VOLTAGE SOURCE CURRENTS
    NAME          CURRENT
    VCC          -1.013E+00

    TOTAL POWER DISSIPATION   3.04E+01  WATTS

    ****       OPERATING POINT INFORMATION       TEMPERATURE =   27.000 DEG C
 **** BIPOLAR JUNCTION TRANSISTORS
NAME         Q1           Q2
MODEL        QN           QN
IB           1.90E-04     2.10E-04
IC           5.70E-03     6.30E-03
VBE          5.81E-01     5.84E-01
VBC         -2.04E+00    -6.69E+00
VCE          2.62E+00     7.27E+00
BETADC       3.00E+01     3.00E+01
BETAAC       3.00E+01     3.00E+01

    ****      INITIAL TRANSIENT SOLUTION        TEMPERATURE =   27.000 DEG C
NODE    VOLTAGE      NODE    VOLTAGE    NODE    VOLTAGE    NODE    VOLTAGE
(    1)  19.4310  (    2)   20.0120  (    3)   22.0520  (    4)    30.0000
(    7)  21.4680  (    8)   28.7410

    VOLTAGE SOURCE CURRENTS
    NAME          CURRENT
    VCC          -1.013E+00
```

Fig. 10.31

PROBLEMS

10.1 The test circuits of Figs. 10.1 and 10.3 are designed to use a typical *npn* transistor. Using data for the 2N3251 *pnp* transistor ($h_{FE} = 180$), produce sets of output and input characteristics. Design an input file that will create the traces in Probe. Provide identifying labels for each of the curves.

10.2 (a) The circuit of Fig. 10.32 has $h_{FE} = 100$. Find the Q point using PSpice; then compare the results with your calculations assuming $V_{BE} = 0.7$ V. (b) In the PSpice analysis assume that $h_{FE} = 50$ and find the Q point.

Fig. 10.32

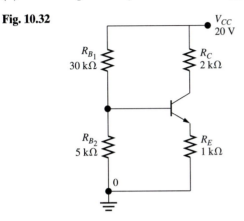

10.3 Determine the Q point for the circuit shown in Fig. 10.33 assuming that $h_{FE} = 60$ and $V_{BE} = 0.7$ V. Verify your calculations with a PSpice analysis using the built-in transistor model.

Fig. 10.33

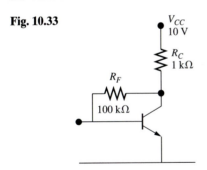

10.4 The circuit in Fig. 10.34 is to be used as a *CE* amplifier. It is desired that the Q point will allow maximum swing in collector current without undue distortion. The transistor has $h_{FE} = 50$.
(a) Find the quiescent collector current and voltage using PSpice.
(b) Run a PSpice/Probe analysis with a sinusoidal input v_i, and determine the practical limit of the input-voltage swing. What is the collector-current swing under this condition?

10.5 A *CE* amplifier with an unbypassed R_E is shown in Fig. 10.35. The transistor has $h_{FE} = 100$. The input signal has a peak value of 0.2 V. Using PSpice/Probe, show the output waveform and determine the voltage gain.

Fig. 10.34

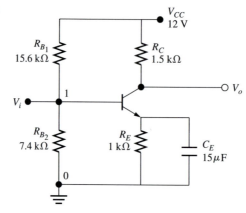

Fig. 10.35

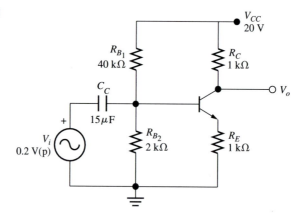

10.6 An emitter-coupled circuit is shown in Fig. 10.36. Use a PSpice analysis to find the quiescent collector currents and voltages for Q_1 and Q_2. Each transistor has $h_{FE} = 100$.

Fig. 10.36

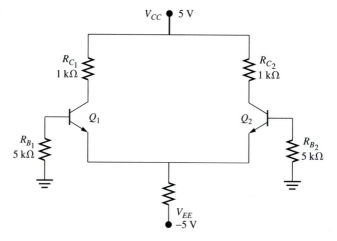

The Field-Effect Transistor

The built-in models for FETs in PSpice are designated with names beginning with *J* (for function FETs), *M* (for MOSFETs), and *B* (for GaAsFETs). Before using any of the devices, it is desirable to obtain sets of characteristic curves, so that the operating-point voltages and currents are properly predicted.

OUTPUT CHARACTERISTICS FOR THE JFET

The evaluation version comes with two *n*-channel JFETs in the library *EVAL.LIB*. The *J2N3819* has been chosen to obtain a useful set of output characteristics. The circuit of Fig. 11.1 yields this input file:

```
Output Characteristics for JFET J2N3819
VGS 1 0 0V
VDD 2 0 12V
JFET 2 1 0 J2N3819
.DC VDD 0 12V 0.2V VGS 0 -4V 1V
.PROBE
.LIB EVAL.LIB
.END
```

The nested loop for *.DC* will allow for up to five traces, with V_{GS} taking on integer values between 0 and -4 V. Run the analysis and observe that only four traces are shown. Refer to Fig. 11.2. Since the top trace is for $V_{GS} = 0$ V, the other traces are for -1 V, -2 V, and -3 V. There is no trace for $V_{GS} = -4$ V, since this is below the pinch-off value. It is now obvious that pinch off occurs at a value of -3 V. Now we are in a position to design a biasing circuit based on this JFET, since we know what values of V_{GS} are useful and what the resulting I_D values will be.

Fig. 11.1 Circuit for JFET
characteristics.

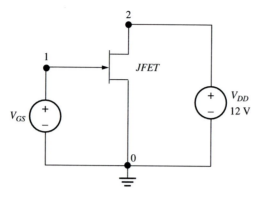

INPUT CHARACTERISTICS FOR THE JFET

For the input characteristics, the nested loop for .DC will use V_{GS} in the outer loop,
giving this as the X-axis variable. Values of V_{DD} will range from 2 V to 10 V in 4-V
steps, giving three traces. If you watch the generation of these on the screen in
Probe, you will see that the first trace, for $V_{DD} = 2$ V, is below the other two, as
expected. Labeling the curves for future use is helpful. Here is the input file:

```
Input Characteristics for JFET
VGS 1 0 0V
```

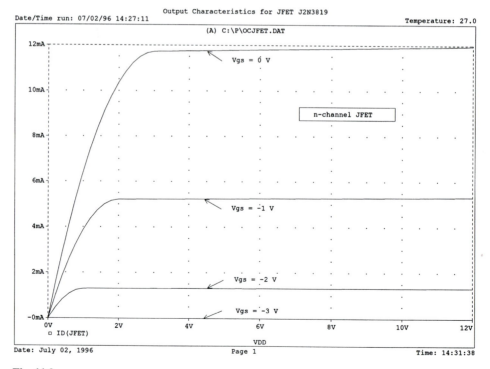

Fig. 11.2

```
VDD 2 0 10V
JFET 2 1 0 J2N3819
.DC VGS −3 0 0.05V VDD 2V 10V 4V
.PROBE
.LIB EVAL.LIB
.END
```

The characteristics are shown in Fig. 11.3, along with appropriate labels.

Since the evaluation library contains only *n*-channel JFETs, if a *p*-channel JFET is needed, you may wish to either insert a *.MODEL* statement in the input file or modify the library *EVAL.LIB* to include one or more such devices. The entry for the *J2N3819* is as follows:

```
.model J2N3819 NJF (Beta=1.304m Betatce=−.5 Rd=1 Rs=1 Lambda=2.25m
+Vto=−3
+Vtotc=−2.5m Is=33.57f Isr=322.4f N=1 Nr=2 Xti=3 Alpha=311.7
+Vk=243.6 Cgd=1.6p M=.3622 Pb=1 Fc=.5 Cgs=2.414p Kf=9.882E−18
+Af=1)
*National pid=50 case=TO92
*88-08-01 rmn BVmin=25
```

Note that $V_{to} = -3$ V is given as the threshold voltage. When a *p*-channel JFET is used, its model should be *PJF* (rather than *NJF*), and a positive value of V_{to} must be used.

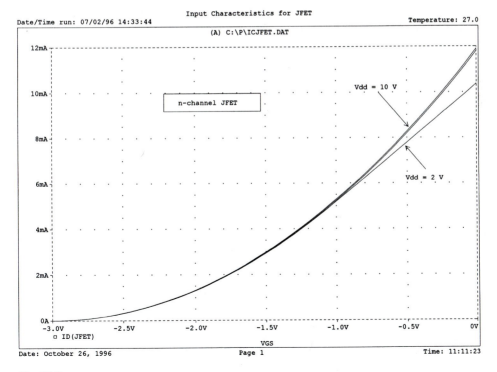

Fig. 11.3

JFET BIASING CIRCUIT

A source self-bias circuit is shown in Fig. 11.4. The built-in model for the *n*-channel JFET is used with several of the default parameters changed as shown in the input file.

```
n-Channel JFET Bias Circuit
VDD 4 0 18V
RG 1 0 0.5MEG
RS 2 0 770
RD 4 3 8.8k
JFET 3 1 2 JM
.MODEL JM NJF(RD=10 RS=10 VTO=-3 BETA=0.2m)
.DC VDD 18V 18V 18V
.OP
.OPT nopage
.PRINT DC I(RD) I(RS) I(RG)
.END
```

The output is shown in Fig. 11.5. In order to see if the PSpice results agree with conventional circuit analysis, the value of I_{DSS} should be known. Run an analysis like the one shown in Fig. 11.2, and verify that for this JFET, $I_{DSS} = 1.78$ mA. Using this, we find

$$g_{mo} = \frac{-2I_{DSS}}{V_P} = \frac{-2(1.78 \text{ mA})}{-3 \text{ V}} = 1.87 \text{ mS}$$

Next, we use the value of I_{DS} from PSpice to find V_{GS}. In the following equation, I_{DS} is the drain current under saturation conditions:

$$I_{DS} = I_{DSS}\left(1 - \frac{V_{GS}}{V_P}\right)^2 = 0.992 \text{ mA} = -1.78 \text{ m A}\left(1 + \frac{V_{GS}}{3}\right)^2$$

Rearranging and solving for V_{GS} gives $V_{GS} = 0.78$ V. Then

$$g_m = g_{mo}\left(1 - \frac{V_{GS}}{V_P}\right) = 1.187 \text{ mS}\left(1 - \frac{0.78}{3}\right) = 0.88 \text{ mS}$$

The values for V_{GS} and g_m are in close agreement with those shown in Fig. 11.5.

Fig. 11.4 JFET self-bias circuit.

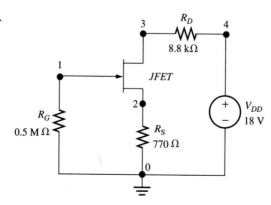

```
n-channel JFET bias circuit

VDD 4 0 18V
RG 1 0 0.5MEG
RS 2 0 770
RD 4 3 8.8k
JFET 3 1 2 JM
.MODEL JM NJF(RD=10 RS=10 VTO=-3 BETA=0.2m)
.DC VDD 18V 18V 18V
.OP
.OPT nopage
.PRINT DC I(RD) I(RS) I(RG)
.END

    ****      Junction FET MODEL PARAMETERS


            JM
            NJF
      VTO   -3
     BETA   200.000000E-06
      RD    10
      RS    10


    ****      DC TRANSFER CURVES               TEMPERATURE =    27.000 DEG C

   VDD       I(RD)       I(RS)       I(RG)

   1.800E+01   9.915E-04   9.915E-04   1.006E-11

    ****      SMALL SIGNAL BIAS SOLUTION      TEMPERATURE =    27.000 DEG C

  NODE   VOLTAGE      NODE   VOLTAGE      NODE   VOLTAGE      NODE   VOLTAGE

(    1) 5.029E-06  (    2)    .7635  (    3)   9.2744  (    4)
18.0000

     VOLTAGE SOURCE CURRENTS
     NAME          CURRENT

     VDD          -9.915E-04

     TOTAL POWER DISSIPATION   1.78E-02   WATTS

    ****      OPERATING POINT INFORMATION      TEMPERATURE =    27.000 DEG C

 **** JFETS


 NAME          JFET
 MODEL         JM
 ID            9.92E-04
 VGS          -7.63E-01
 VDS           8.51E+00
 GM            8.91E-04
 GDS           0.00E+00
 CGS           0.00E+00
 CGD           0.00E+00
```

Fig. 11.5

THE JFET AMPLIFIER

The biasing circuit of the example shown previously can be made into a voltage amplifier with the addition of two capacitors and an ac voltage source, as shown in Fig. 11.6. The input file is designed to show the ac analysis at $f = 5$ kHz.

```
n-Channel JFET Amplifier circuit
VDD 4 0 18V
vi 1a 0 ac 1mV
Cb 1a 1 15uF
Cs 2 0 15uF
RG 1 0 0.5MEG
RS 2 0 770
RD 4 3 8.8k
JFET 3 1 2 JM
.MODEL JM NJF (RD=10 RS=10 VTO=-3V BETA=0.2m)
.DC VDD 18V 18V 18V
.OP
.PRINT DC I(RD) I(RS) I(RG)
.ac lin 1 5kHz 5kHz
.PRINT ac i(RD) v(3) v(1) v(2)
.END
```

The output file is shown in Fig. 11.7. Verify from your analysis that the ac drain voltage V(3) is 7.77 mV, giving a voltage gain of 7.77. This is in agreement with the approximate equation

$$A_V = g_m R_D = (0.891 \text{ mS})(8.8 \text{ k}\Omega) = 7.8$$

JFET Waveshapes

The input file can be modified slightly to produce the sinusoidal waveshapes at the drain and input. In order to produce the sinusoids, the input voltage is changed to

```
vi 1a 0 sin (0 1mV 5kHz)
```

and a transient analysis is performed based on the statement

```
.TRAN 0.02ms 0.6ms
```

which will carry the analysis through three cycles of the 5-kHz wave.

Fig. 11.6   JFET amplifier.

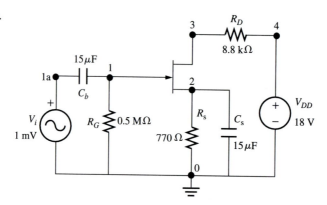

```
n-channel JFET Amplifier circuit

VDD 4 0 18V
vi 1a 0 ac 1mV
Cb 1a 1 15uF
Cs 2 0 15uF
RG 1 0 0.5MEG
RS 2 0 770
RD 4 3 8.8k
JFET 3 1 2 JM
.MODEL JM NJF(RD=10 RS=10 VTO=-3 BETA=0.2m)
.DC VDD 18V 18V 18V
.OP
.OPT nopage
.PRINT DC I(RD) I(RS) I(RG)
.ac lin 1 5kHz 5kHz
.PRINT ac i(RD) v(3) v(1) v(2)
.END


  VDD          I(RD)        I(RS)        I(RG)

   1.800E+01   9.915E-04    9.915E-04    1.006E-11

NODE    VOLTAGE     NODE    VOLTAGE     NODE    VOLTAGE     NODE    VOLTAGE

(    1) 5.029E-06  (    2)    .7635  (    3)    9.2744  (    4)   18.0000
(   1a)    0.0000

     VOLTAGE SOURCE CURRENTS
     NAME            CURRENT

     VDD            -9.915E-04
     vi              0.000E+00

     TOTAL POWER DISSIPATION    1.78E-02   WATTS

**** JFETS

  NAME          JFET
  MODEL         JM
  ID            9.92E-04
  VGS          -7.63E-01
  VDS           8.51E+00
  GM            8.91E-04
  GDS           0.00E+00
  CGS           0.00E+00
  CGD           0.00E+00

  ****     AC ANALYSIS                    TEMPERATURE =    27.000 DEG C

   FREQ         I(RD)       V(3)        V(1)        V(2)

    5.000E+03   8.828E-07   7.768E-03   1.000E-03   1.873E-06
```

Fig. 11.7

Run the simulation and in Probe verify that the drain voltage has a maximum value of 9.282 mV and a minimum value of 9.266 mV. This gives a peak-to-peak value of 15.4 mV, and a peak value of 7.7 mV. The results are in close agreement with the ac analysis previously given. The traces are shown in Fig. 11.8. Note that the cursor has been positioned to show V(3) at its peak value. The input voltage is at a corresponding minimum.

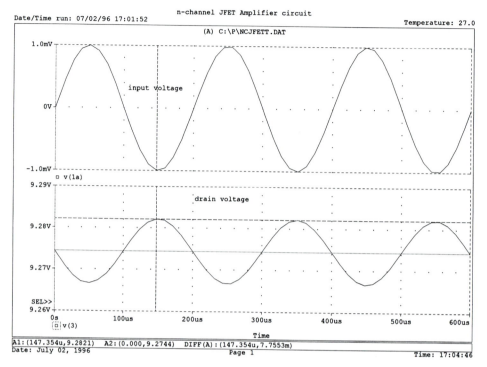

Fig. 11.8

The output file of Fig. 11.9 shows the modification of the input file to include both the transient analysis and a Fourier analysis of the output voltage V(3). The output file shows a dc component of 9.274 V, which is the quiescent collector voltage. The second and higher harmonics are of negligible magnitude, giving a total harmonic distortion of less than 1%.

THE POWER MOSFET

For a case study involving a MOSFET, the *EVAL.LIB* model of such a device will be chosen. This is the *IRF150*, which is an *n*-type power MOSFET. In order to become familiar with its characteristics, we will look at its output and input family of curves.

The Output Characteristics

In order to obtain the output characteristics, the circuit shown in Fig. 11.10 will be used. The input file is

```
n-Channel MOSFET Output Characteristics
VDD 2 0 12V
VGS 1 0 0V
MFET 2 1 0 0 IRF150; drain, gate, source, and substrate
```

```
n-channel JFET Amplifier circuit

VDD 4 0 18V
vi 1a 0 sin(0 1mV 5kHz)
Cb 1a 1 15uF
Cs 2 0 15uF
RG 1 0 0.5MEG
RS 2 0 770
RD 4 3 8.8k
JFET 3 1 2 JM
.MODEL JM NJF(RD=10 RS=10 VTO=-3 BETA=0.2m)
.DC VDD 18V 18V 18V
.OP
.OPT nopage nomod
.TRAN 0.02ms 0.6ms
.PROBE
.FOUR 5kHz V(3)
.END


****      INITIAL TRANSIENT SOLUTION          TEMPERATURE =   27.000 DEG C

  NODE   VOLTAGE     NODE   VOLTAGE     NODE   VOLTAGE     NODE    VOLTAGE

(   1) 5.029E-06  (   2)     .7635  (   3)   9.2744  (   4)    18.0000
(   1a)    0.0000


     VOLTAGE SOURCE CURRENTS
     NAME           CURRENT
     VDD          -9.915E-04
     vi            0.000E+00


     TOTAL POWER DISSIPATION   1.78E-02   WATTS

****      FOURIER ANALYSIS                    TEMPERATURE =   27.000 DEG C

FOURIER COMPONENTS OF TRANSIENT RESPONSE V(3)

 DC COMPONENT =   9.274381E+00

  HARMONIC   FREQUENCY    FOURIER     NORMALIZED     PHASE       NORMALIZED
    NO         (HZ)      COMPONENT    COMPONENT      (DEG)      PHASE (DEG)

     1      5.000E+03    7.679E-03    1.000E+00    -1.797E+02    0.000E+00
     2      1.000E+04    2.155E-05    2.806E-03    -1.014E+02    7.829E+01
     3      1.500E+04    2.311E-05    3.009E-03    -1.076E+02    7.208E+01
     4      2.000E+04    2.231E-05    2.905E-03    -1.139E+02    6.578E+01
     5      2.500E+04    2.154E-05    2.805E-03    -1.189E+02    6.079E+01
     6      3.000E+04    2.067E-05    2.692E-03    -1.247E+02    5.507E+01
     7      3.500E+04    1.949E-05    2.538E-03    -1.300E+02    4.974E+01
     8      4.000E+04    1.848E-05    2.406E-03    -1.352E+02    4.449E+01
     9      4.500E+04    1.723E-05    2.244E-03    -1.399E+02    3.983E+01

     TOTAL HARMONIC DISTORTION =   7.599231E-01 PERCENT
```

Fig. 11.9

```
.DC VDD 0 12V 0.8V VGS 0 8V 1V
.LIB EVAL.LIB
.PROBE
.END
```

The figure shows that the source and substrate are connected together, as
required. The output characteristics are shown in Fig. 11.11. As an example of the

Fig. 11.10   MOSFET circuit for characteristics.

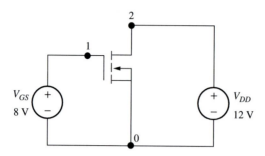

large drain currents involved, it is seen that when $V_{GS} = 5$ V, the saturation current is greater than 7 A. The library entry for the *IRF150* shows $V_{to} = 2.831$ V as the zero-bias threshold voltage. This is a positive voltage for an *n*-channel device.

The Input Characteristics

For the input characteristics, several values of V_{DD} will be used as shown in the following file:

```
Input Characteristic for MOSFET
VGS 1 0 0V
VDD 2 0 10V
MOS 2 1 0 0 IRF150
.DC VGS 0 8V 0.1V VDD 2V 10V 4V
```

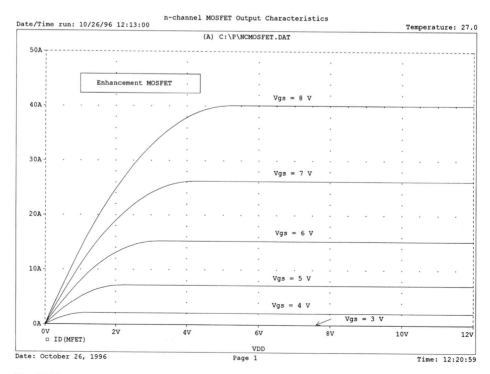

Fig. 11.11

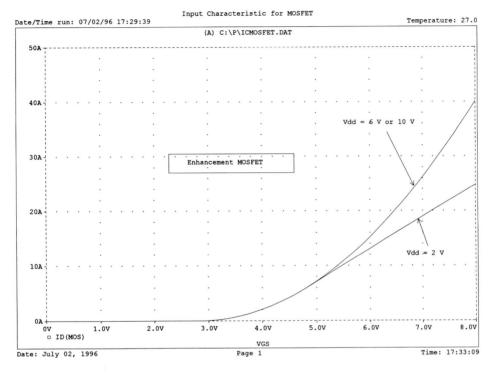

Fig. 11.12

```
.PROBE
.LIB EVAL.LIB
.END
```

The resulting plot is shown in Fig. 11.12. It can be seen that the threshold value of V_{GS} is slightly below 3 V. Also note that the family of curves for $V_{DD} = 6$ V or more will be indistinguishable.

Fig. 11.13 Power MOSFET amplifier.

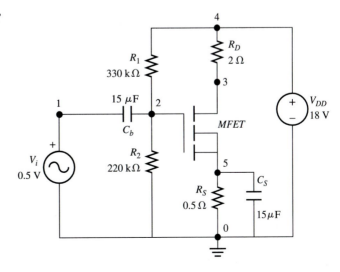

```
n-channel Power MOSFET Amplifier
VDD 4 0 18V
vi 1 0 ac 0.5V
R1 4 2 330k
R2 2 0 220k
Rd 4 3 2
Rs 5 0 0.5
Cb 1 2 15uF
Cs 5 0 15uF
MFET 3 2 5 5 IRF150
.DC VDD 12V 12V 12V
.OP
.PRINT DC i(RD) I(R1) I(R2) I(Rs)
.ac lin 1 5kHz 5kHz
.PRINT ac i(Rd) v(2) v(3)
.LIB EVAL.LIB
.END


     ****      MOSFET MODEL PARAMETERS
     IRF150

                  NMOS
          LEVEL    3
              L    2.000000E-06
              W    .3
            VTO    2.831
             KP    20.530000E-06
          GAMMA    0
            PHI    .6
             RD    1.031000E-03
             RS    1.624000E-03
             RG    13.89
            RDS    444.400000E+03


    VDD          I(RD)        I(R1)        I(R2)        I(Rs)
     1.200E+01   1.781E+00    2.182E-05    2.182E-05    1.781E+00


   NODE   VOLTAGE    NODE   VOLTAGE    NODE   VOLTAGE    NODE   VOLTAGE
   (   1)   0.0000   (   2)   7.2000   (   3)   7.8271   (   4)   18.0000
   (   5)   2.5432


      VOLTAGE SOURCE CURRENTS
      NAME          CURRENT

      VDD          -5.086E+00
      vi            0.000E+00


   TOTAL POWER DISSIPATION   9.16E+01   WATTS

**** MOSFETS
NAME          MFET
MODEL         IRF150
ID            5.09E+00
VGS           4.66E+00
VDS           5.28E+00
VBS           0.00E+00
VTH           2.83E+00
VDSAT         1.82E+00
GM            5.60E+00


   ****      AC ANALYSIS                    TEMPERATURE =    27.000 DEG C
    FREQ         I(Rd)        V(2)         V(3)
     5.000E+03    7.536E-01    4.999E-01    1.507E+00
```

Fig. 11.14

The MOSFET Amplifier

A power amplifier using the *IRF150* is shown in Fig. 11.13. Since large source and drain currents will be involved, the values of R_d and R_s are 2 Ω and 0.5 Ω, respectively. A voltage divider is provided using R_1 and R_2 to give a value of $V_{GS} = 4.7$ V. The input file is

```
n-Channel Power MOSFET Amplifier
VDD 4 0 18V
vi 1 0 ac 0.5V
R1 4 2 330k
R2 2 0 220k
Rd 4 3 2
Rs 5 0 0.5
Cb 1 2 15uF
Cs 5 0 15uF
MFET 3 2 5 5 IRF150
.DC VDD 12V 12V 12V
.OP
.PRINT DC I(RD) I(R1) I(R2) I(Rs)
.ac lin 1 5kHz 5kHz
.PRINT ac i(Rd) v(2) v(3)
.LIB EVAL.LIB
.END
```

The output file is shown in Fig. 11.14. Both dc and ac results are shown. From

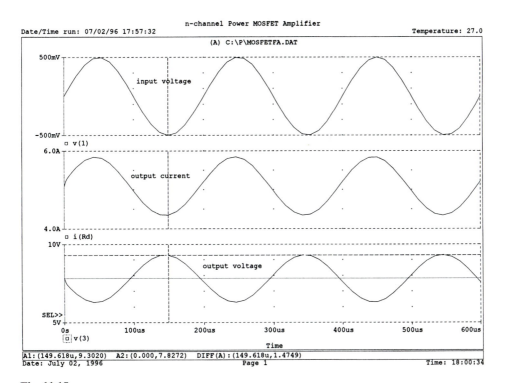

Fig. 11.15

```
n-channel Power MOSFET Amplifier, Fourier analysis

VDD 4 0 18V
vi 1 0 sin(0 0.5V 5kHz)
R1 4 2 330k
R2 2 0 220k
Rd 4 3 2
Rs 5 0 0.5
Cb 1 2 15uF
Cs 5 0 15uF
MFET 3 2 5 5 IRF150
.DC VDD 12V 12V 12V
.opt nopage nomod
.TRAN 0.02ms 0.6ms
.PROBE
.FOUR 5kHz v(3)
.LIB EVAL.LIB
.END

    ****      INITIAL TRANSIENT SOLUTION         TEMPERATURE =   27.000 DEG C

    NODE    VOLTAGE    NODE    VOLTAGE     NODE    VOLTAGE    NODE    VOLTAGE
    (   1)   0.0000    (   2)   7.2000     (   3)   7.8271    (   4)  18.0000
    (   5)   2.5432

        VOLTAGE SOURCE CURRENTS
        NAME            CURRENT

        VDD          -5.086E+00
        vi            0.000E+00

        TOTAL POWER DISSIPATION   9.16E+01   WATTS

    ****      FOURIER ANALYSIS               TEMPERATURE =   27.000 DEG C

FOURIER COMPONENTS OF TRANSIENT RESPONSE V(3)

    DC COMPONENT =   7.819569E+00

    HARMONIC   FREQUENCY    FOURIER     NORMALIZED     PHASE       NORMALIZED
      NO         (HZ)      COMPONENT    COMPONENT      (DEG)      PHASE (DEG)

       1       5.000E+03   1.490E+00   1.000E+00    -1.703E+02    0.000E+00
       2       1.000E+04   7.816E-03   5.246E-03     1.286E+02    2.989E+02
       3       1.500E+04   3.212E-04   2.156E-04    -1.040E+02    6.630E+01
       4       2.000E+04   1.882E-04   1.263E-04    -8.023E+01    9.005E+01
       5       2.500E+04   1.502E-04   1.008E-04    -7.562E+01    9.465E+01
       6       3.000E+04   1.972E-04   1.323E-04    -7.245E+01    9.782E+01
       7       3.500E+04   1.758E-04   1.180E-04    -1.008E+02    6.944E+01
       8       4.000E+04   4.582E-05   3.075E-05    -3.885E+01    1.314E+02
       9       4.500E+04   1.703E-04   1.143E-04    -3.659E+01    1.337E+02

       TOTAL HARMONIC DISTORTION =   5.257215E-01 PERCENT
```

Fig. 11.16

the dc portion of the results, the quiescent drain current (and source current) is $I_D = 1.781$ A, giving a drain voltage V(3) = 7.827 V and a source voltage V(5) = 2.543 V.

The ac analysis shows an input voltage $v_i = 0.5$ V and an output voltage at the drain v(3) = 1.5 V, giving a voltage gain of 3. The ac output current has a value $i_D = 0.7536$A. All these are peak values.

The Waveshapes

The input file may be modified slightly to allow for traces of the input and output voltages and the output current. As in the previous example, the input voltage will be shown as a sine wave using

```
vi 1 0 sin (0 0.5V 5kHz)
```

and a transient analysis will be performed along with a Fourier analysis. Run the simulation and use Probe to plot v(3), i(Rd), and v(1). The results should agree with Fig. 11.15. Use the cursor mode to find the peak value of the output voltage. Although each of the peaks has a slightly different value, due to the transient nature of the trace, the third peak is at 9.3188 V and the quiescent value is 7.8272 V. This gives a peak value of 1.4916 V, which is in close agreement with the ac voltage shown in the previous analysis, affirming the voltage gain of *3*.

The changes in the circuit file along with the output file are shown in Fig. 11.16. Note that there is a small second harmonic, giving a total distortion of just above 0.5%. The dc component of the output voltage is 7.819 V, differing slightly from the quiescent value at node 3.

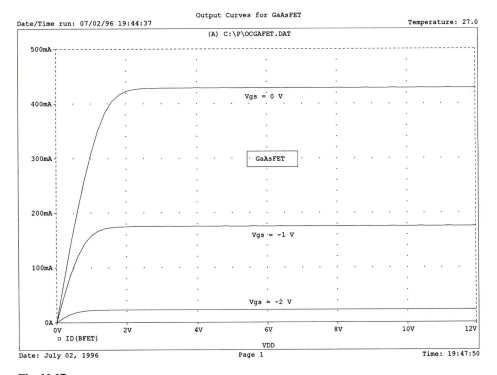

Fig. 11.17

THE GALLIUM ARSENIDE FET

PSpice includes a build-in model for the *n*-channel GaAsFET. The device name begins with *B*. Although no entries are included in the evaluation library, you may specify model parameters or simply use the default values, which are shown in Appendix D. The default value of the pinch-off voltage $V_{to} = -2.5$ V. A sample input file, used to obtain the output characteristics, is shown:

```
Output Curves for GaAsFET
VDD 2 0 12V
VGS 1 0 0V
BFET 2 1 0 B1; nodes are drain, gate, and source
.MODEL B1 GAsFET (Vto=-2.5 B=0.3 Rg=1 Rd=1 Rs=1 Vbi=0.5V)
.DC VDD 0 12V 0.2V VGS 0 -3V 1V
.PROBE
.END
```

Run the simulation in PSpice, then use Probe to obtain the traces of ID(BFET) as shown in Fig. 11.17. Verify that $I_{DSS} = 429$ mA.

PROBLEMS

Note: In SPICE, the JFET parameter *BETA* is found as

$$\beta = \frac{I_{DSS}}{V_P^2}$$

11.1 Using PSpice, determine the drain current I_D and the drain voltage V_{DS} for the JFET circuit shown in Fig. 11.18. Known values are $V_{PO} = 2$ V and $I_{DSS} = 5$ mA.

Fig. 11.18

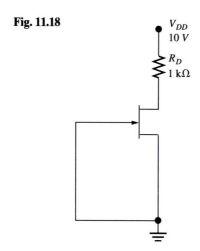

11.2 Find the *Q*-point values of I_D and V_{DS} for the JFET circuit shown in Fig. 11.19. The JFET has the same characteristics as in the previous problem.

Fig. 11.19

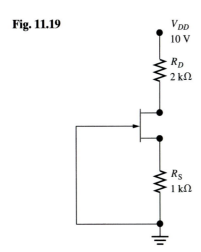

11.3 The circuit in Fig. 11.20 is for a depletion-type MOSFET with $I_{DSS} = 5$ mA and $V_{PO} = 2$ V. Find the values of I_D, V_{GS}, and V_{DS} from a PSpice analysis.

Fig. 11.20

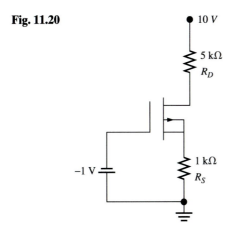

11.4 In the JFET circuit in Fig. 11.21, $I_{DSS} = 8$ mA and $V_{PO} = 5.0$ V. At the operating point $g_d = 0.3$ mS. Find the voltage gain v_o/v_i at low frequencies using a PSpice analysis.

Fig. 11.21

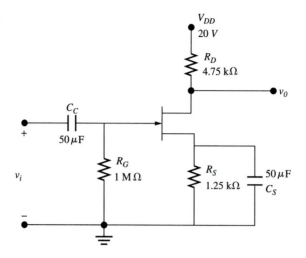

11.5 A JFET amplifier is shown in Fig. 11.22. Known values are $r_d = 100\ k\Omega$ and $g_m = 2850\ \mu S$. Use PSpice to find the voltage gain v_o/v_s.

Fig. 11.22

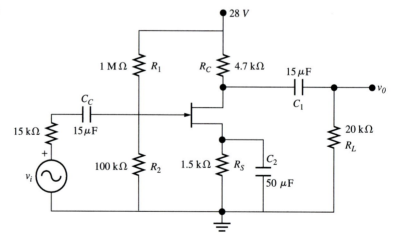

11.6 The MOSFET amplifier in Fig. 11.23 has $V_T = 2.5$ V, $\beta = 0.6$ A/V^2, and $r_d = 120\ k\Omega$. Using PSpice, find the voltage gain v_o/v_s.

Fig. 11.23

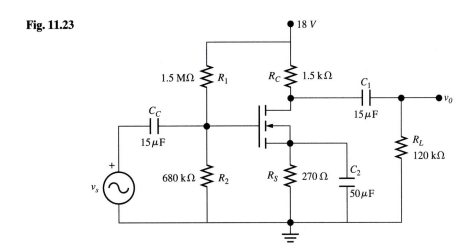

11.7 A chopper circuit is shown in Fig. 11.24. A 1-kHz sine wave is applied as v_i. Its magnitude is less than V_{PO}. The control voltage is a square wave with a 2-kHz frequency. Use a PSpice/Probe analysis to show the output voltage v_o.

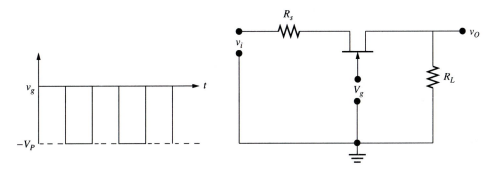

Fig. 11.24

12

Two-Port Networks and Passive Filters

There are occasions when a network may be viewed as a black box, with a pair of terminals at the input and another pair of terminals at the output. The components inside the box may be either unknown or unnecessary to know in order for a circuit analysis to be performed. These networks, called *two-port networks*, might be a set of resistors, a transmission line, and filters, and they might even contain active devices.

TWO-PORT PARAMETERS

Two-port networks have two input terminals and two output terminals, with the input terminals on the source side and the output terminals on the load side of the network. These networks may be analyzed by first finding a set of parameters that define the network and then using equations that employ these parameters. This method of analysis is especially helpful when the source and load change but the network remains the same. We will look at various examples involving the y, z, h, and $ABCD$ parameters.

FINDING THE y PARAMETERS

The two-port admittance parameters are based on the equations

$$I_1 = y_{11}V_1 + y_{12}V_2$$
$$I_2 = y_{21}V_1 + y_{22}V_2$$

Fig. 12.1   Two-port network.

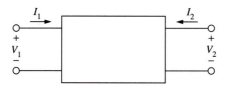

Figure 12.1 shows a two-port network, with the reference directions for the currents and sense directions for the voltages. By setting $V_2 = 0$, it is seen that

$$y_{11} = \left.\frac{I_1}{V_1}\right|_{V_2=0}$$

$$y_{21} = \left.\frac{I_2}{V_1}\right|_{V_2=0}$$

Thus y_{11} is found as the ratio of I_1 to V_1 with $V_2 = 0$, and y_{21} is found as the ratio of I_2 to V_1 with $V_2 = 0$. Also

$$y_{12} = \left.\frac{I_1}{V_2}\right|_{V_1=0}$$

$$y_{22} = \left.\frac{I_2}{V_2}\right|_{V_1=0}$$

PSpice can be used to find these y parameters, which are called the *short-circuit admittance parameters* of the two-port network. A simple network of resistors will be used as an example.

Figure 12.2 shows a T network of three resistors. In order to find y_{11} and y_{21}, we will short-circuit the output terminals (on the right), making $V_2 = 0$. On the input side a 1-V dc source is used for V_1. The input file is

```
Input and Transfer Admittances
V1  1  0  1V
R1  1  2  12
R2  0  2  3
R3  2  0  6
.DC V1  1V  1V  1V
.PRINT DC  I(R1)  I(R2); for y11 and y21
.END
```

Fig. 12.2   *T* network.

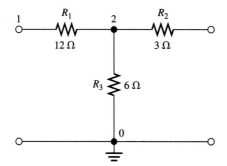

Note that the *R2* statement shows the nodes in the order 0, 2. This will give the proper direction for the current I_2, as shown in Fig. 12.3. Run the PSpice analysis to find I_1 and I_2. The results are

$$I(R1) = 71.43 \text{ mA} \quad \text{and} \quad I(R2) = -47.62 \text{ mA}$$

Since V_1 was chosen as a 1-V source, I_1 has the same value as y_{11}, and I_2 has the same value as y_{21}. Thus

$$y_{11} = 71.43 \text{ mS} \quad \text{and} \quad y_{21} = -47.62 \text{ mS}$$

The other *y* parameters may be found by using a 1-V source for V_2 while making $V_1 = 0$. The latter is done by short-circuiting the input terminals. The input file is

```
Output and Transfer Admittances
V2 2 0 1V
R1 0 1 12
R2 2 1 3
R3 1 0 6
.DC V2 1V 1V 1V
.PRINT DC I(R1) I(R2); for y12 and y22
.END
```

Since V_2 was chosen as a 1-V source, I_1 has the same value as y_{12}, and I_2 has the same value as y_{22}. Run the analysis and verify that

$$y_{12} = -47.62 \text{ mS} \quad \text{and} \quad y_{22} = 142.9 \text{ mS}$$

Note that $y_{12} = y_{21}$, since this is a bilateral network.

If the negative value for $y_{12} = y_{21}$ is a cause for concern, remember that the *y* parameters do not in themselves represent physical elements. However, it is easily shown that the π network of Fig. 12.4 is equivalent to the network containing the *y* parameters, and it is therefore equivalent to the original network, whatever it might have been. In our example

$$y_a = y_{11} + y_{12} = 23.81 \text{ mS}$$
$$y_b = y_{22} + y_{12} = 95.28 \text{ mS}$$
$$y_c = -y_{12} = 47.62 \text{ mS}$$

Fig. 12.3 *T* network with output shorted.

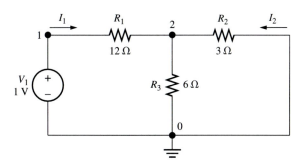

Fig. 12.4 *y*-parameter equivalent circuit.

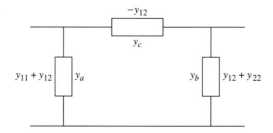

If these are converted to z values (actually R values in this case) by taking reciprocals, we have $z_a = 42\ \Omega$, $z_b = 10.5\ \Omega$, and $z_c = 21\ \Omega$.

Another equivalent network involving the y parameters is shown in Fig. 12.5. This circuit employs two voltage-dependent current sources and follows directly from the original equations that define the y parameters. Recall that the SPICE symbol for this type of source begins with the letter G.

Using the *y* Parameters to Solve a Circuit

It is difficult to see what practical use we can find for the y parameters in a typical situation like that shown in Fig. 12.6. The two-port network is one for which the y parameters have been found, but now a voltage source and a load resistance have been added. The original equations that define the y parameters cannot be used directly to find the load voltage V_2 and the load current $-I_2$, since these equations would be ideally suited for the situation when V_1 and V_2 were known. Analysis shows that

$$\frac{V_2}{V_s} = \frac{-y_{21}G_s}{(y_{11} + G_s)(y_{22} + G_L) - y_{12}y_{21}}$$

where $G_s = 1/R_s$ and $G_L = 1/R_L$. Use the y parameters from the preceding example along with $V_s = 10$ V, $R_s = 5\ \Omega$, and $R_L = 10\ \Omega$ to find V_2/V_s. Verify that the result is $V_2/V_s = 0.1496$.

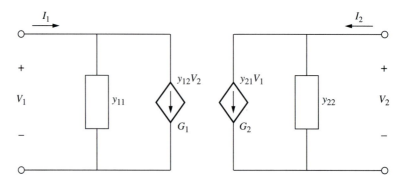

Fig. 12.5 *y*-parameter equivalent circuit with dependent sources.

Fig. 12.6 Practical circuit with source and load.

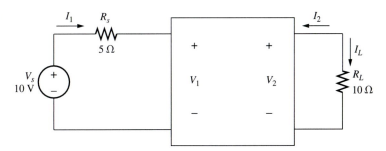

This can be checked by running a PSpice analysis on the original circuit, shown in Fig. 12.7. As an exercise find the ratio V(4)/Vs = 0.1496 using PSpice. Prepare an input file using the entire circuit shown in this figure.

y PARAMETERS OF NETWORK WITH DEPENDENT SOURCE

The previous example was simple enough to solve by ordinary circuit analysis, but when networks become more complicated, PSpice can be used to advantage. In the next example a dependent current source is part of the network, which is shown in Fig. 12.8. In order to find y_{11} and y_{21}, the output will be short-circuited, but a 0-V source will be included in the circuit to allow for a measurement of I_2. See Fig. 12.9 for the modified circuit. The input file is

```
Input and Transfer Admittances with Dependent Source
V1 1 0 1V
F 3 2 V1 -3
V0 0 3 0V
R1 1 2 4
R2 2 0 2
R3 2 3 2
.DC V1 1V 1V 1V
.PRINT DC I(R1) I(V0); to find I1 and I2
.END
```

The input current I_1 will be the current through R_1, and the output current I_2 will be the current through V_0. Run the analysis and verify that

Fig. 12.7 Original *T* circuit with source and load.

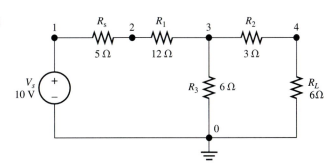

Fig. 12.8 Network with
dependent source.

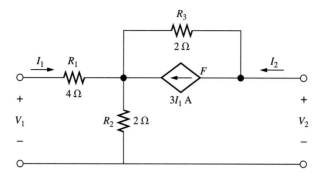

$$I(R1) = 125 \text{ mA} \quad \text{and} \quad I(V0) = 125 \text{ mA}$$

which, because of the 1-V source voltage, means that

$$y_{11} = 125 \text{ mS} \quad \text{and} \quad y_{21} = 125 \text{ mS}$$

In order to find y_{12} and y_{22}, a voltage source V_2 is connected to the output terminals, and the input terminals are shorted through a 0-V source as shown in Fig. 12.10. The input file is

```
Output and Transfer Admittances with Dependent Source
V2 2 0 1V
F 2 1 V0 -3
V0 1a 0 0V
R1 1a 1 4
R2 1 0 2
R3 1 2 2
.DC V2 1V 1V 1V
.PRINT DC I(R1) I(V2); for currents I1 and I2
.END
```

Run the analysis and verify these results:

$$I(R1) = -62.5 \text{ mA} \quad \text{and} \quad I(V2) = -187.5 \text{ mA}$$

This means that $y_{12} = -62.5$ mS and $y_{22} = 187.5$ mS.

Fig. 12.9 Network with output
shorted.

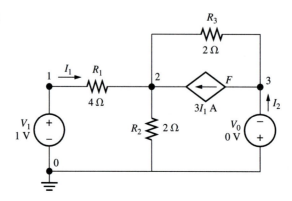

Fig. 12.10 Network with input shorted.

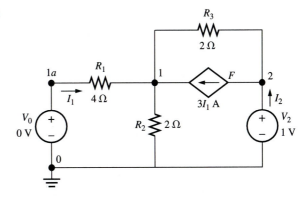

Note that y_{22} is positive although I(V2) is negative. From the circuit diagram you should be able to discover the reason for this.

THE OPEN-CIRCUIT IMPEDANCE PARAMETERS

When the currents in a two-port network are the independent variables, we may write the following equations:

$$V_1 = z_{11}I_1 + z_{12}I_2$$
$$V_2 = z_{21}I_1 + z_{22}I_2$$

from which we obtain

$$z_{11} = \frac{V_1}{I_1}\bigg|_{I_2=0}$$

$$z_{21} = \frac{V_2}{I_1}\bigg|_{I_2=0}$$

$$z_{12} = \frac{V_1}{I_2}\bigg|_{I_1=0}$$

$$z_{22} = \frac{V_2}{I_2}\bigg|_{I_1=0}$$

We will use the simple π network of Fig. 12.11 to introduce the method of solution using PSpice. The first analysis, which sets $I_2 = 0$, is used to find z_{11} and z_{21}. A source current $I_1 = 1$ A is applied to the input terminals with the output open-circuited. The input file is

```
Finding Open-Circuit Impedance Parameters z11 and z21
I1 0 1 1A
R1 1 0 42
R2 1 2 21
R3 2 0 10.5
.TF V(2) I1
.END
```

Fig. 12.11 π network.

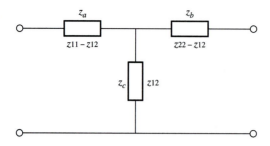

Run the analysis and obtain the following:

INPUT RESISTANCE AT I1 = 18 Ω

This gives $z_{11} = 18\ \Omega$. The output file shows $V(2) = 6$ V. Since the input current is 1 A, this is the same value as the transfer impedance; thus $z_{21} = 6\ \Omega$. The output file also shows

OUTPUT RESISTANCE AT V(2) = 9 Ω

Because the input source is an independent current source, PSpice considers this as an open circuit when computing the output resistance. Therefore $z_{22} = 9\ \Omega$.

The only z parameter remaining to be found is z_{12}. Since this is a bilateral network, $z_{12} = z_{21} = 6\ \Omega$.

As an exercise, verify the values of z_{12} and z_{22} by using a 1-A source as I_2 at the output terminals while the input terminals are open-circuited.

The z parameters do not in themselves represent physical elements of an equivalent circuit. However, it is easily shown that the T network of Fig. 12.12 is equivalent to the z-parameter network and thereby equivalent to the original two-terminal network. In the present example

$$z_a = z_{11} - z_{12} = 12\ \Omega$$

$$z_b = z_{22} - z_{12} = 3\ \Omega$$

$$z_c = z_{12} = 6\ \Omega$$

Fig. 12.12 z-parameter equivalent circuit.

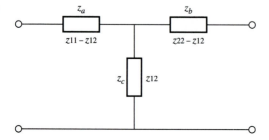

Another circuit may be used to represent the equivalent of the z-parameter network. This circuit, which involves two current-dependent voltage sources, is shown in Fig. 12.13.

THE z PARAMETERS FOR AN AC CIRCUIT

The z parameters for an ac circuit, such as the one shown in Fig. 12.14, can be found using PSpice. We will find these open-circuit parameters for this circuit at a frequency $f = 500$ Hz. It is convenient to use a source current of 1 A at zero degrees to drive the circuit. The input file is

```
Find z parameters for ac circuit
I1 0 1 ac 1A
R1 1 3 20
R2 4 2 10
R3 3 0 50
L1 1 4 6.366mH
C1 3 2 12.73uF
C2 3 0 3.183uF
.ac lin 1 500Hz 500Hz
.PRINT ac v(1) vp(1) v(2) vp(2)
.END
```

Run the analysis and see that the results are

$$V(1) = 5.199E + 01, VP(1) = -2.523E + 01, V(2) = 5.600E + 01,$$
$$VP(2) = -4.030E + 01$$

from which $z_{11} = 52\underline{/-25.23°}\ \Omega$ and $z_{21} = 56\underline{/-40.3°}\ \Omega$.

Finding the other z parameters involves using a 1-A source current I_2 at the output terminals. The input file will not be shown, since it is similar to the previous one, but you should run the analysis and verify that

$$V(1) = 5.600E + 01, VP(1) = -4.030E + 01, V(2) = 7.325E + 01,$$
$$VP(2) = -3.463E + 01$$

from which $z_{12} = 56\underline{/-40.3°}\ \Omega$ and $z_{22} = 73.25\underline{/-34.63°}\ \Omega$.

Since only linear elements are used, this is a bilateral circuit, and $z_{12} = z_{21}$.

Fig. 12.13 z-parameter equivalent circuit with dependent sources.

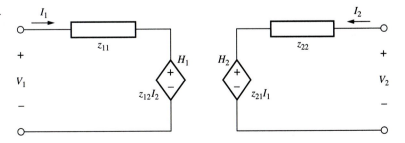

Fig. 12.14 Ac network.

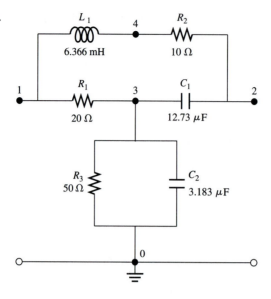

Using the z Parameters to Solve a Circuit

The typical circuit has a source with internal impedance at the sending end and a load impedance at the receiving end as shown in Fig. 12.15. It can be shown that

$$\frac{V_2}{V_s} = \frac{z_{21}Z_L}{(z_{11} + Z_s)(z_{22} + Z_L) - z_{12}z_{21}}$$

Several of the problems at the end of this chapter are related to the use of this and similar equations.

THE *ABCD* PARAMETERS

Another set of parameters, one that is widely used in power-system analysis, is the *ABCD* parameters. These are based on the equations

$$V_1 = AV_2 - BI_2$$
$$I_1 = CV_2 - DI_2$$

Fig. 12.15 Network with source and load.

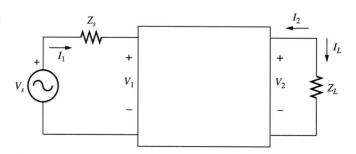

The minus signs are used to make these equations consistent with those of other two-port parameters, where I_2 is directed inward rather than toward the load impedance. From the defining equations it is seen that

$$A = \left.\frac{V_1}{V_2}\right|_{I_2=0}$$

$$C = \left.\frac{I_1}{V_2}\right|_{I_2=0}$$

$$B = -\left.\frac{V_1}{I_2}\right|_{V_2=0}$$

$$D = -\left.\frac{I_1}{I_2}\right|_{V_2=0}$$

Thus it is seen that A and C are open-circuit parameters, whereas B and D are short-circuit parameters.

A power transmission line is often represented as a T section, such as that shown in Fig. 12.16, where the series impedance is represented by resistance and inductance, and the shunt impedance is shown as resistance and capacitance. In order to find A and C, the output will be open-circuited, and the input will have a source voltage of 1 V at 60 Hz applied. The input file is

```
Circuit to find A and C parameters
V1 1 0 ac 1V
L1 1 2a 0.24525H
R1 2a 3 19.35
R3 3 0 4444
C1 3 0 3.06uF
.ac LIN 1 60Hz 60Hz
.PRINT ac v(3) vp(3) i(R1) ip(R1)
.END
```

Fig. 12.16 *T*-section representation of transmission line.

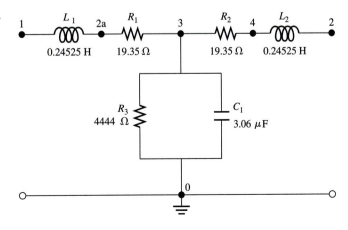

The elements R_2 and L_2 do not appear in this file, since they are hanging without a return path for current. Thus voltage V_3 will be the same as the desired voltage V_2. Run the analysis, which should give

$$V(3) = 1.113E + 00, VP(3) = -2.750E + 00,$$
$$I(R1) = 1.308E - 03, IP(R1) = 7.621E + 01$$

Since A is found from the ratio V_1/V_2, use a calculator to find $A = 0.8985\underline{/2.75°}$. The parameter C is found from the ratio I_1/V_2. This value is $1.175\underline{/78.95°}$ mS.

The parameters B and D are found by short-circuiting the output. Assuming that a 1-V source is used at the input terminals, this input file is

```
Circuit to find B and D parameters
V1  1 0 ac 1V
L1  1 2a 0.24525H
R1  2a 3 19.35
R2  4 3 19.35
L2  0 4 0.24525H
R3  3 0 4444
C1  3 0 3.06uF
.ac LIN 1 60Hz 60Hz
.PRINT ac i(R2) ip(R2) i(R1) ip(R1)
.END
```

The output file gives

$$I(R2) = 5.577E-03, IP(R2) = 1.005E+01,$$
$$I(R1) = 5.012E-03, IP(R1) = -7.673E+01$$

Under the short-circuit conditions, B and D are found using a calculator and are

$$B = -\frac{V_1}{I_2} = 179.3\underline{/79.5°} \ \Omega$$

$$D = -\frac{I_1}{I_2} = 0.8987\underline{/2.77°}$$

It is seen that A and D are equal. This will always be the case when linear elements are involved and the network contains no sources.

The defining equations are used directly to find the voltage and current at the sending end of a transmission line when conditions at the load are known. Problems at the end of the chapter illustrate this method.

When conditions at the sending end of a transmission line are known, the defining equations are more useful when rearranged to solve for V_2 and I_2. It is easily shown that

$$V_2 = \frac{DV_1 - BI_1}{AD - BC}$$

$$I_2 = \frac{CV_1 - AI_1}{AD - BC}$$

It can also be shown that

$$AD - BC = 1$$

giving the final form of the equations for receiving-end voltage and current as

$$V_2 = DV_1 - BI_1$$
$$I_2 = CV_1 - AI_1$$

THE HYBRID PARAMETERS

When the input current and the output voltage are chosen as the independent variables, the two-port equations are

$$V_1 = h_{11}I_1 + h_{12}V_2$$
$$I_2 = h_{21}I_1 + h_{22}V_2$$

It is because of the mix (current and voltage) of independent variables that the hybrid parameters get their name. These are the familiar parameters that are often used to characterize bipolar-junction transistors. Although it is possible to find the h parameters for various dc networks and ac networks, they are used only to a limited extent except with BJTs. From the defining equations we have

$$h_{11} = \left.\frac{V_1}{I_1}\right|_{V_2=0}$$

$$h_{21} = \left.\frac{I_2}{I_1}\right|_{V_2=0}$$

$$h_{12} = \left.\frac{V_1}{V_2}\right|_{I_1=0}$$

$$h_{22} = \left.\frac{I_2}{V_2}\right|_{I_1=0}$$

Since the h-parameter values for the BJT are covered in the chapter on transistor circuits, no more examples will be given here. In terms of the double-subscript notation, compare Fig. 12.17 with Fig. 3.5.

ANOTHER SET OF HYBRID PARAMETERS

Although not called hybrid parameters (to avoid confusion with the h parameters), another set of parameters is defined by allowing the input voltage and the output current to be the independent variables. Thus

$$I_1 = g_{11}V_1 + g_{12}I_2$$
$$V_2 = g_{21}V_1 + g_{22}I_2$$

Fig. 12.17 *h*-parameter equivalent circuit.

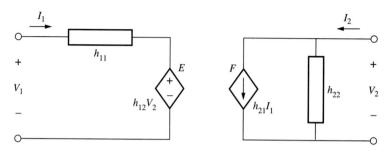

These are called the *g* parameters, but *g* does not mean that they are all conductances. In a dc network, only g_{11} represents a conductance. This is easily verified by noting the dimensions of the various terms in the defining equations. The general equivalent circuit involving the *g* parameters is easily obtained from these equations and is shown in Fig. 12.18. Also it is seen that

$$g_{11} = \left. \frac{I_1}{V_1} \right|_{I_2=0}$$

$$g_{21} = \left. \frac{V_2}{V_1} \right|_{I_2=0}$$

$$g_{12} = \left. \frac{I_1}{I_2} \right|_{V_1=0}$$

$$g_{22} = \left. \frac{V_2}{I_2} \right|_{V_1=0}$$

TRANSMISSION LINES

Although there is a PSpice device called *T* (for transmission line), it is of limited use because it does not take line losses into account. We would prefer to use a model for the transmission line that does include losses, and involves *R*, *L*, *G*, and *C*.

Fig. 12.18 *g*-parameter equivalent circuit.

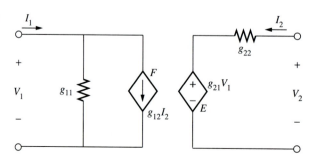

A Long Telephone Line

A certain telephone line uses 104-mil-diameter copper conductors that are spaced 18 in. apart on insulators. The measured parameters for the line are given in terms of *per-loop-mile*. They are

$$R = 10.15 \ \Omega$$
$$L = 3.93 \ \text{mH}$$
$$G = 0.29 \ \mu\text{S}$$
$$C = 0.00797 \ \mu\text{F}$$

The line is 200 mi long. When operated at $\omega = 5000$ rad/s, we would like to see how the voltage and current attenuate as a function of line length when the line is terminated in its characteristic impedance Z_o.

The characteristic impedance is found as $Z_o = \sqrt{z/y}$, where $z = R + j\omega L$ and $y = G + j\omega C$. The propagation constant is found as $\gamma = \sqrt{zy} = \alpha + j\beta$. At the prescribed angular frequency these are calculated to be

$$Z_o = 445\underline{/-13.45°} \ \Omega = (724.567 - j173.285) \ \Omega$$

and

$$\gamma = 0.0297\underline{/76.13°} = 0.00712 + j0.0288$$

Our approach to the solution will be to decide on a reasonable segment length of line that can be represented by lumped parameters and to use the elements of this segment as a model in a subcircuit. Since the line is 200 mi long, we will choose 20 mi as the segment length, representing this segment as a lumped-parameter T section. The per-mile values for R, L, G, and C are to be multiplied by 20, and the resulting values for R and L will then be split in half for each portion of the T. The results are shown in Fig. 12.19 and are incorporated into a subcircuit. Verify the elements shown in subcircuit TLINE.

The transmission line will be fed from a 1-V source. Small sensing resistors will be included at the connections between segments of the transmission line. This will allow for voltage and current measurements to be made at these points. The line is terminated in Z_o, where the value of $-173.285 \ \Omega$ (capacitive reactance) is shown as 1.154 μF, based on the given frequency. Refer to Fig. 12.20 for the node designations. The input file is

```
Transmission-Line Representation
V  1  0  AC  1V
R1  1  2  0.01
R2  3  4  0.01
R3  5  6  0.01
R4  7  8  0.01
R5  9  10  0.01
R6  11  12  0.01
R7  13  14  0.01
R8  15  16  0.01
R9  17  18  0.01
R10  19  20  0.01
```

Fig. 12.19   Portion of a
long telephone line.

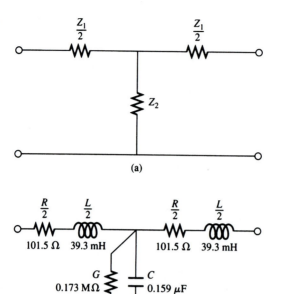

(a)

(b)

```
RL 21 22 724.567
CL 22 0 1.154uF
X1 2 0 3 TLINE
X2 4 0 5 TLINE
X3 6 0 7 TLINE
X4 8 0 9 TLINE
X5 10 0 11 TLINE
X6 12 0 13 TLINE
X7 14 0 15 TLINE
X8 16 0 17 TLINE
```

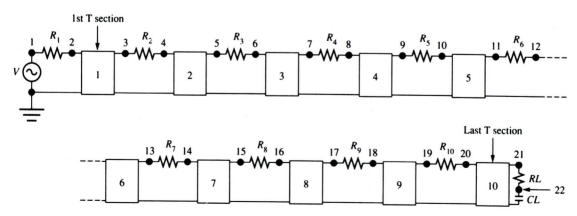

Fig. 12.20   Telephone line consisting of 10 T sections, each representing a 20-mi length.

```
X9 18 0 19 TLINE
X10 20 0 21 TLINE
.subckt TLINE 1 2 6
 R 1 3 101.5
 R1 4 5 101.5
 L 3 4 39.3mH
 L1 5 6 39.3mH
 Rs 4 2 0.172Meg
 C 4 2 0.159uF
.ends
.AC LIN 1 795.8Hz 795.8Hz
.PRINT AC I(R1) I(R2) I(R3) I(R4) I(R5) I(R6) I(R7) I(R8) I(R9) I(R10) I(RL)
.PRINT AC V(2) V(4) V(6) V(8) V(10) V(12) V(14) V(16) V(18) V(20) V(21)
.END
```

Run the analysis and from the output file verify that the sending-end current is 1.392 mA, the receiving-end current is 0.3104 mA, and receiving-end voltage is 0.2312 V. Plot the current and voltage as functions of positions down the length of the transmission line. An exponential decay of these quantities will be evident.

You may also observe the phase shift that occurs with position along the line. Simply run the analysis and print IP(R1), IP(R2), and so forth. Or print VP(2), VP(4), and so forth. Verify that VP(4) = −33.3°. This represents a phase shift in a 20-mi segment of the telephone line and corresponds to 1.665° per mile. From β = 0.0288 rad/mi, you see that these values are in close agreement. Figure 12.21 shows the output file that includes the currents, voltages, and phases of the voltages.

CONSTANT-k FILTER

The constant-k filter is ideally made up of pure reactances. In its simplest form, it might represent either a low-pass or a high-pass filter. A low-pass filter as a T section is shown in Fig. 12.22. The elements chosen for this example are L = 0.04 H and C = 0.1 μF. Such a filter is usually terminated in its characteristic impedance as given by

$$Z_{oT} = \sqrt{Z_1 Z_2 + \frac{Z_1^2}{4}}$$

where $Z_1 = j\omega L$ and $Z_2 = 1/(j\omega C)$.

When a frequency of f = 1592 Hz is chosen, Z_{oT} is calculated to be 600 Ω as a pure resistance. In Fig. 12.22, a voltage source with an internal resistance R = 0.01 Ω is connected on the left, and the value of load resistance is R_L = 600 Ω. The PSpice analysis will find input and output currents and voltages. The input file is

```
Constant-k Filter
V 1 0 AC 1V
L 2 3 0.02H
L1 3 4 0.02H
C 3 0 0.1uF
R 1 2 0.01
RL 4 0 600
.AC LIN 1 1592Hz 1592Hz
```

```
Transmission-Line Representation
V 1 0 AC 1V
R1 1 2 0.01
R2 3 4 0.01
R3 5 6 0.01
R4 7 8 0.01
R5 9 10 0.01
R6 11 12 0.01
R7 13 14 0.01
R8 15 16 0.01
R9 17 18 0.01
R10 19 20 0.01
RL 21 22 724.567
CL 22 0 1.154uF
X1 2 0 3 TLINE
X2 4 0 5 TLINE
X3 6 0 7 TLINE
X4 8 0 9 TLINE
X5 10 0 11 TLINE
X6 12 0 13 TLINE
X7 14 0 15 TLINE
X8 16 0 17 TLINE
X9 18 0 19 TLINE
X10 20 0 21 TLINE
.subckt TLINE 1 2 6
  R 1 3 101.5
  R1 4 5 101.5
  L 3 4 39.3mH
  L1 5 6 39.3mH
  Rs 4 2 0.172Meg
  C 4 2 0.159uF
.ends
.opt nopage
.AC LIN 1 795.8Hz 795.8HZ
.PRINT AC I(R1) I(R2) I(R3) I(R4) I(R5) I(R6) I(R7) I(R8) I(R9) I(R10) I(RL)
.PRINT AC V(2) V(4) V(6) V(8) V(10) V(12) V(14) V(16) V(18) V(20) V(21)
.PRINT AC VP(2) VP(4) VP(6) VP(8) VP(10) VP(12) VP(14) VP(16) VP(18) VP(20) VP(21)
.END


FREQ         I(R1)        I(R2)        I(R3)        I(R4)        I(R5)
7.958E+02   1.392E-03    1.202E-03    1.038E-03    8.953E-04    7.693E-04
FREQ         I(R6)        I(R7)        I(R8)        I(R9)        I(R10)
7.958E+02   6.608E-04    5.709E-04    4.967E-04    4.308E-04    3.678E-04
FREQ         I(RL)
7.958E+02   3.104E-04
FREQ         V(2)         V(4)         V(6)         V(8)         V(10)
7.958E+02   1.000E+00    8.613E-01    7.412E-01    6.390E-01    5.528E-01
FREQ         V(12)        V(14)        V(16)        V(18)        V(20)
7.958E+02   4.784E-01    4.117E-01    3.518E-01    3.015E-01    2.626E-01
FREQ         V(21)
7.958E+02   2.312E-01
FREQ         VP(2)        VP(4)        VP(6)        VP(8)        VP(10)
7.958E+02  -1.676E-04   -3.330E+01   -6.671E+01   -1.002E+02   -1.337E+02
FREQ         VP(12)       VP(14)       VP(16)       VP(18)       VP(20)
7.958E+02  -1.669E+02    1.601E+02    1.268E+02    9.283E+01    5.873E+01
FREQ         VP(21)
7.958E+02   2.568E+01
```

Fig. 12.21

Fig. 12.22 Constant-k, low-pass filter.

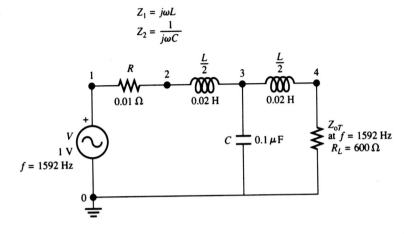

$Z_1 = j\omega L$

$Z_2 = \dfrac{1}{j\omega C}$

```
.PRINT AC I(R) I(RL) I(C) V(2) V(3) V(4) VP(2) VP(4)
.END
```

Run the analysis and obtain a printed copy of the output file. In interpreting the results, recall that at the frequency $f = 1592$ Hz, the characteristic impedance is resistance. The frequency is in the pass band of frequencies, where there will be no attenuation ($\alpha = 0$). This simply means that the input and output currents should be the same. Verify that the input current I(R) and the output current I(RL) are both 1.667 mA. The phase shift for the filter is given by

$$\beta = 2 \tan^{-1}\left(\frac{\sqrt{A}}{\sqrt{1-A}}\right)$$

where

$$A = \left|\frac{Z_1}{4Z_2}\right|$$

The calculated value for the phase shift is 36.88°, which is in agreement with the PSpice results showing VP(4) = –36.88°.

The low-pass filter has a cutoff frequency given by

$$f_c = \frac{1}{\pi\sqrt{LC}}$$

which for the elements chosen gives $f_c = 5033$ Hz. For comparison the MathCAD calculations for the constant-k filter in the pass band are given in Fig. 12.23.

Stop-Band Behavior of the Constant-k Filter

We continue the example for the low-pass filter. Choosing $f = 6$ kHz will mean that this frequency should not be passed without attenuation. To keep the filter properly terminated, the value of Z_{oT} at 6 kHz must be calculated. This is found to be $Z_{oT} = j410.47\ \Omega$. This gives an inductance value for the load of $L = 10.888$ mH.

Fig. 12.23

MathCAD solution of Constant-k filter for f = 1592 Hz
This is a low-pass filter with a cut-off fc = 5033 Hz

$L := 0.04 \quad C := 0.1 \cdot 10^{-6}$ $j := \sqrt{-1}$ $f := 1592$

The cut-off frequency is $fc := \dfrac{1}{\pi \cdot \sqrt{L \cdot C}}$ $fc = 5.033 \cdot 10^3$

$\omega := 2 \cdot \pi \cdot f$ $Z1 := j \cdot \omega \cdot L$ $Z1 = 400.113i$

$Z2 := \dfrac{1}{j \cdot \omega \cdot C}$ $Z2 = -999.717i$

$\qquad\qquad\qquad\qquad\qquad A := \dfrac{Z1}{4 \cdot Z2}$ $A = -0.1$

$ZoT := \sqrt{Z1 \cdot Z2 + \dfrac{Z1^2}{4}}$ $ZoT = 599.981$

$a := |A|$ $a = 0.1$

$\beta := 2 \cdot \text{atan}\left(\dfrac{\sqrt{a}}{\sqrt{1-a}}\right)$ $\beta = 0.644$ $b := \beta \cdot \dfrac{180}{\pi}$ $b = 36.881$

Now look at filter response for $f = 6$ kHz, which is in the stop band of frequencies. The modified input file is

```
Constant-k Filter, Stop-Band
V 1 0 AC 1V
L 2 3 0.02H
L1 3 4 0.02H
C 3 0 0.1uF
R 1 2 0.01
LL 4 0 10.888mH
.AC LIN 1 6000Hz 6000Hz
.PRINT AC I(R) I(LL) I(C) V(2) V(3) V(4) VP(2) VP(4)
.END
```

Run the analysis and obtain a copy of the output file. Verify that the input current $I(R) = 2.436$ mA and that the output current $I(LL) = 0.7187$ mA. The phase shift β is found as $VP(4) = -180°$. The propagation constant is given by

$$\gamma = \ln\left(\frac{I_{\text{in}}}{I_{\text{out}}}\right) = \alpha + j\beta$$

From our results, $\gamma = \ln(3.3895\underline{/180°})$. The value of α is found as the log of the magnitude of γ. This gives $\alpha = 1.22$ nepers. The formula is

$$\alpha = 2\ln(\sqrt{B-1} + \sqrt{B})$$

where

$$B\underline{/\pm\pi} = \left|\frac{Z_1}{4Z_2}\right|$$

This gives a calculated value of $\alpha = 1.22$ nepers, in agreement with the PSpice results. The neper is a fundamental measure of attenuation and corresponds to a current ratio of 2.71728. If a conversion is appropriate, 1 neper = 8.686 dB. Figure 12.24 shows the output files for both the pass-band and the stop-band examples. The MathCAD calculations for the stop band are given in Fig. 12.25.

Lossless Transmission Line

The constant-k filter can also serve as a useful model for a lossless transmission line. Figure 12.26 shows a segment of such a line, using $L = 2\,\text{mH}$ and $C = 50\,\text{nF}$. Assume that the model represents an actual length of line equal to 1 m. The values of L and

```
Constant-k Filter, Pass Band Frequency (1592 Hz)

****      CIRCUIT DESCRIPTION

V 1 0 AC 1V
L 2 3 0.02H
L1 3 4 0.02H
C 3 0 0.1uF
R 1 2 0.01
RL 4 0 600
.OPT nopage
.AC LIN 1 1592Hz 1592Hz
.PRINT AC I(R) I(RL) I(C) V(2) V(3) V(4) VP(2) VP(4)
.END

     ****      AC ANALYSIS                    TEMPERATURE =   27.000 DEG C

   FREQ         I(R)        I(RL)        I(C)       V(2)        V(3)
   1.592E+03    1.667E-03   1.667E-03   1.054E-03   1.000E+00   1.054E+00

   FREQ         V(4)        VP(2)       VP(4)
   1.592E+03    1.000E+00  -2.884E-08  -3.688E+01



Constant-k Filter, Stop-band Frequency (6000 Hz)

****      CIRCUIT DESCRIPTION

V 1 0 AC 1V
L 2 3 0.02H
L1 3 4 0.02H
C 3 0 0.1uF
R 1 2 0.01
LL 4 0 10.8875mH
.OPT nopage
.AC LIN 1 6000Hz 6000Hz
.PRINT AC I(R) I(LL) I(C) V(2) V(3) V(4) VP(2) VP(4)
.END

   FREQ         I(R)        I(LL)        I(C)       V(2)        V(3)
   6.000E+03    2.436E-03   7.187E-04   3.155E-03   1.000E+00   8.369E-01

   FREQ         V(4)        VP(2)       VP(4)
   6.000E+03    2.950E-01   1.396E-03  -1.800E+02
```

Fig. 12.24

Fig. 12.25

MathCAD solution of Constant-k filter for f = 6000 Hz
This is a low-pass filter with a cut-off fc = 5033 Hz

$$L := 0.04 \quad C := 0.1 \cdot 10^{-6} \quad j := \sqrt{-1} \quad f := 6000$$

The cut-off frequency is $\quad fc := \dfrac{1}{\pi \cdot \sqrt{L \cdot C}} \quad fc = 5.033 \cdot 10^3$

$$\omega := 2 \cdot \pi \cdot f \qquad Z1 := j \cdot \omega \cdot L$$
$$Z1 = 1.508 \cdot 10^3 \, i$$

$$Z2 := \dfrac{1}{j \cdot \omega \cdot C} \qquad Z2 = -265.258i$$

$$ZoT := \sqrt{Z1 \cdot Z2 + \dfrac{(Z1)^2}{4}} \qquad ZoT = 410.474i$$

$$B := \dfrac{Z1}{4 \cdot Z2} \qquad B = -1.421 \qquad b := |B| \qquad b = 1.421$$

$$\alpha := 2 \cdot \ln\left(\sqrt{b - 1} + \sqrt{b}\right) \qquad \alpha = 1.221$$

Alpha is the attenuation (in nepers) in the stop band

C then become series inductance per meter and shunt capacitance per meter, respectively. The cutoff frequency for this line is readily found and is $f_c = 31.8$ kHz. The analysis will involve $f = 10$ kHz, a frequency that is well within the pass band.

In order to properly terminate the line, you must solve for Z_{oT}. Verify that $Z_{oT} = 189.874 \underline{/0°}$ Ω. Using the method described in the previous section, you can find the phase shift β of a section of this line. Verify that β = 36.62°. Since the elements were designated as representing 1 m of line length, the phase shift represents 36.62°/m. Figure 12.27 shows the MathCAD calculations for this constant-k filter.

Fig. 12.26 Section of a lossless transmission line.

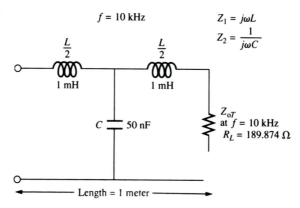

Fig. 12.27

MathCAD solution of Lossless Transmission Line Represented as a series of T sections. This is a constant-k filter representation with a cut-off frequency of 31.83 kHz.

$L := 0.002$ $C := 50 \cdot 10^{-9}$ $j := \sqrt{-1}$ $f := 10 \cdot 10^{3}$

The cut-off frequency is $fc := \dfrac{1}{\pi \cdot \sqrt{L \cdot C}}$ $fc = 3.183 \cdot 10^{4}$

$\omega := 2 \cdot \pi \cdot f$ $Z1 := j \cdot \omega \cdot L$ $Z1 = 125.664i$ $Z2 := \dfrac{1}{j \cdot \omega \cdot C}$

$Z2 = -318.31i$

$ZoT := \sqrt{Z1 \cdot Z2 + \dfrac{Z1^{2}}{4}}$ $ZoT = 189.874$ $A := \dfrac{Z1}{4 \cdot Z2}$

$A = -0.099$ $a := |A|$ $a = 0.099$

$\beta := 2 \cdot atan\left(\dfrac{\sqrt{a}}{\sqrt{1-a}}\right)$ $\beta = 0.639$ radian

$b := \beta \cdot \dfrac{180}{\pi}$ $b = 36.62$ degrees

For a preliminary investigation, create an input file to verify some of the findings. The input file is

```
Transmission Line as Lumped Elements
v 1 0 sin(0 1 10kHz)
L 1 2 1mH
L1 2 3 1mH
C 2 0 50nF
R 3 0 189.874
.tran 1us 100us
.probe
.end
```

Run the analysis and in Probe plot v(1) and v(3). Obtain a printed copy of this plot for further study. The synthesized output-voltage wave appears to have a higher amplitude than the input-voltage wave. Move beyond the positive peaks to the negative peaks and verify that the negative peak of v(1) is at 76 μs, while the corresponding peak of v(3) is at 86 μs. Record the peak magnitude of v(3), which is 1.008 V, for future use. What interpretation can be given to the 10-μs time interval between the two waves? The wave length of a transmission line is $\lambda = 360°/\beta$, which for this example is $360/36.62 = 9.83$ m. For a 10-kHz frequency, its velocity will be $v = f\lambda = 98.3$ km/s.

There is, of course, a simple relationship between time and distance for a transmission line. In our example, we conclude that a line that is 98.3 km in length is a *one-second* line. That is, it takes a wave 1 s to travel 98.3 km down the line. A 1-μs length of line would be 0.0983 m long. The 10-μs time interval between waves v(1) and v(3) is equivalent to (10)(0.0983) = 0.983 m. Since the *T* section represents 1 m of line, the results are in close agreement.

Looking carefully at the plots of v(1) and v(3), the delay of v(3) in beginning its sine-wave form is explained in terms of this time delay of 10 μs. If you sketch v(3) as a true sine wave toward its beginning, you will see that it crosses the *X*-axis at about the 10-μs point. Probe simply uses a curve fit to produce the graph, thereby obscuring this detail. The traces of v(1) and v(3) are shown in Fig. 12.28.

Remove the plots of voltage and plot i(R) for the line segment. Verify that the peak value (use the negative peak) is 5.3 mA. The magnitude of the load impedance is $v/i = 1.008/0.0053 = 190.2 \ \Omega$. (The voltage was recorded earlier.) Since these two waves are exactly in phase, the 190.2 Ω represents a pure resistance. This is in close agreement with the value of $Z_{oT} = 189.874\underline{/0°} \ \Omega$.

The graphs are plotted over a time interval of 100 μs so that the sinusoidal forms will be more evident, but this line is only 1 m in length, which as you know corresponds to 10 μs.

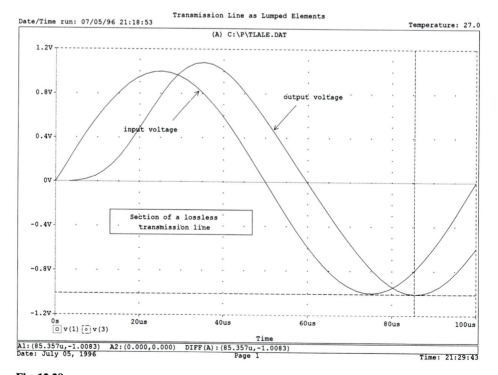

Fig. 12.28

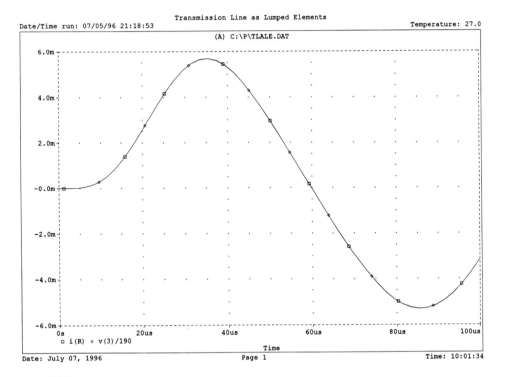

Fig. 12.29

An even more convincing graph is obtained by removing the current trace and plotting v(3)/i(R). Observe that this is a *flat* trace. In the cursor mode, verify that the characteristic impedance $Z_{oT} = 189.9 \, \Omega$.

Now plot together i(R) and v(3)/190. What do you get, and why? See Fig. 12.29 for these traces.

Lossless Line Composed of Several Sections

We may extend the analysis of the constant-k representation of a lossless transmission line to include any number of sections. As an example, let us use five sections, as shown in Fig. 12.30. At the sending end is a 1-V, 10-kHz source. Between the segments small resistors are inserted, so that we may find currents as well as voltages.

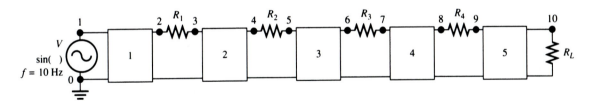

Fig. 12.30 Transmission line with five sections.

The input file is

```
Transmission Line with 5 Sections
v 1 0 sin(0 1 10kHz)
R1 2 3 0.001
R2 4 5 0.001
R3 6 7 0.001
R4 8 9 0.001
RL 10 0 189.874
X1 1 0 2 LC
X2 3 0 4 LC
X3 5 0 6 LC
X4 7 0 8 LC
X5 9 0 10 LC
.subckt LC 1 2 3
 L 1 a 1mH
 L1 a 3 1mH
 C a 2 50nF
.ends
.tran 1us 200us
.probe
.end
```

Run the analysis, and in Probe plot v(1), v(3), v(5), v(7), v(9), and v(10). Each wave is shifted from its adjacent wave by the time required for the wave to pass through one section of line. See Fig. 12.31 for these traces.

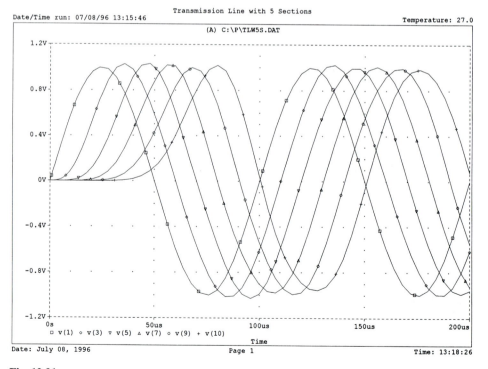

Fig. 12.31

In order to make measurements, remove these traces and plot only v(1) and v(10). Observe where each curve crosses the *X*-axis going negative. Verify that for v(1) this is at $t = 50$ μs and for v(10) this is at $t = 100$ μs. This means that the delay of the entire line is 50 μs. Although the plots are taken for 200 μs and the line is only 50 μs in length, the sinusoidal plots give a clear picture of a traveling wave on the transmission line.

INPUT IMPEDANCE AT POINTS ALONG THE LINE

When a transmission line is properly terminated, the input impedance should be equal to its characteristic impedance regardless of whether the line is one or more sections in length. An ac analysis will readily indicate the results if we call for voltage and current magnitudes and phases. Continuing the previous example, the input file is modified to become

```
Transmission Line with 5 Sections Modified
v 1 0 ac 1
R1 2 3 0.001
R2 4 5 0.001
R3 6 7 0.001
R4 8 9 0.001
RL 10 0 189.874
X1 1 0 2 LC
X2 3 0 4 LC
X3 5 0 6 LC
X4 7 0 8 LC
X5 9 0 10 LC
.subckt LC 1 2 3
 L 1 a 1mH
 L1 a 3 1mH
 C a 2 50nF
.ends
.ac lin 1 10kHz 10kHz
.print ac v(10) i(RL) vp(10) ip(RL)
.print ac v(9) i(R4) vp(9) ip(R4)
.print ac v(7) i(R3) vp(7) ip(R3)
.print ac v(5) i(R2) vp(5) ip(R2)
.print ac v(3) i(R1) vp(3) ip(R1)
.end
```

Run the analysis and look at the output file. At the receiving end, V(10) = 1 V and I(RL) = 5.267 mA. The two waves are in phase with a 176.92° phase shift. This gives $Z = 189.86\underline{/0°}$ Ω, which is the characteristic impedance. The input impedance at the next section is found from V(9) = 1 V and I(R4) = 5.276 mA along with VP(9) = −146.5° and IP(R4) = −146.5°. The voltage and current magnitudes are the same as before, and since the waves are still in phase, the impedance is again equal to the characteristic impedance. Note that at each section of line the voltage values remain the same in magnitude, and the current values are also the same. Also the phase shift between sections is 36.6°. Refer to Fig. 12.32 for the output file.

The results clearly indicate a flat line, that is, a line that will have no standing waves. This is typical of transmission lines that are terminated in their characteristic impedance.

```
Transmission Line with 5 Sections Modified

v 1 0 ac 1
R1 2 3 0.001
R2 4 5 0.001
R3 6 7 0.001
R4 8 9 0.001
RL 10 0 189.874
X1 1 0 2 LC
X2 3 0 4 LC
X3 5 0 6 LC
X4 7 0 8 LC
X5 9 0 10 LC
.subckt LC 1 2 3
  L 1 a 1mH
  L1 a 3 1mH
  C a 2 50nF
.ends
.opt nopage
.ac lin 1 10kHz 10kHz
.print ac v(10) i(RL) vp(10) ip(RL)
.print ac v(9) i(R4) vp(9) ip(R4)
.print ac v(7) i(R3) vp(7) ip(R3)
.print ac v(5) i(R2) vp(5) ip(R2)
.print ac v(3) i(R1) vp(3) ip(R1)
.end

****     AC ANALYSIS                    TEMPERATURE =   27.000 DEG C

  FREQ        V(10)       I(RL)      VP(10)      IP(RL)
  1.000E+04   1.000E+00   5.267E-03  1.769E+02   1.769E+02

  FREQ        V(9)        I(R4)      VP(9)       IP(R4)
  1.000E+04   1.000E+00   5.267E-03  -1.465E+02  -1.465E+02

  FREQ        V(7)        I(R3)      VP(7)       IP(R3)
  1.000E+04   1.000E+00   5.267E-03  -1.099E+02  -1.099E+02

  FREQ        V(5)        I(R2)      VP(5)       IP(R2)
  1.000E+04   1.000E+00   5.267E-03  -7.324E+01  -7.324E+01

  FREQ        V(3)        I(R1)      VP(3)       IP(R1)
  1.000E+04   1.000E+00   5.267E-03  -3.662E+01  -3.662E+01
```

Fig. 12.32

A Band-Pass Filter

A more elaborate passive filter is shown in Fig. 12.33. Both the series elements and the shunt elements contain capacitance and inductance. Formulas for the elements are found in Ware and Reed, *Communication Circuits*, p. 166, and are shown here for reference:

$$C_2 = \frac{1}{\pi R_o (f_o^2 - f_o^1)}$$

$$L_1 = \frac{R_o}{\pi (f_o^2 - f_o^1)}$$

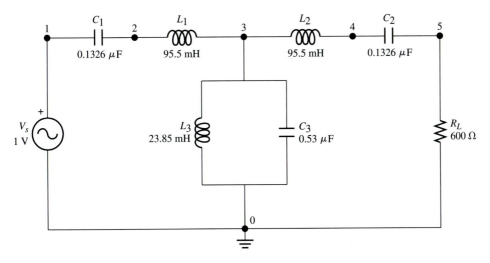

Fig. 12.33 Band-pass filter.

$$C_1 = \frac{f_o^2 - f_o^1}{4\pi f_o^1 f_o^2 R_o}$$

$$L_2 = C_1 R_o^2 = \frac{R_o(f_o^2 - f_o^1)}{4\pi f_o^1 f_o^2}$$

The filter is matched to a 600-Ω line for a pass band between 1 kHz and 2 kHz. Our input file is designed for use with Probe:

```
Band-pass Filter Using Passive Elements
Vs 1 0 ac 1V
C1 1 2 0.1326uF
C2 4 5 0.1326uF
C3 3 0 0.53uF
L1 2 3 95.5mH
L2 3 4 95.5mH
L3 3 0 23.85mH
RL 5 0 600
.ac DEC 50 100Hz 10kHz
.PROBE
.END
```

In Probe, plot the attenuation as shown in Fig. 12.34. Since the attenuation is so large outside the pass band, change the Y-axis by setting the range from –50 to 10. Note that there is no attenuation near the center of the pass band and that due to the resonance properties of the circuit, the output voltage rises near the limits of the pass band. As an exercise, find the gain at each of the peaks. Verify that it is 3.62 dB at the first peak and 3.67 dB at the second peak. Also find the attenuation at $f = 2.4$ kHz.

Practical filter elements, especially inductors, contain an amount of resistance. A problem at the end of the chapter addresses this matter.

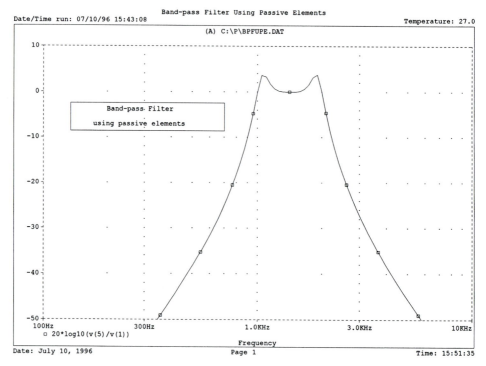

Fig. 12.34

BAND-ELIMINATION FILTER

When the *T* section of the previous study uses parallel inductance and capacitance in the series arms and series elements in the shunt branch, the filter may be designed for band elimination. The design is again based on formulas from Ware and Reed, with an elimination band extending from 2 kHz to 3 kHz. The equations are

$$L_1 = \frac{R_o(f_o^2 - f_o^1)}{\pi f_o^1 f_o^2}$$

$$C_1 = \frac{1}{4\pi R_o(f_o^2 - f_o^1)}$$

$$L_2 = \frac{R_o}{4\pi(f_o^2 - f_o^1)}$$

$$C_2 = \frac{f_o^2 - f_o^1}{\pi f_o^1 f_o^2 R_o}$$

The elements are shown in Fig. 12.35 and the input file is

```
Band-Elimination Filter Using Passive Elements
Vs 1 0 ac 1V
```

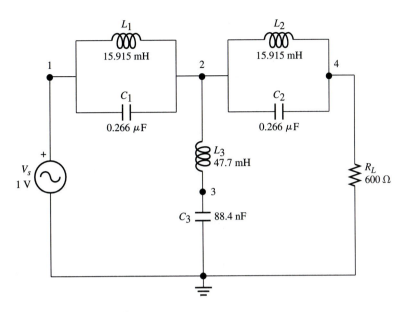

Fig. 12.35 Band-elimination filter.

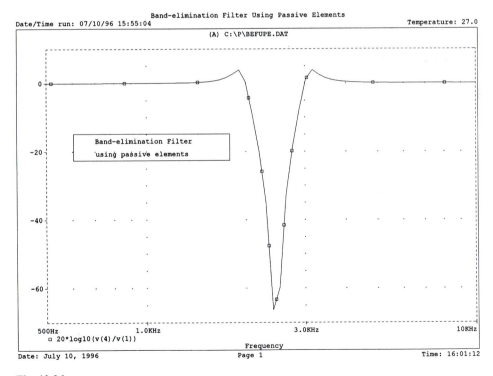

Fig. 12.36

```
L1 1 2 15.915mH
L2 2 4 15.915mH
C1 1 2 0.266uF
C2 2 4 0.266uF
L3 2 3 47.7mH
C3 3 0 88.4nF
RL 4 0 600
.ac DEC 50 100Hz 10kHz
.PROBE
.END
```

In Probe, obtain the dB plot of the ratio of output voltage to input voltage. Change the X range and Y range as shown in Fig. 12.36. Verify that the maximum attenuation occurs in the stop band at $f = 2.4$ kHz where the attenuation is 66.23 dB.

PROBLEMS

12.1 Use PSpice to find the y parameters of the circuit shown in Fig. 12.37. In this and other problems, plan your work so that a minimum amount of pencil-and-paper calculations will be required.

Fig. 12.37

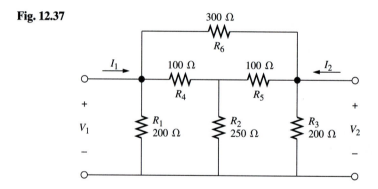

12.2 In Fig. 12.38, $R_s = 50$ Ω and $R_L = 200$ Ω. The network in the box is that of Problem 12.1. Use the y parameters found in this problem to solve for the transfer function V_2/V_s.

Fig. 12.38

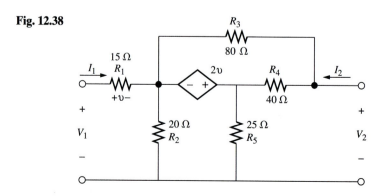

12.3 Use PSpice to find the z parameters of the circuit shown in Fig. 12.37.

12.4 In Fig. 12.6, using $R_s = 50\ \Omega$ and $R_L = 200\ \Omega$ and the z parameters of Problem 12.3, find the transfer function V_2/V_s. Compare the results with your answer to Problem 12.2.

12.5 Use PSpice to find the y parameters of the circuit shown in Fig. 12.38. Note that the circuit contains a dependent-voltage source.

12.6 The circuit in Fig. 12.39 is the π representation of a transmission line. Find its $ABCD$ parameters at $f = 60$ Hz using PSpice.

Fig. 12.39

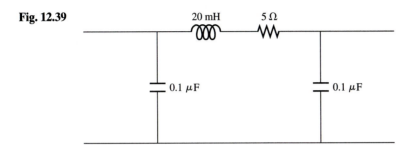

12.7 When the π circuit of Problem 12.6 is terminated with $Z_L = (20 + j20)\ \Omega$, the receiving-end current is $I_L = 3.89\underline{/-45°}$ A. Use the $ABCD$ parameters to find V_1 and I_1, the voltage and current at the sending end.

12.8 In the discussion of a long telephone line, the lumped parameters were shown as a T section. An alternative representation is the π section as shown in Fig. 12.40. Using the same values as those given in the text example, devise a sub-circuit for the 20-mile segment based on the π-section representation. Modify the input file and run the analysis. Compare the results with those obtained using the T-section representation.

Fig. 12.40

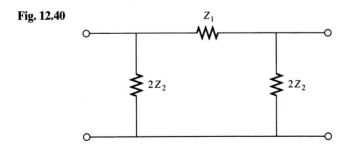

12.9 A constant-k high-pass filter has a cutoff frequency $f_o = 1$ kHz and $Z_o = 600\ \Omega$ (purely resistive) at infinite frequency. The elements of the filter are shown in Fig. 12.41. The design equations give $C = 0.1326\ \mu$F and $L = 47.7$ mH. Perform an analysis like the one shown in the text at (a) $f = 2$ kHz and (b) $f = 500$ Hz.

Fig. 12.41

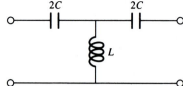

12.10 In the discussion of the lossless transmission line, a T section was used. An alternative form is the π section as shown in Fig. 12.42. To find the characteristic impedance of this section, you may use

$$Z_{o\pi} = \frac{Z_1 Z_2}{Z_{oT}}$$

Fig. 12.42

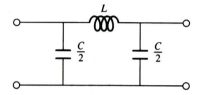

Rework the example given in the text based on the π-section rather than the T-section representation of the lossless transmission line.

13

Nonlinear Devices

In many applications, the elements of an electrical circuit may behave in a nonlinear fashion. The obvious examples include diodes and transistors, which have already been used in numerous examples. There are nonlinear resistors, such as the filament of a lamp, and there are nonlinear magnetic circuits, such as iron-core transformers, and so forth. Can PSpice handle these? The answer is a qualified *yes*.

THE NONLINEAR RESISTOR

A nonlinear resistor or other passive element can be simulated by using a dependent source. In Fig. 13.1 the basic circuit consists of a voltage source and two resistors R_i and R_{L1}. The current through R_{L1} is to be a function of the voltage across it, so that the basic form of Ohm's law, $v_1 = R_{L1}i$, does not apply unless you assume that R_{L1} is not constant. If a copy of R_{L1} is placed in a loop with a dependent source, the volt-ampere response of this resistor can be of various shapes. If you use the polynomial form for the dependent source, you can let the response curve be almost anything that you can predict in terms of a curve fit. Recall that the polynomial is of the form

$$k_0 + k_1x + k_2x^2 + k_3x^3 + \dots$$

If you can assign values to the coefficients, you can predict the response. This is not always easy to do, but for some cases the relationship might be simple to state. Figure 13.1 contains two types of dependent sources. One is E, and you can let its value be determined by the voltage v_2 across R_{L1}. The other is F, and you can let its value be a function of the current through some branch of the circuit. Choose to let

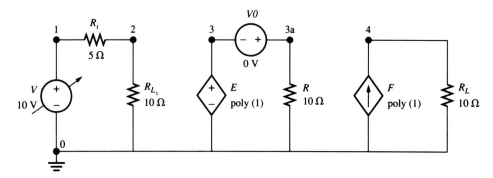

Fig. 13.1   Variable-resistor simulator.

F be a function of the current through R. This example introduces no new concepts, and its input file is

```
Variable Resistor Simulator
V 1 0 10V
Ri 1 2 5
RL1 2 0 10
E 3 0 POLY(1) 2,0 0 0.5 0.1
VO 3A 3 0V
R 3A 0 10
F 0 4 POLY(1) VO 0 -0.5 0.5
RL 4 0 10
.DC V 0 14V 1V
.PROBE
.END
```

Run the analysis and in Probe plot v(2), v(3), and v(4). Because the resistors are actually linear, the current plots will obviously have the same shape as the voltage plots. Note that only the plot of v(2) is linear, while the other two have shapes that are determined by their respective polynomials. See Fig. 13.2 for these traces.

The same polynomial technique will apply to other elements such as capacitors and inductors as well.

THE IRON-CORE INDUCTOR

In any electric circuit where there is a current, there is also a magnetic field. The property of the magnetic field that is directly proportional to the current I is the magnetic field intensity H. The two quantities are related by a constant that is a function of the circuit configuration. An example is a coil of wire of a certain size and shape. The simple equation $H = kI$ applies, although it is often difficult to find an exact value for k.

The magnetic flux density is related to the field intensity by the equation $B = \mu H$. In free space the permeability is given the designation μ_o and is equal to $4\pi \times 10^{-7}$ newtons/ampere^2.

When the magnetic field is in a medium other than free space, a relative permeability μ_r is introduced such that $\mu = \mu_o \mu_r$. The relative permeability is often not

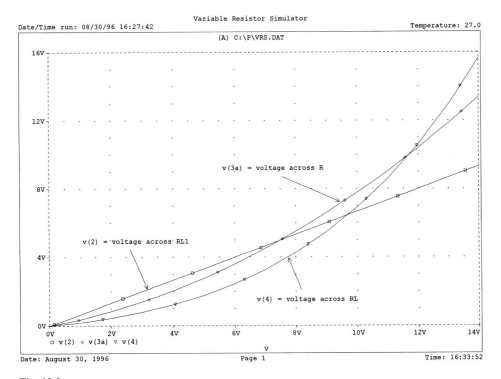

Fig. 13.2

constant but is a function of the current. As the magnetic material begins to reach saturation, further increases in H produce little increase in B. When the current begins to decrease, the retentivity of the magnetic material prevents the B and H relationship from following the same pattern as when the current was increasing. This produces the familiar BH characteristic curve with its hysteresis cycle.

PSpice uses a model for the iron-core inductor based on the Jiles-Atherton treatment for the magnetic domains. It is beyond the scope of this text to describe this model completely; however, we can investigate the BH curve for various conditions and look at what happens to voltage and current waves in transformers when saturation occurs.

The *BH* Curve

The circuit of Fig. 13.3 contains a ferromagnetic coil with $R_L = 10 \ \Omega$ containing 20 turns. Note that the statement for the inductor is

```
L1  1  0  20
```

where the *20* represents *turns* and not 20 *henries*. This is in connection with the model statement containing the key word *core*. If the model were not used, the *20* would represent 20 henries. The four current generators are used to produce low-frequency (1-Hz) sine waves. The first current has a peak value of 0.1 A beginning at $t = 0$.

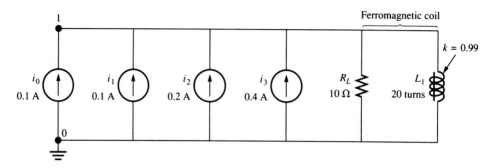

Fig. 13.3   Circuit to drive an iron-core inductor.

Then at $t = 1$ s the next current is introduced. It also has a peak value of 0.1 A. Then a third and fourth sine wave are added during the second and third seconds, respectively. The sine waves are of increasing amplitude in order to demonstrate the effects of saturation. The .MODEL statement uses the key word *core* and allows for the nonlinear magnetic parameters of the core model to take effect. The entire input file is

```
This is the sample magnetic core problem
i0 0 1 sin(0 0.1A 1Hz 0) ; no time delay for i0
i1 0 1 sin(0 0.1A 1Hz 1) ; another current added at 1 s
i2 0 1 sin(0 0.2A 1Hz 2) ; larger current added at 2 s
i3 0 1 sin(0 0.4A 1Hz 3) ; larger current added at 3 s
RL 1 0 10
L1 1 0 20 ; turns=20, not 20 henries since a model is used
K1 L1 0.99 KT ; coefficient of coupling
.model KT Core(MS=420E3 A=26 K=18 C=1.05 AREA=1.17 PATH=8.49)
.options itl5=0
*  Iteration parameter ITL5=0 gives ITL5=infinity
.tran 0.1 4
.probe
.end
```

Run the Probe analysis; then plot B(K1) as a function of time. This shows the nonlinear magnetic flux density in the core over the period from 0 to 4 s. Note that the first time periods show little nonlinearity compared with the later times. Verify that the first peak of B is at 1864 oersteds, the second is for $B = 2965$ oersteds, the third is for $B = 3989$ oersteds, and the final peak is at $B = 4593$ oersteds. Refer to Fig. 13.4 for this trace.

In order to produce the standard *BH* curve, change the *X*-axis to represent H(K1). This is the magnetic field intensity in the core, which is directly proportional to the current. The *Y*-axis still represents B(K1). See Fig. 13.5 for these traces. The four hysteresis loops are for the four levels of current. Verify where the peak values shown on the previous trace appear on this plot.

You might want to try changing the number of turns on the coil and running the analysis again for comparison with the previous results.

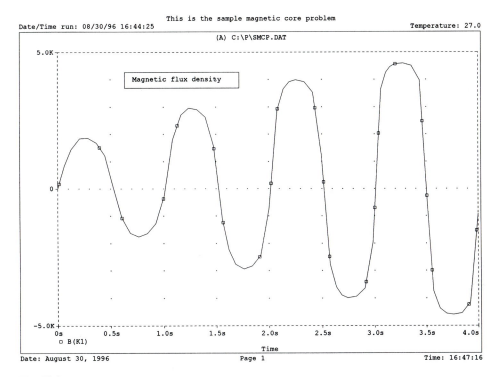

Fig. 13.4

THE IRON-CORE TRANSFORMER

When a transformer with a magnetic core is used, the presence of the iron core will affect the shape of the current wave in the secondary. To illustrate this, consider the circuit of Fig. 13.6, which shows a current-driven transformer. The resistor R_1 is a resistor in parallel with the current source as required. The number of turns on the primary and secondary windings is to be 150 each. The input file is

```
Iron-Core Transformer
i 0 1 sin(0 1A 60Hz)
R1 1 0 1k
L1 1 0 150 ; turns = 150 on primary
L2 2 0 150 ; turns = 150 on secondary
R2 2 0 1
K1 L1 L2 0.9999 KT
.model KT core ; use default values for the core model
.options ITL5=0
.tran 1ms 16.67ms
.probe
.end
```

Run the analysis and in Probe plot i(R2) and i(L1). Observe that although the primary current is a true sine wave, the secondary current is badly distorted. These traces are shown in Fig. 13.7.

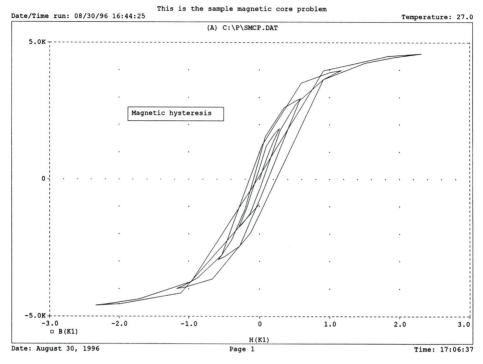

Fig. 13.5

You may want to change the value of R_2 and/or the number of turns on each winding and compare the results with those obtained here. To demonstrate what happens when there is less saturation, use the following input file:

```
Iron-Core Transformer
i 0 1 sin(0 1A 60Hz)
R1 1 0 1k
L1 1 0 10
L2 2 0 150
R2 2 0 1
K1 L1 L2 0.9999 KT
```

Fig. 13.6 An iron-core transformer.

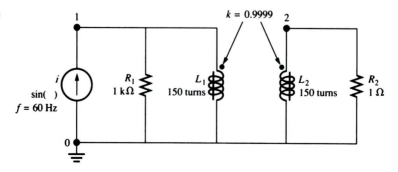

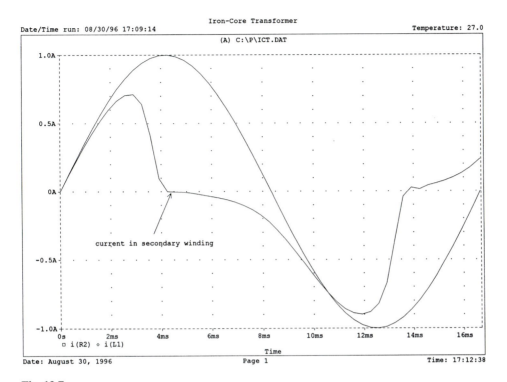

Fig. 13.7

```
.model KT core
.options ITL5=0
.tran 1ms 16.67ms
.probe
.end
```

Run the analysis and in Probe plot i(R2) and i(L1)/20. The latter plot is scaled to be comparable to the former plot. Here you will see that both curves are almost true sine waves. The secondary current still shows some distortion, however. See Fig. 13.8 for these curves.

You may want to try several other combinations of resistance and turns to become more familiar with how the core model works. You will discover that for some combinations, PSpice is unable to complete the analysis.

VOLTAGE-CONTROLLED SWITCH FOR VARIABLE RESISTOR

Another way to achieve a variation in resistance is by using either a voltage-controlled switch or a current-controlled switch. The switch can be made to open or close, depending on the value of voltage or current in another part of the circuit.

Consider Fig. 13.9, which shows the voltage-controlled switch in a series circuit with $V = 10$ V, $R_i = 50$ Ω, and $R_L = 50$ Ω. If you choose V as the controlling voltage, you can allow the switch to close when the voltage reaches a certain value.

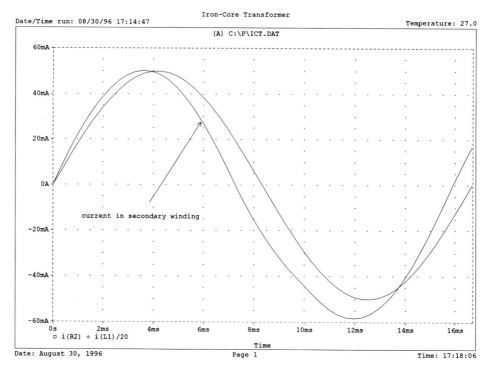

Fig. 13.8

The switch will have nominal resistance values of $RON = 1\ \Omega$ (switch closed) and $ROFF = 1\ M\Omega$ (switch open). The latter value is necessary to prevent a floating node at the switch. The model requires the mode type *vswitch*. In order to see the effects of the switch in both the off and on states, select $VON = 3$ V and use the default value $VOFF = 0$. The required input file is

Fig. 13.9   Voltage-controlled switch.

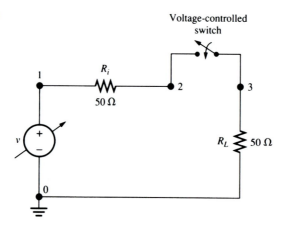

```
Voltage-Controlled Switch
v 1 0 10V
Ri 1 2 50
RL 3 0 50
S 2 3 1 0 S1 ; vcs must begin with S
.model S1 vswitch(RON=1 ROFF=1E6 VON=3V VOFF=0)
.dc v 0 10V 0.05V
.probe
.end
```

Run the analysis and plot i(Ri) Notice that the curve shows almost no current until the input voltage nears 2 V. Then by the time the input voltage has reached $VON = 3$ V, the slope of the curve is correct for the closed-switch condition. The total loop resistance with the switch closed is 101 Ω, which includes the resistance of the switch. Refer to Fig. 13.10 for this plot.

Change the value of VON to 8 V and run the analysis again. Observe the variations of the vi curve in the lower regions. The current begins to rise in the vicinity of 4 V. Remember that the slope of the curve is inversely proportional to the loop resistance. Note that the slope of the curve gradually changes; there is no abrupt change at the value of VON. This must be taken into account if you are to use this type of switch in your circuits. It is advisable to obtain a vi curve such as the one given here before employing the voltage-controlled switch in an elaborate circuit. Refer to Fig. 13.11 for this trace.

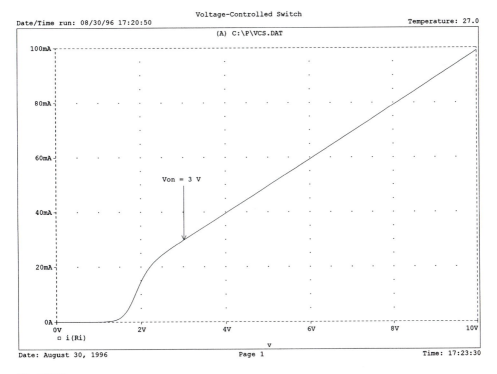

Fig. 13.10

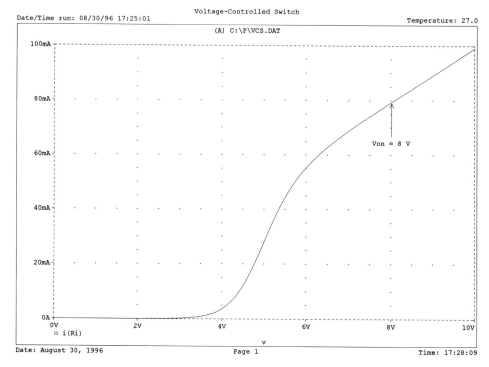

Fig. 13.11

CURRENT-CONTROLLED SWITCH

As an alternative to the voltage-controlled switch, the current-controlled switch may be used. In this case, the closing of a switch is brought about by some predefined current being present in another part of the circuit. This is shown in Fig. 13.12, where there is a current source supplying two branches, each of which contains a 100-Ω resistor. The branch on the right contains the switch W. This branch has high resistance until the switch closes, with $ROFF = 1\ M\Omega$. When the predefined current $ION = 10$ mA is present in the branch on the left, the switch closes. ION uses the default value of zero. Beyond the 10-mA point, the resistance of the branch on the right is 101 Ω, since $RON = 1\ \Omega$. Current-controlled switches must have names beginning with W. The .MODEL statement must use the model type $ISWITCH$. The input file is

```
Current-Controlled Switch
i 0 1 40mA
V0 1 1A 0V
Ri 1A 0 100
RL 2 0 100
W 1 2 V0 W1
.MODEL W1 ISWITCH(ION=10mA RON=1 ROFF=1E6)
.DC i 0 40mA 1mA
.PROBE
.END
```

Fig. 13.12 Current-controlled switch.

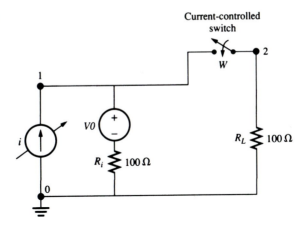

Run the analysis and plot i(RL) as a function of *i*. Since a smooth change of resistance takes place in the circuit, the current through R_L does not have a linear slope until it is slightly greater than 15 mA. Thus for currents in this branch greater than 15 mA, the resistance of the branch is 101 Ω. See Fig. 13.13 for this trace.

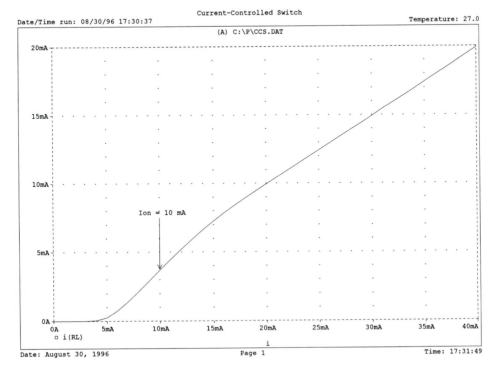

Fig. 13.13

NEW PSPICE STATEMENTS USED IN THIS CHAPTER

S[*name*] <+*switch node*><−*switch node*><+*controlling node*>
<−*controlling node*><*model name*>

For example,

```
S 2 3 1 0 S1
```

means that there is a voltage-controlled switch between nodes *2* and *3*. The switch is normally open (by default), but when the controlling voltage (between nodes *1* and *0*) reaches a certain value, the switch will close. The *S* statement requires a .MODEL statement to account for *on* resistance, *off* resistance, and controlling-voltage values. In this case, the model is identified as *S1*. This identification must begin with the letter *S*. Refer to Appendix D for a full description.

W[*name*] <+*node*><−*node*><*vname*><*model*>

For example,

```
W 1 2 V0 W1
```

means that there is a current-controlled switch between nodes *1* and *2*. The switch is normally open (by default), but when the controlling current passing through the source voltage V0 reaches a certain value, the switch will close. The *W* statement requires a .MODEL statement similar to that required for the voltage-controlled switch described above. In the model statement the model must begin with the letter *W*. Refer to Appendix D for a full description.

NEW DOT COMMAND

.MODEL <*name*><*type*> ([<*parameter name*>=<*value*>]*)

For example,

```
.MODEL KT core
```

When a model is for inductor coupling, the name begins with *K*. If the model statement also contains the word *core*, a nonlinear model is used. The *BH* curve for this nonlinear device will be similar to that shown in Fig. 13.5.

PROBLEMS

13.1 In the discussion of the nonlinear resistor, we pointed out that the resistors are not actually nonlinear, but that the dependent sources were the nonlinear elements. Modify the circuit shown in Fig. 13.1 to produce a voltage V(3) that is approximately equal to the voltage *V* raised to the 1.5 power.

13.2 For the circuit shown in Fig. 13.14, $L_1 = L_2 = 25$ mH, $C_1 = C_2 = 50$ nF, $R_s = 1$ Ω, $R_L = 1$ kΩ, and $M = 1$ mH. The statement for the transformer has the form

```
K1 L1 L2 value
```

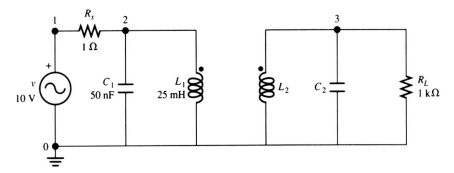

Fig. 13.14

where *value* is the coefficient of coupling. Create an input file to produce a plot of voltage across R_L in the vicinity of the resonant frequency. From the plot determine whether the coupling is less than, equal to, or greater than critical. Justify your answer.

13.3 What is the value of critical coupling in Problem 13.2? Run an analysis to demonstrate that critical coupling gives maximum power transfer to R_L.

13.4 The circuit shown in Fig. 13.15 uses an iron-core transformer (default model). The inductor L_1 contains 150 turns, while L_2 has 300 turns. Perform an analysis at $f = 4.5$ kHz to determine the load-resistor voltage and current.

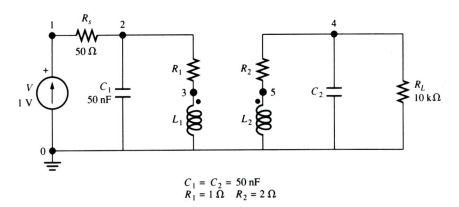

$$C_1 = C_2 = 50 \text{ nF}$$
$$R_1 = 1 \, \Omega \quad R_2 = 2 \, \Omega$$

Fig. 13.15

13.5 Using the same figure as in Problem 13.4, remove the .model statement and use inductive values for L_1 and L_2 instead. In order to produce approximately the same results as previously obtained, begin with $L_1 = 5$ mH and $L_2 = 10$ mH. Run an analysis and print the ac voltages V(2) and V(4). The results should be V(2) = 0.978 V and V(4) = 1.367 V. Select other values for L_1 and L_2 to obtain results that are in closer agreement with those obtained in Problem 13.4. Run the analysis several times using selected values.

13.6 A voltage-controlled switch is shown in Fig. 13.9. A design is required such that the switch will appear to have resistance of 1 kΩ when open and 1 Ω when closed. Let $R_i = 50$ Ω and $R_L = 100$ Ω. In the beginning the switch should be closed. The switch is to open when the input voltage v reaches 5 V. Prepare the input file, run the analysis, and verify your results with a Probe plot.

13.7 Again refer to Fig. 13.9. Use the resistance values given in the figure. The switch should have a resistance of 1 kΩ when open and 1 Ω when closed. In the beginning the switch should be closed. The switch is to open when the voltage across R_i reaches 0.25 V. Prepare the input file, run the analysis, and verify your results with a Probe plot.

Note that the switch statement must give the dependent nodes in the proper order for the analysis to be correct. Run the analysis to determine the proper order of these nodes. You may be surprised! In Probe verify that the current through R_i becomes significant when the source voltage v exceeds 0.55 V.

14

Schematics

MicroSim Schematics provides a medium whereby designers may place parts on a drawing board, or computer screen, in the same way that would draw a circuit for laboratory or production use. The parts available constitute a wide assortment of components such as power supplies, passive devices, active devices, and a variety of special parts.

MicroSim provides libraries of parts, with each category of parts placed in its own library. In the evaluation version of Schematics, the libraries have such names as *analog, breakout, eval, source,* and *special.* When the user selects a part from one of the libraries, it may be placed anywhere on the drawing board, rotated into position as necessary, then connected to other parts until a complete circuit is drawn. Then, rather than creating a circuit file to perform a circuit simulation, the Schematics program does the job instead.

A DC SERIES CIRCUIT

A simple dc circuit consisting of a voltage source and three resistors might be described in the familiar listing shown:

```
Series Circuit with Source and Three Resistors
V1 1 0 24V
R1 1 2 50
R2 2 3 100
R3 3 0 80
.END
```

Working backward, this listing could be used to construct a circuit diagram like that of Fig. 1.1. On the other hand, Schematics gives us a method of producing a circuit file (and completing the simulation) by starting with the circuit diagram. Let us explore how this is done.

CREATING A SCHEMATIC

Select the Schematics icon in the MicroSim work group to obtain the on-screen drawing board as shown in Fig. 14.1. The first time you use Schematics you may see a vertical line on the drawing board, as shown. This divides page 1 from page 2. Use the left arrow at the bottom of the screen as necessary to take you to the beginning of page 1. The title line at the top of the screen identifies Schematics as the program. Until we name the file, the title of the drawing is <new1> and p. 1 shows that we are working with page 1. File names should be chosen with the circuit description in mind; for example *threeres* might be chosen for our first series circuit. The extension *.sch* will be added automatically.

The drawing will be done using *parts* that are available in several *libraries*. To begin the drawing, select Draw from the menu bar, then Get New Part . . . A menu lists the full list of parts available in the Parts Browser Basic. The parts are listed in numerical/alphabetical sequence, and since numbers are at the top of the list, you see such things as diodes and *7400* logic building blocks. Because it will be more convenient to select a particular library, select the Libraries . . . button; this will pro-

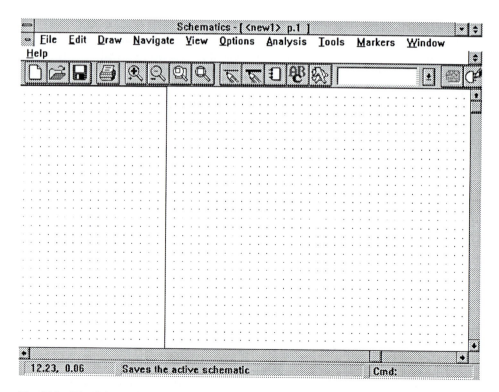

Fig. 14.1   The Schematics drawing board.

duce a list of available libraries (on the right) and their corresponding parts (on the left). See Fig. 14.2 for both of these menus.

Begin with the dc voltage source by selecting *source.slb* as the library, then arrow down to the bottom of the parts list and select VDC. Note that the part name and description "Simple DC voltage source" are shown in boxes at the top of the Library Browser. Click OK to confirm the selection and close the Parts Browser. Using the mouse, move the source to a location near the top left of the drawing board (about 2 in. from the top and 2 in. from the left edge). Click the left mouse button, then move the mouse away from its present location. Note that the mouse is still dragging the source symbol with it; since we do not need another source, click the right button, and the attached symbol disappears.

The resistors are contained in another library and may be obtained by selecting Draw, Get New Part . . . , Libraries. Choose *analog.slb*. This library contains passive circuit elements such as *R, L,* and *C*, and dependent sources. Select *R* and follow the same procedure as before to remove the menus from the screen so that the three resistors may be placed on the drawing board. Put one above and to the right of the source, another opposite the source, and the last one below the first one as shown in Fig. 14.3. After placing the last resistor, click the right button (clk-rt) to remove the *R* symbol from the mouse as before.

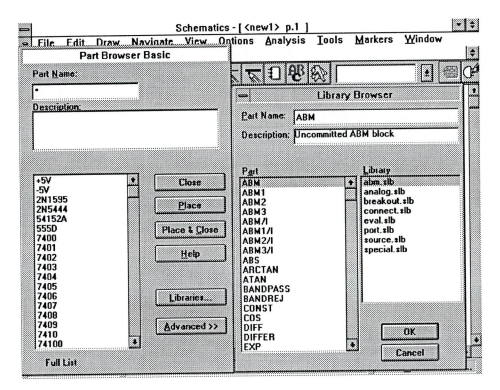

Fig. 14.2 The Parts Browser and a listing of the available Libraries.

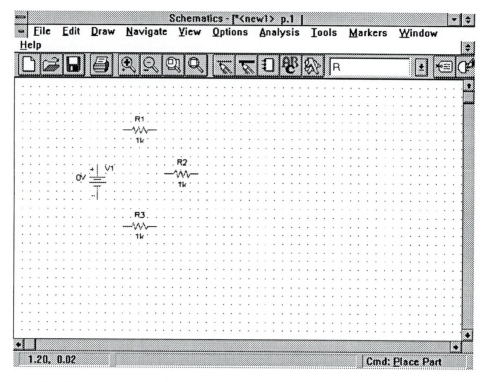

Fig. 14.3   The beginning of a dc circuit with three resistors.

Resistor *R2* will be more easily managed if it is rotated to a vertical position. Left-click on the symbol for *R2* and note that when selected it turns red. Select Edit, Rotate, and *R2* rotates 90°. Incidentally, the pull-down menu shows *Ctrl + R* as the shortcut method of producing rotation. Remembering this will make the task easier. The elements have been placed so that there is working space among them, and now the circuit needs wiring to complete the loop. Choose Draw, Wire and note that the mouse pointer becomes a pencil. Begin at the top of the source wire by clicking at that point and moving to the left end of the *R1* symbol. Click again to complete the wire segment. Move to the other side of *R1* and continue in like fashion until the loop has been completed. Finally clk-rt to remove the pencil symbol. Now select File, Save . . . and name the drawing *threeres.sch*. (It is not necessary to type the extension *.sch*; it is added automatically.)

Although the original circuit file shown at the beginning of this section listed only four elements (source and three resistors), we need a ground point. In the circuit file the line

```
V1  1  0  24V
```

made it obvious that the negative terminal of the source was grounded. We will confirm this in our drawing by selecting the library *port.slb* and the part *AGND*. Place the ground at the bottom left of the drawing.

Now the drawing is complete, but the values of the components are incorrect. In Schematics these are set by selecting each element, then double clicking the mouse to obtain the Part Name menu. Begin with the dc source. The Part Name: VDC window will appear. Select the DC = 0V field and in the <u>V</u>alue field type "24V," then select <u>S</u>ave Attr, OK. Repeat the process for each *R*. For example, with *R1*, select the "Value = 1k, then type "50" for its value. Always remember to choose <u>S</u>ave Attr. When you are done, the circuit should look like Fig. 14.4. (If the value of an element is too close to the symbol, select the value, then drag it to a new location.)

Analyzing the Circuit

In Schematics select <u>A</u>nalysis, <u>S</u>imulate to begin the process. If there are no errors, the familiar PSpice window appears, with the screen telling us that the circuit *threeres.sch* is being simulated in file *threeres.cir* and the results are being placed in the file *threeres.out*. Actually there are five *threeres* files with the following extensions:

.sch

.cir

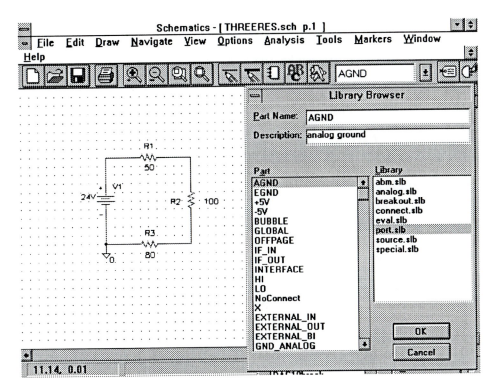

Fig. 14.4   Completed dc circuit with three resistors in series.

.net

.als

.out

We used the name *threeres.sch* when the file was created in Schematics. During the analysis the files with the other extensions were created automatically. (If you try to analyze a schematic without a name, you will be prompted to choose one.) The file *threeres.cir* does not contain the listing shown as a circuit file at the beginning of this chapter as you might expect; instead it contains

```
*  C:P\THREERFS.SCH

*  Schematics Version 6.3 - April 1996
*  Mon Sep 02 14:27:25 1996

** Analysis setup **
.OP

*  From [SCHEMATICS NETLIST] section of msim.ini:
.lib nom.lib

.INC "THREERES.net"
.INC "THREERES.als"

.probe
.END
```

It is instructive to learn the meaning of each of these lines. The ones beginning with an asterisk are comment lines and are self-explanatory. The line containing *.lib nom.lib* refers to the library *nom.lib*. This is the sample standard device library in the evaluation version of PSpice. This library calls *.lib "eval.lib"* and *.lib "breakout.lib"* if they are needed for such devices as diodes and transistors. The lines beginning with .INC are to allow the simulation to insert (include) other files. In the present case they are the *threeres.net* and *threeres.als* files. These files contain the essential information defining *V1, R1, R2,* and *R3.* We will see their entire contents in the output file *threeres.out.*

The Output File in Schematics

In PSpice at the conclusion of the simulation you may choose File, Examine Output, to see the results of the analysis. This should invoke the MicroSim Text Editor and load the output file automatically. In some computers you may get a dreaded GPF (General Protection Fault). This will cause the computer to lock up, and only a reboot will allow you to continue. MicroSim is aware of this problem when the Microsoft IntelliPoint mouse driver is being used; it occurs in other cases, however. This problem may be avoided by (1) using Word for Windows or another word processor to look at the various text files or (2) trying again to use the MicroSim Text Editor. (We have had good results with this method.) Once the Text Editor is in use, do not Exit but toggle among the programs by using *Alt-Tab* to avoid a GPF.

Study Fig. 14.5, which contains the contents of the file *threeres.out.* This file has been edited to eliminate unwanted lines and page feeds. The text is Courier New (TrueType). The file *threeres.net* contains the Schematics Netlist:

```
   * C:\P\THREERES.SCH

   ****        CIRCUIT DESCRIPTION

 * Schematics Version 6.3 - April 1996
 * Mon Sep 02 14:37:46 1996

 ** Analysis setup **
 .OP

 * From [SCHEMATICS NETLIST] section of msim.ini:
 .lib nom.lib

 .INC "THREERES.net"

 **** INCLUDING THREERES.net ****
 * Schematics Netlist *

 V_V1          $N_0001 0 24V
 R_R1          $N_0001 $N_0002  50
 R_R2          $N_0003 $N_0002  100
 R_R3          0 $N_0003  80

 **** RESUMING THREERES.CIR ****
 .INC "THREERES.als"

 **** INCLUDING THREERES.als ****
 * Schematics Aliases *

 .ALIASES
 V_V1              V1(+=$N_0001 -=0 )
 R_R1              R1(1=$N_0001 2=$N_0002 )
 R_R2              R2(1=$N_0003 2=$N_0002 )
 R_R3              R3(1=0 2=$N_0003 )
 .ENDALIASES

 **** RESUMING THREERES.CIR ****

 .probe

 .END

   * C:\P\THREERES.SCH

   ****        SMALL SIGNAL BIAS SOLUTION       TEMPERATURE =   27.000 DEG C

 NODE    VOLTAGE      NODE    VOLTAGE      NODE    VOLTAGE     NODE    VOLTAGE
 ($N_0001)   24.0000                   ($N_0002)   18.7830
 ($N_0003)    8.3478

     VOLTAGE SOURCE CURRENTS
     NAME        CURRENT
     V_V1        -1.043E-01

     TOTAL POWER DISSIPATION   2.50E+00   WATTS

 * C:\P\THREERES.SCH
```

Fig. 14.5   A dc series circuit.

```
V_V1              $N_0001 0 24V
R_R1              $N_0001 $N_0002 50
R_R2              $N_0003 $N_0002 100
R_R3              0 $N_0003 80
```

Compare the first line with the usual PSpice notation for the voltage source:

```
V 1 0 24V
```

The Schematics notation is a bit more complicated, but it is easily understood. The usual PSpice notation for the first resistor is

```
R1 1 2 50
```

In Schematics again note the more complicated designation. The second resistor in PSpice was described as

```
R2 2 3 100
```

In Schematics the order of the nodes has been reversed (3, 2) rather than (2, 3). Note that if you want to change the order of the nodes in Schematics, you can simply rotate the resistor. (We rotated *R2* from horizontal to vertical, which caused a ccw rotation; two more rotations would place the other end at the top.) Resistor *R3* also has the order of the nodes reversed compared with the original circuit description. This could also be changed by rotating the resistor twice. These reversals will not affect the outcome of the analysis, of course. This point is mentioned only for the purpose of considering such factors as current directions through components.

The file *threeres.als* contains Schematic Aliases:

```
.ALIASES
V_V1          V1(+ =$N_0001      -=0 )
R_R1          R1(1=$N_0001      2=$N_0002 )
R_R2          R2(1=$N_0003      2=$N_0002 )
R_R3          R3(1=0    2=$N_0003 )
.ENDALIASES
```

The aliases explain the node ordering in more detail. For example *V1* has its "+" node at node *1* and its "−" node at node *0*. Resistor *R1* has its first node at node *1* (actually node $N_0001) and its second node at node *2*. The "$N" designation for each node avoids any conflict with the customary node designation using numbers or alphabetic characters.

Printing the Results

Finally, the small-signal bias solution is shown at the end of the *threeres.out* file. Figure 14.5 containing the output file has been edited to omit unneeded page feeds and blank lines. If you print this file for your records you should do likewise. You will also want to print the schematic diagram. In Schematics use the mouse to outline the circuit (click at the top left and drag to the bottom right, forming a box), then select File, Print. From the menu select *User-definable zoom factor* and type "150" for the percent; select *Portrait* and also select *Only Print Selected Area*. The results should look like Fig. 14.6. You can now label the nodes 0, 1, 2, and 3 for easy identification.

Fig. 14.6 A schematic for a simple dc circuit.

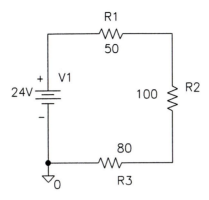

DRAWING A TEE CIRCUIT

Construct the circuit shown in Fig. 14.7 using Schematics. This circuit may be drawn using the techniques introduced in the previous section. The only parts needed are *VDC, R,* and *AGND*. These parts may be found in the Part Browser by simply selecting Draw, Get New Part . . . and typing the name (such as *VDC*) in the "Part Name:" field. After all the parts have been placed and rotated as necessary, double click (dbl-clk) on each part to set the desired values. Use Draw, Wire to connect the parts and complete the circuit. Before attempting a simulation you must name the circuit. Choose the name *tee.sch*.

To begin the simulation, select Analysis, Simulate. After the successful completion of the analysis, examine the output file by selecting File, Examine Output in PSpice. A portion of this output file, along with the circuit in Schematics, is shown in Fig. 14.8. Use your wordprocessor program to produce the listing of *tee.out* as shown in Fig. 14.9. Remember to use the Courier New font, 10 points, and delete unwanted lines. You should be able to get everything you need for proper documentation of your results on a single page. Also print the circuit from Schematics; Fig. 14.7 was produced in Schematics.

Fig. 14.7 The schematic of a Tee (T) circuit.

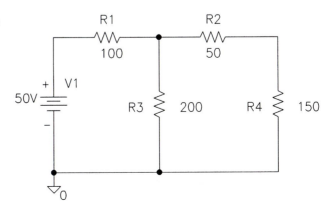

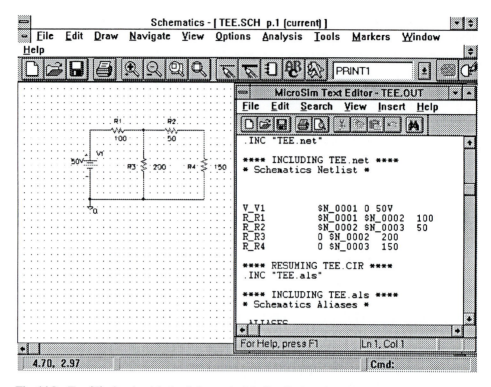

Fig. 14.8   Tee (T) circuit with the Schematics Netlist displayed in the MicroSim Text Editor.

DEPENDENT SOURCES IN SCHEMATICS

Dependent sources are more complicated in Schematics than in PSpice. In SPICE, the dependent source is shown as a two-terminal device in the circuit sketch, but in Schematics, the dependent source is shown as a four-terminal device. This allows for the dependency to be shown in the circuit rather than being stated on the line describing the device in the input file.

Voltage-Dependent Voltage Source

The voltage-dependent voltage source was introduced in Chapter 1. Refer to Fig. 1.17 as an example, Recall that the symbol E was used for this type source. In this example the line describing E was

```
E  3  0  2  0  2
```

the first two numbers ($3\ 0$) mean the dependent source was placed between node 3 (+) and node 0 (−). The next pair of numbers ($2\ 0$) refer to the two nodes upon which the E is dependent. That is, the value of E is a function of the voltage drop V_a across nodes 2 and 0. The last number on the line describing E was 2 also. This was a scale factor such that $V_{2,0}$ appeared doubled in E. It is our desire to convert this information to PSpice in Schematics. Unfortunately, the diamond symbol (the cus-

```
* C:\P\TEE.sch

 ****       CIRCUIT DESCRIPTION

* Schematics Version 6.3 - April 1996
* Thu Jul 11 09:31:59 1996

** Analysis setup **
.OP

* From [SCHEMATICS NETLIST] section of msim.ini:
.lib nom.lib

.INC "TEE.net"

**** INCLUDING TEE.net ****
* Schematics Netlist *

V_V1          $N_0001 0 50V
R_R1          $N_0001 $N_0002   100
R_R2          $N_0002 $N_0003   50
R_R3          0 $N_0002   200
R_R4          0 $N_0003   150

**** RESUMING TEE.CIR ****
.INC "TEE.als"

**** INCLUDING TEE.als ****
* Schematics Aliases *

.ALIASES
V_V1          V1(+=$N_0001 -=0 )
R_R1          R1(1=$N_0001 2=$N_0002 )
R_R2          R2(1=$N_0002 2=$N_0003 )
R_R3          R3(1=0 2=$N_0002 )
R_R4          R4(1=0 2=$N_0003 )
.ENDALIASES

**** RESUMING TEE.CIR ****

.probe

.END

 * C:\P\TEE.sch

 ****       SMALL SIGNAL BIAS SOLUTION      TEMPERATURE =   27.000 DEG C

NODE    VOLTAGE      NODE   VOLTAGE      NODE    VOLTAGE      NODE    VOLTAGE

($N_0001)   50.0000                   ($N_0002)   25.0000
($N_0003)   18.7500

    VOLTAGE SOURCE CURRENTS
    NAME          CURRENT

    V_V1          -2.500E-01

    TOTAL POWER DISSIPATION   1.25E+01  WATTS
```

Fig. 14.9 Output file for Tee (T) circuit.

tomary symbol for a dependent source) is not available for this purpose in Schematics. The symbol will be a square box with two terminals on the left and two terminals on the right.

Construct the circuit shown in Fig. 14.10, using $R_1 = 250\ \Omega$, and $R_2 = 1\ k\Omega$. Next, place E, then $R_3 = 40\ \Omega$, and $R_L = 100\ \Omega$. (These values are not the same as in Fig. 1.17.) The circle in the box represents the two E terminals (as in PSpice), and the *plus* and *minus* symbols on the left side of the box must be connected to the dependent-voltage points, which in the present case will be across the terminals of R_2. Connect the rest of the circuit, then dbl-clk on the E box. Fill in Gain = "2", and elect to display the name and value. Your circuit should look like the one shown in the figure. Save the drawing as *vcontrol.sch*.

Run the simulation and compare your results with those shown. The node voltages are easily verified by hand calculations. Compare the netlist statement.

```
E_E1              $N_0003   0   $N_0002   0   2
```

with the alias statement

```
E_E1              E1(3=$N_0003   4=0   1=$N_0002   2=0 )
```

The alias statement shows four numbered terminals. It is obvious that terminals *3* and *4* are on the right, while terminals *1* and *2* are on the left of the *E* box in Schematics. Think of it this way: The output terminals are for the *E* part itself, and the input terminals are used to show the dependency. Thus we see why the symbol was changed from a diamond to a box.

Current-Dependent Current Source

The transistor biasing circuit of Fig. 3.2 provides a practical example of a current-dependent current source. We will use the same component values as those given in the first example of Chapter 3, with $R_2 = 5\ k\Omega$, $R_E = 100\ \Omega$, F (gain to be set later), $R_C = 1\ k\Omega$, $VA = 0.7\ V$ (representing V_{BE} in the active region), $V_{CC} = 12\ V$, and $R_1 = 40\ k\Omega$. The parts were placed in the order shown, producing the node-number sequence shown in Fig. 14.11. There will be five nodes (in addition to *AGND*) in this circuit compared with four nodes shown in Fig. 3.2.

Compare the two circuits, with the first one (Fig. 3.2) being used to produce the PSpice input file, and the second one being used in Schematics. Because *F* is dependent on a current somewhere in the circuit, the input terminals of *F* must be placed in the loop containing the independent current. Thus the current through *VA* passes through terminals *1* and *2* of the current-dependent current source box. The output terminals of the box are in the path containing the collector current.

Assign the various component values, then dbl-clk on the *F1* box. The gain is set to the value *80*, and the display is set to show both name and value. Save the drawing as *icontrol.sch*.

Run the simulation and compare your results with those shown in Fig. 14.11. In the output file the node voltages are the same as those found in Chapter 3. The nodes have been marked by hand for easy identification. The bias-point solution produces the source currents, the *VF_F1* current is the base current of 50.49 μA,

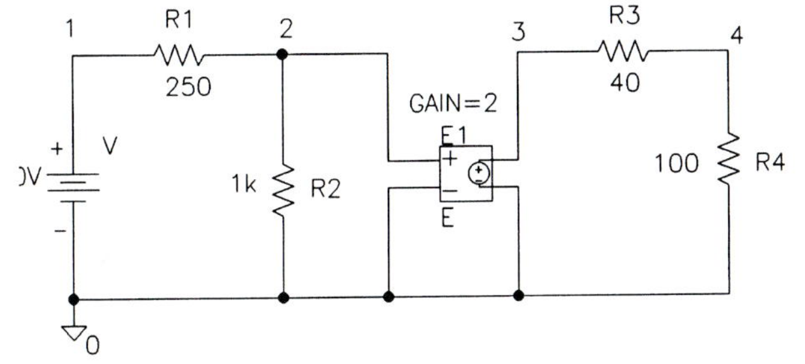

```
* C:\P\VCONTROL.sch
** Analysis setup **
.OP
* From [SCHEMATICS NETLIST] section of msim.ini:
.lib nom.lib
.INC "VCONTROL.net"
**** INCLUDING VCONTROL.net ****
* Schematics Netlist *

V_V          $N_0001 0 10V
R_R1         $N_0001 $N_0002  250
R_R2         $N_0002 0  1k
E_E1         $N_0003 0 $N_0002 0 2
R_R3         $N_0003 $N_0004  40
R_R4         $N_0004 0  100

**** RESUMING VCONTROL.CIR ****
.INC "VCONTROL.als"
**** INCLUDING VCONTROL.als ****
* Schematics Aliases *
.ALIASES
V_V          V(+=$N_0001 -=0 )
R_R1         R1(1=$N_0001 2=$N_0002 )
R_R2         R2(1=$N_0002 2=0 )
E_E1         E1(3=$N_0003 4=0 1=$N_0002 2=0 )
R_R3         R3(1=$N_0003 2=$N_0004 )
R_R4         R4(1=$N_0004 2=0 )
.ENDALIASES
.probe
.END

 NODE   VOLTAGE      NODE   VOLTAGE      NODE   VOLTAGE      NODE   VOLTAGE
($N_0001)   10.0000                   ($N_0002)    8.0000
($N_0003)   16.0000                   ($N_0004)   11.4290

    VOLTAGE SOURCE CURRENTS
    NAME           CURRENT
    V_V            -8.000E-03

    TOTAL POWER DISSIPATION   8.00E-02   WATTS

**** VOLTAGE-CONTROLLED VOLTAGE SOURCES
NAME           E_E1
V-SOURCE       1.600E+01
I-SOURCE       -1.143E-01
```

Fig. 14.10 Schematic and output file for voltage-dependent voltage source.

```
* C:\P\ICONTROL.SCH
** Analysis setup **
.OP
* From [SCHEMATICS NETLIST] section of msim.ini:
.lib nom.lib
.INC "ICONTROL.net"
**** INCLUDING ICONTROL.net ****
* Schematics Netlist *
R_R2            $N_0001 0   5k
R_RE            $N_0002 0   100
F_F1            $N_0004 $N_0002 VF_F1 80
VF_F1           $N_0003 $N_0002 0V
R_RC            $N_0005 $N_0004  1k
V_VA            $N_0001 $N_0003 0.7V
V_VCC           $N_0005 0  12V
R_R1            $N_0005 $N_0001  40k
.INC "ICONTROL.als"
**** INCLUDING ICONTROL.als ****
* Schematics Aliases *
.ALIASES
R_R2            R2(1=$N_0001 2=0 )
R_RE            RE(1=$N_0002 2=0 )
F_F1            F1(3=$N_0004 4=$N_0002 )
VF_F1           F1(1=$N_0003 2=$N_0002 )
R_RC            RC(1=$N_0005 2=$N_0004 )
V_VA            VA(+=$N_0001 -=$N_0003 )
V_VCC           VCC(+=$N_0005 -=0 )
R_R1            R1(1=$N_0005 2=$N_0001 )
.ENDALIASES
.probe
.END


  NODE   VOLTAGE     NODE   VOLTAGE      NODE   VOLTAGE     NODE   VOLTAGE
 ($N_0001)   1.1089                    ($N_0002)     .4089
 ($N_0003)    .4089                    ($N_0004)    7.9610
 ($N_0005)  12.0000


    VOLTAGE SOURCE CURRENTS
    NAME            CURRENT
    VF_F1           5.049E-05
    V_VA            5.049E-05
    V_VCC          -4.311E-03


    TOTAL POWER DISSIPATION   5.17E-02  WATTS

**** CURRENT-CONTROLLED CURRENT SOURCES
NAME            F_F1
I-SOURCE        4.039E-03
```

Fig. 14.11 Schematic and output file for current-dependent current source.

which is the same as the *V_VA* current. The *I-SOURCE* current is the collector current through R_C of 4.039 mA.

AN AC CIRCUIT

In order to analyze the ac circuits of the type dealt with in Chapter 2 (sinusoidal steady-state), we will need *VAC* from the library *source.slb*; *R, L,* and *C* from *analog.slb*; and *AGND* from *port.slb*. Refer to Fig. 2.1, which shows a circuit with an ac source along with a resistor and an inductor in a series loop. Draw the circuit in Schematics using *VAC, R,* and *L,* along with *AGND.* Set the attributes of R1 and L1 by double-clicking on their symbols. See Fig. 14.12 for the completed circuit diagram. Note the pull-down window on the top right (showing *AGND*) that may be used for easy access to parts we have previously used. In order to set the attributes of the ac source, dbl-clk on its symbol to produce the window shown in Fig. 14.12. Select *ACMAG*, then in the Value field type "1V", Save Attr, OK. After setting the values for *R1* and *L1*, you must convey to Schematics the information contained in an .AC (sweep) statement. Recall that in Chapter 2, we used the following line in the input (circuit) file

```
.AC LIN 1 60Hz 60Hz
```

We wish to do the equivalent of this in Schematics. Here is what brings it about.

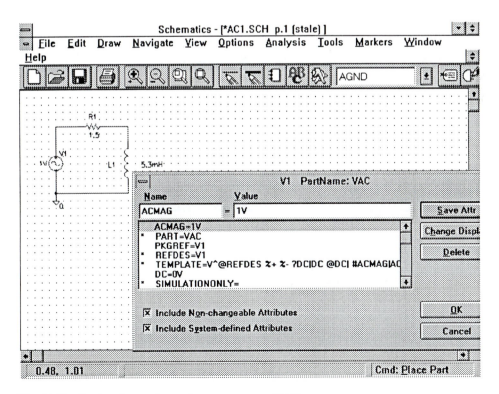

Fig. 14.12 Setting the attributes for an ac source, VAC.

Enabling an AC Sweep

Select Analysis, Setup in Schematics, then press the AC Sweep . . . button on the set-up window. Another window appears with the title AC Sweep and Noise Analysis. Select AC Sweep Type: Linear, and for the Sweep Parameters, Total Pts.: "1", Start Freq.: "60Hz", End Freq.: "60Hz". Click OK to close the windows. Refer to Fig. 14.13. Save the drawing with the name *ac1.sch*. Now, finally, we are ready to perform the analysis. Select Analysis, Simulate. The simulation opens the PSpice window; when the analysis is successfully completed, you will be taken directly to Probe.

There is not much to be seen in Probe. The horizontal axis shows frequency, with 60 Hz in the middle. You can select Trace, Add . . . and look at V(V1:+), the positive terminal of the source; then trace V(L1:2), the voltage at the top end of L1 (the top is its second-named node). You might remove these traces and choose to look at I(L1), which is the current throughout the loop. Although these (point) traces might satisfy your curiosity, they are hardly worth the trouble it has taken to draw and analyze the circuit.

Adding More Statements to the Circuit File

Doubtless we could have produced quicker, more complete results by avoiding Schematics and using PSpice directly after creating a circuit file, just as we did

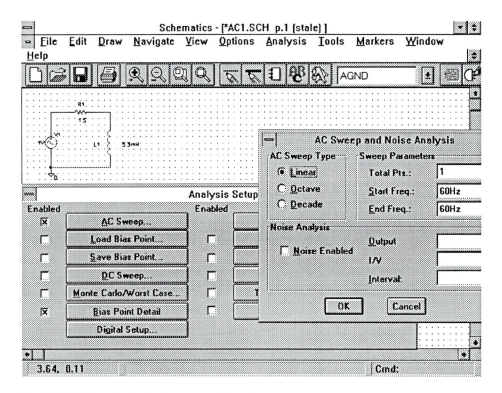

Fig. 14.13 Using Analysis, Setup to enable an ac sweep.

throughout the earlier chapters of the book. Is it worthwhile to use Schematics for ac, steady-state circuit analysis? You may want to answer this question for yourself after you have simulated several other circuits, but at this point the answer appears to be no.

There is a simple solution to our dilemma, awkward though it may seem. Take a look at the file *ac1.out*, which shows the following Schematics Netlist:

```
V_V1          $N_0001   0   DC   0V   AC   1V
R_R1          $N_0001   $N_0002   1.5
L_L1          0   $N_0002 5.3 mH
```

Recognizing how each element is identified, as well as how the nodes are numbered, will be helpful when we add statements to the circuit file. So that the file may be edited, load the file *ac1.cir* into Notepad. Move the cursor to a point just below the .ac LIN statement and type

```
.print ac v(L_L1)   vr(L_L1)   vi(L_L1)   vp(L_L1)
.print ac i(R_R1)   ir(R_R1)   ii(R_R1)   ip(R_R1)
```

Also add an .OPT nopage line.

Now we are ready to go directly to the PSpice icon and run the simulation again. Note that we have asked for the magnitude and the real and imaginary parts of the inductor voltage along with its phase angle. We have also asked for similar information about the current through the resistor. Examine the output file *ac1.out* in your word-processor program, remembering to use the Courier New font with unwanted lines deleted. Your results should look like Fig. 14.14.

Ordering of the Nodes

Pay particular attention to the phasor of the inductor voltage. In polar form it is 0.7997 $\underline{/-143.1°}$. Why is the angle not shown as $+39.9°$, as we would expect? Note that the inductor is described with the order of the nodes given as $(0, 2)$ rather than $(2, 0)$. In Chapter 2, the inductance was listed as

```
L  2  0  5.3mH
```

We could force Schematics to follow the same convention by rotating the *L* symbol not once (to place it in a vertical position) but three times, swapping it end for end. Recall that the first terminal of a passive element is on the left (in the horizontal position), and the second terminal is on the right. When the element is rotated, it moves *ccw*; thus a single rotation moves the first terminal to the bottom (in the vertical position). It may appear to be nit-picking to mention this, but it can cause problems when we need to know either the polarity of voltages or the direction of currents. Note that the current through the resistor is referenced from left to right (cw), corresponding to the current out of the positive terminal of the source. What would the results have been if we had printed the inductor current instead?

There may be something a bit awkward about forcing the file *ac1.cir* to produce more complete results by modifying the file and running PSpice again. However, unless we want to avoid Schematics altogether, this can be a useful tool.

```
* C:\P\AC1.SCH

** Analysis setup **
.ac LIN 1 60Hz 60Hz
.print ac v(L_L1) vr(L_L1) vi(L_L1) vp(L_L1)
.print ac i(R_R1) ir(R_R1) ii(R_R1) ip(R_R1)
.OPT nopage

* From [SCHEMATICS NETLIST] section of msim.ini:
.lib nom.lib

.INC "AC1.net"

**** INCLUDING AC1.net ****
* Schematics Netlist *

V_V1            $N_0001 0 DC 0V AC 1V
R_R1            $N_0001 $N_0002  1.5
L_L1            0 $N_0002  5.3mH

**** RESUMING AC1.CIR ****
.INC "AC1.als"

**** INCLUDING AC1.als ****
* Schematics Aliases *

.ALIASES
V_V1            V1(+=$N_0001 -=0 )
R_R1            R1(1=$N_0001 2=$N_0002 )
L_L1            L1(1=0 2=$N_0002 )
.ENDALIASES

**** RESUMING AC1.CIR ****

.probe

.END

****      AC ANALYSIS                        TEMPERATURE =   27.000 DEG C

  FREQ        V(L_L1)      VR(L_L1)     VI(L_L1)     VP(L_L1)
  6.000E+01   7.997E-01   -6.396E-01   -4.801E-01   -1.431E+02

  FREQ        I(R_R1)      IR(R_R1)     II(R_R1)     IP(R_R1)
  6.000E+01   4.002E-01    2.403E-01   -3.201E-01   -5.310E+01
```

Fig. 14.14 An ac circuit created using Schematics after the circuit file has been modified.

If we return to Schematics and perform the analysis, a new *ac1.cir* file will be created. This will overwrite the modified file and may not be what we want to do. In order to avoid this, save the file in Schematics with a new name, for example *ac1a.sch*. Then when the analysis is performed, *ac1a.cir* will be produced along with the *ac1a.als*, *ac1a.net*, *ac1a.dat*, *ac1a.out*, and *ac1a.prb* files.

SINE-WAVE REPRESENTATION FOR AC ANALYSIS

Before we begin, note that in the study of ac circuits it is customary to use phasor representation, in which a source voltage might be shown as $V_S = 1\underline{/0°}$ V. This means that the source is sinusoidal, with an rms value of 1 V. The sine-wave form of this voltage would have a peak value of $1\sqrt{2} = 1.414$ V. Before we begin to look at the sine-wave form of voltages and currents in Probe, we need to mention that it is more convenient to convert between rms and peak after the waves are displayed. Thus our $V_S = 1\underline{/0°}$ V will be traced as a voltage with a peak value of 1 V simply because it is easier to work with this form. Just remember that the value you read as a peak is actually an rms value. If you feel uncomfortable with this, you may elect to convert (with a calculator) from rms to peak before the analysis. Unless otherwise stated, our values will be given as rms and traced using these values as peak.

In Schematics, begin a new drawing using an ac source with a resistor and inductor in series as in the previous example. This time in place of VAC the source will be shown as VSIN. The symbols for the parts appear the same in the drawing, but they are described differently. Complete the drawing using VSIN, R, L, and AGND. Assign the values $R1 = 1.5$ Ω and $L1 = 5.3$ mH. Rotate L1 three times so that its first terminal is on top. This will give the proper angles on inductor voltage and current, as explained in the previous example. Save the drawing as *ac1sine.sch*.

Select part *V1* and dbl-clk to bring up the part-name menu as shown in Fig. 14.15. Set values for VOFF = "0", VAMPL = "1 V", and FREQ = "60 Hz". Save each attribute as you enter its value. Note that you have the option C$\underline{h}$ange Display for such items as amplitude, frequency, and phase. In the figure, amplitude and frequency are displayed.

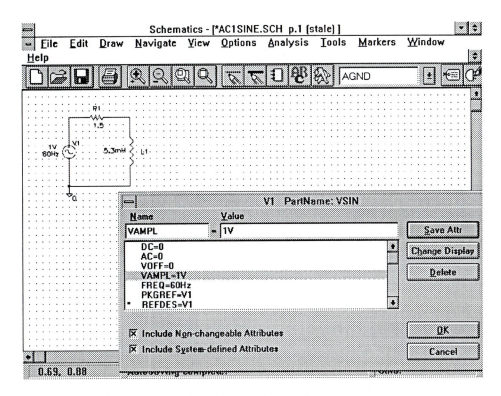

Fig. 14.15 Showing ac source as VSIN for transient analysis.

The analysis requires that you now select <u>A</u>nalysis, Se<u>t</u>up, then the <u>Tran</u>-sient . . . button. This brings up the menu shown in Fig. 14.16. Based on our frequency of 60 Hz, choose a <u>P</u>rint Step of 1 ms, a <u>F</u>inal Time of 30 ms, and a Step Ceiling of 0.0167 ms. After these values are set, select <u>A</u>nalysis, <u>S</u>imulate. At the successful conclusion of the simulation you will be taken into Probe. Trace V(V1:+), the source voltage at node *1*, and V(L1:1), the voltage at the junction between *R1* and *L1* at node *2*. Refer to Fig. 14.17. It looks like the voltage traces begin together, but since V(L1:1) is affected by the initial transient (and no IC was set), move to *t* = 16.667 ms and look at the relationship between the two traces at that time. The trace of V(L1:1) crosses the *X*-axis at *t* = 14.981 ms. This converts to an angle of 36.4°, the angle by which the inductor voltage leads the source voltage. Actually this angle should be 36.9°, but considering our transient-type solution, the agreement is good.

Plotting Current with Voltages

We can look at the current along with the voltages by selecting <u>P</u>lot, Add <u>Y</u> Axis. This gives another vertical axis, which initially has the same scale as the original.

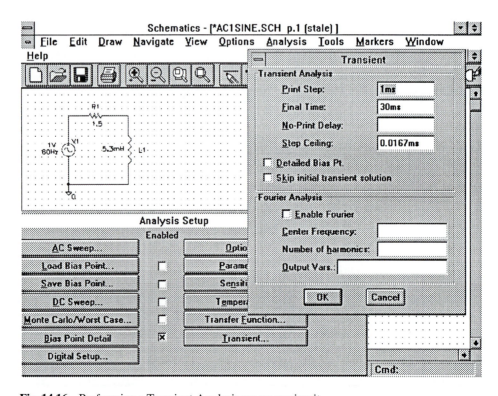

Fig. 14.16 Performing a Transient Analysis on an ac circuit.

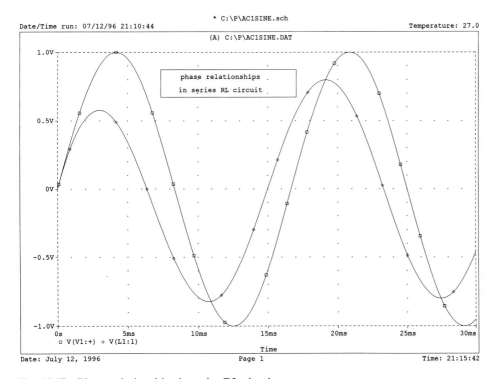

Fig. 14.17 Phase relationships in series RL circuit.

If we now trace I(R1), the leftmost vertical axis keeps its 1-V range, while the axis to the right (marked *2*) adopts a 500-mA range. This technique is especially helpful when the numerical values of voltage and current differ greatly. See Fig. 14.18 for these traces. The current sine wave crosses the *X*-axis at 19.116 ms, which means the current lags the applied voltage by 52.9°. This is close to the true value of 53.1°.

SERIES CIRCUIT WITH *R* AND *C*

The second example of Chapter 2 contains an ac source in series with a resistor and a capacitor. The analysis is performed at $f = 318$ Hz. Construct a circuit similar to this in Schematics, but before you begin, make a note of our desire to rotate the capacitor three times (so that the first terminal will be at the top). Use *VAC, R, C,* and *AGND* in that order. The completed circuit should be like the one shown in Fig. 14.19 (top). Name the drawing *ac2.sch*. Remember to call for an ac sweep at $f = 318$ Hz. Refer to the previous section for details of how this is done. Examine the output file to see how the circuit elements are referenced. Your capacitor should have the following listing in the netlist:

```
C_C1              $N_0002   0     100uF
```

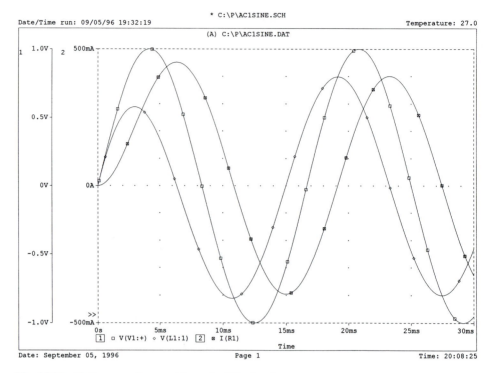

Fig. 14.18   Voltages and current in series RL circuit.

The order of the nodes (*2, 0*) will be in agreement only if you rotated the capacitor three times. Node *2* in the circuit diagram is at the top of the capacitor (between *R1* and *C1*) and this is the first terminal of the capacitor.

Printed Documentation of the Circuit

Figure 14.19 contains the circuit (from Schematics) along with the output file. If you are using a sheet-feed printer (such as a LaserJet or an ink jet) you can print the circuit diagram near the top of the page, then run the page through the printer again. On the second pass, skip the first 14 or so lines before printing *ac2.out*. This will produce the desired documentation. Since we have not added print statements to the file *ac2.cir*, the output file contains no ac analysis. This time we will use Probe to give us the voltage across the capacitor.

Select the Probe icon, then open the file *ac2.dat*. When the graph appears on the screen, the frequency $f = 318$ Hz should be at the middle of the *X*-axis. Select Trace, Add . . . and choose V(C1:1). This will produce a point (actually a narrow line) on the screen; you may use the cursor to see that this point is at 0.707 V. This is the magnitude of the capacitor voltage. Next, select Trace, Add . . . and type "r(V(C1:1))". This produces a point corresponding to the real part of the capacitor voltage. Finally produce a trace of img(V(C1:1)), which is the imaginary part of the capacitor voltage. Use the cursor to verify that these values are (0.500, −0.500) V.

Fig. 14.19 Schematic and output file for series RC circuit.

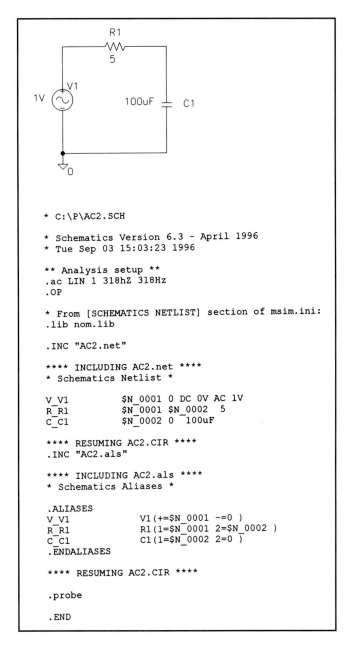

```
* C:\P\AC2.SCH

* Schematics Version 6.3 - April 1996
* Tue Sep 03 15:03:23 1996

** Analysis setup **
.ac LIN 1 318hZ 318Hz
.OP

* From [SCHEMATICS NETLIST] section of msim.ini:
.lib nom.lib

.INC "AC2.net"

**** INCLUDING AC2.net ****
* Schematics Netlist *

V_V1          $N_0001 0 DC 0V AC 1V
R_R1          $N_0001 $N_0002  5
C_C1          $N_0002 0  100uF

**** RESUMING AC2.CIR ****
.INC "AC2.als"

**** INCLUDING AC2.als ****
* Schematics Aliases *

.ALIASES
V_V1          V1(+=$N_0001 -=0 )
R_R1          R1(1=$N_0001 2=$N_0002 )
C_C1          C1(1=$N_0002 2=0 )
.ENDALIASES

**** RESUMING AC2.CIR ****

.probe

.END
```

Figure 14.20 shows the Probe plot of these values with the cursor displaying the magnitude of the capacitor voltage, 0.707 V.

Delete the voltage traces and trace the components of the resistor current. Verify that $I(R1) = 0.141$ A, $r(I(R1)) = 0.1$ A, and $img(I(R1)) = 0.1$ A.

Thus we have seen two methods of finding ac steady-state phasor values: The first used additional statements inserted in the circuit file, while the second used

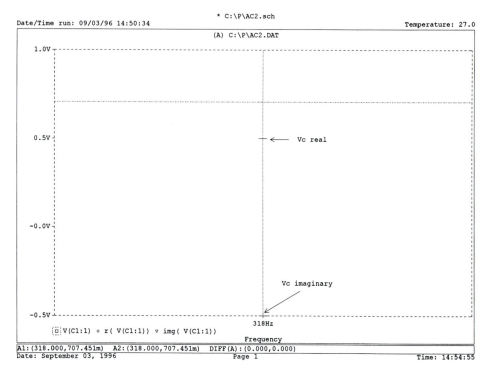

Fig. 14.20 Components of voltage in series RC circuit.

Probe to achieve the same results. There are obvious advantages and disadvantages to each method. Creating a circuit file from a sketch is easy and unambiguous, and the element and node labeling is simple. On the other hand, by using Schematics, we avoid having to create a circuit file, since the program does it for us.

We conclude that for most ac steady-state solutions it is easier to create a circuit file and use PSpice for the analysis, avoiding the more laborious method of drawing the circuit in Schematics, then calling for the sweep analysis.

MAXIMUM POWER TO LOAD IMPEDANCE

Figure 2.9 (Chapter 2) shows a series circuit designed to provide maximum power to the load impedance. Use Schematics to draw the circuit. Begin with *VAC* giving *V1*, next *R1*, then *L1, R2*, and *C1*, and finally *AGND* giving the zero node. Rotate *R2* and *C1* each three times, so that your analysis will agree with the one shown in this example. Figure 14.21 shows the placing of the parts before the actual values have been assigned. Name the circuit *maxpo.sch*. After assigning the component values, use <u>A</u>nalysis, Se<u>t</u>up . . . <u>A</u>C Sweep . . . , and use a linear sweep of one point for $f = 1$ kHz.

Finally choose <u>A</u>nalysis, <u>S</u>imulate to complete the simulation. In order to get a more complete picture of the details of the analysis, go back to Schematics (before running Probe, use Alt-Tab) and print the circuit. Compare your circuit with Fig.

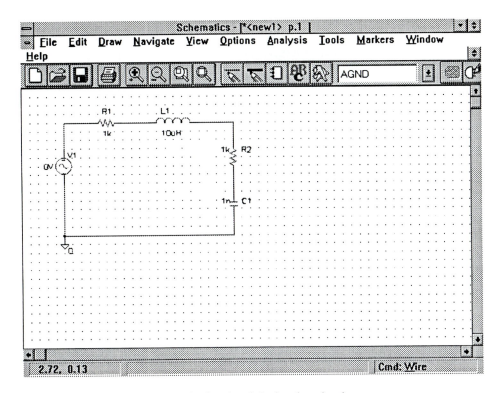

Fig. 14.21   Maximum Power study showing default values for the parts

14.22. Now print the file *maxpo.out* after using Courier New font and removing
unwanted lines. This file is shown in Fig. 14.23. Based on the contents of the file
maxpo.net (as shown in *maxpo.out*) assign node numbers (*0, 1, 2, 3,* and *4*) to your
circuit drawing. Now return to Probe (Alt-Tab) and use Trace, Add . . . to produce
the traces shown in Fig. 14.24. The voltage levels have been shown using the Tools,

Fig. 14.22   Schematic for
Maximum Power to load
impedance.

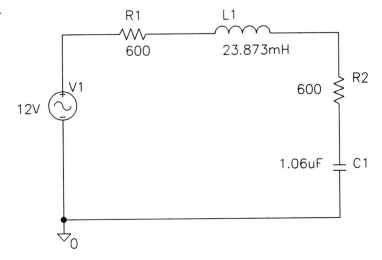

Fig. 14.23 Output file for Maximum Power to load impedance.

```
* C:\P\MAXPO.sch

  ****      CIRCUIT DESCRIPTION

* Schematics Version 6.3 - April 1996
* Wed Sep 04 11:12:43 1996

** Analysis setup **
.ac LIN 1 1kHz 1kHz
.OP

* From [SCHEMATICS NETLIST] section of msim.ini:
.lib nom.lib

.INC "MAXPO.net"

**** INCLUDING MAXPO.net ****
* Schematics Netlist *

V_V1          $N_0001 0 DC 0V AC 12V
R_R1          $N_0001 $N_0002   600
L_L1          $N_0002 $N_0003   23.873mH
R_R2          $N_0003 $N_0004   600
C_C1          $N_0004 0  1.06uF

**** RESUMING MAXPO.CIR ****
.INC "MAXPO.als"

**** INCLUDING MAXPO.als ****
* Schematics Aliases *

.ALIASES
V_V1          V1(+=$N_0001 -=0 )
R_R1          R1(1=$N_0001 2=$N_0002 )
L_L1          L1(1=$N_0002 2=$N_0003 )
R_R2          R2(1=$N_0003 2=$N_0004 )
C_C1          C1(1=$N_0004 2=0 )
.ENDALIASES

**** RESUMING MAXPO.CIR ****

.probe

.END
```

Label, Text . . . command. Next, indicate these voltages at their proper points (nodes) on the circuit drawing. Now the location of each of the various voltages in the circuit becomes clear. For example V(L1:2) is the voltage at node *3* with respect to ground. Thus V(3) = 6.185 V, in agreement with the results shown in Chapter 2. Remove the traces in Probe and trace p(V(L1:2)). Use the cursor to verify that the results show an angle of −14.042°. An alternative way of obtaining printed results of voltages and currents is to go into the file *maxpo.cir* and insert the desired *.PRINT* statements and then going directly to PSpice for the analysis.

SERIES RESONANCE

In Schematics draw the circuit shown in Fig. 14.25. Use parts *VAC, R, L, C,* and *AGND*. If both *L*1 and *C*1 are rotated three times, your nodes and terminals will

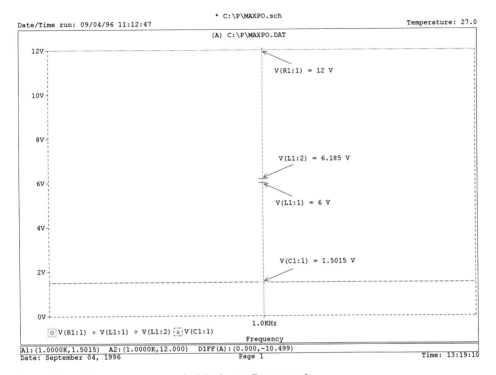

Fig. 14.24 Voltage components in Maximum Power study.

agree with those used in the text. The values are $V1 = 1$ V, $R1 = 50$ Ω, $L1 = 20$ mH, and $C1 = 150$ nF, the same values used for the example of Chapter 2. This circuit is resonant at $f_o = 2905.8$ Hz, and we would like to perform an ac sweep extending from 100 Hz to 5000 Hz. Figure 14.26 shows the screen for the sweep, using Analysis, Setup . . . AC Sweep. A linear sweep with 101 points was used. You may want to print the circuit diagram and the file *resonant.out*, both of which are shown in Fig. 14.25. In Probe plot V(L1:2), which is the voltage at node *3* (shown as V(3) in Chapter 2) and I(R1). Compare your results with those given in Chapter 2. Figure 14.27 shows three traces: (1) r(V(L1:2), the real part of the voltage at node *3* (between *L1* and *C1*); this voltage becomes zero at f_o. (2) img(V(L1:2), the imaginary part of the voltage at node *3*; this voltage reaches a negative peak of 7.238 V at f_o. (3) img(V(L1:1), the imaginary part of the voltage across both *L1* and *C1*; this voltage is zero at f_o.

The Probe Voltage and Current Notation

You may want to experiment with other traces of voltage and current before leaving Probe. Using x to represent a certain part, find the various components by using *V(x:1)* for the voltage at point *x:1* with respect to ground, *r(V(x:1)* for its real component, and *img(V(x:1)* for its imaginary component. Use *I(x)* to find current traces for the current through part *x* from its first node to its second node, *r(I(x))* for its real component, and *img(I(x))* for its imaginary component.

Fig. 14.25 Schematic and output file for series resonance circuit.

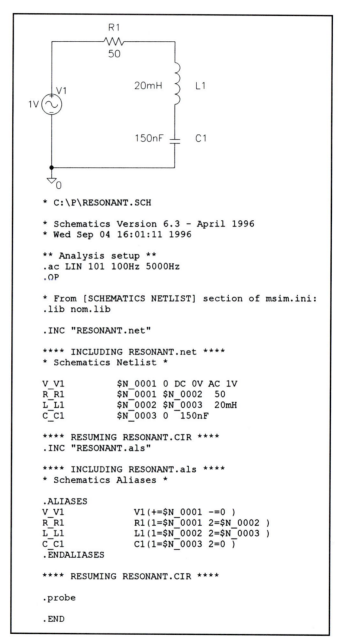

```
* C:\P\RESONANT.SCH

* Schematics Version 6.3 - April 1996
* Wed Sep 04 16:01:11 1996

** Analysis setup **
.ac LIN 101 100Hz 5000Hz
.OP

* From [SCHEMATICS NETLIST] section of msim.ini:
.lib nom.lib

.INC "RESONANT.net"

**** INCLUDING RESONANT.net ****
* Schematics Netlist *

V_V1            $N_0001 0 DC 0V AC 1V
R_R1            $N_0001 $N_0002  50
L_L1            $N_0002 $N_0003  20mH
C_C1            $N_0003 0  150nF

**** RESUMING RESONANT.CIR ****
.INC "RESONANT.als"

**** INCLUDING RESONANT.als ****
* Schematics Aliases *

.ALIASES
V_V1            V1(+=$N_0001 -=0 )
R_R1            R1(1=$N_0001 2=$N_0002 )
L_L1            L1(1=$N_0002 2=$N_0003 )
C_C1            C1(1=$N_0003 2=0 )
.ENDALIASES

**** RESUMING RESONANT.CIR ****

.probe

.END
```

MULTIPLE-SOURCE AC NETWORK

The multiple-source ac network of Chapter 2 will be revisited in this analysis. Create the circuit shown in Fig. 14.28 in Schematics using the name *multisrc.src*. The order of the nodes used in Fig. 2.29 may be preserved if the parts are entered in the following sequence: *V1, C, L, R, V2, V3, AGND*. The capacitor name is changed from

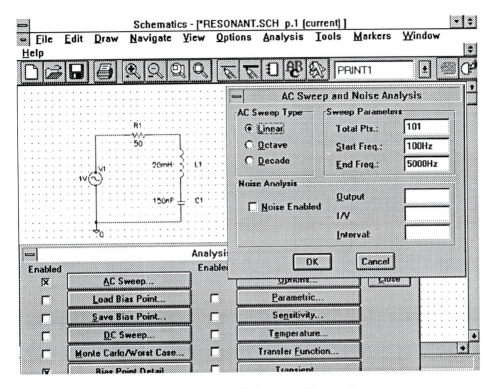

Fig. 14.26   The Series Resonance with *RLC* Circuit for Chapter 2.

the default *C1* to *C* by selecting the name (dbl-clk) and in the "Edit Reference Designator" window typing "C". The parts *L1* and *R1* are renamed in the same way. Indicate the magnitude and phase angle for each of the voltage sources. In order to display the phase angle, after setting the angle click on Change Display and select "Both name and Value". Your drawing should be like that of Fig. 14.28. The simulation should be set for an ac linear sweep at 60 Hz. Run the analysis then document the results by listing the file *multisrc.out*. It is always important to know the location and order of the nodes; label them on the circuit for further study.

In Chapter 2 you were asked to find the current through each of the elements *C, L,* and *R* and to find the voltage V(2). We will find these values using Probe. In Probe obtain traces and verify that: V(C:2) = 35.535 V, r(V(C:2)) = 32.09 V, img(V(C:2)) = −15.261 V, p(V(C:2)) = −25.4°. You may prefer to find only the real and imaginary parts of this voltage and then use the calculator to find the polar form = 35.5/−25.4°. Note that this is V(2) using the customary SPICE notation (the voltage at node 2). Remove the voltage traces, then find I(C) = 4.8663 A, r(I(C)) = −3.8144, img(I(C)) = −3.0218, p(I(C)) = 141.6°.

On your circuit diagram verify that this current is to be shown (with a current arrow) from node *1* to node *2* through *C*. Find the inductor and resistor currents in Probe and show all currents in either polar or rectangular form, with current arrows, on your circuit diagram. The solution is incomplete without the current arrows.

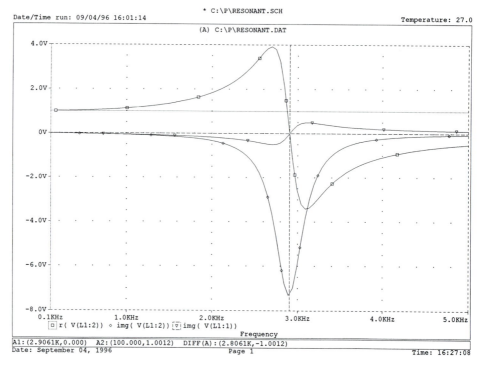

Fig. 14.27   Series resonance in RLC circuit.

SINE-WAVE REPRESENTATION OF MULTISOURCE AC

We will now simulate the previous problem by using *VSIN* for the voltage sources *V1*, *V2*, and *V3* rather than by using *VAC*. This calls for a transient-type solution to the problem as an alternative way of looking at the results. The analysis is more involved and has certain limitations, which will be mentioned as the work proceeds.

Begin a new drawing in Schematics, placing part *VSIN* in the position for *V1*. Refer to Fig. 14.28 for the placement of the parts. Next place *C, L, R, V2,* and *V3* using *VSIN* for each voltage source. Complete the circuit with *AGND* and the necessary wiring. Select *V1* and set VOFF = 0, VAMPL = 20 V, FREQ = 60 Hz, PHASE = 0. Follow the same steps for *V2* and *V3* giving them their proper values. Save the drawing as *tmulti.sch*.

After all parts have been given their proper values and names, the type analysis must be chosen. Use Analysis, Setup . . . , Transient . . . , Print Step: "1.5 ms", Final Time: "30 ms", and "Step Ceiling: "0.0167 ms". This will allow the transient analysis to proceed when you select Analysis, Simulate. The analysis will take you into Probe, where you may trace various voltages and currents.

Figure 14.29 shows V(C:1), which is the source voltage *V1*, and V(C:2), which is the voltage at V(2), using PSpice notation for the node. The latter is the voltage at

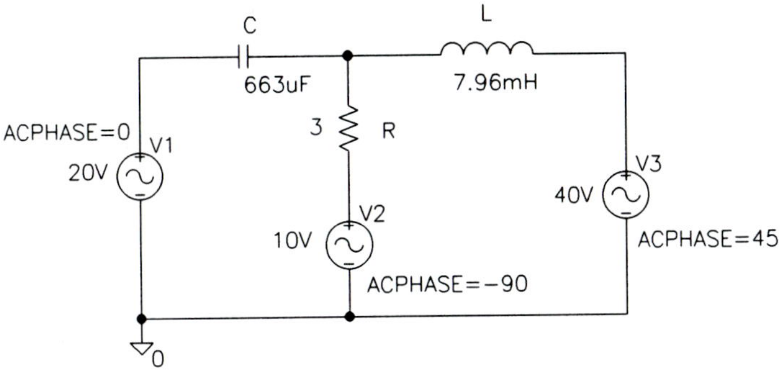


```
* C:\P\MULTISRC.SCH

* Schematics Version 6.3 - April 1996
* Wed Sep 04 19:12:51 1996

** Analysis setup **
.ac LIN 1 60Hz 60Hz
.OP

* From [SCHEMATICS NETLIST] section of msim.ini:
.lib nom.lib

.INC "MULTISRC.net"

**** INCLUDING MULTISRC.net ****
* Schematics Netlist *

V_V1          $N_0001 0 DC 0V AC 20V 0
C_C          $N_0001 $N_0002  663uF
L_L          $N_0002 $N_0003  7.96mH
R_R          $N_0002 $N_0004  3
V_V2          $N_0004 0 DC 0V AC 10V -90
V_V3          $N_0003 0 DC 0V AC 40V 45

**** RESUMING MULTISRC.CIR ****
.INC "MULTISRC.als"

**** INCLUDING MULTISRC.als ****
* Schematics Aliases *

.ALIASES
V_V1            V1(+=$N_0001 -=0 )
C_C             C(1=$N_0001 2=$N_0002 )
L_L             L(1=$N_0002 2=$N_0003 )
R_R             R(1=$N_0002 2=$N_0004 )
V_V2            V2(+=$N_0004 -=0 )
V_V3            V3(+=$N_0003 -=0 )
.ENDALIASES

**** RESUMING MULTISRC.CIR ****
```

Fig. 14.28 Schematic and output file for multisource ac circuit.

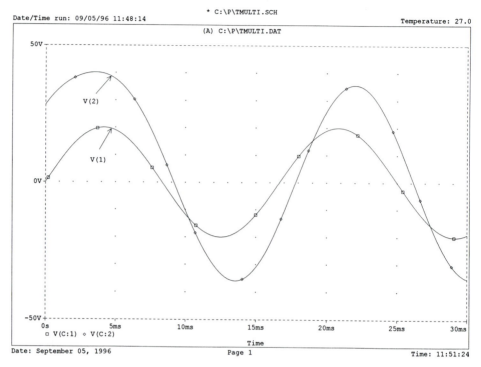

Fig. 14.29 Multisource ac circuit.

the junction of *C, L,* and *R*. Find the point near 16.667 ms where *V1* crosses the *X*-axis rising; then find the point beyond this where V(2) crosses the *X*-axis rising. Verify that this is at 17.819 ms. This means that V(2) lags *V1* by 1.152 ms. When this value is converted to degrees (360° = 16.667 ms), it gives the lagging angle as 24.88°. This is close to the angle of −25.4° found in the previous example. These angles should not be expected to agree exactly.

The transient of V(2) is clearly distorted in the beginning of the plot. In the laboratory, an oscilloscope would show these voltages without their initial transients, which require several cycles to settle down. The second peak of V(2) is at 35.326 V, not quite in agreement with the peak of 35.535 V found previously, for the same reason. You may want to extend the final time of the analysis beyond the chosen 30 s, allowing you to look at a full cycle beyond the first cycle. In the printed file *tmulti.out* the initial transient solution values are of little interest, except to confirm that V(2) begins at 28.284 V on the plot.

Sine Waves of Currents

While you are still in Probe remove the voltage traces and plot each of the currents in the circuit. Remember to show reference directions for all the currents on the circuit diagram. Look at the capacitor and inductor currents after they have passed

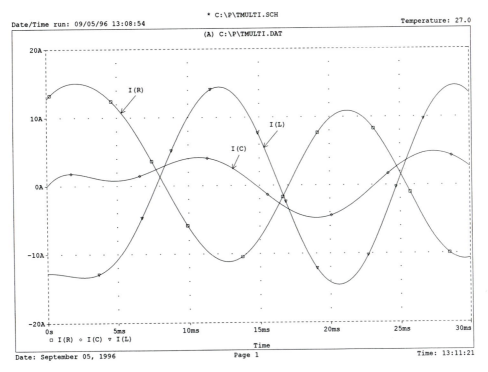

Fig. 14.30 Currents in multisource circuit.

their initial transient period in order to determine amplitudes and phases. We are not actually interested in the transient response of this ac circuit but rather in what we might see in the laboratory using an oscilloscope. Figure 14.30 shows these traces.

TRANSFORMERS

We will use the transformer circuit of Fig. 2.30 to illustrate how this type circuit is drawn in Schematics. Figure 14.31 shows the desired form of the circuit. Begin with VAC for *V*, then R for *R1*, L (rotate three times) for *L1*; repeat for *L2*; R for *R2*; repeat for *RL* (rotate three times); and C (rotate three times) for *CL*. The required part to show the coupling is *K_Linear* in the *analog.slb* library. Place this symbol at a convenient location; it is shown above and between the inductors. In our circuit, using the values from Fig. 2.30, $M = 20$ mH, and with $L1 = L2 = 25$ mH, $k = 0.8$. Double-click on the *K* box, and the window the K1 Part Name: *K_Linear* should appear. Select the line for *L1* and make its value "L1", as shown in Fig. 14.32. Save this attribute and repeat a like process for *L2*. After assigning all other values, set the ac sweep for the single frequency of 1 kHz. Save the drawing as *transfmr.sch*.

Fig. 14.31 Schematic and output file for transformer.

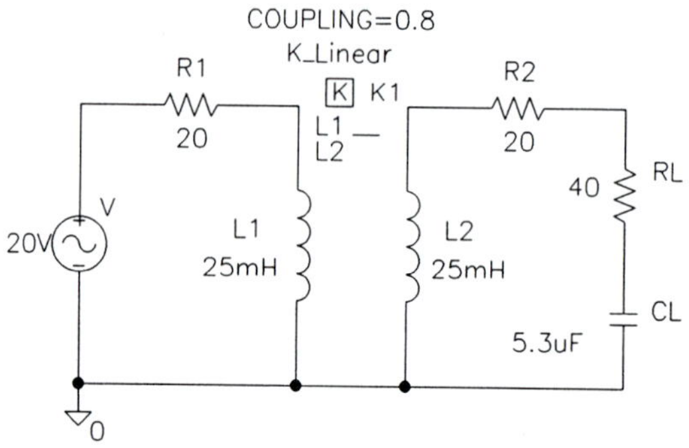

```
* C:\P\TRANSFMR.sch

* Schematics Version 6.3 - April 1996
* Thu Sep 05 17:11:20 1996

** Analysis setup **
.ac LIN 1 1kHz 1kHz
.OP

* From [SCHEMATICS NETLIST] section of msim.ini:
.lib nom.lib

.INC "TRANSFMR.net"

**** INCLUDING TRANSFMR.net ****
* Schematics Netlist *

V_V           $N_0001 0 DC 0V AC 20V
R_R1          $N_0001 $N_0002   20
L_L1          $N_0002 0  25mH
L_L2          $N_0003 0   25mH
R_R2          $N_0003 $N_0004   20
R_RL          $N_0004 $N_0005   40
C_CL          $N_0005 0  5.3uF
Kn_K1         L_L1 L_L2       0.8

**** RESUMING TRANSFMR.CIR ****
.INC "TRANSFMR.als"

**** INCLUDING TRANSFMR.als ****
* Schematics Aliases *

.ALIASES
V_V              V(+=$N_0001 -=0 )
R_R1             R1(1=$N_0001 2=$N_0002 )
L_L1             L1(1=$N_0002 2=0 )
L_L2             L2(1=$N_0003 2=0 )
R_R2             R2(1=$N_0003 2=$N_0004 )
R_RL             RL(1=$N_0004 2=$N_0005 )
C_CL             CL(1=$N_0005 2=0 )
Kn_K1            K1()
.ENDALIASES

**** RESUMING TRANSFMR.CIR ****
```

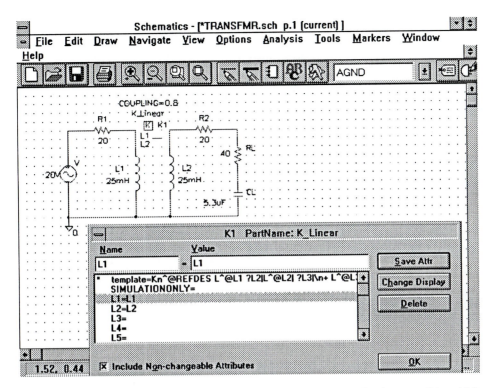

Fig. 14.32 Setting the attributes of K_Linear, the coefficient of coupling between L1 and L2.

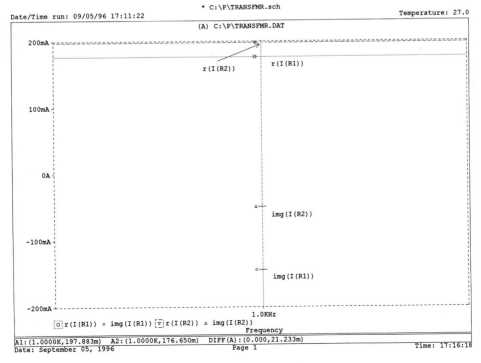

Fig. 14.33 Components of currents in transformer circuit.

Now perform the simulation. At its completion, in Probe trace the real and imaginary parts of the currents in both R1 and R2 for comparison with the results in Chapter 2. The values should be I(R1) = (0.176, −0.144) A and I(R2) = (0.198, −0.049) A. These tracepoints are shown in Fig. 14.33 with cursor indicators at the real part of each current.

Coefficient of Coupling

Pay particular attention to the schematics netlist as shown in the output file of Fig. 14.31. In Chapter 2 the line

```
K L1 L2 0.8
```

described the coefficient of coupling. In Schematics this becomes

```
Kn_K1        L_L1 L_L2     0.8
```

Note that *Kn* is the general name for *k*, and *K1* is our particular *k* (which we could call simply *K* or something else). The other parts listings should be self-evident.

Transistor Circuits in Schematics

Chapter 10 dealt with the PSpice model of the BJT. In the evaluation version of PSpice, there are four BJTs (*Q2N2222, Q2N2907A, Q2N3904,* and *Q2N3906*), two of which are *NPN* and the other two are *PNP* transistors. In order to show some of the features of these parts, we will begin with an example using the *Q2N3904*.

Output Characteristics of *Q2N3904*

Refer to Fig. 10.1 for the desired circuit. Begin with *IDC,* then *R* (for *R_B*), then *R* again (for *R_C*), then *VDC,* and *AGND*. Next, select the *Q2N3904* from the library *eval.slb*. Assign names and component values and use connecting wires to complete the circuit. For this example in Chapter 10, the resistor *RC* was described as

```
RC 4 3 0.01
```

The ordering of the nodes (4, 3) assured that the resistor current would be positive, when referenced from right to left, that is, nodes *4* to *3*. We would like the same convention to apply to our Schematics analysis. Select *RB* and rotate it twice to bring this about. Name the file *bjtchar.sch*. Now we are ready to perform the analysis setup.

Recall that the PSpice analysis used a statement

```
.dc VCC 0 10V 0.05V IB 5uA 25uA 5uA
```

to accomplish the sweep. In Schematics this is done by using Analysis, Setup . . . DC Sweep. . . . In the DC Sweep box select Voltage Source for the type sweep, then Name: "VCC", Start Value: "0 V", End Value: "10 V", and Increment: "0.05 V". See Fig. 15.1 for this step.

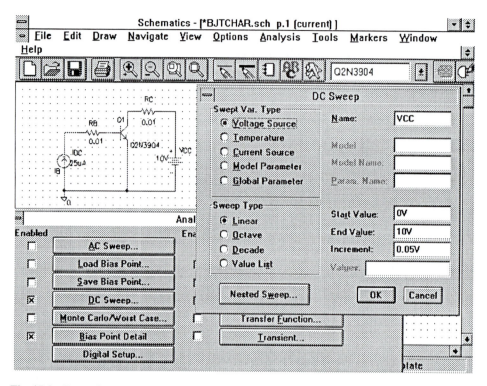

Fig. 15.1   Preparing for a nested sweep of transistor characteristics.

Then click on the Nested Sweep ... button, bringing up another menu. Select Current Source for the type sweep, and Name: "IB", Start Value: "5 uA", End Value: "25 uA", and Increment: "5 uA". Finally, click on Enable Nested Sweep (placing an x in the box), as shown in Fig. 15.2.

Now we are ready to perform the simulation. Compare your results with those shown in Fig. 15.3. Use the cursor to show that for $V_{CE} = 4$ V and $I_B = 25$ μA, $I_C = 4$ mA, giving $\beta_{dc} = 160$. (Select the curve with the mouse.) Also see the file *bjtchar.out*, shown along with the circuit diagram in Fig. 15.4. Note that resistor RC has the desired order of the nodes $(4, 3)$, since it was rotated twice in Schematics. In the netlist the sweep statement is

```
.DC LIN V_VCC 0V 10V 0.05V LIN I_IB 5uA 25uA 5uA
```

Compare this with the sweep statement used in the similar example of Chapter 10.

Input Characteristics of *Q2N3904*

Following the circuit layout of Fig. 10.3 to obtain the input characteristics of the transistor, use IDC (for I_{BB}), R (for R_S) and R again (for R_L) VDC (for V_{CC}), then Q2N3904 for the transistor. Name the file *bjtichar.sch*. The analysis will require a

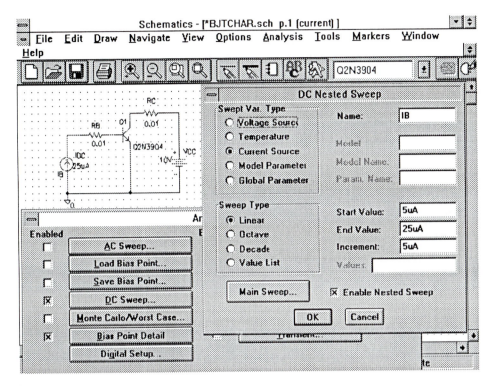

Fig. 15.2 The nested sweep menu being used for the transistor output characteristics.

nested sweep, but this time the outer sweep will use the input current *IBB*. Start at 0 μA, end at *100* μA, using 1-μA increments. For the nested sweep use the output voltage *VCC*. Start at *0* V, end at *10* V, with 2-*V* increments. See Fig. 15.5 for the outer sweep details.

In Probe choose the *X*-axis variable as V(Rs:1), the voltage at node *1*, (the base voltage). Trace I(BB), the base current. This family of curves shows all but the first, for $V_{CE} = 0$, clustered together. These curves are shown in Fig. 15.6. The circuit drawn in Schematics along with the file *bjtichar.out* are shown in Fig. 15.7. The nesting is shown in the sweep statement as

```
.DC LIN I_IBB 0uA 100uA 1uA LIN V_VCC 0V 10V 2V
```

CE BJT CASE STUDY

A biasing case study was presented in Chapter 10, with the original circuit shown in Fig. 10.7. Duplicate this circuit in Schematics, being careful to place the parts in the order that will preserve the original node numbering. This is not an absolute requirement, but it will make the comparisons much easier. Begin with R_2, then R_1, R_C, R_E, V_{CC}, and Q_1. The transistor is to be the same as that of Fig. 10.7, the *2N2222*,

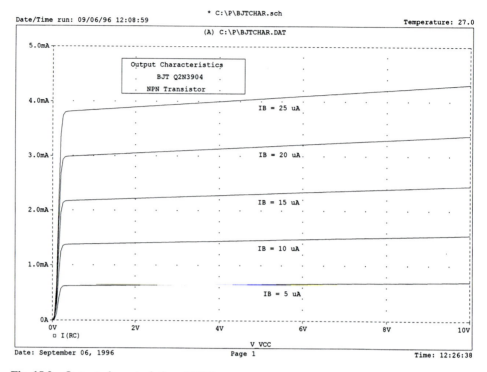

Fig. 15.3 Output characteristics of BJT.

found in Schematics as *Q2N2222*. Rotate the vertical resistors three times, as you have in the previous examples. Save the work with the file name *bjtcase.sch*, perform the simulation and look at the results in the output file. Do your answers agree with those found in Chapter 10? Refer to Fig. 15.8 for the output listing along with the circuit drawings from Schematics. The only current given in the results is the voltage-source current

```
NAME        CURRENT
V_VCC       -1.391E-3
```

This is the (positive) current from the source V_{CC}. We could find the various currents by including a dc sweep in our setup, as follows.

Producing DC-Current Values in Schematics

After having run a successful analysis on the preceding circuit, return to Schematics and call for a dc sweep in the analysis setup. The sweep begins and ends at *12* V, with a *12*-V increment, just as we did in Fig. 10.8. Now, when the simulation occurs, you will be taken into Probe, where you may trace the currents as points with the *X*-axis showing V_{CC} (12 V). Verify the values that were given in Fig. 10.8. The currents are shown in Probe as I(RC), I(R1), I(R2), and I(RE). Figure 15.9 shows the graph, with

Fig. 15.4 Schematic and output file for transistor output characteristics.

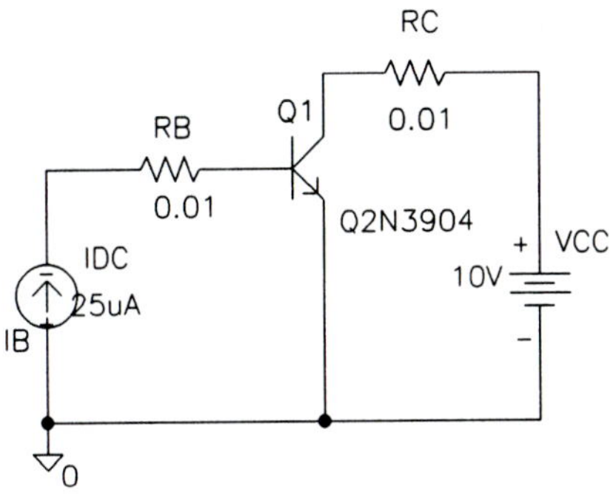

```
* C:\P\BJTCHAR.sch
** Analysis setup **
.DC LIN V_VCC 0V 10V 0.05V
+ LIN I_IB 5uA 25uA 5uA
.OP
* From [SCHEMATICS NETLIST] section of msim.ini:
.lib nom.lib
.INC "BJTCHAR.net"
**** INCLUDING BJTCHAR.net ****
* Schematics Netlist *
I_IB         0 $N_0001 DC 25uA
R_RB         $N_0001 $N_0002  0.01
R_RC         $N_0004 $N_0003  0.01
V_VCC        $N_0004 0 10V
Q_Q1         $N_0003 $N_0002 0 Q2N3904
**** RESUMING BJTCHAR.CIR ****
.INC "BJTCHAR.als"
**** INCLUDING BJTCHAR.als ****
* Schematics Aliases *
.ALIASES
I_IB              IB(+=0 -=$N_0001 )
R_RB              RB(1=$N_0001 2=$N_0002 )
R_RC              RC(1=$N_0004 2=$N_0003 )
V_VCC             VCC(+=$N_0004 -=0 )
Q_Q1              Q1(c=$N_0003 b=$N_0002 e=0 )
.ENDALIASES
**** RESUMING BJTCHAR.CIR ****
.probe
.END
****       BJT MODEL PARAMETERS
               Q2N3904
               NPN
         IS    6.734000E-15
         BF    416.4
**** BIPOLAR JUNCTION TRANSISTORS
NAME         Q_Q1
MODEL        Q2N3904
IB           2.50E-05
IC           4.31E-03
VBE          7.02E-01
VBC          -9.30E+00
VCE          1.00E+01
BETADC       1.72E+02
BETAAC       1.87E+02
```

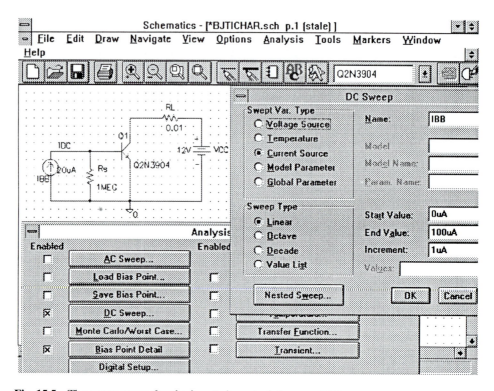

Fig. 15.5   The outer sweep for the input characteristics uses IBB.

12 V (the dc sweep voltage) displayed along the *X*-axis. Use the cursor to find the value of each current. By pressing *Ctrl+rt. arrow* move the cursor to each successive trace.

To find the directions of the currents you must label the nodes on your circuit diagram, then draw arrows in the directions that agree with the schematics netlist (or aliases). For example, node *2* should be at the top of R_C and node *3* at the bottom of R_C. The schematics netlist of Fig. 15.8 shows the node order for RC as (*2, 3*). Show the current arrow on your circuit diagram in the corresponding direction. This might appear to be a trivial matter, but it is most important.

If you need hard-copy verification of the bias currents, you may want to go to the input file *bjtcase.cir* and add a print statement such as

```
.PRINT DC I(R_RC) I(R_R1) I(R_R2) I(R_RE)
```

then run the PSpice analysis. The desired values will appear in the output file much like that of Fig. 10.8. These values appear like this:

```
V_VCC     I(R_RC)   I(R_R1)    I(R_R2)    I(R_RE)
1.200E+01 1.114E-03 2.777E-04 2.707E-04 1.121E-03
```

Remember that in the circuit file (produced by Schematics) the proper notation for

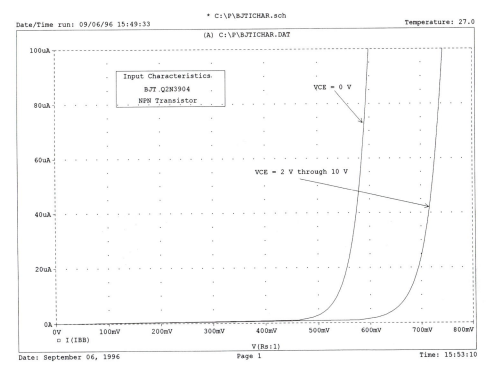

Fig. 15.6   Input characteristics for BJT.

a current is, for example, I(R_RC), whereas in Probe the same current is shown as I(RC).

Producing DC Node Voltages and Voltage Drops in Schematics

Node voltages are already available when you perform the simulation. The Bias Point Detail feature of the analysis provides for these. These are shown in the *bjtcase.out* file of Fig. 15.8 as node voltage ($N_0001) = 0.8933 V, node voltage ($N_0002) = 12.000 V, node voltage ($N_0003) = 6.7651 V, and node voltage ($N_0004) = 0.2466 V. It is customary to simply print the output file to provide a written record of these bias-point voltages. In addition, if you have performed a dc sweep, you can look at these node voltages in Probe. As shown in Fig. 15.10, these are called for by name, although they do not appear in the Trace, Add . . . list. In the figure, using the cursor, you can read V($N_0001) = 0.893325 V, V($N_0002) = 12.000 V, and so forth.

However, using Probe to trace the voltages listed in Trace, Add . . . will give the voltages in a different form. For this example the dc voltages available in Probe are V(R2:1) = 0.893 V, which is V(1) using PSpice notation; V(R1:1) = 12 V, which is V(2); V(Q1:c) = 6.76 V, which is V(3); V(Q1:e) = 0.247 V, which is V(4); and V(R2:2) = 0 V. Verify these values in Probe.

Fig. 15.7 Schematic and output file for BJT input characteristics.

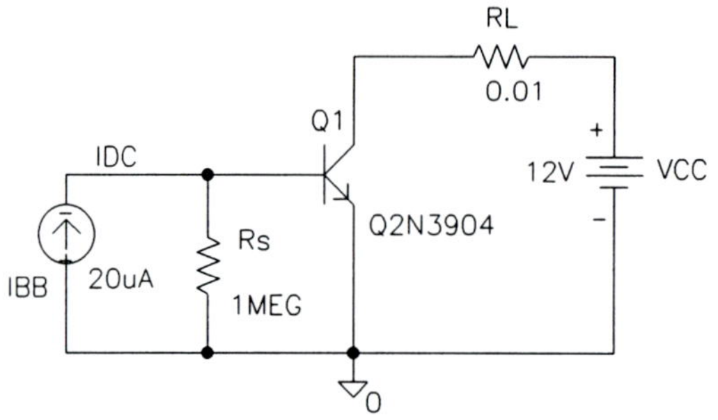

```
* C:\P\BJTICHAR.sch
** Analysis setup **
.DC LIN I_IBB 0uA 100uA 1uA
+ LIN V_VCC 0V 10V 2V
.OP
* From [SCHEMATICS NETLIST] section of msim.ini:
.lib nom.lib
.INC "BJTICHAR.net"
**** INCLUDING BJTICHAR.net ****
* Schematics Netlist *
Q_Q1            $N_0002 $N_0001 0 Q2N3904
R_RL            $N_0002 $N_0003  0.01
I_IBB            0 $N_0001 DC 20uA
V_VCC           $N_0003 0 12V
R_Rs            $N_0001 0  1MEG
**** RESUMING BJTICHAR.CIR ****
.INC "BJTICHAR.als"
**** INCLUDING BJTICHAR.als ****
* Schematics Aliases *
.ALIASES
Q_Q1            Q1(c=$N_0002 b=$N_0001 e=0 )
R_RL            RL(1=$N_0002 2=$N_0003 )
I_IBB           IBB(+=0 -=$N_0001 )
V_VCC           VCC(+=$N_0003 -=0 )
R_Rs            Rs(1=$N_0001 2=0 )
.ENDALIASES
.probe
.END
****        BJT MODEL PARAMETERS
                Q2N3904
                NPN
        IS      6.734000E-15
        BF  416.4
**** BIPOLAR JUNCTION TRANSISTORS
NAME            Q_Q1
MODEL           Q2N3904
IB              1.93E-05
IC              3.33E-03
VBE             6.94E-01
VBC             -1.13E+01
VCE             1.20E+01
BETADC          1.72E+02
BETAAC          1.90E+02
```

```
* C:\P\BJTCASE.SCH
** Analysis setup **
.OP
* From [SCHEMATICS NETLIST] section of msim.ini:
.lib nom.lib
.INC "BJTCASE.net"
**** INCLUDING BJTCASE.net ****
* Schematics Netlist *
R_R2          $N_0001 0  3.3k
R_R1          $N_0002 $N_0001  40k
R_RC          $N_0002 $N_0003  4.7k
R_RE          $N_0004 0  220
V_VCC         $N_0002 0 12V
Q_Q1          $N_0003 $N_0001 $N_0004 Q2N2222
**** RESUMING BJTCASE.CIR ****
.INC "BJTCASE.als"
**** INCLUDING BJTCASE.als ****
.probe
.END
****      BJT MODEL PARAMETERS
              Q2N2222
              NPN
        IS   14.340000E-15
        BF   255.9
        NF   1
        VAF  74.03
   NODE   VOLTAGE      NODE   VOLTAGE      NODE   VOLTAGE      NODE   VOLTAGE
  ($N_0001)    .8933          ($N_0002)   12.0000
  ($N_0003)   6.7651          ($N_0004)     .2466
     VOLTAGE SOURCE CURRENTS
     NAME          CURRENT
     V_VCC        -1.391E-03
     TOTAL POWER DISSIPATION   1.67E-02  WATTS
****        OPERATING POINT INFORMATION      TEMPERATURE =   27.000 DEG C
**** BIPOLAR JUNCTION TRANSISTORS
NAME          Q_Q1
MODEL         Q2N2222
IB            6.96E-06
IC            1.11E-03
VBE           6.47E-01
VBC          -5.87E+00
VCE           6.52E+00
BETADC        1.60E+02
BETAAC        1.77E+02
```

Fig. 15.8 Schematic and output file for BJT case study.

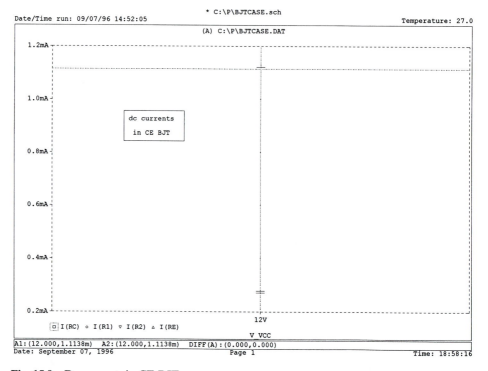

Fig. 15.9   Dc currents in CE BJT.

If you want hard copy for voltage *drops,* rather than just node voltages, you may want to include another print statement in the file *bjtcase.cir* before running the PSpice analysis again:

```
.PRINT DC V(R_RC) V(R_R1) V(R_R2) V(R_RE)
```

This statement follows the same format as the print statement for the currents. It will produce these results in the output file *bjtcase.out:*

```
V_VCC          V(R_RC)        V(R_R1)        V(R_R2)        V(R_RE)
1.200E+01      5.235E+00      1.111E+01      8.933E-01      2.466E-01
```

When dealing with voltages you will need to know which nodes are involved, for example, voltage V(R_RC) is voltage $V_{2,3}$, that is $V_2 - V_3$. If you label the nodes on the circuit diagram using conventional PSpice notation, it becomes clear which voltage drop this represents: It is the difference in potential from the top node of R_C to the bottom node. Be sure that you can explain what all the other voltage drops represent. They are not single-node voltages but double-node voltages, that is, voltage drops.

In summary, you can use add-trace requests such as V($N_0003) or V(Q1:c) to trace node voltages in Probe, but requests for traces such as V(R_RC) will not work. The latter statement is available only if you modify the circuit file to include the requests as shown above.

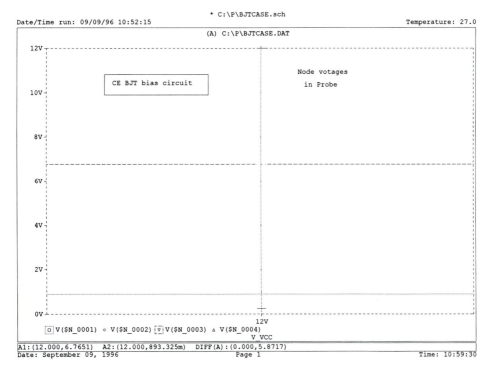

Fig. 15.10 CE BJT bias circuit.

The AC Analysis

Beginning with the circuit *bjtcase.sch,* we wish to add the components shown in Fig. 10.11, making this a common-emitter amplifier if the output is taken at the collector. Add V_s, (using *VAC*), R_s, C_b, and C_e. Instead of a dc sweep, use an ac sweep based on f = 5 kHz as in the example of Chapter 10. Providing for the sweep allows you to trace ac voltages and currents in Probe. The extended circuit is shown in Fig. 15.11, along with the output file *bjtcase.out*. In Probe verify that i(RC) = 388 µA, i(Rs) = 5.52 µA, and i(RE) = 3.77 µA. Also trace and verify v(R2:1) = 9.72 mV, which is v(1); v(Rs:2) = 9.72 mV, which is V(1b); v(RC:2) = 1.827 V, which is v(3); and v(RE:1) = 829.9 µV, which is v(4). Lowercase *i* and *v* are used to make it clear that these are ac values. Use the cursor to locate and record these values. The "which is . . ." values refer to the node designations of Chapter 10. See Fig. 15.12 for the Probe display of ac currents and voltages. Each value may be found by using the cursor and writing down the results as you move from one trace to another (press *Ctrl+rt. arrow*).

The Transient Analysis

Continuing the ac analysis of Fig. 10.9, we would like to look at the base and collector waveforms, which were shown in Fig. 10.11. This calls for a transient analysis,

```
      * C:\P\BJTCASE.SCH
      ** Analysis setup **
      .ac LIN 1 5kHz 5kHz
      .OP

      * From [SCHEMATICS NETLIST] section of msim.ini:
      .lib nom.lib
      .INC "BJTCASE.net"

      **** INCLUDING BJTCASE.net ****
      * Schematics Netlist *
      R_R2          $N_0001 0  3.3k
      R_R1          $N_0002 $N_0001   40k
      R_RC          $N_0002 $N_0003   4.7k
      R_RE          $N_0004 0  220
      V_VCC          $N_0002 0 12V
      Q_Q1          $N_0003 $N_0001 $N_0004 Q2N2222
      V_Vs          $N_0005 0 DC 0V AC 10mV
      R_Rs          $N_0005 $N_0006   50
      C_Cb          $N_0006 $N_0001   15uF
      C_Ce          $N_0004 0  15uF

      **** RESUMING BJTCASE.CIR ****
      .INC "BJTCASE.als"

      **** INCLUDING BJTCASE.als ****
      * Schematics Aliases *
      .ALIASES
      R_R2          R2(1=$N_0001 2=0 )
      R_R1          R1(1=$N_0002 2=$N_0001 )
      R_RC          RC(1=$N_0002 2=$N_0003 )
      R_RE          RE(1=$N_0004 2=0 )
      V_VCC         VCC(+=$N_0002 -=0 )
      Q_Q1          Q1(c=$N_0003 b=$N_0001 e=$N_0004 )
      V_Vs          Vs(+=$N_0005 -=0 )
      R_Rs          Rs(1=$N_0005 2=$N_0006 )
      C_Cb          Cb(1=$N_0006 2=$N_0001 )
      C_Ce          Ce(1=$N_0004 2=0 )
      .ENDALIASES

      **** RESUMING BJTCASE.CIR ****

      .probe

      .END
```

Fig. 15.11   Schematic and output file for ac analysis.

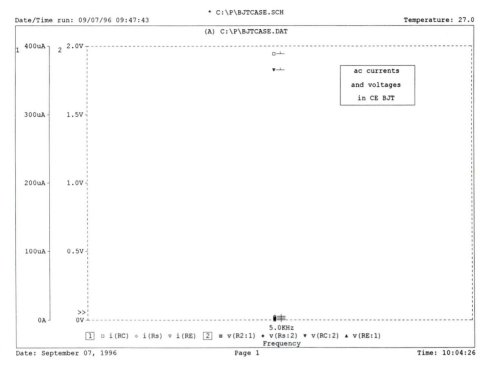

Fig. 15.12 Ac currents and voltages in CE BJT.

which means that you will need to setup for this in Schematics. You should be able to do this following the guidelines given in the previous chapter.

Replace *VAC* with *VSIN* and run the transient analysis for 0.6 ms, as was done for Fig. 10.12. Set $V_s = 10$ mV, which will actually be its peak value, but we will think of it as an rms value to make the analysis a bit simpler. Use File, Save As . . . to rename the circuit *bjtcaset.sch*.

Run the simulation, then plot V(RC:2), which is the voltage at the collector of Q_1 (node *3*), then on the same screen plot V(R1:2), which is the voltage at the base of Q_1 (node *1*). These plots should agree with the results obtained in Chapter 10. The amplitude of the base voltage is 9.72 mV, and the amplitude of the collector voltage is 1.807 V. The voltage gain is thus 186 from base to collector. As shown in Fig. 15.13, the dc level of the output voltage is 6.765 V; the dc level of the input voltage is 0.893 V. The values are the same as those shown in the dc bias results.

Modifying the Transistor Parameters (Using Edit, Model . . .)

The *Q2N2222* transistor part has been used in the previous examples as being typical of what might be found in an actual circuit. If you are working in the laboratory with a transistor whose h_{FE} is considerably less than that of the available part model, you can modify your circuit to obtain results more in keeping with your expectations.

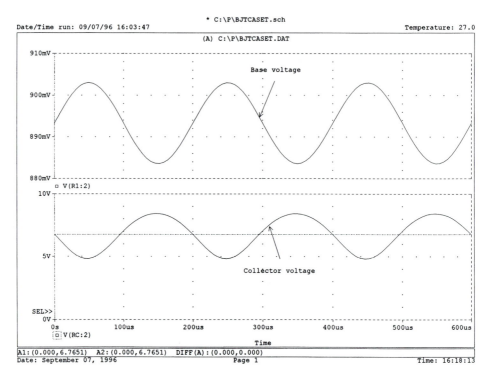

Fig. 15.13   Transient analysis of BJT circuit.

Continue working with the schematic *bjtcase* but rename it *bjtcasea.sch,* then select the transistor and choose Edit, Model . . . , Edit Instance Model (Text). . . . The window that now appears will allow you to modify any of the parameters shown in the listing. Change the value of *Bf* to 100 by using the mouse to select the desired item. The results are shown in Fig. 15.14. Notice that the model name changed when the window appeared on the screen and is now *Q2N2222-X.* The *X* means that you will (or may) modify some of the parameters of the original transistor. At the top left of the window, the "Copied From" library is given as *c:\p\bjtcasea.lib.* At the top right of the window, the "Save To" library is automatically shown as the same. Although you could put the transistor with the modified parameters in another library, we will not elect to do so. When you return to the drawing, you will be ready to run the simulation again. The output file, with the modified BJT model shown as *Q2N2222-X,* along with warnings, is shown in Fig. 15.15. The node voltages have changed from those produced when *Bf* was 255.9, as expected.

After running the simulation, in Probe trace the following and compare your results with those shown here: i(Rc) = 0.36 mA, i(Rs) = 7.48 μA, i(RE) = 3.5 μA, v(R2:1) = 9.63 mV, v(Rs:2) = 9.63 mV, v(RC:2) = 1.69 V, and v(RE:1) = 0.775 mA. These are ac values, with the results obtained from the single-frequency sweep at *f* = 5 kHz.

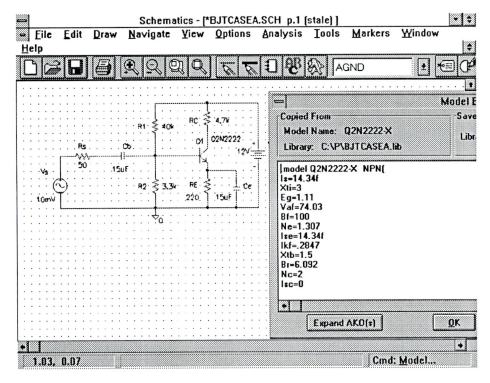

Fig. 15.14 Changing the h_{FE} for the Q2N2222.

The libraries referred to in the output file are *nom.lib* and *bjtcasea.lib*. The latter is a new library created when we chose to edit the selected model. If you look at the input file *bjtcasea.cir*, you will find the statements

```
.LIB BJTCASE.lib
.INC "BJTCASEA.net"
.INC "BJTCASEA.als"
```

These files were created when the simulation took place. The *bjtcase.lib* file contains the type of listing you would expect to find in the evaluation library. However it will show the modified transistor

```
.model Q2N2222-X NPN(Is=14.34f Xti=3 Eg=1.11 Vaf=74.03 Bf=100 Ne=1.307
+Ise=14.34f Ikf=.2847 Xtb=1.5 Br=6.092 Nc=2 Isc=0 Ikr=0 Rc=1 Cjc=7.306p
+Mjc=.3416 Vjc=.75 Fc=.5 Cje=22.01p Mje=3.77 Vje=.75 Tr=46.91n Tf=411.1p
+Itf=.6 Vtf=1.7 Xtf=3 Rb=10)
*       National         pid=19 case=TO18
*       88-09-07 bam        creation
```

Note that the transistor is now called *Q2N2222-X* with *Bf* = 100. This modified transistor is available only in the schematic *bjtcasea.sch*.

In the output file listing the warnings simply remind us that changes in the library and index files will be made.

```
* C:\P\BJTCASEA.SCH
** Analysis setup **
.ac LIN 1 5kHz 5kHz
.OP
.LIB BJTCASEA.lib
.lib nom.lib
.INC "BJTCASEA.net"
**** INCLUDING BJTCASEA.net ****
* Schematics Netlist *
R_R2            $N_0001 0   3.3k
R_R1            $N_0002 $N_0001   40k
R_RC            $N_0002 $N_0003   4.7k
R_RE            $N_0004 0   220
V_VCC           $N_0002 0 12V
Q_Q1            $N_0003 $N_0001 $N_0004 Q2N2222-X
V_Vs            $N_0005 0 DC 0V AC 10mV
R_Rs            $N_0005 $N_0006   50
C_Cb            $N_0006 $N_0001   15uF
C_Ce            $N_0004 0   15uF
.INC "BJTCASEA.als"
* Schematics Aliases *
.ALIASES
R_R2            R2(1=$N_0001 2=0 )
R_R1            R1(1=$N_0002 2=$N_0001 )
R_RC            RC(1=$N_0002 2=$N_0003 )
R_RE            RE(1=$N_0004 2=0 )
V_VCC           VCC(+=$N_0002 -=0 )
Q_Q1            Q1(c=$N_0003 b=$N_0001 e=$N_0004 )
V_Vs            Vs(+=$N_0005 -=0 )
R_Rs            Rs(1=$N_0005 2=$N_0006 )
C_Cb            Cb(1=$N_0006 2=$N_0001 )
C_Ce            Ce(1=$N_0004 2=0 )
.ENDALIASES
.probe
.END
WARNING -- Unable to find index file (BJTCASEA.ind) for library file BJTCASEA.lib
WARNING -- Making new index file (BJTCASEA.ind) for library file BJTCASEA.lib
Index has 2 entries from 1 file(s).
****      BJT MODEL PARAMETERS
              Q2N2222-X
              NPN
         IS   14.340000E-15
         BF   100
         NF   1
NODE    VOLTAGE    NODE   VOLTAGE     NODE   VOLTAGE    NODE    VOLTAGE
($N_0001)    .8768                 ($N_0002)   12.0000
($N_0003)   7.1059                 ($N_0004)    .2318
($N_0005)   0.0000                 ($N_0006)   0.0000
    VOLTAGE SOURCE CURRENTS
    NAME           CURRENT
    V_VCC        -1.319E-03
    V_Vs          0.000E+00
    TOTAL POWER DISSIPATION   1.58E-02   WATTS
**** BIPOLAR JUNCTION TRANSISTORS
NAME            Q_Q1
MODEL           Q2N2222-X
IB              1.24E-05
IC              1.04E-03
VBE             6.45E-01
VBC            -6.23E+00
VCE             6.87E+00
BETADC          8.40E+01
BETAAC          8.83E+01
```

Fig. 15.15 Output file for circuit with modified parameters.

USING THE *h*-PARAMETER MODEL

In Chapter 3 the *h* parameters for a transistor were used to show how an academic model for the BJT is treated in PSpice. The model required two dependent sources, *E* and *F*. When this circuit is drawn in Schematics it becomes hardly recognizable, since *E* and *F* are shown as four-terminal boxes with input terminals on the left and output terminals on the right. In Fig. 3.7 a *CE* amplifier was shown using a *1*-mV signal. Although the signal was shown with an ac symbol, it was pointed out that we could *fool* PSpice into giving us a great deal of useful information by merely performing a dc analysis, then interpreting the results as ac. This saves time and effort as long as no reactive elements are involved in the circuit.

We can now begin the circuit in Schematics, using a dc source for $V_s = 1$ mV, then placing $R_s = 1$ kΩ, $R_i = 1.1$ kΩ, *E1*, *F1*, $R_O = 40$ kΩ, and $R_L = 10$ kΩ. Since *F1* must sense current I_b, its input terminals are in series with R_s and R_i along with the output terminals of *F1*. The input terminals of *E1* must be across the terminals of R_O and are shown this way in the circuit. Refer to Fig. 15.16 to see how this is done. It is no longer necessary to use V_0 as in Fig. 3.7, because the output terminals of *E1* take its place. The circuit is given the name *hparmod.sch*, the gain of *F1* is set at 50 (for h_{fe}), the gain of *E1* is set at 2.5E − 4 (for h_{re}) and the analysis is run.

The Output File

In Fig. 15.16 the nodes have been labeled by hand to aid in the discussion and understanding of the results. Note that the dependent source *E_E1* is described by

```
E_E1 $N_0005 0 $N_0004 0 2.5E−4
```

The first two terminals (5, 0) are the output terminals showing the placing of the dependent source in the circuit, while the input terminals (4, 0) indicate where the independent voltage (upon which *E* is dependent) is located, across R_o.

The dependent source F_F1 is described by

```
F_F1 $N_0004 0 VF_F1 50
```

The first two terminals (4, 0) are the output terminals showing where *F* is placed in the circuit. The input terminals are connected in a series loop with components that carry the independent current (upon which *F* is dependent). In the *F_F1* statement, this dependence is shown by naming a voltage source in that loop. This is implied when we draw the loop containing the current I_b to include the voltage *E1*. Refer to the circuit diagram in order to see this more readily.

In the schematics netlist there is an entry

```
VF_F1      N_0003 $N_0005   0V
```

This line was produced by the program to take the place of the listing for *V0* that was needed in Fig. 3.7 in conjunction with the *F* listing that was used in PSpice.

Remember that our results are to represent ac values, rms if you prefer, and note the following:

```
* C:\P\HPARMOD.sch
.OP
.INC "HPARMOD.net"
**** INCLUDING HPARMOD.net ****
* Schematics Netlist *
V_Vs          $N_0001 0 1mV
R_Rs          $N_0001 $N_0002  1k
R_Ri          $N_0002 $N_0003  1.1k
E_E1          $N_0005 0 $N_0004 0 2.5E-4
F_F1          $N_0004 0 VF_F1 50
VF_F1         $N_0003 $N_0005 0V
R_Ro          $N_0004 0  40k
R_RL          $N_0004 0  10k
**** RESUMING HPARMOD.CIR ****
.INC "HPARMOD.als"
**** INCLUDING HPARMOD.als ****
* Schematics Aliases *
.ALIASES
V_Vs          Vs(+=$N_0001 -=0 )
R_Rs          Rs(1=$N_0001 2=$N_0002 )
R_Ri          Ri(1=$N_0002 2=$N_0003 )
E_E1          E1(3=$N_0005 4=0 1=$N_0004 2=0 )
F_F1          F1(3=$N_0004 4=0 )
VF_F1         F1(1=$N_0003 2=$N_0005 )
R_Ro          Ro(1=$N_0004 2=0 )
R_RL          RL(1=$N_0004 2=0 )
.ENDALIASES
**** RESUMING HPARMOD.CIR ****
.probe
.END
****      SMALL SIGNAL BIAS SOLUTION        TEMPERATURE =   27.000 DEG C
NODE   VOLTAGE     NODE   VOLTAGE     NODE   VOLTAGE     NODE   VOLTAGE
($N_0001)    .0010                  ($N_0002) 500.0E-06
($N_0003)-50.00E-06                 ($N_0004)   -.2000
($N_0005)-50.00E-06
    VOLTAGE SOURCE CURRENTS
    NAME          CURRENT
    V_Vs         -5.000E-07
    VF_F1         5.000E-07
    TOTAL POWER DISSIPATION   5.00E-10  WATTS
**** VOLTAGE-CONTROLLED VOLTAGE SOURCES
NAME        E_E1
V-SOURCE   -5.000E-05
I-SOURCE    5.000E-07
**** CURRENT-CONTROLLED CURRENT SOURCES
NAME        F_F1
I-SOURCE    2.500E-05
```

Fig. 15.16 Schematic and output file for h-parameter model.

The voltage-source current through VF_F1 = 5.000E − 7 A. This is the base current. It is easily verified using other known values:

$$I_b = \frac{V_{1,2}}{R_s} = \frac{1 \text{ mV} - 0.5 \text{ mV}}{1 \text{ k}\Omega} = 0.5 \text{ } \mu A$$

The *VOLTAGE-CONTROLLED VOLTAGE SOURCES* item *V-SOURCE* in Fig. 15.16 is the voltage at node 3 = −50 μV, and the item *I-SOURCE* is the current in the *E1* (output) loop. This is also current I_b.

The *CURRENT-CONTROLLED CURRENT SOURCES* item *I-SOURCE* is the current in the output loop of *F1*. Since *F1* has a gain of 50, this current is $50 \cdot I_{b,} = 25$ mA. By current division, the current through R_L is (4/5) (25 μA) = 20 μA. This current is directed upward in the figure and should be shown as such on your circuit diagram. The voltage at node *4* is (−20 μA) (10 kΩ) = −0.2 V, confirming the value given in the output file. It is a negative voltage in keeping with the phase re-versal of the output voltage with respect to V_s.

In summary, creating the circuit diagram using Schematics has been a much more lengthly process than the PSpice analysis of Chapter 3. The extra work may not be justified, but the Schematics method brings out some important points.

FIELD-EFFECT TRANSISTOR CHARACTERISTICS

The evaluation version of the MicroSim software has parts *J2N3819* and *J2N4393* as models for *n*-channel JFETs. In order to obtain a set of output characteristics, draw the circuit shown in Fig. 15.17 and use a setup calling for a nested sweep. The voltage source *VDD* may be swept from 0 to 12 V, in 0.2-V increments, and the voltage source *VGS* may be swept from 0 to 4 V, in 1-V increments. Save the circuit using the name *jfetch.sch.* Run the analysis, and in Probe trace ID(J1). On the screen you will see a family of curves representing drain currents for each of the specified values of V_{GS}. The curve showing the largest currents is for V_{GS} = 0. The next is for V_{GS} = −1 V, and so forth. The pinch-off voltage is at V_{GS} = −3 V. These are shown in Fig. 15.18.

The output-file listing includes a few of the model parameters: *VTO* = −3 is called the threshold (pinch-off) voltage, *BETA* is the transconductance coefficient, and so forth. Appendix D shows all the model parameters for *J (Junction FET)*. The node voltages shown in the output file correspond to the source voltages shown on the drawing. The voltage source currents are shown for those voltages also. The node voltages are slightly different from those shown in Fig. 11.9, because the JFETs are not identical.

Figure 15.19 shows the PSpice window at the completion of the analysis. At the lower part of the window the values 0, 4, 4 refer to the nested sweep values for V*GS;* the values 0, 12, 12 refer to the sweep values for *VDD.*

THE JFET AMPLIFIER

The JFET amplifier circuit of Fig. 11.6 uses the built-in model for the device. As explained in that example, the lines describing such a device might be

```
* C:\P\JFETCH.SCH
** Analysis setup **
.DC LIN V_VDD 0 12V 0.2V
+ LIN V_VGS 0 4V 1V
.OP
* From [SCHEMATICS NETLIST] section of msim.ini:
.lib nom.lib
.INC "JFETCH.net"
**** INCLUDING JFETCH.net ****
* Schematics Netlist *
J_J1          $N_0002 $N_0001 0 J2N3819
V_VDD         $N_0002 0 12V
V_VGS         0 $N_0001 1V

.INC "JFETCH.als"
**** INCLUDING JFETCH.als ****
* Schematics Aliases *
.ALIASES
J_J1          J1(d=$N_0002 g=$N_0001 s=0 )
V_VDD         VDD(+=$N_0002 -=0 )
V_VGS         VGS(+=0 -=$N_0001 )
.ENDALIASES
.probe
.END
****      Junction FET MODEL PARAMETERS
J2N3819
              NJF
        VTO   -3
       BETA   1.304000E-03
     LAMBDA   2.250000E-03
         RD   1
         RS   1

NODE   VOLTAGE      NODE   VOLTAGE      NODE   VOLTAGE      NODE   VOLTAGE
($N_0001)   -1.0000                    ($N_0002)   12.0000
VOLTAGE SOURCE CURRENTS
        NAME          CURRENT
        V_VDD         -5.328E-03
        V_VGS         -4.329E-10
        TOTAL POWER DISSIPATION   6.39E-02   WATTS
**** JFETS
NAME          J_J1
MODEL         J2N3819
ID            5.33E-03
VGS           -1.00E+00
VDS           1.20E+01
```

Fig. 15.17 Schematic and output file for FET characteristics.

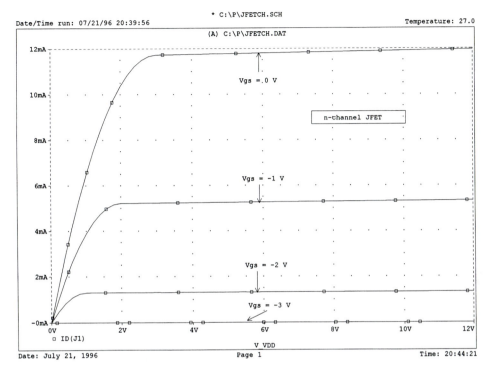

(A) C:\P\JFETCH.DAT

Fig. 15.18 Drain currents for n-channel JFET.

```
JFET 3 1 2 JM
.MODEL JM NJF (RD=10 RS=10 VTO=3V BETA=0.2m)
```

This represents a generic JFET, which we chose to call simply *JM*. If we create this circuit using Schematics we cannot choose a part *JFET;* instead, we may choose one of the available JFETs by name. We can then modify the model by changing its parameters to suit our requirements.

Draw the circuit shown in Fig. 11.6 using *VAC* (for V_i), *C* (for C_b), *R* (for R_g), *J2N3819* (for the *JFET*), *R* (for R_d), *R* (for R_s), *C* (for C_s), and *VDC* (for V_{DD}). When the circuit is completed, it should be like the one shown in Fig. 15.20. Save this circuit as *jfetampl.sch*. Provide for an ac sweep at the single frequency of 5 kHz.

In the example of Chapter 11 the values of some of the JFET parameters were set as shown in the preceding PSpice statement. We need to change some of the parameters of *J2N3819* to match these as closely as possible.

Changing the Parameters of a JFET

Select the *JFET,* then Edit, Model . . . , and click on Edit Instance Model (Text). . . . This will open the window shown in Fig. 15.21. Using the mouse, move to the values that are to be changed and type in the new numbers. In our example *Beta, Rd,* and *Rs* are changed. While the window is open note that a model name, *J2N3819-X,* is used along with a new library, *c:\p\jfetampl.lib*. We will accept these designations, although we could change them if we so desired.

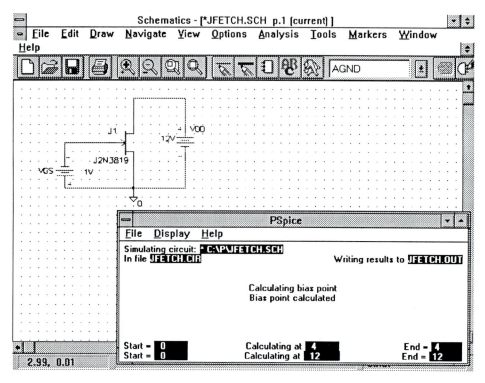

Fig. 15.19   Output characteristics for JFET J2N3819.

Fig. 15.20   The JFET amplifier.

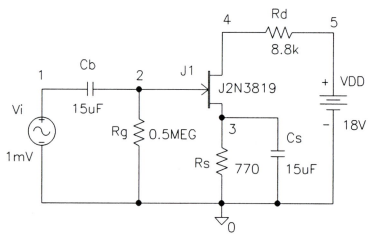

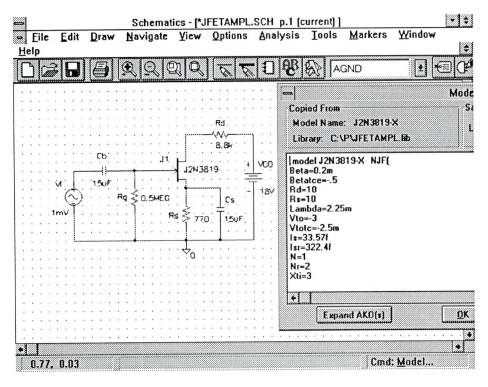

Fig. 15.21 Changing some of the model parameters in Schematics.

After entering the new values, close the window, and run the simulation. In Probe trace and verify the following: I(Rd) = 0.876 μA; V(Cb:2) = 1 mV, which is V(2); V(Rd:1) = 7.73 mV, which is V(4); V(Rs:1) = 1.8 μV, which is V(3). The node numbers have been added by hand to Fig. 15.20. Note that the node numbers of this figure are not the same as those of Fig. 11.6. The results, however, are in close agreement with those shown in Fig. 11.7.

When the PSpice analysis is completed, the PSpice window shows a warning message. See Fig. 15.22, which shows the screen with this message. This does not interfere with the simulation, but it does alert us to look for warnings in the output file. The output file is shown in Fig. 15.23. There you will find the following:

```
WARNING—Unable to find index file (JFETAMPL.ind) for library file JFETAMPL.lib
WARNING—Making new index file (JFETAMPL.ind) for library file JFETAMPL.lib
Index has 1 entries from 1 file(s).
```

These warnings serve to remind us that at the time the analysis is first performed, there is no library file *jfetampl.lib*. There will be one, however, when the analysis is done, along with the file *jfetampl.ind*. The new library is in the *p* directory and contains the following entry:

```
.model J2N3819-X    NJF(Beta=0.2m Betatce=.5 Rd=10 Rs=10 Lambda=2.25m
+Vto=-3
```

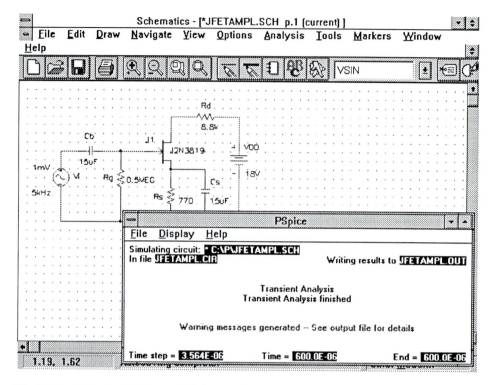

Fig. 15.22   After the PSpice analysis is completed, warning messages may be generated.

```
+Vtotc=-2.5m Is=33.57f Isr=322.4f N=1 Nr=2 Xti=3 Alpha=311.7 Vk=243.6
+Cgd=1.6p M=.3622 Pb=1 Fc=.5 Cgs=2.414p Kf=9.882E-18 Af=1)
*           National        pid=50      case=TO92
*           88-08-01 rmn    Bvmin=25
```

This is the same type of listing that is found in *c:\msimpr63\eval\lib\eval.lib.* The entire evaluation library file contains almost 200 pages of listings for various decades. If you elect to view it in a word processor, be careful to close it without modification, or save it as an ASCII file.

Our new library *jfetampl.lib* reflects the new JFET model, *J2N3819-X,* as well as the new parameter values for *Beta, Rd,* and *Rs.* The new model is called a local model and is available for use only in the schematic *jfetampl.sch.*

The Transient Analysis (JFET Waveshapes)

In order to observe the JFET waveshapes and compare our results with those shown in Fig. 11.8, it will be necessary to replace *VAC* with *VSIN* for *Vi.* Assign the following values: offset voltage = 0, f = 5 kHz, voltage amplitude = 1 mV. Assign values in the analysis setup for a print step of 1 μs, final time of 600 μs, and step ceiling of 1 μs. Run the analysis and in Probe trace V(Rd:1), which is V(4) the drain voltage, and V(Cb:2), which is V(2) the gate voltage. Verify that the output voltage

```
* C:\P\JFETAMPL.SCH
** Analysis setup **
.ac LIN 1 5kHz 5kHz
.OP
.LIB JFETAMPL.lib
* From [SCHEMATICS NETLIST] section of msim.ini:
.lib nom.lib
.INC "JFETAMPL.net"
**** INCLUDING JFETAMPL.net ****
* Schematics Netlist *
V_Vi          $N_0001 0 DC 0V AC 1mV
C_Cb          $N_0001 $N_0002  15uF
R_Rg          $N_0002 0  0.5MEG
J_J1          $N_0004 $N_0002 $N_0003 J2N3819-X
R_Rd          $N_0004 $N_0005  8.8k
R_Rs          $N_0003 0  770
C_Cs          $N_0003 0  15uF
V_VDD         $N_0005 0 18V
.INC "JFETAMPL.als"
**** INCLUDING JFETAMPL.als ****
* Schematics Aliases *
.ALIASES
V_Vi          Vi(+=$N_0001 -=0 )
C_Cb          Cb(1=$N_0001 2=$N_0002 )
R_Rg          Rg(1=$N_0002 2=0 )
J_J1          J1(d=$N_0004 g=$N_0002 s=$N_0003 )
R_Rd          Rd(1=$N_0004 2=$N_0005 )
R_Rs          Rs(1=$N_0003 2=0 )
C_Cs          Cs(1=$N_0003 2=0 )
V_VDD         VDD(+=$N_0005 -=0 )
.ENDALIASES
.probe
.END
WARNING -- Unable to find index file (JFETAMPL.ind) for library file JFETAMPL.lib
WARNING -- Making new index file (JFETAMPL.ind) for library file JFETAMPL.lib
Index has 1 entries from 1 file(s).
****      Junction FET MODEL PARAMETERS
               J2N3819-X
               NJF
        VTO   -3
        BETA  200.000000E-06
        RD    10
        RS    10
   NODE   VOLTAGE      NODE   VOLTAGE      NODE   VOLTAGE      NODE   VOLTAGE
  ($N_0001)    0.0000                    ($N_0002) 605.8E-09
  ($N_0003)    .7719                     ($N_0004)    9.1779
  ($N_0005)   18.0000

     VOLTAGE SOURCE CURRENTS
     NAME          CURRENT
     V_Vi          0.000E+00
     V_VDD        -1.003E-03

     TOTAL POWER DISSIPATION   1.80E-02  WATTS
**** JFETS
NAME       J_J1
MODEL      J2N3819-X
ID         1.00E-03
VGS       -7.72E-01
VDS        8.41E+00
```

Fig. 15.23 Output file for JFET with modified parameters.

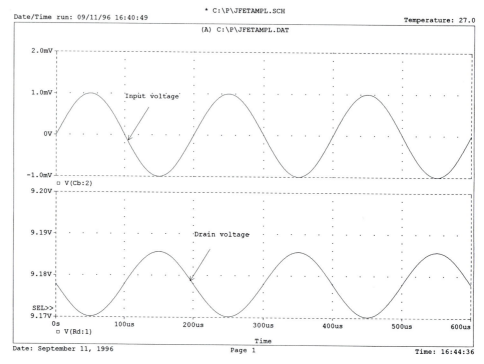

Fig. 15.24   Transient analysis of JFET.

has a peak value of 1.186 mV and a valley value of 9.17 mV. This gives a peak-to-peak value of 15.6 mV, which is 7.8 mV peak. These traces are shown in Fig. 15.24. The values are close to those of Fig. 11.8.

FREQUENCY RESPONSE OF BJT

MicroSim transistor part *Q2N3904* has characteristics that closely resemble those of an actual transistor. Using schematics, draw the circuit of Fig. 15.25, which is based on the circuit of Fig. 10.13 (the current-sensing resistor R_B has been omitted). No attempt was made to preserve the original node sequence. Use *VAC* for V_s. The set-up provided for an ac sweep using 50 points/decade, beginning at 100 kHz and ending at 100 Mhz. The *Q2N3904* model was edited for a β value of 80.

Run the analysis and trace V(Rc:1), the output voltage at the collector. Verify that the midfrequency output voltage is 8.8 mV. Next, obtain a trace of

$$20*log10(V(Rc:1)/8.8mV)$$

Thus the midfrequency gain from the source to the collector is 8.8. Verify that the 3 dB frequency is at about 40.2 MHz. The circuit, PSpice analysis, and trace are shown in Fig. 15.26.

```
* C:\P\HIFREQSC.SCH
.ac DEC 50 100kHz 100MEGHz
.OP
.LIB HIFREQSC.lib
.lib nom.lib
.INC "HIFREQSC.net"
* Schematics Netlist *
Q_Q1          $N_0002 $N_0001 $N_0003 Q2N3904-X
R_R1          $N_0001 $N_0004  40k
R_R2          0 $N_0001  5k
R_Rc          $N_0002 $N_0004  1k
R_Re          0 $N_0003  100
V_Vcc         $N_0004 0 12V
V_Vs          $N_0005 0 DC 0V AC 1mV
C_C1          $N_0006 $N_0001  15uF
R_Rs          $N_0005 $N_0006  100
.INC "HIFREQSC.als"
.probe
****     BJT MODEL PARAMETERS
              Q2N3904-X
              NPN
        IS    6.734000E-15
        BF    80
        CJE   4.493000E-12
        MJE    .2593
        CJC   3.638000E-12
        MJC    .3085
```

NODE	VOLTAGE	NODE	VOLTAGE	NODE	VOLTAGE	NODE	VOLTAGE
($N_0001)	1.0751			($N_0002)	8.2939		
($N_0003)	.3764			($N_0004)	12.0000		
($N_0005)	0.0000			($N_0006)	0.0000		

```
**** BIPOLAR JUNCTION TRANSISTORS
NAME       Q_Q1
MODEL      Q2N3904-X
IB         5.81E-05
IC         3.71E-03
VBE        6.99E-01
VBC       -7.22E+00
VCE        7.92E+00
BETADC     6.38E+01
GM         1.37E-01
CBE        4.78E-11
CBC        1.76E-12
CBX        0.00E+00
CJS        0.00E+00
BETAAC     6.39E+01
```

Fig. 15.25 Schematic and output file for frequency response of BJT.

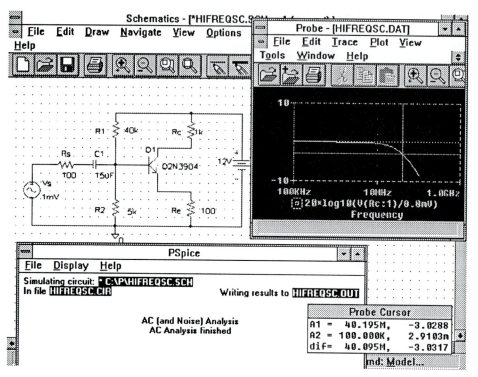

Fig. 15.26 Frequency response of the Q2N3904 (modified) in a *CE* circuit.

16

Operational Amplifiers in Schematics

The ideal op amp was introduced in Chapter 5, Fig. 5.1. It is almost trivial to use this model in Schematics, but we will repeat the problem illustrated in Fig. 5.4 for an introduction to more elaborate models.

Noninverting Ideal Op Amp

Using Schematics, reproduce the circuit of Fig. 5.4, the noninverting ideal op amp, which should appear as shown in Fig. 16.1. The ideal op amp has two components, E and R_i. The voltage-controlled voltage source E has a gain of 200,000 and an input resistance $R_i = 1$ GΩ. Begin with VDC for V_s, then use R for the three resistors, then E for $E1$. Save the drawing as *idealopn.sch*. Run the simulation, then look at the output file. Recall that the ratio of output-to-input voltage is given by $v_o/v_s = 1 + R_2/R_1$. In Chapter 5 we called for the transfer function V(3)/VS, but this ratio is not shown in the output file here. However, since $V_S = 1$ V, the desired gain is the same as the voltage V(3). Verify that this is 9.9995 V. The nodes have marked by hand.

Under the heading VOLTAGE-CONTROLLED VOLTAGE SOURCES, the *V-SOURCE* line shows 10 V under *E_E1*. This refers to the voltage at the output terminals of *E1,* the terminals on the right of the *E* box. The *I-SOURCE* line shows −1 mA under *E_E1*. This refers to the current through the output terminals of *E1*. The minus sign on the current means that the current is in the direction minus to plus inside *E1*. The branches carrying the 1-mA current are identified with current arrows, hand-drawn, in Fig. 16.1. Note that the source current through V_s is negligible.

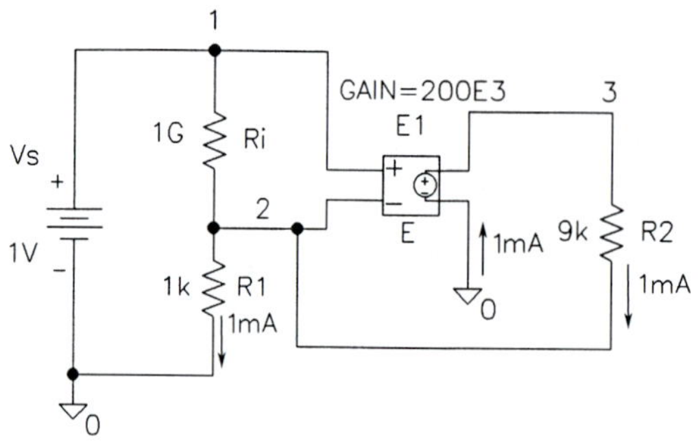

```
* C:\P\IDEALOPN.sch
* Schematics Version 6.3 - April 1996
* Sat Sep 14 17:13:36 1996
** Analysis setup **
.OP
* From [SCHEMATICS NETLIST] section of msim.ini:
.lib nom.lib
.INC "IDEALOPN.net"
**** INCLUDING IDEALOPN.net ****
* Schematics Netlist *
V_Vs          $N_0001 0 1V
R_Ri          $N_0001 $N_0002   1G
R_R1          $N_0002 0  1k
R_R2          $N_0003 $N_0002   9k
E_E1          $N_0003 0 $N_0001 $N_0002 200E3
**** RESUMING IDEALOPN.CIR ****
.INC "IDEALOPN.als"
**** INCLUDING IDEALOPN.als ****
* Schematics Aliases *
.ALIASES
V_Vs          Vs(+=$N_0001 -=0 )
R_Ri          Ri(1=$N_0001 2=$N_0002 )
R_R1          R1(1=$N_0002 2=0 )
R_R2          R2(1=$N_0003 2=$N_0002 )
E_E1          E1(3=$N_0003 4=0 1=$N_0001 2=$N_0002 )
.ENDALIASES
**** RESUMING IDEALOPN.CIR ****
.probe
.END
 NODE    VOLTAGE      NODE    VOLTAGE      NODE    VOLTAGE      NODE    VOLTAGE
 ($N_0001)    1.0000                            ($N_0002)    1.0000
 ($N_0003)    9.9995
    VOLTAGE SOURCE CURRENTS
    NAME          CURRENT
    V_Vs          -5.000E-14
    TOTAL POWER DISSIPATION   5.00E-14   WATTS
**** VOLTAGE-CONTROLLED VOLTAGE SOURCES
NAME          E_E1
V-SOURCE      1.000E+01
I-SOURCE      -1.000E-03
```

Fig. 16.1 Schematic and output file for noninverting op amp.

Op Amp for Voltage-Difference Output

We will use the example of Fig. 5.6 for another example involving the ideal op amp. The node sequence is preserved by placing the elements in this order: $V_a = 3$ V, $R_1 = 5$ kΩ, $R_i = 1$ GΩ, $R_3 = 5$ kΩ, $V_b = 10$ V, $R_2 = 10$ kΩ, $E1$ with a gain of 200,000, and $R_4 = 10$ kΩ. Name the drawing *idealdif.sch* and run the simulation. Recall that in this example the output voltage is supposed to be 2 ($Vb - Va$). The completed circuit is shown in Fig. 16.2 along with the output file. Nodes have been added to the circuit drawing. The results are the same as those shown in Fig. 5.7. Based on node voltages, calculate the current in each resistor.

As an exercise show all nodes on your drawing (they may differ from those shown in this solution), show the voltage at each node, and show magnitudes and directions of all currents.

FREQUENCY RESPONSE OF THE OP AMP

The op amp model of Fig. 5.8 is simple enough to use in Schematics and has the advantage of being a good academic model for understanding the role of a typical op amp in a circuit analysis. We will use the complete circuit of Fig. 5.9 as the first example.

Construct the op amp circuit using the parts and values given in Fig. 5.9 and repeated here: $v_s = 1$ mV, EG with a gain of 1E5, E with a gain of 1, $C = 15.92$ μF, $R_1 = 10$ kΩ, $R_{in} = 1$ MΩ, $R_{i1} = 1$ kΩ, $R_2 = 240$ kΩ, and $RO = 50$ Ω. The Analysis Setup is for a sweep beginning at 100 Hz and ending at 1 MHz, using 40 points/decade. Name the circuit *opampsc.sch*. Figure 16.3 shows the circuit and the output file *opampsc.out*. The output terminal is at the node between $R2$ and RO, which is $R2:2$ in Probe. Trace the gain in decibels as

$$20*\log10(V(R2:2))/V(Vs:+))$$

Note that the Trace, Add ... list in the Probe does not include (Vs:+), which is the same as V(Rin:1). It is helpful to hand-label the nodes for identification as shown in the figure. The results of the trace are shown in Fig. 16.4 and can easily be compared with those of Fig. 5.10.

ACTIVE FILTER

The op amp model introduced above can be used for any of the circuits analyzed in Chapter 5. For the second example, refer to Fig. 5.22 which is a low-pass Butterworth filter. The analysis uses an ideal op amp, consisting of E with a gain $A = 200,000$ and $R_{in} = 1$ MΩ. Use the component values given in Fig. 5.22, saving the file as *butrwrth.sch*. The circuit for Schematics is shown in Fig. 16.5. After looking at the output file, we labeled the nodes by hand. In the output file the reference to E is

```
E_E1      $N_0005 0 $N_0004 $N_0003  −2E5
```

Because the reference to the independent terminals is reversed from that shown in

```
* C:\P\IDEALDIF.sch
.OP
* From [SCHEMATICS NETLIST] section of msim.ini:
.lib nom.lib
.INC "IDEALDIF.net"
**** INCLUDING IDEALDIF.net ****
* Schematics Netlist *
V_Va          $N_0001 0 3V
R_R1          $N_0001 $N_0002  5k
R_Ri          $N_0002 $N_0003  1G
R_R3          $N_0004 $N_0003  5k
V_Vb          $N_0004 0 10V
R_R2          $N_0002 $N_0005  10k
E_E1          $N_0005 0 $N_0002 $N_0003 200E3
R_R4          $N_0003 0  10k
**** RESUMING IDEALDIF.CIR ****
.INC "IDEALDIF.als"
**** INCLUDING IDEALDIF.als ****
* Schematics Aliases *
.ALIASES
V_Va                Va(+=$N_0001 -=0 )
R_R1                R1(1=$N_0001 2=$N_0002 )
R_Ri                Ri(1=$N_0002 2=$N_0003 )
R_R3                R3(1=$N_0004 2=$N_0003 )
V_Vb                Vb(+=$N_0004 -=0 )
R_R2                R2(1=$N_0002 2=$N_0005 )
E_E1                E1(3=$N_0005 4=0 1=$N_0002 2=$N_0003 )
R_R4                R4(1=$N_0003 2=0 )
.ENDALIASES
**** RESUMING IDEALDIF.CIR ****
.probe
.END
NODE    VOLTAGE    NODE    VOLTAGE    NODE    VOLTAGE    NODE    VOLTAGE
($N_0001)    3.0000                 ($N_0002)    6.6667
($N_0003)    6.6667                 ($N_0004)   10.0000
($N_0005)   14.0000
     VOLTAGE SOURCE CURRENTS
     NAME        CURRENT
     V_Va        7.333E-04
     V_Vb       -6.667E-04
     TOTAL POWER DISSIPATION    4.47E-03   WATTS
**** VOLTAGE-CONTROLLED VOLTAGE SOURCES
NAME        E_E1
V-SOURCE    1.400E+01
I-SOURCE   -7.333E-04
```

Fig. 16.2 Schematic and output file for voltage-difference output.

```
* C:\P\OPAMPSC.SCH
** Analysis setup **
.ac DEC 40 100 1MegHz
.OP
* From [SCHEMATICS NETLIST] section of msim.ini:
.lib nom.lib
.INC "OPAMPSC.net"
**** INCLUDING OPAMPSC.net ****
* Schematics Netlist *
V_Vs            $N_0001 0 DC 0V AC 1mV
E_E1            $N_0003 0 $N_0002 $N_0001 1E5
E_E2            $N_0005 0 $N_0004 0 1
C_C             0 $N_0004  15.92uF
R_R1            0 $N_0002  10k
R_Rin           $N_0001 $N_0002  1Meg
R_Ri1           $N_0003 $N_0004  1k
R_R2            $N_0002 $N_0006  240k
R_RO            $N_0005 $N_0006  50
**** RESUMING OPAMPSC.CIR ****
.INC "OPAMPSC.als"
**** INCLUDING OPAMPSC.als ****
* Schematics Aliases *
.ALIASES
V_Vs            Vs(+=$N_0001 -=0 )
E_E1            E1(3=$N_0003 4=0 1=$N_0002 2=$N_0001 )
E_E2            E2(3=$N_0005 4=0 1=$N_0004 2=0 )
C_C             C(1=0 2=$N_0004 )
R_R1            R1(1=0 2=$N_0002 )
R_Rin           Rin(1=$N_0001 2=$N_0002 )
R_Ri1           Ri1(1=$N_0003 2=$N_0004 )
R_R2            R2(1=$N_0002 2=$N_0006 )
R_RO            RO(1=$N_0005 2=$N_0006 )
.ENDALIASES
.probe
.END
```

Fig. 16.3 Schematic and output file for frequency response.

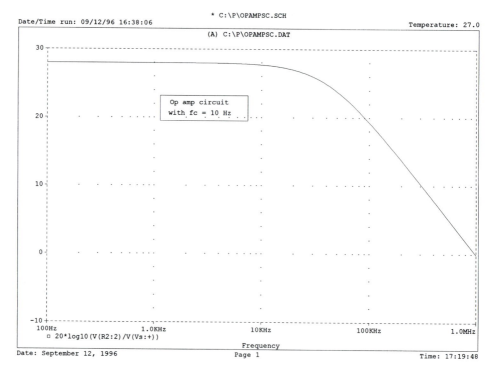

* C:\P\OPAMPSC.SCH

Temperature: 27.0

(A) C:\P\OPAMPSC.DAT

Op amp circuit
with fc = 10 Hz

□ 20*log10(V(R2:2)/V(Vs:+))

Frequency

Date: September 12, 1996   Page 1   Time: 17:19:48

Fig. 16.4 Op amp circuit with f_e = 10 Hz.

Fig. 5.22, the gain is shown with the minus sign for consistency. In Probe trace V(R2:2), which is the output voltage. Its value is 1.586 mV. Then trace

$$20*\log10(V(R2:2)/1.586mV)$$

This plot will be identical with that of Fig. 5.24 and is shown in Fig. 16.6. If you plot instead

$$20*\log10(V(R2:2)/(V(Vi:+)*1.586mv))$$

which is similar to the expression used in Chapter 5, you will not get the expected results. The plot will be shifted on the Y-axis by 60 dB!

Active Resonant Band-Pass Filter

We will use the circuit in Fig. 5.30 as another active filter example. In Schematics draw the circuit using the components shown in the figure. Represent the op as ideal, using E with a gain of 200,000 and R_{in} = 1 MΩ. After completing the drawing, compare yours with the one shown in Fig. 16.7. Save the file as *actvbpfr.sch,* then set up for an ac sweep using 40 points/decade beginning at f = 1 kHz and ending at f = 1 MHz. In Probe decide which voltages represent output and input, then obtain a dB plot. Compare your plot with Fig. 16.8. At midfrequency, f_o = 11.22 kHz, the filter shows a gain of 5.994 dB. The schematics netlist shows the output and input nodes as 5 and 1, respectively.

Fig. 16.5 Schematic and output file for active filter.

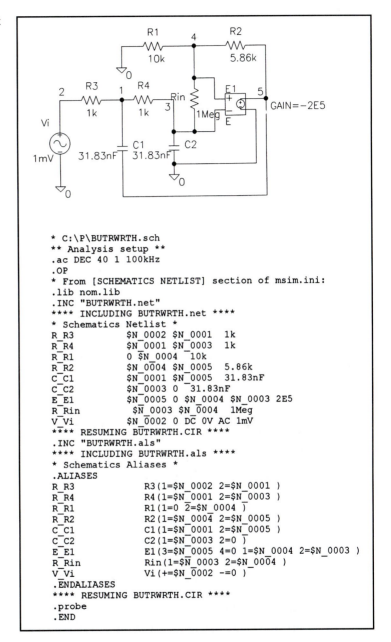

```
* C:\P\BUTRWRTH.sch
** Analysis setup **
.ac DEC 40 1 100kHz
.OP
* From [SCHEMATICS NETLIST] section of msim.ini:
.lib nom.lib
.INC "BUTRWRTH.net"
**** INCLUDING BUTRWRTH.net ****
* Schematics Netlist *
R_R3          $N_0002 $N_0001  1k
R_R4          $N_0001 $N_0003  1k
R_R1          0 $N_0004  10k
R_R2          $N_0004 $N_0005  5.86k
C_C1          $N_0001 $N_0005  31.83nF
C_C2          $N_0003 0  31.83nF
E_E1          $N_0005 0 $N_0004 $N_0003 2E5
R_Rin         $N_0003 $N_0004  1Meg
V_Vi          $N_0002 0 DC 0V AC 1mV
**** RESUMING BUTRWRTH.CIR ****
.INC "BUTRWRTH.als"
**** INCLUDING BUTRWRTH.als ****
* Schematics Aliases *
.ALIASES
R_R3          R3(1=$N_0002 2=$N_0001 )
R_R4          R4(1=$N_0001 2=$N_0003 )
R_R1          R1(1=0 2=$N_0004 )
R_R2          R2(1=$N_0004 2=$N_0005 )
C_C1          C1(1=$N_0001 2=$N_0005 )
C_C2          C2(1=$N_0003 2=0 )
E_E1          E1(3=$N_0005 4=0 1=$N_0004 2=$N_0003 )
R_Rin         Rin(1=$N_0003 2=$N_0004 )
V_Vi          Vi(+=$N_0002 -=0 )
.ENDALIASES
**** RESUMING BUTRWRTH.CIR ****
.probe
.END
```

PART *uA741*

In Fig. 5.9 we used our own model for the op amp in order to test its frequency response. The model is very good for frequency-sensitive studies, but it does not include parts for many of the components actually contained in a commercial op amp. Refer to a text op operational amplifiers, such as Coughlin and Driscoll, and

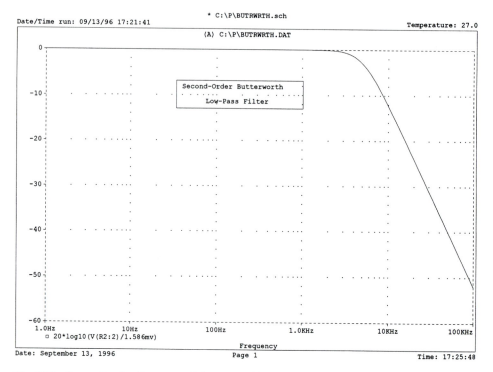

* C:\P\BUTRWRTH.sch

Fig. 16.6   Second-order Butterworth low-pass filter.

find the schematic of an actual op amp. You will see that it would be impractical to attempt to show its entire circuit.

Part *uA741,* available in PSpice and Schematics, is a reasonably accurate model that we might prefer to use instead of our own model. It will require the use of a pair of dc sources in addition to the other external components.

Frequency Response of the *uA741*

We will use the values used in the example at the beginning of this chapter again so that we may compare our model with the more complete model of the *uA741*. In Schematics, begin by selecting part *uA741* in the library *eval.slb*. When the part appears on the drawing board, you will see that there are seven terminals and they have *already* been numbered. This is obviously a puzzle when encountered for the first time and may remain a point of unnecessary confusion.

Subroutine-Node Designation

It will help if you are aware from the beginning that these numbers are contained in a subroutine and that they do not apply to the main circuit numbers. Refer to the section in *Using a Subcircuit for the Op Amp* in Chapter 5 for a review of this topic. Also note in Fig. 5.12 the use of nodes *a, b,* and *c* in the subcircuit but not in

Fig. 16.7 Schematic and output file for active resonant band-pass filter.

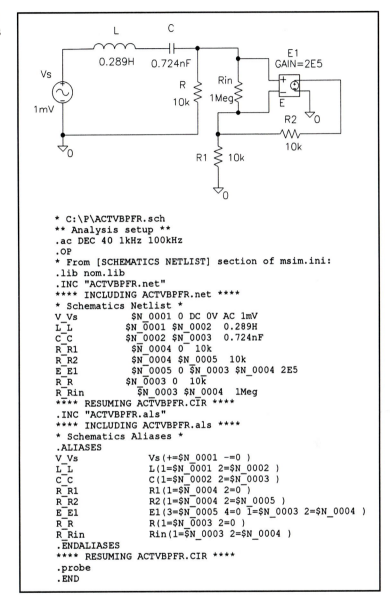

```
* C:\P\ACTVBPFR.sch
** Analysis setup **
.ac DEC 40 1kHz 100kHz
.OP
* From [SCHEMATICS NETLIST] section of msim.ini:
.lib nom.lib
.INC "ACTVBPFR.net"
**** INCLUDING ACTVBPFR.net ****
* Schematics Netlist *
V_Vs          $N_0001 0 DC 0V AC 1mV
L_L           $N_0001 $N_0002  0.289H
C_C           $N_0002 $N_0003  0.724nF
R_R1          $N_0004 0  10k
R_R2          $N_0004 $N_0005  10k
E_E1          $N_0005 0 $N_0003 $N_0004 2E5
R_R           $N_0003 0  10k
R_Rin         $N_0003 $N_0004  1Meg
**** RESUMING ACTVBPFR.CIR ****
.INC "ACTVBPFR.als"
**** INCLUDING ACTVBPFR.als ****
* Schematics Aliases *
.ALIASES
V_Vs          Vs(+=$N_0001 -=0 )
L_L           L(1=$N_0001 2=$N_0002 )
C_C           C(1=$N_0002 2=$N_0003 )
R_R1          R1(1=$N_0004 2=0 )
R_R2          R2(1=$N_0004 2=$N_0005 )
E_E1          E1(3=$N_0005 4=0 1=$N_0003 2=$N_0004 )
R_R           R(1=$N_0003 2=0 )
R_Rin         Rin(1=$N_0003 2=$N_0004 )
.ENDALIASES
**** RESUMING ACTVBPFR.CIR ****
.probe
.END
```

the main file listing. Specifically, the nodes shown on the *uA741* (nodes 1 through 7) will not be the nodes in the actual circuit file.

Now, continue to place parts in the circuit as shown in Fig. 16.9, using *VAC* for V_s, *VDC* for $V+$ and $V-$, and *R* for R_1 and R_2. When wiring the circuit be sure that there is simply a crossing of wires at the left side of R_2 rather than a connection. Compare your drawing with that of Fig. 16.9, then save it with the name *opamp.sch*. Set the analysis for an ac sweep using 40 points/decade, between 100 Hz and 1 MHz. Run the simulation and plot

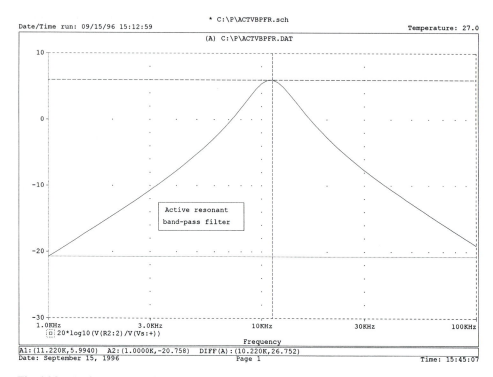

Fig. 16.8 Active resonant band-pass filter.

$$20*\log10(V(U1{:}OUT)/V(Vs{:}+))$$

Compare this plot with the one obtained in the previous example using our own model in Schematics. Verify that the midfrequency gain is 27.957 dB. The results are shown in Fig. 16.10. Identification of the output and input terminals was easy enough, but there are some things about the simulation worthy of further study.

The nodes that were created by placing the parts in the drawing have been labeled by hand and placed in circles. This will distinguish the actual circuit nodes from the subroutine nodes that came from using the *uA741* symbol. Incidentally, we see that nodes *2* and *4* are the same in the output listing and on the op amp symbol. In the output file *opamp.out* the op amp is described in the netlist as

```
X_U1     $N_0001 $N_0002 $N_0003 $N_0004 $N_0005 uA741
```

Nodes *1* through *5* are our nodes (shown in circles), not those placed with the symbol. The first two (*1, 2*) are for the noninverting and inverting inputs, respectively. The next two (*3, 4*) are for the plus and minus dc supplies, respectively. The last (*5*) is for the output terminal. This is followed by the identifying symbol *uA741*. The alias statement for the op amp is

```
X_U1     U1(+=$N_0001  -=$N_0002 V+=$N_0003 v-=$N_0004 OUT=$N_0005)
```

```
* C:\P\OPAMP.SCH
** Analysis setup **
.ac DEC 40 100 1MegHz
.OP
* From [SCHEMATICS NETLIST] section of msim.ini:
.lib nom.lib
.INC "OPAMP.net"
**** INCLUDING OPAMP.net ****
* Schematics Netlist *
X_U1          $N_0001 $N_0002 $N_0003 $N_0004 $N_0005 uA741
V_Vs          $N_0001 0 DC 0V AC 1mV
V_V+          $N_0003 0 15V
V_V-          0 $N_0004 15V
R_R1          0 $N_0002  10k
R_R2          $N_0002 $N_0005  240k
**** RESUMING OPAMP.CIR ****
.INC "OPAMP.als"
**** INCLUDING OPAMP.als ****
* Schematics Aliases *
.ALIASES
X_U1             U1(+=$N_0001 -=$N_0002 V+=$N_0003 V-=$N_0004 OUT=$N_0005 )
V_Vs             Vs(+=$N_0001 -=0 )
V_V+             V+(+=$N_0003 -=0 )
V_V-             V-(+=0 -=$N_0004 )
R_R1             R1(1=0 2=$N_0002 )
R_R2             R2(1=$N_0002 2=$N_0005 )
.ENDALIASES
**** RESUMING OPAMP.CIR ****
.probe
.END
****      Diode MODEL PARAMETERS
****       BJT MODEL PARAMETERS
**** VOLTAGE-CONTROLLED CURRENT SOURCES
**** VOLTAGE-CONTROLLED VOLTAGE SOURCES
**** CURRENT-CONTROLLED CURRENT SOURCES
**** CURRENT-CONTROLLED VOLTAGE SOURCES
```

Fig. 16.9 Schematic and output file uA741 op amp.

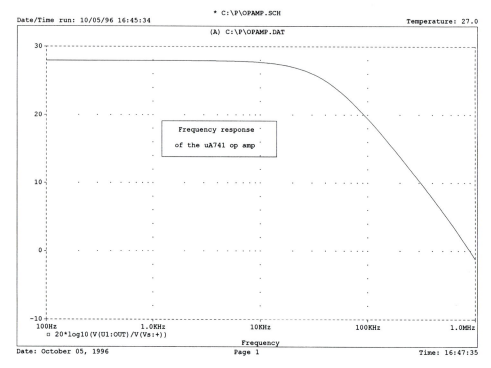

Fig. 16.10   Frequency response of the uA741 op amp.

The *X* notation refers to the subroutine that develops the model for *U1*, the plus and minus symbols refer to the input terminals, and so forth. Only a small part of the output file is shown in Fig. 16.9, indicating that diodes, transistors, voltage-controlled current sources (*G*), voltage-controlled voltage sources (*E*), current-controlled current sources (*F*), and current-controlled voltage sources (*H*) are all involved in the op amp model.

It is simpler to use the model shown in Fig. 5.9 for the op amp when frequency response is a factor. The ideal op amp, using *E* and R_i was shown in Fig. 5.2(b) and elsewhere in Chapter 5.

The *uA741* as a Level Detector

The circuit in Fig. 16.11 is used as a level detector for the input voltage *V1*. Draw this circuit in Schematics, beginning with *VPWL* for *V1*, *VDC* for *Vref*, *V+*, and *V−*. Then add *RL* and the circuit ground. Name the circuit *leveldet.sch.*

Dbl-clk on the *V1* symbol, producing a window into which time and voltage pairs (up to 10) are entered. Enter the pairs as follows: (*0s, 0V*), (*0.2s, 3V*), (*0.4s,5V*), (*0.6s, −5V*), (*0.8s, −3V*), (*1s, 0V*). In order to test the circuit response, use a transient analysis with 1-ms steps to a final time of 1 s.

Analyze the circuit and in Probe trace both the input voltage V(V1:+) and the output voltage V(U1:OUT). Refer to Fig. 16.12 and note that the cursor has been placed just ahead of where the input voltage reaches 3 V. Here the output voltage is

```
* C:\P\LEVELDET.SCH
** Analysis setup **
.tran 1ms 1s 0 1ms
.OP
* From [SCHEMATICS NETLIST] section of msim.ini:
.lib nom.lib
.INC "LEVELDET.net"
**** INCLUDING LEVELDET.net ****
* Schematics Netlist *
V_V1          $N_0001 0
+PWL 0s 0V 0.2s 3V 0.4s 5V 0.6s -5V 0.8s -3V 1s 0V
V_Vref        $N_0002 0 3V
V_V+          $N_0003 0 9V
V_V-          0 $N_0004 9V
X_U1          $N_0002 $N_0001 $N_0003 $N_0004 $N_0005 uA741
R_RL          0 $N_0005 4.8k
**** RESUMING LEVELDET.CIR ****
.INC "LEVELDET.als"
**** INCLUDING LEVELDET.als ****
* Schematics Aliases *
.ALIASES
V_V1          V1(+=$N_0001 -=0 )
V_Vref        Vref(+=$N_0002 -=0 )
V_V+          V+(+=$N_0003 -=0 )
V_V-          V-(+=0 -=$N_0004 )
X_U1          U1(+=$N_0002 -=$N_0001 V+=$N_0003 V-=$N_0004 OUT=$N_0005 )
R_RL          RL(1=0 2=$N_0005 )
.ENDALIASES
**** RESUMING LEVELDET.CIR ****
.probe
.END
****      Diode MODEL PARAMETERS
             X_U1.dx
****      BJT MODEL PARAMETERS
             X_U1.qx
```

NODE	VOLTAGE	NODE	VOLTAGE	NODE	VOLTAGE	NODE	VOLTAGE
($N_0001)	0.0000			($N_0002)	3.0000		
($N_0003)	9.0000			($N_0004)	-9.0000		
($N_0005)	8.6136			(X_U1.10)	2.3597		

Fig. 16.11 Schematic and output file for uA741.

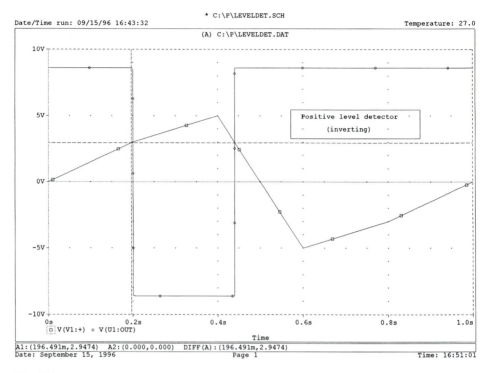

Fig. 16.12   Positive level detector (inverting).

8.6136 (slightly less than V+ = 9 V). When the input voltage rises above 3 V, the output voltage drops to −8.6136 V, remaining at that level until the input voltage falls below 3 V, where the process is repeated. Since the input voltage V_i is connected to the inverting input of the op amp, when the input exceeds *Vref,* the output voltage drops.

The nodes have again been hand-marked and placed in circles to distinguish them from the terminals of the op amp. Remember that these terminal numbers are for the op amp subcircuit, not the main input file. The lines in the schematics netlist describing *V1* are

```
V_V1      $N_0001 0
+PWL 0s 0v 0.2 3V 0.4s 5V 0.6s −5V 0.8s −3V 1s 0V
```

Check the time, voltage pairs for agreement with our setup requirements. The customary parentheses enclosing the pairs are missing, but they are not necessary. The output file shows the node voltages at the beginning of the transient analysis. Note that V(5) = 8.6136 V, as was verified using Probe and the cursor.

Op Amp Phase Shifter

An op amp phase shifter may be constructed from a *uA741* using resistors and a capacitor, as shown in Fig. 16.13. Draw the circuit in Schematics, using *VSIN* for *Vi* in order to obtain a transient plot in Probe. The angle of phase shift is given by

```
    * C:\P\PHSHIFTR.sch
    ** Analysis setup **
    .tran 20us 2ms 0 2us
    .OP
    * From [SCHEMATICS NETLIST] section of msim.ini:
    .lib nom.lib
    .INC "PHSHIFTR.net"
    **** INCLUDING PHSHIFTR.net ****
    * Schematics Netlist *
    V_Vi        $N_0001 0
    +SIN 0V 2V 1kHz 0 0 0
    R_R1        $N_0001 $N_0002  100k
    R_R2        $N_0002 $N_0003  100k
    R_R3        $N_0001 $N_0004  15.9k
    R_RL        $N_0003 0  4.8k
    C_C1        $N_0004 0  0.01uF
    X_U1        $N_0004 $N_0002 $N_0005 $N_0006 $N_0003 uA741
    V_V+        $N_0005 0 12V
    V_V-        0 $N_0006 12V
    **** RESUMING PHSHIFTR.CIR ****
    .INC "PHSHIFTR.als"
    **** INCLUDING PHSHIFTR.als ****
    * Schematics Aliases *
    .ALIASES
    V_Vi            Vi(+=$N_0001 -=0 )
    R_R1            R1(1=$N_0001 2=$N_0002 )
    R_R2            R2(1=$N_0002 2=$N_0003 )
    R_R3            R3(1=$N_0001 2=$N_0004 )
    R_RL            RL(1=$N_0003 2=0 )
    C_C1            C1(1=$N_0004 2=0 )
    X_U1            U1(+=$N_0004 -=$N_0002 V+=$N_0005 V-=$N_0006 OUT=$N_0003 )
    V_V+            V+(+=$N_0005 -=0 )
    V_V-            V-(+=0 -=$N_0006 )
    .ENDALIASES
    **** RESUMING PHSHIFTR.CIR ****
    .probe
    .END
```

Fig. 16.13 Schematic and output file for op amp phase shifter.

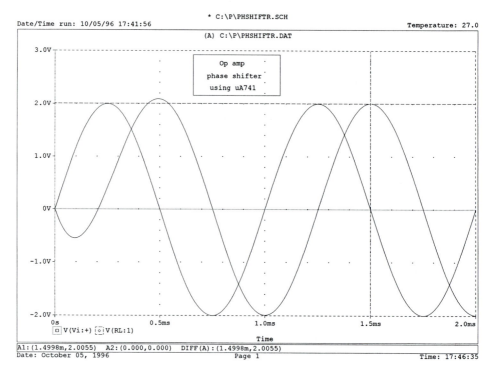

Fig. 16.14   Op amp phase shifter using μA741.

$$\theta = -2 \arctan 2\pi f R_1 C_1$$

The value of R_3 is related to the other elements by

$$R_3 = - \tan \frac{(\theta/2)}{2\pi f C_1}$$

For this example, a phase shift of $-90°$ is desired—that is, the output voltage should lag the input voltage by 90°. Using $C_1 = 0.01$ μF and $f = 1$ kHz gives $R_3 = 15.9$ kΩ. The values for R_1 and R_2 should be the same; a convenient value of 100 kΩ is chosen to complete the circuit. In Analysis, Setup . . . provide for an ac sweep on two full cycles. The file is saved with the name *phshiftr.sch*, and the simulation yields the results shown in Fig. 16.14. To check the phase shift, go beyond the first cycle and note that the peak of the input is at $t \approx 1.24$ ms, whereas the peak of the output is at $t \approx 1.5$ ms, which corresponds to 90°. Because a transient analysis was performed, the output wave contains some distortion. Note the overshoot on the first positive cycle.

As an exercise, print the schematic of this circuit along with the schematics netlist and aliases, then label the nodes (*1, 2*, etc.) in the main circuit. The node order may vary from the given list, depending on which parts are entered first in Schematics.

Fig. 16.15 Schematic and output file for phase shifter.

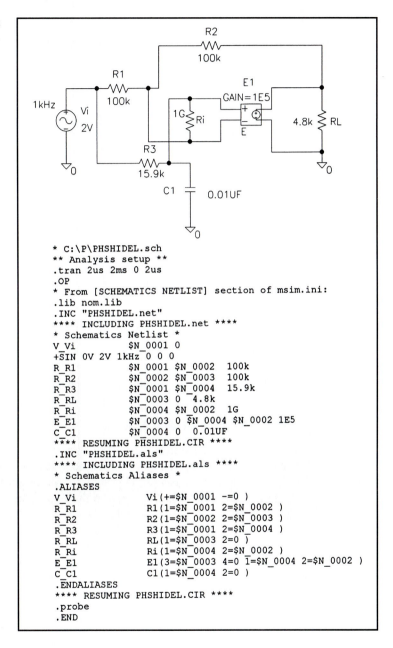

```
* C:\P\PHSHIDEL.sch
** Analysis setup **
.tran 2us 2ms 0 2us
.OP
* From [SCHEMATICS NETLIST] section of msim.ini:
.lib nom.lib
.INC "PHSHIDEL.net"
**** INCLUDING PHSHIDEL.net ****
* Schematics Netlist *
V_Vi           $N_0001 0
+SIN 0V 2V 1kHz 0 0 0
R_R1           $N_0001 $N_0002  100k
R_R2           $N_0002 $N_0003  100k
R_R3           $N_0001 $N_0004  15.9k
R_RL           $N_0003 0  4.8k
R_Ri           $N_0004 $N_0002  1G
E_E1           $N_0003 0 $N_0004 $N_0002 1E5
C_C1           $N_0004 0  0.01UF
**** RESUMING PHSHIDEL.CIR ****
.INC "PHSHIDEL.als"
**** INCLUDING PHSHIDEL.als ****
* Schematics Aliases *
.ALIASES
V_Vi           Vi(+=$N_0001 -=0 )
R_R1           R1(1=$N_0001 2=$N_0002 )
R_R2           R2(1=$N_0002 2=$N_0003 )
R_R3           R3(1=$N_0001 2=$N_0004 )
R_RL           RL(1=$N_0003 2=0 )
R_Ri           Ri(1=$N_0004 2=$N_0002 )
E_E1           E1(3=$N_0003 4=0 1=$N_0004 2=$N_0002 )
C_C1           C1(1=$N_0004 2=0 )
.ENDALIASES
**** RESUMING PHSHIDEL.CIR ****
.probe
.END
```

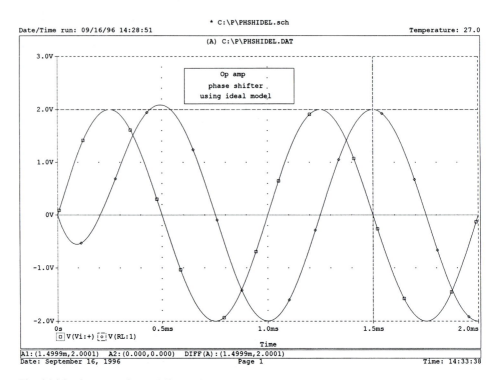

Fig. 16.16   Op amp phase shifter using ideal model.

Phase Shift Using an Ideal Op Amp

The simple phase-shifting circuit does not require the use of the actual *uA741* in Schematics. To keep the analysis simple, you may prefer to use the circuit shown in Fig. 16.15, which is based on Fig. 5.8. Use this circuit to perform the same simulation as that given above. You will see in the Probe that plots of V(Vi: +) and V(RL:1) gives traces are virtually identical with the *uA741* analysis. The new plot is shown in Fig. 16.16.

17

Other Topics in Schematics

Several other topics may be of interest to the user of PSpice and Schematics. Some of these are more useful, however, in the production version of the MicroSim software, as is the case with the Stimulus Editor.

THE STIMULUS EDITOR

Various stimuli, either voltages or currents, are used in PSpice. Voltage stimuli consisting of exponential, pulse, piecewise-linear, frequency-modulated, and sine-wave sources were introduced in Chapter 4. All these are available in the evaluation version of the software. The Stimulus Editor offers a handy method of choosing a stimulus, then setting its attributes and displaying its waveshape on the screen. The attributes of the stimulus can be easily modified for various conditions, and the effect on the waveshape can be seen immediately. However, in the evaluation version of the software, only the sine-wave stimulus can be edited by using the Stimulus Editor.

For a simple example, begin to draw a circuit in Schematics by choosing Draw, Get New Part . . ., then select *VSTIM* (for a voltage stimulus). Place the part on the screen, then select the part with a dbl-clk. You will be given a chance to set the attributes only after the new circuit is given a name. Choose *stimcase.sch,* and continue. Two windows will appear on the screen with the Stimulus Editor in the background. The foreground window will allow you to set the Stimulus Attributes. Note that the type stimulus is shown as *sin*. This is the only stimulus that can be edited in this fashion using the Stimulus Editor. Set the following: Offset Value: "1 V", Amplitude: "1 V", Frequency: "1 kHz", Time Delay: "0", Damping Factor "0", and

Phase Angle: "90". When you select the *Apply* button, a sample of the sine wave will appear on the screen. Verify that it meets the required specifications. Refer to Fig. 17.1 which shows the stimulus source, the editor, and the attributes. You may add other parts to this ac circuit if you desire, but we will study the Stimulus Editor by using the circuit of Fig. 2.1.

A Circuit Example

Begin a new drawing by selecting the part *VSTIM*. Place the part on the drawing, then add a resistor and an inductor as shown in Fig. 17.2. Values are $R = 1.5\ \Omega$, $L = 5.3$ mH. The stimulus is to be a sine wave with an amplitude of 1 V at $f = 60$ Hz. Use the Stimulus Editor to set the attributes after naming the drawing *stimulrl.sch*. The use of a sine wave for the source voltage requires that we perform a transient analysis. Set the final time at 20 ms or greater, using a print step and print ceiling of your choice.

   In Probe trace V(V1:+), which is the source voltage; V(L:1), which is the inductor voltage; and I(R), which is the circuit current (in the cw direction). Refer to Fig. 17.3. Near the beginning of the second cycle verify the *Y*-axis crossings: V(V1:+) at 16.667 ms, V(L:1) at 14.985 ms, and I(R) at 19.123 ms. Draw a phasor diagram of these three quantities based on converting these *times* to *angles*. Use the source phasor as the reference at 0°. Refer to Fig. 2.2 for a sample phasor diagram.

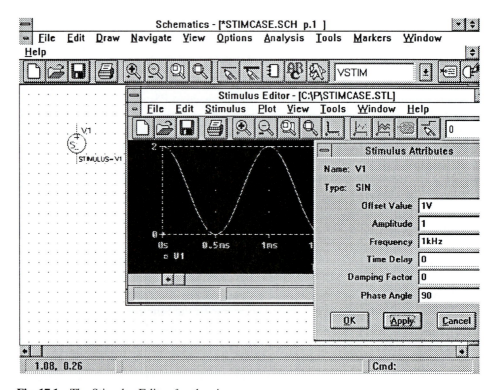

Fig. 17.1   The Stimulus Editor for the sine-wave source.

Fig. 17.2 Schematic and output file using the Stimulus Editor.

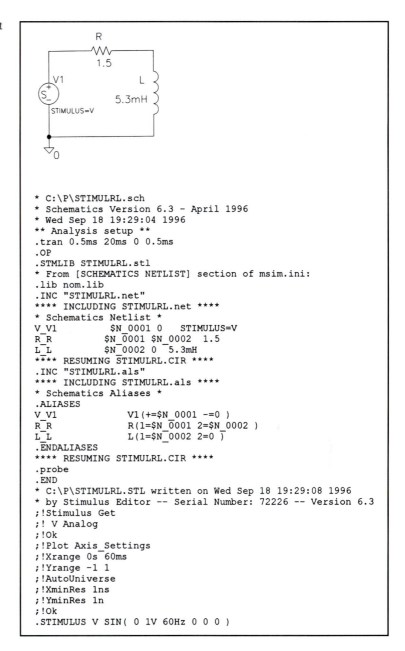

```
* C:\P\STIMULRL.sch
* Schematics Version 6.3 - April 1996
* Wed Sep 18 19:29:04 1996
** Analysis setup **
.tran 0.5ms 20ms 0 0.5ms
.OP
.STMLIB STIMULRL.stl
* From [SCHEMATICS NETLIST] section of msim.ini:
.lib nom.lib
.INC "STIMULRL.net"
**** INCLUDING STIMULRL.net ****
* Schematics Netlist *
V_V1          $N_0001 0     STIMULUS=V
R_R           $N_0001 $N_0002  1.5
L_L           $N_0002 0   5.3mH
**** RESUMING STIMULRL.CIR ****
.INC "STIMULRL.als"
**** INCLUDING STIMULRL.als ****
* Schematics Aliases *
.ALIASES
V_V1              V1(+=$N_0001 -=0 )
R_R               R(1=$N_0001 2=$N_0002 )
L_L               L(1=$N_0002 2=0 )
.ENDALIASES
**** RESUMING STIMULRL.CIR ****
.probe
.END
* C:\P\STIMULRL.STL written on Wed Sep 18 19:29:08 1996
* by Stimulus Editor -- Serial Number: 72226 -- Version 6.3
;!Stimulus Get
;! V Analog
;!Ok
;!Plot Axis_Settings
;!Xrange 0s 60ms
;!Yrange -1 1
;!AutoUniverse
;!XminRes 1ns
;!YminRes 1n
;!Ok
.STIMULUS V SIN( 0 1V 60Hz 0 0 0 )
```

Figure 17.2 includes the output file listing. The last line of the listing is

```
.STIMULUS V SIN(0 1V 60Hz 0 0 0 )
```

This describes the stimulus as a voltage, a sine-wave source with zero offset, an amplitude of 1 V, a frequency of 60 Hz, zero time delay, damping factor, and phase. The output file shows

```
.STMLIB STIMULRL.stl
```

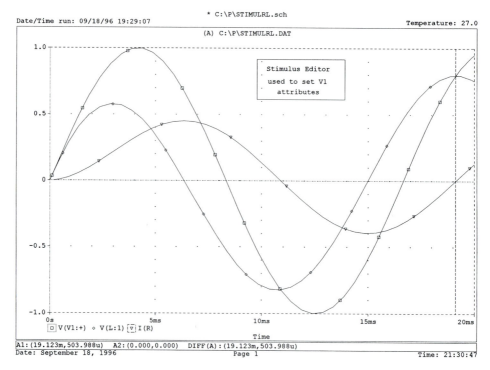

Fig. 17.3   Stimulus Editor used to set VI attributes.

which references the new library. The content of this library is shown toward the end of the output file. It also shows when it was created. The information in the stimulus file shows the type stimulus, the *X*-range and the *Y*-range, among other things.

In summary, the Stimulus Editor is useful when you want to look at the stimulus and possibly make changes before running an analysis. It also provides a convenient means of modifying the stimulus for another simulation.

Using a Bubble

The familiar circuit of Fig. 2.1 is repeated in Fig. 17.4. The source is VSIN (not created in the Stimulus Editor) = 1 V at f = 60 Hz, R = 1.5 Ω, and L = 5.3 mH. The circuit contains only one thing new, the *BUBBLE*. Use Draw, Get New Part . . . for this part, rotate it three times, and place it at the junction between *R* and *L*. The purpose of the bubble is to give this node a special name, which in this case is chosen to be *Vout*. Save this drawing as *plainrl.sch*. In Analysis, Setup . . . call for a transient analysis with print step = 0.5 ms, final time = 20 ms, and a step ceiling = 0 .2 ms. Run the simulation and in Probe use Trace, Add . . . and note that *Vout* is listed. Now look at the output file in Fig. 17.4 and notice the lines for *R* and *L*:

```
R_R      $N_0001 Vout 1.5
L_L      Vout 0 5.3mH
```

The node that would otherwise have been called *$N0002* is simply called *Vout* instead. This designation is shown in both the netlist and the aliases. Designating

Fig. 17.4 Schematic and output file using a BUBBLE.

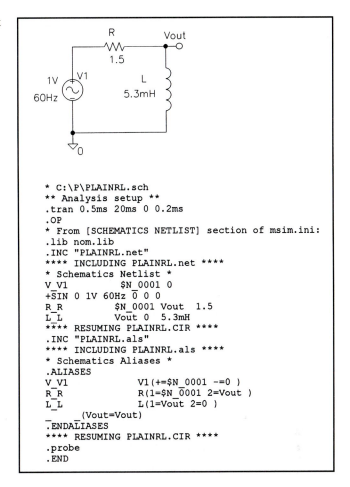

```
* C:\P\PLAINRL.sch
** Analysis setup **
.tran 0.5ms 20ms 0 0.2ms
.OP
* From [SCHEMATICS NETLIST] section of msim.ini:
.lib nom.lib
.INC "PLAINRL.net"
**** INCLUDING PLAINRL.net ****
* Schematics Netlist *
V_V1          $N_0001 0
+SIN 0 1V 60Hz 0 0 0
R_R           $N_0001 Vout  1.5
L_L           Vout 0  5.3mH
**** RESUMING PLAINRL.CIR ****
.INC "PLAINRL.als"
**** INCLUDING PLAINRL.als ****
* Schematics Aliases *
.ALIASES
V_V1               V1(+=$N_0001 -=0 )
R_R                R(1=$N_0001 2=Vout )
L_L                L(1=Vout 2=0 )
       _(Vout=Vout)
.ENDALIASES
**** RESUMING PLAINRL.CIR ****
.probe
.END
```

nodes in this fashion has the obvious advantage of letting you identify points of interest that are to be used in Probe. Thus you might now plot V(Vout) rather than V(L:1), although either expression would produce the same results.

Labeling a Wire Segment

In addition to using a bubble to identify a node, you may label a wire segment with a name. Dbl-clk on a wire segment to bring up the Set Attribute Value window. For example, in the *RL* circuit dbl-clk on a wire segment on the left side of *R*. In the window text box type "Pt_1". This label will show on the drawing and will be available when the simulation takes place. Now instead of *$N_0001,* you will see the node called *Pt_1* in the netlist.

A Temperature Sweep

Draw the circuit shown in Fig. 17.5, which includes a dc voltage source, $R_1 = 4.8$ kΩ, and the *D1N4002* diode. The purpose of this analysis is to show the effect of tem-

```
* C:\P\DIODESWP.SCH
** Analysis setup **
.DC LIN V_V1 0 30V 0.1
+ LIN TEMP 17 47 10
.OP
* From [SCHEMATICS NETLIST] section of msim.ini:
.lib nom.lib
.INC "DIODESWP.net"
**** INCLUDING DIODESWP.net ****
* Schematics Netlist *
V_V1          $N_0001 0 20V
R_R1          $N_0001 $N_0002   4.8k
D_D           $N_0002 0 D1N4002
**** RESUMING DIODESWP.CIR ****
.INC "DIODESWP.als"
**** INCLUDING DIODESWP.als ****
* Schematics Aliases *
.ALIASES
V_V1          V1(+=$N_0001 -=0 )
R_R1          R1(1=$N_0001 2=$N_0002 )
D_D           D(1=$N_0002 2=0 )
.ENDALIASES
**** RESUMING DIODESWP.CIR ****
.probe
.END
****        Diode MODEL PARAMETERS
                 D1N4002
            IS   14.110000E-09
             N   1.984
            ISR  100.000000E-12
            IKF  94.81
             BV  100.1
            IBV  10
             RS    .03389
****        SMALL SIGNAL BIAS SOLUTION        TEMPERATURE IS SWEPT
   NODE   VOLTAGE     NODE   VOLTAGE     NODE   VOLTAGE     NODE   VOLTAGE
  ($N_0001)   20.0000                 ($N_0002)     .6445
     VOLTAGE SOURCE CURRENTS
     NAME          CURRENT
     V_V1          -4.032E-03
     TOTAL POWER DISSIPATION   8.06E-02  WATTS
****  DIODES
 NAME          D_D
 MODEL         D1N4002
 ID            4.03E-03
 VD            6.45E-01
 REQ           1.27E+01
 CCAP          3.74E-07
```

Fig. 17.5   Schematic and output file for temperature sweep.

perature on the circuit. In Analysis, Setup ... provide for a voltage sweep of *V1* from 0 to 30 V in 0.1-V increments, then provide for a nested sweep of temperature beginning at 17 C, ending at 47 C, in increments of 10 C. Figure 17.6 shows the window for the temperature sweep. Save the circuit as *diodeswp.sch*.

Run the simulation and in Probe let the *X*-axis represent V(D:1), then trace I(D). A family of four curves will be produced. The one on the left is clearly for the highest temperature, while the one on the right is for the lowest temperature.

The input file *diodeswp.cir* contains the sweep statement

```
.DC LIN V_V1 0 30V 0.1
+ LIN TMEP 17 47 10
```

After the simulation, the results tell us SMALL SIGNAL BIAS SOLUTION TEMPERATURE IS SWEPT, and the node voltages show the single-temperature result (*27* C implied) for V(2) = 0.6445 V and a current of *4.032* mA. In Probe change the *X*-axis variable to V(D:1), then obtain a trace of I(D). It is easily verified that when I(D) = 4.03 mA, V(D:1) = 0.644 V. Click on the third curve from the left to move the cursor to that region of the plot. The plot, with modified *X*- and *Y*- axis ranges, is shown in Fig. 17.7.

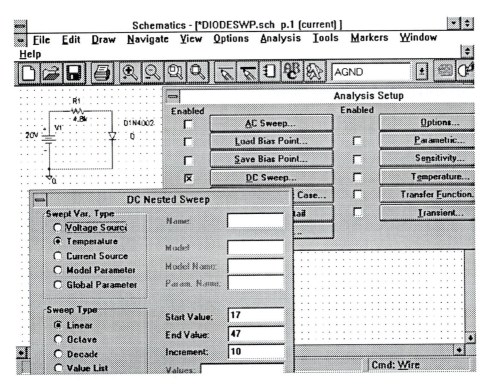

Fig. 17.6 Diode characteristics with temperature sweep of 17, 27, 37, and 47 degrees Celsius.

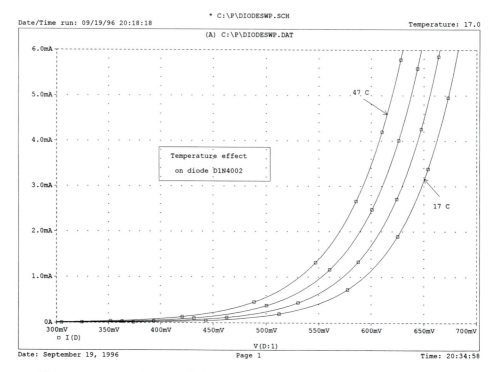

Date/Time run: 09/19/96 20:18:18   * C:\P\DIODESWP.SCH   Temperature: 17.0

(A) C:\P\DIODESWP.DAT

Date: September 19, 1996   Page 1   Time: 20:34:58

Fig. 17.7 Temperature effect on diode.

Changing the Zener-Breakdown Voltage

Because only one zener diode, the *1N750*, is available in the evaluation version of PSpice, you will probably want to change its breakdown voltage. This will allow you to effectively substitute another zener diode into your circuit for analysis purposes.

In Schematics, draw the circuit shown in Fig. 17.8. Save the schematic with the name *zener.sch*. Select the zener symbol and modify its breakdown voltage by choosing Edit, Model ... Edit Instance Model (Text). ... Move down in the window until the value of *Bv* appears on the screen. Type in the new value "4.8 V" that will be used in the simulation. See Fig. 17.9 for the Model Editor window. In order to test the results, set up the analysis for a linear dc sweep of *V1* beginning at −1 V and ending at 15 V, in 0.05-V increments.

Run the simulation, and in Probe, change the *X*-axis for a plot of V(D:2). This is the voltage between node *2* and ground. Obtain a trace of I(R), the current (cw) in the loop. The resulting plot is shown in Fig. 17.10. The breakdown voltage, around 4.8 V, is clearly shown in the results. In the output file, the warning messages indicate that this circuit has been previously, perhaps with different diode parameters, which were stored in the file *zener.lib*.

Now, if you have a more elaborate circuit, such as the diode-ended clipper using avalanche diodes, shown in Fig. 9.14, you can return to the schematic *zener.sch*, add the necessary parts, remove any unwanted parts, then carry out the simulation.

```
                                    * C:\P\ZENER.SCH
                                    * Schematics Version 6.3 - April 1996
                                    * Sat Sep 21 15:07:26 1996
                                    ** Analysis setup **
                                    .DC LIN V_V1 -1V 15V 0.05
                                    .OP
                                    .LIB ZENER.lib
                                    * From [SCHEMATICS NETLIST] section of msim.ini:
                                    .lib nom.lib
                                    .INC "ZENER.net"
                                    **** INCLUDING ZENER.net ****
* Schematics Netlist *
V_V1            $N_0001 0 15V
R_R             $N_0001 $N_0002  500
D_D             0 $N_0002 D1N750-X
**** RESUMING ZENER.CIR ****
.INC "ZENER.als"
**** INCLUDING ZENER.als ****
* Schematics Aliases *
.ALIASES
V_V1                V1(+=$N_0001 -=0 )
R_R                 R(1=$N_0001 2=$N_0002 )
D_D                 D(1=0 2=$N_0002 )
.ENDALIASES
**** RESUMING ZENER.CIR ****
.probe
.END
WARNING -- Library file ZENER.lib has changed since index file ZENER.ind was
created.
WARNING -- The timestamp changed from Sun Jul 28 17:12:26 1996 to Sat Sep 21
15:17:40 1996.
WARNING -- Making new index file (ZENER.ind) for library file ZENER.lib
Index has 1 entries from 1 file(s).
****      Diode MODEL PARAMETERS
              D1N750-X
          IS   880.500000E-18
         ISR   1.859000E-09
          BV   4.8
         IBV   .020245
         NBV   1.6989
        IBVL   1.955600E-03
        NBVL   14.976
          RS   .25
         CJO   175.000000E-12
          VJ   .75
           M   .5516
        TBV1   -21.277000E-06
  NODE   VOLTAGE     NODE   VOLTAGE     NODE   VOLTAGE     NODE   VOLTAGE
($N_0001)   15.0000                 ($N_0002)    4.8011
     VOLTAGE SOURCE CURRENTS
     NAME         CURRENT
     V_V1         -2.040E-02
     TOTAL POWER DISSIPATION   3.06E-01  WATTS
**** DIODES
NAME         D_D
MODEL        D1N750-X
ID           -2.04E-02
VD           -4.80E+00
REQ          2.35E+00
CAP          5.80E-11
```

Fig. 17.8 Schematic and output file for zener diode.

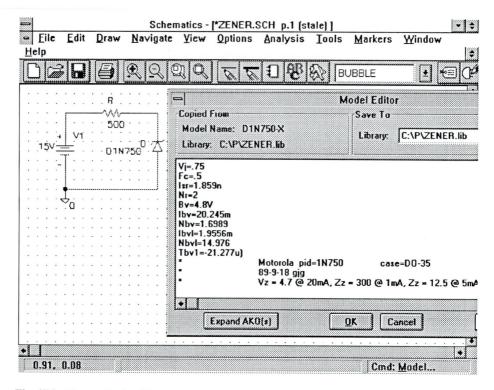

Fig. 17.9 Zener diode with modified breakdown voltage.

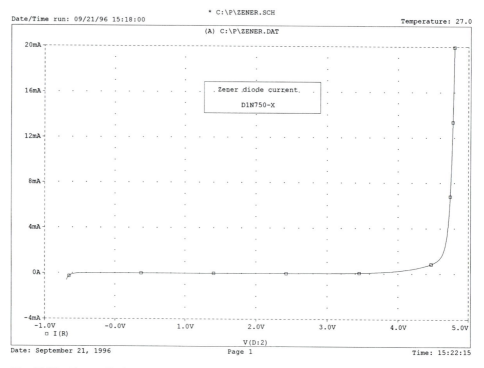

Fig. 17.10 Zener diode current.

Using the Breakout Zener Diode

In the previous example, the *1N750* zener diode was used with a modified breakdown voltage. MicroSim offers another means of modifying parameters of parts through the use of "breakout" parts. In Schematics, select Draw, Get New Part . . . Libraries . . ., then select *breakout.slb* for the library. The Library Browse shows a parts listing of devices, most of which involve the (partial) word "break," as shown in Fig. 17.11. For the zener diode breakout device, select "DbreakZ", and place this symbol on a new drawing. It will have the name *DBreak,* which is to be changed momentarily. Save the drawing with the name *zenerd.sch,* and with the diode selected, choose Edit, Model . . ., Edit Instance Model. In the Model Editor window you will see

```
.model Dbreak-X D
```

which identifies this as a breakout diode. Change this line to read

```
.model Dz3_5 D (BV=3.5V)
```

Click OK to leave the editor. At this time you have created a new library, *zenerd.lib,* that contains the entry as you have just described. For more information, select Analysis, Library and Include Files . . . and note that the window Library Files includes our library *zenerd.lib* among its listings as shown in Fig. 17.12. This simply

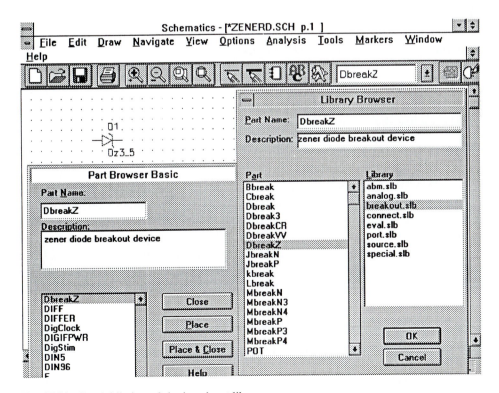

Fig. 17.11 Partial listing of the breakout library.

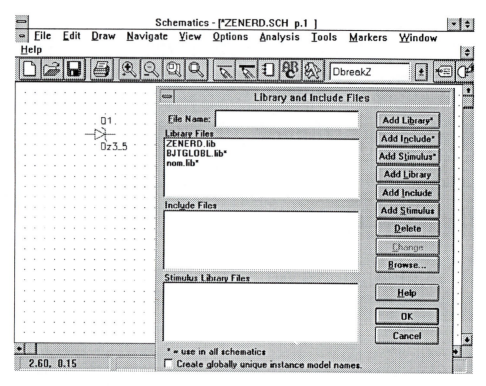

Fig. 17.12   The Library and Include Files window.

means that if we continue to build a circuit in the drawing *zenerd.sch,* the library containing the new zener diode will be available. Accordingly, the output file listing will show a line that reads

```
.LIB zenerd.lib
```

So far, this procedure is similar to that used in other examples where parts such as *D1N750* and *Q2N3904* have been modified for use in a particular schematic. The breakout parts differ in that they can be given new model names as well as certain parameters when we use "Edit Instance Model (text). . . ." Parameters that we do not specify will assume default values. It is helpful to give the breakout parts descriptive names; for example "Dz3_5" suggests a zener diode with a breakdown voltage of 3.5 V. The further advantage of breakout parts is that we can create other schematics and use the new parts in them as well.

Using the Breakout Model in Another Schematic

Construct the circuit shown in Fig. 17.13 using the part *DbreakZ* for the zener diode. After the parts are in place, name the file *zbreak.sch.* Select the diode, then Edit, Model . . ., Change Model Reference. . . . Type "Dz3_5", which is the name of the

```
                  R1
                 /\/\/\
                  880
     +   V1         D1
12V ═══         ═════      * C:\P\ZBREAK.sch
     ─                     ** Analysis setup **
                           .DC LIN V_V1 -1V 15V 0.05V
        Dz3_5              .OP
                           .LIB zenerd.lib
                           .LIB spcbreak.lib
   ▽                       .LIB ZBREAK.lib
   0                       * From [SCHEMATICS NETLIST] section of msim.ini:
                           .lib BJTGLOBL.lib
                           .lib nom.lib
                           .INC "ZBREAK.net"
                           **** INCLUDING ZBREAK.net ****

* Schematics Netlist *
V_V1            $N_0001 0 12V
R_R1            $N_0001 $N_0002  880
D_D1            0 $N_0002 Dz3_5
**** RESUMING ZBREAK.CIR ****
.INC "ZBREAK.als"
**** INCLUDING ZBREAK.als ****
* Schematics Aliases *
.ALIASES
V_V1            V1(+=$N_0001 -=0 )
R_R1            R1(1=$N_0001 2=$N_0002 )
D_D1            D1(1=0 2=$N_0002 )
.ENDALIASES
**** RESUMING ZBREAK.CIR ****
.probe
.END
WARNING -- Unable to find index file (zenerd.ind) for library file zenerd.lib
WARNING -- Making new index file (zenerd.ind) for library file zenerd.lib
Index has 1 entries from 1 file(s).

    ****      Diode MODEL PARAMETERS
                 Dz3_5
            IS    10.000000E-15
            BV    3.5

   NODE  VOLTAGE    NODE  VOLTAGE     NODE   VOLTAGE     NODE    VOLTAGE
 ($N_0001)  12.0000                 ($N_0002)   3.9741
      VOLTAGE SOURCE CURRENTS
      NAME          CURRENT
      V_V1          -9.120E-03

      TOTAL POWER DISSIPATION   1.09E-01  WATTS

**** DIODES
NAME          D_D1
MODEL         Dz3_5
ID            -9.12E-03
VD            -3.97E+00
REQ           2.84E+00
CAP           0.00E+00
```

Fig. 17.13 Schematic and output file for breakout diode.

model defined just prior to this example. Next, just to see what the device characteristics are, choose Edit, Model . . ., Edit Instance Model (Text). . . . An attempt will be made to find the model, and when it cannot be found, you will be taken back to the circuit drawing. The reason for this is that we must first provide for the library to be referenced in this schematic.

Select Analysis, Library and Include Files . . ., then in the File Name window: type "zenerd.lib". Do not press the Enter key, but rather, click the mouse on Add Library, then OK. This means that our schematic zbreak.sch can use any of the parts in the library zenerd.lib. Although there is only one part in this library now, more parts can be added at any time.

To complete a simple analysis, use a dc sweep of V1 beginning at −1 V and ending at 15 V, with an increment of 0.05 V. After a successful simulation you may want to trace the zener diode characteristic, as we did previously with a similar circuit. Figure 17.13 shows the output file. Note that among the libraries referenced we find zenerd.lib, which is the defining library for the diode Dz3_5.

The Global Libraries

In the example just completed, we selected Analysis, Library and Include Files . . . to add the library zenerd.lib to the library file list. The button Add Library was chosen after the file name was inserted. Figure 17.12 shows another button, Add Library*, that we may choose instead of or in addition to the former button. The asterisk is used to indicate that the File Name is intended to be global. Whenever we perform a simulation, global libraries will automatically be included in the file listings, and a search of these libraries will take place so that any referenced parts may be located. We could accomplish the same thing by inserting the appropriate line in the circuit file just before running the analysis in PSpice by selecting the PSpice icon.

Noise Analysis

In a typical ac circuit, noise is produced by random molecular activity in the resistors, diodes, and transistors. The resistor and semiconductor models used in PSpice are designed with this in mind. For an example, draw the circuit of Fig. 17.14 in Schematics using VAC for the source with a magnitude of 10 mV and Q2N3904 for the transistor. Modify the attributes of the transistor such that $h_{FE} = 100$. The input point for the circuit is the ac source VS, and the output point is at the bubble Vout.

To prepare for the noise analysis select Analysis, Setup . . . and begin with the AC Sweep . . . button. The window is titled AC Sweep and Noise Analysis. Use these values: choose Decade sweep, Pts/Decade: "20", Start Freq: "10 Hz", End Freq: "100 MegHz", Output: "V(Vout)", I/V: "Vs", Interval: "100", and select Noise Enabled. These are shown in Fig. 17.15. Save the circuit as selfbs1.sch.

Now we are ready to perform the simulation. When the analysis is completed, trace V(ONOISE), then add another Y-axis and trace V(INOISE). Compare your results with those shown in Fig. 17.16. Note that in the useful range of the circuit, near our sample frequency of 5 kHz, the output noise is 171.6 nV, and the input noise is 1.136 nV. The latter value is not the noise associated with the source Vs but

Fig. 17.14 Schematic and output file for noise analysis.

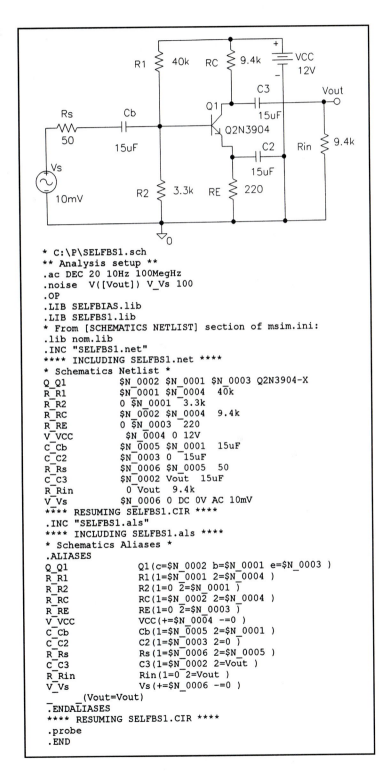

```
* C:\P\SELFBS1.sch
** Analysis setup **
.ac DEC 20 10Hz 100MegHz
.noise V([Vout]) V_Vs 100
.OP
.LIB SELFBIAS.lib
.LIB SELFBS1.lib
* From [SCHEMATICS NETLIST] section of msim.ini:
.lib nom.lib
.INC "SELFBS1.net"
**** INCLUDING SELFBS1.net ****
* Schematics Netlist *
Q_Q1            $N_0002 $N_0001 $N_0003 Q2N3904-X
R_R1            $N_0001 $N_0004   40k
R_R2            0 $N_0001   3.3k
R_RC            $N_0002 $N_0004   9.4k
R_RE            0 $N_0003   220
V_VCC           $N_0004 0 12V
C_Cb            $N_0005 $N_0001   15uF
C_C2            $N_0003 0   15uF
R_Rs            $N_0006 $N_0005   50
C_C3            $N_0002 Vout   15uF
R_Rin           0 Vout   9.4k
V_Vs            $N_0006 0 DC 0V AC 10mV
**** RESUMING SELFBS1.CIR ****
.INC "SELFBS1.als"
**** INCLUDING SELFBS1.als ****
* Schematics Aliases *
.ALIASES
Q_Q1               Q1(c=$N_0002 b=$N_0001 e=$N_0003 )
R_R1               R1(1=$N_0001 2=$N_0004 )
R_R2               R2(1=0 2=$N_0001 )
R_RC               RC(1=$N_0002 2=$N_0004 )
R_RE               RE(1=0 2=$N_0003 )
V_VCC              VCC(+=$N_0004 -=0 )
C_Cb               Cb(1=$N_0005 2=$N_0001 )
C_C2               C2(1=$N_0003 2=0 )
R_Rs               Rs(1=$N_0006 2=$N_0005 )
C_C3               C3(1=$N_0002 2=Vout )
R_Rin              Rin(1=0 2=Vout )
V_Vs               Vs(+=$N_0006 -=0 )
        (Vout=Vout)
.ENDALIASES
**** RESUMING SELFBS1.CIR ****
.probe
.END
```

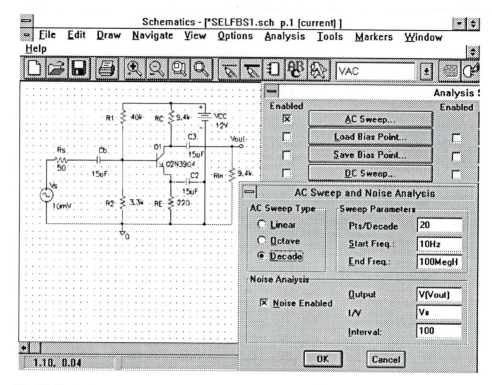

Fig. 17.15 Performing a noise analysis on a transistor amplifier circuit.

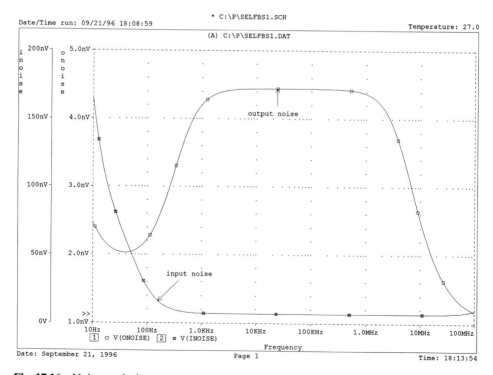

Fig. 17.16 Noise analysis.

represents the equivalent noise from a source at the location of *Vs* that would produce the output noise if the circuit itself were noiseless.

The output and input voltages can be traced in like manner. Begin another plot, this time using V(Vout) and V(Vs:+). This produces traces of the output and input voltages over the selected range of frequencies. At the typical operating frequency of 5 kHz, it is seen that the output-voltage magnitude is 1.51 V compared with the input-voltage magnitude of 10 mV, as shown in Fig. 17.17. Obviously, the output voltage falls at low and high frequencies.

Only the netlist and aliases are shown in Fig. 17.14. Another portion of the output file is shown in Fig. 17.18. The noise analysis is tabulated only for *f* = 10 Hz and *f* = 1 MHz. This was controlled by the Interval: "100" setting in the noise analysis. If this value had been made 10 instead, then the noise analysis tabulation would include *f* = 10 Hz, 316 Hz, 1 kHz, 3.16 kHz, and so forth, producing *36* pages of output! If the interval value is set at 20, the noise analysis tabulation includes *f* = 10 Hz, 100 Hz, 1 kHz, 10 kHz, and so forth.

It is difficult to evaluate the results of a noise analysis on a simple circuit. Unless there are multiple-stage circuits or other circuits that will be used for comparison, the values listed for noise voltages will have uncertain meaning. Note that both transistor-squared noise voltages and resistor-squared noise voltages are produced for each chosen frequency. Also, the listing contains total output noise voltage as well as the transfer function value *Vout/Vs*. The last item shown is equivalent input noise at the source, which was previously mentioned.

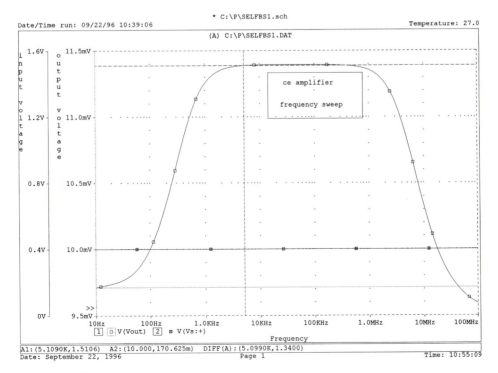

Fig. 17.17 CE amplifier frequency sweep.

```
****        BJT MODEL PARAMETERS
            Q2N3904-X
            NPN
        IS    6.734000E-15
        BF   100
**** BIPOLAR JUNCTION TRANSISTORS
NAME            Q_Q1
MODEL           Q2N3904-X
IB              1.39E-05
IC              9.36E-04
VBE             6.63E-01
VBC            -2.33E+00
VCE             3.00E+00
BETADC          6.73E+01
BETAAC          7.14E+01
****        NOISE ANALYSIS                TEMPERATURE =    27.000 DEG C
    FREQUENCY =  1.000E+01 HZ
**** TRANSISTOR SQUARED NOISE VOLTAGES (SQ V/HZ)
            Q_Q1
RB      5.570E-17
RC      1.250E-24
RE      0.000E+00
IBSN    1.900E-15
IC      1.505E-16
IBFN    0.000E+00
TOTAL   2.107E-15
**** RESISTOR SQUARED NOISE VOLTAGES (SQ V/HZ)
            R_R1       R_R2       R_RC       R_RE       R_Rs       R_Rin
TOTAL   1.361E-16  1.650E-15  3.817E-17  1.176E-15  2.413E-16  3.865E-17
**** TOTAL OUTPUT NOISE VOLTAGE         =  5.387E-15 SQ V/HZ
                                        =  7.339E-08 V/RT HZ

        TRANSFER FUNCTION VALUE:
        V(Vout)/V_Vs                    =  1.706E+01
        EQUIVALENT INPUT NOISE AT V_Vs =  4.301E-09 V/RT HZ
    FREQUENCY =  1.000E+06 HZ
**** TRANSISTOR SQUARED NOISE VOLTAGES (SQ V/HZ)
            Q_Q1
RB      3.773E-15
RC      6.866E-22
RE      0.000E+00
IBSN    3.552E-16
IC      5.682E-15
IBFN    0.000E+00
TOTAL   9.810E-15
**** RESISTOR SQUARED NOISE VOLTAGES (SQ V/HZ)
            R_R1       R_R2       R_RC       R_RE       R_Rs       R_Rin
TOTAL   2.283E-17  2.767E-16  3.342E-17  1.932E-22  1.826E-14  3.342E-17
**** TOTAL OUTPUT NOISE VOLTAGE         =  2.844E-14 SQ V/HZ
                                        =  1.686E-07 V/RT HZ

        TRANSFER FUNCTION VALUE:
        V(Vout)/V_Vs                    =  1.484E+02
        EQUIVALENT INPUT NOISE AT V_Vs =  1.136E-09 V/RT HZ
```

Fig. 17.18 Noise analysis continued.

As an exercise run the analysis again using an interval of 10 in the noise analysis, then load the output file *selfbs1.out* into a word processor. Print only the tabulated results for $f = 10$ kHz, and compare your results with those of Fig. 17.19. At this typical operating frequency compare the noise voltage levels of the transistor and resistors with those shown at $f = 10$ Hz and $f = 1$ MHz in Fig. 17.18. Also note that the ratio *Vout/Vs* = 151.4 agrees with the results obtained in Probe.

```
FREQUENCY =  1.000E+04 HZ
 **** TRANSISTOR SQUARED NOISE VOLTAGES (SQ V/HZ)
            Q_Q1
  RB        3.926E-15
  RC        4.921E-23
  RE        0.000E+00
  IBSN      3.701E-16
  IC        5.912E-15
  IBFN      0.000E+00
  TOTAL     1.021E-14
 **** RESISTOR SQUARED NOISE VOLTAGES (SQ V/HZ)
            R_R1        R_R2        R_RC        R_RE        R_Rs       R_Rin
  TOTAL    2.376E-17  2.880E-16  3.483E-17  2.010E-18  1.900E-14  3.483E-17
 **** TOTAL OUTPUT NOISE VOLTAGE           =   2.959E-14 SQ V/HZ
                                           =   1.720E-07 V/RT HZ

       TRANSFER FUNCTION VALUE:
         V(Vout)/V_Vs                      =   1.514E+02
       EQUIVALENT INPUT NOISE AT V_Vs =    1.136E-09 V/RT HZ
```

Fig. 17.19 Noise analysis, second run.

Harmonic Content in Output Voltage

Continuing our study of the amplifier in the drawing *selfbs1.sch*, we would like to compare the input sine-wave voltage with the output sine-wave to see whether there is any clipping or other form of distortion. In order to carry out the analysis, change the source voltage from *VAC* to *VSIN*. Set the offset voltage to zero, the amplitude to 10 mV, and the frequency to 5 kHz. Display the values on the drawing as shown in Fig. 17.20. Use the File, Save As . . . option to rename the file *selfbs2.sch*. In Analysis Setup . . . select Transient . . . and provide for a print step of 20 ms, a final time of 0.2 ms, and a step ceiling of 100 ms. Next, under Fourier Analysis, select Enable Fourier with Center Frequency: "5 kHz", Number of harmonics: "5", and Output Vars.: "V(Vout)".

Run the simulation and in Probe trace V(Vout) and V(Vs:+). After appropriate labeling, compare the results with Fig. 17.21. At first glance, the output seems to be a replica of the input, with 180° phase reversal. Use Probe to find the first negative peak and the first positive peak of the output voltage. These are −1.61 V and 1.372 V, respectively. They differ because of the fact that we are looking at the first cycle of a transient response.

In the laboratory, an oscilloscope would not display the transients, and we would see only the distortion. This distortion is indicative of harmonic content and is best documented in the output file, a portion of which is shown in Fig. 17.20. Harmonic no. 1 (fundamental) is at $f = 1$ kHz, with a Fourier component of 1.491 V. Comparing this magnitude with those of the second through the fifth harmonics, we see that higher harmonics have little influence. If we simply add the magnitudes of the listed harmonics, the result is 1.61 V. In the earlier analysis using *VAC* for the source type, use found that Vout = 1.51 V. The 1.61 V value is obviously not correct for the output voltage, since it neglects the phase angles of the various harmonics. Note that the total harmonic distortion is less than 7.7%.

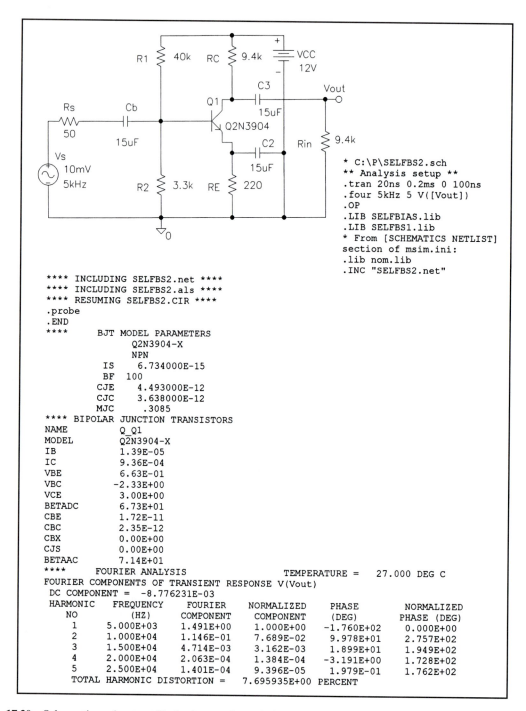

```
                                              + ⎓ VCC
     R1 ⋛ 40k    RC ⋛ 9.4k              ⎓ 12V
                                          ─
                              C3              Vout
                      Q1      ┤├─────────────○
  Rs      Cb                  15uF
  ─WW──────┤├────●──┤ ╲ Q1
  50              │    ╲ Q2N3904
  Vs     15uF     │      ┤ C2          Rin ⋛ 9.4k
 (∿)              │      ┤├───
  10mV            │      15uF
  5kHz    R2 ⋛ 3.3k    RE ⋛ 220
  ─────────────────●──────●──────●
                   ▽ 0
```

* C:\P\SELFBS2.sch
** Analysis setup **
.tran 20ns 0.2ms 0 100ns
.four 5kHz 5 V([Vout])
.OP
.LIB SELFBIAS.lib
.LIB SELFBS1.lib
* From [SCHEMATICS NETLIST]
section of msim.ini:
.lib nom.lib
.INC "SELFBS2.net"

```
**** INCLUDING SELFBS2.net ****
**** INCLUDING SELFBS2.als ****
**** RESUMING SELFBS2.CIR ****
.probe
.END
****       BJT MODEL PARAMETERS
                 Q2N3904-X
                   NPN
        IS    6.734000E-15
        BF   100
       CJE    4.493000E-12
       CJC    3.638000E-12
       MJC    .3085
**** BIPOLAR JUNCTION TRANSISTORS
NAME       Q_Q1
MODEL      Q2N3904-X
IB         1.39E-05
IC         9.36E-04
VBE        6.63E-01
VBC       -2.33E+00
VCE        3.00E+00
BETADC     6.73E+01
CBE        1.72E-11
CBC        2.35E-12
CBX        0.00E+00
CJS        0.00E+00
BETAAC     7.14E+01
****       FOURIER ANALYSIS                    TEMPERATURE =   27.000 DEG C
FOURIER COMPONENTS OF TRANSIENT RESPONSE V(Vout)
 DC COMPONENT = -8.776231E-03
 HARMONIC   FREQUENCY    FOURIER    NORMALIZED     PHASE        NORMALIZED
    NO         (HZ)     COMPONENT   COMPONENT      (DEG)       PHASE (DEG)
     1      5.000E+03   1.491E+00   1.000E+00   -1.760E+02     0.000E+00
     2      1.000E+04   1.146E-01   7.689E-02    9.978E+01     2.757E+02
     3      1.500E+04   4.714E-03   3.162E-03    1.899E+01     1.949E+02
     4      2.000E+04   2.063E-04   1.384E-04   -3.191E+00     1.728E+02
     5      2.500E+04   1.401E-04   9.396E-05    1.979E-01     1.762E+02
     TOTAL HARMONIC DISTORTION =   7.695935E+00 PERCENT
```

Fig. 17.20 Schematic and output file for harmonic analysis.

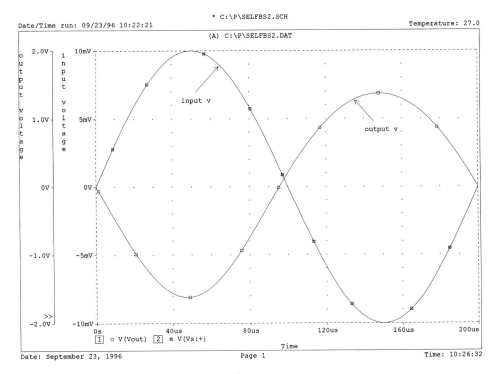

Fig. 17.21 Harmonic content in output voltage.

Using a Variable Parameter

Construct the circuit shown in Fig. 17.22 using the following values: $V = 20$ V, $R_1 = 300$ Ω, $R_2 = 300$ Ω, $R_3 = 10$ kΩ, $R_L = 2.5$ kΩ. The value for R_L is shown differently in the figure in anticipation of a dc sweep, where its value will vary. Dbl-clk on the symbol for R_L, then for its value substitute "{Rvar}". The braces are used to signify that the value is not fixed; the name *Rvar* could be anything of our choosing.

The next step involves choosing a new part. Choose Draw, Get New Part . . . and type in "param". Place this symbol anywhere on the drawing, then note that it becomes "PARAMETERS:" Dbl-clk on this word and the window shown in Fig. 17.23 will appear. Select the NAME1 = line, and in the Value field type in "Rvar"; note that the braces are not used here. The VALUE1 = field must have a value; "2.5 k" is chosen, in agreement with our original selection.

Finally, choose Analysis, Setup . . ., DC Sweep . . .. Select the following: Swept Var. Type: "Global Parameter," Sweep Type: "Linear," Name: "Rvar," Start Value: "500," End Value: "5 k," and Increment: "500." These values are shown in Fig. 17.24.

Run the simulation and in Probe plot the power delivered to the load resistor, which is V(RL:1)*I(RL). In the output file, it is seen that RL:1 is at node *3*, which is at the top of *RL*. Using the cursor, verify that when $RL = 2.5$ kΩ, $PRL = 98.64$ mW,

```
                    PARAMETERS:
                    Rvar    2.5k

        R1          R2
       ___         ___
      |   |       |   |
       ‾‾‾         ‾‾‾
       300         300
                              RL
   +   V        R3           {Rvar}
  ___          10k
  ___
   -   20V

  ▽
  0
        * C:\P\TSECTVA.sch
        .PARAM          Rvar=2.5k
        ** Analysis setup **
        .DC LIN PARAM Rvar 500 5k 500
        .OP
        * From [SCHEMATICS NETLIST] section of msim.ini:
        .lib nom.lib
        .INC "TSECTVA.net"
        **** INCLUDING TSECTVA.net ****

        * Schematics Netlist *
        V_V           $N_0001 0 20V
        R_R1            $N_0001 $N_0002   300
        R_R2            $N_0002 $N_0003   300
        R_RL            $N_0003 0  {Rvar}
        R_R3            $N_0002 0  10k
        **** RESUMING TSECTVA.CIR ****
        .INC "TSECTVA.als"
        **** INCLUDING TSECTVA.als ****

        * Schematics Aliases *
        .ALIASES
        V_V             V(+=$N_0001 -=0 )
        R_R1            R1(1=$N_0001 2=$N_0002 )
        R_R2            R2(1=$N_0002 2=$N_0003 )
        R_RL            RL(1=$N_0003 2=0 )
        R_R3            R3(1=$N_0002 2=0 )
        .ENDALIASES

        **** RESUMING TSECTVA.CIR ****
        .probe
        .END

        NODE   VOLTAGE    NODE   VOLTAGE    NODE   VOLTAGE   NODE   VOLTAGE
        ($N_0001)   20.0000                       ($N_0002)   17.5880
        ($N_0003)   15.7040

            VOLTAGE SOURCE CURRENTS
            NAME          CURRENT
            V_V           -8.040E-03

            TOTAL POWER DISSIPATION   1.61E-01  WATTS
```

Fig. 17.22   Schematic and output file for variable RL.

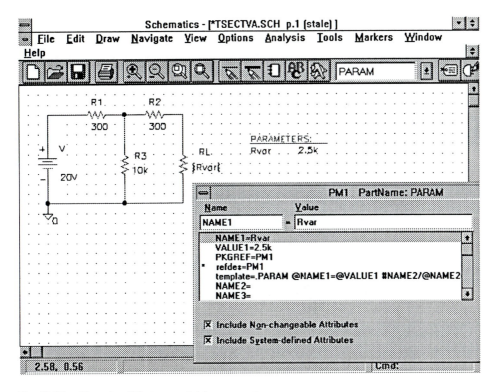

Fig. 17.23 Changing RL to a variable parameter.

as shown in Fig. 17.25. As a check of this value, note in the output file that V(3) = 15.704 V. This is the value when R_L = 2.5 kΩ. Use V^2/R_L in the calculation for verification of the previous value of P_{RL}.

USING DEVICE TOLERANCES

Construct the circuit shown in Fig. 17.26 in Schematics. The transistor used in the circuit is the Q2N2222. The source voltage is *VSIN,* with an amplitude of 10 mV, and *f* = 5 kHz. Use the values shown for resistors and capacitors. Suppose that the transistor has h_{FE} tolerance of ±25%. The tolerance can be set as follows: Select Edit, Model . . ., Edit Instance Model (Text) . . .. On the line displaying "Bf = 255.9" add "Dev = 25%". This parameter deviation will apply to *Bf* only. Save the circuit as *bridgcir.sch.*

Monte Carlo Analysis

The effect of this change in h_{FE} can be seen both graphically and statistically if we perform a Monte Carlo analysis on the circuit. Select Analysis, Setup . . ., Monte Carlo/Worst Case and select the options shown in Fig. 17.27. A total of 10 Monte

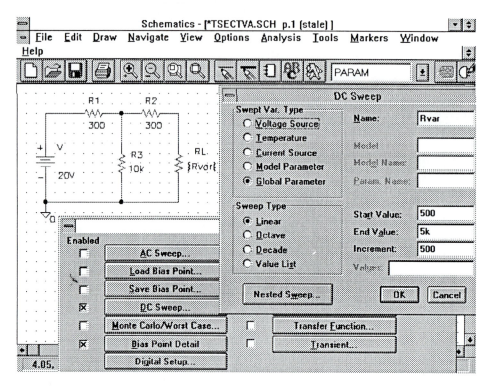

Fig. 17.24 Setting up a Global Parameter sweep for a resistor.

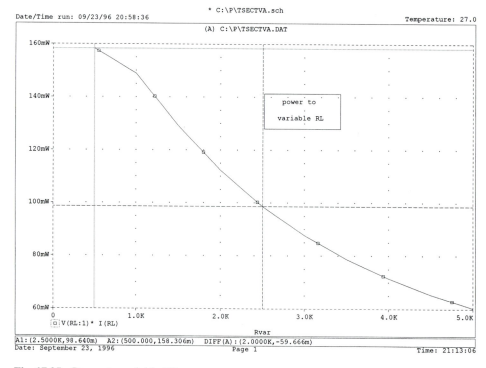

Fig. 17.25 Power to variable RL.

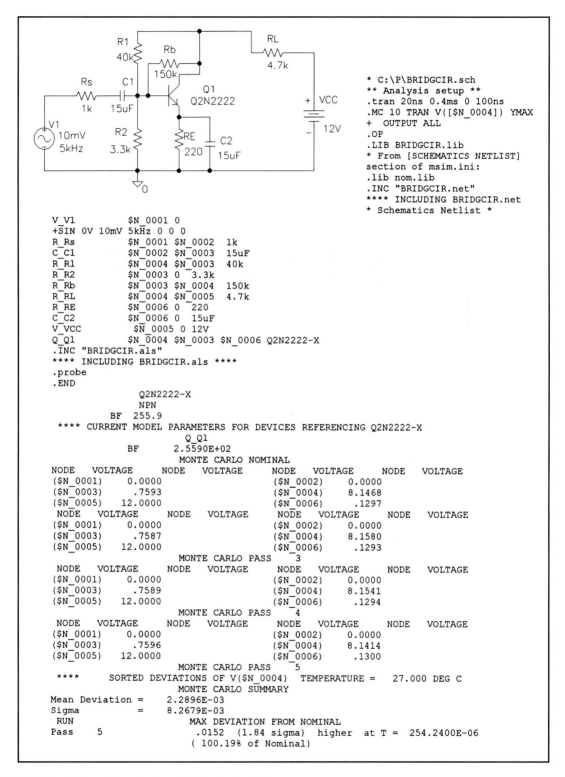

```
                                            * C:\P\BRIDGCIR.sch
                                            ** Analysis setup **
                                            .tran 20ns 0.4ms 0 100ns
                                            .MC 10 TRAN V([$N_0004]) YMAX
                                            + OUTPUT ALL
                                            .OP
                                            .LIB BRIDGCIR.lib
                                            * From [SCHEMATICS NETLIST]
                                            section of msim.ini:
                                            .lib nom.lib
                                            .INC "BRIDGCIR.net"
                                            **** INCLUDING BRIDGCIR.net
                                            * Schematics Netlist *

          V_V1          $N_0001 0
          +SIN 0V 10mV 5kHz 0 0 0
          R_Rs          $N_0001 $N_0002   1k
          C_C1          $N_0002 $N_0003   15uF
          R_R1          $N_0004 $N_0003   40k
          R_R2          $N_0003 0  3.3k
          R_Rb          $N_0003 $N_0004   150k
          R_RL          $N_0004 $N_0005   4.7k
          R_RE          $N_0006 0  220
          C_C2          $N_0006 0  15uF
          V_VCC         $N_0005 0 12V
          Q_Q1          $N_0004 $N_0003 $N_0006 Q2N2222-X
          .INC "BRIDGCIR.als"
          **** INCLUDING BRIDGCIR.als ****
          .probe
          .END

                    Q2N2222-X
                       NPN
                 BF   255.9
          ****  CURRENT MODEL PARAMETERS FOR DEVICES REFERENCING Q2N2222-X
                           Q_Q1
                    BF     2.5590E+02
                       MONTE CARLO NOMINAL
     NODE   VOLTAGE    NODE   VOLTAGE    NODE   VOLTAGE    NODE   VOLTAGE
     ($N_0001)   0.0000                 ($N_0002)   0.0000
     ($N_0003)    .7593                 ($N_0004)   8.1468
     ($N_0005)  12.0000                 ($N_0006)    .1297
     NODE   VOLTAGE    NODE   VOLTAGE    NODE   VOLTAGE    NODE   VOLTAGE
     ($N_0001)   0.0000                 ($N_0002)   0.0000
     ($N_0003)    .7587                 ($N_0004)   8.1580
     ($N_0005)  12.0000                 ($N_0006)    .1293
                         MONTE CARLO PASS     3
     NODE   VOLTAGE    NODE   VOLTAGE    NODE   VOLTAGE    NODE   VOLTAGE
     ($N_0001)   0.0000                 ($N_0002)   0.0000
     ($N_0003)    .7589                 ($N_0004)   8.1541
     ($N_0005)  12.0000                 ($N_0006)    .1294
                         MONTE CARLO PASS     4
     NODE   VOLTAGE    NODE   VOLTAGE    NODE   VOLTAGE    NODE   VOLTAGE
     ($N_0001)   0.0000                 ($N_0002)   0.0000
     ($N_0003)    .7596                 ($N_0004)   8.1414
     ($N_0005)  12.0000                 ($N_0006)    .1300
                         MONTE CARLO PASS     5
        ****     SORTED DEVIATIONS OF V($N_0004)  TEMPERATURE =   27.000 DEG C
                       MONTE CARLO SUMMARY
     Mean Deviation =    2.2896E-03
     Sigma          =    8.2679E-03
      RUN              MAX DEVIATION FROM NOMINAL
     Pass    5             .0152  (1.84 sigma)  higher  at T =  254.2400E-06
                       ( 100.19% of Nominal)
```

Fig. 17.26 Schematic and output file for device tolerances.

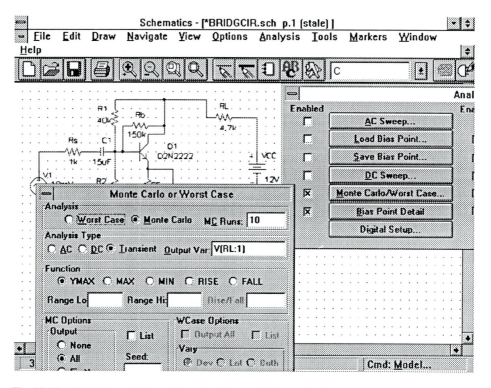

Fig. 17.27 The Monte Carlo settings for the amplifier analysis.

Carlo runs will be used to illustrate the procedure, although a much larger number might sometimes be used for the design of critical circuits. The output variable is V(RL:1), which is node *4* at the collector of the transistor. The choice of *YMAX* yields the greatest differences from the nominal h_{FE}. After this window is completed, the final setup option is to provide for a transient analysis. You may select your own values here; a final time of 0.4 ms allows for two full cycles of the 5-kHz sine wave to be displayed.

Run the analysis and in Probe trace V(Rs:1) and V(RL:1) using two *Y*-axis ranges. Note that the input voltage is retraced a total of 10 times on the screen, for the 10 Monte Carlo runs. Because there is no deviation in the input voltage, these sinusoids trace one over the other. Using Tools, Options . . ., Use Symbols, select "Never" so that the traces will not be covered with markers. Note that as the output traces are drawn some will appear larger than the expected, or normal, value, whereas others will appear smaller. These are the result of random choices of h_{FE} within the ±25%. Refer to Fig. 17.28 for traces. In Probe use the cursor to find the value of each of the *second* peaks of output voltage. They should be 8.3551 V, 8.3649 V, and so forth. On the traces shown here the minimum and maximum values were 8.3501 V and 8.3667 V.

A small portion of the output file is shown in Fig. 17.26. The netlist will be helpful in identifying the nodes; the modified transistor is shown as *Q2N2222-X*

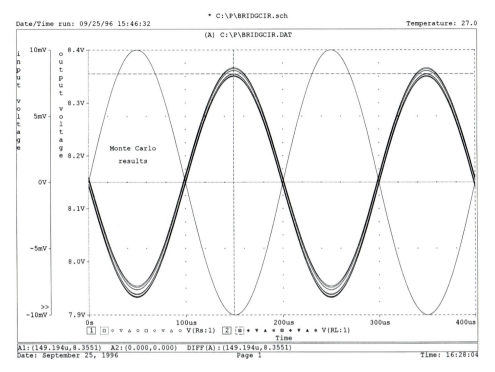

Fig. 17.28 Monte Carlo analysis.

with its nominal *BF* of 255.9. The Monte Carlo nominal node voltages are given next; these values are obtained using the nominal BF. If we had not chosen to use "Dev = 25%" for the deviation from the normal, this is the only set of voltages that would be given. At the bottom of the output file, after the last Monte Carlo results are shown, there is a section showing the sorted deviations of the voltage at node *4*, which is the voltage at the collector. It was called V(RL:1) in our Monte Carlo set-up. The values given represent mean and standard deviation. The $t = 254.24$ μs represents the time at which the maximum deviation occurred and its percentage of the nominal value.

Worst-Case Analysis

In the previous simulation, we ran a Monte Carlo analysis by setting up the conditions in the Monte Carlo or Worst Case window. The same window may be used for the worst-case analysis by selecting <u>W</u>orst Case rather than <u>M</u>onte Carlo in this window, as shown in Fig. 17.29. A transient analysis is still chosen for the analysis type. Also, under Function select "MAX," under WCase Options select "Output All," and under Vary choose "Dev." Thus instead of using a random variation of h_{FE} we will simply use the worst-case value that is 25% above normal.

Run the simulation and note in the PSpice window that there are three runs taking place. The first is for sensitivity "NOMINAL", which means that the nominal

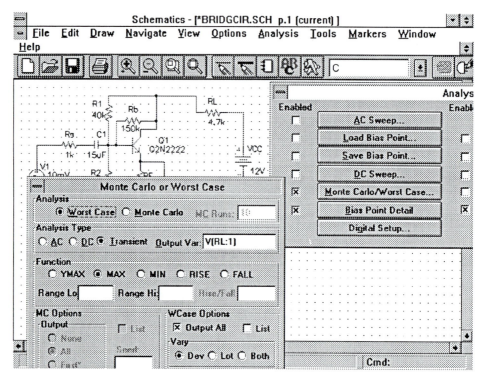

Fig. 17.29 Preparing for a Worst Case analysis of an amplifier circuit.

value of h_{FE} will be used in the transient analysis. The second is for sensitivity "Q_Q1 Q2N2222-X BF", which means that transistor tolerance is used in determining the effect on the output voltage (that is, its sensitivity). The third is for worst case "ALL DEVICES". Because only the transistor tolerance is involved, the term *all devices* is applied only to it. The PSpice window for this analysis is shown in Fig. 17.30.

In Probe trace V(Rs:1) noting that three sinusoids are traced. Also trace V(RL:1), where again three waves are traced. Figure 17.31 shows the input and output sine waves along with the dc voltage level at the collector. As shown in Fig. 17.32, you may use Tools, Options . . ., Use Symbols Always to see which curve is associated with which run. Using the cursor, verify the bias-voltage levels at node *4* for each of the runs. Also find the peak-to-peak output voltage for each run. On the output waveform for runs 1 and 2, the peak is 8.3551 V and the valley is 7.9394 V, giving a peak-to-peak swing of 0.4157 V. This means the ac magnitude of the output voltage is 0.20785 V. When compared with the input voltage of 10 mV, the resulting voltage gain is 20.785.

Some of the output file is shown in Fig. 17.33. At the output node V(4) = 8.1468 V for the nominal value. In the sensitivity run, V(4) = 8.3551 V using an h_{FE} within its deviation range. This is the maximum value of V(4). On the final run for worst-case conditions, V(4) = 8.3479 V.

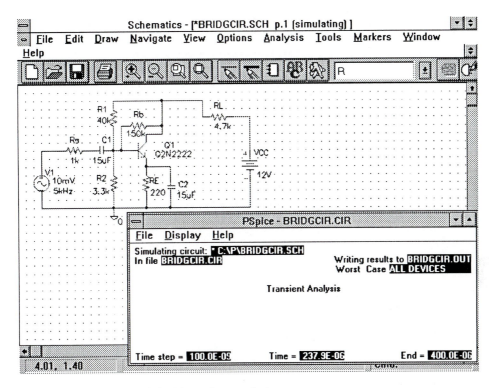

Fig. 17.30 The last run of the Worst Case analysis.

In summary, the deviation of h_{FE} made little difference on the performance of this stable amplifier circuit.

Effect of Resistor Tolerance on Worst-Case Analysis

In the analysis just concluded, only the transistor h_{FE} was allowed to vary. What would be the effect on the worst-case analysis if resistor tolerance were a factor? To simplify matters, only the value of R_L will be modified. Remove the present R_L from the circuit *bridgcir.sch* and replace it with a new part, "Rbreak". Then select the new resistor and choose Edit, Model . . ., Edit Instance Model (Text) . . .. The window identifies the resistor as *Rbreak-X*, assuming that a parameter modification will take place. Just below the line

```
.model Rbreak-X RES
```

insert the following

```
R=1 DEV=20%
```

The "R = 1" means that the resistance multiplier is unity; the "DEV = 20%" allows the resistor to have a tolerance of 20%. Save this circuit as *bridgeca.sch*. Now we are ready to perform the worst-case analysis in the same fashion as in the preceding

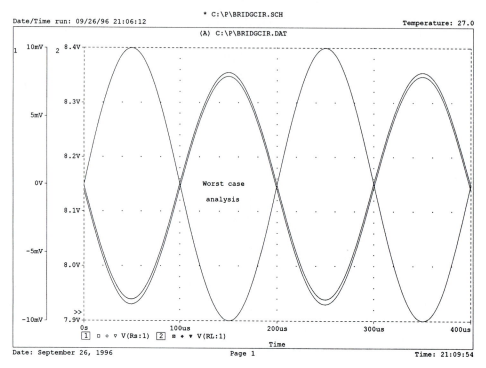

Fig. 17.31   Worst Case analysis.

example. Recall that the transistor h_{FE} and R_L will now both be subject to tolerances. The modified circuit is shown in Fig. 17.34 along with a portion of the output file.

Run the simulation and note that four runs take place in PSpice, as follows: (1) sensitivity *NOMINAL,* (2) sensitivity *Q_Q1 Q2N2222-X BF,* (3) sensitivity *R_RL Rbreak-X R,* and (4) worst case *ALL DEVICES.*

In Probe, plot V(Rs:1) and V(RL:1) as before. A total of eight traces will appear on the screen. The significant difference in this set of traces compared with those previously obtained is a shifted output-voltage plot. Refer to Fig. 17.35 for these traces. Using the cursor verify that the lower output curve has a dc level at 8.1454 V, while the upper output curve has a dc level at 8.4605 V. With the Use Symbols Always option identify each of the output curves by run number.

In the output file the 8.1454-V level is V(4) for the sensitivity *R_RL* run, whereas the 8.4605-V level is V(4) for the worst-case analysis. Note that in the previous analysis V(4) was in the 8.14-V range. The worst-case summary using the maximum value gives V(4) = 8.6676 V at $t = 149.34$ μs.

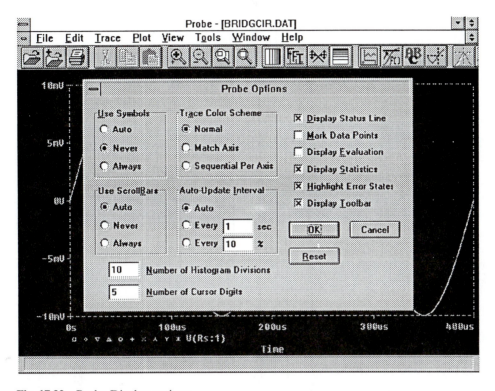

Fig. 17.32 Probe Display options.

DIGITAL SCHEMATICS

In Schematics you will find a large assortment of digital devices. Use the Draw, Get New Part ... command to look at the assortment in *eval.slb,* beginning with 7400, a 2-input positive-NAND gate. If you arrow-down through the list you will see NAND gates, NOR gates, inverters, AND-OR-inverters, JK flip-flops, master-slave flip-flops, 2-bit binary full adders, XOR gates, and so forth. All the listed devices are available in the evaluation version of the MicroSim software.

The NOR Gate

The last example of Chapter 7 dealt with the 7402 2-input NOR gate. The sources V_1 and V_2 were piecewise-linear voltage sources, with waveshapes in the form of pulse trains representing zeros and ones. The same circuit may be shown in Schematics, as in Fig. 17.36. Save the schematic as *norgate.sch.* For each source select *VPLW* and insert the time, voltage pairs shown in the file *norgate.out.* For V_1 these begin with "0s", "0 V", then "0.1 ms", "1 V", and so forth. To provide for a label on the output, dbl-clk on the wire and use the name *Vout.*

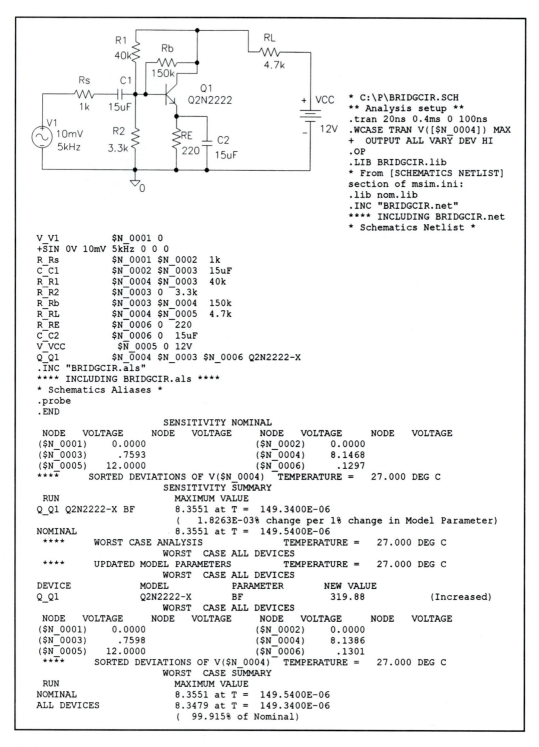

```
* C:\P\BRIDGCIR.SCH
** Analysis setup **
.tran 20ns 0.4ms 0 100ns
.WCASE TRAN V([$N_0004]) MAX
+   OUTPUT ALL VARY DEV HI
.OP
.LIB BRIDGCIR.lib
* From [SCHEMATICS NETLIST]
section of msim.ini:
.lib nom.lib
.INC "BRIDGCIR.net"
**** INCLUDING BRIDGCIR.net
* Schematics Netlist *
```

```
V_V1            $N_0001 0
+SIN 0V 10mV 5kHz 0 0 0
R_Rs            $N_0001 $N_0002   1k
C_C1            $N_0002 $N_0003   15uF
R_R1            $N_0004 $N_0003   40k
R_R2            $N_0003 0   3.3k
R_Rb            $N_0003 $N_0004   150k
R_RL            $N_0004 $N_0005   4.7k
R_RE            $N_0006 0   220
C_C2            $N_0006 0   15uF
V_VCC           $N_0005 0   12V
Q_Q1            $N_0004 $N_0003 $N_0006 Q2N2222-X
.INC "BRIDGCIR.als"
**** INCLUDING BRIDGCIR.als ****
* Schematics Aliases *
.probe
.END
                    SENSITIVITY NOMINAL
  NODE   VOLTAGE   NODE   VOLTAGE   NODE   VOLTAGE   NODE   VOLTAGE
 ($N_0001)   0.0000                ($N_0002)   0.0000
 ($N_0003)    .7593                ($N_0004)   8.1468
 ($N_0005)   12.0000               ($N_0006)    .1297
 ****      SORTED DEVIATIONS OF V($N_0004)  TEMPERATURE =   27.000 DEG C
                    SENSITIVITY SUMMARY
  RUN                   MAXIMUM VALUE
 Q_Q1 Q2N2222-X BF      8.3551 at T =  149.3400E-06
                    (   1.8263E-03% change per 1% change in Model Parameter)
 NOMINAL               8.3551 at T =  149.5400E-06
  ****        WORST CASE ANALYSIS            TEMPERATURE =   27.000 DEG C
                    WORST  CASE ALL DEVICES
  ****        UPDATED MODEL PARAMETERS       TEMPERATURE =   27.000 DEG C
                    WORST  CASE ALL DEVICES
 DEVICE            MODEL         PARAMETER     NEW VALUE
 Q_Q1              Q2N2222-X        BF          319.88             (Increased)
                    WORST  CASE ALL DEVICES
  NODE   VOLTAGE   NODE   VOLTAGE   NODE   VOLTAGE   NODE   VOLTAGE
 ($N_0001)   0.0000                ($N_0002)   0.0000
 ($N_0003)    .7598                ($N_0004)   8.1386
 ($N_0005)   12.0000               ($N_0006)    .1301
 ****      SORTED DEVIATIONS OF V($N_0004)  TEMPERATURE =   27.000 DEG C
                    WORST  CASE SUMMARY
  RUN                   MAXIMUM VALUE
 NOMINAL               8.3551 at T =  149.5400E-06
 ALL DEVICES           8.3479 at T =  149.3400E-06
                    (  99.915% of Nominal)
```

Fig. 17.33   Schematic and output file for Worst Case analysis.

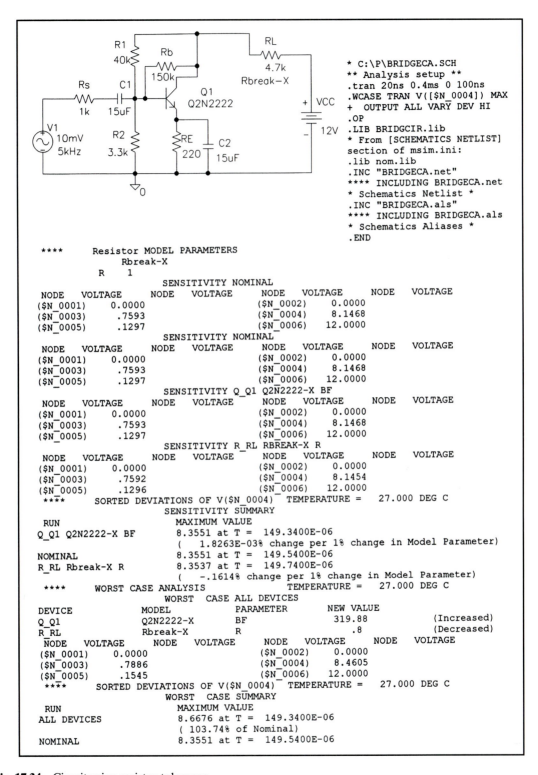

```
                                                        * C:\P\BRIDGECA.SCH
                                                        ** Analysis setup **
                                                        .tran 20ns 0.4ms 0 100ns
                                                        .WCASE TRAN V([$N_0004]) MAX
                                                        +  OUTPUT ALL VARY DEV HI
                                                        .OP
                                                        .LIB BRIDGCIR.lib
                                                        * From [SCHEMATICS NETLIST]
                                                        section of msim.ini:
                                                        .lib nom.lib
                                                        .INC "BRIDGECA.net"
                                                        **** INCLUDING BRIDGECA.net
                                                        * Schematics Netlist *
                                                        .INC "BRIDGECA.als"
                                                        **** INCLUDING BRIDGECA.als
                                                        * Schematics Aliases *
                                                        .END
```

```
****          Resistor MODEL PARAMETERS
                  Rbreak-X
              R     1
                                SENSITIVITY NOMINAL
    NODE   VOLTAGE    NODE   VOLTAGE    NODE   VOLTAGE    NODE   VOLTAGE
 ($N_0001)  0.0000                   ($N_0002)   0.0000
 ($N_0003)   .7593                   ($N_0004)   8.1468
 ($N_0005)   .1297                   ($N_0006)  12.0000
                                SENSITIVITY NOMINAL
    NODE   VOLTAGE    NODE   VOLTAGE    NODE   VOLTAGE    NODE   VOLTAGE
 ($N_0001)  0.0000                   ($N_0002)   0.0000
 ($N_0003)   .7593                   ($N_0004)   8.1468
 ($N_0005)   .1297                   ($N_0006)  12.0000
                          SENSITIVITY Q_Q1 Q2N2222-X BF
    NODE   VOLTAGE    NODE   VOLTAGE    NODE   VOLTAGE    NODE   VOLTAGE
 ($N_0001)  0.0000                   ($N_0002)   0.0000
 ($N_0003)   .7593                   ($N_0004)   8.1468
 ($N_0005)   .1297                   ($N_0006)  12.0000
                          SENSITIVITY R_RL RBREAK-X R
    NODE   VOLTAGE    NODE   VOLTAGE    NODE   VOLTAGE    NODE   VOLTAGE
 ($N_0001)  0.0000                   ($N_0002)   0.0000
 ($N_0003)   .7592                   ($N_0004)   8.1454
 ($N_0005)   .1296                   ($N_0006)  12.0000
 ****       SORTED DEVIATIONS OF V($N_0004)  TEMPERATURE =   27.000 DEG C
                          SENSITIVITY SUMMARY
    RUN                   MAXIMUM VALUE
 Q_Q1 Q2N2222-X BF         8.3551 at T =  149.3400E-06
                           (  1.8263E-03% change per 1% change in Model Parameter)
 NOMINAL                   8.3551 at T =  149.5400E-06
 R_RL Rbreak-X R           8.3537 at T =  149.7400E-06
                           (  -.1614% change per 1% change in Model Parameter)
 ****       WORST CASE ANALYSIS              TEMPERATURE =   27.000 DEG C
                          WORST  CASE ALL DEVICES
 DEVICE                MODEL           PARAMETER       NEW VALUE
 Q_Q1                  Q2N2222-X       BF                319.88       (Increased)
 R_RL                  Rbreak-X        R                    .8        (Decreased)
    NODE   VOLTAGE    NODE   VOLTAGE    NODE   VOLTAGE    NODE   VOLTAGE
 ($N_0001)  0.0000                   ($N_0002)   0.0000
 ($N_0003)   .7886                   ($N_0004)   8.4605
 ($N_0005)   .1545                   ($N_0006)  12.0000
 ****       SORTED DEVIATIONS OF V($N_0004)  TEMPERATURE =   27.000 DEG C
                          WORST  CASE SUMMARY
    RUN                   MAXIMUM VALUE
 ALL DEVICES               8.6676 at T =  149.3400E-06
                           ( 103.74% of Nominal)
 NOMINAL                   8.3551 at T =  149.5400E-06
```

Fig. 17.34 Circuit using resistor tolerance.

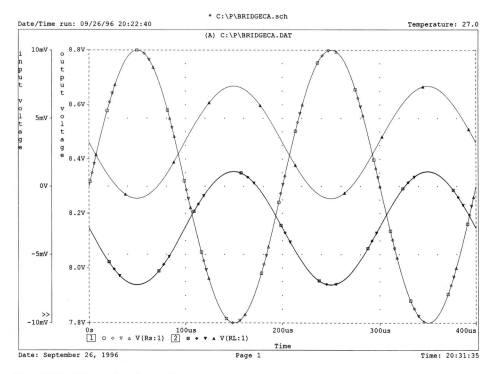

Fig. 17.35   Effect of resistor tolerance.

Perform a transient analysis, using a print step of 0.01 ms and a final time of 5 s. In Probe trace both input voltages along with the output voltage. First trace V(V1:+), then add another plot and trace V(V2:+). Without adding another plot you may trace *Vout.* Compare your results with Fig. 17.37. As you might expect, there will be a large amount of information in the output file, especially because a-to-d and d-to-a interfaces must be created in order to ensure compatibility between the analog and digital devices. Only a small amount of this output file is shown in Fig. 17.36.

A Half-Adder Circuit

It is not necessary to use *VPWL* to provide a pulse pattern for a digital circuit. The *source.lib* library contains *DigStim*, the symbol for which is shown in Fig. 17.38, along with two other parts from *eval.slb*, the 7486 2-input XOR gate and the 7408 2-input AND gate. A short wire segment is placed at the output of each gate. The upper gate is given the label *D*, and the lower gate is labeled *C*. Place the parts in Schematics, naming the drawing *halfaddr.sch*, then dbl-clk on the *DSTM1* symbol. A window will appear, calling for an attribute value. Enter the value "A", which becomes the stimulus name. Then the Stimulus Editor will appear in a window, fol-

```
* C:\P\NORGATE.sch
** Analysis setup **
.tran 0.01ms 5s
.OP
* From [SCHEMATICS NETLIST] section of msim.ini:
.lib nom.lib
.INC "NORGATE.net"
**** INCLUDING NORGATE.net ****
* Schematics Netlist *
V_V1          $N_0001 0
+PWL 0s 0V 0.1ms 1V 1s 1V 1.0001s 0V 2s 0V 2.0001s 1V 3s 1V 3.0001s 0V 4s 0V
+   4.0001s 1V
V_V2          $N_0002 0
+PWL 0s 0V 1.5s 0V 1.50001s 1V 2.5s 1V 2.50001s 0V 3.5s 0V 3.50001s 1V 3.7s 1V
+   3.70001s 0V 5s 0V
X_U1A         $N_0001 $N_0002 Vout $G_DPWR $G_DGND 7402 PARAMS:
+ IO_LEVEL=0 MNTYMXDLY=0
**** RESUMING NORGATE.CIR ****
.INC "NORGATE.als"
**** INCLUDING NORGATE.als ****
* Schematics Aliases *
.probe
.END
**** Generated AtoD and DtoA Interfaces ****
```

Fig. 17.36   Schematic and output file for NOR gate.

lowed by another window calling for settings of the stimulus attributes. See Fig. 17.39 and note that the Name: "A" and Type: "Clock" appear in this window. Type in the values shown with frequency: "1 kHz" and a Duty Cycle of "0.5". This creates a clock operating at 1 kHz, with the upper- and lower-level values of the same duration, 0.5 ms.

Select *DSTM2* and follow a similar procedure using f = "2 kHz" and a duty cycle of "0.5". These two input stimuli will be used to produce a truth table for the half-adder. The final requirement is to set up the transient analysis. A convenient print step of 0.2 ms and a final time of 2 ms may be used. Run the simulation and in Probe trace *TM1:OUT0, TM2:OUT0, D,* and *C.* As is customary, *D* represents the digit and *C* the carry. Use the cursor to move along the time axis and note that the state of the traces changes between *ones* and *zeros*. For example, in Fig. 17.40 at 0.8 ms, *TM1* (the A stimulus) is 1, *TM2* (the B stimulus) is 1, *D* is 0 and *C* is 1. Look at

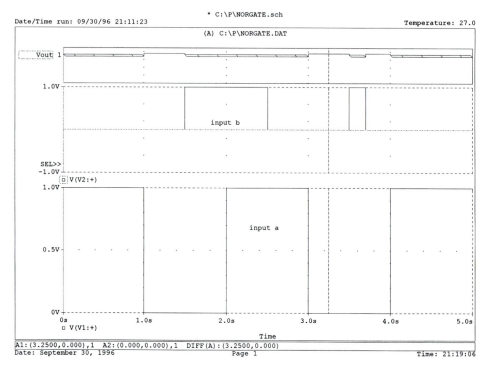

Fig. 17.37   NOR gate input and output.

the waves at any other time and verify that the states of D and C are in keeping with the expected truth-table results. Note that the plot does not fill the entire space of the graph. There is no vertical scale. This graph, as the result of the digital stimuli, allows for observing a large number of logic states rather than just the four we need for this circuit.

A portion of the output file is shown in Fig. 17.38. There was no need to list a-to-d and d-to-a interfaces, since digital stimuli were used. The warning is self-explanatory. In the schematics netlist, the *U* parts are for the digital stimuli, and the *X* references are for subcircuits.

A Circuit for Simplification

The digital circuit shown in Fig. 17.41 consists of a pair of stimuli, one NAND gate, and two NOR gates. Place the parts as shown, then save the circuit as *mixgate.sch*. As an academic exercise find the truth table for the circuit, then as a pencil-and-paper exercise write the Boolean expression for the circuit and simplify it. The stimuli should be the same as in the previous example, with one clock (DSTM1) at $f =$

```
                                    U1A
DSTM1        1
[S  ⊓⊔ ⊐                              3   D
STIMULUS=A   2

                                    7486
DSTM2                               U2A
[S  ⊓⊔ ⊐     1
STIMULUS=B                           3   C
             2

                                    7408
```

```
                          * C:\P\HALFADDR.sch
                          ** Analysis setup **
                          .tran 0.2ms 2ms
                          .OP
                          .STMLIB HALFADDR.stl
                          * From [SCHEMATICS NETLIST] section of msim.ini:
                          .lib nom.lib
                          .INC "HALFADDR.net"
                          **** INCLUDING HALFADDR.net ****

* Schematics Netlist *
U_DSTM1        STIM(1,0) $G_DPWR $G_DGND $N_0001 IO_STM STIMULUS=A
U_DSTM2        STIM(1,0) $G_DPWR $G_DGND $N_0002 IO_STM STIMULUS=B
X_U1A         $N_0001 $N_0002 D $G_DPWR $G_DGND 7486 PARAMS:
+ IO_LEVEL=0 MNTYMXDLY=0
X_U2A         $N_0001 $N_0001 C $G_DPWR $G_DGND 7408 PARAMS:
+ IO_LEVEL=0 MNTYMXDLY=0
**** RESUMING HALFADDR.CIR ****
.INC "HALFADDR.als"
**** INCLUDING HALFADDR.als ****
* Schematics Aliases *
.probe
.END
* C:\P\HALFADDR.STL written on Tue Oct 01 11:32:13 1996
* by Stimulus Editor -- Serial Number: 72226 -- Version 6.3
;!Stimulus Get
;! A Digital B Digital
;!Ok
;!Plot Axis_Settings
;!Xrange 0s 4ms
;!AutoUniverse
;!XminRes 1ns
;!YminRes 1n
;!Ok
.STIMULUS B STIM (1, 1) ;! CLOCK 2kHz 0.5 0 0
+    +0s 0
+    +250us 1
+    Repeat Forever
+        +250us 0
+        +250us 1
+    EndRepeat
.STIMULUS A STIM (1, 1) ;! CLOCK 1kHz 0.5 0 0
+    +0s 0
+    +500us 1
+    Repeat Forever
+        +500us 0
+        +500us 1
+    EndRepeat
.STIMULUS A STIM (1, 1) ;! CLOCK 1kHz 0.5 0 0
+    +0s 0
+    +500us 1
+    Repeat Forever
+        +500us 0
+        +500us 1
+    EndRepeat
WARNING -- No analog devices -- Small-Signal analysis ignored
```

Fig. 17.38 Schematic and output file for half-adder.

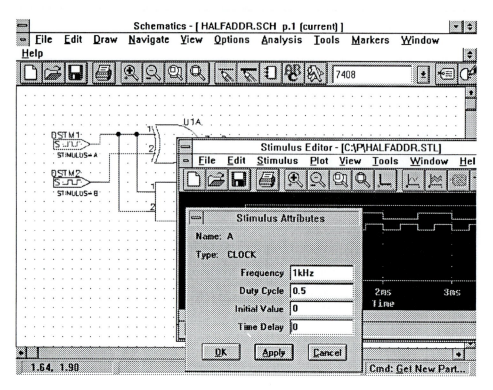

Fig. 17.39 Setting the Stimulus Attributes for a digital stimulus.

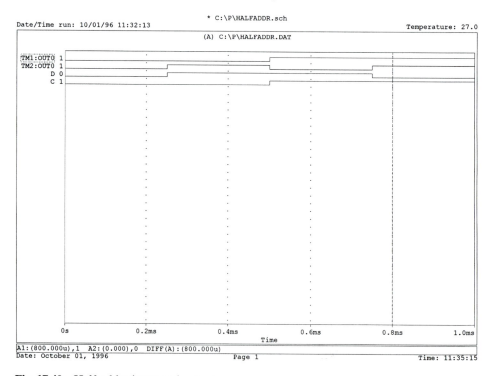

Fig. 17.40 Half-adder input and output.

```
                                                    * C:\P\MIXGATE.sch
                                                    ** Analysis setup **
                                                    .tran 0.2ms 2ms
                                                    .STMLIB MIXGATE.stl
                                                    * From [SCHEMATICS NETLIST]
                                                    section of msim.ini:
                                                    .lib nom.lib
                                                    .INC "MIXGATE.net"
                                                    **** INCLUDING MIXGATE.net
                                                    * Schematics Netlist *
U_DSTM1          STIM(1,0) $G_DPWR $G_DGND $N_0001 IO_STM STIMULUS=A
U_DSTM2          STIM(1,0) $G_DPWR $G_DGND $N_0002 IO_STM STIMULUS=B
X_U2A       $N_0001 $N_0002 $N_0003 $G_DPWR $G_DGND 7400 PARAMS:
+ IO_LEVEL=0 MNTYMXDLY=0
X_U1A       $N_0001 $N_0002 $N_0004 $G_DPWR $G_DGND 7402 PARAMS:
+ IO_LEVEL=0 MNTYMXDLY=0
X_U3A       $N_0004 $N_0003 Vout $G_DPWR $G_DGND 7402 PARAMS:
+ IO_LEVEL=0 MNTYMXDLY=0
**** RESUMING MIXGATE.CIR ****
.INC "MIXGATE.als"
.probe
.END
* C:\P\MIXGATE.STL written on Tue Oct 01 16:58:51 1996
* by Stimulus Editor -- Serial Number: 72226 -- Version 6.3
;!Stimulus Get
;! A Digital B Digital
;!Ok
;!Plot Axis_Settings
;!Xrange 0s 4ms
;!AutoUniverse
;!XminRes 1ns
;!YminRes 1n
;!Ok
.STIMULUS B STIM (1, 1) ;! CLOCK 2kHz 0.5 0 0
+    +0s 0
+    +250us 1
+    Repeat Forever
+       +250us 0
+       +250us 1
+    EndRepeat
.STIMULUS A STIM (1, 1) ;! CLOCK 1kHz 0.5 0 0
+    +0s 0
+    +500us 1
+    Repeat Forever
+       +500us 0
+       +500us 1
+    EndRepeat
.STIMULUS A STIM (1, 1) ;! CLOCK 1kHz 0.5 0 0
+    +0s 0
+    +500us 1
+    Repeat Forever
+       +500us 0
+       +500us 1
+    EndRepeat
```

Fig. 17.41   Schematic and output file for a circuit to be simplified.

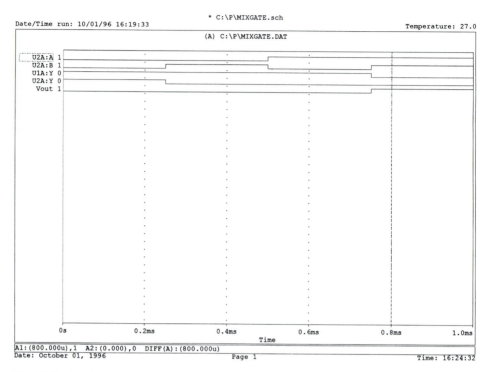

Fig. 17.42   Timing diagram for NAND–NOR circuit.

1 kHz, and the other (DSTM2) at $f = 2$ kHz. Label the output wire *Vout*. The setup may be for a transient analysis with a print step of 0.01 ms and a final time of 2 ms.

Run the simulation and in Probe trace all available variables as shown in Fig. 17.42; then construct a truth table showing inputs *A* and *B* and outputs Y_1 for the first NOR gate, Y_2 for the NAND gate, and *Vout* for the second NOR gate. Verify that at $t = 0.8$ ms $A = 1, B = 1, Y_1 = 0, Y_2 = 0$, and $Vout = 1$, as shown in Fig. 17.42.

The D Flip-Flop

The 7474 in Schematics is described as a *D*-type positive edge–triggered flip-flop with preset and clear. Draw the circuit shown in Fig. 17.43 using this part. Save the schematic as *dflip.sch*. The *DigStim* part is used for *PS, D,* and *CL,* and *DigClock* is used for the clock. Set the attributes for *PS* with $f = 1$ kHz, duty cycle = 0.5, initial value = 1, and time delay = 0. The respective values for *D* are (1 kHz, 0.5, 1, and 0.75 ms), for *CL* they are (0.8 kHz, 0.5, 0, and 0). The waveshapes for the digital stimuli are shown in Fig. 17.44. The *DigClock* settings are delay = 0, ontime = 0.4 ms, offtime = 0.6 ms, and startval = 0. Set the transient analysis to run for 2 ms with a print time of 0.2 ms.

```
DSTM1
S ⎍
STIMULUS=PS

DSTM2                        4    U1A
S ⎍                          PRE
STIMULUS=D              2 ─┤D   Q├ 5

DSTM4                   3 ─┤>CLK Q̄├ 6
CLK ⎍                        CLR
                        1   7474
DSTM3
S ⎍
STIMULUS=CL
```

```
* C:\P\DFLIP.sch
* Schematics Version 6.3 - April 1996
* Wed Oct 02 14:35:41 1996
** Analysis setup **
.tran 0.2msd 2ms
.STMLIB DFLIP.stl
* From [SCHEMATICS NETLIST] section of msim.ini:
.lib nom.lib
.INC "DFLIP.net"
**** INCLUDING DFLIP.net ****
* Schematics Netlist *
U_DSTM1           STIM(1,0) $G_DPWR $G_DGND $N_0001 IO_STM STIMULUS=PS
U_DSTM2           STIM(1,0) $G_DPWR $G_DGND $N_0002 IO_STM STIMULUS=D
U_DSTM3           STIM(1,0) $G_DPWR $G_DGND $N_0003 IO_STM STIMULUS=CL
U_DSTM4           STIM(1,1) $G_DPWR $G_DGND $N_0004 IO_STM IO_LEVEL=0
+ 0 0
+ +0 1
+REPEAT FOREVER
+ +0.4ms 0
+ +0.6ms 1
+ ENDREPEAT
X_U1A             $N_0003 $N_0002 $N_0004 $N_0001 $N_0005 $N_0006 $G_DPWR $G_DGND
+ 7474 PARAMS:
+ IO_LEVEL=0 MNTYMXDLY=0
**** RESUMING DFLIP.CIR ****
.INC "DFLIP.als"
**** INCLUDING DFLIP.als ****
.probe
.END
* C:\P\DFLIP.STL written on Wed Oct 02 14:36:11 1996
* by Stimulus Editor -- Serial Number: 72226 -- Version 6.3
;!Stimulus Get
;! PS Digital D Digital CL Digital
;!Ok
;!Plot Axis_Settings
;!Xrange 0s 6ms
;!AutoUniverse
;!XminRes 1ns
;!YminRes 1n
;!Ok
.STIMULUS CL STIM (1, 1) ;! CLOCK 0.8kHz 0.5 0 0
+    +0s 0
+    +625us 1
+    Repeat Forever
+       +625us 0
+       +625us 1
+    EndRepeat
.STIMULUS D STIM (1, 1) ;! CLOCK 1kHz 0.5 1 0.75ms
+    +0s 1
+    +750us 0
+    Repeat Forever
+       +500us 1
+       +500us 0
+    EndRepeat
.STIMULUS PS STIM (1, 1) ;! CLOCK 1kHz 0.5 1 0
+    +0s 1
+    +500us 0
+    Repeat Forever
+       +500us 1
+       +500us 0
+    EndRepeat
```

Fig. 17.43 The D flip-flop.

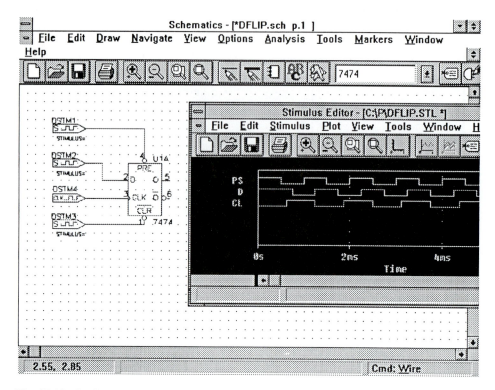

Fig. 17.44 Setting the stimuli values as displayed in the Stimulus Editor.

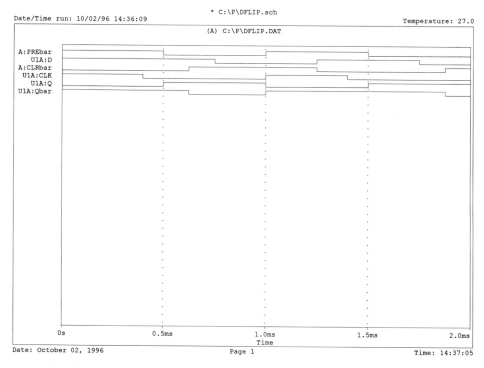

Fig. 17.45 Timing diagram for the D flip-flop.

In Probe trace all the available waveshapes, and compare your results with those shown in Fig. 17.45. Verify from your knowledge of the operation of this flip-flop that the results are correct. Why are there periods of time when Q and $Qbar$ are not complementary? In a portion of the output file, as shown in Fig. 17.38, you can see the clock parameters for the various stimuli.

A

Brief Summary of PSpice Statements

The statements shown here are given in quick-reference form. This will prove helpful if you need to look up a statement that you have seen or used previously. More detailed information is given in Appendix B and Appendix D and at the end of each chapter.

General notes:

Uppercase and lowercase alphabetic characters may be used interchangeably.

< > means required information.

[ ] means optional information.

* indicates a comment line in the PSpice input file.

; shows a comment, generally following a statement on the same line.

.AC[LIN][OCT][*dec*]<*points*> <*f start*> <*f end* >; for ac sweep

B[*name*]<*drain*> <*gate*> <*source*> <*model name*> [*area value*]; for GaAsFET

C[*name*]<*+node*> <*–node*>[*model name*]<*value*> [IC = initial value]; for capacitor

D[*name*]<*+node*> <*–node*> <*model name*>[*area value*]; for diode

.DC[LIN][OCT][DEC]<*sweep variable*> <*start*> <*end*> <*increment*>[LIST]; for dc sweep

E[*name*]<*+node*> <*–node*> <*+controlling node*> <*–controlling node*> <*gain*>; VCVS

E[*name*]<*+node*> <*–node* >POLY(*value*)<*+controlling node*> <*–controlling node*> <*polynomial coefficient values*>; VCVS

.END; indicates the end of the circuit input file

.ENDS *<subcircuit name>*; indicates the end of a subcircuit

F[*name*]*<+node> <−node> <controlling V device name> <gain>*;CCCS

F[*name*]*<+node> <−node>*POLY(*value*) *<controlling V device name> <polynomial coefficient values>*; CCCS

.FOUR*<frequencies> <output variable>*; for Fourier analysis

G[*name*]*<+node> <−node> <+controlling node> <−controlling node> <transconductance>*; VCCS

G[*name*]*<+node> <−node>*POLY(*value*) *<+controlling node> <−controlling node> <polynomial coefficient values>*; VCCS

H[*name*]*<+node> <−node> <controlling V device name> <transresistance>*; CCVS

H[*name*]*<+node> <−node>*POLY(*value*) *<controlling V device name> <polynomial coefficient values>*; CCVS

I[*name*]*<+node> <−node>* [[*DC*]*<value>*] [*AC<magnitude>*[*phase*]] [*transient specification*]; for independent current source

.IC*<Vnode = value>*; shows an initial node voltage for transient analysis

.INC*<file name>*; inserts another file

J[*name*]*<drain node> <gate node> <source node> <model name>* [*area*]; for JFET

K[*name*] L[*name*] [L[*name*]] *<coupling value>*; for inductor coupling

K[*name*] L[*name*] [L[*name*]] *<coupling value> <model name>*[*size value*]; for inductor coupling model

L[*name*] *<+node> <−node>*[*model name*]*<value>*[IC = *value*]; for inductor

.LIB *<file name>*; references a model or subcircuit library in another file. The default file is NOM.LIB.

.MC[#*runs*] [DC] [AC] [TRAN] [*output variable*] YMAX; for Monte Carlo analysis

.MODEL[*name*] [*type*]; describes a built-in model

M[*name*]*<drain node> <gate node> <source node> <bulk/substrate node> <model name>*[*parameter value*]; for MOSFET

.NODESET*<Vnode = value>*; gives initial guess for node voltage

.NOISE *<Vnode>*[*,node*] *<name>*[*internal value*]; gives noise analysis along with ac analysis

.OP; gives detailed bias-point information

.OPTIONS *<option name>*; sets options for analysis

.PLOT[DC] [AC] [NOISE] [TRAN] [*output variable*]; gives printer-type plot

.PRINT[DC] [AC] [NOISE] [TRAN] [*output variable*]; produces a listing in the output file

.PROBE [*output variable*]; creates PROBE.DAT file for graphics analysis

Q[*name*] <*collector node*> <*base node*> <*emitter node*> [*substrate node*] <*model name*> [*area value*]; for BJT

R[*name*] <+*node*> <−*node*> [*model name*] <*value*>; for resistor

S[*name*] <+*switch node*> <−*switch node*> <+*controlling node*> <−*controlling node*> <*model name*>; for voltage-controlled switch

.SENS <*output variable*>; used for the sensitivity analysis

.SUBCKT <*name*> [*node (s)*]; marks the beginning of a subcircuit

T[*name*] <+A *port node*> <−A *port node*> <+B *port node*> <−B *port node*> <ZO = *value*> [TD = *value*] [F = *value*] [NL = *value*]; for ideal transmission line

.TEMP <*value*>; set the temperature for the analysis in Celsius

.TF <*output variable*> <*input source*>; for transfer function

.TRAN <*step value*> <*final value*> [*step ceiling value*] [UIC]; for transient analysis

V[*name*] <+*node*> <−*node*> [[DC]<*value*>][AC <*magnitude*> [*phase*]] [*transient specification*]; for independent voltage

W[*name*] <+*switch node*> <−*switch node*> <*controlling V device name*> <*model name*>; for current controlled switch

.WIDTH = <*value*>; sets the number of chracters per line of output

X[*name*] <[*nodes*]> <*subcircuit name*>; to specify a subcircuit

PSpice Devices and Statements

PSPICE DEVICES

B device—GaAsFET

General form:

B*<name>* *<d>* *<g>* *<s>* *<model>*[*<area>*]

Examples:

```
BIN 100  1  0 GFAST
B13  22 14 23 GNOM 2.0
```

C device—Capacitor

General form:

C*<name>* *<+node>* *<−node>*[*<model>*]*<value>*[IC = *<initial>*]

Examples:

```
CLOAD 15  0 20pF
CFDBK  3 33 CMOD 10pF IC=1.5v
```

d device—Diode

General form:

D*<name>* *<+node>* *<−node>* *<model>*[area]

Examples:

```
DCLAMP 14  0 DMOD
D13    15 17 SWITCH 1.5
```

E device—(Voltage-) Controlled Voltage Source

General forms:

E*<name>* *<+node>* *<−node>* *<+control>* *<−control>* *<gain>*

E*<name>* *<+node>* *<−node>*POLY(*<value>*)*<<+control>* *<−control>>**
*<<coeff>>**

E*<name>* *<+node>* *<−node>*VALUE={*<exp>*}

E*<name>* *<+node>* *<−node>*TABLE{*<exp>*}*<(inval),(outval)>**

E*<name>* *<+node>* *<−node>*LAPLACE{*<exp>*}{*<sexp>*}

E*<name>* *<+node>* *<−node>*FREQ{*<exp>*}*<(freq,magdb,phasedeg)>**

Examples:

```
EBUFF   1    2 10 11 1.0
EAMP    13   0 POLY(1) 26 0 500
ENLIN  100 101 POLY(2) 3 0 4 0 0.0 13.6 0.2 0.005
ESQRT   10   0 VALUE = {SQRT(V(5))}
ETAB    20   5 TABLE {V(2)} (−5v,5v) (0v,0v) (5v,−5v)
E1POLE  10   0 LAPLACE {V(1)} {1 / (1 + s)}
EATTEN  20   0 FREQ {V(100)} (0,0,0 10,−2,−5 20,−6,−10)
```

F device—Current-Controlled Current Source

General forms:

F*<name>* *<+node>* *<−node>* *<vname>* *<gain>*

F*<name>* *<+node>* *<−node>*POLY(*<value>*)*<vname>>**<coeff>>**

Examples:

```
FSENSE  1    2 VSENSE 10.0
FAMP    13   0 POLY(1) VIN 500
FNLIN  100 101 POLY(2) V1 v2 0.0 0.9 0.2 0.005
```

G device—(Voltage-) Controlled Current Source

General forms:

G*<name>* *<+node>* *<−node>* *<+control>* *<−control>* *<gain>*

G*<name>* *<+node>* *<−node>*POLY(*<value>*)*<<+control>* *<−control>>**
*<<coeff>>**

G*<name>* *<+node>* *<−node>*VALUE=[*<exp>*]

G*<name>* *<+node>* *<−node>*TABLE[*<exp>*]=*<(inval),(outval)>**

G*<name>* *<+node>* *<−node>*LAPLACE[*<exp>*][*<sexp>*]

G*<name>* *<+node>* *<−node>*FREQ[*<exp>*]*<(freq,magdb,phasedeg)>**

Examples:

```
GBUFF    1    2 10 11 1.0
GAMP    13    0 POLY(1) 26 0 500
GNLIN  100 101 POLY(2) 3 0 4 0 0.0 13.6 0.2 0.005
GSQRT   10    0 VALUE = {SQRT(V(5))}
GTAB    20    5 TABLE{V(2)} = (-5v,5v) (0v,0v) (5v,-5v)
G1POLE  10    0 LAPLACE [V(1)] [1 / (1 + s)]
GATTEN  20    0 FREQ [V(100)] (0,0,0 10,-2,-5 20,-6,-10)
```

H device—Current-Controlled Voltage Source

General forms:

H*<name>* *<+node>* *<−node>* *<vname>* *<gain>*

H*<name>* *<+node>* *<−node>*POLY(*<value>*)*<<vname>>*<<coeff>>**

Examples:

```
HSENSE   1    2 VSENSE 10.0
HAMP    13    0 POLY(1) VIN 500
HNLIN  100 101 POLY(2) V1 V2 0.0 0.9 0.2 0.005
```

I device—Current Source

General form:

I*<name>* *<+node>* *<−node>*[[DC]*<value>*][AC*<mag>*[*<phase>*]][*<transient>*]

Transient specifications:

  EXP(i1 ipk rdelay rtc fdelay ftc)

  PULSE(i1 i2 td trise tfall pw per)

  PWL(t1 i1 t2 i2 . . . tn fn)

  SFFM(ioff iampl fc mod fm)

  SIN(ioff iampl freq td df phase)

Examples:

```
IBIAS 13 0 2.3mA
IAC    2 3 AC .001
IACPHS 2 3 AC .001 90
IPULSE 1 0 PULSE(-1mA 1mA 2ns 2ns 2ns 50ns 100ns)
I3 26 77   DC .002 AC 1 SIN(.002 .002 1.5MEG)
```

J device—Junction FET

General form:

J*<name>* *<d>* *<g>* *<s>* *<model>*[*<area>*]

Examples:

```
JIN 100  1  0 JFAST
J13  22 14 23 JNOM 2.0
```

K device—Inductor Coupling

General forms:

K*<name>*L*<name>*<L*<name>*>*<coupling>

K*<name>*<L*<name>*>*<coupling> *<model>*[*<size>*]

Examples:

```
KTUNED L3OUT L4IN  .8
KXFR1  LPRIM LSEC  .99
KXFR2  L1 L2 L3 L4 .98 KPOT_3C8
```

L device—Inductor

General form:

L*<name>* <+node> <−node>[model]*<value>*[IC=*<initial>*]

Examples:

```
LLOAD   15  0 20mH
L2       1  2 .2e−6
LCHOKE  3 42 LMOD .03
LSENSE  5 12 2uH IC=2mA
```

M device—MOSFET

General form:

M*<name>* *<d>* *<g>* *<s>* *<sub>* *<mdl>*[L=*<value>*][W=*<value>*]
[AD=*<value>*][AS=*<value>*][PD=*<value>*][PS=*<value>*]
[NRD=*<value>*][NRS=*<value>*]
[NRG=*<value>*][NRB=*<value>*]

Examples:

```
M1   14 2  13   0 PNOM L=25u W=12u
M13 15 3    0   0 PSTRONG
M2A  0 2 100 100 PWEAK L=33u w=12u
+ AD=288p AS=288p PD=60u PS=60u NRD=14 NRS=24 NRG=10
```

N device—Digital Input

General form:

N*<name>* *<inode>* *<lonode>* *<hinode>* *<model>*[SIGNAME=*<name>*][IS=*<init>*]

Examples:

```
NRESET  7 15  16 FROM_TTL
N12     18  0 100 FROM_CMOS SIGNAME=VCO_GATE IS=0
```

O device—Digital Output

General form:

O*<name>* *<iface>* *<ref>* *<model>*[SIGNAME=*<name>*]

Examples:

```
OVCO 17   0 TO_TTL
O5   22 100 TO_CMOS SIGNAME=VCO_OUT
```

Q device—Bipolar Transistor

General form:

Q*<name> <c> <b> <e>*[*<subs>*]*<model>*[*<area>*]

Examples:

```
Q1   14 2 13 PNPNOM
Q13 15 3  0 1 NPNSTRONG 1.5
Q7   VC 5 12 [SUB] LATPNP
```

R device—Resistor

General form:

R*<name> <+node> <−node>*[*<model>*]*<value>*

Examples:

```
RLOAD 15 0 2k
R2    1 2 2.4e4
```

S device—Voltage-Controlled Switch

General form:

S*<name> <+node> <−node> <+control> <−control> <model>*

Examples:

```
S12 13 17 2 0 SMOD
SRESET 5 0 15 3 RELAY
```

T device—Transmission Line

General form:

T*<name> <A+> <A−> <B+> <B−> <Z0=value>*[TD=*<val>*]
    [F=*<val>*[NL=*<val>*]]

Examples:

```
T1 1 2 3 4 Z0=220 TD=115ns
T2 1 2 3 4 Z0=50 F=5MEG NL=0.5
```

U device—Digital

General form:

U*<name> <type> <parms> <node>**[*<parm>=<val>*]**

Types: BUF, INV, AND, NAND, OR, NOR, XOR, NXOR, BUF3, INV3, AND3,

OR3, NOR3, XOR3, NXOR3, JKFF, DFF, PULLUP, PULLDN, STIM.

STIM Syntax:

U*<name>*STIM(*<width>,<radices>*)*<node>***<iomodel>*
  [TIMESTEP=*stepsize*]<*<time>,<value>*>|
  <*<time>*GOTO*<label><n>*TIMES>|
  <*<time>*GOTO*<label><rv><val>*>|
  <*<time>*INCR BY*<val>*>
  <*<time>*DECR BY*<val>*>**<rv>*=UNTIL GT|GE|LT|LE

Examples:

```
U7 XOR() INA INB OUTXOR DEFGATE DEFIO
U101 STIM( 1, 1 ) IN1 STMIO TIMESTEP=10ns
+ (LABEL=STARTLOOP) (+10c, 0)(+5ns, 1)
+ (+40c GOTO STARTLOOP 1 TIMES)
```

V device—Voltage Source

General form:

V*<name>* <+*node>* <−*node>*[[DC]*<value>*][AC*<mag>*[*<phase>*]][*<transient>*]

Transient specifications:

      EXP(iv vpk rdelay rtc fdelay ftc)

      PULSE(v1 v2 td trise tfall pw per)

      PWL(t1 v1 t2 v2 . . . tn vn)

      SFFM(voff vampl fc mod fm)

      SIN(voff vampl freq td df phase)

Examples:

```
VBIAS  13  0 2.3mV
VAC     2  3 AC .001
VACPHS  2  3 AC .001 90
VPULSE  1  0 PULSE(-1mV 1mV 2ns 2ns 2ns 50ns 100ns)
V3     26 77 DC .002 AC 1 SIN(.002 .002 1.5MEG)
```

W device—Current-Controlled Switch

General form:

W*<name>* <+*node>* <−*node>* *<vname>* *<model>*

Examples:

```
W12 13 17 VC WMOD
WRESET 5 0 VRESET RELAY
```

X device—Subcircuit Call

General form:

X*<name>*[*<node>*]**<sname>*[PARAMS:<*<par>*=*<val>**>]

Examples:

```
X12 100 101 200 201 DIFFAMP
XBUFF 13 15 UNITAMP
```

PSPICE STATEMENTS AS LISTED IN PSPICE.HLP

.AC—AC Analysis

General form:

.AC[LIN][OCT][DEC]<*points*><*start*><*end*>

Examples:

```
.AC LIN 101 10Hz 200Hz
.AC OCT  10 1KHz 16KHz
.AC DEC  20 1MEG 100MEG
```

.DC—DC Analysis

General forms:

.DC[LIN]<*varname*><*start*><*end*><*incr*>[<*nest*>]

.DC[OCT][DEC]<*varname*><*start*><*end*><*points*>[<*nest*>]

.DC<*varname*>LIST<*value*>*[<*nest*>]

Examples:

```
.DC VIN −.25 .25 .05
.DC LIN I2 5mA −2mA 0.1mA
.DC VCE 0v 10v .5v IB 0mA 1mA 50uA
.DC RES RMOD(R) 0.9 1.1 .001
.DC DEC NPN QFAST(IS) 1e−18 1e−14 5
.DC TEMP LIST 0 20 27 50 80
```

.DISTRIBUTION—User-Defined Dist

General form:

.DISTRIBUTION<*name*><<*dev*><*prob*>>*

Example:

```
.DISTRIBUTION bimodal (−1,1)(−.5,1)(−.5,0)(.5,0)(.5,1)(1,1)
```

.END—End Circuit

.ENDS—End Subcircuit

General forms:

.END

.ENDS[<*name*>]

Examples:

```
.END
.ENDS
.ENDS 741
```

.FOUR—Fourier Analysis

General form:

.FOUR*<freq><output var>**

Examples:

```
.FOUR 10KHz v(5) v(6,7)
```

.FUNC—Define Function

General form:

.FUNC*<name>*([*arg**])*<body>*

Examples:

```
.FUNC DR(D) D/57.296
.FUNC E(X) EXP(X)
.FUNC APBX(A,B,X) A+B*X
```

.IC—Initial Transient Conditions

General form:

.IC<*<vnode>*=*<value>*>*

Examples:

```
.IC V(2)=3.4 V(102)=0
```

.INC—Include File

General form:

.INC*<name>*

Examples:

```
.INC SETUP.CIR
.INC C:\PSLIB\VCO.CIR
```

.LIB—Library File

General form:

.LIB[*<name>*]

Examples:

```
.LIB
```

```
.LIB OPNOM.LIB
.LIB C:\\PSLIB\\QNOM.LIB
```

.MC—Monte Carlo Analysis

General form:

.MC<#*runs*>[DC][AC][TRAN]<*opvar*><*func*><*option*>*

Examples:

```
.MC 10 TRAN V(5) YMAX
.MC 50   DC IC(Q7) MIN LIST
.MC 20  AC VP(13,5)RISE_EDGE(1.0) LIST OUTPUT ALL
```

.WCASE—Worst-Case Analysis

General form:

.WCASE<*analysis*><*opvar*><*func*><*option*>*

Examples:

```
.WCASE DC V(4,5) YMAX
.WCASE TRAN V(1) FALL_EDGE(3.5v) VARY BOTH BY RELTOL DEVICES RL
```

.MODEL—Model

General form:

.MODEL<*name*><*type*>[<*param*>=<*value*>[<*tol*>]]*

Typename	Devname	Devtype
CAP	Cxxx	capacitor
IND	Lxxx	inductor
RES	Rxxx	resistor
D	Dxxx	diode
NPN	Qxxx	*npn* bipolar
PNP	Qxxx	*pnp* bipolar
LPNP	Qxxx	lateral PNP
NJF	Jxxx	*n*-channel JFET
PJF	Jxxx	*p*-channel JFET
NMOS	Mxxx	*n*-channel MOSFET
PMOS	Mxxx	*p*-channel MOSFET
GASFET	Bxxx	*n*-channel GaAsFET
CORE	Kxxx	nonlinear core
VSWITCH	Sxxx	v/c switch
ISWITCH	Wxxx	c/c switch
DINPUT	Nxxx	digital i/p
DOUTPUT	Oxxx	digital o/p

Examples:

```
.MODEL RMAX RES (R=1.5 TC=.02 TC2=.005)
.MODEL QDRIV NPN (IS=1e−7 BF=30)
.MODEL DLOAD D (IS=1e−9 DEV 5% LOT 10%)
```

.NODESET—Nodeset

General form:

.NODESET<<*node*>=<*value*>>*

Examples:

```
.NODESET V(2)=3.4 V(3)=−1V
```

.NOISE—Noise Analysis

General form:

.NOISE<*opvar*><*name*>[<*ival*>]

Examples:

```
.NOISE V(5) VIN
.NOISE V(4,5) ISRC 20
```

.OP—Bias Point

General form:

.OP

Examples:

```
.OP
```

.OPTIONS—Options

General form:

```
.OPTIONS[<fopt>*][<vopt>=<value>*]
```

Flag Options:

ACCT summary & accounting
EXPAND show subcircuit expansion
LIBRARY list lines from library files
LIST output summary
NODE output netlist
NOECHO suppress listing
NOMOD suppress model param listing
NOPAGE suppress banners
OPTS output option values

Value Options:

ABSTOL	best accuracy of currents
CHGTOL	best accuracy of charges
CPTIME	CPU time allowed
DEFAD	MOSFET default AD
DEFAS	MOSFET default AS
DEFL	MOSFET default L
DEFW	MOSFET default W
GMIN	min conductance, any branch
ITL1	DC & bias pt blind limit
ITL2	DC & bias pt guess limit
ITL4	transient per-point limit
ITL5	transient total, all points
LIMPTS	max for print/plot
NUMDGT	#digits output
PIVREL	rel mag for matrix pivot
PIVTOL	abs mag for matrix pivot
RELTOL	rel accuracy of V's and I's
TNOM	default temp
TRTOL	transient accuracy adjustment
VNTOL	best accuracy of voltages
WIDTH	output width

Examples:

```
.OPTIONS NOECHO NOMOD RELTOL=.01
.OPTIONS ACCT DEFL=12u DEFW=8u
```

.PARAM—Global Parameter

General form:

.PARAM<<*name*>=<*value*>>*

Examples:

```
.PARAM pi=3.14159265
.PARAM RSHEET=120, VCC=5V
```

.PLOT—Plot

General form:

.PLOT[DC][AC][NOISE][TRAN][[<*opvar*>*][(<*lo*>,<*hi*>)]]*

Examples:

```
.PLOT DC V(3) V(2,3) V(R1) I(VIN)
.PLOT AC VM(2) VP(2) VG(2)
.PLOT TRAN V(3) V(2,3) (0,5V) ID(M2) I(VCC) (−50mA,50mA)
```

.PRINT—Print

General form:

.PRINT[DC][AC][NOISE][TRAN][*<opvar>**]

Examples:

```
.PRINT DC V(3) V(2,3) V(R1) IB(Q13)
.PRINT AC VM(2) VP(2) VG(5) II(7)
.PRINT NOISE INOISE ONOISE DB(INOISE)
```

.PROBE—Probe

General forms:

.PROBE[/CSDF]

.PROBE[/CSDF][*<opvar>**]

Examples:

```
.PROBE
.PROBE v(2) I(R2) VBE(Q13) VDB(5)
```

.PROBE/CSDF

.SENS—Sensitivity Analysis

General form:

.SENS*<opvar>**

Examples:

```
.SENS V(9) V(4,3) I(VCC)
```

.STEP—Stepped Analysis

General forms:

.STEP[LIN]*<varname>* *<start>* *<end>* *<incr>*

.STEP[OCT][DEC]*<varname>* *<start>* *<end>* *<points>*

.STEP*<varname>*LIST*<value>**

.STEP PARAM X 1 5 0.1

Examples:

```
.STEP VIN −.25 .25 .05
.STEP LIN I2 5mA −2mA 0.1mA
```

```
.STEP RES RMOD(R) 0.9 1.1 .001
.STEP TEMP LIST 0 20 27 50 80
```

.SUBCKT—Subcircuit Definition

General form:

.SUBCKT<*name*>[<*node*>*][PARAMS:<*par*>[=<*val*>]*]

Examples:

```
.SUBCKT OPAMP 1 2 101 102
.SUBCKT FILTER IN OUT PARAMS: CENTER, WIDTH=10 KHz
```

.TEMP—Temperature

General form:

.TEMP<*value*>*

Examples:

```
.TEMP 125
.TEMP 0 27 125
```

.TF—Transfer Function

General form:

.TF<*opvar*> <*ipsrc*>

Examples:

```
.TF V(5) VIN
.TF 1(VDRIV) ICNTRL
```

.TRAN—Transient Analysis

General form:

.TRAN[/OP]<*pstep*> <*ftime*>[<*noprint*>[<*ceiling*>]]][UIC]

Examples:

```
.TRAN 1ns 100nS
.TRAN/OP 1nS 100nS 20ns UIC
.TRAN 1nS 100nS 0nS .1nS
```

.WIDTH—Width

General form:

.WIDTH OUT=<*val*>

Example:

```
.WIDTH OUT=80
```

OUTPUT VARIABLES

This section describes the types of output variables that can be used in both the
.PRINT and .PLOT statements. Each such statement may have up to eight output
variables.

DC Sweep and Transient Analysis

V(<*node*>)
V(<+*node*>,<−*node*>)
V(<*name*>)
Vx(<*name*>)
Vxy(<*name*>)
Vz(<*name*>)
I(<*name*>)
Ix(<*name*>)
Iz(<*name*>)

The following is an abbreviated list of the two-terminal device types for which the
dc sweep and transient analysis applies.

Devtypes: C/D/E/F/G/H/I/L/R/V

For the Vx, Vxy, Ix forms, <*name*> must be a three- or four-terminal device and x
and y must each be a terminal abbreviation. In abbreviated form these are

xy: D/G/S (B)
xy: D/G/S (J)
xy: D/G/S/B (M)
xy: C/B/E/S (Q)
z: A/B

AC Analysis

Suffixes:

M   magnitude
DB   magnitude
P   phase
G   group delay
R   real
I   imaginary

The following is an abbreviated list of devices through which currents are available:

Devtypes: C/I/L/R/T/V

For other devices, you must put a zero-valued voltage source in series with the device (or terminal) of interest.

Noise Analysis

INOISE

ONOISE

DB(INOISE)

DB(ONOISE)

COMMON SOURCES OF ERROR IN PSPICE INPUT FILES

Floating nodes have no dc path to ground. There are three frequent causes of trouble:

1. The two ends of a transmission line do not have a dc connection between them.
2. Voltage-controlled sources do not have a dc connection between their controlling nodes.
3. There is an error in the circuit description.

Assuming that this circuit is correct, the solution is to connect the floating node to ground via a large-value resistor.

PSpice checks for zero-resistance loops. These may be caused by independent voltage sources (V), controlled voltage sources (E and H), and inductors (L); or there may be an error in the circuit description.

Assuming the circuit to be correct, the solution is to add series resistance into the loop.

Convergence problems may occur in the dc sweep, in bias-point calculations, and in transient analysis:

DC Sweep—The most frequent problem is attempting to analyze circuits with regenerative feedback (e.g., Schmitt trigger). Try doing a Transient Analysis instead of the dc Sweep. Use a piecewise-linear voltage source to generate a slow ramp. You can sweep up and down again in the same analysis.

Bias Point—Use the .NODESET statement to help PSpice find a solution. Nodes such as the outputs of op amps are good candidates for .NODESET.

Transient Analysis—Unrealistic modeling of circuits with switches but no parasitic capacitance can cause problems, for example, circuits containing diodes and inductors but no parasitic resistance or capacitance.

It may be necessary to relax RELTOL from .001 to .01.

Using the "uic" modifier causes the Transient Bias-Point calculation to be skipped, causing Transient Analysis convergence problems. Use .IC or .NODESET instead.

With high voltages and currents, it may be necessary to increase VNTOL and ABSTOL. For voltages in the kV range, raise VNTOL to 1 mV. For currents in the amps range, raise ABSTOL to 1 nA. For currents in the kA range, raise ABSTOL to 1 uA.

PSpice's accuracy is controlled by the RELTOL, VNTOL, ABSTOL, and CHGTOL parameters of the .OPTIONS statement. The most important is RELTOL, which controls the relative accuracy of all voltages and currents that are calculated. RELTOL defaults to 0.1%. VNTOL sets best accuracy for voltages. ABSTOL sets best accuracy for currents. CHGTOL sets best accuracy for charge/flux.

Global nodes begin with the prefix "$G_". Examples are $G_VCC $G_COMMON.

Predefined digital nodes are $D_HI,$D_LO,$D_NC,$D_X.

PSpice will accept expressions in most places where a numeric value is required. This includes component values, model parameter values, subcircuit parameters, initial conditions, and so forth. An expression is contained within { } and must fit on one line.

Components of an expression include numbers, operators $+-*/$, parameter names, and functions (sin, cos, exp, etc.) For example, a resistor value could be defined in terms of a global parameter RSHEET:

```
rel 20 21 {rsheet*1.10}
```

Expressions may be used for global parameters values, but these expressions may not contain parameter names.

Expressions used in the extended controlled sources may additionally refer to node voltages, currents, and the swept variable "time."

Global parameters are defined with the .PARAM statement. They can then be used in expressions for device values, and so forth. For example,

```
.param pi=3. 14159265
c1 2 0 {1/ (2*pi*10khz*10k)}
```

Subcircuit parameters supply default values for subcircuits. The defaults can be overridden when the subcircuit is called. The values given to subcircuit parameters can be expressions. In addition to the normal components of an expression, subcircuit parameter expressions may refer to the names of a subcircuit's own parameters (if any).

If a global parameter and a subcircuit parameter have the same name, the subcircuit parameter definition is used. For example, here is the definition of a parasitic node:

```
.subckt para 1 params:r=1meg,c=1pf
rl 10{r}
cl 10{c}
.ends
```

and here is the subcircuit being used:

```
xparal 27 para params: c=5pf
```

C

Installing the MicroSim Software

At the time of this writing, the MicroSim evaluation software version 6.3, revision 2 was the latest available version. The MicroSim Corporation has given permission for the publisher to include this (or a later version) of the software on CD-ROM with this text. In File Manager for Windows 3.x, when you view the contents of the MicroSim CD, you will see the directories shown in Fig. C.1. The folders shown with plus signs have additional subdirectories. As you can see, there are 127 Mbytes (packed) on this CD. When this window is open, in File Manager you may dbl-clk on the *setup.exe* icon to begin the installation, or use the following procedure.

INSTALLATION FOR WINDOWS 3.1X

In Windows 3.1X from the Program Manager, select File, Run . . . and type

d:\setup

where *d* represents the letter assigned to the CD-ROM drive. The installation options allow you to choose the regular evaluation software and PLSyn evaluation software. For our purposes only the regular evaluation software will be chosen, as shown in Fig. C.2. If you choose also to install the full on-line documentation, you will need almost 56 Mbytes of storage on your hard-disk drive; the minimal installation requires considerably less. Figure C.3 shows a typical set of icons for the MicroSim Evaluation work group.

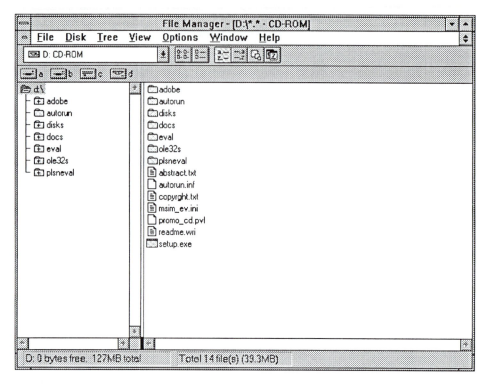

Fig. C.1 The directories contained on the MicroSim evaluation software CD-ROM.

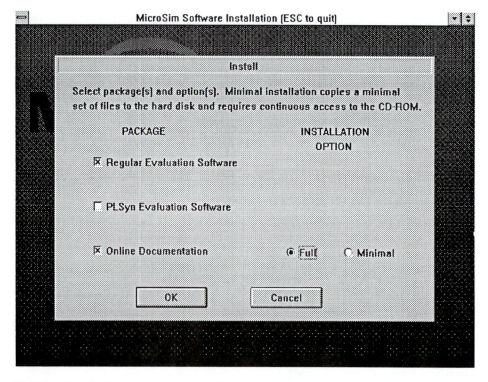

Fig. C.2 Installation options for the evaluation software.

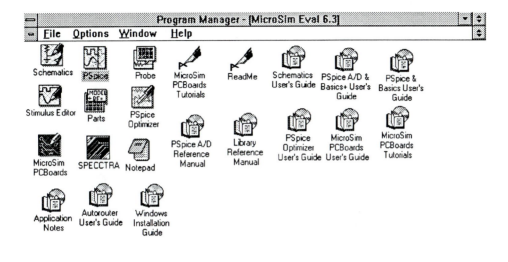

Fig. C.3   The MicroSim Program Group in Windows 3.1x.

Setting the Program Item Properties

Using the icons for PSpice, Schematics, and Probe will be made more simple if you change the working directory for each of these programs. As an example, select the icon for PSpice, then in Program Manager choose File, Properties . . . and in the Program Item Properties window make the Working Directory *c:\p*. Repeat this process for the Schematics and Probe icons. The process is illustrated in Fig. C.4.

Using Notepad

Notepad is found in Windows in the Accessories workgroup. Select the Notepad icon, then in Program Manager choose File, Copy . . . and in the Copy Program Item window select "MicroSim Eval 6.3" as the To Group. This will place a copy of the Notepad icon in the MicroSim workgroup for easy access. See Fig. C.5, which shows how this is done and incidentally shows the Notepad icon in both workgroups.

INSTALLATION FOR WINDOWS 95

If you are using Windows 95, rather than Windows 3.1x, install the MicroSim evaluation software by opening the Windows Explorer, then rt-clk the CD-ROM icon,

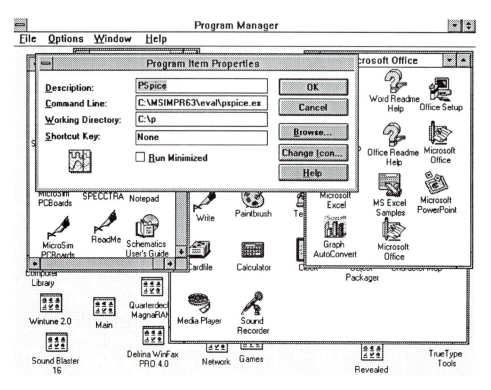

Fig. C.4 Setting the Program Item Properties.

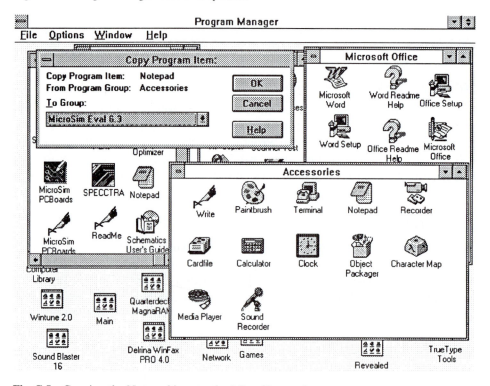

Fig. C.5 Copying the Notepad icon to the MicroSim workgroup.

and select Autoplay. This will cause the CD-ROM drive to activate and read the *set-up.exe* file. The screen display will be as shown in Fig. C.6. Select the regular evaluation software package with either full or minimal on-line documentation. At the completion of the installation, the MicroSim Evaluation Program Group should appear as shown in Fig. C.7.

Copy the Microsoft Notepad program to the MicroSim Eval 6.3 program group, or simply keep Notepad available for use whenever it is needed. This is done by first opening Notepad, then when you have finished using it, make it inactive by clicking on the left control button. The three control buttons are at the top right of the window. They are used to inactivate (or minimize) the application, change between maximized and floating windows, and close an application (from left to right). Figure C.8 shows the MicroSim Eval 6.3 window; note the control buttons at the top right of the window. Also see that Notepad appears on the bottom line (to the right of the Start button).

In order to run the various MicroSim programs in Windows 95 the path shown in Fig. C.9 should be used. Begin with the Start button, select Programs, MicroSim Eval 6.3, then select from the list shown in Fig. C.9.

Note: Do not attempt to run Schematics using the Microsoft Explorer route shown in Fig. C.10. In this figure there is an icon on the right called *Psched.exe*. It has the correct symbol for Schematics and is indeed the Schematics program icon.

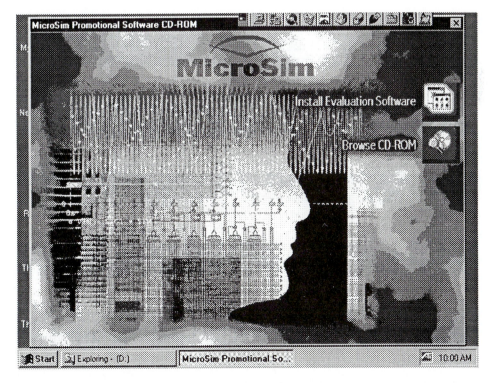

Fig. C.6 The Start-up Screen for MicroSim in Windows 95.

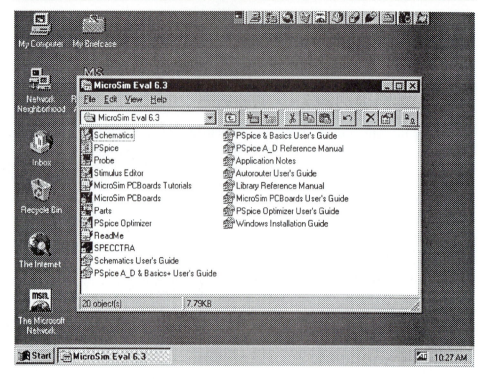

Fig. C.7 MicroSim Folder in Windows 95.

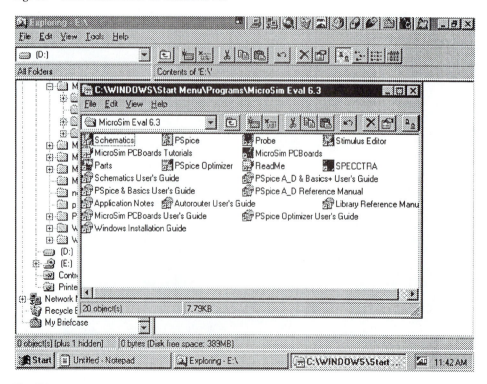

Fig. C.8 The MicroSim Folder in Windows 95.

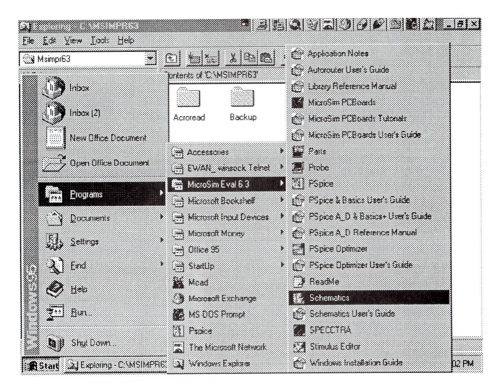

Fig. C.9   The path to Schematics in Windows 95.

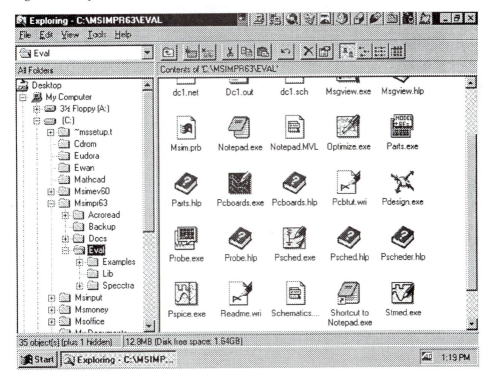

Fig. C.10   Folders in the MicroSim directory.

567

It will not properly run Schematics because it does not invoke the *msim_ev.ini file,* which is necessary for the MicroSim libraries to be made available.

The PSpice A/D Reference Manual

If you have questions about any of the features available in PSpice, the PSpice A/D Reference Manual is an invaluable aid in finding answers. This manual is included on the CD-ROM and is readily available if you have installed the on-line documentation. When you click on the proper icon, you will see the title page for the Adobe Acrobat Reader, which provides the link to the on-line manuals, as shown in Fig. C.11. In a moment the beginning of the reference manual will appear on the screen.

      The row of icons just below the menu provides a method for moving to various portions of the manual and so forth. This title page is shown in Fig. C.12. The two icons on the far left allow you to choose between a split view (with bookmarks) and a full-page view. The next icon allows you to choose quickly from among three successive pages, as shown in Fig. C.13. At the bottom of the screen, 75% magnification has been selected. This is helpful when an overview of each page is desired. In order to clearly see the text on a printed page, 150% magnification is a good choice.

Fig. C.11   The Acrobat Reader is used for loading MicroSim on-line manuals.

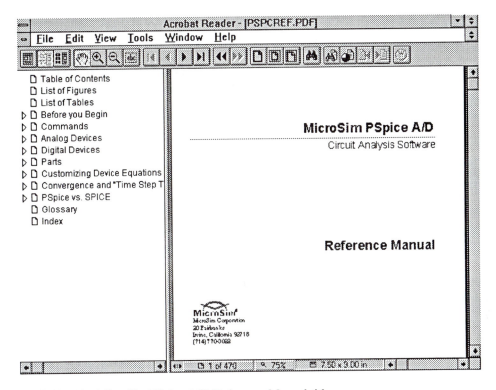

Fig. C.12   The MicroSim PSpice A/D Reference Manual title page.

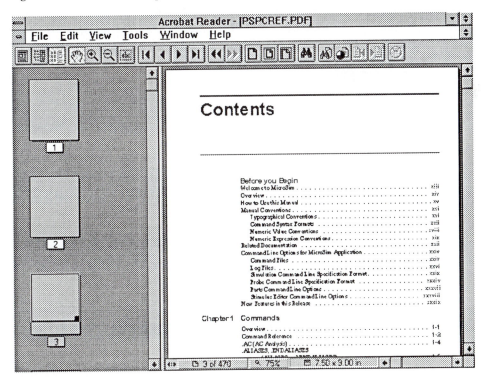

Fig. C.13   Multipage view selection in the Acrobat Reader.

There are several other on-line reference manuals that are included on the evaluation CD-ROM. The *Library Reference Manual* contains a listing of all the parts available in the production version and will be of limited use if you do not have this version of the software. You may want to refer to the *PSpice & Basics User's Guide* for an introduction to the on-line manuals. Note the limitations of the Evaluation Version as shown in Fig. C.14.

How to Begin

In the MicroSim workgroup, select Notepad (dbl-clk) in order to enter a circuit file. The PSpice Overview chapter shows a file for a simple dc circuit. The title line is "Resistive Circuit with Voltage Source." There is another line for each element in the circuit, consisting of a voltage source and three resistors. Refer to Fig. C.15 to see how the completed file looks. After all lines have been completed, use File, Save, and name the file *preview.cir.* You may close Notepad, or simply move it to the side, as shown in the figure.

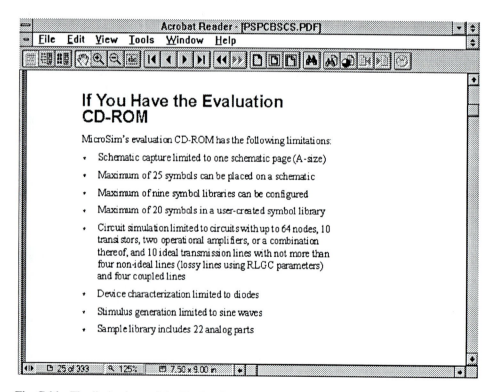

Fig. C.14 The limitations of the Evaluation Version of PSpice.

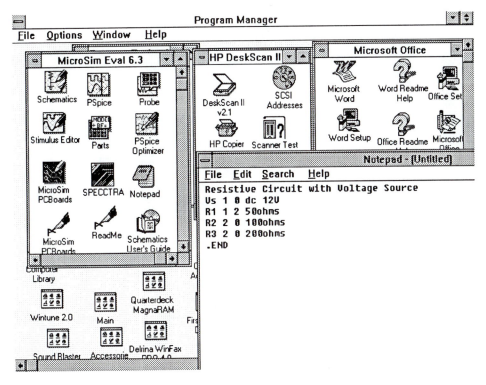

Fig. C.15 Using Notepad to produce a circuit listing. The file will be saved as *preview.cir.*

Simulating the Circuit

Select the PSpice icon (dbl-clk) in the MicroSim workgroup, then use File, Open. . . . You will see the beginning of a list of all the circuit files (which have the extension cir). Either select *preview.cir* from the list or type the name *preview* in the File Name box. A PSpice information window will appear, and you should see the message "Simulation Completed Successfully." When you click on OK, the PSpice screen shows "Writing results to PREVIEW.out." The output file contains the circuit file listing as well as the results of the simulation. It may be viewed by selecting File, Examine Output in PSpice, or by specifying the file *preview.out* in Notepad or in a word-processing program.

Several of the on-line reference manuals show in diagramatic form the steps involved in circuit simulation. In Fig. C.16 the box on the left shows the process beginning with Schematics that produces a netlist, simulation directives, and a circuit file set. The first 13 chapters of this text do not rely on Schematics to produce the circuit simulation. The method of analysis simply begins with a circuit file (cre-

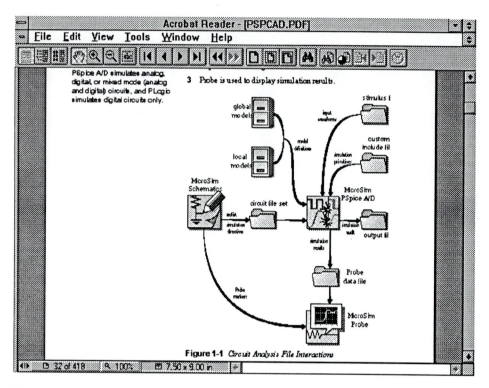

Fig. C.16   A page from the PSpice A/D & Basics+ User's Guide.

ated in Notepad); the circuit file is then submitted to the PSpice program (shown at the center of Fig. C.16). This allows for the analysis to proceed with the creation of an output file and a Probe data file if requested.

Refer to the Overview chapter at the beginning of the text for other simple PSpice examples, then continue with Chapter 1, DC Circuit Analysis.

D

PSpice Devices and Model Parameters

< >* indicates that an item may be repeated.

B GaAsFET

B<*name*><*drain node*><*gate node*><*source node*><*model name*><*[area]*>

Model Parameters		Default Value	Units
LEVEL	model type(1 = Curtice, 2 = Raytheon)	1	
VTO	threshold voltage	–2.5	volts
ALPHA	tanh constant	2	volts^{-1}
B	doping tail extending parameter	0.3	
BETA	transconductance coef.	0.1	A/V^2
LAMBDA	channel-length modulation	0	volt^{-1}
RG	gate ohmic resistance	0	ohm
RD	drain ohmic resistance	0	ohm
RS	source ohmic resistance	0	ohm
IS	gate *pn* saturation current	1E–14	ampere
M	gate *pn* grading coefficient	0.5	
N	gate *pn* emission coefficient	1	
VBI	gate *pn* potential	1	volt
CGD	gate-drain zero-bias *pn* cap.	0	farad
CGS	gate-source zero-bias *pn* cap.	0	farad
CDS	drain-source capacitance	0	farad

TAU	transit time	0	sec
FC	forward-bias dep. cap. coef.	0.5	
VTOTC	VTO temperature coef.	0	volt/°C
BETATCE	BETA exponential temp. coef.	0	%/°C
KF	flicker noise coef.	0	
AF	flicker noise exponent	1	

[*area*] is the relative device area and defaults to 1.

    The GaAsFET, as shown in Fig. D.1, is modeled as an intrinsic FET with ohmic resistance RD in series with the drain. Another ohmic resistance RS is in series with the source, and another ohmic resistance RG is in series with the gate.

C Capacitor

C*<name>< +node><−node>*[*model name*]*<value>*[IC=*<initial value>*]

Model Parameters		Default Value	Units
C	capacitance multiplier	1	
VC1	linear voltage coefficient	0	volts^{-1}
VC2	quadratic voltage coefficient	0	volts^{-2}
TC1	linear temperature coefficient	0	°C^{-1}
TC2	quadratic temperature coefficient	0	°C^{-2}

If [*model name*] is left out, then *<value>* is the capacitance in farads. If [*model name*] is given, then the capacitance is

$$<value>\cdot C(1+VC1\cdot V+VC2\cdot V^2)(1+TC1(T\text{-}T_{nom})+TC2(T\text{-}T_{nom})^2)$$

Fig. D.1   GaAsFET model.

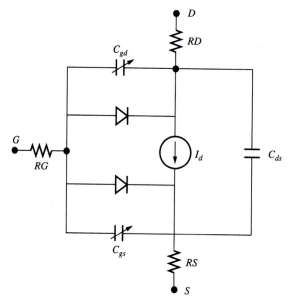

T_{nom} is the nominal temperature which is set with the TNOM option.

D Diode

D*<name><+node><−node><model name>[area]*

Model Parameters		Default Value	Units
IS	saturation current	1E–14	ampere
N	emission coefficient	1	
RS	parasitic resistance	0	ohm
CJO	zero-bias *pn* capacitance	0	farad
VJ	*pn* potential	1	volt
M	*pn* grading coefficient	0.5	
FC	forward-bias depletion cap. coef.	0.5	
TT	transit time	0	s
BV	reverse breakdown voltage	infinite	volts
IBV	reverse breakdown current	1E–10	ampere
EG	bandgap voltage (barrier height)	1.11	eV
XTI	IS temperature exponent	3	
KF	flicker noise coefficient	0	
AF	flicker noise exponent	1	

The diode, which is shown in Fig. D.2, is modeled as an ohmic resistance RS in series with an intrinsic diode.

E Voltage-Controlled Voltage Source

E*<name><+node><−node><+controlling node><−con. node><gain>*
E*<name><+node><−node>*POLY(*<value>*)
  <<+controlling node><−con. node>><<*polynomial coefficient value>>**

F Current-Controlled Current Source

F*<name><+node><−node><controlling V device name><gain>*

Fig. D.2 Diode model.

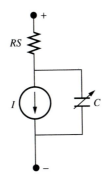

F*<name><+node><−node>*POLY(*<value>*)*<controlling V device name>*<<polynomial coefficient value>>**

G Voltage-Controlled Current Source

G*<name><+node><−node><+controlling node>*
  <−controlling node><transconductance>

G*<name><+node><−node>*POLY(*<value>*)
  <<+controlling node><−controlling node>*
  <<polynomial coefficient value>>*

H Current-Controlled Voltage Source

H*<name><+node><−node><controlling V device name>*
  <transresistance>

H*<name><+node><−node>*POLY(*<value>*)
  <controlling V device name>*<<polynomial coefficient value>>*

I Independent Current Source

I*<name><+node><−node>*[[DC*<value>*]
  [AC*<magnitude value>*[*phase value*]][*transient specification*]

If present, [*transient specification*] must be one of these:

EXP<>,PULSE<>,PWL<>,SFFM<>,or SIN<>

J Junction FET

J*<name><drain node><gate node><source node><model name>*[*area*]

Model Parameters		Default Value	Units
VTO	threshold voltage	−2.0	volts
BETA	transconductance coefficient	1E–4	A/V^2
LAMBDA	channel-length modulation	0	volt^{-1}
RD	drain ohmic resistance	0	ohm
RS	source ohmic resistance	0	ohm
IS	gate *pn* saturation current	1E–14	ampere
PB	gate *pn* potential	1	volt
CGD	gate-drain zero-bias *pn* capac.	0	farad
CGS	gate-source zero-bias *pn* capac.	0	farad
FC	forward-bias depletion cap. coef.	0.5	
VTOTC	VTO temperature coefficient	0	V/°C
BETATCE	BETA exponential temp. coef.	0	%/°C
KF	flicker noise coefficient	0	
AF	flicker noise exponent	1	

The JFET, as shown in Fig. D.3, is modeled as an intrinsic FET with an ohmic resis-

Fig. D.3 JFET model.

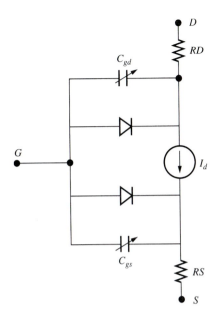

tance RD in series with the drain. Another ohmic resistance RS is in series with the source.

K Inductor Coupling (Transformer Core)

K*<name>*L*<inductor name>*<L*<inductor name>*>*<coupling value>

K*<name>*<L*<inductor name>*>*<coupling value><model name>[size]

Model Parameters (for Nonlinear Only)		**Default Value**	**Units**
AREA	mean magnetic cross section	0.1	cm^2
PATH	mean magnetic path length	1	cm
GAP	effective air-gap length	0	cm
PACK	pack (stacking) factor	1	
MS	magnetization saturation	1E+6	A/m
ALPHA	mean field parameter	0.001	
A	shape parameter	1000	A/m
C	domain wall flexing constant	0.2	
K	domain wall pinning constant	500	

K*<name>* couples two or more inductors. Use the dot convention to give a dot on the first(positive) node of each inductor.

   If *<model name>* is given, then (a) the inductor is a nonlinear device with a magnetic core; (b) the *BH* characteristics are based on the Jiles-Atherton model; (c) the *L* values indicate windings, with the value indicating the number of turns; and (d) a model statement is needed to specify model parameters.

L Inductor

L*<name><+node><−node>*[*model name*]*<value>*[IC=*initial value*]

Model Parameters		Default Value	Units
L	inductance multiplier	1	
IL1	linear current coefficient	0	ampere^{-1}
IL2	quadratic current coefficient	0	ampere^{-2}
TC1	linear temperature coefficient	0	°C^{-1}
TC2	quadratic temperature coefficient	0	°C^{-2}

If [*model name*] is omitted, then *<value>* is the inductance in henries. If [*model name*] is present, then the inductance is

$$<value>\cdot L(1+IL1\cdot I+IL2\cdot I^2)(1+TC1(T\text{-}T_{nom})+TC2(T\text{-}T_{nom})^2)$$

T_{nom} is the nominal temperature which is set with the TNOM option.

M MOSFET

M*<name><drain node><gate node><source node><bulk/substrate node>*
 <model name>[L=*<value>*][W=*<value>*][AD=*<value>*][AS=*<value>*]
 [PD=*<value>*][PS=*<value>*][NRD=*<value>*][NRS=*<value>*]
 [NRG=*<value>*][NRB=*<value>*]

Model Parameters		Default Value	Units
LEVEL	model type (1, 2, or 3)	1	
L	channel length	DEFL	meter
W	channel width	DEFW	meter
LD	lateral diffusion (length)	0	meter
WD	lateral diffusion (width)	0	meter
VTO	zero-bias threshold voltage	0	volt
KP	transconductance	2E–5	A/V^2
GAMA	bulk threshold parameter	0	volt$^{1/2}$
PHI	surface potential	0.6	volt
LAMBDA	channel-len. mod.(LEVEL 1 or 2)	0	volt^{-1}
RD	drain ohmic resistance	0	ohm
RS	source ohmic resistance	0	ohm
RG	gate ohmic resistance	0	ohm
RB	bulk ohmic resistance	0	ohm
RDS	drain-source shunt resistance	infinite	ohms
RSH	drain-source diff. sheet res.	0	ohm/sq.
IS	bulk *pn* saturation current	1E–14	A
JS	bulk *pn* sat. current/area	0	A/m^2
PB	bulk *pn* potential	0.8	volt
CBD	bulk-drain zero-bias *pn* cap.	0	farad
CBS	bulk-source zero-bias *pn* cap.	0	farad
CJ	bulk *pn* zero-bias bot. cap./area	0	F/m^2

CJSW	bulk *pn* zero-bias perimeter cap./length	0	F/m
MJ	bulk *pn* bottom grading coefficient	0.5	
MJSW	bulk *pn* sidewall grading coefficient	0.33	
FC	bulk *pn* forward bias capacitance coefficient	0.5	
CGSO	gate-source overlap capacitance/channel width	0	F/m
CGDO	gate-drain overlap capacitance/channel width	0	F/m
CGBO	gate-bulk overlap capacitance/channel length	0	F/m
NSUB	substrate doping density	0	cm^{-3}
NSS	surface state density	0	cm^{-2}
NFS	fast surface state density	0	cm^{-2}
TOX	oxide thickness	infinite	meter
TPG	gate material type	+1	
	+1 = opposite of substrate		
	−1 = same as substrate		
	0 = aluminum		
XJ	metallurgical junction depth	0	meter
UO	surface mobility	600	cm^2/Vs
UCRIT	mobility degradation critical field (LEVEL=2)	1E4	V/cm
UEXP	mobility degradation exponent (LEVEL=2)	0	
UTRA	(not used) mobility degradation transverse field coef.		
VMAX	maximum drift velocity	0	m/s
NEFF	channel charge coefficient (LEVEL=2)	1	
XQC	fraction of channel charge attributed to drain	1	
DELTA	width effect on threshold	0	
THETA	mobility modulation (LEVEL=3)	0	$volt^{-1}$
ETA	static feedback (LEVEL=3)	0	
KAPPA	saturation field factor (LEVEL=3)	0.2	
KF	flicker noise coefficient	0	
AF	flicker noise exponent	1	

The MOSFET, which is shown in Fig. D.4, is modeled as an intrinsic MOSFET with ohmic resistance RD in series with the drain, ohmic resistance RS in series with the source, ohmic resistance RG in series with the gate, and ohmic resistance RB in series with the (bulk) substrate. A shunt resistance RDS is in parallel with the (drain-source) channel.

Q Bipolar Transistor

Q<*name*><*collector node*><*base node*>
<*emitter node*><[*substrate node*]<*model name*>[*area value*]

Fig. D.4   MOSFET model.

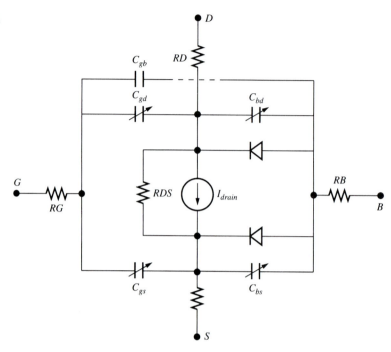

Model Parameters		Default Values	Units
IS	*pn* saturation current	1E–16	A
BF	ideal maximum forward beta	100	
NF	forward current emission coefficient	1	
VAF (VA)	forward Early voltage	infinite	V
IKF (IK)	corner for fwd beta high-cur roll off	infinite	A
ISE (C2)	base-emitter leakage saturation current	0	A
NE	base-emitter leakage emission coefficient	1.5	
BR	ideal maximum reverse beta	1	
NR	reverse current emission coefficient	1	
VAR (VB)	reverse Early voltage	infinite	V
IKR	corner for rev beta hi-cur roll off	infinite	A
ISC (C4)	base-collector leakage saturation current	0	A
NC	base-collector leakage emission coefficient	2.0	
RB	zero-bias (maximum) base resistance	0	ohm
RBM	minimum base resistance	RB	ohm
RE	emitter ohmic resistance	0	ohm
RC	collector ohmic resistance	0	ohm
CJE	base-emitter zero-bias *pn* capacitance	0	F
VJE (PE)	base-emitter built-in potential	0.75	V
MJE (ME)	base-emitter *pn* grading factor	0.33	
CJC	base-collector zero-bias pn capacitance	0	F

VJC (PC)	base-collector built-in potential	0.75	V
MJC (MC)	base-collector *pn* grading factor	0.33	
XCJC	fraction of Cbc connected int to Rb	1	
CJS (CCS)	collector-substrate zero-bias pn capacitance	0	F
VJS (PS)	collector-substrate built-in potential	0.75	
MJS (MS)	collector-substrate *pn* grading factor	0	
FC	forward-bias depletion capacitor coefficient	0.5	
TF	ideal forward transit time	0	s
XTF	transit time bias dependence coefficient	0	
VTF	transit time dependency on Vbc	infinite	V
ITF	transit time dependency on Ic	0	A
PTF	excess phase @ $1/(2\pi TF)$ Hz	0	°C
TR	ideal reverse transit time	0	s
EG	band-gap voltage (barrier height)	1.11	eV
XTB	forward and reverse beta temp coefficient	0	
XTI (PT)	IS temperature effect exponent	3	
KF	flicker noise coefficient	0	
AF	flicker noise exponent	1	

The bipolar transistor, as shown in Fig. D.5, is modeled as an intrinsic transistor with ohmic resistance RC in series with the collector, a variable resistance Rb in series with the base, and an ohmic resistance RE in series with the emitter. The substrate node is optional, defaulting to ground unless otherwise specified.

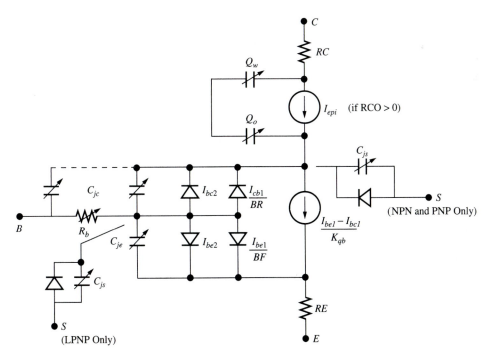

Fig. D.5 Bipolar transistor model.

R Resistor

R<*name*><+*node*><−*node*>[*model name*]<value>

<table>
<tr><td>**Model Parameters**</td><td></td><td>**Default Values**</td><td>**Units**</td></tr>
<tr><td>R</td><td>resistance multiplier</td><td>1</td><td></td></tr>
<tr><td>TC1</td><td>linear temperature coefficient</td><td>0</td><td>°C^{-1}</td></tr>
<tr><td>TC2</td><td>quadratic temperature coefficient</td><td>0</td><td>°C^{-2}</td></tr>
<tr><td>TCE</td><td>exponential temperature coefficient</td><td>0</td><td>%/°C</td></tr>
</table>

If [*model name*] is included and TCE is not specified, then the resistance is

$$<value> \cdot R(1+TC1(T\text{-}T_{nom})+TC2(T\text{-}T_{nom})^2)$$

If [*model name*] is included and TCE is specified, then the resistance is

$$<value> \cdot R \cdot 1.01^{TCE(T\text{-}Tnom)}$$

T_{nom} is the nominal temperature.

Noise is calculated assuming a 1-Hz bandwidth. The resistor generates thermal noise with this power density:

$$i^2 = \frac{R}{4kT}$$

S Voltage-Controlled Switch

S<*name*><+*switch node*><−*switch node*><+*controlling node*>
<−*cont. node*><*model name*>

<table>
<tr><td>**Model Parameters**</td><td></td><td>**Default Value**</td><td>**Units**</td></tr>
<tr><td>RON</td><td>*on* resistance</td><td>1</td><td>ohm</td></tr>
<tr><td>ROFF</td><td>*off* resistance</td><td>1E6</td><td>ohms</td></tr>
<tr><td>VON</td><td>control voltage for *on* state</td><td>1</td><td>volt</td></tr>
<tr><td>VOFF</td><td>control voltage for *off* state</td><td>0</td><td>volt</td></tr>
</table>

Note that the resistance varies continuously between RON and ROFF.

T Transmission Line

T<*name*><+*A port node*><−*A port node*><+*B port node*>
<−*B port node*>Z0=<>[TD=<>][F=<>[NL=<>]]

Z0 is the characteristic impedance, *F* is frequency, and *NL* is relative wavelength (with a default value of 0.25 (*F* then becomes the 1/4-wavelength *f*).

The transmission line, as shown in Fig. D.6, is modeled as a bidirectional delay line with two ports. The port A is shown on the left with nodes *1* and *2*; the port B is shown on the right with nodes *3* and *4*.

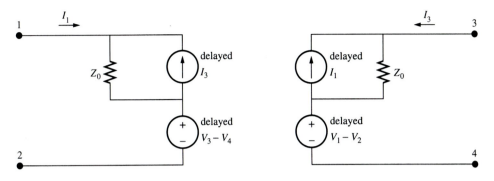

Fig. D.6 Transmission-line model.

V Independent Voltage Source

V<*name*><+*node*><−*node*>[[DC]<>][AC<*magnitude*>[*phase*]][*transient*]

If [*transient*] is specified, it must be one of these:

EXP<>,PULSE<>,PWL<>,SFFM<>,or SIN<>

W Current-Controlled Switch

W<*name*><+*switch node*><−*switch node*>
<*controlling V device name*><*model*>

Model Parameters		Default Value	Units
RON	*on* resistance	1	ohm
ROFF	*off* resistance	1E6	ohms
ION	control current for *on* state	0.001	ampere
IOFF	control current for *off* state	0	ampere

Note that the resistance varies continuously between RON and ROFF.

X Subcircuit Call

X<*name*>[node]*<*subcircuit name*>

There must be the same number of nodes in the call as in the subcircuit definition.

E

Sample Standard Device Library

This is a reduced version of MicroSim's standard parts libraries. Some components from several types of component libraries have been included here.

The following is a summary of parts in this library:

Part name	Part type
Q2N2222	NPN bipolar transistor
Q2N2907A	PNP bipolar transistor
Q2N3904	NPN bipolar transistor
Q2N3906	PNP bipolar transistor
D1N750	zener diode
MV2201	voltage-variable capacitance diode
D1N4002	power diode
D1N4148	switching diode
MBD101	switching diode
J2N3819	N-channel junction field-effect transistor
J2N4393	N-channel junction field-effect transistor
IXGH40N60	N-channel insulated gate bipolar transistor
LM324	linear operational amplifier
LF411	linear operational amplifier
UA741	linear operational amplifier
LM111	voltage comparator
K3019PL_3C8	ferroxcube pot magnetic core
K502T300_3C8	ferroxcube pot magnetic core
K528T500_3C8	ferroxcube pot magnetic core

KRM8PL_3C8	ferroxcube pot magnetic core
IRF150	N-type power MOS field effect transistor
IRF9140	P-type power MOS field effect transistor
PAL20RP4B	Programmable logic device
A4N25	optocoupler
2N1595	silicon controlled rectifier
2N5444	Triac
555D	555 timer subcircuit Sw_tOpen,Sw_tClose time-dependent switch models
P/L2C	Coupled, equal, lumped T-section tline
P/L2C_A	Coupled, unequal, lumped T-section tline
P/LS	Uncoupled (single), lumped tline
P/T2C	Coupled, equal, distributed tline
P/T2C_A	Coupled, unequal, distributed(asymmetrical) tline
P/TS	Uncoupled (single), distributed tline
ESC2_B	Pentium mercury set IBIS I/O model
54152A	Multiplexer/data selector 8-1 line
7400	Quadruple 2-input positive-NAND gates
7401	Quadruple 2-input positive-NAND gates with open-collector outputs
7402	Quadruple 2-input positive-NOR gates
7403	Quadruple 2-input positive-NAND gates with open-collector outputs
7404	Hex inverters
7405	Hex inverters with open-collector outputs
7406	Hex inverter buffers/drivers with open-collector high-voltage outputs
7407	Hex buffers/drivers with open-collector high-voltage outputs
7408	Quadruple 2-input positive-AND gates
7409	Quadruple 2-input positive-AND gates with open-collector outputs
7410	Triple 3-input positive-NAND gates
74100	8-Bit bistable latches
74107	Dual J-K flip-flops with clear
74109	Dual J-KBar positive-edge-triggered flip-flops
7411	Triple 3-input positive-AND gates
74S11	S-series TTL triple 3-input positive-AND gates
74110	And-gated J-K master-slave flip-flops with data lockout
74111	Dual J-K master-slave flip-flops with data lockout
7412	Triple 3-input positive-NAND gates with open-collector outputs
74121	Nonretriggerable monostable multivibrator with schmitt-trigger inputs
74122	Retriggerable monostable multivibrator
74123	Retriggerable monostable multivibrator
74125	Quadruple bus buffer with 3-state outputs
74126	Quadruple bus buffer with 3-state outputs

74128	Line drivers
7413	Dual 4-input positive-NAND schmitt triggers
74132	Quadruple 2-input positive-NAND schmitt trigger
74136	Quadruple 2-input exclusive-OR gates with open-collector outputs
7414	Hex schmitt-trigger inverters
74147	Priority encoder 10-4 line
74148	Priority encoder 8-3 line
74151A	Multiplexer/data selector 8-1 line
74153	Dual 4-line to 1-line data selectors/multiplexers
74154	Decoder/demultiplexer 4-16 line
74155	Decoder/demultiplexer 2-4 line
74156	Decoder/demultiplexer 2-4 line with open collector outputs
74157	Quadruple 2-line to 1-line data selectors/multiplexers
74159	Decoder/demultiplexer 4-16 line with open-collector outputs
7416	Hex inverter buffers/drivers with open-collector high-voltage outputs
74160	Synchronous 4-bit decade counters with asynchronous clear
74161	Synchronous 4-bit binary counter with direct clear
74162	Synchronous 4-bit decade counters with synchronous clear
74163	Synchronous 4-bit binary counter
74164	8-bit parallel-out serial shift registers
7417	Hex buffers/drivers with open-collector high-voltage outputs
74173	Registers D-type 4-bit with 3-state outputs
74174	Hex D-type flip-flops with clear
74175	Quadruple D-type flip-flops with clear
74176	35 MHz presettable decade and binary counter/latch
74177	35 MHz presettable decade and binary counter/latch
74178	4-bit parallel-access shift register
74179	4-bit parallel-access shift register
74180	Parity generator/checker odd/even 9-bit
74181	ALU/function generator
74182	Look-ahead carry generator
74184	BCD-to-binary converters
74185A	Binary-to-BCD converters
74194	4-bit bidirectional universal shift registers
74195	4-bit parallel-access shift registers
74196	4-bit presettable decade counter/latch
74197	4-bit presettable binary counter/latch
7420	Dual 4-input positive-NAND gates
7422	Dual 4-input positive-NAND gates with open-collector outputs
7423	Dual 4-input NOR gates with strobe
74246	Decoder/driver BCD-7 segment with open-collector outputs
74248	Decoder/driver BCD-7 segment with internal pullups
74249	Decoder/driver BCD-7 segment with open-collector outputs
7425	Dual 4-input NOR gates with strobe

74251	Multiplexer/data selector 8-1 line with 3-state outputs
74259	8-bit addressable latches
7426	High-voltage interface positive-NAND gates
74265	Quad. complementary-output elements
7427	Triple 3-input positive-NOR gates
74273	Octal D-type edge-triggered flip-flops with clear
74276	Quadruple J-K flip-flops
74278	Priority registers 4-bit cascadable
74279	Quadruple SBAR-RBAR latches
7428	Quadruple 2-input positive-NOR buffers
74283	4-bit binary full adders with fast carry
74290	Counter decade 4-bit, asynchronous
74293	Counter binary 4-bit, asynchronous
74298	Multiplexers quad 2-input with storage
7430	8-input positive-NAND gates
7432	Quadruple 2-input positive-OR gates
7433	Quadruple 2-input positive-NOR buffers with open-collector outputs
74351	Dual data selector/multiplexer with 3-state outputs
74365A	Hex bus drivers with 3-state outputs
74366A	Hex bus drivers with 3-state outputs
74367A	Hex bus drivers with 3-state outputs
74368A	Hex bus drivers with 3-state outputs
7437	Quadruple 2-input positive-NAND buffers
74376	Quadruple J-K flip-flops
7438	Quadruple 2-input positive-NAND buffers with open-collector outputs
7439	Quadruple 2-input positive NAND buffers with open-collector outputs
74390	Counter decade 4-bit, asynchronous
74393	Counter binary 4-bit, asynchronous
7440	Dual 4-input positive-NAND buffers
74425	Quadruple bus buffers with 3-state outputs
74426	Quadruple bus buffers with 3-state outputs
7442A	Decoder BCD-decimal 4-10 line
7443A	Decoder excess-3-decimal 4-10 line
7444A	Decoder gray-decimal 4-10 line
7445	Decoder/driver BCD-decimal with open-collector outputs
7446A	Decoder/driver BCD-7 segment with open-collector outputs
7448	Decoder/driver BCD-7 segment with internal pullups
7449	Decoder/driver BCD-7 segment with open-collector outputs
74490	Counter decade 4-bit, asynchronous
7450	Dual 2-wide 2-input AND-OR-invert gates
7451	AND-OR-invert gates
7453	Expandable 4-wide AND-OR-invert gates
7454	4-wide AND-OR-invert gates

7460	Dual 4-input expanders
7470	AND-gated J-K positive-edge-triggered flip-flops with preset and clear
7472	AND-gated J-K master-slave flip-flops with preset and clear
7473	Dual J-K flip-flops with clear
7474	Dual D-type positive-edge-triggered flip-flops with preset and clear
7475	4-bit bistable latches (dual 2-bit common clock 4-bit bistable latches)
7476	Dual J-K flip-flops with preset and clear
7477	4-bit bistable latches
7482	2-bit binary full adders
7483A	4-bit binary full adders with fast carry
7485	4-bit magnitude comparator
7486	Quadruple 2-input exclusive-OR gates
7491A	8-bit shift registers
7492A	Counter divide-by-12 4-bit, asynchronous
7493A	Counter binary 4-bit, asynchronous
7494	4-bit shift registers
7495A	4-bit parallel shift registers
7496	8-bit parallel-out serial shift registers

LIBRARY OF BIPOLAR TRANSISTOR MODEL PARAMETERS

This is a reduced version of MicroSim's bipolar transistor model library. The parameters in this model library were derived from the data sheets for each part. Each part was characterized using the Parts option.

Devices can also be characterized without Parts as follows:

NE, NC	Normally set to 4
BF, ISE, IKF	These are adjusted to give the nominal beta vs. collector current curve. BF controls the midrange beta. ISE/IS controls the low-current roll-off. IKF controls the high-current roll-off.
ISC	Set to ISE.
IS, RB, RE, RC	These are adjusted to give the nominal VBE vs. IC and VCE vs. IC curves in saturation. IS controls the low-current value of VBE. RB + RE controls the rise of VBE with IC. RE + RC controls the rise of VCE with IC. RC is normally set to 0.
VAF	The voltages specified on the data sheet are used to set VAF to give the nominal output impedance (RO on the .OP printout) on the data sheet.
CJC, CJE	The voltages specified on the data sheet are used to set CJC and CJE to give the nominal input and output capacitances (CPI and CMU on the .OP printout; Cibo and Cobo on the data sheet).
TF	Using the voltages and currents specified on the data sheet for FT, TF is adjusted to produce the nominal value of FT on the .OP printout.

TR   The rise- and fall-time circuits on the data sheet are used to adjust
                      TR (and if necessary TF) to give a transient analysis that shows
                      the nominal values of the turn-on delay, rise time, storage time,
                      and fall time.

KF, AF   These parameters are set only if the data sheet has a spec for
                      noise. Then, AF is set to 1 and KF is set to produce a total noise
                      at the collector that is greater than the generator noise at the col-
                      lector by the rated number of decibels.

```
.model Q2N2222   NPN(Is=14.34f Xti=3 Eg=1.11 Vaf=74.03 Bf=255.9 Ne=1.307
+                Ise=14.34f Ikf=.2847 Xtb=1.5 Br=6.092 Nc=2 Isc=0 Ikr=0 Rc=1
+                Cjc=7.306p Mjc=.3416 Vjc=.75 Fc=.5 Cje=22.01p Mje=.377 Vje=.75
+                Tr=46.91n Tf=411.1p Itf=.6 Vtf=1.7 Xtf=3 Rb=10)
                 National    pid=19           case=TO18
                 88-09-07 bam      creation

.model Q2N2907A PNP(Is=650.6E-18 Xti=3 Eg=1.11 Vaf=115.7 Bf=231.7 Ne=1.829
+                Ise=54.81f Ikf=1.079 Xtb=1.5 Br=3.563 Nc=2 Isc=0 Ikr=0 Rc=.715
+                Cjc=14.76p Mjc=.5383 Vjc=.75 Fc=.5 Cje=19.82p Mje=.3357 Vje=.75
+                Tr=111.3n Tf=603.7p Itf=.65 Vtf=5 Xtf=1.7 Rb=10)
                 National    pid=63           case=TO18
                 88-09-09 bam      creation

.model Q2N3904   NPN (Is=6.734f Xti=3 Eg=1.11 Vaf=74.03 Bf=416.4 Ne=1.259
+                Ise=6.734f Ikf=66.78m Xtb=1.5 Br=.7371 Nc=2 Isc=0 Ikr=0 Rc=1
+                Cjc=3.638p  Mjc=.3085  Vjc=.75  Fc=.5  Cje=4.493p  Mje=.2593
                 Vje=.75
+                Tr=239.5n Tf=301.2p Itf=.4 Vtf=4 Xtf=2 Rb=10)
                 National    pid=23           case=TO92
                 88-09-08 bam      creation

.model Q2N3906   PNP(Is=1.41f Xti=3 Eg=1.11 Vaf=18.7 Bf=180.7 Ne=1.5 Ise=0
+                Ikf=80m Xtb=1.5 Br=4.977 Nc=2 Isc=0 Ikr=0 Rc=2.5 Cjc=9.728p
+                Mjc=.5776 Vjc=.75 Fc=.5 Cje=8.063p Mje=.3677 Vje=.75 Tr=33.42n
+                Tf=179.3p Itf=.4 Vtf=4 Xtf=6 Rb=10)
                 National    pid=66           case=TO92
                 88-09-09 bam      creation
```

LIBRARY OF DIODE MODEL PARAMETERS

This is a reduced version of MicroSim's diode model library.

The parameters in this model library were derived from the data sheets for
each part. Most parts were characterized using the Parts option.

Devices can also be characterized without Parts as follows:

IS   Nominal leakage current
RS   For zener diodes: nominal small-signal impedance at specified operating cur-
      rent
IB   For zener diodes: set to nominal leakage current
IBV   For zener diodes: at specified operating current IBV is adjusted to give the
      rated zener voltage

Zener Diodes

"A" suffix zeners have the same parameters (e.g., 1N750A has the same parameters
as 1N750).

```
.model D1N750     D(Is=880.5E-18 Rs=.25 Ikf=0 N=1 Xti=3 Eg=1.11 Cjo=175p
M=.5516
+         Vj=.75 Fc=.5 Isr=1.859n Nr=2 Bv=4.7 Ibv=20.245m Nbv=1.6989
+         Ibvl=1.9556m Nbvl=14.976 Tbvl=-21.277u)
          Motorola    pid=1N750   case=DO-35
          89-9-18 gjg
          Vz = 4.7 @ 20mA, Zz = 300 @ 1mA, Zz = 12.5 @ 5mA, Zz =2.6 @ 20mA
```

Voltage-Variable Capacitance Diodes

The parameters in this model library were derived from the data sheets for each part. Each part was characterized using the Parts option.

```
.model MV2201   D(Is=1.365p Rs=1 Ikf=0 N=1 Xti=3 Eg=1.11 Cjo=14.93p M=.4261
+         Vj=.75 Fc=.5 Isr=16.02p Nr=2 Bv=25 Ibv=10u)
          Motorola    pid=MV2201  case=182-03
          88-09-22 bam        creation
```

Switching Diodes

```
.model D1N4148 D(Is=2.682n N=1.836 Rs=.5664 Ikf=44.17m Xti=3 Eg=1.11
+Tt=11.54n) Cjo=4p M=.3333 Vj=.5 Fc=.5 Isr=1.565n Nr=2 Bv=100 Ibv=100u

.model MBD101    D(Is=192.1p Rs=.1 Ikf=0 N=1 Xti=3 Eg=1.11 Cjo=893.8f
+M=98.29m Vj=.75 Fc=.5 Isr=16.91n Nr=2 Bv=5 Ibv=10u)
          Motorola    pid=MBD101  case=182-03
          88-09-22 bam        creation
```

Power Diode

```
+.MODEL D1N4002 D (IS=14.11E-9  N=1.984  RS=33.89E-3   IKF=94.81   XTI=3
+ EG=1.110   CJO=51.17E-12  M=.2762  VJ=.3905  FC=.5  ISR=100.0E-12
+ NR=2   BV=100.1  IBV=10   TT=4.761E-6)
```

LIBRARY OF JUNCTION FIELD-EFFECT TRANSISTOR (JFET) MODEL PARAMETERS

This is a reduced version of MicroSim's JFET model library.

The parameters in this model library were derived from the data sheets for each part. Each part was characterized using the Parts option.

```
.model J2N3819     NJF(Beta=1.304m Betatce=-.5 Rd=1 Rs=1 Lambda=2.25m
Vto=-3
+         Vtotc=-2.5m Is=33.57f Isr=322.4f N=1 Nr=2 Xti=3 Alpha=311.7
+         Vk=243.6 Cgd=1.6p M=.3622 Pb=1 Fc=.5 Cgs=2.414p Kf=9.882E-18
+         Af=1)
          National    pid=50            case=TO92
          88-08-01 rmn      BVmin=25

.model J2N4393     NJF(Beta=9.109m Betatce=-.5 Rd=1 Rs=1 Lambda=6m
Vto=-1.422
+         Vtotc=-2.5m Is=205.2f Isr=1.988p N=1 Nr=2 Xti=3 Alpha=20.98u
+         Vk=123.7 Cgd=4.57p M=.4069 Pb=1 Fc=.5 Cgs=4.06p Kf=123E-18
```

```
+           Af=1)
            National   pid=51           case=TO18
            88-07-13 bam     BVmin=40
```

LIBRARY OF INSULATED GATE BIPOLAR TRANSISTOR (IGBT) MODEL PARAMETERS

The parameters in this model library were derived from data sheets.

This part was characterized using the Parts program and the Optimizer program.

```
.MODEL IXGH40N60 NIGBT
+ TAU=287.56E-9
+ KP=50.034
+ AREA=37.500E-6
+ AGD=18.750E-6
+ VT=4.1822
+ KF=.36047
+ CGS=31.942E-9
+ COXD=53.188E-9
+ VTD=2.6570
```

LIBRARY OF LINEAR IC DEFINITIONS

This is a reduced version of MicroSim's linear subcircuit library.

The parameters in the op amp library were derived from the data sheets for each part. The macromodel used is similar to the one described in Boyle, Graeme, Barry Cohn, Donald Pederson, and James Solomon. 1974. Macromodeling of integrated circuit operational amplifiers. *IEEE Journal of Solid-State Circuits* SC-9, no. 6 (December).

Differences from the reference cited occur in the output limiting stage, which was modified to reduce internally generated currents associated with output voltage limiting, as well as short-circuit current limiting.

The op amps are modeled at room temperature and do not track changes with temperature. This library file contains models for nominal, not worst-case, devices.

```
connections:    non-inverting input
                 | inverting input
                 | | positive power supply
                 | | | negative power supply
                 | | | | output
                 | | | | |
.subckt LM324   1 2 3 4 5
  c1    11 12 2.887E-12
  c2     6  7 30.00E-12
  dc     5 53 dx
  de    54  5 dx
  dlp   90 91 dx
  dln   92 90 dx
  dp     4  3 dx
  egnd  99  0 poly(2) (3,0) (4,0) 0 .5 .5
  fb     7 99 poly(5) vb vc ve vlp vln 0 21.22E6 -20E6 20E6 20E6 -20E6
  ga     6  0 11 12 188.5E-6
  gcm    0  6 10 99 59.61E-9
```

```
  iee    3  10 dc 15.09E-6
  hlim  90   0 vlim 1K
  q1    11   2 13 qx
  q2    12   1 14 qx
  r2     6   9 100.0E3
  rc1    4  11 5.305E3
  rc2    4  12 5.305E3
  re1   13  10 1.845E3
  re2   14  10 1.845E3
  ree   10  99 13.25E6
  ro1    8   5 50
  ro2    7  99 25
  rp     3   4 9.082E3
  vb     9   0 dc 0
  vc     3  53 dc 1.500
  ve    54   4 dc 0.65
  vlim   7   8 dc 0
  vlp   91   0 dc 40
  vln    0  92 dc 40
.model dx D(Is=800.0E-18 Rs=1)
.model qx PNP(Is=800.0E-18 Bf=166.7)
.ends

connections:   non-inverting input
                  |   inverting input
                  |   |   positive power supply
                  |   |   |   negative power supply
                  |   |   |   |   output
                  |   |   |   |   |
.subckt uA741     1  2  3  4  5
  c1    11  12 8.661E-12
  c2     6   7 30.00E-12
  dc     5  53 dx
  de    54   5 dx
  dlp   90  91 dx
  dln   92  90 dx
  dp     4   3 dx
  egnd  99   0 poly(2) (3,0) (4,0) 0 .5 .5
  fb     7  99 poly(5) vb vc ve vlp vln 0 10.61E6 -10E6 10E6 10E6 -10E6
  ga     6   0 11 12 188.5E-6
  gcm    0   6 10 99 5.961E-9
  iee   10   4 dc 15.16E-6
  hlim  90   0 vlim 1K
  q1    11   2 13 qx
  q2    12   1 14 qx
  r2     6   9 100.0E3
  rc1    3  11 5.305E3
  rc2    3  12 5.305E3
  re1   13  10 1.836E3
  re2   14  10 1.836E3
  ree   10  99 13.19E6
  ro1    8   5 50
  ro2    7  99 100
  rp     3   4 18.16E3
  vb     9   0 dc 0
  vc     3  53 dc 1
  ve    54   4 dc 1
  vlim   7   8 dc 0
  vlp   91   0 dc 40
  vln    0  92 dc 40
.model dx D(Is=800.0E-18 Rs=1)
```

```
.model qx NPN(Is=800.0E-18 Bf=93.75)
.ends

connections:    non-inverting input
                  |   inverting input
                  |   |   positive power supply
                  |   |   |   negative power supply
                  |   |   |   |   output
                  |   |   |   |   |
.subckt LF411     1   2   3   4   5
  c1    11  12  4.196E-12
  c2     6   7  10.00E-12
  css   10  99  1.333E-12
  dc     5  53  dx
  de    54   5  dx
  dlp   90  91  dx
  dln   92  90  dx
  dp     4   3  dx
  egnd  99   0  poly(2) (3,0) (4,0) 0 .5 .5
  fb     7  99  poly(5) vb vc ve vlp vln 0 31.83E6 -30E6 30E6 30E6 -30E6
  ga     6   0  11 12 251.4E-6
  gcm    0   6  10 99 2.514E-9
  iss   10   4  dc 170.0E-6
  hlim  90   0  vlim 1K
  j1    11   2  10 jx
  j2    12   1  10 jx
  r2     6   9  100.0E3
  rd1    3  11  3.978E3
  rd2    3  12  3.978E3
  ro1    8   5  50
  ro2    7  99  25
  rp     3   4  15.00E3
  rss   10  99  1.176E6
  vb     9   0  dc 0
  vc     3  53  dc 1.500
  ve    54   4  dc 1.500
  vlim   7   8  dc 0
  vlp   91   0  dc 25
  vln    0  92  dc 25
.model dx D(Is=800.0E-18 Rs=1m)
.model jx NJF(Is=12.50E-12 Beta=743.3E-6 Vto=-1)
.ends
```

VOLTAGE COMPARITORS

The parameters in this comparator library were derived from data sheets for each part. The macromodel used was developed by MicroSim Corporation and is produced by the Parts option to PSpice.

Although we do not use it, another comparator macromodel is described in Getreu, Ian, Andreas Hadiwidjaja, and Johan Brinch. 1976. An integrated-circuit comparator macromodel. *IEEE Journal of Solid-State Circuits* SC-11, no. 6 December.

This reference covers the considerations that go into duplicating the behavior of voltage comparators.

The comparators are modeled at room temperature. The macromodel does not track changes with temperature. This library file contains models for nominal, not worst-case, devices.

```
connections:   non-inverting input
                   |   inverting input
                   |   |   positive power supply
                   |   |   |   negative power supply
                   |   |   |   |   open collector output
                   |   |   |   |   |   output ground
                   |   |   |   |   |   |
.subckt LM111    1   2   3   4   5   6
   f1     9   3  v1  1
   iee    3   7  dc  100.0E-6
   vil   21   1  dc  .45
   vi2   22   2  dc  .45
   q1     9  21   7  qin
   q2     8  22   7  qin
   q3     9   8   4  qmo
   q4     8   8   4  qmi
.model qin  PNP(Is=800.0E-18 Bf=833.3)
.model qmi  NPN(Is=800.0E-18 Bf=1002)
.model qmo  NPN(Is=800.0E-18 Bf=1000 Cjc=1E-15 Tr=118.8E-9)
   e1    10   6   9   4   1
   v1    10  11  dc  0
   q5     5  11   6  qoc
.model   qoc    NPN(Is=800.0E-18   Bf=34.49E3   Cjc=1E-15   Tf=364.6E-12
+Tr=79.34E-9)
   dp     4   3  dx
   rp     3   4  6.122E3
.model dx   D(Is=800.0E-18 Rs=1)
.ends
```

LIBRARY OF MAGNETIC CORE MODEL PARAMETERS

This is a reduced version of MicroSim's magnetic core library.

The parameters in this model library were derived from the data sheets for each core. The Jiles-Atherton magnetics model is described in Jiles, D. C. and D. L. Atherton. 1986, Theory of ferromagnetic hysteresis. *Journal of Magnetism and Magnetic Materials* 61:48–60.

Model parameters for ferrite material (Ferroxcube 3C8) were obtained by trial simulations, using the B-H curves from the manufacturer's catalog. The library was then compiled from the data sheets for each core geometry. Notice that only the geometric values change once a material is characterized.

Example use: `K2 L2 .99 K1409PL_3C8`

Notes:

1. Using a K device (formerly only for mutual coupling) with a model reference changes the meaning of the L device: The inductance value becomes the number of turns for the winding.
2. K devices can "get away" with specifying only one inductor, as in the preceding example, to simulate power inductors.

Example circuit file:

```
+
|Demonstration of power inductor B-H curve
| To view results with Prove (B-H curve):
| 1) Add Trace for B(K1)
| 2) set X-axis variable to H(K1)
| Probe x-axis unit is Oersted
| Probe y-axis unit is Gauss
|.tran .1 4
|igen0 0 1 sin(0 .1amp 1Hz 0) ; Generator: starts with 0.1 amp sinewave,
then
|igen1 0 1 sin(0 .1amp 1Hz 1) ;   +0.1 amps, starting at 1 second
|igen2 0 1 sin(0 .2amp 1Hz 2) ;   +0.2 amps, starting at 2 seconds
|igen3 0 1 sin(0 .8amp 1Hz 3) ;   +0.4 amps, starting at 3 seconds
|RL 1 0 1ohm              ; generator source resistance
|L1 1 0 20                ; inductor with 20 turns
|K1 L1 .9999 K528T500_3C8    ; Ferroxcube torroid core
|.model K528T500_3C8    CORE(Ms=415.2K A=44.82 C=.4112 K=25.74)
|+              AREA=1.17 PATH=8.49)
|.options itl5=0
|.probe
|.end
+
```

Ferroxcube Pot Cores: 3C8 Material

```
.model K3019PL_3C8      Core(MS=415.2K A=44.82 C=.4112 K=25.74
+                       Area=1.38 Path=4.52)
```

Ferroxcube Square Cores: 3C8 Material

```
.model KRM8PL_3C8     Core(MS=415.2K A=44.82 C=.4112 K=25.74
+                     Area=.630 Path=3.84)
```

Ferroxcube Toroid Cores: 3C8 Material

```
.model K502T300_3C8     Core(MS=415.2K A=44.82 C=.4112 K=25.74
+                       Area=.371 Path=7.32)
```

```
.model K528T500_3C8     Core(MS=415.2K A=44.82 C=.4112 K=25.74
+                     Area=1.17 Path=8.49)
```

LIBRARY OF MOSFET MODEL PARAMETERS (FOR "POWER" MOSFET DEVICES)

This is a reduced version of MicroSim's power MOSFET model library.

The parameters in this model library were derived from the data sheets for each part. Each part was characterized using the Parts option.

Devices can also be characterized without Parts as follows:

LEVEL	Set to 3 (short-channel device)
TOX	Determined from gate ratings
L, LD, W, WD	Assume L = 2u. Calculated from input capacitance
XJ, NSUB	Usual technology assumed

IS, RD, RB	Determined from "source-drain diode forward voltage" specification or curve (Idr vs. Vsd)
RS	Determined from Rds(on) specification
RDS	Calculated from Idss specification or curves
VTO, UO, THETA	Determined from "output characteristics" curve family (Ids vs. Vds, stepped Vgs)
ETA, VMAX, CBS	Set for null effect
CBD, PB, MJ	Determined from "capacitance vs. Vds" curves
RG	Calculated from rise/fall time specification or curves
CGSO, CGDO	Determined from gate-charge, turn-on/off delay and rise-time specifications

Note: When specifying the instance of a device in your circuit file, BE SURE to have the source and bulk nodes connected together, as this is the way the real device is constructed. DO NOT include values for L, W, AD, AS, PD, PS, NRD, or NDS. The PSpice default values for these parameters are taken into account in the library model statements. Of course, you should NOT reset the default values using the .OPTIONS statement, either.

Example use: `M17    15 23 7 7      IRF150`

The "power" MOSFET device models benefit from relatively complete specification of static and dynamic characteristics by their manufacturers. The following effects are modeled: DC transfer curves in forward operation, gate drive characteristics and switching delay, "on" resistance, reverse-mode "body-diode" operation.

The factors not modeled include maximum ratings (e.g., high-voltage breakdown), safe operating area (e.g., power dissipation), latch-up, noise.

For high-current switching applications, we advise that you include series inductance elements, for the source and drain, in your circuit file. In doing so, voltage spikes due to di/dt will be modeled. According to the 1985 International Rectifier databook, the following case styles have lead inductance values of

TO-204 (modified TO-3)	source = 12.5 nH	drain = 5.0 nH
TO-220	source = 7.5 nH	drain = 3.5–4.5 nH

```
.model IRF150       NMOS(Level=3 Gamma=0 Delta=0 Eta=0 Theta=0 Kappa=0
+Vmax=0 Xj=0
+           Tox=100n Uo=600 Phi=.6 Rs=1.624m Kp=20.53u W=.3 L=2u Vto=2.831
+           Rd=1.03m Rds=444.4K Cbd=3.229n Pb=.8 Mj=.5 Fc=.5 Cgso=9.027n
+           Cgdo=1.679n Rg=13.89 Is=194E-18 N=1 Tt=288n)
            Int'l Rectifier    pid=IRFC150 case=TO3
            88-08-25 bam       creation

.model IRF9140      PMOS(Level=3 Gamma=0 Delta=0 Eta=0 Theta=0 Kappa=0
Vmax=0 Xj=0
+           Tox=100n  Uo=300  Phi=.6  Rs=70.6m  Kp=10.15u  W=1.9  L=2u
+           Vto=-3.67
+           Rd=60.66m Rds=444.4K Cbd=2.141n Pb=.8 Mj=.5 Fc=.5 Cgso=877.2p
+           Cgdo=369.3p Rg=.811 Is=52.23E-18 N=2 Tt=140n)
            Int'l Rectifier    pid=IRFC9140 case=TO3
            88-08-25 bam       creation$
```

DIGITAL COMPONENTS

7400 Quadruple 2-Input Positive-Nand Gates

Source: The *TTL Data Book,* Vol. 2, 1985, Texas Instruments.

```
.subckt 7400  A  B  Y
+     optional: DPWR=$G_DPWR DGND=$G_DGND
+     params: MNTYMXDLY=0 IO_LEVEL=0
U1 nand(2) DPWR DGND
+     A  B   Y
+     D_00 IO_STD MNTYMXDLY={MNTYMXDLY}   IO_LEVEL={IO_LEVEL}
.ends

.model D_00 ugate (
+     tplhty=11ns tplhmx=22ns
+     tphlty=7ns  tphlmx=15ns
+     )
```

7401 Quadruple 2-Input Positive-Nand Gates with Open-Collector Outputs

Source: The *TTL Data Book,* Vol. 2, 1985, Texas Instruments.

```
.subckt 7401  A  B  Y
+     optional: DPWR=$G_DPWR DGND=$G_DGND
+     params: MNTYMXDLY=0 IO_LEVEL=0
U1 nand(2) DPWR DGND
+     A  B   Y
+     D_01 IO_STD_OC MNTYMXDLY={MNTYMXDLY}   IO_LEVEL={IO_LEVEL}
.ends

.model D_01 ugate (
+     tplhty=35ns tplhmx=55ns
+     tphlty=8ns  tphlmx=15ns
+     )
```

7402 Quadruple 2-Input Positive-Nor Gates

Source: The *TTL Data Book,* Vol. 2, 1985, Texas Instruments.

```
.subckt 7402  A  B  Y
+     optional: DPWR=$G_DPWR DGND=$G_DGND
+     params: MNTYMXDLY=0 IO_LEVEL=0
U1 nor(2) DPWR DGND
+     A  B   Y
+     D_02 IO_STD MNTYMXDLY={MNTYMXDLY}   IO_LEVEL={IO_LEVEL}
.ends

.model D_02 ugate (
+     tplhty=12ns tplhmx=22ns
+     tphlty=8ns  tphlmx=15ns
+     )
```

7403 Quadruple 2-Input Positive-Nand Gates with Open-Collector Outputs

Source: The *TTL Data Book,* Vol. 2, 1985, Texas Instruments.

```
.subckt 7403 A B Y
+     optional: DPWR=$G_DPWR DGND=$G_DGND
```

```
+      params: MNTYMXDLY=0 IO_LEVEL=0
U1 nand(2) DPWR DGND
+      A  B    Y
+      D_03 IO_STD_OC MNTYMXDLY={MNTYMXDLY}   IO_LEVEL={IO_LEVEL}
.ends

.model D_03 ugate (
+      tplhty=35ns tplhmx=45ns
+      tphlty=8ns  tphlmx=15ns
+      )
```

7404 Hex Inverters

Source: The *TTL Data Book*, Vol. 2, 1985, Texas Instruments.

```
.subckt 7404   A Y
+      optional: DPWR=$G_DPWR DGND=$G_DGND
+      params: MNTYMXDLY=0 IO_LEVEL=0
U1 inv DPWR DGND
+      A    Y
+      D_04 IO_STD MNTYMXDLY={MNTYMXDLY}   IO_LEVEL={IO_LEVEL}
.ends

.model D_04 ugate(
+      tplhty=12ns tplhmx=22ns
+      tphlty=8ns  tphlmx=15ns
+      )
```

7405 Hex Inverters with Open-Collector Outputs

Source: The *TTL Data Book*, Vol. 2, 1985, Texas Instruments.

```
.subckt 7405   A Y
+      optional: DPWR=$G_DPWR DGND=$G_DGND
+      params: MNTYMXDLY=0 IO_LEVEL=0
U1 inv DPWR DGND
+      A    Y
+      D_05 IO_STD_OC MNTYMXDLY={MNTYMXDLY}   IO_LEVEL={IO_LEVEL}
.ends

.model D_05 ugate (
+      tplhty=40ns tplhmx=55ns
+      tphlty=8ns  tphlmx=15ns
+      )
```

7406 Hex Inverter Buffers/Drivers with Open-Collector High-Voltage Outputs

Source: The *TTL Data Book*, Vol. 2, 1985, Texas Instruments.

```
.subckt 7406   A Y
+    optional: DPWR=$G_DPWR DGND=$G_DGND
+    params: MNTYMXDLY=0 IO_LEVEL=0
U1 inv DPWR DGND
+      A    Y
+      D_06 IO_STD_OC MNTYMXDLY={MNTYMXDLY}   IO_LEVEL={IO_LEVEL}
.ends

.model D_06 ugate (
+      tplhty=10ns tplhmx=15ns
```

```
+       tph1ty=15ns tph1mx=23ns
+       )
```

7407 Hex Buffers/Drivers with Open-Collector High-Voltage Outputs

Source: The *TTL Data Book,* Vol. 2, 1985, Texas Instruments.

```
.subckt 7407   A Y
+       optional: DPWR=$G_DPWR DGND=$G_DGND
+       params: MNTYMXDLY=0 IO_LEVEL=0
U1 buf DPWR DGND
+       A    Y
+       D_07 IO_STD_OC MNTYMXDLY={MNTYMXDLY}   IO_LEVEL={IO_LEVEL}
.ends

.model D_07 ugate (
+       tp1hty=6ns   tp1hmx=10ns
+       tph1ty=20ns tph1mx=30ns
+       )
```

7408 Quadruple 2-Input Positive-And Gates

Source: The *TTL Data Book,* Vol. 2, 1985, Texas Instruments.

```
.subckt 7408   A B Y
+       optional: DPWR=$G_DPWR DGND=$G_DGND
+       params: MNTYMXDLY=0 IO_LEVEL=0
U1 and(2) DPWR DGND
+       A B    Y
+       D_08 IO_STD MNTYMXDLY={MNTYMXDLY}   IO_LEVEL={IO_LEVEL}
.ends

.model D_08 ugate (
+       tp1hty=17.5ns        tp1hmx=27ns
+       tph1ty=12ns tph1mx=19ns
+       )
```

7409 Quadruple 2-Input Positive-And Gates with Open-Collector Outputs

Source: The *TTL Data Book,* Vol. 2, 1985, Texas Instruments.

```
.subckt 7409   A B Y
+       optional: DPWR=$G_DPWR DGND=$G_DGND
+       params: MNTYMXDLY=0 IO_LEVEL=0
U1 and(2) DPWR DGND
+       A B    Y
+       D_09 IO_STD_OC MNTYMXDLY={MNTYMXDLY}   IO_LEVEL={IO_LEVEL}
.ends

.model D_09 ugate (
+       tp1hty=21ns tp1hmx=32ns
+       tph1ty=16ns tph1mx=24ns
+       )
```

7410 Triple 3-Input Positive-Nand Gates

Source: The *TTL Data Book,* Vol. 2, 1985, Texas Instruments.

```
.subckt 7410   A B C Y
+       optional: DPWR=$G_DPWR DGND=$G_DGND
```

```
+      params: MNTYMXDLY=0 IO_LEVEL=0
U1 nand(3) DPWR DGND
+      A B C   Y
+      D_10 IO_STD MNTYMXDLY={MNTYMXDLY}   IO_LEVEL={IO_LEVEL}
.ends

.model D_10 ugate (
+      tplhty=11ns tplhmx=22ns
+      tphlty=7ns  tphlmx=15ns
+      )
```

7411 Triple 3-Input Positive-And Gates

Source: 1989 National Semiconductor.

```
.subckt 7411  A B C Y
+      optional: DPWR=$G_DPWR DGND=$G_DGND
+      params: MNTYMXDLY=0 IO_LEVEL=0
U1 and(3) DPWR DGND
+      A B C   Y
+      D_11 IO_STD MNTYMXDLY={MNTYMXDLY}   IO_LEVEL={IO_LEVEL}
.ends

.model D_11 ugate (
+      tplhmx=27ns
+      tphlmx=19ns
+      )
```

7412 Triple 3-Input Positive-Nand Gates with Open-Collector Outputs

Source: The *TTL Data Book,* Vol. 2, 1985, Texas Instruments.

```
.subckt 7412  A B C Y
+      optional: DPWR=$G_DPWR DGND=$G_DGND
+      params: MNTYMXDLY=0 IO_LEVEL=0
U1 nand(3) DPWR DGND
+      A B C   Y
+      D_12 IO_STD_OC MNTYMXDLY={MNTYMXDLY}   IO_LEVEL={IO_LEVEL}
.ends

.model D_12 ugate (
+      tplhty=35ns tplhmx=45ns
+      tphlty=8ns  tphlmx=15ns
+      )
```

7413 Dual 4-Input Positive-Nand Schmitt Triggers

Source: The *TTL Data Book,* Vol. 2, 1985, Texas Instruments.

```
.subckt 7413  A B C D Y
+      optional: DPWR=$G_DPWR DGND=$G_DGND
+      params: MNTYMXDLY=0 IO_LEVEL=0
```

Note: These devices are modeled as simple NAND gates. Hysteresis is modeled in the AtoD interface.

```
U1 nand(4) DPWR DGND
+      A B C D   Y
```

```
+      D_13 IO_STD_ST MNTYMXDLY={MNTYMXDLY}   IO_LEVEL={IO_LEVEL}
.ends

.model D_13 ugate (
+      tplhty=18ns tplhmx=27ns
+      tphlty=15ns tphlmx=22ns
+      )
```

7414 Hex Schmitt-Trigger Inverters

Source: The *TTL Data Book,* Vol. 2, 1985, Texas Instruments.

```
.subckt 7414   A Y
+      optional: DPWR=$G_DPWR DGND=$G_DGND
+      params: MNTYMXDLY=0 IO_LEVEL=0
```

Note: These devices are modeled as simple inverters. Hysteresis is modeled in the AtoD interface.

```
U1 inv DPWR DGND
+      A   Y
+      D_14 IO_STD_ST MNTYMXDLY={MNTYMXDLY}   IO_LEVEL={IO_LEVEL}
.ends

.model D_14 ugate (
+      tplhty=15ns tplhmx=22ns
+      tphlty=15ns tphlmx=22ns
+      )
```

7420 Dual 4-Input Positive-Nand Gates

Source: The *TTL Data Book,* Vol. 2, 1985, Texas Instruments.

```
.subckt 7420   A B C D Y
+      optional: DPWR=$G_DPWR DGND=$G_DGND
+      params: MNTYMXDLY=0 IO_LEVEL=0
U1 nand(4) DPWR DGND
+      A B C D   Y
+      D_20 IO_STD MNTYMXDLY={MNTYMXDLY}   IO_LEVEL={IO_LEVEL}
.ends

.model D_20 ugate (
+      tplhty=12ns tplhmx=22ns
+      tphlty=8ns  tphlmx=15ns
+      )
```

7427 Triple 3-Input Positive-Nor Gates

Source: The *TTL Data Book,* Vol. 2, 1985, Texas Instruments.

```
.subckt 7427   A B C Y
+      optional DPWR=$G_DPWR DGND=$G_DGND
+      params: MNTYMXDLY=0 IO_LEVEL=0
U1 nor(3) DPWR DGND
+      A B C   Y
+      D_27 IO_STD MNTYMXDLY={MNTYMXDLY}   IO_LEVEL={IO_LEVEL}
.ends
```

```
.model D_27 ugate (
+       tplhty=10ns tplhmx=15ns
+       tphlty=7ns  tphlmx=11ns
+       )
```

7451 And-Or-Invert Gates

Source: The *TTL Data Book,* Vol. 2, 1985, Texas Instruments.

```
.subckt 7451   A B C D Y
+       optional: DPWR=$G_DPWR DGND=$G_DGND
+       params: MNTYMXDLY=0 IO_LEVEL=0
U1 aoi(2,2) DPWR DGND
+       A B C D    Y
+       D_51 IO_STD MNTYMXDLY={MNTYMXDLY}   IO_LEVEL={IO_LEVEL}
.ends
```

7470 And-Gated J-K Positive-Edge-Triggered Flip-Flops with Preset and Clear

Source: The *TTL Data Book,* Vol. 2, 1985, Texas Instruments.

```
.subckt 7470   CLK PREBAR CLRBAR J1 J2 JBAR K1 K2 KBAR Q QBAR
+       optional: DPWR=$G_DPWR DGND=$G_DGND
+       params: MNTYMXDLY=0 IO_LEVEL=0
U1V inva(3) DPWR DGND
+       CLK JBAR KBAR    CLKBAR J3 K3
+       D0_GATE IO_STD IO_LEVEL={IO_LEVEL}
U2A anda(3,2) DPWR DGND
+       J3 J1 J2 K3 K1 K2    J K
+       D0_GATE IO_STD IO_LEVEL={IO_LEVEL}
U3 jkff(1) DPWR DGND
+       PREBAR CLRBAR CLKBAR    J K    Q QBAR
+       D_70 IO_STD MNTYMXDLY={MNTYMXDLY}   IO_LEVEL={IO_LEVEL}
.ends
```

7473 Dual J-K Flip-Flops with Clear

Source: The *TTL Data Book,* Vol. 2, 1985, Texas Instruments.

```
.subckt 7473   CLK CLRBAR J K Q QBAR
+       optional: DPWR=$G_DPWR DGND=$G_DGND
+       params: MNTYMXDLY=0 IO_LEVEL=0
UIBUF bufa(3) DPWR DGND
+       CLRBAR J K    CLRBAR_BUF J_BUF K_BUF
+       D0_GATE IO_STD IO_LEVEL={IO_LEVEL}
U2BUF buf DPWR DGND
+       CLK    CLK_BUF
+       D_73_4 IO_STD MNTYMXDLY={MNTYMXDLY}   IO_LEVEL={IO_LEVEL}
U1 inva(3) DPWR DGND
+       CLK_BUF J_BUF K_BUF    CLKBAR JB KB
+       D0_GATE IO_STD
U2A ao(3,2) DPWR DGND
+       J_BUF QBAR_BUFD K_BUF J_BUF KB $D_HI    W1
+       D_73_3 IO_STD MNTYMXDLY={MNTYMXDLY}
U2B ao(3,2) DPWR DGND
+       J_BUF K_BUF Q_BUFD $D_HI JB K_BUF    W2
+       D_73_3 IO_STD MNTYMXDLY={MNTYMXDLY}
U3 srff(1) DPWR DGND
+       $D_HI CLRBAR_BUF CLK_BUF    W1 W2    Y YB
```

```
+      D_73_1 IO_STD MNTYMXDLY={MNTYMXDLY}
U4 srff(1) DPWR DGND
+      $D_HI CLRBAR_BUF CLKBAR   Y YB   QBUF QBAR_BUF
+      D_73_2 IO_STD MNTYMXDLY={MNTYMXDLY}
UOBUF bufa(2) DPWR DGND
+      QBUF QBAR_BUF    Q QBAR
+      D_73_3 IO_STD MNTYMXDLY={MNTYMXDLY}   IO_LEVEL={IO_LEVEL}
UBUF bufa(2) DPWR DGND
+      QBUF QBAR_BUF   Q_BUFD QBAR_BUFD
+      D_73_3 IO_STD MNTYMXDLY={MNTYMXDLY}
.ends
```

7474 Dual D-Type Positive-Edge-Triggered Flip-Flops with Preset and Clear

Source: The *TTL Data Book,* Vol. 2, 1985, Texas Instruments.

```
.subckt 7474  1CLRBAR 1D 1CLK 1PREBAR 1Q 1QBAR
+      optional: DPWR=$G_DPWR DGND=$G_DGND
+      params: MNTYMXDLY=0 IO_LEVEL=0
UFF1 dff(1) DPWR DGND
+      1PREBAR 1CLRBAR 1CLK   1D   1Q 1QBAR
+      D_74 IO_STD MNTYMXDLY={MNTYMXDLY}   IO_LEVEL={IO_LEVEL}
.ends

.model D_74 ueff (
+      twpclmn=30ns     twclklmn=37ns
+      twclkhmn=30ns    tsudclkmn=20ns
+      thdclkmn=5ns     tppcqlhmx=25ns
+      tppcqhlmx=40ns   tpclkqlhty=14ns
+      tpclkqlhmx=25ns  tpclkqhlty=20ns
+      tpclkqhlmx=40ns
+      )
```

I/O MODELS, DIGITAL POWER SUPPLY, STIMULUS MODELS, ETC.—FROM DIG_IO.LIB

Source: Copyright 1989, 1990, 1991, 1992 by MicroSim Corporation.

The parameters in this model library were derived from The *TTL Data Book,* vol. 2, 1985, Texas Instruments, 1-21 to 1-28, 3-4 to 3-9, and 3-79 to 3-81.

AtoD and DtoA Subcircuits

The subcircuits in this library are used to convert analog signals into digital signals (AtoD) and digital signals into analog signals (DtoA). The PSpice Digital Simulation Option creates "X" devices that reference these subcircuits whenever it needs to convert a digital or analog signal. You will usually not need to use these subcircuits directly. However, if you need to add new AtoD or DtoA subcircuits, the interface nodes must be in the following order, and have the following parameters:

AtoD:

```
.subckt <name> <analog-node> <dig-node> <dig-pwr> <dig-gnd>
+ params: CAPACITANCE = 0
```

DtoA:

```
.subckt <name> <dig-node> <analog-node> <dig-pwr> <dig-gnd>
+ params: DRVL = 0 DRVH = 0 CAPACITANCE = 0
```

I/O Models

I/O models specify the names of the AtoD and DtoA subcircuits PSpice must use to convert analog signals to digital signals or vice versa. (I/O models also describe driving and loading characteristics.) Up to four AtoD and DtoA subcircuit names each may be specified in an I/O model, using parameters AtoD1 through AtoD4, and DtoA1 through DtoA4. The subcircuit that PSpice actually uses depends on the value of the IO_LEVEL parameter in a subcircuit reference.

As implemented in this library, the levels have the following definitions:

IO_LEVEL	Definition
1	AtoD generates X, R, and F between VIL max and VIH min
2	AtoD transitions directly between 0 and 1 at Vt
3	Unused (same as level 1)
4	Unused (same as level 2)

Note that Schmitt-trigger inputs always transition directly between 0 and 1.

For example, to specify the basic interface without an intermediate X value, you would use

```
X1 in out 74LS04 PARAMS: IO_LEVEL=2
```

If the IO_LEVEL is not specified for a device, the default IO_LEVEL is used. The default level is controled by the .OPTION parameter DIGIOLVL, which defaults to 1.

Switching Times

The I/O models include switching-time parameters for low-to-high, and high-to-low transitions (TSWLHn and TSWHLn). There is a different pair of switching times for each IO_LEVEL value. These times are subtracted from the propagation delay times for devices that have a DtoA subcircuit created at their output. The switching time is the time it takes the output of the DtoA to change its output voltage from steady state to the logic threshold.

The switching-time values are selected so that inserting a DtoA/AtoD pair in a logic path does not change the overall propagation delay. (Assuming that no additional load is placed on the analog signal.)

Power Supplies

The I/O models also specify the name of a digital power supply subcircuit. These subcircuits are called by PSpice in the event any AtoD/DtoA interfaces are created.

Digital Power Supplies

PSpice calls a power supply subcircuit as a consequence of AtoD or DtoA interface creation. The resulting digital power supply nodes are used by the AtoD/DtoA interfaces. The name of the power supply subcircuit is specified in the technology's I/O models. Currently, these power supplies are

Device Type   Subcircuit Name   Nodes Created
TTL   DIGIFPWR $G_DPWR $G_DGND

PSpice always passes node 0 as the required analog reference node "GND". By default, the nodes created by the subcircuit call are global nodes ($G_xxx) that are used throughout the device library for that family.

The default power supply voltage for TTL (and compatible CMOS) devices is 5.0 V.

TTL/CMOS power supply

```
.subckt DIGIFPWR   AGND
+      optional: DPWR=$G_DPWR DGND=$G_DGND
+      params:   VOLTAGE=5.0v REFERENCE=0v

VDPWR    DPWR DGND  {VOLTAGE}
R1       DPWR AGND  1MEG
VDGND    DGND AGND  {REFERENCE}
R2       DGND AGND  1MEG
.ends
```

Stimulus Device Models and Subcircuits

Stimulus I/O Models

```
.model IO_STM uio (
+      drvh=0       drvl=0
+      DtoA1="DtoA_STM"   DtoA2="DtoA_STM"
+      DtoA3="DtoA_STM"   DtoA4="DtoA_STM"
+      DIGPOWER="DIGIFPWR"
+      )

.model IO_STM_OC uio (
+      drvh=1MEG   drvl=0
+      DtoA1="DtoA_STM_OC"      DtoA2="DtoA_STM_OC"
+      DtoA3="DtoA_STM_OC"      DtoA4="DtoA_STM_OC"
+      DIGPOWER="DIGIFPWR"
+      )
```

Stimulus DtoA Subcircuit

```
.subckt DtoA_STM   D A   DPWR DGND
+      params: DRVL=0 DRVH=0 CAPACITANCE=0

N1   A DGND DPWR DINSTM DGTLNET=D IO_STM
C1   A DGND {CAPACITANCE+0.1pF}
.ends
```

Stimulus Open-Collector DtoA Subcircuit

```
.subckt DtoA_STM_OC   D A   DPWR DGND
+      params: DRVL=0 DRVH=0 CAPACITANCE=0

N1   A DGND DPWR DINSTM_OC DGTLNET=D IO_STM_OC
C1   A DGND {CAPACITANCE+0.1pF}
.ends
```

Stimulus Digital Input/Output Models

We use 0.5 Ω and a 500-ps transition time, on the assumption that this will be a "strong" signal source with a "fast" switching time in most systems that use this library. Change the tsw's and/or the rlow and rhi values if these don't work for your system.

```
.model DINSTM dinput (
+     s0name="0"  s0tsw=0.5ns s0rlo=.5    s0rhi=1k
+     s1name="1"  s1tsw=0.5ns s1rlo=1k    s1rhi=.5
+     s2name="X"  s2tsw=0.5ns s2rlo=0.429 s2rhi=1.16 ; .313ohm, 1.35v
+     s3name="R"  s3tsw=0.5ns s3rlo=0.429 s3rhi=1.16 ; .313ohm, 1.35v
+     s4name="F"  s4tsw=0.5ns s4rlo=0.429 s4rhi=1.16 ; .313ohm, 1.35v
+     s5name="Z"  s5tsw=0.5ns s5rlo=1MEG  s5rhi=1MEG
+     )

.model DINSTM_OC dinput (
+     s0name="0"  s0tsw=0.5ns s0rlo=.5    s0rhi=1k
+     s1name="1"  s1tsw=0.5ns s1rlo=1MEG  s1rhi=1MEG
+     s2name="X"  s2tsw=0.5ns s2rlo=0.429 s2rhi=1.16 ; .313ohm, 1.35v
+     s3name="R"  s3tsw=0.5ns s3rlo=0.429 s3rhi=1.16 ; .313ohm, 1.35v
+     s4name="F"  s4tsw=0.5ns s4rlo=0.429 s4rhi=1.16 ; .313ohm, 1.35v
+     s5name="Z"  s5tsw=0.5ns s5rlo=1MEG  s5rhi=1MEG
+     )
```

Default Models and Subcircuits Default I/O Models

```
.model IO_DFT uio (
+     drvh=50     drvl=50
+     AtoD1="AtoD_STD"   AtoD2="AtoD_STD_NX"
+     AtoD3="AtoD_STD"   AtoD4="AtoD_STD_NX"
+     DtoA1="DtoA_STD"   DtoA2="DtoA_STD"
+     DtoA3="DtoA_STD"   DtoA4="DtoA_STD"
+     DIGPOWER="DIGIFPWR"
+     )

.model IO_DFT_OC uio (
+     drvh=1MEG   drvl=50
+     AtoD1="AtoD_STD"   AtoD2="AtoD_STD"
+     AtoD3="AtoD_STD"   AtoD4="AtoD_STD"
+     DtoA1="DtoA_STD_OC"    DtoA2="DtoA_STD_OC"
+     DtoA3="DtoA_STD_OC"    DtoA4="DtoA_STD_OC"
+     DIGPOWER="DIGIFPWR"
+     )
```

Default AtoD Subcircuit

```
.subckt AtoDDEFAULT  A D  DPWR DGND
+     params: CAPACITANCE=0

O1  A DGND DO74 DGTLNET=D IO_DFT
.ends
```

Default DtoA Subcircuit

```
.subckt DtoADEFAULT  D A  DPWR DGND
+     params: DRVL=0 DRVH=0 CAPACITANCE=0

N1  A DGND DPWR DIN74 DGTLNET=D IO_DFT
```

```
C1   A DGND {CAPACITANCE+0.1pF}
.ends
```

74/54 Family (standard TTL)

7400 I/O Models

```
.model IO_STD uio (
+       drvh=96.4    drvl=104
+       AtoD1="AtoD_STD"    AtoD2="AtoD_STD_NX"
+       AtoD3="AtoD_STD"    AtoD4="AtoD_STD_NX"
+       DtoA1="DtoA_STD"    DtoA2="DtoA_STD"
+       DtoA3="DtoA_STD"    DtoA4="DtoA_STD"
+         tswhl1=1.373ns         tswlh1=3.382ns
+         tswhl2=1.346ns         tswlh2=3.424ns
+         tswhl3=1.511ns         tswlh3=3.517ns
+         tswhl4=1.487ns         tswlh4=3.564ns
+       DIGPOWER="DIGIFPWR"
+       )


.model IO_STD_ST uio (
+       drvh=96.4    drvl=104
+       AtoD1="AtoD_STD_ST"       AtoD2="AtoD_STD_ST"
+       AtoD3="AtoD_STD_ST"       AtoD4="AtoD_STD_ST"
+       DtoA1="DtoA_STD"    DtoA2="DtoA_STD"
+       DtoA3="DtoA_STD"    DtoA4="DtoA_STD"
+         tswhl1=1.373ns            tswlh1=3.382ns
+         tswhl2=1.346ns            tswlh2=3.424ns
+         tswhl3=1.511ns            tswlh3=3.517ns
+         tswhl4=1.487ns            tswlh4=3.564ns
+       DIGPOWER="DIGIFPWR"
+       )


.model IO_STD_OC uio (
+       drvh=1MEG    drvl=104
+       AtoD1="AtoD_STD"    AtoD2="AtoD_STD_NX"
+       AtoD3="AtoD_STD"    AtoD4="AtoD_STD_NX"
+       DtoA1="DtoA_STD_OC"       DtoA2="DtoA_STD_OC"
+       DtoA3="DtoA_STD_OC"       DtoA4="DtoA_STD_OC"
  tsw values measured with 330 ohm pull up
+         tswhl1=2.617ns            tswlh1=1.432ns
+         tswhl2=2.598ns            tswlh2=1.460ns
+         tswhl3=2.747ns            tswlh3=1.589ns
+         tswhl4=2.732ns            tswlh4=1.615ns
+       DIGPOWER="DIGIFPWR"
+       )
```

7400 Standard AtoD Subcircuits

```
.subckt AtoD_STD  A D  DPWR DGND    params: CAPACITANCE=0

o0  A DGND DO74 DGTLNET=D IO_STD
C1  A DGND {CAPACITANCE+0.1pF}
D0          DGND        a          D74CLMP
D1          1           2          D74
D2 2        DGND        D74
R1          DPWR        3          4k
Q1 1 3 A 0  Q74 ; substrate should be DGND
.ends
```

```
.subckt AtoD_STD_NX   A D   DPWR DGND
+      params: CAPACITANCE=0

O0   A DGND DO74_NX DGTLNET=D IO_STD
C1   A DGND {CAPACITANCE+0.1pF}
D0             DGND           a             D74CLMP
D1             1             2             D74
D2 2           DGND          D74
R1             DPWR          3             4k
Q1 1 3 A 0   Q74 ; substrate should be DGND
.ends
```

7400 Standard DtoA Subcircuit

```
.subckt DtoA_STD   D A   DPWR DGND
+      params: DRVL=0 DRVH=0 CAPACITANCE=0

N1   A DGND DPWR DIN74 DGTLNET=D IO_STD
C1   A DGND {CAPACITANCE+0.1pF}
.ends
```

7400 Open-Collector DtoA Subcircuit

```
.subckt DtoA_STD_OC   D A   DPWR DGND
+      params: DRVL=0 DRVH=0 CAPACITANCE=0
N1   A DGND DPWR DIN74_OC DGTLNET=D IO_STD_OC
C1   A DGND {CAPACITANCE+0.1pF}
.ends
```

7400 Digital Input/Output Models

```
.model DIN74 dinput (
+      s0name="0"  s0tsw=3.5ns s0rlo=7.13  s0rhi=389 ; 7ohm,     0.09v
+      s1name="1"  s1tsw=5.5ns s1rlo=467   s1rhi=200 ; 140ohm,   3.5v
+      s2name="X"  s2tsw=3.5ns s2rlo=42.9  s2rhi=116 ; 31.3ohm, 1.35v
+      s3name="R"  s3tsw=3.5ns s3rlo=42.9  s3rhi=116 ; 31.3ohm, 1.35v
+      s4name="F"  s4tsw=3.5ns s4rlo=42.9  s4rhi=116 ; 31.3ohm, 1.35v
+      s5name="Z"  s5tsw=3.5ns s5rlo=200K  s5rhi=200K
+      )

.model DIN74_OC dinput (
+      s0name="0"  s0tsw=3.5ns s0rlo=7.13  s0rhi=389 ; 7ohm,     0.09v
+      s1name="1"  s1tsw=5.5ns s1rlo=200K  s1rhi=200K
+      s2name="X"  s2tsw=3.5ns s2rlo=42.9  s2rhi=116 ; 31.3ohm, 1.35v
+      s3name="R"  s3tsw=3.5ns s3rlo=42.9  s3rhi=116 ; 31.3ohm, 1.35v
+      s4name="F"  s4tsw=3.5ns s4rlo=42.9  s4rhi=116 ; 31.3ohm, 1.35v
+      s5name="Z"  s5tsw=5.5ns s5rlo=200K  s5rhi=200K
+      )

.model DO74 doutput (
+      s0name="X"  s0vlo=0.8   s0vhi=2.0
+      s1name="0"  s1vlo=-1.5  s1vhi=0.8
+      s2name="R"  s2vlo=0.8   s2vhi=1.4
+      s3name="R"  s3vlo=1.3   s3vhi=2.0
+      s4name="X"  s4vlo=0.8   s4vhi=2.0
+      s5name="1"  s5vlo=2.0   s5vhi=7.0
+      s6name="F"  s6vlo=1.3   s6vhi=2.0
+      s7name="F"  s7vlo=0.8   s7vhi=1.4
+      )
```

```
.model DO74_NX doutput (
+      s0name="0"  s0vlo=-1.5  s0vhi=1.35
+      s2name="1"  s2vlo=1.35  s2vhi=7.0
+      )

.model DO74_ST doutput (
+      s0name="0"  s0vlo=-1.5  s0vhi=1.7
+      s1name="1"  s1vlo=0.9   s1vhi=7.0
+      )
```

TTL device models

These parameter values are taken from Hodges, David A., and Horace G. Jackson. 1983. *Analysis and Design of Digital Integrated Circuits* New York: McGraw-Hill, 301.

```
.model D74 d (
+      is=1e-16    rs=25 cjo=2pf
+      )

.model D74S d (
+      is=1e-12    vj=.7 rs=25 cjo=2pf
+      )

.model D74CLMP d (
+      is=1e-15    rs=2  cjo=2pf
+      )

.model D74SCLMP d (
+      is=1e-11    vj=.7 rs=2  cjo=2pf
+      )

.model Q74 npn (
+      ise=1e-16   isc=4e-16
+      bf=49 br=.03
+      cje=1pf     cjc=.5pf
+      cjs=3pf     vje=0.9v
+      vjc=0.8v    vjs=0.7v
+      mje=0.5     mjc=0.33
+      mjs=0.33    tf=0.2ns
+      tr=10ns     rb=50
+      rc=20
+      )

.model Q74S npn (
+      ise=1e-16   isc=4e-16
+      bf=49 br=33
+      cje=1pf     cjc=.5pf
+      cjs=3pf     vje=0.9v
+      vjc=0.8v    vjs=0.7v
+      mje=0.5     mjc=0.33
+      mjs=0.33    tf=0.2ns
+      tr=10ns     rb=50
+      rc=20
+      )
```

74S11 Triple 3-Input Positive-And Gates

Source: The *TTL Data Book,* Vol. 2, 1985, Texas Instruments.

```
.subckt 74S11   A  B  C  Y
+      optional: DPWR=$G_DPWR DGND=$G_DGND
+      params: MNTYMXDLY=0 IO_LEVEL=0
U1 and(3) DPWR DGND
+      A  B  C    Y
+      D_S11 IO_S MNTYMXDLY={MNTYMXDLY}   IO_LEVEL={IO_LEVEL}
.ends
```

Note: The file *EVAL.LIB* contains many more devices than those shown in the preceding subset.

Index